# SOURCES OF CHRISTIAN THEOLOGY IN AMERICA

# SOURCES OF CHRISTIAN THEOLOGY IN AMERICA

Edited by
Mark G. Toulouse and
James O. Duke

Abingdon Press
Nashville

SOURCES OF CHRISTIAN THEOLOGY IN AMERICA

*Copyright © 1999 by Abingdon Press*

*This book is printed on recycled, acid-free, elemental-chlorine–free paper.*

**Library of Congress Cataloging-in-Publication Data**

Sources of Christian theology in America / edited by Mark G. Toulouse
and James O. Duke.
    p.  cm.
    Includes bibliographical references and index.
    ISBN 0-687-02524-9 (alk. paper)
    1. Theology, Doctrinal—United States.  I. Toulouse, Mark G.,
1952–    . II. Duke, James O.
BT30.U6S68    1999
230'.0973—dc21                              99-15042
                                                        CIP

Scripture quotations, unless otherwise indicated, are from the King James Version of the Bible.

Scripture quotations noted DV are from the Douay-Rheims Version of the Bible.

Scripture quotations noted RSV are from the Revised Standard Version of the Bible, copyright 1946, 1952, 1971 by the Division of Christian Education of the National Council of the Churches of Christ in the USA. Used by permission.

"History as Apocalypse" by Thomas J. J. Altizer is reprinted from *Deconstruction and Theology*, edited by Thomas J. J. Altizer et al., copyright 1982, published by The Crossroad Publishing Company.

"Authority" is reproduced from *The Case for Orthodox Theology* by Edward John Carnell. © W. L. Jenkins MCMLIX. Used by permission of Westminster John Knox Press.

"God as Creative-Responsive Love" is reproduced from *Process Theology* by John B. Cobb, Jr., and David Ray Griffin. © 1976 The Westminster Press. Used by permission of Westminster John Knox Press.

"The Content and Method of Black Theology" by James H. Cone is reprinted from *The Journal of Religious Thought* (Fall 1975).

"Christian Discourse About God" is reprinted with the permission of Simon & Schuster from *Naming the Whirlwind* by Langdon Gilkey. Copyright © 1969 by Langdon Gilkey.

*This copyright page continues on page 605.*

99 00 01 02 03 04 05 06 07 08—10 9 8 7 6 5 4 3 2 1

MANUFACTURED IN THE UNITED STATES OF AMERICA

To
Jeffica and Jeanne

# PREFACE

This collection of readings is intended to aid students, teachers, and others seeking to understand Christianity in America. Understanding any religion well, even within the confines of a specific geographical region and time span, is a challenge for believers and outsiders alike. The aid being offered here is ready access to an assortment of texts by thinkers formative of Christian theology in America from colonial to recent times.

Anthologies of theological literature like this one are traditional tools for teaching and learning in undergraduate, seminary, and graduate education. Their value is better measured by their use and usefulness than by what their editors say about them in advance. Even so, an introduction to this reworking of a tradition, one of many in flux and in some dispute today, may serve both to alert readers to its aim, focus, and design and to orient them to its contents.

Since the goal is to foster an understanding of Christianity in America, it is appropriate to say at the outset that the path taken here is only one of many possible and desirable, each attempting in its own way to cast some light on a multifaceted subject. It should perhaps also be said that this gathering together of theological writings is meant to be instructive, not celebratory of theology as queen of the sciences, the achievements of this land's theologians, the canon of theological truths, or the editors' top sixty favorite thinkers. It does reflect several convictions and values, as well as hosts of decisions, regarding both Christianity in America and serious study of it, among them: theology is an integral element of Christian faith; it is a force in as well as a product of its time and place; and attention to *its* history provides—especially in comparing and contrasting it to other developments—a larger grasp of Christianity and American history than can be gained by ignoring it. To these must be added the desires that students of Christianity encounter its theological thinking firsthand (preferably sooner than later), and engage at least a number of sources which together record main currents and some strong countercurrents of thought going into the making of Christian theology in America.

The record of swirling crosscurrents compiled here is in substance a retelling, through primary source material, of a story already told in

*Makers of Christian Theology in America* (Abingdon, 1997) by scholars who sketched intellectual portraits of ninety-one thinkers formative of Christian theological discussion during their lifetimes and thereafter. The two books are meant to serve, then, as companion pieces, although each is designed to stand on its own.

Like all twice-told tales, this one involves certain expansions and contractions. Expansion comes in providing more or less extensive selections of works which contributors to *Makers,* asked to say what they judged important to say in exceedingly brief space, had to summarize or mention only in passing. Gain there necessitates cutbacks elsewhere—narrowing the scope of coverage for a single volume of reasonable size. Of chief concern in selecting theologians and texts for inclusion has been their fitness for duty as representatives of main movements and critical turns of theological thinking over the course of time. While much of the diversity of Christian thought is displayed, comprehensiveness is an impossible dream. Emphasis falls here on theologians and theologies with reach considerably beyond their denominational, regional, ethnic, or "school" support bases. The outcome in view is not *the* sampler "everyone" agrees upon but one with selections of the sort standard and revisionist histories *alike* have cause to take into account in their field surveys.

Two other editorial decisions weigh heavily in the shaping of this anthology. One is focus on the tradition(s) of "scholarly Christian church theology." The phrase goes in quote marks because its terms—*scholarly, Christian, church,* and *theology*—carry historically variable and often contested meanings. This focus is historically descriptive rather than theologically normative, and hence not exclusive in a cookie-cutter fashion, but rather a highlighting of theologies illustrative of combinations of the four traits or concerns, albeit in differing measure. Yet it is only honest and otherwise right to say that a reader with another focus, for instance, theological scholarship, devotional classics, "orthodox" doctrine, ethics, or diversity of "religious opinion" per se, would and should come out differently.

The second decision is pedagogical: a preference for selections offering access to substantive content at some substantial length, and as complete and self-contained as practicable, instead of snippets. Here, too, trade-offs are inevitable. Accessibility means at times choosing a popularized presentation of views argued elsewhere in technical, detailed fashion. Substantiveness means occasionally featuring the most learned and polished formulations of thought by some theologians who customarily deliver their thought in more of a homespun style. Selections do vary in length, but factors in addition to editorial estimates of all-star ratings do enter into play. Each theologian receives space to express at least one point of vital concern. The breadth, depth, and effect of some thinkers are simply too vast to represent by excerpts. In such instances, ample time is granted for the development of a key theme, or maybe two.

Selections are in the main "continuous cuts" in the sense of complete *sections* of chapters, sermons, essays, treatises, et cetera. On occasion, however, it seemed wise to cover a running train of thought or line of argument by making some internal excisions rather than reproduce merely its start, midsection, or finale. Editorial omissions are indicated by ellipses. Due diligence is given to issues of textual reliability; nonetheless, it is worth remembering that selected readings should lead to, not substitute for, close study of unabridged writings in scholarly critical editions.

Christian theology's history in America unfolds here through four eras, as though it were a play in four acts: the colonial, early national, post–Civil War to World War I, and twentieth century development. These divisions are standard in surveys of American Christianity, in keeping with historical studies generally, though they are at root and in effect more "political" than "Christian-theological." Such boundary markers are best understood as conveniences, because the flows of continuities and changes in history are too complex to channel into hard-and-fast compartments. Assigning readings to their "proper" era is often simple and noncontroversial, but not always. Theology's players appear here in rough chronological order; the very few exceptions—somewhat early or late entries, so to speak—are timed by the character and impact of their thought instead of the calendar or clock.

With all such endeavors, editors accumulate debts of gratitude. In this case, we appreciate suggestions provided by scholars who worked with us on the *Makers* volume. Further thanks are due both Brite Divinity School and Texas Christian University. Brite supported the project through summer research support and in other meaningful ways. TCU provided a study carrel in the library. We were beneficiaries of strong support from Brite staff in the form of Robin Gray, who was an assistant in this project from beginning to end, and Chris Arrequin. Shonda Jones and Joan Copeland, two students at Brite Divinity School, provided aid as well. For the efforts of all these people, we are grateful. Finally, we dedicate this volume to our spouses Jeffica and Jeanne, two women who value education, Christian theology, and the stories of history as much as we do.

9

# CONTENTS

# CONTENTS

# INTRODUCTION

## MARK G. TOULOUSE AND JAMES O. DUKE

People in the newly formed United States of America at the end of the eighteenth century were familiar with the word *theology*. Then, as now, almost everyone in America recognized that the word had to do with "God" and was an apt label for convictions, beliefs, ideas, accounts, studies, and other things relating to nature, will, and ways of God. Uses of the word in ordinary language were many and varied, depending on the context of discussion.

In the context of colonial America's churches, *theology, theological,* and *theologian* were terms with multiple historic associations, formed in the main in the course of transplanting Christian traditions to "new world" soil. Christianity's message of God and things of God—the divinely revealed truths of faith—was theology. So too were the belief-ful grasp and appropriation of those truths; the spiritual and intellectual disciplines that led to awareness and understanding of "divinity"; the body of church teachings (doctrines) that set forth the objects of Christian faith, hope, and love; and the customary forms or genres of discourse that dealt with these topics, such as creeds, articles and confessions of faith, catechisms, handbooks, sermons, and treatises.

Two other associations went with and cut across the common church uses of the term. First, while it was understood that Christians should learn and affirm faith's truths, public teaching of the faith within and in the name of the church was a weighty responsibility of church leadership—a task of ministry entrusted to persons well-equipped and duly authorized to undertake it. Second, study in theology extended to higher learning beyond the reach of most Christians. As taught in the universities of Europe, it presupposed knowledge of the "arts and sciences," involved mastery of the skills of reasoning, and addressed the most perplexing issues of faith and often philosophy as well.

15

This short list of related but distinct meanings of *theology* calls attention to key planks of the framework for Christian theology's development in America. Within this framework appeared many and diverse formulations of the *fides quae creditur* (the faith that is to be believed), and many disputes and divisions over understanding faith's sources, character, contents, and implications rightly. Theology's ingredients were the grand themes of scripture and church tradition. Chief among them were God, Jesus Christ, the Spirit, creation, providence, fall, sin, grace, law, gospel, salvation, the nature and purpose of the church, and the fulfillment of God's intentions at the "end of the world." In dealing with these themes, theologies were at the same time pondering humanity's perennial questions, both basic and profound. The work of the theologian included queries into the origin and destiny (the *telos* or goal) of the universe, the meaning of life and death, the significance of human history, and the adequacy of governing standards regulating human activity and social order.

Theology was not, strictly speaking, the whole of life, or even the whole of the Christian religion. Vast numbers of Christians were simple believers with scant learning in theology per se. But theology's themes embraced the whole of life, and pervaded colonial culture along with Christianity itself, leaving a legacy of rhetoric that still contributes to shaping the most basic cultural understandings of the American self. Little if anything in colonial times ever failed to reflect or trigger a measure of theological concern. The question of the union or separation of church and state, for example, was at once theological and political, and epitaphs on churchyard tombstones witnessed in their own way to theological convictions just as scholarly tomes on divinity did in theirs. Yet, as a general rule, the historic associations of the word imported from the "old world" that, whatever else was said about it, theology par excellence was the work of theologians, that is, the church's minister-teachers and their teachers, who were devoted to advanced learning in Christian doctrine.

This rule was by no means universal or tension-free. Christians interpreted it in different ways. Implementing it was especially difficult under frontier conditions in America. Waves of immigrants, accompanied by few leaders, founded churches by transporting overseas the theologies embedded in the liturgy or pattern of worship, confessional standards, and other homeland traditions. Most weathered some time of transition from foreign-born to indigenous theological leadership. Although adaptations to changed circumstances were inevitable, and some were quick and striking, inherited ways of thinking about "God and things of God" were slow to change. Those ways were not always tied or limited to "official" church teachings. Many colonists brought with them other views and folkways relating to "divinity" too: experiments with magic and fortune-telling, the occult, and other attempts to contact, avoid, or manipulate supernatural forces exemplified yet another aspect of early American religious life, more pervasive than often realized. In short, theologies were plentiful but theologians of the sort found across the Atlantic were few and far between, and home schooling took time and resources as well as talent.

Whether it was more blessed to replicate "old world" ways or revise and improve them was a disputed question within the churches. The answers were as likely to turn on love-hate relations with heritage and immediate needs and opportunities as on deliberative weightings of theological options. In any case, Christian theology in America was never so isolated that it escaped the currents, movements, schools, challenges, and conflicts encountered or established by theology elsewhere.

The new nation's vast expanse meant opportunity for the wide variety of splintered post-Reformation Christian groupings. Representatives of what contemporary historians call the major traditions—Anglican, Reformed, Lutheran, "Radical," and Roman Catholic—gained a foothold in the colonies. Of them, those among the Reformed were the first to gather numbers and strength to carry on "learned" church theology comparable to that of Europe's theologians. Puritan settlements of New England, unlike the other struggling immigrant or mission churches, included a sizable contingent of Old England's young, and well-schooled minister-theologians dedicated to preserving and advancing the cause of Reformed church theology. This is one reason the Puritans and streams of thought flowing from New England's colonial headwaters still command a place in histories of theology larger than that due them in studies of countless other facets of Christianity in America.

The Puritan movement arose amid the turbulent course of the Reformation in England. Puritans, anxious to place Reformed ideas on a fast track within the church life of England, helped transform Henry VIII's convenient Protestantism of the 1530s into a full-blown Protestant program by 1600. Complex and amorphous as it was, Puritanism's theological taproot was nourished by visions of a Reformed church, as "evangelical" (gospel-oriented) as Lutheranism, but distinctive with respect to doctrine, worship practices, views of the sacraments, and forms of church polity and discipline conducive of faithful living. From its Swiss homelands Reformed Christianity spread widely in Europe, and found forceful expression in the theology of John Calvin, who worked to make Geneva a model Christian commonwealth and staging area for Reformation elsewhere. Those in England of more or less like mind with Calvin and his continental allies fought for the soul—and control—of the Church of England from the mid-sixteenth to the late seventeenth centuries. Puritans sought to rid the church of "popish" traditions and adopt pure, apostolic precepts and practices. They went on in time to uphold broadly "Calvinist" views of doctrine, polity, and moral discipline.

In the end, the Puritan movement in England developed three large but internally fractious dissenting churches—Presbyterians, Congregationalists, and Baptists—and countless smaller bodies, the most long-lived being the Society of Friends, or Quakers. It also caused the Church of England to define itself more clearly than ever before as a distinct "Anglican" communion, neither Roman Catholic, Lutheran, Puritan, nor sect, although housing many sympathetic to Reformed ways and still others who were repelled by doctrinal pettiness and strife.

Puritanism's theological themes were transported to the American shores beginning in the 1630s. Thoroughly Reformed, Puritans emphasized the divine initiative as the only sure foundation of salvation. Human beings are helpless without God. Redemption rests firmly upon God's activity in human history. This is why John Cotton's catechism has the young Christian, right from the start, making a clear affirmation of what God has done: "God hath made me, He keepeth me, and he can save me." Related to this affirmation is the Puritan emphasis on human sinfulness. Sinners cannot save themselves (see also the sixth article of Cotton's "Twelve Fundamental Articles"). As expressed in this catechism, the wages of sin are "death and damnation." Salvation rests in Jesus Christ and comes only as the Spirit begets faith in the sinner "to receive Him, prayer to call upon Him, repentance to mourn after Him, and new obedience to serve Him." For the Puritan, all initiative pertaining to salvation rests solely with God.

In like manner, as Thomas Hooker shows, Puritans described God as the "Principall cause and Institutour of a visible church." As a result of God's initiative, the church, with Christ as its head, is established. The relationship between God and the church illustrates a second dimension of Puritan theology, its emphasis on divine covenants. When talking of salvation, most Puritans emphasized the covenant of grace, a covenant stressing God's activities rather than human responsibilities. For Cotton, the church represented a congregation of saints joined together through the bond of this covenant of grace. Though Cotton and Hooker shared this Puritan theological emphasis on covenantal theology, Hooker stressed the role of human participation within the covenant somewhat more freely than Cotton, especially in relationship to the work of the church. Hooker's covenant theology, as it touched church life, was more congregational than presbyterian. As a result, Hooker emphasized the covenant that visible saints made with one another to form the fellowship of faith and to help one another walk in obedience to Christ. Many other Puritans occasionally applied the language of covenant to God's special relationship to the nation, a theme later generations transformed into a doctrine of manifest destiny.

Another key theme of Puritan theology in early America was the unique authority of scripture. Good Puritans lived their lives according to the dictates of the Bible. The problem, of course, was that even good Puritans differed in their interpretations of what the Bible actually said. Anne Hutchinson and Roger Williams illustrate this problem well. Leaders of Puritan Massachusetts Bay colony used scripture to make their cases against them, and both defendants answered these charges by using the Bible to accuse their accusers.

As the lives of English Puritans amply demonstrated, Puritan theology also contained a strong reforming tendency. Whether in England or New England, Puritans believed that God had a plan for society and they intended to do their part to implement it. This belief often led to the kind of persecution that Hutchinson and Williams experienced. At the same time, however, it provided the prophetic insight that drove most of Puritanism's better social accomplishments. The Puritan confidence that if only Christians "would set themselves to devise good, a world of good might be done" found very clear expression in the work of many early Puritans. Cotton Mather's essay represents it well.

The turn of the eighteenth century was a time of theological transitions. Its full-blown results were to dominate the scene long thereafter. The catchwords for these rising forces are *Pietism* and *Enlightenment,* each an umbrella term for a multitude of phenomena. Some pietist emphases—faith as heartfelt devotion to God, intense personal awareness of God's mercy in Christ for repentant sinners, and commitment to righteous living—were hardly new or markedly controversial. But the "founder" of Pietism within German Lutheranism, Philip Jakob Spener, drew upon Christian mystical writings, Reformed thought, including the Puritans', and the Scriptures even while insisting—in response to home-church confessionalists and other critics—that his views were Lutheran loyalism. Pietists elsewhere were to make similar avowals of church loyalty, among them those who spearheaded an Evangelical Revival in Great Britain and a First Great Awakening in America. Reformation of life, not doctrine, was their avowed aim. Even so, pietistic impulses, once unleashed, were not easily subjected to doctrinal control.

Indeed, the call for such reform itself turned on the conviction there was something more to truly authentic faith than the church's established teachings, teachers, and means of grace (doctrinally sound preaching, sacraments, participation in worship and church life) were able to deliver. Orthodoxy's theologians wanted to know: What was this thing called revivalism, and why should anyone think that it supplied the one thing missing but needful in human life? What did it accomplish through its momentarily wrenching "conversion experiences" (often of baptized, believing Christians), or its tests, programs, and strategies of spiritual-moral improvement? It was then not so much the ends as it was the means to those ends that divided colonial churches into pro- and anti-pietist parties.

This division, however, was itself a theological concern for both parties. Even the pietists who denied no historic church doctrines effectually recast them all. Faith, which the Reformers called trust or reliance on the promises of God, became synonymous with inwardly warm feelings for God and things of God; salvation by grace alone became receiving—or accepting—the power of the Spirit in a born-again flash; and so on. To many staunch confessionalists, pietist expositions of doctrine looked lax and subjective, and their de-emphasis on intellectual rigor in the name of piety seemed especially dangerous.

The Enlightenment, on the other hand, emphasized the capacity of humans by the use of reason to discover the way and workings of the universe. It was fueled by the advance of modern science, graphically evident in the success of scientific astronomy from Copernicus to Sir Isaac Newton but underway in other fields as well. Parallel to these developments were the new, modern philosophies exalting critical reason, both rationalistic (as in the cases of René Descartes and G. W. Leibniz) and empiricist (in the cases of Francis Bacon and John Locke). All told, this new learning challenged traditional accounts of the operations of the natural world and explained many things once called mysteries and acts of God. The modern scientific worldview that emerged forced many thoughtful Christians to reconsider the intelligibility and validity of faith's revealed truths. It also forced them to reconsider the role, and limits, of free inquiry and critical reasoning in biblical and theological studies. Last but not least, rising amid the ashes of wars of religion, emphasis on the light of reason conveyed a less technical and more everyday meaning as well: reasonableness. Balance, harmony, moderation in all things, tolerance, self-control, and virtue were among the movement's watchwords.

Christian responses to the Enlightenment were diverse, as complex and differentiated as the new thinking and new ethos itself. Most condemned those who took the method and philosophy to the extreme of a comprehensive materialism that "reduced" the universe to matter and motion containing no God or immortal soul. Deist thought also posed a threat, one which advocated, on the basis of the well-ordered design of nature and nature's universal laws, a "natural religion" of belief in a wise and benevolent Creator combined with an emphasis on the practice of virtue. Yet few Christians considered it possible, much less desirable, to claim that Christian faith meant committing to an altogether unenlightened, unreasoning, and unreasonable life, hostile to any advance in learning.

Few Americans, therefore, were drawn either to an extreme fideism that emphasized a faith incompatible with reason, or to a rationalism so extreme that it had no need of faith. Instead, most Americans drawn to Enlightenment thought were attracted to the more moderate forms of it, those, for example, expressed in the writings of John Locke in England. Among educated colonists, as in England, categories of thought of the sort ably expressed by Locke held widespread appeal. Locke supported greater religious toleration as a healthy solution for strife-weary England—a view of increasing influence in eighteenth-century America. He urged the examination of all claims to truth fairly and impartially, testing each in terms of its basis in human experience and sound reasoning. Science and philosophy, he held, were, through reason, to discern the structure and workings of the natural order.

But Locke also acknowledged certain limits of reason. The realm of things "above nature," the super-natural world, was beyond its scope. Information regarding supernatural truths came by divine revelation, conveyed in the case of the truths of the Christian religion, in the Bible. Therefore, faith or belief held a place within this more moderate style of Enlightenment, provided they were not demonstrably contrary to reason. The conflicting truth-claims of theologies should be evaluated, much like courtroom procedure, on the basis of the credibility of those making them and the intelligibility of their testimony. Charles Chauncy, an opponent of the revivalistic culture beginning to sweep across eighteenth-century America, stressed this style of rational religion as a counter measure to emotional excess and "unreasonable" beliefs and behavior.

This framework and attitude of thinking, more than the specifics of Locke's own position, proved of vast consequence for enlightened religion. The model—adducing evidences from experience and reason for the credibility of theology's authoritative sources and then focusing on the intelligibility of theology's credible truth-claims—seemed at once profound in its simplicity and yet infinitely adaptable. It figured in a wide variety of theologies sharing little if anything in common other than a "rational supernaturalism," a quest to show that the Christian message of God and things of God is at points beyond reason's power to confirm or deny but by no means arbitrary or absurd. The supernatural "points" might vary considerably. The intelligibility of some doctrines—Trinity, incarnation, and predestination—was not at all readily demonstrable, and so it is perhaps not surprising that so many who ended their careers as Socinians, Unitarians, Arians, Universalists, "free will" Christians, and Deists started out as orthodox Anglicans, Presbyterians, and Congregationalists with inquiring minds. By the same token, appeals to "rational evidences" for the divine origin of the Scriptures or the New Testament or the fundamentals of Christianity became a near-standard feature of theology in America, more popular in the nineteenth century than the eighteenth even among expressly anti-Enlightenment theologians.

Jonathan Edwards managed to combine many of the attributes of the trinity of influences that operated upon him: Reformed (Calvinist) orthodoxy, pietism, and the moderate Enlightenment. His work synthesized the content of Reformed themes (the utter sinfulness of humanity combined with an absolute dependence upon the grace of God) with the spiritual concerns of the pietist (an awe-filled reverence for both the majesty of God and the absolute beauty of holiness, and a profound ability to describe the authentic piety of the Christian who sees both for what they are). In addition, the rational commitments of the Enlightenment were evident in his work, as, for example, in his consistent and rigorous application of the scientific method to his analysis of Christian conversion. Therefore, his pietism was as intellectually sharp and as self-consciously Calvinist as any of the writings of theologians who wrote as anti-pietistic rationalists. Edwards, though well ahead of his time in so many ways as a theologian, clearly wrote as a theologian who was influenced by all the cultural and intellectual trends of his time.

Edwards's unique approach to theology gave rise to a new school of American theology often referred to as New Divinity. These younger theologians (most had been students of Edwards) expressed their Calvinism with an American twist. Chief among the early New Divinity theologians was Samuel Hopkins, who spent his life attempting to articulate a Calvinism that took seriously the idea of personal moral accountability. Hopkins and a few others developed an indigenous American theology striving to weave together in one theological system their commitments to both divine sovereignty and human responsibility.

As the glowing embers of the Great Awakening cooled, American Christians turned increasingly toward dealing with issues of independence, revolution, the formation of a national government. The tasks of organizing (or reorganizing) their church polities and keeping up with the tidal waves of migration pouring into the east and spilling over into the western frontier followed. Though welcome to many and acceptable to many more, the Constitution's first amendment guarantees of freedom of worship and separation of church and state betokened threat as well as promise. So too were postwar ecclesiastical reorganization and frontier expansion. Internal schism (sparked by church-political and ethnic as well as doctrinal discord) combined with the growth of once tiny groups and the entry of scores of newcomers to turn "theology in America" from colonial heterogeneity to unbridled proliferation. The frontier might be "lost" to indifference, immorality, or (equally repugnant in the predominantly Protestant culture) Roman Catholicism.

But potential gains were massive as well, especially if true Christians could win the hearts and minds of the people for true religion. Since the truths of the Christian religion were theology's primary concern, emphatic conviction and clarity were critical. Yet many debated whether all the doctrines handed down as tradition, along with the formulations and forms in which they had been delivered, were really essentials of the faith. Reformulation, as well as modifications, additions, or subtractions, might well be called for. Such thoughts prompted searching and scholarly reappraisals of Christianity's doctrinal tradition as well as experiments with options leading far afield from Christian theology and its history. Another thought occurred to many: perhaps the best way to win the hearts and minds of the people was to concentrate on concerns other than those the "theologians" considered so important.

Within Christian theology in antebellum America, two larger waves of thought flooded in from across the Atlantic, Scottish Common-Sense Thought and post-Kantian romanticism. The first arose in the mid-eighteenth century, at the height of the Enlightenment in Scotland. It was an empirical philosophy, building upon the works of Francis Bacon, celebrated as the founder of the modern scientific method, and Locke. Thomas Reid, one of its earliest theorists, worked to defend and, as necessary, to clarify and correct Locke's theory of knowledge. An updating of the basic principle that all knowledge was based on ideas arising from sense perception seemed necessary. This was especially true because, after Locke, there had developed schools of idealism, sensationalism, and, in David Hume, skepticism, each in its own way questioning the idea that perceptions produced knowledge of objects existing independently of ideas in the external world. Scottish Common-Sense thinkers insisted on a dual basis for knowledge, sense perception (the material world) and ideas (the mental or spiritual world). They also insisted on the firm, common-sense link between the two. The observations, experiments, and inductive method of science were, then, capable of attaining genuine knowledge.

This philosophy of "Realism" took root in America with the appointment of John Witherspoon to the presidency of Princeton College (then the College of New Jersey) in 1798. But some American leaders had already drawn upon its resources to help justify the American Revolution. England's colonial policy seemed to violate every dictate of American common sense. Quickly spreading across the colonies along with English, Scottish, and Scots-Irish immigrants, Common-Sense Realism became the standard for schooling throughout antebellum America and the lingua franca of Protestant theology. Presbyterianism was its chief stronghold, but its use in education and its adaptability in theology commended it for widespread use. It gave rational supernaturalism new life: just as the ideas of science were based on the facts of the natural world, so the ideas of theology were based on facts about the supernatural truths found in the Scriptures.

Common-Sense thought played a role in America's most prominent school of theology in the early national era, New Haven theology. The New Haven theologians at Yale, beginning with Timothy Dwight and flourishing under his student Nathaniel W. Taylor and his allies, combined Scottish Common-Sense Realism, the Reformed (Calvinist) heritage, and religious revivals into a mighty force extending the staying power of America's Second Great Awakening. Emphasis on conversion from sin by the direct power of the Spirit was one side of their program; rationally persuasive accounts of the religious truths set forth in the

Scriptures, Calvin, and Edwards was another. In stump preaching and lengthy theological systems and treatises, representatives of the New Haven school recast the legacy of Edwards for fresh service. Building on the work of Samuel Hopkins, greater room and weight were placed on the responsibility of each individual for sin, which, though inevitable, is not inescapably predetermined by God. These theologians also emphasized a human ability to plead for God's aid to overcome sinning, to strengthen the resolve to sin no more, and to obey the duties of Christian living. Lemuel Haynes, an African American Congregationalist minister, in his eloquent sermon that extols the ruling providence of God while at the same time it calls for human resolve to serve as God's instruments to accomplish God's purposes, illustrates well the extensive influence of the message of this New Haven school.

Whether this New Haven message represented minor modifications necessary for a loyal restatement of tradition or a covert total betrayal of it became a matter of controversy right away. The "new measures" of revivalism introduced by Charles G. Finney, including advance planning and publicity, fiery preaching, appeals to fears of God's wrath on hard-hearted sinners and rewards for righteousness, now and in the hereafter, and front-row benches for people mourning their sins and anxious for salvation, intensified the debate. Formal division resulted in some church bodies; ongoing partisan discord in many others. Yet none could overlook the popularity of the message and the means, and over time very few churches were able in conscience to repudiate "revivalistic religion" in toto, with or without distinctive New Haven features.

Even the Lutherans found a leader amenable to revivalistic principles. Samuel Schmucker, educated in the orthodox corridors of Princeton Seminary, became an advocate of making Lutheranism more at home in America. He worked within interdenominational circles and provided his support to the more activist features of American Protestantism, including the Sunday school and antislavery movements, and involvement in American Protestantism's virulent anti-Catholic biases. Though he upheld a limited role for a modified Augsburg Confession, he openly encouraged Lutherans to modify traditional beliefs in light of the Christian's personal experience of conversion. In most ways, he shared more in common with those Protestants sympathetic to the revivalism of Finney than with other Lutherans. Those Lutherans more in tune with the old-world style of Lutheranism had a strong representative in Charles Porterfield Krauth. His theological work defended the practices and confessions of historical Lutheranism and urged American Lutherans to resist the aberrations of an Americanized church.

Edwards had spoken of the Northampton revival and the First Great Awakening as a "surprising work of God." After the Second Great Awakening the work was no longer so utterly surprising, but had become a constituent feature of "evangelical" Protestantism. The newer revivals were still considered a work of God, one that involved preaching law and gospel, sinners dead in sin, and conversion by the Spirit. But there was much emphasis on the point that sinners were dead in sin only because they, rather than God, made themselves that way. And they were not so dead that they could not actively seek or, with the powers of human choice still available to them, choose to accept the way of salvation. The protests and the accommodations to this line of thinking makes the New Haven school paradigmatic rather than directly causative of far-reaching developments in theology. Its thought did come to define, for a long time, the meaning of *Calvinism* in the popular mind. And against this development both self-avowed "true" Calvinists and anti-Calvinists (Roman Catholics, Lutherans, "Arminian" Episcopalians and Methodists, direct heirs of the Radical Reformation, and many others, like Baptists, who themselves were divided by their mixed Reformed and radical lineage) had to contend.

New Haven leadership in antebellum America's Awakenings also directs attention to the early makings of trends, tensions, and conflicts in Protestant theology that come to the fore long after and far beyond that school's direct spheres of influence. Converts to basic, simple biblical truths might follow where their heads or their hearts led—to theological study, personal holiness, the sanctification of the world by social activism, or some combination of the three. They might also set out in quest of yet other, perhaps more profound and lasting, conversion experiences. Or, alternatively, they might seek some religious path more satisfying to the heart or the head than evangelical, commonsense faith. In short, the coalescence of historic doctrines, whether generically or genuinely Reformed, with a commonsense commitment to sound reasoning in science and theology, ethical imperatives of individual and social duty, and emphasis on stirrings of the heart (the source of New Haven theology's great strength), was not to be sustained easily, or for long.

Scottish Common-Sense Realism played an even more decisive role in the Princeton School Theology than in the New Haven school. For well over a century, from Archibald Alexander (1772–1851) to the departure of J. Grescham Machen (1881–1937), teaching focused on the defense of an orthodox doctrine derived from scripture, propounded in the Calvinist Westminster Confession of Faith, and altogether compatible with and commended by the principles of Common-Sense reason and genuine scientific inquiry. Charles Hodge, the most erudite and influential of the school's thinkers, integrated many elements in his lectures on systematic theology into a Presbyterian confessionalism that granted critics and opponents no quarter. That integration included the Westminster Confession, the dogmatics of Reformed Scholasticism (especially of Francis Turretin), and the "modern" scientific method of Scottish philosophy. Over against the uses of Scottish Common-Sense Thought by "liberals," Hodge sought a clear and well-defined reassertion of Reformation orthodoxy. Learning at Princeton—among the first institutions of post-graduate theological study in America and sponsor of the scholarly journal *The Biblical Repertory and Princeton Review*— was impressive, though very conventional.

Nathan Bangs and Phoebe Palmer represented several different facets of the Methodist stream, one which flowed in directions other than the New England schools of Calvinism, but shared in some of the currents of Scottish Common-Sense Realism. Bangs's theology presented a Methodist alternative to Calvinist ideas about salvation. Over against the New Divinity work of Hopkins and others, Bangs defended the universality of Christ's life and work. All human beings were capable of responding to Christ and by this means could receive the aid of the Spirit to become faithful. Crafting theological arguments that blended scripture and the philosophical leanings of commonsense reasoning, Bangs led Methodism into the theological arena traditionally dominated by other denominations. His theological interests did not, however, divert him from maintaining his interest in communicating with the people in the pew. Phoebe Palmer, for her part, worked to recover a concern for Christian perfection. Her theology described the immediacy of Christian sanctification and the role of the Christian in nourishing it toward Christian perfection.

The second wave of thought that brought about massive transformations of theology in America was post-Kantian romanticism. Like Scottish Realism, it was a response to the Enlightenment in the last half of the eighteenth century, but one by design (as it were) as well as in effects far more difficult to define. That is, the first appearances of broadly romantic responses to the Enlightenment, in literature more than philosophy or theology, were noteworthy as impulses of emotion that clashed with enlightened reason's calm quest for certainty, order, and harmony. And at its broadest, in its late as well as early forms, the term *Romanticism* is even more varied, multifaceted, and frankly amorphous than a label given to the wider extension of any particular school of thought. Romantics placed emphasis on the heights and depths of feeling, imaginative creativity, dynamic historical development, the organic relatedness of things, the sublime beauty of nature, and the nobility of artistic and ethical endeavor. Such emphases were as applicable to the uncanny, bizarre, and weird as they were to gushy sentimentalism. Romanticism, then, ends up pointing to an era (the "Romantic age"), diverse trends and traits (romantic music, art, literature, etc.), and a tenor or mood, including wistfulness and moodiness.

In terms of philosophy per se, Romanticism's point of departure was the "Copernican revolution" of Immanuel Kant. Kant sought in his own way, as Common-Sense thinkers in theirs, to respond to Hume's skepticism. Studies of the natural world (natural philosophy, the physical sciences) and the moral world (moral philosophy, ethics) focus on phenomena. These phenomena might be described as finite objects of human experience which are what they are because of a prior ordering of mind (e.g., Reason) that sets them in time and space and in cause-effect relations, and so forth. What things there are in the noumenal world, that is, the realm of objects as they are before or beyond the phenomenal world, is simply unknowable by "pure reason." So-called metaphysical proofs of the existence of God, for example, are, so far as Kant is concerned, only inconclusive speculations. God, freedom, and immortality belong to the noumenal realm, and so are beyond empirical verification; a faith in them can be justified only on the basis that they are necessary postulates of moral experience.

Motifs of Kant's thought were of more import to post-Kantian and Romantic thinkers than its details were. The lasting motifs included delineations of the noumenal realm (infinite and beyond the human senses) and the phenomenal realm of sensory experience (the finite). Kant's legacy also included the role of "higher" Reason in organizing the world of sensory and moral experience, the human self as a living point of contact between Infinite Spirit and human spirit, and the urging to turn from external, scientific "proofs" of God to inward evidences. Post-Kantian philosophy moved toward idealistic accounts of reality, speaking of God—the divine, the Infinite, the Absolute—as Mind or Spirit unfolding itself in the creation of the universe and returning to full self-awareness over the course of history through the highest aspirations of the human spirit. Far more widespread, since no special philosophical or theological training was necessary, were interminglings of post-Kantian and romantic themes. The striving, yearning, and longing for an awareness of the Infinite, which was beyond human senses yet already and always near at hand if only one had eyes to see and ears to hear, found expression in literature and the other arts. So too did romantic visions of times past and of a future yet to come, one where people realized oneness with God and one another. Romantic sensibilities grew in favor among cultured and genteel circles. Theology's early encounters with the "new" thought developing in Germany since the French Revolution, however, were typically "nasty, brutish, and short."

The Kantian revolution and the development of Romantic thought first had significant impact on the scholarly church theology of America in the 1830s. The best known of romanticism's manifestations were the Transcendentalists, led by Ralph Waldo Emerson, whose Divinity School Address at Harvard roiled New England Unitarianism by attacking the precepts of rational theology as outmoded, sterile, and lifeless. Emerson called for a theology of the future. Margaret Fuller, an antebellum feminist theologian, shared Emerson's vision and, like him, worked to shift the operating theological paradigm away from arguments about divine revelation to discussions about revelatory experiences of God, the latter providing considerably more solid footing for an appreciation of the equality of women.

William Channing's work represented that wing of Unitarianism Emerson opposed. Channing and his colleagues were, at heart, rational supernaturalists, who sought to free Christian faith from irrational and mistaken traditions of the past and to blend it anew with the dignity and potential they saw within humanity. They shared a high regard for scripture, and articulated a supernaturalism that focused on Christian revelation for its content. For the next several decades civil war raged within Unitarianism, dividing the rational supernaturalists of English-Scots empiricism and the younger generation fond of the German paradigm. Emerson himself had already resigned his pastorate in 1832, devoting himself to a ministry at large through his writings and lectures. Other Transcendentalists, however, aimed at transforming Unitarianism from within, and by the late half of the nineteenth century it had become much more diversified than the body of "liberal Christians" Channing and his associates had cultivated.

Two sparks flying from the Boston debates proved of consequence for Roman Catholic theology in America—Orestes Brownson and Isaac Hecker. Brownson's theological pilgrimage led him to Channing, and to

Unitarian and Universalist connections, on to Transcendentalism, and at length to the Roman Catholic Church. His Catholic conversion is indicative of the wider reach of Romanticism. So too was that of Isaac Hecker, Brownson's friend, Transcendentalist colleague, and fellow pilgrim. In Europe after the French Revolution, longings for the Infinite prompted fresh interest in the rich, enduring continuities of the catholic heritage. Among Roman Catholics, these promptings fostered, on the one hand, romantic love for church teachings and ways of pre-Reformation and pre-modern times or, on the other hand, romantic hope for a revitalization of ancient traditions along lines ushering in a new age of faith.

Similar interests—the conservative sort—arose within the Church of England in the 1830s, with the Oxford or Tractarian movement led by John Keble, Edward B. Pusey, and John Henry Newman, its foremost theologian. There was, then, a certain parallel in the fact that Newman, like Brownson and Hecker, entered the Roman Catholic Church and all three contributed to the development of nineteenth-century Catholic thinking, the first (Newman) as priest and bishop, the second (Brownson) as a lay intellectual, and the third (Hecker) as priest and founder of a new religious order.

The Oxford Movement itself, despite the departure of Newman and others, survived as a revival of catholicism within the Church of England, with significant effects on the liturgy, worship, and sensibilities of American Episcopalians as well as Anglicans in Britain during the second half of the century. One detects in the theological writings of many Episcopalians after the Civil War, such as William P. DuBose, the expression of the church's historic doctrines in distinctly Romantic tones.

The presence within Christian churches of theologians whose language and conceptual frame of reference was too foreign and radical even for "anti-Trinitarian rationalists" of the house of Channing to tolerate alarmed many other theologians. The Christian Transcendentalism represented in, but not exhausted by, the work of Emerson and Fuller seemed, to many theologians, to take confidence in both reason and human experience a bit too far. Thanks to Common-Sense thought, both the most confessionalist and the most revivalist advocates of evangelical faith had made their peace with what they considered truly right and good with respect to enlightened, critical thinking about Christian theology and to "modern" philosophy and science.

The pay-out benefits of these accords for the churches were high, and rising during the mid-nineteenth century. A re-shaking of the foundations seemed neither necessary nor desirable. Glances at trends in Europe, especially Germany, seemed only to justify George Washington's early warnings against American involvements in foreign conflicts. American Christians found there, under the umbrella of a union of church, state, and university, "theological" scholars of the church engaged in speculative fancy, questioning the reliability of biblical accounts of history and calling them legends, sagas, myths, and symbols, and freely reconstructing—or discarding—historic doctrine in the name of critical inquiry.

Factors such as these go at least partway in explaining the odd situation of the church theologians who applied the methods and results of ongoing, critical inquiry to the life and thought of the Protestant churches, as well as the controversies their theologies generated. Two of the most prominent were John Williamson Nevin (1803–1886) and Philip Schaff (1819–1893), who during the 1840s joined forces at the one struggling seminary, at Mercersburg, Pennsylvania, of the small German Reformed Church in America to develop the "Mercersburg Theology." Nevin was conversant with both the contemporary German theology and the trends of the Oxford Movement in England. Further, trained at Princeton, he possessed a strong sense of both the Reformed tradition and the conservative uses of the Common-Sense Realism represented in the theology of Charles Hodge, one of his teachers.

In his own work, Nevin took a more "mystical" approach to scripture, one based more securely in the intuition than in the inclinations of commonsense reasoning. Following Friedrich Schleiermacher's lead, Nevin expressed a profound interest in the human experience of God and in the spiritual growth related to it. But he strongly opposed the forms of it he found in the styles of "new measure revivalism" introduced by Finney and other New Haven evangelists. Instead, he mixed his concerns for the Reformed church heritage prior to the rise of "modern Puritanism" and for spiritual growth with a high doctrine of Christ and the church, one with particular emphasis on the sacraments as means of grace and the continuity between the theology of the Reformation and the formulations of the ancient creeds.

Another theologian with progressivist views during these years was Horace Bushnell. He helped to pioneer a new paradigm in the theological life of Congregationalists by stimulating and exemplifying uses of romantic views in theology and church life. Viewed by later generations as a key figure in the birth of Protestant liberalism, Bushnell led Congregationalists and others into the world of post-Kantian Romanticism.

Borrowing from both the Romanticism of Samuel Taylor Coleridge and the theology of Schleiermacher, Bushnell presented a more experiential approach to theology, one offering assurance that the presence and power of God was found intuitively in the midst of human experience. Over against the dominant tradition of Common-Sense Realism, Bushnell argued that, because of the imprecision of human language, no one could approach theology entirely scientifically or logically. Instead, he wrote of the metaphorical character of language. Words could only point in the direction of truth. They could not capture it completely. Thus, he had no sympathy for the propositional approach to truth found in the theological circles fond of Scottish Common-Sense Realism. In its place, he developed a theological method committed to openness and the search for religious truth wherever such openness might lead him.

After Bushnell, the varieties of Protestant liberalism soon exploded into a multitude of options. Though one could argue that all strands were deeply indebted to Bushnell, the one most clearly following in his steps was evangelical liberalism. Sharing Bushnell's proclivity to mediate faith and culture, these theologians were devoted to a christocentric focus and an ethical activism that would later develop into a full-blown social-gospel orientation. Among the first of this second generation of mediating theologians was Henry Boynton Smith. Just thirteen years younger than Bushnell, and living only one year longer, Smith was among the first of America's evangelical Protestants to travel to Germany for study. His theological education there caused him to question the adequacy of Scottish Common-Sense Realism and led him to affirm the methods being developed on the Continent. This shift lessened the importance placed on theological debates about the relationship between divine initiative and human agency and spurred a new interest in the social context of Christian living and the place of the life and teachings of Christ within it.

Prior to the Civil War, most theologians were also pastors. Those who taught in seminaries also ministered in churches. There were very few career theologians. Intellectual developments in the world of scholarship after the Civil War brought increased complexity to the vocation of theological endeavors. Charles Darwin's *Origin of the Species* immediately challenged traditional Christian conceptions of human beginnings and endings. In its wake, the relationship between religion and science took on new meaning. Serious theologians had to take the methods and results of science much more seriously than ever before. The main streams of American Protestantism worked toward bringing science and religion together in ways that would sacrifice the integrity of neither. Theologians integrated the scientific disciplines into their religious reflection in creative ways and became more aware of the changing nature of thinking about religious truth itself. Antoinette Brown Blackwell, the first woman ordained by mainstream Protestants, for example, felt it necessary to remind her readers that human beings tended to take themselves much too seriously and in the process misunderstood much of nature's law.

Liberalism grew into a dominant force among the Protestant churches of America in the late nineteenth and early twentieth centuries. Its influence was so widespread and its variations so many that the term, like so many of similar scope, defies strict definition. Various of its important characteristics are noted as a list of distinct emphases—religious experience; God's immanence in world and history; a historical approach to religion, including the historical-critical study of the Scriptures and the life and teachings of Jesus Christ; efforts to free the Christian doctrinal tradition of claims shown false or antiquated by advances in the sciences, the humanities, and culture at large; concern for the moral betterment of society as well as its individual members; and missionary activities devoted to extending the "blessings" of Protestant faith and modern civilization around the world. Interests such as these were often expressed as inspiring, ennobling ideals that were to find progressive realization on earth through dedication to the cause of Christ. The social base for liberalism's emphases was America's rising middle classes, increasingly well educated, prosperous, and involved in turning frontier communities into robust towns and towns into cities noteworthy for economic, cultural, and moral attainment. Liberal theology grew as its base grew, especially in northern states, which after the Civil War enjoyed opportunities and faced problems unlike those of the old Confederacy. Its church base rested in the "evangelical" churches, which despite their differences, shared common roots in the teachings of the magisterial Reformation (Reformed, Anglican, and Lutheran), and even before the Civil War had sought to unite forces against "sects," "infidels," and Roman Catholics.

Saying even this much about liberalism en masse sheds some light on its still disputed place in the history of Christian theology in America. The transition "from sect to church" that moved a number of Christian groups from marginal to "mainstream" status typically involved shifts in theology along liberal lines. By the same token, opponents of liberalism were a mixed company, including the strictest post-Reformation confessionalists, those least "blessed" by or admiring of where the nation was going, the most independent of independent churches, and vast numbers within and outside "old evangelicalism" beholden to the simple but bottom-line truths conveyed by revivalistic Christianity.

The rise of liberalism in these churches was judged quite differently by different people. Some viewed it as a compromise, perhaps abandonment, of Christian tradition; others, as a wholesome sifting of that tradition utterly necessary for its survival and vitality. The latter view was that of the largest camp of liberals—the evangelical, classical, or christocentric liberals with their new theology, progressive orthodoxy, and (in some cases) social-gospel messages. Like Horace Bushnell and Henry Boynton Smith, they were self-consciously mediating theologians, drawing upon contemporary resources in order to identify those elements of the Christian heritage of lasting value for the greatest needs and highest aspirations of the contemporary world. One of the most important questions asked by William Newton Clarke and other evangelical liberals was "How does God work in human life?"

The movement's characteristic emphases were outgrowths of a pattern of reasoning developed in the wake of Kant's Copernican revolution in philosophy and in the idiom of romanticism. The Christian faith, like every religious faith, is at root profound awareness of the living presence of God—the divine, the Infinite—in finite life. This presence, perfectly embodied and exemplified in the life of Jesus Christ, is shared by all of his true followers, renewing their lives and calling them to manifest a loving concern for the world like that which God made manifest in Christ. Both the language and the good works of faith arise as human responses to the divine life and its call. At their best, they are heartfelt and telling, but they are by their very nature only finite symbols of "God and things of God" cast in forms fit for their times and hence in need of recasting to serve their purposes in other contexts. Understanding the Scriptures involves probing behind the texts in order to grasp the original experiences of God being expressed there; preaching and teaching involve drawing out the abiding truths of those original experiences and expressing those truths anew in terms meaningful to people today. Theology is at root reflection on religious experience, and at its height a scholarly examination, appraisal, and—where apt—reformulation of church doctrine. Within this context, William P. DuBose and Newman Smyth worked as biblical scholars attempting to reinterpret Christian doctrine in light of historical-critical methodology.

Another distinct brand of liberalism, following in the school of evangelical liberalism but differing from it somewhat in its passion to apply the gospel specifically to social situations, came to be known as the social gospel. The main systematizer of this theological perspective was, of course, Walter Rauschenbusch. A trained church historian and theologian, Rauschenbusch shared with other evangelical liberals a desire to build a bridge between church and culture. In addition, he combined social-scientific methodology with theology to present a revolutionary Christ whose life contained profound implications for the social and political order. An emphasis on social themes was not limited, however, to liberal Protestants. The work of Frances Elizabeth Willard, national president of the Woman's Christian Temperance Union, illustrates the fact that segments of conservative evangelicalism found ways to participate actively in the various reform movements of the period. Most who did were transformed significantly in the process.

Many theologians attempted to hold the line against the kinds of transformations occasioned by either liberal styles of activism or liberal dependence on human experience instead of scripture. Particularly illustrative of these conservative tendencies were the next generation's theological standard-bearers for the Reformed Scholasticism of Charles Hodge. Chief among these was Benjamin Breckenridge Warfield, who held the fort as long as he could at Princeton Seminary. Throughout his career, he upheld the old alliance between Reformed orthodoxy and Scottish Common-Sense Realism well into the twentieth century. Ultimately, the battle was lost there, and new schools like Westminster Seminary in Philadelphia were founded to defend the rational Calvinism of the old Princeton school.

Several terms—*experience, history, loving concern,* and *scholarship*—are handy bridges to follow in tracking liberalism's broader currents. Religious experience invited explorations other than those that launched classical liberalism. It figured in studies of comparative religions and the history of (world) religions, which developed during the nineteenth century. Lydia Child, known for her work in abolitionism and women's rights, struggled to satisfy her own longings for spiritual truth. In the process, she wrote a very early theological analysis of other religions without succumbing to the temptation of privileging Christianity. Such studies would become increasingly prominent toward the end of the nineteenth century and beyond.

Liberalism's concern for human experience also stood many black theologians well in their efforts to address the hypocrisy of the American experiment with slavery and the resulting social problems caused by racial prejudice. Frederick Douglass's own life experience enabled him to make a powerful theological witness against the oppression of those forms of Christianity that tried to justify the unjustifiable. Alexander Crummell, though imbued with a liberal's confidence in the inevitability of progress, was able to encourage blacks to develop self-love and their own inner character as ways to defeat the prejudice and racism they encountered in the larger culture. Bishop Henry McNeal Turner, on the other hand, rejected the Eurocentric American confidence in progress, and provided a precedent for the black theology of the twentieth century when he declared without any qualification that "God is a Negro."

Religious experience also proved of vital interest to those in the budding fields of the social sciences, especially empirical psychology, and to the philosophers, among them the pioneering pragmatists and naturalists. With or without explicit church affiliation, such scholars were not "teachers of the church" intending to contribute to the doctrinal tradition. They wrote as sociologists, psychologists, historians, and philosophers of religion, and with the expansion and differentiation of scholarly disciplines, it was customary for them—and others—to announce that they were not "theologians."

Their research, however, would have massive influence on liberal theology, and at least some of their writings addressed issues of theology so knowledgeably and insightfully that they put the "theologians" to shame. Among those in this group must be counted both William James and Josiah Royce. They took the connection between science and religion to new heights and began an empirical study of religious experience that influenced later theology to a considerable degree.

The theology of Borden Parker Bowne illustrates a use of the social sciences and philosophy designed for church service. He combined a social-scientific methodology with strands of Romanticism and neo-Kantianism and a scientific approach to the Bible to develop a personalist theology. The philosophical result provided Methodist theology with a scientifically credible response to American tendencies toward materialism and cast the Methodist concern for human responsibility in entirely new expressions. Personalism joined the accumulation of the data of personal experience with the methods of scientific research in order to posit an understanding of the nature of the world and the place of human beings within it. In some ways, Bowne's work depended upon the earlier efforts of Daniel D. Whedon, who developed an indigenous form of Methodism. Whedon continued the more traditional Methodist theological focus upon the relationship between human freedom and divine sovereignty. But he also provided Methodist tradition with a liberal twist by giving greater attention to human experience than to scripture. By doing so, he helped to bring Methodist theology into line with the American democratic liberalism of the mid-nineteenth century and paved the way for the kind of developments represented in Bowne's theological endeavors.

Another development of the early twentieth century is represented in the work of the scientific modernists. This empirical school had little use for philosophical idealism and preferred the more functional approach represented in the writings of John Dewey. These thinkers pushed beyond the borders of developing Christian liberalism. Their work relied more completely on sociohistorical methodology and transformed the theological enterprise into an analysis of how purposefulness could be found within the human experience. When uncovered by scientific analysis, and revealed to be consistent and coherent, this purposefulness demonstrated the empirical reality of God that must stand behind it. These modernists, represented early by Shailer Mathews and other members of the faculty at the University of Chicago Divinity School (hence the name of the "Chicago School"), provided a style of empirical and social research that served many theologians well over the next several generations. This empirical strand was continued in the theological work of both Douglas C. Macintosh of Yale and Henry Nelson Wieman of Chicago. Macintosh reflected more traditional concern with the themes of theology than did Wieman. He developed empirically based arguments on behalf of what he and many others regarded as the central tenets of Christian faith. Wieman's empiricism represented a more explicit brand of theocentric naturalism. He found God in the natural workings of the universe toward a progressive integration.

The decade of the 1920s found the party of liberals or "modernists" and that of their opponents (allied under the banner of fundamentalism) in power struggles for institutional control of the Protestant churches dominant in America. Liberal successes on that front sparked further church separations. These, combined with highly publicized controversies like the Scopes trial, a Pyrrhic victory for the anti-Darwin cause, brought fundamentalism into discredit. A season of demoralization, disarray, and serious reevaluation followed, first after World War II and then, more powerfully, after the war in Vietnam, before conservative survivors of the "old" church battles regrouped. Their theologians developed quite different attitudes toward both theological tradition and contemporary life than their predecessors and took in new allies, ultimately rising to renewed popularity as representatives of "(neo-)evangelical Christianity." Its more popular forms surfaced first in the revivalism of Billy Graham and later in the youth movements associated with Youth for Christ and Campus Crusade. Its scholarly forms were represented in the theological writings of Carl F. H. Henry and Edward J. Carnell.

For churches noted for liberalism (a term fast becoming ever more generic and theologically vague), the future that for a brief time had seemed secure was to be the opposite. The "liberal" label would stick, sometimes and in some quarters used as badge of honor for purposes of self-identification but, more and more over the decades, as a concession to common use in sociology and the news media rather than as a crisp description of theological conviction or idiom.

Theologically, however, "liberalism" entered—as early as the 1920s—times of trial from which it never fully recovered, at the end no longer a groundbreaking advance but a "classical" moment of theology's history. This "ironic" turn was primarily due to insurgencies within its own camp. The first was led by younger theologians, well schooled and church committed. They judged liberalism's optimism about human goodness, the realization of Christian "ideals" by goodwill and good works, and the march of civilization to be a naive and shallow response to the horrors of World War I and the problems arising in its aftermath. The names given to this development and its outcomes reflect its variety—dialectical, neo-Reformation, neoorthodox, or crisis theology; "Barthianism"; and, especially in its American forms, Christian realism.

The first forms of its appearance harken back to various early postwar contacts between independent-minded thinkers including Karl Barth, Emil Brunner, Rudolf Bultmann, and Paul Tillich. These discussions highlighted dialectical thinking as a mark distinguishing the new lines of thought, moving over time in quite different directions, from those typical of both liberalism and its critics alike. God and things of God defy encapsulation in simple, straightforward terms; instead, they are to be understood and stated by juxtaposing statements and counter statements, which remain unresolved paradoxes to reason and relativities of human history. So, too, Christian faithfulness to God is not unqualified commitment to either the march or the halt of "progress," but a ("existential," "crisis") faith-decision made at each moment amid ever-changing, complex, ambiguous, and difficult circumstances.

A "recovery" of the most paradoxical themes both of scripture (especially the writings of Paul) and the reformers Luther and Calvin was another striking feature of the new trends. Emphasis and sustained dialectical reflection on the divine initiative in revelation, the unique character and content of the biblical message, God's "otherness" and sovereignty, the meaning and scope of sin, the gospel of Christ crucified, grace, and other elements of faith's "distinctive language" warranted the names neo-Reformation or neoorthodox. The latter seems now on its way to becoming the standard umbrella term in histories of theology, and is helpful so long as stress is on "neo" and note is made that "the movement's" finest minds sought in notably different ways to reexamine and reformulate Christianity's biblical-doctrinal heritage not in order to (re-)gain a lost orthodoxy but in order to draw from it insights on the objects and life of faith all too often missed, forgotten, or dismissed by traditional liberalism.

Here the names Reinhold and H. Richard Niebuhr are the most prominent, though the second brother listed here differed from the classical neoorthodoxy of the first. Reinhold stressed the realities of power and offered an assessment of the human condition before God that took seriously both the possibilities of human potential and the perils of human sin. By way of his thorough treatment of a self-styled "objective relativism," H. Richard offered a more confessional approach to theology than Reinhold. He held that human beings could only approach knowledge of the universal from a historically limited point of view. Rather than taking the skeptical turn of contemporary postmodernism, he preferred to confess his relativism and then proceed confidently to examine the nature of God and reality from that point of view.

The temper of the new theologies, varied as they were, was even perhaps more disconcerting to liberals and modernists than the substance they represented, and in retrospect that seems altogether apt. Their substance shared the liberal preference for a christocentric approach, always appreciative of free and open inquiry in the arts, humanities, and sciences, supportive of critical scholarship in theology, and concerned for social, economic, and political as well as ecumenical issues. American Fundamentalists who first took heart at word of brilliant young scholars in Europe who challenged the liberal thinking of their teachers did not rejoice long after a closer look. At midcentury the signature themes of neoorthodox, realistic thought had extended far beyond its original base, embracing not only multiple schools of theology but movements in biblical theology, church history, Christian education, worship, ecumenism, and ethics. They cut across the Protestant theological spectrum, laying claim to a broad center.

Georgia Harkness, for example, fashioned the critical realism of

Reinhold Niebuhr, the social-gospel commitments of Walter Rauschenbusch, and the personalism of Borden Parker Bowne into her own brand of liberal evangelicalism. Martin Luther King, Jr., put personalism to more pragmatic and prophetic uses. He taught a generation of blacks by his example and his message what it meant to be given the worthy and God-given gift of human personhood. Though he found his liberalism tempered by the corrective that neoorthodoxy offered concerning human nature, King never felt fully at home in either theological camp, preferring instead to live out his theology through his commitment to right the wrongs of social injustice. King's commitment to the civil religious themes of American life, sounded often to demonstrate how far short of their ideals the American people fell, was not shared by all other black theologians in the twentieth century. Marcus Garvey promoted an early version of liberation theology, preaching liberation from the American civil religion that oppressed all black people through his own commitment to black nationalism.

That center of liberal brands of theology seemed to expand with the election of John F. Kennedy as the first Roman Catholic President of the United States, the civil rights movement, and, most especially, through Vatican II. The theology of John Courtney Murray marks a new maturity in Catholic theology, one fully at home in the culture of the American democratic experiment. His work represented a distinctively Catholic approach to theology while at the same time engaging the theology of the Protestant ecumenical church with a creative appreciation for the meaning of modern religious pluralism. The pluralism in America also grew to embrace the work of theologians representing Eastern Orthodoxy. This acceptance owed no small debt of gratitude to the ecumenical commitments found in the theological reflections of Georges Florovsky and John Meyendorff.

Among Protestants, process thought emerged as an option for interpreting the church's doctrinal tradition and serving the interests of practical theology and ministry. Process philosophy was not itself new, having arrived in America with Alfred North Whitehead when he moved from Cambridge to assume a chair in philosophy at Harvard and having gained adherents between World War I and World War II. Process philosophy emphasized that all of human life was experientially complex, dynamic, developmental, evolutionary. Whitehead's philosophy found a theological home at the University of Chicago in the work of the philosopher of religion Charles Hartshorne and theologians such as Bernard Meland and Bernard Loomer and, later, Daniel Day Williams.

Of special appeal to a number of Christian theologians was process thought's commitment to a metaphysical grounding for claims to truth in science, philosophy—and theology. Reality as process allowed for diverse, interrelated, and changing relations within experience and nonetheless justified claims about reality, rooted in and tested by analyses of actual experience, rather than merely subjective feelings or dictates of authority. The concept of the dipolarity of God, one pole unchanging and the other pole actually affected by the unfolding of the events of the universe and human history, was also significant for theologians. It offered, in view of some, a via media between naturalist, pragmatist, and functionalist accounts of the "idea of God" on the one hand and the revival of "supernaturalism" among neoorthodox thinkers on the other.

The popularity of the movement, however, increased early in the second half of the twentieth century as theologians applied process categories to church doctrines in addition to the nature of God and the "metaphysical" relationship between God and the world. The movement remained a distinctly "liberal" alternative to neoorthodoxy, but through engagement with a range of themes of scripture and church tradition as well as self-conscious efforts to bring process thinking into dialogue with existentialist, neoorthodox, and realist positions, it gained standing in seminary and graduate school studies as a resource for church theologians.

The career and writings of John Cobb, a philosophical theologian forthright about his concerns for the church generally and his own Methodist connections in particular, were at once illustrations of and influences on these developments.

But the later 1960s and 70s were to dispel any illusions of a theological middle ground, however broad. *Ferment, pluralism, creativity,* and *chaos* are the terms most frequently used to speak of Christian theology at the century's end, each term obviously a value-laden judgment. Perhaps, then, it is most apt to suggest that the most common and persistent feature of the multifarious theologies of recent times has been a preoccupation, implicit even when not explicit, with the relationship(s) between particularities and generalities.

This characterization itself, a summary overview, is as likely to illustrate as it is to pinpoint the "problem" at issue. It tries to capture, in only a phrase, a multitude of particular theologies and theologians, as though the particularities of each and differences among them can be embraced by singling out some "common" characteristic that is presumably more basic or otherwise important than the particularities and differences themselves. But who is it that dares make such a generalized claim, and with what right, on what grounds, and for what aims does one dare to do so? Such questioning is by no means altogether new in the history of Christian theology, but it arises in new forms and with new force in current theological discussion. How to handle the gains and the losses, and their unequal distribution, that attend every attempt to speak of "God and things of God" has moved to the forefront of theology's agenda.

Concern for dynamic interpretations of God and world have figured prominently in black theology and feminist theology, as it has in liberation theologies worldwide, and in other movements that draw nourishment from rootage in the particularities of identity—ethnic, national, economic, sexual, and cultural. It is characteristic for such theologies to focus on the biblical themes of liberation and justice, protesting against the still ongoing history of discriminations, injustices, and oppressions by which one group maintains its privileges at the expense of others and pressing for aggressive action to alter the status quo. They are in one sense a resurgence and expansion of the tradition of moral and social reform that has played a major role in the history of theology in America. But they are in another sense a questioning and reworking of that tradition as well as the rest of theology's history.

It is characteristic of such theologies to break apart and then reconfigure the categories, the "generalities," used to state the church's faith, its life, and its theology. These efforts are more than updating theology's ideas and language or adding to the list of Christian moral and social concerns. There emerges instead a realization that the churches and their theologies have created generalizations about what faith, scripture, doctrine, and church mean, as though what it has meant to them, and for them, is its true meaning. As a result, conversation about theology itself has been structured so that those "other" than themselves have been excluded from it.

Absent the insights into the meaning of faith that these "others" have gained from the particularities of their experiences of scripture and church heritage over the course of their history, theology itself has perpetuated multiple systems of oppression despite—and even during—its self-avowedly "good faith" efforts to resist evil and promote good. James Cone's powerful book of 1969, *Black Theology and Black Power,* marked a significant turn both in the terms and the tenor of theology in America. His demand that the theology of African Americans be heard and his showing of the theological productivity of the results represented a paradigm shift in thinking that was reflected also in writings by feminist theologians like Mary Daly, Rosemary Ruether, and Sallie McFague, womanist theologians like Jacqueline Grant and Delores Williams, and other liberationists.

A notable feature of these movements is a refusal to treat even liberation and justice as "generalities." The notion that the themes of scripture and doctrine carry some single, self-enclosed, and suprahistorical meaning is illusory. They were understood differently at their origins, exposited in one way by oppressors and in other ways by the oppressed. Neither routine historical-critical nor philosophical nor doctrinal analyses have adequately probed the ramifications of historical rationales for patriarchy, racism, and other forms of injustice built into the very fabric of theology's sources, authorities, methods, and contents. Hence reconstruction of theology is radical transformation rather than mere conceptual revision. Finally, it is not to be expected that the end product of theology will be an account of what faith means everywhere, always, and to all. The Christian message of liberation is discovered, recovered, understood, and worked out differently by different peoples and groups and in the context of ongoing struggles for freedom, dignity, and justice.

Likewise reflective of concern for the handling of particularities and generalities in the last third of the century are myriad inquiries and proposals regarding theological method, the language of religion itself and Christian theology especially, hermeneutics, and interdisciplinary as well as interfaith issues. Diverse liberation theologies, as noted, have engaged such issues, and in so doing have illustrated as well as contributed to the revived, at times radical, reconsideration of method that is a hallmark of theology at the end of this century. The focus of attention in the theologies that come in discussion here, however, is not any one or more of theology's themes but questions of the rationale and aims of theology itself and the approach to be taken in theological reflection.

In this regard, like quite a few others in American history the decade of the sixties was a turning point. Even as the lines of thought developed by Barth, Bultmann, Tillich, and Reinhold and H. Richard Niebuhr reached their apex, many of their students as well as others grappled with the "meaningfulness" and validity of key elements of those theological projects, such as revelation, the "mighty acts of God," "the Christ of faith," "the kerygma," emerging ecumenical "consensus," and "realistic" solutions to contemporary problems. Dramatic in their breadth, such themes were also "generalities" in need of ever-increasing qualification in light of diversity, exceptions, details—in a word, differences.

What had been a "center" in the sense of a midrange of more or less neoorthodox and liberal positions along a spectrum did not so much collapse as much as it dispersed into units now free-floating without unity. Quests for revised or radically new approaches to theology were one result.

It is not unusual for theologians at work on such issues to make heavy use of insights and resources from other fields of scholarship, for instance, movements in German, French, or Anglo American philosophy, linguistics, literary theory, anthropology, sociology, or psychology, to name but a few. The results of such uses—both borrowings and sustained conversations—are in some cases highly specialized and in others strikingly eclectic efforts to handle particularities and generalities within theology. And, not surprisingly, they represent or lead to a wide variety of theological positions, not infrequently characterized as revivals of theology's historic tradition (as some have cast the work of George Lindbeck), or as bold departures from that tradition (as some have described the work of Thomas J. J. Altizer).

The truth of such claims is to be tested in each particular instance. But to generalize—as though these diverse particulars are not in every respect unlike—it might be said that theology in recent times continues to explore Christian theology's perennial issues: if theology has to do with God and things of God, how is it possible for humans to speak of these matters, what do they mean when they do so, and how are they to measure the adequacy of their statements?

# THE COLONIAL ERA

(1607–1789)

# Thomas Hooker

*The* writings of Thomas Hooker (1586–1647), along with
John Cotton's that follow, are samples of "the marrow of divinity"
taught by early New England Puritans. A leader of the Puritan party in
the Church of England with an M.A. from Cambridge University,
Hooker escaped persecution by flight to the Massachusetts Bay Colony.
Arriving in 1633, he helped found the Hartford colony, draft Connecticut's constitution (Fundamental Orders, 1638), and form a New England Confederation. His thought commanded international attention.

Puritanism's quest of a reformed church, sound in its doctrine, worship,
order, and discipline, was the vital center of Hooker's work. The selection
here is a digest of his understanding of the elements constituting the church
on earth, as presented in A Survey of the Summe of Church Discipline. His
analysis of the church in terms of scholastic categories (efficient, material,
and formal causes) is illustrative not only of Puritan emphasis on the theme
of covenant but also of the rational handling of "biblical doctrine" typical
of Reformed orthodoxy in post-Reformation Protestant scholasticism.
Hooker's arguments with opponents have been excised so that his own
constructive view of the church can unfold more directly and fully.

## A SURVEY OF THE SUMME OF CHURCH DISCIPLINE

*Chap. II The Constitution of a visible Church*
*in the Causes thereof: The Efficient and Matter.*[1]

. . .

We now come to enquire of the *visible Church in her first constitu-*
*tion and gathering.*

And in the handling of this, we shall take into consideration such speciall Questions, wherein there appears any difference betwixt us, and
our Reverend and very learned Brethren, desirous to propound things,
wherein difficulties yet appear unto us, hoping some further evidence

47

may be given for the manifestation of the truth, which we only seek, if we know what we seek: and therefore would live and learn; only while we thus beleeve, we thus speak.

*The causes of a visible Church,* which will make most for the clearing of the subject we have in hand, are the *Efficient,* As also the *Materiall,* and *Formall.*

### Of the Efficient

Concerning the *Principall cause* and Institutour of a visible Church, there is a common concurrence of all sides, so far as I can reade, and therefore I shall ease the Reader of all large discourse in this behalf.

It shall be enough to point out the truth, as it is expressed in Scripture: namely, The institution of the Church issues from the speciall appointment of *God the Father, thorow* [through] *the Lord Jesus Christ,* as the head thereof, *by the holy Ghost,* sent and set on work for that end. So the Apostle speaks most pregnantly and plainly, *Heb.3.31. For this man* (meaning *Christ) was counted worthy of more honour then Moses, inasmuch as he that hath builded the house, hath more honour then the house. Christ is set over the Church,* which is, *the house of God, as the Sonne, Moses as a servant.* He the master-builder, *Moses* as an Inferiour and underworkman. And *vers.4. For every house is builded by some man, but he that buildeth all things is God.* This *ALL* is to referred to the things that went before, to wit, the *things of the house.*

What ever belongs to the Church hath God in Christ the Authour of it. And hence in the old Testament it was given in charge to *Moses,* that as *he saw* all presented before him *in the Mount,* in a lively manner, so he must be cautious and conscientious to hold himself to that patern, not to swerve an hairs breadth there-from, or to adde any thing of his own devising. And hence our Saviour claims this as his prerogative royall, *Mat. 16. Upon this rock I will build my Church.* It is his house, and he knows his own minde, and therefore he only will fashion it thereunto. And from hence it is, that in the time wherein *Ezekiel* would limme out, and that unto the life, the *Temple* to be erected in the *new Testament,* he there laies out all the particulars by Gods speciall appointment; The *Outgoings* and *Incomings, Forms, Fashions, Laws* thereof, and the *Ordinances* thereof.[2]

Touching *the Inferiour helping cause,* viz, *The Civil Magistrate,* how farre he may be said to have a hand in the erecting of Churches, It is that which hath exercised the heads and pens of the most judicious, and is too large for this place, and our purpose, we willingly passe it by, being not yet perswaded that the chief Magistrate should stand a Neuter, and tolerate all Religions.

Of the Matter

Proceed we to make enquiry of the *Matter,* and there (though it hath not so much Art in it, yet because it hath more use, and indeed more evidence, in regard of all, to whom we addresse this our enquiry; sith it concerns all, who seek the good of Church-fellowship, as all need it, if they were worthy to share therein). Our first conclusion is negative.

Conclusion 1.

*Parish precincts, or the abode and dwelling within the bounds and liberties of such a place, doth not give a man right, or make him matter fit for a visible Congregation.*

Reason 1. *No civil rule can properly convey over an Ecclesiasticall right.* The rules are *in specie* distinct, and their works and ends also, and therefore cannot be confounded.

*Civil power* hath a *nourishing* and *preserving* faculty of Ecclesiastical Orders, Officers, and their serverall operations. *Kings shall be nursing Fathers,* &c. But in their *proper constitutions,* they cannot meet. *Imperare* and *praedicare* are not compatible, hath been a ruled case, admitting no contradiction in an ordinary way: one is compleat, and hath all the causes without the other, and therefore one doth not receive his constitution in whole or in part from the other. Civil power may compell Ecclesiasticall persons to do, what they ought in their offices, but doth not confer their Offices upon them. The Kingdom of Christ is spirituall, and not of this world. That *Proposition* then is beyond controul. The *second* is open to experience.

*But the taking up an abode or dwelling in such a place or precincts is by the rule of policy and civility.* A man hath it by inheritance from his parents, or purchaseth it by his money, or receives it by gift or exchange. *Ergo, This can give him no Ecclesiasticall right to Church-fellowship.*

Reason 2. *That right which any man hath in Church-fellowship, Excommunication out of a Church can, nay doth take away.* For Excommunication is, according to the intent of the Word, The *cutting off* from all Church-communion: and what ever right before he had in his admission, is now disanulled by his Excommunication. *Let him be as an Heathen,* Mat. 18.

*But Excommunication doth not, nor can take away a mans civil right* to the house and land, the civil priviledges he doth posesse, or remove him from the right of his habitation, civil office or authority, he is invested in.

*Ergo, That is no Ecclesiasticall right.*

*Reas.*3. If Parish Precincts should have right to Church-fellowship, then Atheists, Papists, Turks and profane ones, who are enemies to the truth and Church, yea men of strange Nations and languages, who neither know, nor be able to do the duties of Church members, should be fit matter for a Church, because they have abode in such places: yea those should have right to whom Christ hath denied right, *Revel.*21.27.

Much more might here be added, but that the tenet is so grosse, that I suppose any, seriously judicious, will see the errour of it.

We shall come nearer home then, and our

2d Conclusion is,

*Visible Saints only are fit Matter appointed by God to make up a visible Church of Christ.*

The *terms* shall be, 1. *Opened.* 2. *The Question stated.* 3. *The Conclusion proved.*

*Saints* as they are taken in this controversie, and in the currant expressions of Scripture, which look this way, and speak to this subject *(Saints at Corinth, Saints at Philippi, at Rome, in Caesars house)* were members of the Churches, comprehending the Infants of confoederate believers under their Parents Covenant, according to 1 *Cor.*7.14. and such constant expressions of Saintship do intimate, that either *they were such,* or at least conceived to be *such in view* and *in appearance.* I say in *appearance*: for when the Scripture so terms and stiles men, we must know that *Saints* come under a double apprehension. *Some* are *such* according to *Charity: Some* according *to truth. Saints* according to *charity* are such, who in their practice and profession (if we look at them in their course, according to what we see by experience, or receive by report and testimony from others, or lastly, look we at their expressions) *they favour so much, as though they had been with Jesus. From all which,* as farre as *rationall charity* directed *by rule* from *the Word,* a man cannot but conclude, That *there may be some seeds of some spirituall work of God in the soul. These* we call *visible Saints* (leaving *secret things to God*) in our view, and according to the reach of rationall charity, which can go no further, then to hopefull fruits. We say and *hope,* and so are *bound* to *conceive they are Saints*: though such be the secret conveyances, and hidden passages of hypocrisie, that they may be gilt, not gold, seemingly such only, not savingly, known to God and their own hearts, not known to others. So *Judas, Demas, Simon Magus, Ananias,* &c. And therefore our Saviour proceeds with such, not *as God* who knows the heart, but in a *Church-way,* as those who judge the tree by the fruit. *De occultis non judicat Ecclesia,* That which the Church doth not see, it cannot censure. *Some mens sins go before, & some come after,* 1 *Tim.*5.24.

*The STATE* then of the *QUESTION* is this. Persons, though they be hypocrites inwardly, yet if their conversations and expressions be such, so blamelesse and inoffensive, that according to *reason* directed by the

*Word,* we cannot conclude, but in *charity* there *may be, and is some speciall spirituall good* in them; *These are fit matter of a visible Church* appointed and allowed by Christ: and that for these Reasons.

*Reason 1.*

From the *nature of a visible Church* rightly constituted,

It is truly stiled, and truly judged by Scripture light to be the *visible body of Christ,* over whom he is a *Head,* by *Politicall Government* and guidance, which he lends thereunto, 1 *Cor.* 12.12. And that it is a visible politick body, appears quite thorow the whole Chapter, but especially, *v.*27,28. Because in *that Church God sets Orders and Officers, Some Apostles, Teachers, Helpers, Governments.* The like to this, *Ephes.*4.12.13. Where these *Officers* are, it is supposed there be *visible* concurrences of many *Saints* consenting, both to *choose* such, and to *subject* unto such being chosen. Whence the Argument proceeds,

*The members of Christs body are fit alone to be members of a true Church,* because that is the body of Christ, *ex concessis.*

*But only visible Saints, who according to the rules of reasonable charity may be conceived to have some speciall good in them, are only members of Christs body.*

For to have a member, which nor doth, nor ever did receive any power or vertual impression of any operation in the kinde of it from the head, is not onely against reason, but *against that reference and correspondence, which the members have to the head.* Now visible Saints onely, according to former explication, can be said by the rules of reasonable charity, to have some vertuall influence of some spirituall operation from Christ as a Head.

Therefore *Such onely are members of a Church.*

Reason. 2.

*Those are fit to be members of Christs Church, that are subjects in Christs Kingdome.*

The *Church is the visible kingdome* in which *Christ* reigns, by the scepter of his word and ordinances, and the execution of discipline. *To whomsoever* he is a *Head,* over them he *will be King.* He is *our King;* He is *our lawgiver.* The *Church* is his *House,* and he is *Master* and *Ruler* of it. They who carry themselves, in *professed rebellion,* they are *Traitors,* not subjects. The members of the *Body* are under the *motion* and guidance of the *Head. Wolves* and *Cancers* are contrary to it. Members are in *subordination,* Wolves and Cancers are in *opposition* to the Head.[3]

*But visible Saints* (as formerly described) *are onely subjects in this kingdome.*

51

Christ is the *King of Saints* (not of drunkards and whoremongers, Atheists, *&c.*) they alone proclaim subjection in their practice: They onely attend to know and doe the will and command of God, or in case they swerve aside, and be carried unawares and unwittingly into conspiracie, yet are they willing to see, ready to yeeld, and come in again. But such, who cry, *hail Master, kisse Christ* and *betray him*: that in words professe the truth, but in *deeds deny* it, and are to *every good work reprobate, Sonnes of Belial,* who can bear no yoke, but *break all cords,* and *cast all commands behinde their backs,* these are *convicted rebells,* but are not *subjects* of Christs kingdome.

As a *Generall* of the field, he will overpower these, and *destroy* them *as* his *enemies,* but not *govern* them as *leige people,* and therefore he professeth to such, as would not have him to rule over them, that they were his enemies. *Bring hither mine enemies, and slay them before mine eyes.*
*Reason. 3.*

If those who be visible Saints, be not those that are only fit to be members, then those who are not visible Saints, that is such who in the judgement of rationall charity, are gracelesse persons for the present, and give up themselves to the swinge of their distempers, they may be members.

The consequence is beyond dispute, for contradicents divide the breadth of being.

*If visible Saints onely be not;*
*Then non-visible may be.*

*But this draws many absurdities with it:* For then such who to the judgement of charity are *members of the devil,* may be conceived *members of Christ. Those,* who to the eye of reason, are *servants to sin,* may be *servants of righteousnesse* and of Christ: and those, who are under the *kingdome of darknesse* by the rule of reasonable charity, by *the same rule,* at *the same time,* they may be judged under the *kingdome of light.* Those may be counted fit to *share in the covenant* and the priviledges thereof, as Sacraments and Church society, who are *strangers from the covenant, and without God in the world.* All which are absurdities, that common sense will not admit.

If it be replied, that all these may be verified of cunning hypocrites not yet discovered.

I answer: The Argument leaves no place for the appearance of such an objection: for the terms in open expression are pointed directly against such, that in the judgement of charity were not Saints: and then the difference is exceeding wide. *Those that are darknesse,* and the *servants of sin inwardly,* may to the *view of charity* seem to *be light,* and servants of

Christ *outwardly*, and yet in *charity* be led by light. But that he who in his outward practice should appear to be a slave to sin, and subject to the kingdome of darknesse, should yet be conceived to be a servant to God and subjected to his kingdome: Surely *charity* must not onely pluck out her eies to see by anothers spectacles, but loose eies and spectacles and all, and cease to be *charity*; yea be turned into *folly* and madnes.

*Reason.* 4.

*Those* who by God are *excluded* from *his convenant* and medling with *that*, as *unfit*, they are *not fit* to have *communion* with the *Church*: For to *that* all the *holy things of God* do in an especiall manner *appertain*.

Its *Gods house*, and there all Gods treasury lies: The *keyes of the kingdome* are given to them: To them all *the oracles*, ordinances and priviledges do belong, *&c.*

*But those* who *hate to be reformed*, and *cast away his commands*, God professeth, *they have nothing to do to take his covenant into their mouth*, Psal.50.16,17.

. . .

But before we leave the conclusion, we shall make some *inferences* from it, which may further help us in our proceedings and purpose in hand. Something hence may be collected for the discovery of sundry *mistakes* in the *Separatists*, wherein they *go aside* from the truth. Something observed, for *to clear their* way, wherein they go along with it.

*Inference.* 1.

If *visible Saints* be *fit matter* for to make a Church, *Then Church fellowship presupposeth* them to be *such*, but properly *doth not make* them *such*.

*Inference.* 2.

And hence, such *mistakes* in *judgement* or *practice* that do *not hinder* men from *being visible Saints*, doe not *unfit men* from *being members* of a Church.

*Inference.* 3.

Hence, the *holding* of the *visible Churches in England* to be *true Churches* (suppose it were an *errour*, which *it is not*) doth not *hinder* men from being *fit matter* for a visible Church.

*Inference.* 4.

Hence lastly, the *not being* in a *Church*, doth *not hinder private* Christian *communion*.

The two last inferences, are the *Tenets* of those of the *Separation*, not onely extreamly *rigid*, but very *unreasonable*. For if they be fit matter for publique communion, they are much more fit for private: But men

53

are or should be visible Christians before they come into Church fellowship, and are thereby fitted for it, and therefore much more fitted for private communion.

. . .

### 3. Conclusion,

*Churches constituted of fit matter may be corrupted by the breaking forth of scandals, and pestered with scandalous, persons which may so far be tolerated, until in a judiciall way, the censures of the Church be exercised upon them, according to the rule of Christ, and they thereby reformed or else removed and cut off from the body.*

There be *three branches* in the conclusion, which hold forth evidence of truth at the first sight, and therefore we shall not stay long upon proof.

That *Churches rightly constituted may soon be corrupted,* the Scriptures are pregnant which testifie it, and experience is so plain, it is past gainsaying, at *Corinth, Galatia, Sardis, Laodicea,* &c. And above all, this is to be seen in the *Church of the Jews,* the canker of falsenesse in doctrine, and corruption in manners, had so far eaten into the very *essence* of the Church, *Hos.2.2.9.* that the Lord threatned her to give her *a bill of divorce,* and to cast her out of his sight as not his wife.

2. Yet in such declining times, when deseases grow deadly, there is allowed, and *a toleration of necessity must be so far granted, untill* Juridice *by a judiciall preceeding the evil be examined, the parties convinced, censures applied for Reformation.* For the Ordinances of Christ and rules of the Gospel serve, not only for the *constitution* of a Church, but for the *preservation* of it. That is the main scope of our Saviour his government: first, to gain a sinner if it may be, *for he came not to condemn the World* (men can condemn themselves fast enough) *but to save it,* and the censures of the Church are sufficient to recover the sick and defeated, as well as to nourish the sound.

And hence our Saviour requires time of triall, if they may be healed, and untill that be over, they must be tolerated. Cutting off is only used when things come to extremity. *If he will not hear, let him be as an Heathen,* &c. Therefore had he heard and submitted to the censure of the Church, and been gained thereby to repentance and reformation, there had needed no further proceeding.

But in case they prove incorrigeable and irrecoverable by the physick used, they are then to be abandoned. *Purge out the old leaven,* 1 Cor.5. cast out such an one.

And hence it is evident, the corrupting of a Church constituted gives no allowance to bring in corrupt members to the constitution of a

Church, but the contrary, if a pertinacious member should be removed by the rule of the Gospel, then such a one should not be admitted.
. . .

*Chap. IV. Of the Formall cause of a visible
Church, the Church Covenant.*

We have done with the *Materiall* cause of a visible Church: and we have seen such as be *visible Saints* make up that.

We are now come to consider of the *Formall* cause, *that* which *makes* the Church to be that which *it is* and gives the *specificall nature* (as we use to speak) thereunto.

For take *all* the *faithfull* whether they be seemingly or sincerely such, *scattered up and down* the face of the whole earth, these are but like scattered stones in the street, or timber felled in the woods, as yet there is neither *wall* made up, nor frame erected.

They who be *sincere* are truly said to be the *mysticall* body of Christ, built upon him by a saving faith, and so injoy *union* to, and *communion* with the *head*: But they cannot (to common sense) be taught to make up a *visible communion* when they are, not only *severed* from one another, but it may so fall out, as in times of persecution, they may be wholly *unknown* each to the other.

This invisible communion by faith makes up the *Church militant* taken *mystically,* and it is but *one* in all the world: But the *Church* we are to attend, must be *visible: so many as may comely meet together in one place, who as they have the right to all ordinances, so they may enjoy the use of them in Christ his order: and so they must be, and accordingly are stiled many.* The *Churches* of *Judea,* of *Galatia,* &c.

*That* then which gives the *formality* of these Churches we are now to inquire: and the conclusion we maintain this,

*Mutuall covenanting and confoederating of the Saints in the fellowship of the faith according to the order of the Gospel, is that which gives constitution and being to a visible Church.*

We shall consider 1. *What this confoederating is.* 2. *How it is expressed.* 3. *The reasons of the conclusion.*

1.

This confoederating and covenanting implies two things.

1. The *Act* that is performed betwixt some men for the while, and so passeth away in the expression.

2. The *State* arising from the *Act* of obligation, which is nothing else but that *relation* of these persons thus obliged *one to another.*

The *Sum* in short is this. By *mutuall ingagement* each to the other, such persons stand bound in such a *state and condition* to Answer the terms of it, and *to walk in such* waies, as *may attain the end thereof*.

And the right conceiving of the *nature* of the thing, I mean the *incorporating of men together,* will constrain the judgement to yeeld this.

. . .

## 2. How the Covenant may be expressed.

This Covenant is dispensed or acted after a double manner. Either *Explicitely,* or *Implicitely.*

An *Explicite* Covenant is, when there is an *open expression* and *profession* of this ingagement in the face of the Assembly, which persons by mutuall consent undertake in the waies of Christ.

An *Implicite* Covenant is, when in their practice they *do that,* whereby they *make* themselves *ingaged* to walk in such a society, according to such rules of government, which are exercised amongst them, and to submit themselves thereunto: but doe *not* make any *verball profession* thereof.

Thus the people in the *parishes in* England, when there is a *Minister* put upon them by the *Patrone* or *Bishop,* they *constantly* hold them to the *fellowship* of the people in such a place, *attend* all the *ordinances* there used, and the *dispensations* of the *Minister* so imposed upon them, *submit* thereunto, perform all *services* that may give countenance or incouragement to the person in this work of his Ministery. By *such actions,* and a *fixed* attendance upon *all such services* and duties, they declare *that* by their *practices, which* others do hold forth by publike *profession.*

### Notes

1. In *A Survey of the Summe of Church-Discipline* (New York: Arno Press, 1972; reprint edition of the original, published in 1648), pp. 11-28, 45-48.
2. As M R. acknowledgeth 1, 2, p. 10, Ezek.43.11.
3. Isa.33.22.

# John Cotton

Cotton (1584–1652), like Hooker, earned an M.A. from Cambridge and fled to the Bay Colony in 1633 during Archbishop Laud's crackdown on English Puritans. As teacher of Boston's First Church, he played a major, sometimes controversial, role in the colony's religious and political affairs. His defenses of Congregationalism itself and Puritan New England's "church way" in particular circulated widely on both sides of the Atlantic.

Two compact statements of his appear here, each a standard type (genre) of theological literature used for the teaching of the faith. The first is Cotton's catechism, repeatedly reprinted in colonial times, which is a summary of basic doctrine in the form of succinct questions and answers to be learned by young Christians. The second is Cotton's delineation of faith's "fundamental articles," a listing of affirmations that distinguish believers from unbelievers and heretics and identify the nonnegotiable essentials required of any person or group seeking recognition and fellowship among Christians.

## MILK FOR BABES[1]

Q.  What hath God done for you?
A.  God hath made me, He keepeth me, and He can save me.
Q.  Who is God?
A.  God is a Spirit of Himself and for Himself.
Q.  How many gods be there?
A.  There is but one God in three persons, the Father, the Son, and the Holy Ghost.
Q.  How did God make you?
A.  In my first parents holy and righteous.
Q.  Are you then born holy and righteous?
A.  No, my first father sinned, and I in him.
Q.  Are you then born a sinner?

A. I was conceived in sin and born in iniquity.

Q. What is your birth-sin?

A. Adam's sin imputed to me and a corrupt nature dwelling in me.

Q. What is your corrupt nature?

A. My corrupt nature is empty of grace, bent unto sin, and only unto sin, and that continually.

Q. What is sin?

A. Sin is the transgression of the Law.

Q. How many commandments of the Law be there?

A. Ten.

Q. What is the First Commandment?

A. Thou shalt have no other gods but me.

Q. What is the meaning of this commandment?

A. That we would worship the only true God and no other beside Him.

Q. What is the Second Commandment?

A. Thou shalt not make to thyself any graven image, &c.

Q. What is the meaning of this commandment?

A. That we should worship the true God with true worship such as God hath ordained, not such as man hath invented.

Q. What is the Third Commandment?

A. Thou shalt not take the name of the Lord thy God in vain, &c.

Q. What is here meant by the name of God?

A. God Himself and the good things of God, whereby He is known, as a man by his name, as His attributes, worship, Word, and works.

Q. What is it not to take His name in vain?

A. To make use of God and the good things of God to His glory and our good, not vainly, not unreverently, not unprofitably.

Q. What is the Fourth Commandment?

A. Remember that thou keep holy the Sabbath day, &c.

Q. What is the meaning of this commandment?

A. That we should rest from labor and much more from play on the Lord's day, that we may draw nigh to God in holy duties.

Q. What is the Fifth Commandment?

A. Honor thy father and thy mother, that thy days may be long in the land which the Lord thy God giveth thee.

Q. Who are here meant by father and mother?

A. All our superiors, whether in family, school, church, and commonwealth.

Q. What is the honor due to them?

A. Reverence, obedience, and (when I am able) recompense.

Q. What is the Sixth Commandment?

A. Thou shalt do no murder.

Q. What is the meaning of this commandment?

A. That we should not shorten the life or health of ourselves or others but preserve both.

Q. What is the Seventh Commandment?

A. Thou shalt not commit adultery.

Q. What is the sin here forbidden?

A. To defile ourselves or others with unclean lusts.

Q. What is the duty here commanded?

A. Chastity, to possess our vessels in holiness and honor.

Q. What is the Eighth Commandment?

A. Thou shalt not steal.

Q. What is the stealth here forbidden?

A. To take away another man's goods without his leave, or to spend our own without benefit to ourselves or others.

Q. What is the duty here commanded?

A. To get our goods honestly, to keep them safely, and to spend them thriftily.

Q. What is the Ninth Commandment?

A. Thou shalt not bear false witness against thy neighbor.

Q. What is the sin here forbidden?

A. To lie falsely, to think or speak untruly of ourselves or others.

Q. What is the duty here required?

A. Truth and faithfulness.

Q. What is the Tenth Commandment?

A. Thou shalt not covet, &c.

Q. What is the coveting here forbidden?

A. Lust after the things of other men and want of contentment with our own.

Q. Whether have you kept all these commandments?

A. No, I and all men are sinners.

Q. What is the wages of sin?

A. Death and damnation.

Q. How look you then to be saved?

A. Only by Jesus Christ.

Q. Who is Jesus Christ?

A. The eternal Son of God, who for our sakes became man that He might redeem and save us.

Q. How doth Christ redeem and save us?

A. By His righteous life and bitter death and glorious resurrection to life again.

Q. How do we come to have part and fellowship with Christ in His death and resurrection?

A. By the power of His Word and Spirit, which bring us to Christ and keep us in Him.

Q. What is His Word?

A. The Holy Scriptures of the prophets and apostles, the Old and New Testament, Law and Gospel.

Q. How doth the ministry of the Law bring you towards Christ?

A. By bringing me to know my sin and the wrath of God against me for it.

Q. What are you thereby the nearer to Christ?

A. So I come to feel my cursed estate and need of a savior.

Q. How doth the ministry of the Gospel help you in this cursed estate?

A. By humbling me yet more and then raising me up out of this estate.

Q. How doth the ministry of the Gospel humble you more?

A. By revealing the grace of the Lord Jesus in dying to save sinners and yet convincing me of my sin in not believing on Him and of mine utter insufficiency to come to Him, and so I feel myself utterly lost.

Q. How then doth the ministry of the Gospel raise you up out of this lost estate to come unto Christ?

A. By teaching me the value and the virtue of the death of Christ and the riches of His grace to lost sinners, by revealing the promise of grace to such and by ministering the Spirit of grace to apply Christ and His promise of grace unto myself and to keep me in Him.

Q. How doth the Spirit of grace apply Christ and His promise of grace unto you and keep you in Him?

A. By begetting in me faith to receive Him, prayer to call upon Him, repentance to mourn after Him, and new obedience to serve Him.

Q. What is faith?

A. Faith is a grace of the Spirit whereby I deny myself and believe on Christ for righteousness and salvation.

Q. What is prayer?

A. It is a calling upon God in the name of Christ by the help of the Holy Ghost, according to the will of God.

Q. What is repentance?

A. Repentance is a grace of the Spirit whereby I loath my sins and myself for them and confess them before the Lord and mourn after

Christ for the pardon of them and for grace to serve Him in newness of life.

Q. What is newness of life or new obedience?

A. Newness of life is a grace of the Spirit whereby I forsake my former
lusts and vain company, and walk before the Lord in the light of
His Word and in the communion of His saints.

Q. What is the communion of saints?

A. It is the fellowship of the church in the blessings of the Covenant of
Grace and the seals thereof.

Q. What is the church?

A. It is a congregation of saints joined together in the bond of the
Covenant to worship the Lord and to edify one another in all His
holy ordinances.

Q. What is the bond of the Covenant in which the church is joined
together?

A. It is the profession of that Covenant which God hath made with
His faithful people to be a God unto them and to their seed.

Q. What doth the Lord bind His people to in this Covenant?

A. To give up themselves and their seed first to the Lord to be His people and then to the elders and brethren of the church to set forward
the worship of God and their mutual edification.

Q. How do they give up themselves and their seed to the Lord?

A. By receiving, through faith, the Lord and His Covenant to themselves and to their seed, and accordingly walking themselves and
training up their children in the ways of His Covenant.

Q. How do they give up themselves and their seed to the elders and
brethren of the church?

A. By confession of their sins and profession of their faith and of their
subjection to the Gospel of Christ. And so they and their seed are
received into the fellowship of the church and the seals thereof.

Q. What are the seals of the Covenant now in the days of the Gospel?

A. Baptism and the Lord's Supper.

Q. What is done for you in baptism?

A. In baptism the washing with water is a sign and seal of my washing with the blood and Spirit of Christ and thereby of my ingraft-
ing into Christ, of the pardon and cleansing of my sins, of my rising
up out of affliction, and also of my resurrection from the dead at
the last day.

Q. What is done for you in the Lord's Supper?

A. In the Lord's Supper the receiving of the bread broken and the wine

61

poured out is a sign and seal of my receiving the communion of the body of Christ broken for me, and of His blood shed for me, and thereby of my growth in Christ, of the pardon and healing of my sins, of the fellowship of His Spirit, of my Strengthening and quickening in grace, and of my sitting together with Christ on His throne of glory at the Last Judgment.

Q. What is the resurrection from the dead, which was sealed up to you in baptism?

A. When Christ shall come to His Last Judgment, all that are in the graves shall rise again, both the just and the unjust.

Q. What is the Last Judgment which is sealed up to you in the Lord's Supper?

A. At the last day we shall all appear before the judgment seat of Christ to give an account of our works and to receive our reward according to them.

Q. What is the reward that shall then be given?

A. The righteous shall go into life eternal, and the wicked shall be cast into everlasting fire with the devil and his angels.

## THE TWELVE FUNDAMENTAL ARTICLES[2]

*Mr.* John Cotton, *of* Boston *in* New-England, *his twelve Fundamental Articles of Christian Religion? The denial whereof after once or twice Admonition* [he conceives] *makes a man an Heretick.*

1. The first is touching the Persons in the Trinity; that there be Three Persons, Father, Son, and Holy Ghost; and all but One God, this is a known Principle of our Christian Faith, and held forth in every Creed: and that it is of the Foundation, appears by this, 1 Joh. 2 23. *Whosoever denieth the Son, the same hath not the Father*; therefore when a man upon pretence there is but one God, will have no more Persons but One, and the Son he will not have to be as he is, God, this man overthroweth the Foundation of Christian Religion, as *Arius* did, and others after him; the Holy Ghost is joyned together with the rest in our Baptism; *I Baptise thee into the Name of the Father, and of the Son, and of the Holy Ghost*; this is a Profession of part of our Christianity, and a great part of it too, *Mat.* 28. 19,20.

2. It is another Article, and Fundamental Article of Christian Religion, that the Lord hath Made, and doth Govern all the World, and is a Rewarder of Good and Evil. That he is a Rewarder with Blessing of that which is Good, and taketh Vengeance on every one that doth Evil, *Heb.*

11.6. *He that comes to God, must believe that he is, and that he is a Rewarder of them that diligently seek him.* Gen. 1.1. He must know this, he that comes to God must believe this, if he believe not this, there is no hope of Salvation for such an one, *Heb.* 1.3. *Eph.* 1.11. *Rom.* 2. 6. 10.

3. This is another Fundamental Article of our Christian Faith? That this God alone is to be Worshipped, with Religious Worship, *Mat.* 4.10. *Thou shalt Worship the Lord thy God, and him only shalt thou serve*: If a man Worship any other God, besides the Lord, or if a man Worship any other God, the Lord will cut off them that Swear by the Lord, and that Swear by *Malcham*. If a man Worship Angels, he holds not the Head: *Get thee behind me Satan* in such a Case. *Avante.*

4. This is the Fourth. That this Worship of God is to be offered to him according to his Written Word. I say, this Worship that is acceptable to him, is written in his Word; if any man shall worship God by the Precepts of men, it is not according to the Will of God: *To the Law and to the Testimony? If any man speak not according to this word, it is because there is no light in them,* 2 Tim. 2.16,17. the whole Scripture (the written Word of God, is of Divine Inspiration, *and is profitable for Doctrine, for Reproof,* &c. The Scripture is a perfect Rule of Faith and Manners, that is a Foundation of Christian Religion.

5. A Fifth Article is, That for our own part, we have not so Worshipped God, from the Fall of our First Parents. We and our Fathers before us, we have all Sinned, and were Born in Sin from our Mothers Womb. *If any man say, he hath no Sin* (saith the Apostle) *there is no truth in him.* We have not kept the Ordinances and Statutes of the Lord, and so have deceived our selves of that Reward which the Lord hath promised to them that diligently seek him, *Rom.* 3. 10,11,23. And instead of being under a Reward of Blessing, we are under the Curse.

6. The Sixth Article which a man must know; or cannot be saved, (and if he hold against it, and know what he holds, it is impossible there should be any true Grace in him) is, that we of our selves are utterly unable to rescue our selves from this Misery, by any strength of our own; but we are utterly unable to help our selves; It's that which the Prophet *Hosea* speaks to, *Hos.* 13.9. *O Israel, thou hast destroyed thy self, but in me is thy help.* And as we have fallen in our First Parents, so in falling, we are only fit to fall: Where is then our help? It is in God. We were Born not of Blood, nor of the will of the Flesh, nor of the will of Man, but of God; not of Blood, that is, our Conversion to God, comes not by the Blood of our Ancestors; Nor by the Will of the Flesh, not the Will of

Corrupt Nature; Nor by the Will of man, that is, of our most holy Parents, or Ministers, or other Good men.

7. A Seventh Article is, That Jesus Christ, the Son of the Eternal Father, in fulness of time took upon him our Nature, and became man, and hath Redeemed his Church (by his perfect Obedience to his Father) from Sin and Misery: *The Word that was from the Beginning was made flesh, and we saw his glory, as the glory of the only Begotten Son of the Father, full of grace and truth,* Joh. 1.14. This is a Foundation of Christian Religion. *Every Spirit that confesseth not Jesus Christ come in the Flesh, is not of God,* &c, *Christ hath Redeemed us from the Curse of the Law, being made a Curse for us,* Gal 3.13.

8. A Eighth Article is, This Salvation and Redemption of Christ is freely given in the Gospel, unto every Soul that believes in his Name; & Faith is also freely given, that we may believe. I say, this Christ that works this Salvation and Redemption, is given only to such as believe in his Name. *For God so loved the World,* &c. *Joh.* 3.16. *And if you believe not in me,* (saith he) *you have no life in you,* no Salvation by me, *Joh.* 8.24. *If ye believe not that I am he, you shall die in your Sins,* and the Lord in giving you his Son, gives you Faith to believe in his Son, *Eph.* 3.17. and both at the same instant, that if you have not Christ, you have not Faith, and if you have not Faith, you have not Christ, Christ dwells in your heart by Faith; *As many as received him, to them he gave power to become the Sons of God, even to them that believe in his Name,* Joh. 1.12. No man can come to Jesus Christ, that is, believe on him, except the Father draw him: No man can come, there is an impossibility of reaching him, except the Lord put forth his Almighty Power.

9. Those whom the Lord draws by his Word and Spirit to believe on Christ, them he Justifies freely by his Grace in Christ: I say, those whom the Lord draws to Christ by Faith, he justifies freely by his rich Grace in Christ, *Rom.* 3.23,24. This is a Foundation of our Christian Faith also. *By the deeds of the Law, shall no Flesh be justified in his sight*: So then Christ is God and man, he is come, and hath Redeemed us, this Redemption is given to the Faith of his People, this Faith is wrought by the Word and Spirit of God, it is the power of God to Salvation to them that believe. Where this Faith is, there is Justification.

10. Where the Soul is Justified, it is also Regenerated. *Joh.* 3.3. *For except ye be born a-new, ye cannot enter into the Kingdom of God. Except ye Repent, ye shall all likewise perish.* Luk. 13. 5.

11. This Regeneration in us is imperfect, by reason we consist partly of Flesh, and partly of Spirit. I *Cor.* 13.9. *Gal.* 5.17. Therefore gifts of

64

Grace to be given, and Sins to be mortified, it is a fundamental point of Religion. Therefore the Apostle crieth out of his own Misery, that he was not able to wrestle against his own Corruptions.

12. All men shall Rise again at the Last Day, both such as are Regenerated, and such as are riot Regenerate; and both shall be judged according to their works, the Righteous to Everlasting Salvation, the Wicked to Everlasting Damnation. So then put all these things together, and you have all the necessary Points of Christian Religion; which whoso obstinately opposeth, or is ignorant of, he cannot be found in a State of Grace that Accompanies Salvation, this is the Summe of the Articles; and he that overthrows any one of these, and obstinately persisteth therein, brings himself to Eternal Damnation.

Q. *If any man ask, Why we should look at any Fundamental Articles of Christian Religion, besides them that are in the Creed of the twelve Apostles.*

A. I Answer, There be some things there that are not Fundamental Articles, and there are some Fundamental Articles that are left out; as that Christ descended into Hell, it is no Fundamental Article of Christian Religion, though it be taken for his Descending into the Grave; nor do I think this Creed was made by the Apostles, much less that Article, and there are other Fundamental Articles which are not there, as the Word to be a Rule of Faith and Manners; little also is said in the Creed of Justification or Regeneration.

### Notes

1. In *John Cotton*, rev. ed., ed. Everett Emerson (Boston: Twayne Publishers, 1990; originally published as *Milk for Babes, Drawn Out of the Breasts of both Testaments, Chiefly, for the spirituall nourishment of Boston Babes in either England: But may be of like use for any Children*, 1646), pp. 97-101.
2. In *A Library of American Puritan Writings: The Seventeenth Century*, ed. Sacvan Bercovitch, vol. 13, *The Way of Faith* (New York: AMS Press, 1983; original essay published in 1641), pp. 4-9.

# Anne Hutchinson

*The trial and banishment of Hutchinson (1591–1643) by Massachusetts Bay authorities is one of several episodes of colonial Puritanism to enter American folklore as well as historical and theological studies. The case still invites varied analyses and responses. For the history of theology specifically, it brings to the fore at least three disputed questions for Puritans: (1) If salvation is by God's sovereign grace, how can human good works be considered necessary conditions for or signs of divine favor? (2) If God's faithful are reborn, illumined, and upheld by the power of the Spirit within them, how can it be denied that they may receive and witness to spiritual revelations of God and things of God? (3) Since God grants diverse spiritual gifts for diverse church services, how can the church or state justify refusing to permit women with manifest gifts for teaching the faith to do so?*

*Hutchinson sought to become conversant with Puritan teaching, attentive especially to the views of John Cotton, before and after emigrating to New England in 1634. There she was respected by many for her religious zeal, selfless service as a midwife, and ability to recapitulate and elucidate the messages of the ministers at home meetings open to those who missed the services. Rumors that her elucidations included criticizing the clergy for advocating works over grace were among the reasons used to warrant judicial action against her. The legal proceedings are the only extant records of her words. This selection focuses on the question of her right to function as a Christian teacher—in effect, a theologian—and illustrates a typically Puritan dispute over applying scripture to contemporary cases.*

## THE EXAMINATION OF MRS. ANNE HUTCHINSON AT THE COURT OF NEWTOWN[1]

November 1637

*Mr. Winthrop, governor.* Mrs. Hutchinson, you are called here as one of those that have troubled the peace of the commonwealth and the churches here; you are known to be a woman that hath had a great share in the promoting and divulging of those opinions that are causes of this trouble, and to be nearly joined not only in affinity and affection with some of those the court had taken notice of and passed censure upon, but you have spoken divers things as we have been informed very prejudicial to the honour of the churches and ministers thereof, and you have maintained a meeting and an assembly in your house that hath been condemned by the general assembly as a thing not tolerable nor comely in the sight of God nor fitting for your sex, and notwithstanding that was cried down you have continued the same, therefore we have thought good to send for you to understand how things are, that if you be in an erroneous way we may reduce you that so you may become a profitable member here among us, otherwise if you be obstinate in your course that then the court may take such course that you may trouble us no further, therefore I would intreat you to express whether you do not hold and assent in practice to those opinions and factions that have been handled in court already, that is to say, whether you do not justify Mr. Wheelwright's sermon and the petition.

*Mrs. Hutchinson.* I am called here to answer before you but I hear no things laid to my charge.

*Gov.* I have told you some already and more I can tell you. *(Mrs. H.)* Name one Sir.

*Gov.* Have I not named some already?

*Mrs. H.* What have I said or done?

*Gov.* Why for your doings, this you did harbour and countenance those that are parties in this faction that you have heard of. *(Mrs. H.)* That's matter of conscience, Sir.

*Gov.* Your conscience you must keep or it must be kept for you.

*Mrs. H.* Must not I then entertain the saints because I must keep my conscience.

*Gov.* Say that one brother should commit felony or treason and come to his other brother's house, if he knows him guilty and conceals him he is guilty of the same. It is his conscience to entertain him, but if his conscience comes into act in giving countenance and entertainment to him that hath broken the law he is guilty too. So if you do countenance those that are transgressors of the law you are in the same fact.

*Mrs. H.* What law do they transgress?

*Gov.* The law of God and of the state.

*Mrs. H.* In what particular?

*Gov.* Why in this among the rest, whereas the Lord doth say honour thy father and thy mother.

*Mrs. H.* Ey Sir in the Lord. *(Gov.)* This honour you have broke in giving countenance to them.

*Mrs. H.* In entertaining those did I entertain them against any act (for there is the thing) or what God hath appointed?

*Gov.* You knew that Mr. Wheelwright did preach this sermon and those that countenance him in this do break a law.

*Mrs. H.* What law have I broken?

*Gov.* Why the fifth commandment.

*Mrs. H.* I deny that for he saith in the Lord.

*Gov.* You have joined with them in the faction.

*Mrs. H.* In what faction have I joined with them?

*Gov.* In presenting the petition.

*Mrs. H.* Suppose I had set my hand to the petition what then? *(Gov.)* You saw that case tried before.

*Mrs. H.* But I had not my hand to the petition.

*Gov.* You have councelled them. *(Mrs. H.)* Wherein?

*Gov.* Why in entertaining them.

*Mrs. H.* What breach of law is that Sir?

*Gov.* Why dishonouring of parents.

*Mrs. H.* But put the case Sir that I do fear the Lord and my parents, may not I entertain them that fear the Lord because my parents will not give me leave?

*Gov.* If they be the fathers of the commonwealth, and they of another religion, if you entertain them then you dishonour your parents and are justly punishable.

*Mrs. H.* If I entertain them, as they have dishonoured their parents I do.

*Gov.* No but you by countenancing them above others put honor upon them.

*Mrs. H.* I may put honor upon them as the children of God and as they do honor the Lord.

*Gov.* We do not mean to discourse with those of your sex but only this; you do adhere unto them and do endeavour to set forward this faction and so you do dishonour us.

*Mrs. H.* I do acknowledge no such thing neither do I think that I ever put any dishonour upon you.

*Gov.* Why do you keep such a meeting at your house as you do every week upon a set day?

*Mrs. H.* It is lawful for me so to do, as it is all your practices and can you find a warrant for yourself and condemn me for the same thing? The ground of my taking it up was, when I first came to this land because I did not go to such meetings as those were, it was presently reported that I did not allow of such meetings but held them unlawful and therefore in that regard they said I was proud and did despise all ordinances, upon that a friend came unto me and told me of it and I to prevent such aspersions took it up, but it was in practice before I came therefore I was not the first.

*Gov.* For this, that you appeal to our practice you need no confutation. If your meeting had answered to the former it had not been offensive, but I will say that there was no meeting of women alone, but your meeting is of another sort for there are sometimes men among you.

*Mrs. H.* There was never any man with us.

*Gov.* Well, admit there was no man at your meeting and that you was sorry for it, there is no warrant for your doings, and by what warrant do you continue such a course?

*Mrs. H.* I conceive there lyes a clear rule in Titus, that the elder women should instruct the younger and then I must have a time wherein I must do it.

*Gov.* All this I grant you, I grant you a time for it, but what is this to the purpose that you Mrs. Hutchinson must call a company together from their callings to come to be taught of you?

*Mrs. H.* Will it please you to answer me this and to give me a rule for then I will willingly submit to any truth. If any come to my house to be instructed in the ways of God what rule have I to put them away?

*Gov.* But suppose that a hundred men come unto you to be instructed will you forbear to instruct them?

*Mrs. H.* As far as I conceive I cross a rule in it.

*Gov.* Very well and do you not so here?

*Mrs. H.* No Sir for my ground is they are men.

*Gov.* Men and women all is one for that, but suppose that a man should come and say Mrs. Hutchinson I hear that you are a woman that Got hath given his grace unto and you have knowledge in the word of God I pray instruct me a little, ought you not to instruct this man?

*Mrs. H.* I think I may.—Do you think it not lawful for me to teach women and why do you call me to teach the court?

*Gov.* We do not call you to teach the court but to lay open yourself.

*Mrs. H.* I desire you that you would then set me down a rule by which I may put them away that come unto me and so have peace in so doing.

*Gov.* You must shew your rule to receive them.

*Mrs. H.* I have done it.

*Gov.* I deny it because I have brought more arguments than you have.

*Mrs. H.* I say, to me it is a rule.

*Mr. Endicot.* You say there are some rules unto you. I think there is a contradiction in your own words. What rule for your practice do you bring, only a custom in Boston.

*Mrs. H.* No Sir that was no rule to me but if you look upon the rule in Titus it is a rule to me. If you convince me that it is no rule I shall yield.

*Gov.* You know that there is no rule that crosses another, but this rule crosses that in the Corinthians. But you must take it in this sense that elder women must instruct the younger about their business, and to love their husbands and not to make them to clash.

*Mrs. H.* I do not conceive but that it is meant for some publick times.

*Gov.* Well, have you no more to say but this?

*Mrs. H.* I have said sufficient for my practice.

### Note

1. In *The Antinomian Controversy, 1636-1638: A Documentary History,* 2d ed., ed. David D. Hall. (Durham: Duke University Press, 1990; original essay published in 1767), pp. 312-16.

# Cotton Mather

*M*ather *(1663–1728) is this book's first theologian born on American soil, descended from two founding families of Puritan New England and educated (B.A., M.A.) at Harvard. During a long ministry at Boston's North Church (1680 on), he was prominent in both civil and religious affairs. His dedication to the Reformed deposit of truth and traditional values passed down from the colony's origins have virtually typecast him in history as a close-minded reactionary. Orthodox he was, or intended to be. Yet he also took interest in the new science of the Enlightenment, and his own studies in the physical sciences and natural philosophy—most notably his work* The Christian Philosopher *(1720)— gained him membership in England's Royal Academy of Sciences. He also responded with sympathy to the aims and emphases of emergent Pietism.*

*An encyclopedic mind and a prolific writer, Mather dealt with a vast array of topics. Selected here is a portion of one of his more popular works,* Bonifacius, *or* Essays To Do Good. *His Reformed roots are evident, as when he maintains, for instance, that good works are to glorify the Creator and Redeemer. Stress on doing good, however, was common to Puritanism, Pietism, and the Enlightenment, and it is noteworthy that Mather speaks of "reasonable religion" as well as the attitudes or dispositions motivating doers of the good.*

## Essays to Do Good[1]

Such *glorious things are spoken* in the oracles of our good God, concerning them who *devise good,* that A BOOK OF GOOD DEVICES may very reasonably demand attention and acceptance from them that have any impressions of the most *reasonable religion* upon them. I am *devising* such a BOOK; but at the same time offering a sorrowful demonstration, that if men would set themselves to *devise good,* a world of *good* might be done, more than there is, in this *present evil world.* It is very sure, the world has *need enough*. There needs abundance to be done, that the great GOD and His CHRIST may be more known and served in the world; and that the *errors* which are *impediments* to the *acknowledgments* wherewith men ought to glorify their Creator and Redeemer, may be rectified. There needs abundance to be done, that the *evil manners* of the world, by which men are *drowned in perdition,* may be reformed; and mankind rescued from the epidemical corruption and slavery which has overwhelmed it. There needs abundance to be done, that the *miseries* of the world may have *remedies* and *abatements* provided for them; and that miserable people may be relieved and comforted. The world has according to the computation of some, above seven hundred millions of people now living in it. What an ample field among all these, to *do good* upon! In a word, *the kingdom of God* in the world calls for innumerable *services* from us. To do SUCH THINGS is to DO GOOD. Those men DEVISE GOOD, who shape any DEVICES to do things of such a tendency; whether the things be of a *spiritual* importance, or of a *temporal.* You see, Sirs, the general matter, appearing as yet but as a *chaos,* which is to be wrought upon. *Oh! that the good Spirit of God may now fall upon us, and carry on the glorious work which lies before us!* . . .

§7. To the title of GOOD WORKS there do belong, those *essays to do good,* which are now urged for. To produce them, the *first* thing, and indeed the ONE thing, that is *needful,* is, a glorious work of GRACE on the soul, renewing and quickening of it, and *purifying* of the sinner, and rendering him *zealous of good works:* a *workmanship of God* upon us, *creating* us over again, by JESUS CHRIST, *for good works.* And then, there is needful, what will necessarily follow upon such a *work:* that is, a *disposition* to *do good works* upon true, genuine, generous, and evangelical *principles.* Those *principles* are to be *stated,* before we can go any further; when they are *active,* we shall go a great deal further.

It is in the first place, to be taken for granted: that the *end* for which we do *good works* must not be, to afford the matter of our *justification,* before the Law of the holy GOD. Indeed, no *good works* can be done by any man until he be *justified.* Until a man be united unto the glorious CHRIST, who is *our life,* he is a *dead man.* And, I pray, what *good works* to be expected from such a man? They will all be *dead works.* For, "Severed from me ye can do nothing," saith our Saviour. . . . It was an old maxim of the faithful, *Bona opera sequuntur justificatum, non praecedunt justificandum.*[2] It is the *righteousness* of the *good works* done by our Saviour and *Surety,* not our own, that *justifies* us before God, and

72

answers the demands of His Law upon us. We do by *faith* lay hold on those *good works* for our *justifying righteousness* before we arrive to do our own. 'Tis not our *faith* itself, either as doing of *good works,* or as being itself one of them, which entitles us to the *justifying righteousness* of our Saviour. But it is *faith,* only *as* renouncing of our own righteousness, and relying on that of our Saviour, provided for the *chief of sinners,* by which we are *justified.* Sir, all your attempts at *good works* will come to nothing, till a *justifying faith* in your Saviour, shall carry you forth unto them. This was the divinity of the ancients; *Jerome* has well expressed it: *Sine Christo omnis virtus est in vitie.*[3] Nevertheless; first, you are to look upon it, as a glorious truth of the Gospel, that the *moral law* (which prescribes and requires *good works*) must by every Christian alive be made the *rule* of his life. *Do we make void the Law through faith? God forbid. Yea, we establish the Law.* The *rule,* by which we are to *glorify* God, is given us in the law of *good works,* which we *enjoy* (I will express it *so!*) in the *Ten Commandments.* It is impossible for us, to be released from all obligations to glorify God by a conformity to this *rule;* sooner shall we cease to be creatures. The *conformity* to that rule in the *righteousness,* which our Saviour by His obedience to it, has *brought in,* to *justify* us, has forever *magnified the Law, and made it honorable.* Though our Saviour has furnished us, with a perfect and spotless *righteousness,* when His obedience to the *Law,* is placed unto our account; yet it is a *sin* for us at all to fall short in our own obedience to the *Law:* we must always loathe and judge ourselves for the *sin.* We are not under the *Law* as a *covenant of works.* Our own exactness in doing of *good works,* is not now the *condition* of our *entering into life. Woe unto us if it were!* But still, the *Covenant of Grace* holds us to it, as our *duty;* and if we are in the *Covenant of Grace,* we shall make it our *study,* to *do* those *good works* which once were the terms of our *entering into life. Manet lex tota pietatis;*[4] *that was the divinity in Tertullian's days!* There must be such an esteem for the *law* of *good works* retained forever in all the *justified:* a *law* never to be abrogated; never to be abolished! And then, secondly, though we are *justified* by a *precious faith* in the *righteousness of God our Saviour,* yet good works are demanded of us, to *justify* our *faith;* to *demonstrate,* that it is indeed that *precious faith.* A *justifying faith* is a *jewel,* which may be *counterfeited.* But now the *marks* of a *faith,* which is no counterfeit, are to be found in the *good works* whereto a servant of God is inclined and assisted by his *faith.* It is by a *regenerating work* of the Holy Spirit, that *faith* is wrought in the souls of the chosen people. Now the same *work* of God, and of *grace,* which does in a *regeneration* dispose a man to make his flight by *faith,* unto the *righteousness* of his only Saviour, will also dispose him to the *good works* of a *Christian life.* And the same *faith* which goes to the Saviour for a part in His *righteousness,* will also go to Him, for an heart and strength to do the *good works,* which are *ordained, that we should walk in them.* If our *faith* be not such a *faith,* 'tis a *lifeless* one, and it will not bring to *life.* A *workless faith* is a *worthless faith.* My friend, suppose thyself standing before the *Judgment-seat* of the glorious LORD. A needful, a prudent, supposal; it ought to be a very *frequent* one. The *Judge* demands, "What hast thou to plead, for a portion in the blessedness of the righteous?" The plea must be:

"O my glorious Judge, Thou hast been my sacrifice. Oh! Judge of all the earth, give poor dust and ashes leave to say, 'My righteousness is on the bench. Surely in the Lord I have my righteousness. O my Saviour, I have received it, I have secured it, upon Thy gracious offer of it.' "

The *Judge* proceeds:

"But what hast thou to plead, that thy faith should not be rejected, as the faith and hope of the hypocrite?"

Here the plea must be:

"Lord, my faith was Thy work. It was a faith which disposed me to all the good works of Thy holy religion. My faith sanctified me. It carried me to Thee, O my Saviour, for grace to do the works of righteousness. It embraced that for my Lord as well as for my Saviour. It caused me with sincerity to love and keep Thy commandments; with assiduity to serve the interests of Thy Kingdom in the world." Thus you have *Paul* and *James* reconciled. Thus you have *good works* provided for. . . . The believer cannot but inquire, "What shall I render to my Saviour?" The result of the inquiry will be, *with good works to glorify Him.* . . .

These, these are to be our dispositions:

"O my Saviour, hast Thou done so much for me? Now will I do all I can for Thy Kingdom, and people in the world? Oh! What service is there that I may now do for my Saviour, and for His people in the world!"

These are the principles to be proceeded on! And on them, I will observe to you a notable thing. 'Tis worthy of observation, that there are no men in the world, who so abound in *good works,* as the men who have most of all abandoned all pretense to *merit* by their *works.* . . .

74

**Notes**

1. In *Bonifacius: An Essay upon the Good,* ed. David Levin (Cambridge, Massachusetts: The Belknap Press of Harvard University Press, 1966; original essay published in 1710), pp. 17-18, 27-31.
2. "Good works follow justification; they do not precede justification." Levin's translation.
3. "Without Christ, all virtue is vice." Levin's translation.
4. "The entire law of duty (or obedience to God) remains." Levin's translation.

# Roger Williams

*W*illiams *(1603–1683) earned a Cambridge B.A. in 1627
and shortly thereafter joined the Puritan group preparing for emigration
to New England. He arrived in Massachusetts Bay in 1631 and quickly
clashed with other colony leaders because of his "Separatist" view that
truly reformed Christians must dissociate themselves altogether from
England's "corrupt" established church. Banished in 1636, he found
refuge with Native Americans in the place he named Providence, which
became the nucleus for the Rhode Island colony and permitted full freedom of worship. There he waged a lifelong campaign against the
churches of old and New England alike, contending that the "true
church" of God's holy people sought and required—for the sake of spiritual purity and conformity to the law of Christ—a wall of separation
between church and state. Coercion and violence in the name of religion
were in his view greater threats to religious truth and civil order than
tolerance of diverse religious opinion.*

*In many respects the theology of Williams was that of a "seeker" and
illustrates how, for some, impulses and ideals of Reformed faith made
Puritan "orthodoxy" a way station to more radical positions. Founder
of the first Baptist church in the colonies, Williams himself is well
known as one of that body's church theologians, as well as a champion
of religious liberty. His theological defense of that principle, The
Bloudy Tenent of Persecution, has long served as one of the finest
examples of early American Christian thought. Included here are his
initial propositions and most of chapters 36–40, which counter the
views of John Cotton ("The Answerer") on the interpretation of scripture and doctrine.*

## BLOUDY TENENT OF PERSECUTION[1]

First, That the blood of so many hundred thousand soules of *Protestants* and *Papists*, spilt in the *Wars* of *present* and *former Ages*, for their

respective *Consciences*, is not *required* nor *accepted* by *Jesus Christ* the *Prince of Peace.*

Secondly, Pregnant *Scripturs* and *Arguments* are throughout the Worke proposed against the *Doctrine* of *persecution* for *cause* of *Conscience.*

Thirdly, Satisfactorie Answers are given to *Scriptures*, and objections produced by Mr. *Calvin, Beza,* Mr. *Cotton,* and the Ministers of the New English Churches and others former and later, tending to prove the *Doctrine of persecution* for cause of *Conscience.*

Fourthly, The *Doctrine of persecution* for cause of Conscience, is proved guilty of all the *blood* of the *Soules* crying for *vengeance* under the *Altar.*

Fifthly, All *Civill States* with their *Officers* of *justice* in their respective *constitutions* and *administrations* are proved *essentially Civill,* and therefore not *Judges, Governours* or *Defendours* of the *Spirituall* or *Christian state* and *Worship.*

Sixthly, It is the will and command of God, that (since the comming of his Sonne the *Lord Jesus*) a *permission* of the most *Paganish, Jewish, Turkish,* or *Antichristian consciences* and *worships,* bee granted to *all* men in all *Nations* and *Countries*: and they are onely to bee *fought* against with that *Sword* which is only (in *Soule matters*) *able* to *conquer,* to wit, *the Sword of Gods Spirit,* the *Word* of God.

Seventhly, The *state* of the *Land* of *Israel,* the *Kings* and *people* thereof in *Peace & War,* is proved *figurative* and *ceremoniall,* and no *patterne* nor *president* for any *Kingdome* or *civill state* in the *world* to follow.

Eightly, *God* requireth not an *uniformity* of *Religion* to be *inacted* and *inforced* in any *civill state*; which inforced *uniformity* (sooner or later) is the greatest occasion of *civill Warre, ravishing* of *conscience, persecution* of *Christ Jesus* in his servants, and of the *hypocrisie* and *destruction* of *millions* of *souls.*

Ninthly, In holding an inforced *uniformity* of *Religion* in a *civill state,* wee must necessarily *disclaime* our desires and hopes of the *Jewes conversion* to *Christ.*

Tenthly, An inforced *uniformity* of *Religion* throughout a *Nation* or *civill state,* confounds the *Civill* and *Religious,* denies the principles of Christianity and civility, and that *Jesus Christ* is come in the Flesh.

Eleventhly, The permission of other *consciences* and *worships* then a state professeth, only can (according to God) procure a firme and lasting *peace,* (good *assurance* being taken according to the wisdome of the *civill state* for *uniformity* of *civill obedience* from all sorts).

Twelfthly, lastly, true *civility* and *Christianity* may both flourish in a *state* or *Kingdome*, notwithstanding the *permission* of divers and contrary *consciences*, either of *Jew* or *Gentile*. . . .

### Chap. XXXVI

*Peace.* The next Scripture brought against such persecution is *Luke* 9. 54, 55. where the Lord Jesus reproved His Disciples, who would have had fire come downe from Heaven, and devoure those *Samaritanes* that would not receive Him in these words: You know not of what *spirit* you are, the Son of Man is not come to *destroy* mens lives, but to *save* them.

With this Scripture Mr. *Cotton* joynes the fourth, and answers both in one, which is this, 2 *Tim.* 2. 24. The servant of the *Lord* must not strive, but must be gentle toward all men, suffering the *evill men*, instructing them with *meeknesse* that are contrary minded and *oppose* themselves, proving if *God* peradventure will give them *repentance* that they may acknowledge the *truth*, and that they may recover themselves out of the snare of the *Divell* who are taken *captive* by him at his *will*.

Unto both these *Scriptures* it pleaseth him thus to answer: "Both these are *directions* to *Ministers* of the *Gospel* how to deale (not with obstinate offendors in the *Church* who sin against *conscience*, but) either with *men* without as the *Samaritanes* were, and many unconverted *Christians* in *Creet*, whom *Titus* (as an Evangelist) was to seek to convert:

"Or at best with some *Jews* or *Gentiles* in the Church, who though carnall, yet were not convinced of the errour of their way: And it is true it became not the Spirit of the *Gospel* to convert Aliens to the *Faith* (such as the *Samaritanes* were) by fire and brimstone, nor to deale harshly in *publicke Ministery* or private conference with all such severall minded men as either had not yet entred into *Church fellowship*, or if they had did hitherto sin of *ignorance*, not against *Conscience*: But neither of both these Texts doe hinder the *Minister* of the *Gospel* to proceed in a *Church* way against *Church members*, when they became scandalous offenders either in *life* or *doctrine*, much lesse doe they speake at all to the *Civill Magistrate*."

### Chap. XXXVII.

*Truth.* This perplexed and ravelled *Answer*, where in so many things and so doubtfull are wrapt up and intangled together, I shall take in pieces.

First, concerning that of the *Lord Jesus* rebuking his *Disciples* for their rash and ignorant bloudy *zeale* (*Luc.* 9.) desiring *corporall destruction* upon the *Samaritanes* for refusing the *Lord Jesus,* &c. the *Answerer* affirmeth, that hindreth not the *Ministers* of the *Gospell* to proceed in a *Church* way against scandalous offenders, which is not here questioned, but maintained to bee the holy will of the *Lord,* and a sufficient censure and punishment, if no civill offence against the *Civill State* be committed.

Secondly (saith hee) "Much lesse doth this speake at all to the Civill *Magistrate.*"

Where I observe that he implyes that beside the *censure* of the *Lord Jesus,* in the hands of his *spirituall governours,* for any spirituall evill in *life* or *doctrine,* the *Civill Magistrate* is also to inflict *corporall punishment* upon the contrary minded: whereas

First, if the *Civill Magistrate* be a *Christian,* a *Disciple* or follower of the meeke *Lambe* of *God,* he is bound to be far from destroying the *bodies of men,* for refusing to receive the *Lord Jesus Christ,* for otherwise hee should not know (according to this speech of the *Lord Jesus*) what *spirit* he was of, yea and to be ignorant of the sweet end of the comming of the *Son of Man,* which was not to destroy the *bodies of Men,* but to save both *bodies* and *soules, vers.* 55. 56.

Secondly, if the *Civill Magistrate,* being a *Christian,* gifted, *prophesie* in the *Church,* 1 *Corinth.* 1. 14. although the *Lord Jesus Christ,* whom they in their owne persons hold forth, shall be refused, yet they are here forbidden to call for fire from *heaven,* that is, to procure or inflict any corporall *judgment* upon such *offenders,* remembring the end of the *Lord Jesus* his comming, not to *destroy* men's lives, but to *save* them.

Lastly, this also concernes the *conscience* of the *Civill Magistrate,* as he is bound to preserve the *civill peace* and quiet of the *place* and people under him, he is bound to suffer no man to breake the *Civill Peace,* by laying hands of *violence* upon any, though as vile as the *Samaritanes* for not receiving of the *Lord Jesus Christ.*

It is indeed the *ignorance* and blind *zeale* of the second *Beast,* the *false Prophet, Rev.* 13. 13. to perswade the *civill Powers* of the earth to persecute the Saints, that is, to bring fiery *judgements* upon men in a *judiciall way,* and to pronounce that such *judgments* of *imprisonment, banishment, death,* proceed from Gods righteous *vengeance* upon such *Hereticks.* So dealt divers *Bishops* in *France,* and *England* too in Queene *Maries* dayes with the Saints of God at their putting to death, declaiming against them in their Sermons to the people, and proclaiming that these persecutions even unto death were Gods *just judgements from heaven upon these Heretickes.*

*Chap. XXXVIII*

*Peace.* Doubtlesse such fiery spirits (as the Lord Jesus said) are not of God: I pray speake to the second place out of *Timothy,* 2. *Epist.* 25. 26.

*Truth.* I acknowledge this instruction to be meeke and patient, &c. is properly an instruction to the *Ministers* of the Gospel. Yet divers Arguments from hence will truly and fairly be collected, to manifest and evince how farre the *civill Magistrate* ought to bee from dealing with the civill sword in *spirituall cases.*

. . .

*Chap. XXXIX*

*Peace.* But what is there in this Scripture of *Timothy* alledged concerning the civill *Magistracy?*

*Truth.* I argue from this place of *Timothy* in particular, thus.

First, if the *civill Magistrates* bee *Christians,* or members of the *Church,* able to *prophesie in the Church of Christ,* then I say as before, they are bound by this command of *Christ* to suffer opposition to their *doctrine,* with *meeknesse* and *gentlenesse,* and to be so farre from striving to subdue their *opposites* with the *civill sword,* but they are bound with *patience* and *meeknesse* to wait if *God* peradventure will please to grant *repentance* unto their opposites.

So also it pleaseth the Answerer to acknowledge in these words:

"It becomes not the *Spirit* of the *Gospel* to convert *Aliens* to the Faith (such as the *Samaritanes,* and the unconverted *Christians* in *Crete*) with *Fire* and *Brimstone.*"

Secondly, be they *oppositions within,* and *Church members* (as the Answerer speakes) become *scandalous* in *doctrine,* (I speake not of *scandals* against the *civill State,* which the *civill Magistrate* ought to punish) it is the *Lord* onely (as this Scripture to *Timothy* implyes) who is able to give them *repentance,* and recover them out of *Sathans* snare: to which end also he hath appointed those holy and dreadfull *censures* in his *Church* or *Kingdome.* True it is, the *Sword* may make (as once the *Lord* complained, *Isa.* 10.) a whole *Nation* of *Hypocrites:* But to recover a Soule from *Sathan* by *repentance,* and to bring them from *Antichristian doctrine* or *worship,* to the *doctrine* or *worship Christian,* in the least true *internall* or *externall* submission, that only works the *All-powerfull God,* by the *sword* of the Spirit in the hand of his *Spirituall officers.*

What a most wofull proofe hereof have the *Nations* of the Earth given in all *Ages?* And to seeke no further than our *native* Soyle, within a few scores of yeeres, how many wonderfull *changes* in *Religion* hath the *whole Kingdome* made, according to the *change* of the *Governours* thereof, in the severall *Religious* which they themselves imbraced! *Henry* the 7. finds and leaves the *kingdome* absolutely *Popish. Henry* the 8. casts it into a *mould* half *Popish* halfe *Protestant. Edward* the 6. brings forth an *Edition* all *Protestant.* Queen *Mary* within few yeares defaceth *Edwards* worke, and renders the *Kingdome* (after her Grandfather *Hen.* 7. his pattern) all *Popish. Maries* short *life* and *Religion* ends together: and *Elizabeth* reviveth her Brother *Edwards* Modell, all Protestant: And some eminent *Witnesses* of Gods Truth against *Antichrist,* have enclined to believe, that before the downfall of that *Beast,* England must once againe bow down her faire Neck to his proud usurping yoake and foot.

*Peace.* It hath been *Englands* sinfull shame, to fashion & change their *Garments* and *Religions* with wondrous *ease* and *lightnesse,* as a *higher Power,* a *stronger Sword* hath prevailed; after the ancient patterne of *Nebuchadnezzars* bowing the whole world in one most solemne *uniformitie* of *worship* to his *Golden Image,* Dan. 3.

## Chap. XL

But it hath been thought, or said, Shall *oppositions* against the *Truth* escape unpunished? Will they not prove mischievous, &c.

*Truth.* I answer (as before) concerning the blinde Guides (in case there be no *Civill offence* committed) the *Magistrates,* & all men that by the mercy of God to themselves discerne the *miserie* of such *Opposites,* have cause to lament and bewaile that fearfull condition wherein such are entangled, to wit, in the *snares* & *chains* of *Satan,* with which they are so invincibly caught and held, that no power in *Heaven* or *Earth,* but the Right hand of the *Lord* in the meeke and gentle dispensing of the *Word* of *Truth,* can release and quit them.

Those many false Christs (of whom the Lord Jesus forewarnes, *Mat.* 24.) have sutably their false *bodies, faith, spirit, Baptisme,* as the Lord Jesus, hath his true *body, faith, spirit,* &c. *Ephes.* 4. correspondent also are their *weapon*s, and the *successe,* issue, or operation of them. A *carnall weapon* or *sword* of *steele* may produce a *carnall repentance,* a shew, an outside, an *uniformitie* through a State or *Kingdome:* But it hath pleased the Father to exalt the *Lord Jesus* only, to be a Prince (armed with *power* and meanes sufficient) to give *repentance* to *Israel,* Acts 5. 31.

Accordingly an *unbelieving* Soule being dead in sinne (although he be changed from one *worship* to another, like a dead man shifted into severall changes of *apparell*) cannot please *God*, Heb. 11. and consequently, whatever such an *unbelieving* & *unregenerate* person acts in *Worship* or *Religion*, it is but sinne, *Rom.* 14. *Preaching* sinne, *praying* (though without beads or booke) sinne; *breaking of bread*, or *Lords supper* sinne, yea as odious as the oblation of Swines *blood*, a Dog's *neck*, or *killing of a Man*, Isa. 66.

But *Faith* it is that *gift* which proceeds alone from the *Father* of Lights, *Phil.* 1. 29. and till he please to make his *light* arise and open the eyes of blind sinners, their soules shall lie fast asleep (and the faster, in that a *sword* of steele compells them to a *worship* in *hypocrisie*) in the dungeons of *spirituall darknesse* and *Sathans slavery*.

*Peace.* I adde, that a *civill sword* (as wofull experience in all ages hath proved) is so far from bringing or helping forward an *opposite* in *Religion* to *repentance*, that *Magistrates* sinne grievously against the *worke* of *God* and *blood* of Soules, by such proceedings. Because as (commonly) the suffrings of *false* and *Antichristian Teachers* harden their *followers*, who being blind, by this meanes are occasioned to tumble into the *ditch of Hell* after their *blind leaders*, with more inflamed zeale of lying confidence. So, secondly, *violence* and a *sword* of *steele* begets such an *impression* in the sufferers, that certainly they conclude (as indeed that *Religion* cannot be true which needs such *instruments* of *violence* to uphold it so) that *Persecutors* are far from soft and gentle commiseration of the *blindnesse* of others. To this purpose it pleased the *Father* of *Spirits*, of old, to constraine the *Emperour* of *Rome*, *Antoninus Pius*, to write to all the *Governours* of his *Provinces* to forbeare to persecute the *Christians*, because such dealing must needs be so far from converting the *Christians* from their way, that it rather begat in their mindes an opinion of their *crueltie*, &c.

### Note

1. In *The Complete Writings of Roger Williams*, ed. Samuel L. Caldwell, vol. 3 (New York: Russell & Russell, 1963; originally published as *The Bloudy Tenent, of Persecution, for Cause of Conscience, discussed, in A Conference betweene Truth and Peace*, 1644), pp. 3-4, 129-39.

# Charles Chauncy

*T*hroughout his long career at Boston's First Church, beginning *after receipt of his Harvard M.A. (1727), Chauncy (1705–1787) represented the transition toward a rational, moral faith in keeping with the rising education, culture, and prosperity of New England's Puritans. His* Seasonable Thoughts on the State of Religion in New-England *(1743), a rebuttal of Edwards's defense of revivals, assures his place in church history as party leader of the Great Awakening's opponents. It is not without theological interest: Chauncy attacks the revivals, in the name of tradition, for disdaining the ordinary "means of grace" God has established within the churches and, in the name of sound reason and morality, for inciting fanaticism and disorderly conduct.*

*He worked for years, however, on studies so "radical" that he confided his thoughts to few and withheld public statement until late in life. Portions of these studies, from* The Mystery Hid from Ages and Generations, *appear here. The work reflects an elevation of reason in theology as he challenges the common belief in the eternal damnation of the unbelieving and unrighteous: this view, he argues, is logically incompatible with God's moral attributes and saving purposes. Yet Chauncy's respect for the place of revealed truth in Christianity's message and the authority of scripture, rightly interpreted, are everywhere evident. The desire to reproduce biblical teaching in its purity and simplicity, clean of doctrinal overlays that distort its meaning, was deeply rooted in Protestant tradition and manifested itself not only in Chauncy's "liberalism" but also in theologies that were diametrically opposed to his.*

## THE MYSTERY HID FROM AGES AND GENERATIONS

*Chapter I*
*Containing Preliminary Explanations*[1]

As I am desirous of avoiding confusion of method, and would, at the same time, guard, as much as may be, against the undue operation of prejudice in those who may think it worth their while to read the following essay, it may not be amiss to begin with a few particulars, tending to prevent a misconstruction of my meaning, in the proposition I have advanced, and shall endeavour presently to prove, namely, that *all men, according to the scripture-scheme, shall finally and certainly be happy.* And they are these that follow:

I. I would not be understood to mean hereby, that all men will be admitted to the enjoyment of happiness in the state that next succeeds the present. This would be a direct contradiction to the general tenour of the scriptures. Nay, it should seem, from several passages in the New Testament, as though the greater part of mankind would miss of happiness in the state that follows next upon this. To this purpose is that of our Saviour, "Strait is the gate, and narrow the way, which leadeth unto life; and *few* there be that find it."[2] And, when one came to him with that question, "Lord, are there *few* that be saved?" he plainly concedes that it was so, by the reply which he makes in the following verse, "Strive to enter in at the strait gate; for *many,* I say unto you, will seek to enter in, and *shall not be able.*"[3] And it is observable, the conclusion of two of his parables is summed up in these emphatical words, "For many are called, and few are chosen."[4] To these and such like texts it may be owing, that the salvation of comparatively but a few of the human race has been received as an undoubted doctrine of the bible. And I see not, I confess, but that such texts would be a full confirmation of this doctrine, if it were a truth (as has been generally supposed) that the next is the final state of men. But if this, instead of a truth, should turn out a false notion, grounded on mistaken apprehensions of the genuine sense of scripture, the above declarations, importing that many shall not be saved in the next state, are no inconsistencies with the affirmation we have laid down to be proved. . . .

II. Though I affirm, that all men will finally be happy, yet I deny not but that many of them will be miserable in the next state of existence, and to a great degree, and for a long time, in proportion to the moral depravity they have contracted in this. There is no reasonable room for debate here. It is not only plain from the threatenings of God in general, compared with the known characters of men, but from several parables spoken by our Saviour, as well as from the frequent representations that are made of the great, and (as it is commonly called) last judgment, that many, in consequence of their present ill-conduct, will have their next existence in the place of "weeping, and wailing, and gnashing of teeth." Most interpreters, I am aware, suppose this to be a place of everlasting torment. . . . But that the scripture ought not to be interpreted in this sense, we shall take care to make clearly evident afterwards. . . .

III. I would not be understood, when I say, that all men shall be finally happy, to insinuate as though this would ever be their lot, till they are all cured of their moral depravity, and formed to a meetness for heaven, by being brought back to a virtuous temper of mind. Men, who are intelligent and moral agents, cannot be rationally happy, but in the regular exercise of their intellectual and moral powers. While in a degenerate state, they must be miserable. 'Tis impossible in the nature of things it should be otherwise. And if ever they are delivered from their misery, it must be by effecting a change in their moral character. . . .

IV. Upon the whole therefore, what I mean to prove, in the following essay, is, that the scheme of revelation has the happiness of all mankind lying at bottom, as its great and ultimate end; that it gradually tends to this end; and will not fail of its accomplishment, when fully compleated. . . .

This, in general, I take to be the scheme of revelation, with reference to the human kind. And it exhibits the Deity in so amiable and interesting a light, and reflects so much glory on the mediatorial undertaking of Jesus Christ, that every man, one would think, should, beforehand, be disposed to wish it might be well supported from the scriptures. Can the thought be displeasing to any son of Adam, that the whole human race shall finally have entrance ministered to them into the kingdom of heaven, to partake there of joys that flow for ever from God's right hand? Where is the man so destitute of benevolence, so bereft of humanity, as not to bid God-speed to an attempt, intended to establish it as a revealed truth, that this, before the scene of providence is finally shut up, shall be the portion of all men, of whatever nation, character, colour, station, or condition? . . .

Some generally received doctrines, it is confessed, must be given up, if this is admitted to be the scheme of God, with reference to mankind. And it is high time they should be renounced, and others embraced in their room, that are more honorable to the Father of mercies, and comfortable to the creatures whom his hands have formed. I doubt not, it has been a perplexing difficulty to most persons (I am sure, it has been such to me), how to reconcile the doctrine, which dooms so great a number of the human race to eternal flames, with the essential, absolutely perfect, goodness of the Deity. And, perhaps, they contain ideas utterly irreconcilable with each other. . . . Whereas, there is no difficulty of this sort attending the present scheme. All objections to the infinite benevolence of God vanish at once; and this attribute of the divine nature shines even more conspicuous, as viewed in the light of revelation, than in the light of mere reason. Nor is there any scheme that so illustriously sets forth the powerful efficacy, and extensive advantage, of the mediation of Jesus Christ. If mankind universally are the object of his concern; if he died for them all; if he is ascended up to heaven for them all; if he is there acting on their behalf, and managing all things, in the kingdom of grace, with a view to their salvation, and will not give up his ministry, in this kingdom, till he has actually accomplished this great design, and instated the whole human kind in eternal glory;—what more noble idea can we form of his undertaking for us? . . . Whereas, upon the common scheme, the extent of God's benevolence is comparatively small, as well as the advantage of Christ's mediation. For notwithstanding all that has yet been done, or ever will be done, the greatest part of mankind will continue God's enemies, and the devil's slaves; . . . Is there any room for debate, which of these schemes reflects most honor on God, and Jesus Christ, and is most beneficial to men? . . .

*Conclusion*

. . .

And as it is from the BIBLE, that we are furnished with this *evidence;* as it is in this *sacred book,* that the infinitely benevolent God is represented as having set on foot a *scheme* for the *recovery* of the *whole race of Adam,* which scheme he will go on prosecuting by his *Son Jesus Christ,* on whose *blood* and *righteousness* it was founded, till he has instated them *all* in the profession of *everlasting happiness;*—how *thankful* should we be for the *scripture-revelation?* And how very imprudent are such as *voluntarily* put themselves into the state of those who have *no hope,* but what they fetch by their own arguings from the *mere light of nature?* There are great numbers of this kind of persons in the Christian world; and they seem to be upon the increase. . . . Is the prospect which *mere reason* gives us of a *future world* to be compared with *that,* which we may take of it by the help of *revelation?* By no means. . . .

It is, I am verily persuaded, very much owing to the *false light* in which *revelation* has been placed, and by its very good friends too, that so many have been led to *reject* it. And, in truth, if the *sense* of revelation *really* was, what it has too generally been represented to be, even by Christians themselves, I see not that blame could justly be reflected on them. It is impossible *that* should come from God, which is *unworthy of him,* nor would any *external evidence* be sufficient to justify a man in believing him to be the author of *that,* which, in its own nature, is *unreasonable* and *absurd.* . . .

If, conformably to the account we have given from the *scriptures,* God has so loved us as to project a scheme, which, in the final result of its prosecution, will instate us *all* in *heavenly* and *immortal glory;* how powerfully are we herefrom excited to yield to him the intire homage of our hearts? Who but God, who in competition with God, should be the supreme object of our love, hope, confidence, joy, and delight? We may, with infinite reason, take to ourselves the words of the Psalmist, and say, "Whom have we in heaven but thee? There is none on earth we desire besides thee: Our flesh and our heart may fail us: But God is the strength of our heart, and our portion for ever." . . .

### Notes

1. In *The Mystery Hid from Ages and Generations* (New York: Arno Press & The New York Times, 1969; originally published in 1784), pp. 7-15, 358-64.
2. Matt. vii. 14.
3. Luke xiii. 23.
4. Matt. xx. 16.–xxii. 14.

# Jonathan Edwards

*E*ducated at Yale, Edwards (1703–1758) became the Congregationalist minister at Northampton, Massachusetts (1729–1750),
missionary to the Indians in Stockbridge (1751–1757), and, for the final
three months of his life, President of Princeton. His church was the epi-
center of a regional revival of religion in the early 1730s, and a decade
later he took part in the revivals known as the First Great Awakening.
His writings describing and defending revivalism first brought him to
international attention. Theologically, he was a "strict Calvinist" whose
aim was to renew that tradition's teaching of election, bondage of the
will, salvation by grace, and the importance of spiritual and moral discipline within the church. (His exercise of discipline led to his dismissal
from the Northampton church.) Major works of the 1750s and others
published posthumously developed his cases for original sin and against
freedom of the will as well as his reflections on true virtue and ethics in
carefully argued detail. His knowledgeable, creative deployment of post-
Lockean philosophy in defense of historical doctrine are notable features of his work.

It is frankly an impossible task to choose one passage from Edwards
as representative of the whole. The section chosen here, from part 3 of
his Treatise Concerning Religious Affections in Three Parts *(1746), is his
account of the second of twelve distinguishing marks of the holy affections. For Edwards, there is a difference between authentic and inauthentic Christian piety. The former emerged only as the end product of
divine influences, which aroused affections of pure love of God untamed
by human tendencies toward self-interest. The selection exhibits
Edwards's triple concern for Reformed theology, analytical reasoning,
and experiential religion.*

## SHEWING WHAT ARE DISTINGUISHING SIGNS OF TRULY GRACIOUS AND HOLY AFFECTIONS[1]

*Part Three*

. . .

II. The first objective ground of gracious affections, is the transcendently excellent and amiable nature of divine things, as they are in themselves; and not any conceived relation they bear to self, or self-interest.

I say that the supremely excellent nature of divine things, is the first, or primary and original objective foundation of the spiritual affections of true saints; for I do not suppose that all relation which divine things bear to themselves, and their own particular interest, are wholly excluded from all influence in their gracious affections. For this may have, and indeed has, a secondary and consequential influence in those affections that are truly holy and spiritual; as I shall show how by and by.

It was before observed, that the affection of love is as it were the fountain of all affection; and particularly, that Christian love is the fountain of all gracious affections: now the divine excellency and glory of God, and Jesus Christ, the word of God, the works of God, and the ways of God, etc. is the primary reason, why a true saint loves these things; and not any supposed interest that he has in them, or any conceived benefit that he has received from them, or shall receive from them, or any such imagined relation which they bear to his interest, that self-love can properly be said to be the first foundation of his love to these things.

Some say that all love arises from self-love; and that it is impossible in the nature of things, for any man to have any love to God, or any other being, but that love to himself must be the foundation of it. But I humbly suppose it is for want of consideration, that they say so. They argue, that whoever loves God, and so desires his glory, or the enjoyment of him, he desires these things as his own happiness; the glory of God, and the beholding and enjoying his perfections, are considered as things agreeable to him, tending to make him happy; he places his happiness in them, and desires them as things, which (if they were obtained) would be delightful to him, or would fill him with delight and joy, and so make him happy. And so, they say, it is from self-love, or a desire of his own happiness, that he desires God should be glorified, and desires to behold and enjoy his glorious perfections. But then they ought to consider a little further, and inquire how the man came to place his happi-

89

ness in God's being glorified, and in contemplating and enjoying God's perfections. There is no doubt, but that after God's glory, and the beholding his perfections, are become so agreeable to him, that he places his highest happiness in these things, then he will desire them, as he desires his own happiness. But how came these things to be so agreeable to him, that he esteems it his highest happiness to glorify God, etc.? Is not this the fruit of love? A man must first love God, or have his heart united to him, before he will esteem God's good his own, and before he will desire the glorifying and enjoying of God, as his happiness. 'Tis not strong arguing, that because after a man has his heart united to God in love, as a fruit of this, he desires his glory and enjoyment as his own happiness, that therefore a desire of this happiness of his own, must needs be the cause and foundation of his love: unless it be strong arguing, that because a father begat a son, that therefore his son certainly begat him. If after a man loves God, and has his heart so united to him, as to look upon God as his chief good, and on God's good as his own, it will be a consequence and fruit of this, that even self-love, or love to his own happiness, will cause him to desire the glorifying and enjoying of God; it will not thence follow, that this very exercise of self-love, went before his love to God, and that his love to God was a consequence and fruit of that. Something else, entirely distinct from self-love might be the cause of this, viz. a change made in the views of his mind, and relish of his heart; whereby he apprehends a beauty, glory, and supreme good, in God's nature, as it is in itself. This may be the thing that first draws his heart to him, and causes his heart to be united to him, prior to all considerations of his own interest or happiness, although after this, and as a fruit of this, he necessarily seeks his interest and happiness in God.

There is such a thing, as a kind of love or affection, that a man may have towards persons or things, which does properly arise from self-love; a preconceived relation to himself, or some respect already manifested by another to him, or some benefit already received or depended on, is truly the first foundation of his love, and what his affection does wholly arise from; and is what precedes any relish of, or delight in the nature and qualities inherent in the being beloved, as beautiful and amiable. When the first thing that draws a man's benevolence to another, is the beholding those qualifications and properties in him, which appear to him lovely in themselves, and the subject of them, on this account, worthy of esteem and goodwill, love arises in a very different manner, than when it first arises from some gift bestowed by another, or depended on from him, as a judge loves and favors a man that has bribed him; or from the relation he supposes another has to him, as a man who loves another because he looks upon him as his child. When love to another arises thus, it does truly and properly arise from self-love.

That kind of affection to God or Jesus Christ, which does thus properly arise from self-love, cannot be a truly gracious and spiritual love; as appears from what has been said already: for self-love is a principle entirely natural, and as much in the hearts of devils as angels; and therefore surely nothing that is the mere result of it, can be supernatural and divine, in the manner before described.[2] Christ plainly speaks of this kind of love, as what is nothing beyond the love of wicked men, Luke 6:32: "If ye love them that love you, what thank have ye? For sinners also love those that love them." And the devil himself knew that that kind of respect to God which was so mercenary, as to be only for benefits received or depended on (which is all one), is worthless in the sight of God; otherwise he never would have made use of such a slander before God, against Job, as in Job 1:9-10: "Doth Job serve God for nought? Hast thou not made an hedge about him, and about his house?" etc. Nor would God ever have implicitly allowed the objection to have been good, in case the accusation had been true, by allowing that that matter should be tried, and that Job should be so dealt with, that it might appear in the event, whether Job's respect to God was thus mercenary or no, and by putting the proof of the sincerity and goodness of his respect, upon that issue.

'Tis unreasonable to think otherwise, than that the first foundation of a true love to God, is that whereby he is in himself lovely, or worthy to be loved, or the supreme loveliness of his nature. This is certainly what makes him chiefly amiable. What chiefly makes a man, or any creature lovely, is his excellency; and so what chiefly renders God lovely, and must undoubtedly be the chief ground of true love, is his excellency. God's nature, or the divinity, is infinitely excellent; yea 'tis infinite beauty, brightness, and glory itself. But how can that be true love of this excellent and lovely nature, which is not built on the foundation of its true loveliness? How can that be true love of beauty and brightness, which is not for beauty and brightness' sake? How can that be a true prizing of that which is in itself infinitely worthy and precious, which is not for the sake of its worthiness and preciousness? This infinite excellency of the divine nature, as it is in itself, is the true ground of all that is good in God in any respect; but how can a man truly and rightly love God, without loving him for that excellency in him, which is the foundation of all that is in any manner of respect good or desirable in him? They whose affection to God is founded first on his profitableness to them, their affection begins at the wrong end; they regard God only for the utmost limit of the stream of divine good, where it touches them, and reaches their interest; and have no respect to that infinite glory of God's nature, which is the original good, and the true fountain of all good, the first fountain of all loveliness of every kind, and so the first foundation of all true love.

A natural principle of self-love may be the foundation of great affections towards God and Christ, without seeing anything of the beauty and glory of the divine nature. There is a certain gratitude that is a mere natural thing. Gratitude is one of the natural affections of the soul of man, as well as anger; and there is a gratitude that arises from self-love, very much in the same manner that anger does. Anger in men is an affection excited against another, or in opposition to another, for something in him that crosses self-love: gratitude is an affection one has toward another, for loving him, or gratifying him, or for something in him that suits self-love. And there may be a kind of gratitude, without any true or proper love; as there may be anger without any proper hatred, as in parents towards their children, that they may be angry with, and yet at the same time have a strong habitual love to them. This gratitude is the principle which is in exercise in wicked men, in that which Christ declares concerning them, in the 6th of Luke, where he says, "Sinners love those that love them" [Luke 6:32]; and which he declares concerning even the Publicans, who were some of the most carnal and profligate sort of men (Matt. 5:46). This is the very principle that is wrought upon by bribery, in unjust judges; and it is a principle that even the brute beasts do exercise: a dog will love his master that is kind to him. And we see in innumerable instances, that mere nature is sufficient to excite gratitude in men, or to affect their hearts with thankfulness to others for kindnesses received; and sometimes toward them, whom at the same time they have an habitual enmity against. Thus Saul was once and again greatly affected, and even dissolved with gratitude towards David, for sparing his life; and yet remained an habitual enemy to him. And as men, from mere nature, may be thus affected towards men; so they may towards God. There is nothing hinders, but that the same self-love may work after the same manner towards God, as towards men. And we have manifest instances of it in Scripture; as in the children of Israel, who sang God's praises at the Red Sea, but soon forgat God's works; and in Naaman the Syrian, who was greatly affected with the miraculous cure of his leprosy, so as to have his heart engaged thenceforward to worship the God that had healed him, and him only, excepting when it would expose him to be ruined in his temporal interest. So was Nebuchadnezzer greatly affected with God's goodness to him, in restoring him to his reason and kingdom, after his dwelling with the beasts.

Gratitude being thus a natural principle, it renders ingratitude so much the more vile and heinous; because it shows a dreadful prevalence of wickedness when it even overbears, and suppresses the better principles of human nature: as it is mentioned as an evidence of the high degree of the wickedness of many of the heathen, that they were without natural affection (Rom. 2:31). But that the want of gratitude, or natural affection, are evidences of an high degree of vice, is no argument that all gratitude and natural affection, has the nature of virtue, or saving grace.

Self-love, through the exercise of mere natural gratitude, may be the foundation of a sort of love to God many ways. A kind of love may arise from a false notion of God, that men have been educated in, or have some way imbibed; as though he were only goodness and mercy, and no revenging justice; or as though the exercises of his goodness were necessary, and not free and sovereign; or as though his goodness were dependent on what is in them, and as it were constrained by them. Men on such grounds as these, may love a God of their own forming in their imaginations, when they are far from loving such a God as reigns in heaven.

Again, self-love may be the foundation of an affection in men towards God, through a great insensibility of their state with regard to God, and for want of conviction of conscience to make 'em sensible how dreadfully they have provoked God to anger; they have no sense of the heinousness of sin, as against God, and of the infinite and terrible opposition of the holy nature of God against it: and so having formed in their minds such a God as suits them, and thinking God to be such an one as themselves, who favors and agrees with them, they may like him very well, and feel a sort of love to him, when they are far from loving the true God. And men's affections may be much moved towards God, from self-love, by some remarkable outward benefits received from God; as it was with Naaman, Nebuchadnezzar, and the children of Israel at the Red Sea.

Again, a very high affection towards God, may, and often does arise in men, from an opinion of the favor and love of God to them, as the first foundation of their love to him. After awakenings and distress through fears of hell, they may suddenly get a notion, through some impression on their imagination, or immediate suggestion, with or without texts of Scripture, or by some other means, that God loves 'em, and has forgiven their sins, and made them his children; and this is the first thing that causes their affections to flow towards God and Jesus Christ: and then after this, and upon this foundation, many things in God may appear lovely to them, and Christ may seem excellent. And if such persons are asked, whether God appears lovely and amiable in himself? They would perhaps readily answer, Yes; when indeed, if the matter be strictly examined, this good opinion of God was purchased and paid for before ever they afforded it, in the distinguishing and infinite benefits they imagined they received from God; and they allow God to be lovely in himself, no otherwise, than that he has forgiven them, and accepted them, and loves them above most in the world, and has engaged to improve all his infinite power and wisdom in preferring, dignifying and exalting them, and will do for 'em just as they would have him. When once they are firm in this apprehension, 'tis easy to own God and Christ to be lovely and glorious, and to admire and extol them. 'Tis easy for them to own Christ to be a lovely person, and the best in the world, when they are first firm in it, that he, though Lord of the universe, is captivated with love to them, and has his heart swallowed up in them, and prizes 'em far beyond most of their neighbors, and loved 'em from eternity, and died for 'em, and will make 'em reign in eternal glory with him in heaven. When this is the case with carnal men, their very lusts will make him seem lovely: pride itself will prejudice them in favor of that which they call Christ: selfish proud man naturally calls that lovely that greatly contributes to his interest, and gratifies his ambition.

And as this sort of persons begin, so they go on. Their affections are raised from time to time, primarily on this foundation of self-love and a conceit of God's love to them. Many have a false notion of communion with God, as though it were carried on by impulses, and whispers, and external representations, immediately made to their imagination. These things they often have; which they take to be manifestations of God's great love to 'em, and evidences of their high exaltation above others of mankind; and so their affections are often renewedly set agoing.

Whereas the exercises of true and holy love in the saints arise in another way. They don't first see that God loves them, and then see that he is lovely; but they first see that God is lovely, and that Christ is excellent and glorious, and their hearts are first captivated with this view, and the exercises of their love are wont from time to time to begin here, and to arise primarily from these views; and then, consequentially, they see God's love; and great favor to them.[3] The saint's affections begin with God; and self-love has a hand in these affections consequentially, and secondarily only. On the contrary, those false affections begin with self, and an acknowledgment of an excellency in God, and an affectedness with it, is only consequential and dependent. In the love of the true saint God is the lowest foundation; the love of the excellency of his nature is the foundation of all the affections which come afterwards, wherein self-love is concerned as an handmaid: on the contrary, the hypocrite lays himself at the bottom of all, as the first foundation, and lays on God as the superstructure; and even his acknowledgment of God's glory itself, depends on his regard to his private interest.

Self-love may not only influence men, so as to cause them to be affected with God's kindness to them separately; but also with God's kindness to them, as parts of a community: as a natural principle of self-love, without any other principle, may be sufficient to make a man concerned for the interest of the nation to which he belongs: as for instance, in the present war, self-love may make natural men rejoice at the successes of our nation, and sorry for their disadvantages, they being concerned as members of the body. So the same natural principles may extend further, and even to the world of mankind, and might be affected with the benefits the inhabitants of the earth have, beyond those of the inhabitants of other planets; if we knew that such there were, and knew how it was with them. So this principle may cause men to be affected with the benefits that mankind have received beyond the fallen angels. And hence men, from this principle, may be much affected with the wonderful goodness of God to mankind, his great goodness in giving his Son to die for fallen man, and the marvelous love of Christ in suffering such great things for us, and with the great glory they hear God has provided in heaven for us; looking on themselves as persons concerned and interested, as being some of this species of creatures, so highly favored: the same principle of natural gratitude may influence men here, as in the case of personal benefits.

But these things that I have said do by no means imply that all gratitude to God is a mere natural thing, and that there is no such thing as a spiritual gratitude, which is a holy and divine affection: they imply no more, than that there is a gratitude which is merely natural, and that when persons have affections towards God only or primarily for benefits received, their affection is only the exercise of a natural gratitude. There is doubtless such a thing as a gracious gratitude, which does greatly differ from all that gratitude which natural men experience. It differs in the following respects:

1. True gratitude or thankfulness to God for his kindness to us, arises from a foundation laid before, of love to God for what he is in himself; whereas a natural gratitude has no such antecedent foundation. The gracious stirrings of grateful affection to God, for kindness received, always are from a stock of love already in the heart, established in the first place on other grounds, viz. God's own excellency; and hence the affections are disposed to flow out, on occasions of God's kindness. The saint having seen the glory of God, and his heart overcome by it, and captivated into a supreme love to him on that account, his heart hereby becomes tender, and easily affected with kindnesses received. If a man has no love to another, yet gratitude may be moved by some extraordinary kindness; as in Saul towards David. But this is not the same kind of thing, as a man's gratitude to a dear friend, that his heart was before possessed with a high esteem of, and love to; whose heart by this means became tender towards him, and more easily affected with gratitude, and affected in another manner. Self-love is not excluded from a gracious gratitude; the saints love God for his kindness to them, "I love the Lord, because he hath heard the voice of my supplication" (Ps. 116:1). But something else is included; and another love prepares the way, and lays the foundation, for these grateful affections.

2. In a gracious gratitude, men are affected with the attribute of God's goodness and free grace, not only as they are concerned in it, or as it affects their interest, but as a part of the glory and beauty of God's nature. That wonderful and unparalleled grace of God, which is manifested in the work of redemption, and shines forth in the face of Jesus Christ, is infinitely glorious in itself, and appears so to the angels; 'tis a great part of the moral perfection and beauty of God's nature: this would be glorious, whether it were exercised towards us or no; and the saint who exercises a gracious thankfulness for it, sees it to be so, and delights in it as such; though his concern in it serves the more to engage his mind, and raise the attention and affection; and self-love here assists as an handmaid, being subservient to higher principles, to lead forth a mind to the view and contemplation, and engage and fix the attention, and heighten the joy and love: God's kindness to them is a glass that God sets before them, wherein to behold the beauty of the attribute of God's goodness; the exercises and displays of this attribute, by this means, are brought near to them, and set right before them. So that in a holy thankfulness to God, the concern our interest has in God's good-

ness, is not the first foundation of our being affected with it; that was laid in the heart before, in that stock of love which was to God, for his excellency in himself, that makes the heart tender, and susceptive of such impressions from his goodness to us: nor is our own interest, or the benefits we have received, the only, or the chief objective ground of the present exercises of the affection; but God's goodness, as part of the beauty of his nature; although the manifestations of that lovely attribute, set immediately before our eyes, in the exercises of it for us, be the special occasion of the mind's attention to that beauty, at that time, and serves to fix the attention, and heighten the affection.

Some may perhaps be ready to object against the whole that has been said, that text, "We love him, because he first loved us" (1 John 4:19), as though this implied that God's love to the true saints were the first foundation of their love to him.

In answer to this I would observe, that the Apostle's drift in these words, is to magnify the love of God to us from hence, that he loved us, while we had no love to him; as will be manifest to anyone who compares this verse, and the two following, with the 9th, 10th and 11th verses. And that God loved us, when we had no love to him, the Apostle proves by this argument, that God's love to the elect, is the ground of their love to him. And that it is three ways: (1) The saints' love to God, is the fruit of God's love to them; as it is the gift of that love. God gave them a spirit of love to him, because he loved them from eternity. And in this respect God's love to his elect is the first foundation of their love to him, as it is the foundation of their regeneration, and the whole of their redemption. (2) The exercises and discoveries that God has made of his wonderful love to sinful men, by Jesus Christ, in the work of redemption, is one of the chief manifestations, which God has made of the glory of his moral perfection, to both angels and men; and so is one main objective ground of the love of both to God; in a good consistence with what was said before. (3) God's love to a particular elect person, discovered by his conversion, is a great manifestation of God's moral perfection and glory to him, and a proper occasion of the excitation of the love of holy gratitude, agreeable to what was before said. And that the saints do in these respects love God, because he first loved them, fully answers the design of the Apostle's argument in that place. So that no good argument can be drawn from hence, against a spiritual and gracious love in the saints, arising primarily from the excellency of divine things, as they are in themselves, and not from any conceived relation they bear to their interest.

And as it is with the love of the saints, so it is with their joy, and spiritual delight and pleasure: the first foundation of it, is not any consideration or conception of their interest in divine things; but it primarily consists in the sweet entertainment their minds have in the view or contemplation of the divine and holy beauty of these things, as they are in themselves. And this is indeed the very main difference between the joy of the hypocrite, and the joy of the true saint. The former rejoices in himself; self is the first foundation of his joy: the latter rejoices in God. The hypocrite has his mind pleased and delighted, in the first place, with his own privilege, and the happiness which he supposes he has attained, or shall attain. True saints have their minds, in the first place, inexpressibly pleased and delighted with the sweet ideas of the glorious and amiable nature of the things of God. And this is the spring of all their delights, and the cream of all their pleasures; 'tis the joy of their joy. This sweet and ravishing entertainment, they have in the view of the beautiful and delightful nature of divine things, is the foundation of the joy that they have afterwards, in the consideration of their being theirs. But the dependence of the affections of hypocrites is in a contrary order: they first rejoice, and are elevated with it, that they are made so much of by God; and then on that ground, he seems in a sort, lovely to them.

The first foundation of the delight a true saint has in God, is his own perfection; and the first foundation of the delight he has in Christ, is his own beauty; he appears in himself the chief among ten thousand, and altogether lovely: the way of salvation by Christ, is a delightful way to him, for the sweet and admirable manifestations of the divine perfections in it; the holy doctrines of the gospel, by which God is exalted and man abased, holiness honored and promoted, and sin greatly disgraced and discouraged, and free and sovereign love manifested; are glorious doctrines in his eyes, and sweet to his taste, prior to any conception of his interest in these things. Indeed the saints rejoice in their interest in God, and that Christ is theirs; and so they have great reason; but this is not the first spring of their joy: they first rejoice in God as glorious and excellent in himself, and then secondarily rejoice in it, that so glorious a God is theirs: they first have their hearts filled with sweetness, from the view of Christ's excellency, and the excellency of his grace, and the beauty of the way of salvation by him; and then they have a secondary joy, in that so excellent a Saviour, and such excellent grace is theirs.[4]

But that which is the true saint's superstructure, is the hypocrite's foundation. When they hear of the wonderful things of the gospel, of God's great love in sending his Son, of Christ's dying love to sinners, and the great things Christ has purchased, and promised to the saints, and hear these things livelily and eloquently set forth; they may hear with a great deal of pleasure, and be lifted up with what they hear: but if their joy be examined, it will be found to have no other foundation than this, that they look upon these things as theirs, all this exalts them, they love to hear of the great love of Christ so vastly distinguishing some from others; for self-love, and even pride itself, makes 'em affect great distinction from others: no wonder, in this confident opinion of their own good estate, that they feel well under such doctrine, and are pleased in the highest degree, in hearing how much God and Christ makes of 'em. So that their joy is really a joy in themselves, and not in God.

And because the joy of hypocrites is in themselves, hence it comes to pass, that in their rejoicings and elevations, they are wont to keep their eye upon themselves; having received what they call spiritual discoveries or experiences, their minds are taken up about them, admiring their own experiences: and what they are principally taken and elevated with, is not the glory of God, or beauty of Christ, but the beauty of their experiences. They keep thinking with themselves, what a good experience is this! What a great discovery is this! What wonderful things have I met with! And so they put their experiences in the place of Christ, and his beauty and fullness; and instead of rejoicing in Christ Jesus, they rejoice in their admirable experiences: instead of feeding and feasting their souls in the view of what is without them, viz. the innate, sweet, refreshing amiableness of the things exhibited in the gospel, their eyes are off from these things, or at least they view them only as it were sideways; but the object that fixes their contemplation, is their experience; and they are feeding their souls, and feasting a selfish principle with a view of their discoveries: they take more comfort in their discoveries than in Christ discovered, which is the true notion of living upon experiences and frames; and not a using experiences as the signs, on which they rely for evidence of their good estate, which some call living on experiences: though it be very observable, that some of them who do so, are most notorious for living upon experiences, according to the true notion of it.

The affections of hypocrites are very often after this manner; they are first, much affected with some impression on their imagination, or some impulse, which they take to be an immediate suggestion, or testimony from God, of his love and their happiness, and high privilege in some respect, either with or without a text of Scripture; they are mightily taken with this, as a great discovery; and hence arise high affections. And when their affections are raised, then they view those high affections, and call them great and wonderful experiences; and they have a notion that God is greatly pleased with those affections; and this affects them more; and so they are affected with their affections. And thus their affections rise higher and higher, till they sometimes are perfectly swallowed up: and self-conceit, and a fierce zeal rises withal; and all is built like a castle in the air, on no other foundation but imagination, self-love and pride.

And as the thoughts of this sort of persons are, so is their talk; for out of the abundance of their heart, their mouth speaketh. As in their high affections, they keep their eye upon the beauty of their experiences, and greatness of their attainments; so they are great talkers about themselves. The true saint, when under great spiritual affections, from the fullness of his heart, is ready to be speaking much of God, and his glorious perfections and works, and of the beauty and amiableness of Christ, and the glorious things of the gospel; but hypocrites, in their high affections, talk more of the discovery, than they do of the thing discovered; they are full of talk about the great things they have met with, the wonderful discoveries they have had, how sure they are of the love of God to them, how safe their condition is, and how they know they shall go to heaven, etc.

A true saint, when in the enjoyment of true discoveries of the sweet glory of God and Christ, has his mind too much captivated and engaged by what he views without himself, to stand at that time to view himself, and his own attainments: it would be a diversion and loss which he could not bear, to take his eye off from the ravishing object of his contemplation, to survey his own experience, and to spend time in thinking with himself, what an high attainment this is, and what a good story I now have to tell others. Nor does the pleasure and sweetness of his mind at that time, chiefly arise from the consideration of the safety of his state, or anything he has in view of his own qualifications, experiences, or circumstances; but from the divine and supreme beauty of what is the object of his direct view, without himself; which sweetly entertains, and strongly holds his mind.

As the love and joy of hypocrites, are all from the source of self-love; so it is with their other affections, their sorrow for sin, their humiliation and submission, their religious desires and zeal: everything is as it were paid for beforehand, in God's highly gratifying their self-love, and their lusts, by making so much of them, and exalting them so highly, as things are in their imagination. 'Tis easy for nature, as corrupt as it is, under a notion of being already some of the highest favorites of heaven, and having a God who does so protect 'em and favor 'em in their sins, to love this imaginary God that suits 'em so well, and to extol him, and submit to him, and to be fierce and zealous for him. The high affections of many are all built on the supposition of their being eminent saints. If that opinion which they have of themselves were taken away, if they thought they were some of the lower form of saints (though they should yet suppose themselves to be real saints), their high affections would fall to the ground. If they only saw a little of the sinfulness and vileness of their own hearts, and their deformity, in the midst of their best duties and their best affections, it would knock their affections on the head; because their affections are built upon self, therefore self-knowledge would destroy them. But as to truly gracious affections, they are built elsewhere: they have their foundation out of self, in God and Jesus Christ; and therefore a discovery of themselves, of their own deformity, and the meanness of their experiences, though it will purify their affections, yet it will not destroy them, but in some respects sweeten and heighten them.

### Notes

1. In *The Works of Jonathan Edwards: Religious Affections*, ed. John E. Smith, vol. 2 (New Haven: Yale University Press, 1959; originally published in 1746), pp. 240-53.
2. "There is a natural love to Christ, as to one that doth thee good, and for thine own ends; and spiritual, for himself, whereby the Lord only is exalted." Thomas Shepard, *The Parable of the Ten Virgins* (London, 1660), Pt. I, p. 25.
3. "There is a seeing of Christ after a man believes, which is Christ in his love, etc. But I speak of that first sight of him that precedes the second act of faith; and 'tis an intuitive, or real sight of him, as he is in his glory." Shepard, *Parable*, Pt. I, p. 74.
4. Dr. Owen, speaking of a common work of the Spirit, says, "The effects of this work on the mind, which is the first subject affected with it, proceeds not so far, as to give it delight, complacency and satisfaction in the lovely spiritual nature and excellencies of the things revealed unto it. The true nature of saving illumination consists in this, that it give the mind such a direct intuitive insight and prospect into spiritual things, as that in their own spiritual nature they suit, please, and satisfy it; so that it is transformed into them, cast into the mold of them, and rests in them; Rom. 6:17; 12:2; I Cor. 2:13-14; II Cor. 3:18; 4:6. This, the work we have insisted on, reacheth not unto. For notwithstanding any discovery that is made therein of spiritual things unto the mind, it finds not an immediate, direct, spiritual excellency in them; but only with respect unto some benefit or advantage, which is to be attained by means thereof. It will not give such a spiritual insight into the mystery of God's grace by Jesus Christ, called his glory shining in the face of Christ, II Cor. 4:6, as that the soul, in its first direct view of it, should, for what it is in itself, admire it, delight in it, approve it, and find spiritual solace, with refreshment, in it. But such a light, such a knowledge, it communicates, as that a man may like it well in its effects, as a way of mercy and salvation." John Owen, *Pneumatologia or, A Discourse Concerning the Holy Spirit* (London, 1674), Bk. III, ch. 2, sec. 16, pp. 199-200.

# Samuel Hopkins

*H*opkins *(1721–1803) studied for ministry with Edwards following his Yale B.A. (1741), and he sought thereafter in his writings and ministry among New England Congregationalists to uphold and extend his teacher's legacy. Along with other followers of Edwards such as Joseph Bellamy, Nathaniel Emmons, and Jonathan Edwards, Jr., Hopkins combined Edwards's staunch, scholarly Calvinism with revivalistic conversion and concern for moral reform into a mix variously called New Divinity, Edwardseanism, Consistent Calvinism, and Hopkinsianism.*

*His "Application of Redemption" describes humanity's fall into sin and the need for and provision of redemption through union with Jesus Christ. This selection offers his account of regeneration. It was preceded by an introduction stating that regeneration is one side (the divine "cause") of redemption; its other side is conversion (its human effects). As this division suggests, Hopkins aims at stressing both divine and human elements in redemption, and in proper relationship. The success of his efforts was much disputed, some praising his brilliant exposition of the Calvinist-Edwardsean heritage, others detecting in his work subtle but troubling modifications of it. Also surfacing in this excerpt is the controversial Hopkinsian affirmation of the direct (unmediated) work of the Holy Spirit.*

## THE APPLICATION OF REDEMPTION[1]

*Section II. On Regeneration*

It has been observed that mankind, being naturally under the power of sin and total depravity, it is necessary that they should be the subjects of a renovation by the Spirit of God, in order to their union to Christ and being redeemed by him. It is proposed now to attend more particularly to this renovation as it is represented in the Holy Scriptures.

Regeneration and conversion are often used only as two words meaning the same thing; and it is certain that all that can be properly understood by them is that change and renovation, which is expressed in Scripture by being *born again, born of the Spirit of God* and *born of God, created in Christ Jesus unto good works,* etc. Yet, as there are two distinct things included in this change, which it is necessary should be distinguished in order to understand this subject, these words may be properly used to make and keep up this distinction, as many divines have done. In this renovation there is the operation of the cause, which is the work done by the Spirit of God; and there is the effect, which consists in the exercises of the regenerate in which they are active and agents. Though these imply each other, and cannot be separated more than the cause can be separated from the effect, yet they must be distinguished; and the former may properly be called regeneration. In order to explain this, and prevent mistakes concerning it, the following things must be observed:—

1. The Spirit of God is the only agent and cause by whose energy the effect takes place; and, so far as the Spirit of God is the cause and agent, the subject, the heart of man, is passive, being the subject on which, or in which, the effect is wrought. Though the effect be activity, or the exercise of the new heart, in which the renewed person is the agent, yet, in the operation which causes the effect to exist, and, therefore, in the order of nature is antecedent to the effect, the Spirit of God is the only agent, and man is the passive subject.

2. This change, of which the Spirit of God is the cause, and in which he is the only agent, is instantaneous,—wrought not gradually, but at once. The human heart is either a heart of stone—a rebellious heart, or a new heart. The man is either under the dominion of sin, as obstinate and vile as ever, dead in trespasses and sins, or his heart is humble and penitent, he is a new creature, and spiritually alive. There can be no instant of time in which the heart is neither a hard heart nor a new heart and the man is neither dead in trespasses and sins nor spiritually alive. The Spirit of God finds the heart of man wholly corrupt, and desperately wicked,—wholly and strongly, even with all the power he has, opposed to God and his law, and to that renovation which he produces. The enmity of the heart against God continues as strong as ever it was till it is slain by the instantaneous energy of the divine Spirit, and from carnal it becomes spiritual, betwixt which there is no medium, according to Scripture and reason. All the exercises of the hard, impenitent, unrenewed heart are exercises of impenitence and rebellion,—of enmity

against God and his law; whatever the external conduct may be, they are the corrupt fruit of a corrupt, rebellious heart. The exercises and fruit of a heart dead in trespasses and sins are *dead works*. If this were not demonstrably certain from the nature of the case, it is abundantly asserted in the Scripture, and our Savior has decided it in the most express manner. His words are, "Either make the tree good, and his fruit good, or else make the tree corrupt, and his fruit corrupt. A good man, out of the good treasure of his heart, bringeth forth good things; and an evil man, out of the evil treasure, bringeth forth evil things." (Matt. xii. 33, 35.) St. Paul repeatedly asserts the same thing. By a number of quotations from the Old Testament, he proves that all men are, by nature, altogether and to a great degree, corrupt;—that there is nothing morally good in them, or done by them. (Rom. iii.9, etc.) He asserts that, antecedent to regeneration, man does nothing morally good,—that all of this kind is the consequence of it. "We are his workmanship, created in Christ Jesus unto good works." (Eph. ii. 10.) And again he says, "We ourselves also were sometimes foolish, disobedient, deceived, serving divers lusts and pleasures, living in malice and envy, hateful, and hating one another. But after that the kindness and love of God our Savior appeared, not by works of righteousness which we have done, but according to his mercy, he saved us by the washing of regeneration, and renewing of the Holy Ghost." (Tit. iii. 3, 4, 5.) Here he describes their state and moral character, which is the character of all men antecedent to regeneration. He denies their having done any good works, but, on the contrary, says all their works were evil, and gives them a very bad character. He then ascribes all their reformation, and the alteration of their character for the better, to their regeneration, by which, alone, they were washed from their moral pollutions.

3. The subject of this operation, in which this change and effect is wrought, is the will or the heart; that is, the moral and not the natural powers and faculties of the soul. As moral depravity is wholly in the will or heart, the source and seat of all moral actions, the divine operation directly respects the heart, and consists in changing and renewing that. The understanding or intellect, considered as distinct from the will, is a natural faculty, and is not capable of moral depravity. It may be hurt and weakened, and improved to bad purposes, as other natural faculties may, by the moral corruption or sinfulness of the heart; but nothing is necessary, in order to remove the disorders of the intellect, and all the natural powers of the soul, but the renovation of the heart: so far as the will is right, the understanding, considered as a natural faculty, will be

rectified, and do its office well. Therefore, regeneration is in Scripture represented as consisting in giving *a new heart,* a heart to know the Lord, etc. The Scripture, indeed, speaks of the understanding being enlightened, and of its being darkened, and of being without understanding, as criminal; and represents a good understanding, as comprehending all virtue or holiness. But the understanding in these instances is not considered and spoken of as mere intellect, distinct from the will or heart; but as comprehending and principally intending the heart, which is the seat of all moral perception and exercise. In Scripture, the distinction between the understanding and the heart is not often made; but the former is generally spoken of as implying the latter, and consisting in that discerning which is implied in right exercises of heart; and cannot take place any farther than the heart is renewed, and the will is right. Therefore, we read of "a wise and *understanding heart.*" And wisdom and understanding are words frequently used in Scripture as nearly synonymous, and denoting the same thing; but *wisdom* belongs to the heart, and is of a moral nature; and that in which, according to the Scripture, true holiness consists.

All moral, criminal darkness, has its seat in the heart, as all sin has, and the former cannot be distinguished from the latter; and selfishness is the essence of both. And, on the contrary, all true light and understanding, which is of a moral nature, belongs to the heart, and implies real holiness, and cannot be separated, and even distinguished from it, as one necessarily implies and involves the other. This is asserted by our divine Teacher in the following words: "The light of the body is the eye; if, therefore, thine eye be single, thy whole body shall be full of light. But if thine eye be evil, thy whole body shall be full of darkness." (Matt. vi. 22, 23.) The single and evil eye are opposites, and belong to the heart, and consist in the exercises of that. This is said by Christ of the evil eye. "For from within, *out of the heart of men,* proceed evil thoughts, adulteries, fornications, murders, thefts, covetousness, wickedness, deceit, lasciviousness, *an evil eye,* blasphemy, pride, foolishness. All these evil things come from within, and defile the man." (Mark vii. 21-23.) Here an evil eye, which fills the mind with darkness, and is darkness itself, is numbered among the evil things which belong to the corrupt heart, and of which that is the source, and is altogether criminal. And, consequently, the single eye, which is opposite to the evil eye, must also belong to the heart, and consists in that which is real holiness, or which implies it. Where this is, the man is full of light.

Therefore, in regeneration, the heart being changed and renewed,

light and understanding take place; and there is no need of any operation on the understanding, or intellectual faculty of the mind, as distinguished from the heart, or any change in that which does not necessarily
take place, upon the renovation of the will or heart.

As the moral disorder and depravity of man lies wholly in his heart,
the cure and renovation must begin and end there; and when the heart
is perfectly right, the man will be wholly recovered to perfect holiness.

This point is particularly observed and stated, to expose and rectify a
mistake which has been too often made, representing regeneration as consisting chiefly, if not wholly, in renewing the understanding, as distinguished from the will, and letting light into that, antecedent to any change
of the heart, and in order to it; and by which light in the understanding,
the will is inclined and turned from sin to holiness. This is turning this
matter upside down, and has a dangerous and bad tendency. It supposes
that human depravity lies in the understanding, and not in the will; or, at
least, that it has its foundation and beginning in the former; and that,
when that comes right, the will or heart acts right, of course. The consequence is, that there is little or no moral depravity in the heart, that being
ready to do its office well, when the understanding is set right; therefore,
man is not blamable for his depravity, and not being holy, since his blindness, which alone is in the way of his acting right, is not dependent on his
will, or owing to any disorders in that. It is, indeed, impossible to give true
moral light and understanding to the depraved mind of man, by any operation whatsoever, on the intellect, antecedent to the renovation of the will;
for the darkness is in the latter, and consists in the wrong inclination of
that; and, therefore, cannot be removed but by renewing the heart.

Others have supposed that there is in regeneration an operation on
the understanding, or intellect, first, in order to enlighten the mind; and
then by divine energy the will is renewed, and brought to comply with
the light let into the understanding. But this is unscriptural, and contrary
to the nature and order of things; and tends to lead to hurtful mistakes,
as has been often observed. Nothing is necessary but the renovation of
the will, in order to set every thing right in the human soul; and if the
will be not renewed, or a new heart be not given, by an immediate operation, no operation on any other faculty of the soul, and no supposable
or possible change can set the heart right, or renew it in the least degree.
The Scripture makes no such distinction between the faculties of the soul
in treating of this matter; but represents the renovation of the will, or
giving a new heart, as setting the whole soul right in all the powers and
faculties of it.

4. The divine operation in regeneration, of which the new heart is the effect, is immediate, or it is not wrought by the energy of any means as the cause of it, but by the immediate power and energy of the Holy Spirit. It is called a creation, and the divine agency in it is as much without any medium, as in creating something from nothing. Men are not regenerated, in the sense in which we are now considering regeneration, by light or the word of God. This is evident from what has been observed under the last particular. If the evil eye, which is total darkness, and shuts all the light out, be the evil, corrupt heart of man, then this corrupt heart must be renewed, in order to there being any true light in the mind, and previous to it. There must be a discerning heart, which is the same with a new heart, in order to see the light; and, therefore, this cannot be produced by light. The evil eye, which shuts out all the light, cannot be cured, and made a single eye, by seeing the light; and the light cannot have any effect, or answer any end, till they are so far made single as to admit the light. Therefore, that operation which changes the evil eye to a single eye, cannot be by means of light; but must take place antecedent to any light, or any influence or effect that can be produced by it. It is said the Lord opened the heart of Lydia, that she attended unto the things that were spoken by Paul. It would be a contradiction, and very absurd, to say that the word spoken by Paul was that by which her heart was opened; for she knew not what he did speak, until her heart was opened to attend to his words, and understand them. Her heart was first opened, in order to his words having any effect, or giving any light to her. And this must be done by an immediate operation of the Spirit of God on her heart. This was the regeneration now under consideration, by which her heart was renewed, and formed to true discerning, like the single eye.

St. James says, "Of his own will begat he us, *with the word of truth*." (James i. 18.) But here in regeneration he includes the effect wrought, or conversion, and does not mean only the act by which the effect is produced, as distinguished from the effect, which is intended by the regeneration now under consideration. The effect produced by the regenerating energy of the Spirit of God, in the adult, is active conversion, which supposes light and truth in the discerning mind, and exercises answerable to it; which is to be particularly considered, under the next general head.

5. The divine operation in the regeneration of which we are speaking, though very great and powerful, is altogether imperceptible by the subject on whom the work is wrought, and by which he is regenerated.

Nothing is perceived but the effect, which in the adult consists in perception of truth and answerable exercises. The cause is to be learned and
known only by the effect. When Adam was created, he perceived nothing, and was conscious of nothing, but his own existence, perceptions,
and exercises. The divine operation, which was the cause of his existence, was over and finished, before he began to perceive any thing.
Every creature is constantly supported by God, and divine energy
attends and is exerted in all our motions and actions. "For in him we
live, and move, [or, which is more agreeable to the original, *are moved,*]
and have our being." "And the inspiration of the Almighty giveth us
understanding." Yet we perceive nothing but the effect, and argue the
cause from the effect. So it is in this case. "The wind bloweth where it
listeth, and thou hearest the sound thereof, but canst not tell whence it
cometh, and whither it goeth: so is every one that is born of the Spirit."
(John. iii. 8.)

6. The grace granted in regeneration is a sovereign, undeserved, and
unpromised favor.

The sinner, who is the chosen subject of this operation, and object of
this favor, is infinitely ill deserving, and is disposed to go on in rebellion,
till this change is wrought. He is obstinate, and refuses to hearken to the
divine command, to repent and embrace the gospel, and the offer of
mercy, whatever methods have been taken with him to reclaim him.
However much he may be terrified with the fears of threatened destruction, and the evil, dangerous state in which he is; and though he may
have earnest desires to escape misery, and be happy forever, and may
make many prayers, and do many things, he has not the least inclination
to repent, submit to God and accept of offered mercy; but, directly contrary to all this, he with his whole heart abuses every favor granted to
him, rejects the offer of mercy, opposes God, slights Christ, and resists
the Holy Ghost, in all his prayers and in all he does; for still his heart is
a heart of stone, an impenitent, rebellious heart, and is full of enmity
against God. This character is given of all the unregenerate, in the Scripture. Therefore, he is not only undeserving of any favor, and especially
of this, and infinitely ill deserving, but is constantly provoking God to
give him up to utter destruction. When the sinner is in this situation,
God has mercy on him, and by his Spirit gives him a new heart. Surely
this is, in the highest sense *sovereign mercy.* God is infinitely far from
being under obligation to any sinner to do this for him: "Therefore hath
he mercy on whom he will have mercy, and whom he will he hard-
eneth."

And God has not obliged himself by any promise to grant this mercy to any individual person, antecedent to his actually doing it. He has made no promise, in his word, to those who do not accept nor desire the mercy and salvation which he offers, but reject it with their whole heart; which is true of all the unregenerate, as has been observed. There are, indeed, promises made to the church, that God will pour out his Spirit, and regenerate sinners; but no individual, unconverted sinner can claim this promise, as it is not made to him in particular. There are promises made to those who repent and believe the gospel, that they shall be saved, that the Spirit of God shall dwell in them forever, etc., but the regenerating influences of the Spirit, which are antecedent to faith, and the first act of faith, which is the gift of God, are unpromised gifts and favors; and God cannot be under any obligation to those who receive them by promise, or any other way.

7. The divine operation, by which men are regenerated, and a new heart is given, is not in the least degree inconsistent with human liberty, nor does it impede or obstruct it in any respect; but finds and leaves men in the free exercise of all desirable or possible freedom, and wholly blamable for all the exercises of their heart, not conformable to the law of God, and commendable for all right exercises of the new heart; which are as much their own, and as free, as if they had taken place without any divine influences, were this possible.

This is evident and certain, if liberty consists in voluntary action, or in the choice and exercises of the will, and in nothing else. No compulsion can be offered to the will, or the freedom of it be any way affected by any operation or influence on the mind which takes place antecedent to the exercise of the will, and in order to the choice that is made. Man is active only in willing, and in this only consists his moral freedom. And in this he is not capable of compulsion; and no impression that is made upon him, nor any operation whatsoever can take away his liberty in the least degree unless it obstructs and is inconsistent with his acting voluntarily. For so far, and so long, as he does this, and puts forth acts of will, they are his own acts, and he is free, and enjoys and exercises all the freedom of which there can be any consistent conception, or that is possible in the nature of things. Antecedent to regeneration, man acts freely. With great strength of inclination and choice, his heart opposes the law of God, and rejects the gospel, seeking himself wholly. And when the instantaneous, immediate energy of the Holy Spirit renews his heart, he turns about, and loves and chooses what he hated before, and exercises as real freedom in his choice and pursuit of that which he had opposed and rejected.

8. Regeneration is but the beginning of a divine operation which does not wholly renew the heart at once; but from this small beginning the operation continues and goes on to perfection, that is, till the heart is made perfectly clean and holy, which will not be accomplished till death. For God continues to work in the regenerate to will and to do, and they are as dependent on divine influence for every after right exercise of will, as for the first. And God who begins this good work in them will perform it, and go on with it, until the day of Jesus Christ. (Phil. i.6; ii.13.)

**Note**

1. In *The Works of Samuel Hopkins*, vol. 1, American Religious Thought of the 18th and 19th Centuries, ed. Bruce Kuklick (New York: Garland Publishing, 1987; originally published in 1865), pp. 367-74.

# John Woolman

*The life and writings of Woolman (1720–1772) cast light on understandings of faith developed in the context of the Society of Friends, or Quakers, and illustrative as well of spiritual and ethical imperatives that touched the consciences of many Reformed Christians. The Reformed tradition stressed conversion and commitment to righteous living by the power of the Spirit despite its own opposition to Quakerism itself. Woolman, a New Jersey Quaker, consciously chose a plain and simple life, devoting himself to a self-supported itinerant ministry. Concern for those who were "least" in terms of the views and ways of the world—the poor, Native Americans, slaves, and everyone in suffering or despair—was uppermost in his thoughts. His journals have long been regarded as a classic exemplar of religious autobiography.*

*His extended appeal for Christian living,* Plea for the Poor *(printed in 1793 but drafted thirty years before), captures his "radical" view of faithfulness. Its overall theme may be summarized in a phrase: because "the earth is the Lord's," the people of God should undertake selfless service of care toward all creatures. Each chapter applies this message to one or more spheres of human life and society.*

## A Plea for the Poor or A Word of Remembrance and Caution to the Rich[1]

*Chapter Two*

The Creator of the earth is the owner of it. He gave us being thereon, and our nature requires nourishment which is the produce of it. As he is kind and merciful, we as his creatures, while we live answerable to the design of our creation, we are so far entitled to a convenient subsistence that no man may justly deprive us of it. By the agreements and contracts of our fathers and predecessors, and by doings and proceedings of our own, some claim a much greater share of this world than others; and whilst those possessions are faithfully improved to the good of the whole, it consists with equity. But he who with a view to self-exaltation causeth some with their domestic animals to labour immoderately, and with the moneys arising to him therefrom employs others in the luxuries of life, acts contrary to the gracious design of him who is the true owner of the earth; nor can any possessions, either acquired or derived from ancestors, justify such conduct.

Goodness remains to be goodness, and the direction of pure wisdom is obligatory on all reasonable creatures—that laws and customs are no further a standard for our proceedings than as their foundation is on universal righteousness.

Though the poor occupy our estates by a bargain to which they in their poor circumstance agreed, and we ask even less than a punctual fulfilling of their agreement, yet if our views are to lay up riches or to live in conformity to customs which have not their foundation in the Truth, and our demands are such as requires greater toil or application to business in them than is consistent with pure love, we invade their rights as inhabitants of that world of which a good and gracious God is proprietor, under whom we are tenants.

Were all superfluities and the desire of outward greatness laid aside and the right use of things universally attended to, such a number of people might be employed in things useful that moderate labour with the blessing of heaven would answer all good purposes relating to people and their animals, and a sufficient number have leisure to attend on proper affairs of civil society.

. . .

*Chapter Eight*

To labour for an establishment in divine love where the mind is disentangled from the power of darkness is the great business of man's life. Collecting of riches, covering the body with fine-wrought, costly apparel, and having magnificent furniture operates against universal love and tends to feed self, that to desire these things belongs not to the children of the Light.

He who sent ravens to feed Elijah in the wilderness, and increased the poor widow's small remains of meal and oil, is now as attentive to the necessities of his people as ever, that when he numbers us with his people and saith, "Ye are my sons and daughters" [2 Cor. 6:18]—no greater happiness can be desired by them who know how gracious a Father he is.

The greater part of the necessaries of life are so far perishable that each generation hath occasion to labour for them; and when we look toward a succeeding age with a mind influenced by universal love, we endeavour not to exempt some from those cares which necessarily relate to this life, and give them power to oppress others, but desire they may all be the Lord's children and live in that humility and order becoming his family. Our hearts being thus opened and enlarged, we feel content in a use of things as foreign to luxury and grandeur as that which our Redeemer laid down as a pattern.

By desiring wealth for the power and distinction it gives and gathering it on this motive, a person may properly be called a rich man, whose mind is moved by a draft distinguishable from the drawings of the Father and cannot be united to the heavenly society, where God is the strength of their life, before he is delivered from this contrary drawing.

"It is easier," saith our Saviour, "for a camel to go through a needle's eye than for a rich man to enter the kingdom of God" [Mark 10:25]. Here our Lord uses an instructing similitude, for as a camel considered under that character cannot pass through a needle's eye, so a man who trusteth in riches and holds them for the sake of the power and distinction attending them cannot in that spirit enter the kingdom. Now every part of a camel may be so reduced as to pass through a hole as small as a needle's eye, yet such is the bulk of the creature, and the hardness of its bones and teeth, that it could not be completed without much labour. So man must cease from that spirit which craves riches, and be reduced into another disposition, before he inherits the kingdom, as effectually as a camel must cease from the form of a camel in passing through the eye of a needle.

When our Saviour said to the rich youth, "Go sell that thou hast and give to the poor" [Mark 10:21], though undoubtedly it was his duty to have done so, yet to confine this of selling all as a duty on every true Christian would be to limit the Holy One. Obedient children who are entrusted with much outward substance wait for wisdom to dispose of it agreeable to his will, in whom "the fatherless findeth mercy" [Hos. 14:3]. It may not be the duty of every one to commit at once their substance to other hands, but rather from time to time to look round amongst the numerous branches of the great family, as his stewards who said, "Leave thy fatherless children; I will preserve them alive; and let thy widows trust in me" [Jer. 49:11]. But as disciples of Christ, however entrusted with much goods, they may not conform to sumptuous or luxurious living. For if possessing great treasures had been a sufficient reason to make a fine show in the world, then Christ our Lord, who had an unfailing storehouse, and in a way surpassing the common operations in nature supplied thousands of people with food, would not have lived in so much plainness.

What we equitably possess is a gift from God to us; but by the Son all things were created. Now he who forms things out of nothing—who creates and, having created, doth possess—is more truly rich than he who possesseth by receiving gifts from another. If depth of knowledge and a high title had been sufficient reasons to make a splendid show, he would have made it. He told the woman of Samaria sundry things relative to her past life, made mention of the decease of Lazarus, and answered the scribe who accounted him a blasphemer, without information, and having the spirit without measure knew what was in man. The title of Lord he owned, nor was it ever more justly given to any—that in riches and wisdom and greatness there was none on earth equal to him; and as he lived in perfect plainness and simplicity, the greatest in his family cannot by virtue of their station claim a right to live in worldly grandeur without contradicting his doctrine who said: "It is enough for the disciple to be as his master" [Matt. 10:25].

### Note

1. In *The Journal and Major Essays of John Woolman,* ed. Phillips P. Moulton, A Library of Protestant Thought (New York: Oxford University Press, 1971; original essay published in 1793), pp. 239-40, 250-52.

# THE NATIONAL ERA

(1789–1865)

# Nathaniel William Taylor

*Taylor (1786–1858) was schooled at Yale under Timothy Dwight and returned after pastoral work to serve as Professor of Theology in 1822. Following Dwight's lead, he sought to realign the New England tradition of Puritan and Edwardsean Calvinism to the revivalism of the Second Great Awakening and emergent Scottish Common-Sense philosophy. The realignment, which evangelist-theologians like Lyman Beecher and Charles G. Finney promoted in church-and-field revivalism, divided the Presbyterian church and disturbed many others. Yet its practical success was beyond question. One result was a popular, "biblical" Calvinism differing little in substance and less in effect from a grace-oriented Arminianism. Masses converted in revivals of the nineteenth century developed into a generically American "evangelical Protestantism," equally capable of uniting or dividing according to the issue at hand and changing circumstances.*

*Taylor's sermon* Concio ad Clerum *(1828) has frequently served to exemplify not only his thought but the "New Haven School Theology" generally, or at least its initial, classic form. The work has three sections, including a footnote on the "moral government of God" of such length it is equivalent to another section. The first part propounds the New Haven doctrine of sin or moral depravity, attempting to distinguish the "tendency to sin" due to humanity's fallen nature from sin itself: God is not the author of sin; its cause and guilt fall solely on human choice. The second part defends this view by reference to the history of doctrine. The third details applications and implications of the doctrine for church ministry. The initial declamation of the doctrine appears here, as does the note expositing God's moral government. Both themes circulated widely in nineteenth-century American theology.*

117

# Concio Ad Clerum: A Sermon[1]

*On Human Nature, Sin, and Freedom*

*Ephesians 2:3.*
*And were by nature the children of wrath, even as others.*

The Bible is a plain book. It speaks, especially on the subject of sin, directly to human consciousness; and tells us beyond mistake, what sin is, and why we sin. In the text, the Apostle asserts the fact of the moral depravity of mankind, and assigns its cause. To be "the children of wrath" is to possess the character which deserves punishment; in other words, it is to be sinners, or to be entirely depraved in respect to moral character. The text then teaches; THAT THE ENTIRE MORAL DEPRAVITY OF MANKIND IS BY NATURE.

. . .

## I [Moral Depravity Defined]

By the moral depravity of mankind I intend generally, the entire sinfulness of their moral character—that state of the mind or heart to which guilt and the desert of wrath pertain. I may say then negatively,

This depravity does not consist in any essential attribute or property of the soul—not in *any thing created* in man by his Maker. On this point, I need only ask—does God create in men a sinful nature, and damn them for the very nature he creates? Believe this, who can.

Nor does the moral depravity of men consist in a sinful nature, which they have corrupted by being *one* with Adam, and by *acting in his act.* To believe that I am one and the same being with another who existed thousands of years before I was born, and that by virtue of this identity I truly acted in his act, and am therefore as truly guilty of his sin as himself—to believe this, I must renounce the reason which my Maker has given me; I must believe it also, in face of the oath of God to its falsehood, entered upon the record.

Nor does the moral depravity of men consist in any *constitutional propensities* of their nature. Whoever supposed himself or others to be guilty, for being hungry or thirsty after long abstinence from food or drink; or merely for desiring knowledge, or the esteem of his fellow-men, or any other good, abstractly from any choice to gratify such desires? Who does not know that a perfectly holy man must he subject to all these propensities? The man Christ Jesus was subject to every one of them, for he "was *in all points* tempted like as we are, yet without sin."

Nor does any degree of *excitement* in these propensities or desires, not resulting in choice, constitute moral depravity. Suppose them then, in the providence of God, excited in any degree, and yet the man to prefer doing the will of God to their gratification; all will admit that it is the noblest act of obedience conceivable in a moral being. All will agree that the man who always triumphs over excited propensity, who duly subordinates all his desires of inferior good to the will of God, is a perfect man. It is the uniform sentiment of inspired truth, that this ruling of the spirit, this government of himself, imparts unrivalled glory to his character. We add the express declaration of the Apostle: "*Blessed* is the man that *endureth* temptation."

Nor does the moral depravity of men consist in *any disposition or tendency* to sin, which is *the cause of all sin*. It is important on this point to guard against error from the ambiguity of terms. There is an obvious distinction between a *disposition* or tendency to sin, which is prior to *all* sin, and a *sinful* disposition. I am not saying, then, that there is not what with entire propriety may be called a disposition or tendency to sin, which is the cause of *all* sin; nor that there is not, as *a consequence* of *this* disposition or tendency, what with equal propriety may be called a *sinful* disposition, which is the true cause of all *other* sin, itself excepted. But I say, that that which is the cause of *all* sin, is not itself sin. The cause of all sin itself sin! Whence then came the first sin? Do you say, from a previous sin as its cause? Then you say, there is a sin before the first sin. Our first parents and fallen angels were once holy. Tell us now, whence came *their* first sin? Do you still repeat, from a previous sin? And what sort of philosophy, reason, or common sense is this—a sin before the first sin—sin before all sin? Do you say there must be *difficulties* in theology? I ask must there be *nonsense* in theology?[2]

The question then still recurs, what is this moral depravity for which man deserves the wrath of God? I answer—*it is man's own act, consisting in a free choice of some object rather than God, as his chief good— or a free preference of the world and of worldly good, to the will and glory of God.*

In support of these views of the subject, I now appeal to the testimony of some of the ablest divines, of Apostles, and of common sense.

Says Calvin, speaking of our text, "our nature is there characterized, not as it was created by God, but as it was vitiated in Adam; *because* it would be unreasonable to make God the author of death."[3] Again, "natural depravity is not a substantial property originally innate, but can be imputed to none but man himself." He says of sin expressly, "it is voluntary." "If they are convicted of any fault, the Lord justly reproaches them with their own perverseness." "He who sins necessarily, sins no less voluntarily."[4]

The Westminster divines say, that "every sin both original and actual being a transgression of the righteous law of God &c."[5] I ask, is not transgression, action? is it not something done, and done knowingly and voluntarily?

Dr. Bellamy, speaking of the *sinful* propensities of man, says "they are not created by God with the essence of the soul, but result from its native choice, or rather, more strictly, are themselves its native *choice*.— They are not natural in the same sense in which the *faculties* of our souls are; for they are not the workmanship of God but are our native *choice*, and the *voluntary, free, spontaneous* bent of our hearts."[6]

Says President Edwards, "The inferior principles of self-love and natural appetite which were given only to serve, (and which as he also says, 'were in man in innocence') being alone and left to themselves became reigning principles. Man did set up himself (which by the way was doing something) and the objects of his private affections and appetites as *supreme,* and so they took the place of God. Man's love to his own honour, private interest and pleasure which was before wholly subordinate unto love to God and regard to his glory (and while thus, he says also, 'all things were in excellent order and in their proper and perfect state') now disposes him to pursue those objects without regard to God's honour or law." Thus he adds, "it is easy to give an account, how total corruption of heart should follow—without God's putting *any evil* into his heart, or implanting any *bad principle,* or infusing any *corrupt taint,* and *so* becoming the author of depravity."[7] Again, he says, "If the essence of virtuousness or fault does not lie in the nature of the dispositions or *acts of the mind,* then it is certain, it lies no where at all." "That which makes vice hateful—is a certain deformity in that *evil will,* which is the soul of all vice." "If a thing be from us, and not from our *choice,* it has not the nature of blame-worthiness or ill-desert."[8]

What says St. Paul? In the context he describes the nature of human depravity, and I request you to mark the agreement between his description and that of the last named author. He says "ye, who were dead in trespasses and sins, wherein ye *walked.*" You see it was a *walking—living* death. Dead as they were, they did something: "Wherein ye walked according to the course of this world." And what is the course of this world? What is it, but as Edwards says, "Men setting up themselves and the objects of their private affections as supreme, so that these things take the place of God?" What is it, but a world loving the creature more than God the Creator, and acting accordingly. Again says this Apostle, "Among whom we all had our conversation"—our deportment and manner of life, "in the lusts of the flesh, fulfiling the desires of the flesh and the mind." Now what is this, but freely and voluntarily yielding to propensities, which men ought to restrain and govern, and to subordinate to the will of God; what is it but propensities rising into a free preference of their objects, and going out into a free purpose of self-gratification? For how can men walk in the lusts of the flesh and fulfil the desires of the flesh and of the mind without preferring the gratification of these lusts and desires to other good? How live and act thus, without choosing to do it? You see then that the sin which the Apostle describes consists not merely in external action, nor merely in having propensities for natural good, but in acting freely, in yielding to these propensities as a matter of choice and preference.

What saith St. James?—"Let no man say when he is tempted, I am tempted of God," (and was there ever a more fatal tempter than God, if he creates sin in us?)—"for God is not tempted of evil neither tempteth he any man; but every man is tempted when he is drawn away of his own lust and enticed. *Then,* when lust, i. e. strong desire (the same word used by Paul when he says 'I have a *desire* to depart, &c.'—and by our Lord when he says 'with *desire* have I *desired* to eat this passover') *then* when lust hath conceived it bringeth forth sin." Now when does lust or strong desire conceive and bring forth sin? When it rises into a preference of its object, and goes out in action to secure its own gratification.—Or, if you say the lust is itself the sin (though I think this is ascribing to the Apostle the absurdity of asserting sin before sin) yet be it so. What then is the lust which is sin, but *a preference of its object,* a *stronger* affection for it than for God? Interpret then the language of the Apostle either way, and you come to the same result—that all sin consists in freely preferring some inferior good to God. I might add to these many other passages. I only ask what is the import of the most common terms used by Apostles to describe sin in its true nature? I refer to such as these, *minding the flesh, walking in the flesh, living after the flesh, the flesh lusting against the Spirit,* what is this, but freely, voluntarily setting up the gratification of our natural propensities and appetites as our chief good, fixing our supreme affections upon it—setting the heart, when the living God claims it, upon some inferior good?

I now enquire, what says Common Sense? Take then any action which common sense in the common use of language calls a *sinful* action—what is the sin of it? As an example, take the act of murder. Now do we mean by this term in common usage, to denote simply the external act of killing? Clearly not. This may be by accident, or in obedience to a divine law. Do we mean simply the external act, together with the specific volition, to perform the act? Clearly not; for there must be such a volition, though the act were performed in obedience to a divine command. It is only when the circumstances and manner of the action evince a selfish or malicious purpose, a state of mind in which the perpetrator of the deed shows a preference of some private selfish interest to the life of a fellow-being, and to the will of God, that we call it murder. So true is it, that we regard this state of mind as constituting the sin of the action, that could we ascertain independently of external action, the existence of such a preference, we should, as the Bible does, pronounce it murder. This preference then of some private interest, object or end, rather than God, common sense decides to be the sin of all that we call sinful action, and strictly speaking, the sum total of all sin.

But common sense decides the question in another form. And here we come to what I regard as the turning point of the whole controversy. So far as I know, the only argument in support of the opinion, that sin pertains to something which is not preference, is based in a supposed decision of common sense. The decision claimed is, that all particular or specific sins, as fraud, falsehood, injustice, unbelief, envy, pride, revenge, result from a *wicked heart,* from a *sinful disposition,* as the cause or source of such sinful acts. To this fact, I yield unqualified assent, as "the dictate of the universal sense & reason of mankind," and by this universal judgment, I wish the present question to be decided. Let us then look at the fact in its full force and just application. There is a man, then, whose course of life is wholly that of a worldling, his heart and hand shut against human woe, living without prayer, without gratitude, unmindful of God, and rejecting the Saviour of men, devising all, purposing all, doing all, for the sake of this world. Why is it? You say, and *all* say, and say *right,* it is owing to his love of the world—to his worldly disposition—to a heart set on the world. Now while all say this, and are right in saying it, we have one simple question to decide, viz. what do all *mean* by it? Every child can answer. Every child knows that the meaning is, that this man does freely and voluntarily fix his affection on worldly good, in preference to God; that the man has chosen the world as his chief good, his portion, his God. He knows that this is what is meant by *a worldly heart, a worldly disposition,* which leads to all *other*

122

sins. So when we ascribe the sins of the miser to his *avaricious disposition,* we mean his supreme love of money; or the crimes of the hero or conqueror to his *ambitious disposition,* we mean his supreme love of fame, a state of mind which involves *preference* for its object. And whatever previous tendency, or if you will, previous disposition, there is to this state of mind; this state of mind itself and not any previous thing as the cause of it, is the *wicked heart*—the sinful disposition of men. They love the creature more than the Creator, when they can and ought to love the Creator most. This forbidden choice of worldly good, this preference of the low and sordid pleasures of the earth to God and his glory—this love of the world which excludes the love of the Father—*this*—*this* is man's depravity. This is that evil treasure of the heart, from which proceed evil things; this is the fountain, the source of all *other* abominations—man's free, voluntary preference of the world as his chief good, amid the revealed glories of a perfect God.

. . .

[Excursus on Sin, Human Freedom, and God's Moral Government]

The difficulties on this difficult subject as it is extensively regarded, result in the view of the writer from two very common but groundless assumptions—assumptions which so long as they are admitted and reasoned upon, *must* leave the subject involved in insuperable difficulties.

The assumptions are these; First, *that sin is the necessary means of the greatest good and as such, so far as it exists, is preferable on the whole to holiness in its stead.* Secondly, *that God could in a moral system have prevented all sin or at least the present degree of sin.*

In further explanation of the ground taken in answering the above objection, the following enquiries are submitted to the consideration of the candid.

Is not the assumption that the degree of sin which exists, or even any degree of sin, is on the whole preferable to holiness in its stead, inconsistent alike with the benevolence and the sincerity of God? With his benevolence. If such be the nature of God, of man, of holiness, of sin, of all things, that sin is the necessary means of the greatest good, ought it not to be made the subject of precept—would it not be, by a benevolent moral Governor? For how can it be consistent with the benevolence of a moral governor, to require of his subjects that moral conduct which is not on the whole for the best?

If it be said that it is on the whole for the best that *he* should *require* it, but not on the whole for the best that *they* should *perform* it—what is this but to say that it is on the whole for the best that he should prac-

123

tice deception on his subjects? And what then becomes of his *sincerity*? Let us take an example or two. Who would regard the command of a parent as *sincere,* it being known that he prefers on the whole the dis-obedience of the child to his obedience? Who would regard the invita-tion of a friend as *sincere,* being fully apprised that he prefers on the whole its rejection to its acceptance? If it be said that no subjects of God have such knowledge of God's preference of sin to holiness in their own case, then the question is whether their ignorance alters *the fact;* and whether he is truly *sincere,* when he would be justly pronounced *insin-cere* if *the real fact were known?* Besides, after the commission of sin, the fact of such a preference, if there be one, is known. How then does the *sincerity* of God appear when it is placed beyond a doubt by the event, that he did prefer on the whole, the sin committed by the subject to the holiness required in his law? Is it then possible that God should be sincere in his commands and invitations, unless holiness in man be on the whole preferable to sin in its stead?

Further, it is extensively maintained that virtue is founded in utility, i.e. that such is the nature, relations and tendencies of things, that greater happiness will result from virtue or holiness than from vice or sin. How then can sin in the nature of things be the necessary means of the greatest good?

Again, if sin be *the necessary means* of the greatest good, who can reasonably regard the commission of it with sorrow or even regret? What benevolent being duly informed, can ingenuously regret that by sin he has put it in the power of God to produce greater good, than God could otherwise produce? Ought it not rather to be matter of grateful praise that he has sinned, and thus furnished, by what he has done, the necessary means of the greatest possible good? Surely the act considered simply in the relation of the necessary means of such an end, is not a matter for regret; this being the very reason, why God himself is sup-posed to prefer it.

Is it then said, that *the intention* is selfish and sinful? Be it so. Had the subject however been fully apprised of the utility of the deed and the real preference of God (as in the case of the destruction of the Canaanites), his own interest and his duty would have been coincident; and how does it appear that in this case he had not performed the act from a *benevo-lent* intention? And how great is the guilt of a selfish intention which, for aught that appears, is occasioned by deception on the part of the lawgiver? Is it said that the selfish intention is necessary to the action as the means of good? But where is an instance in which the good educed

124

from a sinful action is dependent on the selfish intention of the agent? Is it said, that otherwise God could not shew mercy in its forgiveness? Does God then deceive his subjects in regard to the true nature and tendency of moral acts, and thus occasion their sin that he may have the glory of forgiving it? Is this the glory of his mercy? Besides, how does it appear that the subject did not really *intend* good? The law of God, according to the assumption, is no proof that transgression is not on the whole for the best; indeed the subject knows that all sin will prove to be the necessary means of the greatest good; how then does it appear that with this knowledge he was not truly benevolent in performing the deed? What reason then for sorrow or regret remains?

The second assumption now claims our notice; viz. *that God could have prevented all sin, or at least the present degree of sin, in a moral system.*

If holiness in a moral system be preferable on the whole to sin in its stead, why did not a benevolent God, were it possible to him, prevent all sin and secure the prevalence of universal holiness? Would not a moral universe of perfect holiness, and of course of perfect happiness, be happier and better than one comprising sin and its miseries? And must not infinite benevolence accomplish all the good it can? Would not a benevolent God then, *had it been possible to him in the nature of things,* have secured the existence of universal holiness in his moral kingdom?

Is the reader startled by an enquiry which seems to limit the power of God? But does not *he* equally limit the power of God by supposing, or rather affirming, that God COULD NOT secure the greatest good without the existence of sin? On either supposition there is what may be called a limitation of the power of God by *the nature of things.* In one case, the limitation is supposed to result from *the nature of sin;* in the other, from *the nature of moral agency.* If then one of these suppositions *must* be made, which is the most honourable to God?

Further, does not he who is startled by this supposition, limit *the goodness* of God? Undeniably he does, if it be conceded that holiness is on the whole preferable to sin in its stead. For he who admits this, and maintains that God *could* have secured the existence of holiness instead of sin, must also admit that God is not good enough to accomplish all the good in his power; not good enough to prevent the worst of evils. And who does most reverence to God, he who supposes that God *would* have prevented all sin in his moral universe, but *could* not, or he who affirms that he *could* have prevented it, but *would* not? Or is it more honourable to God to suppose that such is the nature of sin, that he *could not* accomplish the highest good without it, than to suppose that such is the nature of *free agency* that God *could not* wholly prevent its perversion?

But the main enquiry on this point remains—does the supposition that God could not prevent sin in a moral system, limit his power at all? To suppose or affirm that God cannot perform what is *impossible in the nature of things,* is not properly to limit his power. Is there then the least particle of evidence, that the entire prevention of sin in moral beings is possible to God in the nature of things? If not, then what becomes of the very common assumption of such possibility?

All evidence of the truth of this assumption must be derived either from *the nature of the subject,* or from *known facts.* Is there such evidence from *the nature of the subject?* It is here to be remarked, that the prevention of sin by any influence that destroys the *power to sin,* destroys moral agency. Moral agents then must possess the *power to sin.* Who then can prove *a priori* or from the nature of the subject, *that a being who* CAN *sin, will* NOT *sin?* How can it be proved *a priori* or from the nature of the subject, that a thing *will not be,* when for aught that appears, it *may* be? On this point, is it presumptuous to bid defiance to the powers of human reason?

Is there any evidence from *facts?* Facts, so far as they are known to us, furnish no support to the assumption, that God could in a moral system prevent all sin, or even the present degree of sin. For we know of no creature of God, whose holiness is secured without that influence which results either directly or indirectly, from the existence of sin and its punishment. How then can it be shown *from facts,* that God could secure any of his moral creatures in holiness, without this influence; or to what purpose is it to allege instances of the prevention of sin *under* this influence, to prove that God could prevent it *without* this influence? Rather, do not all known facts furnish a strong presumption to the contrary? If God could prevent all sin without this influence, why has he not done it? Be this however as it may, since God has not, so far as we know, prevented sin in a single instance without this influence, how can it be proved *from facts,* that he could have prevented all sin, or even the present degree of sin in a moral system? Had his creatures done what *they* could, then indeed there had been more holiness and less sin. But the question is, what could *God* have done to secure such a result? Had he prevented the sins of one human being to the present time, or had he brought to repentance one sinner more than he has, who can prove that the requisite interposition for the purpose, would not result in a vast increase of sin in the system, including even the apostacy and augmented guilt of that individual? In a word, who is competent to foretell, or authorised even to *surmise* the consequences of the least iota of change in the present system of influence to produce holiness and prevent sin? If no one, then all assumptions on the subject, like that under consideration, are wholly unwarranted. It may be true, that God will secure under the present system of things, the greatest degree of holiness and the least degree of sin, which *it is possible to him in the nature of things* to secure. Neither the *nature of the subject,* nor *known facts,* furnish a particle of evidence to the contrary. The assumption therefore, that God could in a moral system have prevented all sin or the present degree of sin, is wholly gratuitous and unauthorised, and *ought never to be made the basis of an objection or an argument.*

As an apology for this note, the writer would say that the objection alluded to in the discourse, so commonly rises in the mind in connexion with the subject, that it was thought proper to notice it; and while he knows of no refutation except the one given, he was desirous of attempting still further to free the subject from distressing and groundless perplexity. This is done in his own view, simply by dismissing from the mind the two assumptions which have been examined. The mode in which the mind will in this way, be led to view the character and government of God may, it is believed, to be shown to be free from embarrassment by an example.

Suppose then the father of several sons to have foreknown with minute accuracy the various propensities and tendencies of their nature, and *all the possible* conditions or circumstances in which he might place them, with all the results of each condition. Suppose him also to foresee with absolute certainty, that to place them at a public seminary, although he knows it will be, unavoidably to himself, attended with a temporary course of vice on their part, will nevertheless result in greater good than he can secure by placing them in any *other* condition or circumstances. Suppose it to be true, and known to him, that their uniform good conduct at the seminary would be far better on the whole or in every respect than their misconduct. Suppose him now to send them at the proper age, to the place of their education with solemn and unqualified injunctions of uniform good conduct; and all the results to be as foreseen. Now can the procedure of this father be impeached in any respect whatever? Does he not evince wisdom and benevolence in every part of it? Does he not evince the most absolute and perfect sincerity in his injunctions of right conduct? Does he not at the same time furnish by what *he* does, adequate and decisive ground for acquiescence in view of the incidental evil; and is there not equally decisive ground for repentance to his disobedient children in what *they* do? If these things are so in the procedure of this father, why are they not so in the procedure of God?

The writer hopes he shall not be charged *without proof,* with denying what he fully believes—that the providential purposes or decrees of God extend to all actual events, sin not excepted. God may really purpose the existence of sin, whether he purpose it for one reason or for another; he may, as the example shows, as really purpose sin though wholly an evil, considered as *incidental,* so far as his power of prevention is concerned, to the best moral system, as purpose it considered as so excellent in its nature and relations as to be the necessary means of the greatest good. And while the theory now proposed exhibits the providential government of God as the basis of submission, confidence, and joy, under all the evils that befall his dependent creatures; it also presents, as no other theory in the view of the writer does present, the Moral Government of God in its unimpaired perfection and glory, to deter from sin and allure to holiness his accountable subjects.

### Notes

1. In *Theology in America: The Major Protestant Voices from Puritanism to Neo-Orthodoxy,* ed. Sydney E. Ahlstrom (Indianapolis and New York: Bobbs-Merrill, 1967; originally published in *Concio ad Clerum. A Sermon Delivered in the Chapel of Yale College, September 10, 1828,* 1828), pp. 213-22, 242-49.

   Ahlstrom notes that when the sermon was published it was preceded by this statement on another page:

   "The author of this discourse has no reason to believe, that the views which it contains, are in any essential respect diverse from those of his brethren, who heard it. That the general proposition Will meet with the approbation of all who hold the fundamental doctrines of the Gospel, he has no doubt. In regard to some of the more specific statements, he supposes that there is, in some limited degree, the semblance of controversy, rather than real diversity of opinion. It may be proper to remark, that he is not aware of any change in his own views on these points, since he entered the ministry; nor of any departure in any article of doctrinal belief, from his revered instructor in theology, the former President of the College [Timothy Dwight, 1752–1817]. Facts, however, which are extensively known, furnish, it is believed, a sufficient apology for the selection of the topic as well as for the publication of the discourse."

2. The embarrassment which in some minds attends this part of the subject, seems to result from the different senses in which the word *disposition* is used. That this word, like most others, is used in different senses, is undeniable; sometimes denoting simply *tendency* or *bias,* and sometimes, the moral temper, the *governing affection* or *predominant inclination* of the mind. The manner of its use, however, if correct, always shews in which sense it is used. Thus if we speak of *a disposition* to sin, in the way of accounting for *all* sin, the case shews that we

use the word simply in the sense of *tendency;* or as Edwards says, "a prevailing liableness or exposedness to such an event." For by the *very mode* of speaking, the *disposition* and the *sin* are so distinguished as to show that we cannot mean, that the *disposition* is itself sin; it being spoken of as the cause of *all* sin. But if we speak of a *sinful* or *wicked disposition,* or *a worldly disposition,* or *an avaricious disposition,* or of *a disposition* as the cause of specific sinful acts, or if in any other way we imply *its sinfulness* by our mode of speaking, then the predicate shews that we intend a state of mind which includes *preference—a supreme or governing affection of the heart.* Such, it is supposed yond all question, is the *usus loquendi;* a due attention to which would have saved some theologians from no trivial amount of absurdity.

3. John Calvin, *The Institutes of the Christian Religion,* I, 1, 6.
4. Ibid., II, 5, 1.
5. The Westminster Confession of Faith (1646), Chap. VI, Art. 6.
6. Joseph Bellamy, *True Religion Delineated,* Discourse I, Section V, Use I, Subsection 3. Quoted from *Works* (New York Edition, 1808–1809), 1, 201, 202.
7. Jonathan Edwards, *The Great Christian Doctrine of Original Sin Defended,* Part IV, Chap. II. Quoted from *Works* (Worcester Edition, 1808–1809), VI, 430, 431; see also pp. 427-36.
8. Jonathan Edwards, *Freedom of the Will,* Part IV, Section I. Quoted from *Works* (Worcester Edition), V, 220, 222. See also *Religious Affections,* Part I, Doctrine 1; *Works,* IV, 12-16.

129

# Lemuel Haynes

*The ministry of Haynes (1753–1833) had its origins in the revivalist Calvinism that followed the First Great Awakening and reemerged, newly configured, early in the nineteenth century in the Northern sphere of the Second Great Awakening. The son of a black father and white mother, he was reared by New England Presbyterians under conditions of indentured servitude and then studied with New Divinity ministers. Upon ordination to Congregationalist ministry (1785), he became well known among black and white New Englanders for his advocacy of "Hopkinsianism."*

*This excerpted selection exhibits his solidarity with the young Edwardseans. One sees also the theological foundations of his deep concern for the moral character of life, used to good effect in his critique of an American society dedicated to slaveholding. The form of the sermon is New Divinity style, as is his absolute confidence in the ruling providence of God. Equally striking is his insistence that human beings must themselves responsibly serve as "instruments" of God for the fulfillment of God's purposes, including the Christianization of Africa.*

## DIVINE DECREES[1]

By faith, Moses, when he was born, was hid three months of his parents, because they saw he was a proper child; and they were not afraid of the King's commandments.—Hebrews 11:23.

The children of Israel having been in Egypt about one hundred and thirty-four years, the time drew near when God intended their deliverance, which took place eighty years after the birth of Moses. The whole time of their sojourning there was two hundred and fifteen years.

God, in accomplishing his most holy purposes, makes use of means, and those that are in the best manner calculated to exhibit his wisdom, power and goodness; such as to blind mortals do not appear to be adapted to the end designed.—What human sagacity could have thought that the wickedness of Joseph's brethren was to fulfil a prediction to Abraham, one hundred and eighty-four years before, (Gen. 15:13) or to bring the Israelites into Egypt? That the cruel edict of Pharaoh to destroy the Hebrew male children, should be introductory to the emancipation of the chosen tribes, according to divine promise three hundred and forty-two years before? Moses was born at a time most unlikely to be an instrument to effect the above purpose, it being after the children were devoted to death. Aaron, the elder, and the rest of the family were passed by.

Men are naturally blind to divine government; and as this is the great source of happiness and consolation to the people of God, it seems suitable that he should so work that we may plainly see and acknowledge the operations of his hand. Pharaoh's wicked design to destroy the Church of God, was made greatly subservient to its deliverance. Moses is qualified for the important work through the instrumentality of those who were the greatest enemies to it. History informs us, that some of the Seers of Egypt had intimated that a great man was to be raised up from among the Hebrews about this time, who was to be their deliverer, which gave rise to the tyrannical edict of the Egyptian court. Josephus relates that the parents of Moses were informed by divine revelation some way, that this child was designed by God as the deliverer of the children of Israel from their bondage, which is also intimated in my text. They saw something in his looks, perhaps, or by some other means, were made to put confidence in God, that he would preserve him from devoted destruction. They saw he was a *proper child; fair in the sight of God*—as the words are in the original. The conduct of the parents, in consequence of the heavenly vision, is truly remarkable. Their faith was strong, so as to exclude distrust in God, and fear of the King's commandment.

To collect your minds to a general point, I would propose the following observation, viz. That, although pious people believe and confide in the unalterable purpose and providence of God to bring about all events, yet they will diligently use such means as God requires, and that tend to their accomplishment.

It is proposed to shew,

I. That all things are brought about by the fixed purpose and providence of God.

II. That the people of God do believe and trust in his absolute government.

III. Yet they are diligent in the use of such means that are appointed, and necessary to accomplish events.

That there are events constantly transpiring, both in the natural and moral worlds, all allow. That they are the effects of cause is equally evident. 'Tis certain that they had a beginning, and so not self-existent; for there could be nothing in them to operate as the cause of their being before they had any. As nothing can begin to exist without God, so it cannot *continue* without him. 'Tis impossible for Deity to communicate or impart independence to any; this is peculiar to himself; and it would imply the grossest absurdity and contradiction to suppose it of any other being. 'Tis certain that men do not create, or bring about events, only as instruments in the hand of God. Many of them we have no idea about before they take place; and they depend on so many minute circumstances, that we can discover no kind of connexion between the means and the end; so that we can have no design in the matter. Joseph could not discover, while he was telling his dreams, that it was to be the means of saving the house of Israel from perishing in a time of famine, and of bringing them into Egypt. Pharaoh had no design of bringing them out, by passing the cruel edict against the Hebrew children, or by educating Moses. Things are daily taking place contrary to the designs and exertions of man; and they are often defeated in their anxious expectations.

The preservation of the Church amidst such a series of fiery calamities, must certainly be the good will of Him that dwelt in the bush.

That all things depend on God for their existence is a sentiment abundantly taught in the word of God. Rom. 11:36. "For of him, and through him, are *all things.*" I Cor. 8:6. "But to us there is but one God, the Father, of *whom are all things,* and we in him; and one Lord, Jesus Christ, by *whom are all things,* and we by him." II Cor. 5: 18.—"*All things are of God.*" Even the wickedness of men is effected or brought about by the agency or providence of God; such as sending Joseph into Egypt, and the crucifixion of Christ. God brought the Israelites out of Egypt by an high hand, and a stretched out arm, by means of wicked instruments.

Not only events of great, but those of less magnitude, are ascribed to God; even the falling of a sparrow, or a hair of our head. It is difficult for us to distinguish between great and small events; there is not a superfluous link in the whole chain; they all depend on each other. It was necessary that Moses should be born at that time; that the careful parents should lodge him in the flags, by the side of the river, at such a place; that Thermuses, Pharaoh's daughter, should come to such a place to wash; that her eye should be fixed on the spot, and discover something amidst the thicket; that her curiosity should excite her to have it fetched; that little Moses should weep, and excite female compassion; that he should fall into the hands of a tender mother, etc. These things are beyond the wisdom of mortals; and are parts of the ways of the Almighty.

If, then, God effects or brings about all events, he has design or volition agreeably to Eph. 1:11. "Who worketh all things after the *counsel of his own will.*" There is no other way by which the Deity can give existence to things; he is incapable of what is called accidental events; and it is by the effective acts of his will, that he creates, or causes things to exist. Besides, could he work without design, he would not be virtuous or praise-worthy. Indeed, were there any possible events that could take place without God, it might be very difficult for us to find out which they were; and to be in a capacity always to comply with that holy injunction. Prov. 3:6. "In all thy ways acknowledge him." As all things are the effect of divine volition, design or decree, the purposes of God must be eternal and unchangeable. God is incapable of any new design; this would suppose him to increase in knowledge, or that he is growing wiser, and by extending our views back, his knowledge would decrease; admit this, then there was a time when he knew nothing at all.—There can be no alteration in the mind of the Deity, as nothing new can come up to his view, as a ground of such mutation. God eternally saw the propriety of all things taking place just as they do, and has adopted the best possible plan. Some are unwilling to acknowledge the absolute and unlimited providence and agency of God in the production of all things, especially with respect to the existence of moral evil, that it implies wickedness in Jehovah; as though there must be the same in the cause as in the effect: should this be admitted, we must deny God in the greater parts of creation and providence. Would men learn to distinguish between events in their own nature, and the good to which they are made subservient, it would relieve them of many difficulties. However wicked Pharaoh was in devoting the Hebrew children to death, yet good was effected thereby, and the hand of God shone conspicuous. (All will allow that God *permitted* or *suffered* sin to take place; But if; on the whole, it is not promotive or made subservient to the highest possible good, then he cannot be vindicated in *permitting* it to be; but if it is best that sin should have existence, why cannot the divine Character be cleared in *causing* it to take place? Some, to relieve themselves of difficulties, suppose sin to be merely negative, consisting in the want of holiness; But can this be criminal only as implying positive exercises of hatred to God? Should I tell my neighbor who stands by me, that the pen with which I now write is crooked—should he reprove me for my impertinence and deficiency of language, and say I had not declared the thing as it is; for it *wants straitness,* should I gain much philosophical instruction by the remark?) If it be inconsistent with moral rectitude to stir up and employ wicked instruments, as best calculated to bring about his purposes, then the hand of God is not to be seen or acknowledged in sending Joseph into Egypt, and in bringing Israel out, in the destruction of the Babylonish empire, or in the crucifixion of Christ.

II. The people of God do believe, and confide in his absolute government.

It is allowed that the really pious men through want of instruction, and not well understanding all the terms that are made use of to express divine government, appear to oppose it: improper terms may be used on the subject; yet all that love God, will love his holy character. It is not to be supposed, but what there may be much remaining even in the children of God that is not reconciled to his decrees—they are sanctified, but in part; yet, so far as they fear, love, and serve God, they will acknowledge his government. That which distinguishes the righteous from the wicked is, the one loves God, the other hates him. To love God is to be pleased and delighted with his character, as exhibited in his word and works. As the whole of God's moral perfections consist in design, so that will be the principal objects of the Christian's love and joy. The reason why the wicked are so much opposed to the decrees of God, is because they give us so clear a discovery of him. As the moral perfections of God constitute his holiness or goodness, so it is the great object of virtuous affection. The natural perfections of the Deity are no further desirable than they are promotive of goodness. The feet of those are beautiful to the Saints, that bring such good tidings, "THY GOD REIGNETH," Is. 52:7. Zion was glad when she heard that God reigned, and called upon all to rejoice on the occasion, Ps. 97. We find that it has always been the practice of the people of God to acknowledge him: therefore it is that they attend to the external duties of religion, such as the public worship of God, prayer, and praise, by which they express their belief and love of a superintending providence. This was the object of the faith of those mentioned in my text. They had a firm belief in divine purposes concerning Moses, so as to exclude all fear of the King's commandment. The righteous view, and hold communion with God in his works, and repair to his absolute government in times of distress, as their only hid-ing place; Ps. 27. It was God's immutable promises and designs that supported Noah, Abraham, Isaac, Jacob, Moses, David and all God's people in all ages of the world—God has appointed the Lord Jesus Christ to be King on his holy hill of Zion, and has laid the government on his shoulders; the pious are his obedient subjects; and it is their duty to submit to him. They are to have the *mind* of Christ, as they would not forfeit their interest in him; Rom. 8:9. Rejoicing in the absolute dominion and agency of God was an important trait in his character; Luke 10:21. "In that hour, Jesus rejoiced in spirit, and said, I thank thee, O Father, Lord of heaven and earth, that thou hast hid these things from the wise and prudent, and hast revealed them unto babes: even so, Father, for so it seemed good in thy sight."

That the inspired writers were friendly to, and put their trust in the unchangeable purposes, power and wisdom of God, is evident to all that are acquainted with the holy Scriptures. It was in the view of this that they could have rational ground of support and success in their exertions in the cause of God; this has been the great source of consolation to the Church in all ages of the world, and will be to the second coming of Christ.

III. Although the people of God believe and confide in Divine Providence, or unchangeable purposes of God, yet they will be diligent in the use of such means as are necessary to accomplish events.

This idea is remarkably illustrated in the conduct of the parents of Moses, alluded to in the text; they hid him three months. Their care was excited by the full trust they had in God that he designed him for some important work.—Their faith was so great, as to exclude all doubt but what God would take care of the child, and fulfill his own purpose, in spite of all the designs of the enemy: "*They were not afraid of the King's commandment.*" They did not fear to exert themselves to the utmost for the preservation of the child, nor that their measures would not be successful. He was doubtless secreted, and removed from place to place, to elude the search of the enemy. An ark was invented for the security of the helpless infant; every seam carefully secured, with slime and pitch, that the babe might have a dry and safe asylum. It is carried to the river side; deposited among the flags—an unlikely place to be found. She chose a place where the swelling of the Nile would not be likely to carry it away. The ark was not committed to the foaming waters, to be exposed to the voracious monsters of the deep; but as much care was exercised as though the life of the child wholly depended on their vigilance. Miriam, the sister of Moses, must lie in ambush at a suitable dis-

135

tance, to watch every disaster; and often to run and soothe the cries of the solitary infant. But "Moses was not safer when King in Jeshurun, encompassed with the thousands of Israel—was not safer in the mount with God—is not safer within the walls of the new Jerusalem, than in the flags" (Dr. Hunter).

The same spirit of vigilance shone conspicuously among all the people of God in all ages of the world. God revealed unto Abraham his unalterable designs concerning him and his posterity; and yet how diligent was he in using such means as tended to bring the events to pass. By faith he went out. By faith he sojourned in the land of promise, etc. The conduct of Isaac, Jacob, Moses, David, and the prophets, illustrate the same sentiment. Paul, in Acts 27. is a striking instance of the truth now under consideration. When it was revealed to him, that God's purpose was to save all in the ship, yet his diligence in the use of such means as tended to their preservation, exceeded all the mariners. He was evidently encouraged by the purpose of God revealed; yea without means, he tells them plainly, they *cannot be saved.*—No preacher ever held up the decrees of God more clearly, and more frequently than Paul; and none of the Apostles were more laborious; he labored more abundantly than they all; I. Corin. 15:10. We derive similar ideas from the doctrines and examples of him who spake as never man spake. The purposes of God with respect to the deliverance of the Jews from the Babylonish captivity, stirred up the saints to prayer; Dan. 9:2. The certainty of the incarnation of Christ, excited Old Testament Saints to prayer for the accomplishment of it; and this is what God greatly approved. The parents of Moses have a place in the sacred canon—whose faith is highly applauded.

2. Faith, in divine purposes, will excite the people of God to the diligent use of means; as he has appointed them as instruments, by which he will accomplish his designs; and has commanded them to be workers together with him: indeed, without the exertions of men, it is impossible that they should take place. God revealed to Abraham, that his seed should go down into Egypt, and at such a time be delivered; but this supposed a series of second causes, all dependent on the first cause; without them the event could not take place. One was the edict of Pharaoh to destroy the male infants of the Hebrews; that Moses should be born and hid three months; that he should be educated at the expense of the King of Egypt; that the Egyptians should be visited with ten plagues, etc. I might with propriety make the same remark with respect to the deliverance of Israel from the Babylonish captivity, and the birth and death of

Christ. The people of God consider themselves as active instruments to bring about his holy designs; and are, in a good degree, cured of that unreasonable temper of mind, that will deduce unnatural consequences from certain promises, in order to gratify a licentious conduct.

3. The truly pious are pleased with the absolute decrees of God—as what will promote the greatest possible good. If it is desirable that all God's counsels should stand, then it must be pleasing to saints to be in the use of such means as tend to bring them to pass—without which they cannot exist; this makes them *cheerful* in the service of God; as they are seeking the same glorious ultimate object with him. Jachobed, and her husband, doubtless understood that God, by this remarkable child, designed the deliverance of the Church from the iron furnace, which was an animating object; all they did in fitting him for this work, afforded satisfaction.—Although the children of God cannot always see the connexion between means and end, yet they put such confidence in the Divine Being, as delights their souls in persevering in the path of duty—believing that God will effect the greatest good by it.

4. The friends of God delight in *expressing* their obedience to him. The use of means afford them opportunity to glorify God, and commend him to others. If love and obedience are delightful exercises to the saints, then to express them will be pleasing. As God cannot exhibit any true virtue, or moral excellence, without pursuing a plan, so neither can we, unless we regard his will and interest, and are workers together with him.

5. The humble Christian will feel his own weakness and insufficiency to do anything of himself, and will see that all his sufficiency is of God, and his faith and hope will rest on his power and providence to do all; which will be a motive to diligence. This will be the foundation of his trust, and will excite him to "work out his own salvation, with fear and trembling; knowing that it is *God that worketh in him,* both to will and to do of his good pleasure," Phil. 2:12, 13. This supported the parents of Moses amidst all their care about him, and by which "they were not afraid of the King's commandment."

6. Christians will very diligently attend to means, as they will see much to be done. Wherever they turn their eyes, they will behold work laid out for them; and it is criminal to stand idle in the market-place. The good man will see enough to employ his head, his heart, his hands, and his temporal interest, in the service of God. The reason that so many can find but little to do for God, is on account of a slothful and indolent heart, that refuses to labor.

137

*Improvement*

1. The doctrine of the decrees of God, or his absolute government, is a powerful motive to morality and religion.—This idea is abundantly held up in the holy Scriptures. Eccl. 52:14. "I know that whatsoever God doth, it shall be forever: nothing can be put to it, nor any thing taken from it; and God doth it that men should *fear* before him." The same thing is declared in Ps. 33. Men are there exhorted to fear and reverence God, from the consideration that [sic] "that the counsel of the Lord standeth forever; and the thoughts of his heart to all generations." Compare Job 33:13. and on. The absolute dominion of Jehovah is the object and foundation of all true morality; and to withhold this doctrine, or to preach contrary to it, is highly immoral—tending to cherish looseness of sentiment and conduct. Ministers, therefore, are far from falling in with the true dictates of prudence and religion, by keeping back this doctrine, or by explaining it away by vague and indefinite expressions.

2. The agency and government of God is perfectly consistent with the liberty and freedom of men, and with their being the subjects of blame and praise; so that it does not exclude moral good and evil from the system. *That* cannot destroy virtue that is the very essence or foundation of it; nor vice that greatly enhances it. The reason why the wicked must be slain before the face of God is because they oppose his holy government or plan; Luke 19:14. That the providence and agency of God does not destroy our freedom, and so not our criminality, is evident from universal experience. Even Pharaoh and Balaam, though very wicked men, own it; Ex. 9:27; Num. 22:34. If the unchangeable purposes of God destroy human liberty, it will more effect the morality and freedom of the Deity; as he fully sees all things unalterably fixed, and many events he cannot bring about without our agency or instrumentality, any more than we can without his. It is highly absurd to suppose that an agent can have no freedom in prosecuting a wise, holy, and unalterable plan.

That events are constantly taking place, all will allow; and when they come to exist, we know that it was always certain that they would. To say that it was ever possible that they should not come to pass, is as contradictory as to say they have no existence now. It makes no difference as to all things that do take place, as to their fixedness, or certainty, whether we admit that they were decreed or not: so that the liberties of men would be equally effected on any other hypothesis.

3. It argues no imperfection in the Deity that he cannot execute his designs without the intervention of second causes. God exercises no less power than if he used no means; he takes such ways to execute his

decrees that are wisest and best, and can take no other. Creatures are to take nothing to themselves. "Neither is he that planteth any thing, neither he that watereth; but God who giveth the increase;" I Cor. 3:7.

If it is desirable that the purposes of God should be executed; then it is suitable we use such means as he has appointed. This sets human exertions in a very important point of light.

4. Those who live unholy, vicious lives, have not a proper belief of the great doctrines of grace, or the immutable decrees of God. Men, it is true, will try to accommodate them to their lusts, as they do all the doctrines of the Bible; but no man was ever influenced to licentiousness from a true love and faith in these sentiments: so that the doctrines themselves, nor those who preach them, are accountable for the bad use that is made of them; but the corrupt and vicious tempers of men. Review the characters of those who have been advocates for divine government, and you will find that it had a holy and practical influence on all their conduct.

5. We infer the perfect safety of the Church, and in what view it is so. It is founded on the immutable purposes and providence of God. Not all the evil designs of Pharaoh and his wicked courters, could destroy the chosen tribes. Every exertion to prevent their increase was made; heavy burdens were imposed; they were denied wholesome food. It was not uncommon for them, says a Jewish historian, to faint and die under the cruel hands of their task-masters; and they were often denied a burial. But the more they afflicted them, the more they multiplied and grew; "And they were grieved because of the children of Israel;" Exod. 1:12. An attempt to frustrate the divine purpose was subservient to its accomplishment. The wrath of men and devils will praise God. All the good promised to Israel, so many ages before, was brought about, and not one thing failed. These things afford comfort and consolation to the people of God, while they are truly alarming and confounding to the enemies of the church.

6. The subject, so far illustrated sets the design of the Institution to which our attention is particularly called, on the present occasion, in an important point of light. It is to aid pious and needy young men in acquiring Education for the GOSPEL MINISTRY. A remarkable spirit of zeal and liberality in the cause of God has been excited in the minds of the pious, in various parts of the Christian world. Missionaries have been sent out among the heathen, and to our new settlements; and their labors have been crowned with abundant success. People, while watering, have been watered themselves. The conversion of thousands, I

believe, has been the effect of these benevolent exertions. The desert and the solitary wilderness have been made to blossom as the rose. Recent instances of the trophies of divine grace, in some parts of Africa, have made glad the city of our God.—The friends of Christ on both sides of the Atlantic, have united in this glorious cause; but much still remains to be done.

PEOPLE, within our reach, are perishing for lack of spiritual food. The harvest is great—but the laborers are comparatively few. The number of those qualified to carry the bread of life to the dying, are inadequate. Our missionary exertions must be greatly impeded, unless pious, ingenious and learned men be found to engage in the service. Our Evangelical Society virtually embraces the same object of those commonly called Missionary Societies—as necessary and subservient thereto. Whatever funds are raised, unless proper preachers can be obtained, they cannot be rendered useful. That a competent degree of literary acquirements are necessary and indispensable in those who engage in ministerial labors, none will deny, who have the importance of the work on their minds. The patronage of those who love God and the Souls of men, is earnestly solicited. We hope you will not withhold that pecuniary aid which the urgency of the case requires.

I stand here this day, my friends and brethren, to plead for thousands of poor perishing, dying fellow mortals, who need the bread of life; whose cries and distresses call for compassion, beyond the groaning Israelites. Who, that knows the love of God, and the terrors of eternal death, but longs to run to their relief! Satan, the potent and imperious prince of darkness, has long since issued his cruel and bloody edict against the Church of God, to destroy and exterminate it from the earth.

We stand this day to plead the cause of that Jesus, who sits upon the holy hill of Zion, with pardon in his hands, and whose delight is with the sons of men; and who is now calling for your assistance. We plead the promises and predictions of God's word, that may encourage your hope and trust. Be not afraid of the haughty mandate of the prince of darkness, for it shall be made to subserve the interest of Christ's kingdom—God requires exertions as much as he did for the preservation of Moses, or the deliverance of Israel out of Egypt. It is sacrificing the cause of God, and the immortal Souls of men to withhold. Is there not an impropriety in our bearing the name of christians unless the love of Christ constrains us? Is it not an important trait in the characters of the godly, that they *took joyfully the spoiling of their goods?* That they *suffered the loss of all things, that they might win Christ,* and save Souls?

What illustrious examples of benevolence do we find in the word of God; especially in the blessed Savior of the world? *That though he was rich, yet for our sake he became poor, that we, through his poverty, might be rich.* Can there be a more delightful employment, this side heaven, than to wrest Souls from the jaws of death and hell, and to send the blessed news of salvation to a perishing world.

To promote the felicity of the universe is the happiness of the redeemed in glory; and this spirit, among Christians, is heaven begun on earth. If your hearts do not glow with holy affection towards perishing sinners, by which you are disposed to do something for their relief, you have reason to fear and tremble, that you have no inheritance among the Saints in light.

. . .

### Note

1. In *Black Preacher to White America: The Collected Writings of Lemuel Haynes, 1774–1883*, ed. Richard Newman (Brooklyn: Carlson Publishing, 1990; originally published in 1805), pp. 89-100. It was published with the following heading: "Divine Decrees, an Encouragement to the Use of Means. A Sermon Delivered at Granville, (N.Y.) June 25, 1805, before the Evangelical Society, instituted for the purpose of aiding pious and needy young men in acquiring education for the work of the Gospel ministry."

# Samuel Simon Schmucker

*S*chmucker *(1799–1873) worked throughout his life to foster a distinctive identity for American Lutherans, a minority, mainly
immigrant people in a setting far from their faith's homeland. Education
at Princeton Theological Seminary informed his estimates of the
strengths and weaknesses of the Protestantism dominant in the nation,
though he took with him little "Princeton theology" except perhaps an
awareness of the importance of church polity. He was architect of the
new, united Lutheran General Synod's constitution, founder and first
president and professor of Gettysburg Theological Seminary, and translator and author of texts on Lutheran dogmatics and popular theology.*

*Pietist in background, Schmucker was supportive of Protestant
America's emphasis on personal, experiential religion, revivals, and
moral reform. In theology he upheld the position of scholars of Germany's "old Tübingen" school, arguing that Kant's separation of reason and revelation reconfirmed the Reformation's insistence that
"scripture alone" offered knowledge of Christian religious truth. His
proposals to modify the Lutheran confessions in order to minimize conflicts and highlight commonalities among "Evangelicals" reduced his
standing within his church and showed the vitality of his confessionalist opponents. His efforts to form an Evangelical Alliance of churches
did not work out according to plan either but did win him interdenominational recognition and helped pave the way for later ecumenical
developments.*

## DISCOURSE.

### Vocation of the American Lutheran Church[1]

. . .

I. *Since, as eldest sister of the Reformation, our church was first to
express the grand Protestant principle of exclusive, infallible authority
of the Bible, in antithesis to tradition and human authority, and yet was*

*prevented from carrying it out to its legitimate sequences; it is part of her vocation to complete the work so happily begun.*

The sufficiency of a revelation from Heaven, without the auxiliary light of tradition, is the natural corollary of its divinity itself. The very reason which rendered the one necessary, implies the invalidity of the other. If uninspired human teachings had been reliable, as sources of new truth, a revelation would have been superfluous. Hence the fact, that God inspired holy men of old to speak as the Spirit guided them, seems to establish the insufficiency of mere uninspired human deduction. But this word of revelation being admitted as divine, its own declarations must forever settle this point. The same inspired Apostle who declared all Scripture to be divinely inspired (Θεόπνευσος), and able not only to subserve some purposes of the man of God, but to make him *"perfect,"* thoroughly furnished, not only for some, but "for all good works;" has also explicitly pronounced the Holy Scriptures competent to teach us the supreme and vital interests of man, "able to make us wise unto salvation." Whilst he warns us to beware of any and every teacher, even if it were an angel from heaven, who should preach any other doctrine than that taught by himself, (and contained in his epistles,) and whilst he pronounces the curse of God upon him; the disciple whom Jesus loved, in the book placed last in the canonical collection, whether last written or not, adds the fearful menace: "if any one shall add unto these things, God shall add unto him the plagues that are written in this book." Since, then, it is evident that God designed his revelation to be as complete as it is infallible, to be the standing and only certain guide to his church in all ages; we urge the inquiry upon every ingenuous mind, upon every true disciple of our blessed Master, and especially upon ministers of the Gospel, what should be our unflinching determination on this subject? Certainly, that which the noble minded Luther and his Spartan band of coadjutors adopted, to adhere to the word of God, in opposition not only to angels and devils, but to popes, cardinals and councils, whenever, in our judgment, they come in conflict with this divinely authenticated voice of Heaven. "No man (said Luther) can or ought to doubt, that every thing contrary to the commands of God, whether it be living or dying, taking a vow or becoming free, speaking or remaining silent, is to be condemned, and by all means to be abandoned, changed and avoided. For the will of God must be supreme, and must be done in heaven and on earth. Matth. 6:10." And if the professions of any man were ever put to the test, Luther's were at the memorable diet of Worms, when summoned to recant his doctrines before that august court of the empire. His truly sublime answer, synonymous with that of the apostle's to the Jewish Sanhedrim, and given when he expected it would cost his life, has for three centuries been the subject of admiration to the civilized world: "Except I can be convinced by clear and conclusive reasoning, or by proofs taken from the Holy Scriptures, I neither can nor will recant; because it is neither safe nor advisable to do any thing which is against my conscience. Here I stand, I cannot do otherwise, God help me! Amen." The same principle he has expressed in various parts of his works. One or two passages must suffice. "Hitherto," says he, "all cases which arose concerning true and false doctrine, were referred to a council, or to the Pope at Rome, or to the universities, which were to be umpires. But these are not Gilead, they have misled and deceived us. But the Holy Scriptures pronounce the decision, as to whose instructions are correct or erroneous. For although the Holy Ghost instructs every one in his heart, so that he knows what is right; it is still necessary to resort to the Scriptures, in order to prove the accuracy of our views. It is the Scriptures which decide whether our faith is correct or not. Therefore, we can look for no farther evidence, either of the fathers or councils; but must adhere exclusively to the clear declarations of Scripture."[2] Again, "God's word is the only certain rule which cannot deceive us."[3] Once more: "The right of free judgment we must retain, so as not to suffer ourselves to be bound indiscriminately by what the councils or fathers have taught; but we must make this difference: if they have decided and appointed any thing according to God's word, we also receive it, not on their account, but on account of the same divine word, on which they rest, and to which they refer us."[4] Here, then, we have a distinct avowal of the paramount and exclusively infallible authority of the Scriptures, an avowal in direct conflict with the oath which he had taken when he was created Doctor of Divinity, in which he had solemnly *sworn "to obey the church of Rome, and not to teach any doctrines condemned by her."*

And shall it be supposed that he, whose sublime principles thus elevated him above the fate of emperors and kings, and cardinals and popes, contended against popes and bishops only to occupy their station himself, and wield a similar authority? That he who was so evidently guided by the fear of God, when contending against the decrees of councils, the authority of the fathers, and the bulls of popes, did so in order that men should bow to his opinions and make him the subject of similar idolatry? No, he neither did so himself, nor did others attempt it during his lifetime. It was not until more than a quarter of a century after his death, that *not the church* or body of believers; but some *secular princes* usurping authority not confided to them by God, together with some learned and excellent, but mistaken theologians, undertook to prescribe a doctrinal test to ministers in general, and thus dictate to them not only the general and fundamental doctrines of Christianity, but an extended detail of particulars, in one case at least, commanding the belief of a doctrine from which Luther had receded, the ubiquity or omnipresence of Christ's body! Yes, let it ever be remembered that Luther himself was no symbolic Lutheran, and that this whole system of minute confessional servitude, was riveted on the church long after Luther and Melancthon had been translated to a better world.

But although these two distinguished servants of Christ, guided by their supreme reverence for the Bible, accomplished wonders in casting off the major part of the errors and prejudices of their Romish education; they did not live to complete the work, nor had they power to introduce all the reforms, the necessity of which had become clear to their vision. They were therefore alike too wise and too humble, to desire the stadium of their attainments to be the *ne plus ultra* of reform. Against the practice of designating the church of the Reformation by his name, Luther protested in the most energetic manner, alledging it to be a repetition of Corinthian sectarianism, condemned by Paul. "The Papists," says he, "may well have party names, because they are not satisfied with the doctrines and names of Christ, and desire also to be popish. Then let them be called after the Pope, who is their master. *But I am not and will not be any one's master.*" Yet it was not only against this abuse of his name, that the noble-hearted Luther protested; it was far from his desire that his writings should be invested with binding authority on his successors. "If any person," said he in the latter part of his life, (1539,) "desires to have my writings, let him by all means not suffer them to interfere with his study of the scriptures themselves, but treat them as I do the papal decrees, and the works of the sophists, that is, though I occasionally look into them to see what they have done, or to take an account of the history of the times, it is not for the purpose of studying them, as though I must act according to their views."[5] "I have no catalogue of my works, and not even all the books themselves, and I would much rather that men would read the Bible alone, instead of my works."[6] And finally he says, "Read my books, compare them with the writings of our opponents, and both with the scriptures, and then judge them according to this touchstone."[7]

It is therefore the duty of Christians of the present day, and especially of this favored country, where liberty of conscience is our birthright, to act on the noble principles adopted by these reformers, and to reduce them to practice in those cases also, in which their Romish education prevented them from doing so. It is the special vocation of the American Lutheran church to forsake, as she has done, those remnants of Romanism and also those anti-papal superstitions which the church of Rome had borrowed from the earlier fathers, and which the first reformers failed to renounce. It is our vocation to cast off all regard for the authority of the fathers, Nicene and Anti-Nicene, Romish and Protestant, excepting what justly attaches to them on account of the intrinsic force of their arguments, or their character and opportunities as witnesses of facts; for no point in patristic theology is more fully established than the numerous and serious aberrations of even some of the earliest so-called fathers from the truth of God. Yea, it is certain, that the whole of them as a body are not more reliable as expositors of scripture than the same number of respectable authors in the different evangelical churches of our day. It is our duty to do as Luther did, to look up through the long vista of antiquity to the era of the apostles, and from that high standpoint to form a scriptural judgment not only of the corruptions of Rome, but of the doctrines and practice of all past ages. Had Luther acted on the principles of many now bearing his name, he would have founded his Christianity and the organization of his church on the basis of his great theological favorite, *Augustine*. He would have selected one or more of his works, either that entitled *"De Civitate Dei,"* in which he defends the Christian religion against the heathen, or more probably his *"Enchiridion* (or Manual) *ad Laurentium, sive de fide, spe et caritate liber,"* in which he gives an account of his doctrinal views and those of the church. This he would have made symbolical, pledging himself to abide by its contents for life, and binding all who united with his ministry to the same production. And this church he would have baptized as the *Augustinian church*. But no, Luther had not so learned Christ. He could discriminate between inspired and uninspired writings, between the books of God and those of men. Whilst, therefore, he avowed his assent to the three ecumenical creeds, the Apostolic, the Nicene and the Athanasian, which are confined to fundamentals, and are very short, he never adopted as binding any extended creed, nor suffered any human productions to deprive him of that liberty conceded by the word of God. He continued through life to improve his views of doctrine and duty, by the light of scripture, and in the most emphatic language inculcated on others the obligation to do likewise. That he was intolerant to Zwingli, and his followers, belongs to the imperfections of the age and of the man, not to his general principles of action. *Temporum culpa fuit, non ejus.* And were he still living we doubt not, he would hurl his denunciation at the intolerant ultra-Lutherans of our day, as he did at Carlstadt and Zwingli of old, only, by this time, in milder phrase.

How completely our General Synod has fulfilled her vocation in this respect, is evident from the fact that she makes no reference to the fathers, ancient or modern, thus leaving them all to stand on their intrinsic merits as theological authority, and as witnesses to historical facts; whilst the former symbolical books, after having pronounced the fathers fallible, nevertheless cite their views and arguments in multitudes of cases.

### Notes

1. In *The American Lutheran Church* (New York: Arno Press & The New York Times, 1969; original essay published in 1851), pp. 252-57. Omitted here are Schmucker's quotations in Latin.
2. Luther's Works, Walch's edit. vol, 3, p. 754.
3. Vol. 1, p. 1854.
4. Idem, vol. ix. p. 631.
5. Preface to his German Works.
6. Letter to Ursinus.
7. Luther's Works, 3d vol., p. 256.

# Charles Porterfield Krauth

*I*mpulses toward the recovery and revival of historic confessional traditions arose within many American churches during the mid-nineteenth century, 1830–1880. The confessional revival within Lutheranism found especially forceful expression in the theology of Krauth (1823–1883). Krauth graduated from Gettysburg College and then Gettysburg Theological Seminary (1841), where his father, Charles Phillip Krauth, and Samuel Schmucker were among his teachers. A talented pastor-theologian, he became, early in the 1860s, editor of the magazine Lutheran and Missionary, a noted preacher and lecturer, and, in 1864, professor at the newly founded Philadelphia Lutheran Theological Seminary. From 1868 until his death he served as Professor of Philosophy and vice-provost of the University of Pennsylvania.*

*Like Schmucker, Krauth was concerned for American Lutheranism's distinctive theological identity. His response and initiative to this issue moved in directions opposite to those of his former teacher: he sought a confessional, sacramental, and liturgical renewal of tradition in the church. The principles basic to this proposal were set forth in* The Conservative Reformation and Its Theology. *It was no simple summary of early Lutheran doctrine but an account of the three dialectical "moments" (or features) constituting Reformation Lutheranism— catholic substance, progressivism, and reformatory balance maintaining the other two in proper relationship.*

## THE CONFESSIONAL PRINCIPLE OF THE CONSERVATIVE REFORMATION[1]

*The Rule of Faith*

. . . We stand upon the everlasting foundation—the Word of God: believing that the Canonical Books of the Old and New Testament are in their original tongues, and in a pure text, the perfect and only rule of faith. All these books are in harmony, each with itself, and all with each other, and yield to the honest searcher, under the ordinary guidance of the Holy Spirit, a clear statement of doctrine, and produce a firm assurance of faith. Not any word of man, no creed, commentary, theological system, nor decision of Fathers or of councils, no doctrine of Churches, or of the whole Church, no results or judgments of reason, however strong, matured, and well informed, no one of these, and not all of these together, but God's word alone is the rule of faith. No apocryphal books, but the canonical books alone, are the rule of faith. No translations, as such, but the original Hebrew and Chaldee of the Old Testament, and the Greek of the New, are the letter of the rule of faith. No vitiation of the designing, nor error of the careless, but the incorrupt text as it came from the hands of the men of God, who wrote under the motions of the Holy Spirit, is the rule of faith. To this rule of faith we are to bring our minds; by this rule we are humbly to try to form our faith, and in accordance with it, God helping us, to teach others—teaching them the evidences of its inspiration, the true mode of its interpretation, the ground of its authority, and the mode of settling its text. The student of theology is to be taught the Biblical languages, to make him an independent investigator of the word of the Holy Spirit, as the organ through which that Spirit reveals His mind. First of all, as the greatest of all, as the ground-work of all, as the end of all else, we are to teach God's pure word, its faith for faith, its life for life; in its integrity, in its marvellous adaptation, in its divine, its justifying, its sanctifying, and glorifying power. We are to lay, as that without which all else would be laid in vain, the foundation of the Apostles and Prophets—Jesus Christ himself being the chief corner-stone.

### Confession of Faith

Standing really upon the everlasting foundation of this Rule of Faith, we stand of necessity on the faith, of which it is the rule. It is not the truth as it lies, silent and unread, in the Word, but the truth as it enters from that Word into the human heart, with the applying presence of the Holy Ghost, which makes men believers. Faith makes men Christians; but Confession alone marks them as Christians.

The Rule of Faith is God's voice to us; faith is the hearing of that voice, and the Confession, our reply of assent to it. By our faith, we are known to the Lord as his; by our Confession, we are known to each other as His children. Confession of faith, in some form, is imperative. To confess Christ, is to confess what is our faith in him. As the Creed is not, and cannot be the Rule of Faith, but is its Confession merely, so the Bible, because it is the Rule of Faith, is of necessity not its Confession. The Bible can no more be any man's Creed, than the stars can be any man's astronomy. The stars furnish the rule of the astronomer's faith: the Principia of Newton may be the Confession of his faith. If a man were examined as a candidate for the chair of astronomy in a university, and were asked, "What is your astronomical system?" and were to answer, "I accept the teaching of the stars," the reply would be, "You may think you do—so does the man who is sure that the stars move round the world, and that they are not orbs, but 'gimlet-holes to let the glory through.' We wish to know what you hold the teachings of the stars to be? Do you receive, as in harmony with them, the results reached by Copernicus, by Galileo, by Kepler, by Newton, La Place, and Herschel, or do you think the world one great flat, and the sun and moon mere pendants to it?"

"Gentlemen," replies the independent investigator, "the theories of those astronomers are human systems—man-made theories. I go out every night on the hills, and look at the stars, as God made them, through a hole in my blanket, with my own good eyes, not with a man-made telescope, or fettered by a man-made theory; and I believe in the stars and in what they teach me: but if I were to say, or write what they teach, that would be a human creed—and I am opposed to all creeds." "Very well," reply the examiners, "we wish you joy in the possession of a good pair of eyes, and feel it unnecessary to go any further. If you are unwilling to confess your faith, we will not tax your conscience with the inconsistency of teaching that faith, nor tax our own with the hazard of authorizing you to set forth in the name of the stars your own ignorant assumptions about them."

What is more clear than that, as the Rule of Faith is first, it must, by necessity of its being, when rightly used, generate a true faith? But the man who has true faith desires to have it known, and is bound to confess his faith. The Rule cannot really generate two conflicting beliefs; yet men who alike profess to accept the Rule, do have conflicting beliefs; and when beliefs conflict, if the one is formed by the Rule, the other must be formed in the face of it. Fidelity to the Rule of Faith, therefore, fidelity to the faith it teaches, demands that there shall be a Confession of the faith. The firmest friend of the Word is the firmest friend of the Creed. First, the Rule of Faith, next the Faith of the Rule, and then the Confession of Faith.

. . .

150

## Meaning of Subscription to a Confession

. . . The subscription to a Confession is simply a just and easy mode of testifying to those who have a right to ask it of us, that we are what we claim and profess to be. So to sign a Confession as to imply that we are what we are not, or to leave it an open question what we are, is not the just result of the right of private judgment, or of any right whatever, but is utterly wrong. For it is a first element of truth, with which no right, private or public, can conflict, that names shall honestly represent things. What immorality is more patent than the pretence that the right of private judgment is something which authorizes a man to make his whole life a falsehood; is something which fills the world with names, which no longer represent things, fills it with black things, that are called white, with bitter things, that are called sweet, and with lies, that are called truths, with monarchists, who are called republicans, with Socinians, who are called Trinitarians, with Arminians, who are called Calvinists, with Romanists, Rationalists, fanatics, or sectarians, who are called Lutherans?

We concede to every man the absolute right of private judgment as to the faith of the Lutheran Church, but if he have abandoned the faith of that Church, he may not use her name as his shelter in attacking the thing she cherishes, and in maintaining which she obtained her being and her name. It is not enough that you say to me, that such a thing is clear to your private judgment. You must show to my private judgment, that God's word teaches it, before I dare recognize you as in the unity of the faith. If you cannot, we have not the same faith, and ought not to be of the same communion; for the communion is properly one of persons of the same faith. In other words, your private judgment is not to be my interpreter, nor is mine to be yours. If you think me in error, I have no right to force myself on your fellowship. If I think you in error, you have no right to force yourself on mine. You have the civil right and the moral right to form your impressions in regard to truth, but there the right stops. You have not the right to enter or remain in any Christian communion, except as its terms of membership give you that right. So easy is this distinction, and so clearly a part, not of speculation, but of practical morals, that the law of the land recognizes it.
. . .

## Summary of Result

This, then, is a summary of the result we reach: The basis of the Evangelical Lutheran Church is the Word of God, as the perfect and absolute Rule of Faith, and because this is her basis, she rests of necessity on the faith of which that Word is the Rule, and therefore on the Confessions which purely set forth that faith. She has the right rule, she reaches the right results by the rule, and rightly confesses them. This Confession then is her immediate basis, her essential characteristic, with which she stands or falls. The Unaltered Augsburg Confession and its Apology, the Catechisms and Schmalcald Articles, and the Formula of Concord, have been formally declared by an immense majority of the Lutheran Church as their Confession of Faith. . . . They fairly represent the faith of the Church, and simply and solely as so representing it are they named in the statement of the basis of the Evangelical Lutheran Church. The real question, then, is this: Ought the Church to rest unreservedly and unchangeably on this faith as her doctrinal basis? To this question, which is but the first repeated in a new shape, we reply, as we replied to the first, She ought.

### Note

1. In *The Conservative Reformation and Its Theology* (Minneapolis: Augsburg Publishing House, 1963; originally published in 1871), pp. 165-67, 171-72, 179.

# Charles Hodge

*The career of Hodge (1797–1878) was inseparably bound up with "Princeton School Theology," which he learned as a student from Archibald Alexander, exposited and defended throughout his long service on the faculty (from 1822 until his death), and passed on as a legacy to later generations of scholars and students. Amalgamating the Calvinist content of the Westminster Confession of Faith and "old" (late–seventeenth-century) Reformed Orthodoxy with post-Lockean, enlightened, Common-Sense philosophy, Hodge dedicated himself to upholding sound doctrine within the Presbyterian Church. One of the most learned theologians of his day and conversant with (but typically hostile to) the "rationalism," "mysticism," and "innovations" of European scholarship after Kant, he composed numerous influential books, articles, and tracts.*

*His Systematic Theology, published late in his life (1871–1873), was built of lectures delivered over decades of teaching. It represents his chief contribution to Reformed dogmatics. Presented here is a selection from chapter 1, where Hodge speaks not only for himself and his own church but for many other educated Protestants in defining theology as a rigorous "inductive science."*

## ON METHOD[1]

### §1. Theology a Science

In every science there are two factors: facts and ideas; or, facts and the mind. Science is more than knowledge. Knowledge is the persuasion of what is true on adequate evidence. But the facts of astronomy, chemistry, or history do not constitute the science of those departments of knowledge. Nor does the mere orderly arrangement of facts amount to science. Historical facts arranged in chronological order, are mere annals. The philosophy of history supposes those facts to be understood in their causal relations. In every department the man of science is assumed to understand the laws by which the facts of experience are determined; so that he not only knows the past, but can predict the future. The astronomer can foretell the relative position of the heavenly bodies for centuries to come. The chemist can tell with certainty what will be the effect of certain chemical combinations. If, therefore, theology be a science, it must include something more than a mere knowledge of facts. It must embrace an exhibition of the internal relation of those facts, one to another, and each to all. It must be able to show that if one be admitted, others cannot be denied.

The Bible is no more a system of theology, than nature is a system of chemistry or of mechanics. We find in nature the facts which the chemist or the mechanical philosopher has to examine, and from them to ascertain the laws by which they are determined. So the Bible contains the truths which the theologian has to collect, authenticate, arrange, and exhibit in their internal relation to each other. This constitutes the difference between biblical and systematic theology. The office of the former is to ascertain and state the facts of Scripture. The office of the latter is to take those facts, determine their relation to each other and to other cognate truths, as well as to vindicate them and show their harmony and consistency. This is not an easy task, or one of slight importance.

### Necessity for System in Theology.

It may naturally be asked, why not take the truths as God has seen fit to reveal them, and thus save ourselves the trouble of showing their relation and harmony?

The answer to this question is, in the first place, that it cannot be done. Such is the constitution of the human mind that it cannot help endeavoring to systematize and reconcile the facts which it admits to be true. In no department of knowledge have men been satisfied with the possession of a mass of undigested facts. And the students of the Bible can as little be expected to be thus satisfied. There is a necessity, therefore, for the construction of systems of theology. Of this the history of the Church affords abundant proof. In all ages and among all denominations, such systems have been produced.

Second, A much higher kind of knowledge is thus obtained, than by the mere accumulation of isolated facts. It is one thing, for example, to know that oceans, continents, islands, mountains, and rivers exist on the face of the earth; and a much higher thing to know the causes which have determined the distribution of land and water on the surface of our globe; the configuration of the earth; the effects of that configuration on climate, on the races of plants and animals, on commerce, civilization, and the destiny of nations. It is by determining these causes that geography has been raised from a collection of facts to a highly important and elevated science. In like manner, without the knowledge of the laws of attraction and motion, astronomy would be a confused and unintelligible collection of facts. What is true of other sciences is true of theology. We cannot know what God has revealed in his Word unless we understand, at least in some good measure, the relation in which the separate truths therein contained stand to each other. It cost the Church centuries of study and controversy to solve the problem concerning the person of Christ; that is, to adjust and bring into harmonious arrangement all the facts which the Bible teaches on that subject.

Third, We have no choice in this matter. If we would discharge our duty as teachers and defenders of the truth, we must endeavor to bring all the facts of revelation into systematic order and mutual relation. It is only thus that we can satisfactorily exhibit their truth, vindicate them from objections, or bring them to bear in their full force on the minds of men.

Fourth, Such is evidently the will of God. He does not teach men astronomy or chemistry, but He gives them the facts out of which those sciences are constructed. Neither does He teach us systematic theology, but He gives us in the Bible the truths which, properly understood and arranged, constitute the science of theology. As the facts of nature are all related and determined by physical laws, so the facts of the Bible are all related and determined by the nature of God and of his creatures. And as He wills that men should study his works and discover their wonderful organic relation and harmonious combination, so it is his will that we should study his Word, and learn that, like the stars, its truths are not isolated points, but systems, cycles, and epicycles, in unending harmony and grandeur. Besides all this, although the Scriptures do not contain a system of theology as a whole, we have in the Epistles of the New Testament, portions of that system wrought out to our hands. These are our authority and guide.

## §2. Theological Method

Every science has its own method, determined by its peculiar nature. This is a matter of so much importance that it has been erected into a distinct department. Modern literature abounds in works on Methodology, *i.e.*, on the science of method. They are designed to determine the principles which should control scientific investigations. If a man adopts a false method, he is like one who takes a wrong road which will never lead him to his destination. The two great comprehensive methods are the *à priori* and the *à posteriori*. The one argues from cause to effect, the other from effect to cause. The former was for ages applied even to the investigation of nature. Men sought to determine what the facts of nature must be from the laws of mind or assumed necessary laws. Even in our own day we have had Rational Cosmogonies, which undertake to construct a theory of the universe from the nature of absolute being and its necessary modes of development. Every one knows how much it cost to establish the method of induction on a firm basis, and to secure a general recognition of its authority. According to this method, we begin with collecting well-established facts, and from them infer the general laws which determine their occurrence. From the fact that bodies fall toward the centre of the earth, has been inferred the general law of gravitation, which we are authorized to apply far beyond the limits of actual experience. This inductive method is founded upon two principles: First, That there are laws of nature (forces) which are the proximate causes of natural phenomena. Secondly, That those laws are uniform; so that we are certain that the same causes, under the same circumstances, will produce the same effects. There may be diversity of opinion as to the nature of these laws. They may be assumed to be forces inherent in matter; or, they may be regarded as uniform modes of divine operation; but in any event there must be some cause for the phenomena which we perceive around us, and that cause must be uniform and permanent. On these principles all the inductive sciences are founded; and by them the investigations of natural philosophers are guided.

The same principle applies to metaphysics as to physics; to psychology as well as to natural science. Mind has its laws as well as matter, and those laws, although of a different kind, are as permanent as those of the external world.

. . .

## §5. The Inductive Method

It is so called because it agrees in everything essential with the inductive method as applied to the natural sciences.

First, The man of science comes to the study of nature with certain assumptions. (1.) He assumes the trustworthiness of his sense perceptions. Unless he can rely upon the well-authenticated testimony of his senses, he is deprived of all means of prosecuting his investigations. The facts of nature reveal themselves to our faculties of sense, and can be known in no other way. (2.) He must also assume the trustworthiness of his mental operations. He must take for granted that he can perceive, compare, combine, remember, and infer; and that he can safely rely upon these mental faculties in their legitimate exercise. (3.) He must also rely on the certainty of those truths which are not learned from experience, but which are given in the constitution of our nature. That every effect must have a cause; that the same cause under like circumstances, will produce like effects; that a cause is not a mere uniform antecedent, but that which contains within itself the reason why the effect occurs.

Second, The student of nature having this ground on which to stand, and these tools wherewith to work, proceeds to perceive, gather, and combine his facts. These he does not pretend to manufacture, nor presume to modify. He must take them as they are. He is only careful to be sure that they are real, and that he has them all, or, at least all that are necessary to justify any inference which he may draw from them, or any theory which he may build upon them.

Third, From facts thus ascertained and classified, he deduces the laws by which they are determined. That a heavy body falls to the ground is a familiar fact. Observation shows that it is not an isolated fact; but that all matter tends toward all other matter; that this tendency or attraction is in proportion to the quantity of matter; and its intensity decreases in proportion to the square of the distance of the attracting bodies. As all this is found to be universally and constantly the case within the field of observation, the mind is forced to conclude that there is some reason for it; in other words, that it is a law of nature which may be relied upon beyond the limits of actual observation. As this law has always operated in the past, the man of science is sure that it will operate in the future. It is in this way the vast body of modern science has been built up, and the laws which determine the motions of the heavenly bodies; the chemical changes constantly going on around us; the structure, growth, and propagation of plants and animals, have, to a greater or less extent, been ascertained and established. It is to be observed that these laws or general principles are not derived from the mind, and attributed to external objects, but derived or deduced from the objects and impressed upon the mind.

## A. The Inductive Method as Applied to Theology.

The Bible is to the theologian what nature is to the man of science. It is his store-house of facts; and his method of ascertaining what the Bible teaches, is the same as that which the natural philosopher adopts to

157

ascertain what nature teaches. In the first place, he comes to his task with all the assumptions above mentioned. He must assume the validity of those laws of belief which God has impressed upon our nature. In these laws are included some which have no direct application to the natural sciences. Such, for example, as the essential distinction between right and wrong; that nothing contrary to virtue can be enjoined by God; that it cannot be right to do evil that good may come; that sin deserves punishment, and other similar first truths, which God has implanted in the constitution of all moral beings, and which no objective revelation can possibly contradict. These first principles, however, are not to be arbitrarily assumed. No man has a right to lay down his own opinions, however firmly held, and call them "first truths of reason," and make them the source or test of Christian doctrines. Nothing can rightfully be included under the category of first truths, or laws of belief, which cannot stand the tests of universality and necessity, to which many add self-evidence. But self-evidence is included in universality and necessity, in so far, that nothing which is not self-evident can be universally believed, and what is self-evident forces itself on the mind of every intelligent creature.

### Facts to Be Collected.

In the second place, the duty of the Christian theologian is to ascertain, collect, and combine all the facts which God has revealed concerning himself and our relation to Him. These facts are all in the Bible. This is true, because everything revealed in nature, and in the constitution of man concerning God and our relation to Him, is contained and authenticated in Scripture. It is in this sense that "the Bible, and the Bible alone, is the religion of Protestants." It may be admitted that the truths which the theologian has to reduce to a science, or, to speak more humbly, which he has to arrange and harmonize, are revealed partly in the external works of God, partly in the constitution of our nature, and partly in the religious experience of believers; yet lest we should err in our inferences from the works of God, we have a clearer revelation of all that nature reveals, in his word; and lest we should misinterpret our own consciousness and the laws of our nature, everything that can be legitimately learned from that source will be found recognized and authenticated in the Scriptures; and lest we should attribute to the teaching of the Spirit the operations of our own natural affections, we find in the Bible the norm and standard of all genuine religious experience. The Scriptures teach not only the truth, but what are the effects of the truth on the heart and conscience, when applied with saving power by the Holy Ghost.

### The Theologian to Be Guided by the Same Rules as the Man of Science.

In the third place, the theologian must be guided by the same rules in the collection of facts, as govern the man of science.

1. This collection must be made with diligence and care. It is not an easy work. There is in every department of investigation great liability to error. Almost all false theories in science and false doctrines in theology are due in a great degree to mistakes as to matters of fact. A distinguished naturalist said he repeated an experiment a thousand times before he felt authorized to announce the result to the scientific world as an established fact.

2. This collection of facts must not only be carefully conducted, but also comprehensive, and if possible, exhaustive. An imperfect induction of facts led men for ages to believe that the sun moved round the earth, and that the earth was an extended plain. In theology a partial induction of particulars has led to like serious errors. It is a fact that the Scriptures attribute omniscience to Christ. From this it was inferred that He could not have had a finite intelligence, but that the Logos was clothed in Him with a human body with its animal life. But it is also a Scriptural fact that ignorance and intellectual progress, as well as omniscience, are ascribed to our Lord. Both facts, therefore, must be included in our doctrine of his person. We must admit that He had a human, as well as a divine intelligence. It is a fact that everything that can be predicated of a sinless man, is in the Bible, predicated of Christ; and it is also a fact that everything that is predicated of God is predicated of our Lord; hence it has been inferred that there were two Christs,—two persons,— the one human, the other divine, and that they dwelt together very much as the Spirit dwells in the believer; or, as evil spirits dwelt in demoniacs. But this theory overlooked the numerous facts which prove the individual personality of Christ. It was the same person who said, "I thirst;" who said, "Before Abraham was I am." The Scriptures teach that Christ's death was designed to reveal the love of God, and to secure the reformation of men. Hence Socinus denied that his death was an expiation for sin, or satisfaction of justice. The latter fact, however, is as clearly revealed as the former; and therefore both must be taken into account in our statement of the doctrine concerning the design of Christ's death.

### Necessity of a Complete Induction.

Illustrations without end might be given of the necessity of a comprehensive induction of facts to justify our doctrinal conclusions. These facts must not be willfully denied or carelessly overlooked, or unfairly appreciated. We must be honest here, as the true student of nature is honest in his induction. Even scientific men are sometimes led to suppress or to pervert facts which militate against their favorite theories; but the temptation to this form of dishonesty is far less in their case, than in that of the theologian. The truths of religion are far more important than those of natural science. They come home to the heart and conscience. They may alarm the fears or threaten the hopes of men, so that they are under strong temptation to overlook or pervert them. If, however, we really desire to know what God has revealed we must be conscientiously diligent and faithful in collecting the facts which He has made known, and in giving them their due weight. If a geologist should find in a deposit of early date implements of human workmanship, he is not allowed to say they are natural productions. He must either revise his conclusion as to the age of the deposit, or carry back to an earlier period the existence of man. There is no help for it. Science cannot make facts; it must take them as they are. In like manner, if the Bible asserts that Christ's death was a satisfaction to justice, the theologian is not allowed to merge justice into benevolence in order to suit his theory of the atonement. If the Scriptures teach that men are born in sin, we cannot change the nature of sin, and make it a tendency to evil and not really sin, in order to get rid of difficulty. If it be a Scriptural fact that the soul exists in a state of conscious activity between death and the resurrection, we must not deny this fact or reduce this conscious activity to zero, because our anthropology teaches that the soul has no individuality and no activity without a body. We must take the facts of the Bible as they are, and construct our system so as to embrace them all in their integrity.

### Principles to Be Deduced from Facts.

In the fourth place, in theology as in natural science, principles are derived from facts, and not impressed upon them. The properties of matter, the laws of motion, of magnetism, of light, etc., are not framed by the mind. They are not laws of thought. They are deductions from facts. The investigator sees, or ascertains by observation, what are the laws which determine material phenomena; he does not invent those laws. His speculations on matters of science unless sustained by facts, are worthless. It is no less unscientific for the theologian to assume a theory as to the nature of virtue, of sin, of liberty, of moral obligation, and then explain the facts of Scripture in accordance with his theories. His only proper course is to derive his theory of virtue, of sin, of liberty, of obligation, from the facts of the Bible. He should remember that his business is not to set forth his system of truth (that is of no account), but to ascertain and exhibit what is God's system, which is a matter of the greatest moment. If he cannot believe what the facts of the Bible assume to be true, let him say so. Let the sacred writers have their doctrine, while he has his own. To this ground a large class of modern exegetes and theologians, after a long struggle, have actually come. They give what they regard as the doctrines of the Old Testament; then those of the Evangelists; then those of the Apostles; and then their own. This is fair. So long, however, as the binding authority of Scripture is acknowledged, the temptation is very strong to press the facts of the Bible into accordance with our preconceived theories. If a man be persuaded that certainty in acting is inconsistent with liberty of action; that a free agent can always act contrary to any amount of influence (not destructive of his liberty) brought to bear upon him, he will inevitably deny that the Scriptures teach the contrary, and thus be forced to explain away all facts which prove the absolute control of God over the will and volitions of men. If he hold that sinfulness can be predicated only of intelligent, voluntary action in contravention of law, he must deny that men are born in sin, let the Bible teach what it may. If he believes that ability limits obligation, he must believe independently of the Scriptures, or in opposition to them, it matters not which, that men are able to repent, believe, love God perfectly, to live without sin, at any, and all times, without the least assistance from the Spirit of God. If he deny that the innocent may justly suffer penal evil for the guilty, he must deny that Christ bore our sins. If he deny that the merit of one man can be the judicial ground of the pardon and salvation of other men, he must reject the Scriptural doctrine of justification. It is plain that complete havoc must be made of the whole system of revealed truth, unless we consent to derive our philosophy from the Bible, instead of explaining the Bible by our philosophy. If the Scriptures teach that sin is hereditary, we must adopt a theory of sin suited to that fact. If they teach that men cannot repent, believe, or do anything spiritually good, without the supernatural aid of the Holy Spirit, we must make our theory of moral obligation accord with that fact. If the Bible teaches that we bear the guilt of Adam's first sin, that Christ bore our guilt, and endured the penalty of the law in our stead, these are facts with which we must make our principles agree. It would be easy to show that in every department of theology,—in regard to the nature of God, his relation to the world, the plan of salvation, the person and work of Christ, the nature of sin, the operations of divine grace, men, instead of taking the facts of the Bible, and seeing what principles they imply, what philosophy underlies them, have adopted their philosophy independently of the Bible, to which the facts of the Bible are made to bend. This is utterly unphilosophical. It is the fundamental principle of all sciences, and of theology among the rest, that theory is to be determined by facts, and not facts by theory. As natural science was a chaos until the principle of induction was admitted and faithfully carried out, so theology is a jumble of human speculations, not worth a straw, when men refuse to apply the same principle to the study of the Word of God.

## §6. *The Scriptures Contain All the Facts of Theology*

This is perfectly consistent, on the one hand, with the admission of intuitive truths, both intellectual and moral, due to our constitution as rational and moral beings; and, on the other hand, with the controlling power over our beliefs exercised by the inward teachings of the Spirit, or, in other words, by our religious experience. And that for two reasons: First, All truth must be consistent. God cannot contradict himself. He cannot force us by the constitution of the nature which He has given us to believe one thing, and in his Word command us to believe the opposite. And, second, All the truths taught by the constitution of our nature or by religious experience, are recognized and authenticated in the Scriptures. This is a safeguard and a limit. We cannot assume this or that principle to be intuitively true, or this or that conclusion to be demonstrably certain, and make them a standard to which the Bible must conform. What is self-evidently true, must be proved to be so, and is always recognized in the Bible as true. Whole systems of theologies are founded upon intuitions, so called, and if every man is at liberty to exalt his own intuitions, as men are accustomed to call their strong convictions, we should have as many theologies in the world as there are thinkers. The same remark is applicable to religious experience. There is no form of conviction more intimate and irresistible than that which arises from the inward teaching of the Spirit. All saving faith rests on his testimony or demonstrations (1 Cor. ii. 4). Believers have an unction from the Holy One, and they know the truth, and that no lie (or false doctrine) is of the truth. This inward teaching produces a conviction which no sophistries can obscure, and no arguments can shake. It is founded on consciousness, and you might as well argue a man out of a belief of his existence, as out of confidence that what he is thus taught of God is true. Two things, however, are to be borne in mind. First, That this inward teaching or demonstration of the Spirit is confined to truths objectively revealed in the Scriptures. It is given, says the Apostle, in order that we may know things gratuitously given, *i.e.*, revealed to us by God in his Word (1 Cor. ii. 10-16). It is not, therefore, a revelation of new truths, but an illumination of the mind, so that it apprehends the truth, excellence, and glory of things already revealed. And second, This experience is depicted in the Word of God. The Bible gives us not only the facts concerning God, and Christ, ourselves, and our relations to our Maker and Redeemer, but also records the legitimate effects of those truths on the minds of believers. So that we cannot appeal to our own feelings or inward experience, as a ground or guide, unless we can show that it agrees with the experience of holy men as recorded in the Scriptures.

### The Teaching of the Spirit.

Although the inward teaching of the Spirit, or religious experience, is no substitute for an external revelation, and is no part of the rule of faith, it is, nevertheless, an invaluable guide in determining what the rule of faith teaches. The distinguishing feature of Augustinianism as taught by Augustin himself, and by the purer theologians of the Latin Church throughout the Middle Ages, which was set forth by the Reformers, and especially by Calvin and the Geneva divines, is that the inward teaching of the Spirit is allowed its proper place in determining our theology. The question is not first and mainly, What is true to the understanding, but what is true to the renewed heart? The effort is not to make the assertions of the Bible harmonize with the speculative reason, but to subject our feeble reason to the mind of God as revealed in his Word, and by his Spirit in our inner life. It might be easy to lead men to the conclusion that they are responsible only for their voluntary acts, if the appeal is made solely to the understanding. But if the appeal be made to every man's, and especially to every Christian's inward experience, the opposite conclusion is reached. We are convinced of the sinfulness of states of mind as well as of voluntary acts, even when those states are not the effect of our own agency, and are not subject to the power of the will. We are conscious of being sold under sin; of being its slaves; of being possessed by it as a power or law, immanent, innate, and beyond our control. Such is the doctrine of the Bible, and such is the teaching of our religious consciousness when under the influence of the Spirit of God. The true method in theology requires that the facts of religious experience should be accepted as facts, and when duly authenticated by Scripture, be allowed to interpret the doctrinal statements of the Word of

God. So legitimate and powerful is this inward teaching of the Spirit, that it is no uncommon thing to find men having two theologies,—one of the intellect, and another of the heart. The one may find expression in creeds and systems of divinity, the other in their prayers and hymns. It would be safe for a man to resolve to admit into his theology nothing which is not sustained by the devotional writings of true Christians of every denomination. It would be easy to construct from such writings, received and sanctioned by Romanists, Lutherans, Reformed, and Remonstrants, a system of Pauline or Augustinian theology, such as would satisfy any intelligent and devout Calvinist in the world.

The true method of theology is, therefore, the inductive, which assumes that the Bible contains all the facts or truths which form the contents of theology, just as the facts of nature are the contents of the natural sciences. It is also assumed that the relation of these Biblical facts to each other, the principles involved in them, the laws which determine them, are in the facts themselves, and are to be deduced from them, just as the laws of nature are deduced from the facts of nature. In neither case are the principles derived from the mind and imposed upon the facts, but equally in both departments, the principles or laws are deduced from the facts and recognized by the mind.

### Note

1. In *Systematic Theology* (Grand Rapids: Eerdmans, 1975; originally published in 1872), pp. 1-4, 9-17.

# Nathan Bangs

*B*angs *(1778–1862) was Methodism's most prominent theologian during the national era. His calling was to model and encourage the cultivation of theological study and intellectually well-formulated doctrine within the church. Ordained in 1804, a few years after a "typical" revivalist conversion experience, his first—and arguably most theologically substantive—work,* The Errors of Hopkinsianism, *appeared in 1815, written in the course of his pastoral duties. Many others were to follow, among them works on predestination, sanctification, holiness, and Methodist history, doctrine, and polity. As head of the Methodist Book Concern and editor of various church magazines, he helped guide his church into ongoing, active theological dialogue (and debate) about contemporary currents of thought and church affairs.*

The Errors of Hopkinsianism *is, by intention, a polemical piece. Its aim is to meet the arguments for original sin, predestination, human depravity, and other themes of the "New Divinity" with counterarguments on behalf of Methodist "Arminianism" and in terms as learned with respect to scripture, historic doctrine, and Common-Sense philosophy as the Calvinists ("determinists") themselves.*

## REMARKS ON "NATURAL ABILITY" AND "MORAL INABILITY"[1]

One of the most convincing evidences of the truth of any system is, its exact conformity to the moral perfections of God, and its suitableness to the moral condition of man. And whenever this is perceived in any system, we shall, at the same time, perceive a harmony in its several parts, one truth growing out of another, and the various branches of truth mutually depending upon, and supporting each other. And that which recommends Christianity to the consideration of intelligent beings is, that it perspicuously illustrates the divine perfections, exhibits the character of man as our daily experience proves it to be, adapts itself to our moral condition, by the sovereign remedy it has provided for our spiritual disease, and by presenting to the enlightened mind a harmonious system of doctrines and precepts. While, therefore, we contemplate this glorious system, our minds are delighted in beholding, the beauty, order, and sacred harmony, so visibly manifested in every part of it. It is like a well contrived, and a well finished building in which nothing is wanting, nothing superfluous; so that, while we view this sacred edifice, we not only behold a permanent foundation on which it securely rests, but also a superstructure of exquisite workmanship, the lovely harmony of the several parts in which, mutually supporting and strengthening each other, being *fitly framed together, groweth unto an holy temple in the Lord.*

But while we behold this internal evidence of the divine authority of the gospel, in the sacred harmony and exquisite beauty of the Christian building, our minds turn with avidity and disgust from the heterogenius mixture of those materials with which the discordant temple of error is composed. How much so ever the art and ingenuity of men may display themselves, in decorating the external appearance of this confused edifice, its internal deformity, when examined in the light of truth, exhibits convincing evidence of its human origin, and of its defective structure. Instead of beholding that *Zion which is the perfection of beauty, out of which God hath shined,* we perceive evident marks of that gloomy mansion, where the Sun of truth never shines but to reveal the rottenness of its foundation, and the weakness of its superstructure.

We shall see, I trust, these remarks verified while examining Mr. Williston's theory of *natural ability* and *moral inability.* It is true, we have not much to object to his explanation of his views of this subject only as they are connected with other parts of his system: for we grant that every sinner "has powers and faculties which belong to his nature as a rational moral agent, which are sufficient to enable him to do all that which he is commanded." p.230—But we contend that this is only true when the sinner is viewed in relation to the *gospel* representation of Redemption and Salvation, which exhibits the ample provision made by Jesus Christ for the present and eternal salvation of all mankind; for no man can have, either *natural* or *moral* ability, to do an impossibility: but if a part of the human family were eternally reprobated, and thereby excluded from any saving benefits of redemption, their eternal salvation was absolutely and eternally impossible. And have these excluded reprobates *natural* ability to do that which is *naturally* and *absolutely* impossible? If their salvation were *possible,* then the Hopkinsian decree of reprobation is a human decree. If it were *impossible,* then their doctrine of natural ability to love God is worse than human. They may extricate themselves from this dilemma in any way their system will admit. If they break down the first barrier, they annihilate their doctrine of decrees: If the second, they destroy this peculiarity of Hopkinsianism, and confirm the doctrine of the old fashioned Calvinists: But if, with a bolder flight, they leap over them both, they will find themselves happily escaped into the open plains of gospel truth, where rivers of divine love flow to all the human race, which so washes off the defects of *natural ability,* and supplies by its invigorating influence, the deficiency of a *moral inability,* that they may come to Christ, the flowing fountain of eternal life, drink, and live for ever. How absurd it is to suppose that a man has *natural* power to regenerate himself, in direct *opposition* to his *inclination,* and to prepare himself, by loving God with all his heart, for heaven, when at the same time, Christ had no *intention* of *saving* him when he died for him, and his eternal damnation was made unalterably certain by God's irrevocable decree. Therefore, although it is proper to say that men have physical and moral powers to do what God requires of them, when enlightened by the Spirit of truth, and when comprehended in the grand scheme of redemption; yet, it appears extremely absurd to suppose they have natural power to do this in direct *opposition* to the *eternal* purpose, and the *present* agency of God. This would be to invest man with a power to overcome the omnipotent decree of Jehovah, and to do that which was rendered absolutely impossible by an act of God himself. Does any one perceive the beauty of truth in this deformed face of Hopkinsianism?

Moreover, it seems unscriptural to suppose that men have *natural* ability to perceive and understand the way of life and salvation, only as they are enlightened by the word and Spirit of God; for the understandings of men are darkened in consequence of original depravity, their ears are dull of hearing, and they cannot see spiritual objects unless divine illumination is afforded them: how then, can they have *natural,* while they have no *moral power* to love God? We grant, indeed, that all men have sufficient powers of mind to understand, and to do, what God requires them to understand and do, when they are enlightened and empowered by grace; and that this grace is afforded to all men during their probationary state: but this truth grows out of that true proposition of the gospel, (which Hopkinsianism denies in its first principle respecting universal decrees,) namely, that Christ, by his death and suffering has made salvation possible to all men. I know, indeed, that Mr. W. has asserted that Jesus Christ "has put all men into a *salvable* state;"

but we also know, that this assertion can never be reconciled with his doctrine of an eternal, definite, and absolute reprobation: and neither will his plaster of *natural ability* ever heal the wound which the keen razor of truth has made in this limb of his hydra; it being certain that no man has *natural ability* to do that which God, by an immutable decree, has made impossible to be done.

But why is this doctrine of natural ability and moral inability contended for? It is , it would appear, to vindicate the claims of divine justice in the final and perpetual condemnation of those unhappy reprobates, who were eternally condemned in the mind of God; whose *inability* and *ability* with all their effects and causes are in exact conformity to the original intention, and the present existing agency of God. But pray tell us, how does this vindicate the claims of divine justice? If the bow be bent by the marksman in just such a direction as he would have it, so as to answer his purpose precisely; and if from long use, it contract an inclination to that particular direction; is the bow accountable for not altering its inclination? So, if the hearts of these poor reprobates are *inclined* by an Almighty and effective decree to a particular direction, namely, to sin and damnation; and if they perfectly answer the mind of God in all they passively do, must they be eternally condemned for possessing a *moral inability* to alter their *inclination,* and turn themselves about, and save themselves *contrary* to the original design of God? This would seem a hard case indeed. Of what use, now, can this new-fangled doctrine of *natural ability,* and *moral inability* be in vindicating the justice of God in the condemnation of the reprobates? It can serve no other purpose than to hide the real state of the doctrine for which Mr. W. has so zealously contended in the first chapter of his book. . . .

From this scriptural and rational view of the subject under consideration, we perceive the manifest absurdity of the Hopkinsian speculations concerning a *moral inability,* consisting altogether in the perversity of the will, as if that turned the scale in every thing. This unintelligible something, which they sometimes denominate the will, and sometimes a *moral* inability, occupies, as before observed, in their system, precisely the same place, and performs the same functions, which *fate* did in heathenism, and as *decree* does in Calvinism; and appears to have been invented for the purpose of obviating the Arminian objection to the doctrine of Calvinistic reprobation, respecting the injustice of consigning those reprobates to hell for not doing what they never had any power to do. Hence, say the advocates of this phantasm, men have *natural power* to counteract the influence of God's decree, but never do it, because they have no *moral* power; and when you ask them to explain what they mean by this moral power, they tell you it is the *will*—reprobates and devils might love God if they *would*, but they *will* not. But the fact is, a man has no will respecting a particular subject, until that subject is presented to his mind; and then he may will to consider upon it or not; and finally, will to accept or reject, according to his own choice.

Thus, when God calls upon sinners to repent, the subject of Christianity presenting itself to their minds in all its bearings, they deliberate upon it, if they act understandingly, whether it be best to comply with the call or not; and if they conclude it best to comply, their language is, We *will*—We *will* return unto the Lord, *we will* believe in Jesus Christ; they do not say, Our *will* resolves we shall repent, and therefore we must yield a compliance to its lordly dictates. However absurd such language may appear, it is but the legitimate offspring of this mother of inconsistency, that the will is a constituent faculty of the soul, exercising a lordly influence over the whole man. The moment we accommodate our phraseology to the theory we are opposing, respecting the will possessing a preponderating influence over the man, leading him captive to its capricious humour, we see its manifest inconsistency. All those forms of speech, found in the sacred scripture, in moral writers, and in our verbal communications with each other, justify the doctrine for which we plead, that the will is the effect, or result of deliberation, or that which is induced by the presentation of any query or subject, concerning which the mind resolves to deliberate. The first existence, then, of the will in reference to any particular subject, is the first act of the mind respecting that subject—I say in reference to any *particular subject*; because the mind is always active—always *willing* or *nilling* respecting something.

Hence the immaterial spirit of man, is an undefinable something invested by its Creator with sovereign authority (subordinate, however, to the wise and beneficient government of God) over itself, and which thinks, deliberates and acts freely. Of this every man may be conscious if he attend to what passes in his own breast—and the best proof of man is man himself—If he will calmly attend to what passes in his own mind, though he cannot explain *how*, nor assign the reasons *wherefore*, he will find such self-evident demonstrations of his own dominion over himself, as shall completely nullify all the erroneous conclusions drawn from theories which have been adopted to support a favourite system. Every man is conscious of such a principal of action as involves responsibility; and his deliberate judgment tells him that he cannot be responsible for

169

actions which are induced by necessity; but if he be bound by an invincible *moral inability, will, disposition,* or *inclination,* or whatever other name may be given to the controling power, to only one line of conduct, however pleasant it may be to him, neither justice nor goodness can assign any reason why he should be condemned. I say however *pleasant* it may be to him; for if the *disposition* to choose be entirely directed by an Almighty predisposing cause, inducing the sinner either by a secret operation upon his heart, or by the presentation of external motives, to choose as he does, although it may be said that he does as he *pleases,* it alters not the state of the case; because, according to our opponents, all those things came to pass only in consequence of the exciting agency of God upon his heart. These things being considered, pray tell us, ye who have studied this system, how the Hopkinsian theory of natural ability, and moral inability will obviate the Arminian objection against Calvinistic reprobation; or rescue the justice of God from the impeachment of cruelty, in the condemnation of the reprobates? That doctrine says, that the natural ability and moral inability, all the desires of the heart, internal and external motives, all the actions of the life, whether righteous or wicked, are according to God's original decree, and are now produced by the efficient hand of God. Now if this be so, of what use is a natural ability, or a moral inability. Can either the strength of the one, or the feebleness of the other, counteract the immutable decree of heaven, or resist the irresistible influence of the universal divine efficiency? So little do these subtle refinements respecting natural and moral ability, benefit the system they are designed to support.

Upon the whole, therefore, I conclude, that it is not the "words which I have used as making a true representation of their sentiments, which seem to have such a strange clashing with each other, that the inattentive reader would be led to imagine, that none but men more fit for a mad house, than to be Christian teachers, could ever believe and propogate such self-contradictory doctrines," (p. 135.) but it is that *doctrine* of my antagonist that has such a *strange clashing* that the *attentive* reader must perceive that none but those who are extremely puzzled to support a favourite theory, would ever attempt to vindicate. Of this I believe every impartial observer must be convinced who attentively weighs the preceding observations. To suppose that men have natural power to love God with all the heart without grace, and without any disposition, is one of the incredible paradoxes reserved for the perfecting of modern divinity; and it so *clashes* with the *essential doctrines of the reformation,* with the word of the living God, and is so abhorrent to the dictates of common sense, that I believe it would be difficult to persuade even a *mad-man,* much less a *sober man,* to believe it. But when we are further told that these men, who were unconditionally reprobated to eternal burnings by an immutable decree of God, have *natural* power without any *disposition,* to break that decree, regenerate themselves, and be prepared for heaven, we candidly think such absurd notions are more fit for a "mad-house" than for a Christian temple: and that it is high time for the teachers of such "clashing" doctrines to put themselves into the school of sober reason, until they are prepared for the higher branches of scriptural divinity, which exhibits and illustrates the harmonious doctrines of Jesus Christ. They will then learn to proclaim a consistent scheme of divine doctrines, which harmonizes all the divine attributes, presents the Saviour of sinners in the transcendent glories of his character as having atoned for the sin of the world; and also opens a door of mercy to all men, by showing the efficacy of the Holy Spirit, who comes to enlighten the dark minds of sinners, to restrain their evil dispositions, and to enable them to overcome the natural or moral aversion of their hearts, come to Christ and live. Likewise, to exhibit an impartial God, eternally existing in the sacred Unity of Trinity, the plenitude of whose uncreated goodness, is manifested in granting unto all men a probationary state. Yes, they would then unfold the wonderful design of Creating, Redeeming, Pardoning, and Sanctifying love, so eminently exemplified in the grand system of revelation. Guided by this ray of divine light, the mind is enraptured at the view of the unbounded wisdom, the untarnished justice, the unfathomable love, and the impartial goodness of the Triune God, in devising, executing, and revealing the superexcellent and comprehensive system of redemption and salvation. With hearts imbued with this love, with what supreme delight does the tongue proclaim the wonders of redeeming grace! Embracing all mankind in the arms of love, with what sincerity, faith, and unutterable delight may we invite sinners to come to Christ and live. Standing upon this eminence, raised by the dying groans of Jesus Christ, with what holy rapture do we look up to the Throne of God, while we behold the impartial God, demonstrating his love to all the human family; and with what commisseration do we look down upon our lost world, while we call upon them to accept of eternal life. While the heart swells with gratitude to our adored God, from this delightful view of his sacred character, it is drawn forth with the tenderest sympathy toward the human race. Being authorized from this scriptural representation of the divine economy, we joyfully proclaim in the ears of our fellow men, the unsearchable riches of Christ—assuring them upon the most indubitable testimony, that they all have been comprehended in the grand scheme of redemption.

On the other hand—With what truth, with what justice, may we denounce the penalties of God's righteous law against its bold violaters. To such we may say: The law you have unjustly violated: The gospel you have despised: Jesus Christ who died for you, you have neglected: The Holy Spirit you have grieved: In a word, you have slighted, abused, and finally rejected that goodness which the Holy God had mercifully offered unto you. Rejecting the sincere offers of life and salvation you have *treasured up to yourselves wrath against the day of wrath, and the revelation of the righteous judgment of God.* Your condemnation, therefore, originates necessarily, from the nature of your own conduct, from your own voluntary rejection of eternal life.

These are the awfully interesting truths with which Christianity gently assails mankind, and by which it powerfully recommends itself to *every man's conscience in the sight of God.*

And do we perceive any *strange clashing* among these truths? Do we not perceive them all concentrating in the perfections of God; and from thence branching out in various directions, amplifying, and suiting themselves to the various relations, conditions, and characters of men? How diminutive does poor, fallen, and guilty man appear, while this glare of divine light shines upon him! And how transcendently glorious does the Triune God appear, while the mind views Him, through the medium of these sublime, and interesting truths. Not the smallest spot of eternal hatred to one part of the human family, is beheld to darken the divinely glorious character of Jehovah—Not a cloud of reprobating wrath is seen hovering in the luminous atmosphere of gospel truth— until we see them rising from the stagnant pool of human corruption and perversity. All around the divine throne, on which sits the God of power, justice, and goodness, encircled with the bright rays of universal love, we behold, when enlightened by the Sun of truth, evident signs of *good will* to the degraded, suffering, and miserable sons of men: while, in this dark valley of human nature, we see evident tokens of depravity, wrath, variance, and opposition to God and goodness. We see, indeed, the wretched sons of men, madly pursuing their race in folly and wickedness, shutting their ears against the calls of divine mercy, and persisting, in spite of all the signals of coming indignation, in the high road to hell! At this dismal sight, the heart of the philanthropist, filled with godly sorrow, cries out, *Is there no help?* He looks up, and beholds a God—a

172

Saviour—whose impartial love led him to die for those sinners. No sooner does this truth fasten upon the understanding, than the lover of human souls, announces it unto these perishing sinners; urging them by all that is dear to themselves, by the love of God, by the dying groans of Jesus Christ, not madly to rush on to their own destruction, but to return unto God and live.

Armed with these truths, and surrounded by this flood of divine light, the minister of the Lord Jesus, may boldly step forth in the name of his Master, unfolding to a lost world, the sovereign remedy provided for their diseased souls, and the willingness of Almighty God to apply it to them. Now, we think, that all who act under the influence of these harmonious truths of God, will perceive sufficient reason to believe that all men, during their probationary state, have sufficient natural and moral power to repent of their sins, and to believe in Jesus Christ *with a heart unto righteousness.*

### Note

1. In *The Reformer Reformed: Or a Second Part of the Errors of Hopkinsianism Detected and Refuted: Being an Examination of Mr. Seth Williston's "Vindication of Some of the Most Essential Doctrines of the Reformation"* (New York: Printed by John C. Totten, 1818), pp. 316-20, 341-48.

# Phoebe Palmer

*P*almer's *(1807–1874) writings gave special focus for Methodists to the desire for sanctification that was virtually a pan-Protestant concern in the decades prior to the Civil War. The "Tuesday Meetings for the Promotion of Holiness" that she and her sister sponsored as early as the 1830s were in one sense illustrative of new quests for visible signs of righteousness in the age of revivalism and Jacksonian democracy. Her emphasis on entire sanctification, however, was rooted quite specifically in John Wesley's teachings and "mainstream" Methodism: e.g., Nathan Bangs, who attended the Tuesday Meetings, was among the theologians attentive to Palmer's many writings, and the church's bishops in the 1840s urged the faithful to "go on to perfection."*

*Her views on the immediacy of entire sanctification, rather than its lifelong process, was one of the points that later in the nineteenth century divided Methodists and stimulated the growth of the Holiness movement. In this selection from chapter 2 of* Entire Devotion to God *(1845), Palmer defines sanctification, highlights its dependence upon faith and the continuing work of the Holy Spirit, and recognizes the possibility that even the sanctified remain capable of sin.*

## ENTIRE DEVOTION TO GOD[1]

II. What is Gospel Holiness, or Sanctification?

Gospel holiness is that *state* which is attained by the believer when, through *faith* in the infinite merit of the Saviour, body and soul, with every ransomed faculty, are ceaselessly presented, a living sacrifice, to God; the purpose of the soul being steadily bent to know nothing among men, save Christ and Him crucified, and the eye of faith fixed on "the Lamb of God which taketh away the sin of the world." In obedience to the requirement of God, the sacrifice is presented *through* Christ, and the soul at once proves that "He is able to save them to the *uttermost* that come unto God by Him."

Holiness implies salvation from sin, a redemption from *all* iniquity. The soul, through faith, being laid upon the *altar* that *sanctifieth* the gift, experiences *constantly* the all-cleansing efficacy of the blood of Jesus. And through this it knows the blessedness of being presented faultless before the throne, and mingles its triumphant ecstasies with the blood-washed company: "Unto Him that loved us, and washed us from our sins in His own blood, and hath made us kings and priests unto God and His Father, to Him be glory and dominion for ever and ever. Amen."

Though saved from all sin at present, yet the soul that has been brought into the *experience* of this state well knows that it is not saved to the uttermost. If finds that, in the entire surrender of the world, it has but "laid aside every weight." And now, with undeviating purpose and unshackled feet, it runs with increasing rapidity and delight in the way of His commandments, gaining new accessions of wisdom, power, and love, with every other grace, daily.

"Holiness," "sanctification," and "perfect love" are terms intimately related in meaning. The terms *holiness* and *sanctification,* being frequently used by Divine inspiration, we may presume to be most significantly expressive of the state to which it is the duty of every believer to attain.

"Sanctification" being a word of much the same prominence as "holiness" in the blessed Word, it may be well to devote a few moments to its investigation, as it will doubtless throw an increase of light on the endeavour to ascertain the *nature* of the blessing.

As we have frequent occasion to observe in Scripture, the term "sanctify," in its most simple definition, means setting apart for any specified purpose. Thus it was that Moses was commanded to sanctify the children of Israel. "And the Lord said unto Moses, Go unto this people, and sanctify them today and tomorrow, and let them wash their clothes, and be ready against the third day: for the third day the Lord will come down in the sight of all the people upon Mount Sinai" (Exod. xix. 10, 11).

The Israelites also were required to sanctify themselves: "Sanctify yourselves therefore and be ye holy: for I am the Lord your God" (Lev. xx. 7). The Saviour sanctified Himself for the redemption of the world: "And for their sakes I sanctify Myself, that they also might be sanctified through the truth" (John xvii. 19). God also is represented as sanctifying His people: "I am the Lord that doth sanctify you" (Exod. xxxi. 13).

"And the very God of peace sanctify you wholly" (1 Thess. v. 23). "Even as Christ also loved the Church and gave Himself for it, that He might sanctify and cleanse it" (Eph. v. 25, 26). The Saviour prays that His disciples may be sanctified through the truth: "Sanctify them through Thy truth: Thy word is truth" (John xvii. 17). Peter also speaks of the sanctification of the elect, according to the foreknowledge of God, unto obedience and sprinkling of the blood of Jesus (1 Peter i. 2). Paul as above speaks of the sanctification of the Church, cleansed with the washing of water by the Word (Eph. v. 26, 27). The Corinthian brethren are also exhorted to cleanse themselves from all filthiness of the flesh and spirit, by taking hold on the promises (2 Cor. vii. 1). The vessels in the Temple were all, by the special appointment of God, set apart for holy purposes; and though a variety of uses was designated, yet they were sanctified exclusively for the holy service of the sanctuary.

Thus it is that the Christian, redeemed from all iniquity, not with corruptible things, such as silver and gold, but by the precious blood of Jesus, is, by the most explicit *declarations* and *obligations,* required to come out and be separate. "And what agreement hath the temple of God with idols? for ye are the temple of the living God: as God hath said, I will dwell in them, and walk in them; and I will be their God, and they shall be My people. Wherefore come out from among them and be ye separate, saith the Lord, and touch not the unclean thing, and will receive you" (2 Cor. vi. 16, 17). "Go ye out of the midst of her; be ye clean, that bear the vessels of the Lord" (Isaiah lii. 11). "Know ye not that your body is the temple of the Holy Ghost which is in you, which ye have of God, and ye are not your own? For ye are bought with a price: therefore glorify God in your body, and in your spirit, which are God's" (1 Cor. v. 19, 20). "For this is the will of God, even your sanctification" (1 Thess. iv. 3, 4). "If ye were of the world, the world would love his own; but because ye are not of the world, but I have chosen you out of the world, therefore the world hateth you" (John xv. 19). Yet "sanctification," as applied to believers, comprehends inconceivably greater blessedness than a mere nominal setting apart of body and soul, with every power, to God. The sacrifice, or service, however well intended, could not for a moment be acceptable without the washing of regeneration, and the renewing of the Holy Ghost.

And then, in order to be continually washed, cleansed, and renewed after the image of God, the sacrifice must be *ceaselessly* presented. This is implied in the expression, "a *living* sacrifice;" it is thus we are made priests unto God. Through Jesus Christ, the Lamb of God, that taketh

176

away the sins of the world; the Way, the Truth, and the Life, the Door by which we enter in; the Lamb slain from the foundation of the world; the sacrifice ascends unto God a sweet savour of Christ. It is thus that the triumphant believer momentarily realizes the blessed fulfillment of the prayer: "And the very God of peace sanctify you wholly; and I pray God your whole spirit, and soul, and body, be preserved *blameless* unto the coming of our Lord Jesus Christ. Faithful is He that calleth you, who also will do it." Amen. Even so, Lord Jesus.

### Note

1. In *Phoebe Palmer: Selected Writings,* ed. Thomas C. Oden (New York and Mahwah: Paulist Press, 1988; originally published in 1845), pp. 187-90.

# William Ellery Channing

*A Harvard graduate (1798), Channing (1780–1842) began his lifelong ministry at Boston's Federal Street (Congregationalist) Church in 1803. Over the following decades he became the foremost leader of "liberal Christian"—Unitarian—thought in America. The transition was not abrupt. By the turn of the nineteenth century, heirs of New England Puritanism were dividing much along the same lines and for much the same reasons as their "cousins" in Great Britain over issues of the soundness of Calvinist doctrine as judged by Enlightenment norms of clear, intelligible, and rationally well-founded claims to truth. Traditional teachings of the Trinity and christology were the focus of attention; differing appraisals of humanity's nature, limits, and possibilities fueled the controversy.*

*Channing believed scripture and reason alike demonstrated that "Calvinist" theology was a gross misunderstanding of the Christian message of God and things of God and the human condition as well. A rational supernaturalist employing a grammatical-historical (philological) method of biblical interpretation and concerned with cultivating virtuous living, he defended Harvard from Calvinist attack for appointing teachers of "liberal" views and went on—in the sermon "Unitarian Christianity" (1819) and myriad other works—to establish Unitarianism's early theological and moral foundations. "Likeness to God" (1828), condensed here, was a sermon-treatise written in midcareer that conveys the "heart" of Channing's thought.*

## LIKENESS TO GOD[1]

Discourse at the Ordination of the Rev. F. A. Farley, Providence, R.I., 1828.
Ephesians V.I. "Be ye therefore followers of God, as dear children."

To promote true religion is the purpose of the Christian ministry. For this it was ordained. On the present occasion, therefore, when a new teacher is to be given to the church, a discourse on the character of true religion will not be inappropriate. I do not mean that I shall attempt, in the limits to which I am now confined, to set before you all its properties, signs, and operations; for in so doing I should burden your memories with divisions and vague generalities as uninteresting as they would be unprofitable. My purpose is to select one view of the subject which seems to me of primary dignity and importance; and I select this because it is greatly neglected, and because I attribute to this neglect much of the inefficacy and many of the corruptions of religion.

The text calls us to follow or imitate God, to seek accordance with or likeness to him; and to do this not fearfully and faintly, but with the spirit and hope of beloved children. The doctrine which I propose to illustrate is derived immediately from these words, and is incorporated with the whole New Testament. I affirm, and would maintain, that true religion consists in proposing, as our great end, a growing likeness to the Supreme Being. Its noblest influence consists in making us more and more partakers of the Divinity. For this it is to be preached. Religious instruction should aim chiefly to turn men's aspirations and efforts to that perfection of the soul which constitutes it a bright image of God. Such is the topic now to be discussed; and I implore Him whose glory I seek to aid me in unfolding and enforcing it with simplicity and clearness, with a calm and pure zeal, and with unfeigned charity.

I begin with observing, what all indeed will understand, that the likeness to God, of which I propose to speak, belongs to man's higher or spiritual nature. It has its foundation in the original and essential capacities of the mind. In proportion as these are unfolded by right and vigorous exertion, it is extended and brightened. In proportion as these lie dormant, it is obscured. In proportion as they are perverted and overpowered by the appetites and passions, it is blotted out. In truth, moral evil, if unresisted and habitual, may so blight and lay waste these capacities, that the image of God in man may seem to be wholly destroyed.

The importance of this assimilation to our Creator is a topic which needs no labored discussion. All men, of whatever name, or sect, or opinion, will meet me on this ground. All, I presume, will allow that no good in the compass of the universe, or within the gift of omnipotence, can be compared to a resemblance of God, or to a participation of his attributes. I fear no contradiction here. Likeness to God is the supreme gift. He can communicate nothing so precious, glorious, blessed as himself. To hold intellectual and moral affinity with the Supreme Being, to partake his spirit, to be his children by derivations of kindred excellence, to bear a growing conformity to the perfection which we adore,—this is a felicity which obscures and annihilates all other good.

It is only in proportion to this likeness that we can enjoy either God or the universe. That God can be known and enjoyed only through sympathy or kindred attributes, is a doctrine which even Gentile philosophy discerned. That the pure in heart can alone see and commune with the pure Divinity, was the sublime instruction of ancient sages as well as of inspired prophets. It is indeed the lesson of daily experience. To understand a great and good being, we must have the seeds of the same excellence. How quickly, by what an instinct, do accordant minds recognize one another! No attraction is so powerful as that which subsists between the truly wise and good; whilst the brightest excellence is lost on those who have nothing congenial in their own breasts. God becomes a real being to us in proportion as his own nature is unfolded within us. To a man who is growing in the likeness of God, faith begins even here to change into vision. He carries within himself a proof of a Deity, which can only be understood by experience. He more than believes, he feels the Divine presence; and gradually rises to an intercourse with his Maker, to which it is not irreverent to apply the name of friendship and intimacy. The Apostle John intended to express this truth, when he tells us that he in whom a principle of divine charity or benevolence has become a habit and life "dwells in God and God in him."

It is plain, too, that likeness to God is the true and only preparation for the enjoyment of the universe. In proportion as we approach and resemble the mind of God, we are brought into harmony with the creation; for in that proportion we possess the principles from which the universe sprung; we carry within ourselves the perfections of which its beauty, magnificence, order, benevolent adaptations, and boundless purposes are the results and manifestations. God unfolds himself in his works to a kindred mind. It is possible that the brevity of these hints may expose to the charge of mysticism what seems to me the calmest and clearest truth. I think, however, that every reflecting man will feel that likeness to God must be a principle of sympathy or accordance with his creation; for the creation is a birth and shining forth of the Divine Mind, a work through which his spirit breathes. In proportion as we receive this spirit we possess within ourselves the explanation of what we see. We discern more and more of God in every thing, from the frail flower to the everlasting stars. Even in evil, that dark cloud which hangs over the creation, we discern rays of light and hope, and gradually come

180

to see, in suffering and temptation, proofs and instruments of the sublimest purposes of wisdom and love.

I have offered these very imperfect views that I may show the great importance of the doctrine which I am solicitous to enforce. I would teach that likeness to God is a good so unutterably surpassing all other good, that whoever admits it as attainable must acknowledge it to be the chief aim of life. I would show that the highest and happiest office of religion is to bring the mind into growing accordance with God; and that by the tendency of religious systems to this end their truth and worth are to be chiefly tried.

I am aware that it may be said that the Scriptures, in speaking of man as made in the image of God, and in calling us to imitate him, use bold and figurative language. It may be said that there is danger from too literal an interpretation; that God is an unapproachable being; that I am not warranted in ascribing to man a like nature to the divine; that we and all things illustrate the Creator by contrast, not by resemblance; that religion manifests itself chiefly in convictions and acknowledgments of utter worthlessness; and that to talk of the greatness and divinity of the human soul is to inflate that pride through which Satan fell, and through which man involves himself in that fallen spirit's ruin.

I answer that, to me, Scripture and reason hold a different language. In Christianity, particularly, I meet perpetual testimonies to the divinity of human nature. This whole religion expresses an infinite concern of God for the human soul, and teaches that He deems no methods too expensive for its recovery and exaltation. Christianity, with one voice, calls me to turn my regards and care to the spirit within me, as of more worth than the whole outward world. It calls us to "be perfect as our Father in heaven is perfect;" and everywhere, in the sublimity of its precepts, it implies and recognizes the sublime capacities of the being to whom they are addressed. It assures us that human virtue is "in the sight of God of great price," and speaks of the return of a human being to virtue as an event which increases the joy of heaven. In the New Testament, Jesus Christ, the Son of God, the brightness of his glory, the express and unsullied image of the Divinity, is seen mingling with men as a friend and brother, offering himself as their example, and promising to his true followers a share in all his splendors and joys. In the New Testament God is said to communicate his own spirit and all his fulness to the human soul. In the New Testament man is exhorted to aspire after "honor, glory, and immortality;" and Heaven, a word expressing the nearest approach to God and a divine happiness, is everywhere proposed as the end of his being. In truth, the very essence of Christian faith is that we trust in God's mercy as revealed in Jesus Christ, for a state of celestial purity in which we shall grow for ever in the likeness and knowledge and enjoyment of the Infinite Father. Lofty views of the nature of man are bound up and interwoven with the whole Christian system. Say not that these are at war with humility; for who was ever humbler than Jesus, and yet who ever possessed such a consciousness of greatness and divinity? Say not that man's business is to think of his sin and not of his dignity; for great sin implies a great capacity; it is the abuse of a noble nature; and no man can be deeply and rationally contrite but he who feels that in wrong-doing he has resisted a divine voice, and warred against a divine principle in his own soul. I need not, I trust, pursue the argument from revelation. There is an argument from nature and reason which seems to me so convincing, and is at the same time so fitted to explain what I mean by man's possession of a like nature to God, that I shall pass at once to its exposition.

That man has a kindred nature with God, and may bear most important and ennobling relations to him, seems to me to be established by a striking proof. This proof you will understand by considering, for a moment, how we obtain our ideas of God. Whence come the conceptions which we include under that august name? Whence do we derive our knowledge of the attributes and perfections which constitute the Supreme Being? I answer, we derive them from our own souls. The divine attributes are first developed in ourselves, and thence transferred to our Creator. The idea of God, sublime and awful as it is, is the idea of our own spiritual nature, purified and enlarged to infinity. In ourselves are the elements of the Divinity. God, then, does not sustain a figurative resemblance to man. It is the resemblance of a parent to a child, the likeness of a kindred nature.

We call God a Mind. He has revealed himself as a Spirit. But what do we know of mind but through the unfolding of this principle in our own breasts? That unbounded spiritual energy which we call God is conceived by us only through consciousness, through the knowledge of ourselves. We ascribe thought or intelligence to the Deity, as one of his most glorious attributes. And what means this language? These terms we have framed to express operations or faculties of our own souls. The Infinite Light would be for ever hidden from us did not kindred rays dawn and brighten within us. God is another name for human intelligence raised above all error and imperfection, and extended to all possible truth.

. . .

182

The same is true of all the moral perfections of the Deity. These are comprehended by us only through our own moral nature. It is conscience within us which, by its approving and condemning voice, interprets to us God's love of virtue and hatred of sin; and without conscience, these glorious conceptions would never have opened on the mind. It is the law-giver in our own breasts which gives us the idea of divine authority, and binds us to obey it. The soul, by its sense of right, or its perception of moral distinctions, is clothed with sovereignty over itself, and through this alone it understands and recognizes the Sovereign of the universe. . . .

I am aware that it may be objected to these views, that we receive our idea of God from the universe, from his works, and not so exclusively from our own souls. The universe, I know, is full of God. The heavens and earth declare his glory. In other words, the effects and signs of power, wisdom, and goodness, are apparent through the whole creation. But apparent to what? Not to the outward eye; not to the acutest organs of sense; but to a kindred mind, which interprets the universe by itself. It is only through that energy of thought by which we adapt various and complicated means to distant ends, and give harmony and a common bearing to multiplied exertions, that we understand the creative intelligence which has established the order, dependencies, and harmony of nature. We see God around us because He dwells within us. It is by a kindred wisdom that we discern his wisdom in his works. The brute, with an eye as piercing as ours, looks on the universe; and the page, which to us is radiant with characters of greatness and goodness, is to him a blank. In truth, the beauty and glory of God's works are revealed to the mind by a light beaming from itself. We discern the impress of God's attributes in the universe by accordance of nature, and enjoy them through sympathy. I hardly need observe that these remarks in relation to the universe apply with equal if not greater force to revelation.

I shall now be met by another objection, which to many may seem strong. It will be said that these various attributes of which I have spoken exist in God in infinite perfection, and that this destroys all affinity between the human and the divine mind. To this I have two replies. In the first place, an attribute by becoming perfect does not part with its essence. Love, wisdom, power, and purity do not change their nature by enlargement. If they did, we should lose the Supreme Being through his very infinity. Our ideas of him would fade away into mere sounds. For example, if wisdom in God, because unbounded, have no affinity with that attribute in man, why apply to him that term? It must signify nothing. Let me ask what we mean when we say that we discern the marks of intelligence in the universe? We mean that we meet there the proofs of a mind like our own. We certainly discern proofs of no other; so that to deny this doctrine would be to deny the evidences of a God, and utterly to subvert the foundations of religious belief. What man can examine the structure of a plant or an animal, and see the adaptation of its parts to each other and to common ends, and not feel that it is the work of an intelligence akin to his own, and that he traces these marks of design by the same spiritual energy in which they had their origin?

But I would offer another answer to this objection, that God's infinity places him beyond the resemblance and approach of man. I affirm, and trust that I do not speak too strongly, that there are traces of infinity in the human mind; and that, in this very respect, it bears a likeness to God. The very conception of infinity is the mark of a nature to which no limit can be prescribed. This thought, indeed, comes to us not so much from abroad as from our own souls. We ascribe this attribute to God, because we possess capacities and wants which only an unbounded being can fill, and because we are conscious of a tendency in spiritual faculties to unlimited expansion. We believe in the divine infinity through something congenial with it in our own breasts. . . . In truth, the soul is always bursting its limits. It thirsts continually for wider knowledge. It rushes forward to untried happiness. It has deep wants, which nothing limited can appease. Its true element and end is an unbounded good. Thus, God's infinity has its image in the soul; and through the soul, much more than through the universe, we arrive at this conception of the Deity.

In these remarks I have spoken strongly. But I have no fear of expressing too strongly the connection between the divine and the human mind. My only fear is that I shall dishonor the great subject. The danger to which we are most exposed is that of severing the Creator from his creatures. . . . How much of God may be seen in the structure of a single leaf, which, though so frail as to tremble in every wind, yet holds connections and living communications with the earth, the air, the clouds, and the distant sun, and, through these sympathies with the universe, is itself a revelation of an omnipotent mind! God delights to diffuse himself everywhere. Through his energy unconscious matter clothes itself with proportions, powers, and beauties, which reflect his wisdom and love. How much more must He delight to frame conscious and happy recipients of his perfections, in whom his wisdom and love may substantially dwell, with whom He may form spiritual ties, and to whom He may be an everlasting spring of moral energy and happiness! How far the Supreme Being may communicate his attributes to his intelligent offspring, I stop not to inquire. But that his almighty goodness will impart to them powers and glories of which the material universe is but a faint emblem, I cannot doubt. That the soul, if true to itself and its Maker, will be filled with God, and will manifest him more than the sun, I cannot doubt. Who can doubt it, that believes and understands the doctrine of human immorality?

. . .

The greatest use which I would make of the principles laid down in this discourse, is to derive from them just and clear views of the nature of religion. What, then, is religion? I answer, it is not the adoration of a God with whom we have no common properties; of a distinct, foreign, separate being; but of an all-communicating Parent. It recognizes and adores God as a being whom we know through our own souls; who has made man in his own image; who is the perfection of our spiritual nature; who has sympathies with us as kindred beings; who is near us, not in place only like this all-surrounding atmosphere, but by spiritual influence and love; who looks on us with parental interest, and whose great design it is to communicate to us for ever, and in freer and fuller streams, his own power, goodness, and joy. The conviction of this near and ennobling relation of God to the soul, and of his great purposes towards it, belongs to the very essence of true religion; and true religion manifests itself chiefly and most conspicuously in desires, hopes, and efforts, corresponding to this truth. It desires and seeks supremely the assimilation of the mind to God, or the perpetual unfolding and enlargement of those powers and virtues by which it is constituted his glorious image. The mind, in proportion as it is enlightened and penetrated by true religion, thirsts and labors for a godlike elevation. What else, indeed, can it seek if this good be placed within its reach? If I am capable of receiving and reflecting the intellectual and moral glory of my Creator, what else in comparison shall I desire? Shall I deem a property in the outward universe as the highest good, when I may become partaker of the very mind from which it springs, of the prompting love, the disposing wisdom, the quickening power, through which its order, beauty, and beneficent influences subsist? True religion is known by these high aspirations, hopes, and efforts. And this is the religion which most truly honors God. To honor him is not to tremble before him as an unapproachable sovereign, not to utter barren praise which leaves us as it found us. It is to become what we praise. It is to approach God as an

185

inexhaustible fountain of light, power, and purity. It is to feel the quickening and transforming energy of his perfections. It is to thirst for the growth and invigoration of the divine principle within us. It is to seek the very spirit of God. It is to trust in, to bless, to thank him for that rich grace, mercy, love, which was revealed and proffered by Jesus Christ, and which proposes as its great end the perfection of the human soul.

I regard this view of religion as infinitely important. It does more than all things to make our connection with our Creator ennobling and happy; and, in proportion as we want it, there is danger that the thought of God may itself become the instrument of our degradation. That religion has been so dispensed as to depress the human mind, I need not tell you; and it is a truth which ought to be known, that the greatness of the Deity, when separated in our thoughts from his parental character, especially tends to crush human energy and hope. To a frail, dependent creature, an omnipotent Creator easily becomes a terror, and his worship easily degenerates into servility, flattery, self-contempt, and selfish calculation. Religion only ennobles us, in as far as it reveals to us the tender and intimate connection of God with his creatures, and teaches us to see in the very greatness which might give alarm the source of great and glorious communications to the human soul. You cannot, my hearers, think too highly of the majesty of God. But let not this majesty sever him from you. Remember that his greatness is the infinity of attributes which yourselves possess. Adore his infinite wisdom; but remember that this wisdom rejoices to diffuse itself, and let an exhilarating hope spring up at the thought of the immeasurable intelligence which such a Father must communicate to his children. In like manner adore his power. Let the boundless creation fill you with awe and admiration of the energy which sustains it. But remember that God has a nobler work than the outward creation, even the spirit within yourselves; and that it is his purpose to replenish this with his own energy, and to crown it with growing power and triumphs over the material universe. Above all, adore his unutterable goodness. But remember that this attribute is particularly proposed to you as your model; that God calls you, both by nature and revelation, to a fellowship in his philanthropy; that he has placed you in social relations for the very end of rendering you ministers and representatives of his benevolence; that he even summons you to espouse and to advance the sublimest purpose of his goodness, the redemption of the human race, by extending the knowledge and power of Christian truth. It is through such views that religion raises up the soul, and binds man by ennobling bonds to his Maker.

To complete my views of this topic, I beg to add an important caution. I have said that the great work of religion is to conform ourselves to God, or to unfold the divine likeness within us. Let none infer from this language that I place religion in unnatural effort, in straining after excitements which do not belong to the present state, or in any thing separate from the clear and simple duties of life. I exhort you to no extravagance. I reverence human nature too much to do it violence. I see too much divinity in its ordinary operations to urge on it a forced and vehement virtue. To grow in the likeness of God we need not cease to be men. This likeness does not consist in extraordinary or miraculous gifts, in supernatural additions to the soul, or in any thing foreign to our original constitution; but in our essential faculties, unfolded by vigorous and conscientious exertion in the ordinary circumstances assigned by God. To resemble our Creator, we need not fly from society, and entrance ourselves in lonely contemplation and prayer. Such processes might give a feverish strength to one class of emotions, but would result in disproportion, distortion, and sickliness of mind. Our proper work is to approach God by the free and natural unfolding of our highest powers,—of understanding, conscience, love, and the moral will.

Shall I be told that, by such language, I ascribe to nature the effects which can only be wrought in the soul by the Holy Spirit? I anticipate this objection, and wish to meet it by a simple exposition of my views. I would on no account disparage the gracious aids and influences which God imparts to the human soul. The promise of the Holy Spirit is among the most precious in the Sacred Volume. Worlds could not tempt me to part with the doctrine of God's intimate connection with the mind, and of his free and full communications to it. But these views are in no respect at variance with what I have taught, of the method by which we are to grow in the likeness of God. Scripture and experience concur in teaching that, by the Holy Spirit, we are to understand a divine assistance adapted to our moral freedom, and accordant with the fundamental truth that virtue is the mind's own work. By the Holy Spirit, I understand an aid which must be gained and made effectual by our own activity; an aid which no more interferes with our faculties than the assistance which we receive from our fellow-beings; an aid which silently mingles and conspires with all other helps and means of goodness; an aid by which we unfold our natural powers in a natural order, and by which we are strengthened to understand and apply the resources derived from our munificent Creator. This aid we cannot prize too much, or pray for too earnestly. But wherein, let me ask, does it war with the doctrine that God is to be approached by the exercise and unfolding of our highest powers and affections, in the ordinary circumstances of human life?

I repeat it, to resemble our Maker we need not quarrel with our nature or our lot. Our present state, made up as it is of aids and trials, is worthy of God, and may be used throughout to assimilate us to him. For example, our domestic ties, the relations of neighborhood and country, and daily interchanges of thoughts and feelings, the daily occasions of kindness, the daily claims of want and suffering,—these and the other circumstances of our social state form the best sphere and school for that benevolence which is God's brightest attribute; and we should make a sad exchange, by substituting for these natural aids any self-invented artificial means of sanctity. Christianity, our great guide to God, never leads us away from the path of nature, and never wars with the unsophisticated dictates of conscience. We approach our Creator by every right exertion of the powers He gives us. Whenever we invigorate the understanding by honestly and resolutely seeking truth, and by withstanding whatever might warp the judgment; whenever we invigorate the conscience by following it in opposition to the passions; whenever we receive a blessing gratefully, bear a trial patiently, or encounter peril or scorn with moral courage; whenever we perform a disinterested deed; whenever we lift up the heart in true adoration to God; whenever we war against a habit or desire which is strengthening itself against our higher principles; whenever we think, speak, or act, with moral energy and resolute devotion to duty, be the occasion ever so humble, obscure, familiar;—then the divinity is growing within us, and we are ascending towards our Author. True religion thus blends itself with common life. We are thus to draw nigh to God without forsaking men. We are thus, without parting with our human nature, to clothe ourselves with the divine.

. . .

## Note

1. In *The Works of William E. Channing, D.D., With an Introduction* (Boston: American Unitarian Association, 1875), pp. 291-98.

# Ralph Waldo Emerson

*The status as a literary and cultural icon that Emerson (1803–1882) had gained by the end of his life was such that his role in the development of religious thinking generally and Christian theology quite specifically was—and remains—anything but common knowledge. Descended from a long line of ministers, he studied for Unitarian ministry at Harvard but served only briefly, and not especially happily, moving on to a Transcendentalist faith that was more supradenominational than it was inter- or non-denominational, or even distinctly Christian. During the 1830s, however, he was the catalyst for a controversial shift in Christian theological sensibilities which not only transformed the "liberal Christians" called Unitarians but presaged similar shifts that were to come, sooner or later, during the nineteenth century in American Protestantism at large.*

*Shorthand terms for this shift are: in cultural studies, Romanticism; in philosophy, Kantianism and post-Kantian idealism; in theology, "liberalism." In Emerson's case, a trip to England and firsthand encounter with the Romantics there triggered the change from rational supernatural precepts to feelings, presentiments, and inspirations of the immanence of Infinite Spirit within the finite world of nature and human spirits. That this message was "radical" was evident to all. Whether it was an advance in and for—or a leap outside of—Christianity was an open question to be long debated, and at considerable length. Emerson's address to Harvard Divinity School's graduating class of 1838, condensed here, put the question before the public.*

## AN ADDRESS DELIVERED BEFORE THE SENIOR CLASS IN DIVINITY COLLEGE, CAMBRIDGE, SUNDAY EVENING, JULY 15, 1838[1]

. . .

A more secret, sweet, and overpowering beauty appears to man when his heart and mind open to the sentiment of virtue. Then he is instructed

189

in what is above him. He learns that his being is without bound; that to the good, to the perfect, he is born, low as he now lies in evil and weakness. That which he venerates is still his own, though he has not realized it yet. *He ought.* He knows the sense of that grand word, though his analysis fails to render account of it. When in innocency or when by intellectual perception he attains to say,—"I love the Right; Truth is beautiful within and without forevermore. Virtue, I am thine; save me; use me; thee will I serve, day and night, in great, in small, that I may be not virtuous, but virtue;"—then is the end of the creation answered, and God is well pleased.

The sentiment of virtue is a reverence and delight in the presence of certain divine laws. It perceives that this homely game of life we play, covers, under what seem foolish details, principles that astonish. The child amidst his baubles is learning the action of light, motion, gravity, muscular force; and in the game of human life, love, fear, justice, appetite, man, and God, interact. These laws refuse to be adequately stated. They will not be written out on paper, or spoken by the tongue. They elude our persevering thought; yet we read them hourly in each other's faces, in each other's actions, in our own remorse. The moral traits which are all globed into every virtuous act and thought,—in speech we must sever, and describe or suggest by painful enumeration of many particulars. Yet, as this sentiment is the essence of all religion, let me guide your eye to the precise objects of the sentiment, by an enumeration of some of those classes of facts in which this element is conspicuous.

The intuition of the moral sentiment is an insight of the perfection of the laws of the soul. These laws execute themselves. They are out of time, out of space, and not subject to circumstance. Thus in the soul of man there is a justice whose retributions are instant and entire. He who does a good deed is instantly ennobled. He who does a mean deed is by the action itself contracted. He who puts off impurity, thereby puts on purity. If a man is at heart just, then in so far is he God; the safety of God, the immortality of God, the majesty of God do enter into that man with justice. If a man dissemble, deceive, he deceives himself, and goes out of acquaintance with his own being. A man in the view of absolute goodness, adores, with total humility. Every step so downward, is a step upward. The man who renounces himself, comes to himself.

See how this rapid intrinsic energy worketh everywhere, righting wrongs, correcting appearances, and bringing up facts to a harmony with thoughts. Its operation in life, though slow to the senses, is at last as sure as in the soul. By it a man is made the Providence to himself, dispensing good to his goodness, and evil to his sin. Character is always known. Thefts never enrich; alms never impoverish; murder will speak out of stone walls. The least admixture of a lie,—for example, the taint of vanity, any attempt to make a good impression, a favorable appearance,—will instantly vitiate the effect. But speak the truth, and all nature and all spirits help you with unexpected furtherance. Speak the truth, and all things alive or brute are vouchers, and the very roots of the grass underground there do seem to stir and move to bear you witness. See again the perfection of the Law as it applies itself to the affections, and becomes the law of society. As we are, so we associate. The good, by affinity, seek the good; the vile, by affinity, the vile. Thus of their own volition, souls proceed into heaven, into hell.

These facts have always suggested to man the sublime creed that the world is not the product of manifold power, but of one will, of one mind; and that one mind is everywhere active, in each ray of the star, in each wavelet of the pool; and whatever opposes that will is everywhere balked and baffled, because things are made so, and not otherwise. Good is positive. Evil is merely privative, not absolute: it is like cold, which is the privation of heat. All evil is so much death or nonentity. Benevolence is absolute and real. So much benevolence as a man hath, so much life hath he. For all things proceed out of this same spirit, which is differently named love, justice, temperance, in its different applications, just as the ocean receives different names on the several shores which it washes. All things proceed out of the same spirit, and all things conspire with it. Whilst a man seeks good ends, he is strong by the whole strength of nature. In so far as he roves from these ends, he bereaves himself of power, or auxiliaries; his being shrinks out of all remote channels, he becomes less and less, a mote, a point, until absolute badness is absolute death.

The perception of this law of laws awakens in the mind a sentiment which we call the religious sentiment, and which makes our highest happiness. . . .

This sentiment is divine and deifying. It is the beatitude of man. It makes him illimitable. Through it, the soul first knows itself. It corrects the capital mistake of the infant man, who seeks to be great by following the great, and hopes to derive advantages *from another,*—by showing the fountain of all good to be in himself, and that he, equally with every man, is an inlet into the deeps of Reason. When he says, "I ought;" when love warms him; when he chooses, warned from on high, the good and great deed; then, deep melodies wander through his soul from Supreme Wisdom.—Then he can worship, and be enlarged by his worship; for he can never go behind this sentiment. In the sublimest flights of the soul, rectitude is never surmounted, love is never outgrown.

This sentiment lies at the foundation of society, and successively creates all forms of worship. The principle of veneration never dies out. Man fallen into superstition, into sensuality, is never quite without the visions of the moral sentiment. In like manner, all the expressions of this sentiment are sacred and permanent in proportion to their purity. . . .

These general views, which, whilst they are general, none will contest, find abundant illustration in the history of religion, and especially in the history of the Christian church. In that, all of us have had our birth and nurture. The truth contained in that, you, my young friends, are now setting forth to teach. As the Cultus, or established worship of the civilized world, it has great historical interest for us. Of its blessed words, which have been the consolation of humanity, you need not that I should speak. I shall endeavor to discharge my duty to you on this occasion, by pointing out two errors in its administration, which daily appear more gross from the point of view we have just now taken.

Jesus Christ belonged to the true race of prophets. He saw with open eye the mystery of the soul. Drawn by its severe harmony, ravished with its beauty, he lived in it, and had his being there. Alone in all history he estimated the greatness of man. One man was true to what is in you and me. He saw that God incarnates himself in man, and evermore goes forth anew to take possession of his World. He said, in this jubilee of sublime emotion, "I am divine. Through me, God acts; through me, speaks. Would you see God, see me; or see thee, when thou also thinkest as I now think." But what a distortion did his doctrine and memory suffer in the same, in the next, and the following ages! There is no doctrine of the Reason which will bear to be taught by the Understanding. The understanding caught this high chant from the poet's lips, and said, in the next age, "This was Jehovah come down out of heaven. I will kill you, if you say he was a man." The idioms of his language and the figures of his rhetoric have usurped the place of his truth; and churches are not built on his principles, but on his tropes. . . .

He felt respect for Moses and the prophets, but no unfit tenderness at postponing their initial revelations to the hour and the man that now is; to the eternal revelation in the heart. Thus was he a true man. Having seen that the law in us is commanding, he would not suffer it to be commanded. Boldly, with hand, and heart, and life, he declared it was God.

Thus is he, as I think, the only soul in history who has appreciated the worth of man.

1. In this point of view we become sensible of the first defect of historical Christianity. Historical Christianity has fallen into the error that corrupts all attempts to communicate religion. As it appears to us, and as it has appeared for ages, it is not the doctrine of the soul, but an exaggeration of the personal, the positive, the ritual. It has dwelt, it dwells, with noxious exaggeration about the *person* of Jesus. The soul knows no persons. It invites every man to expand to the full circle of the universe, and will have no preferences but those of spontaneous love. But by this eastern monarchy of a Christianity, which indolence and fear have built, the friend of man is made the injurer of man. The manner in which his name is surrounded with expressions which were once sallies of admiration and love, but are now petrified into official titles, kills all generous sympathy and liking. All who hear me, feel that the language that describes Christ to Europe and America is not the style of friendship and enthusiasm to a good and noble heart, but is appropriated and formal,— paints a demigod, as the Orientals or the Greeks would describe Osiris or Apollo. Accept the injurious impositions of our early catechetical instruction, and even honesty and self-denial were but splendid sins, if they did not wear the Christian name. One would rather be

"A pagan, suckled in a creed outworn,"

than to be defrauded of his manly right in coming into nature and finding not names and places, not land and professions, but even virtue and truth foreclosed and monopolized. You shall not be a man even. You shall not own the world; you shall not dare and live after the infinite Law that is in you, and in company with the infinite Beauty which heaven and earth reflect to you in all lovely forms; but you must subordinate your nature to Christ's nature; you must accept our interpretations, and take his portrait as the vulgar draw it.

That is always best which gives me to myself. The sublime is excited in me by the great stoical doctrine, Obey thyself. That which shows God in me, fortifies me. That which shows God out of me, makes me a wart and a wen. There is no longer a necessary reason for my being. Already the long shadows of untimely oblivion creep over me, and I shall decease forever.

The divine bards are the friends of my virtue, of my intellect, of my strength. They admonish me that the gleams which flash across my mind are not mine, but God's; that they had the like, and were not disobedient to the heavenly vision. So I love them. Noble provocations go out from them, inviting me to resist evil; to subdue the world; and to Be. And thus, by his holy thoughts, Jesus serves us, and thus only. To aim to convert a man by miracles, is a profanation of the soul. A true conversion, a true Christ, is now, as always, to be made by the reception of beautiful sentiments. It is true that a great and rich soul, like his, falling among the simple, does so preponderate, that, as his did, it names the world. The world seems to them to exist for him, and they have not yet drunk so deeply of his sense as to see that only by coming again to themselves, or to God in themselves, can they grow forevermore. It is a low benefit to give me something; it is a high benefit to enable me to do somewhat of myself. The time is coming when all men will see that the gift of God to the soul is not a vaunting, overpowering, excluding sanctity, but a sweet, natural goodness, a goodness like thine and mine, and that so invites thine and mine to be and to grow.

The injustice of the vulgar tone of preaching is not less flagrant to Jesus than to the souls which it profanes. The preachers do not see that they make his gospel not glad, and shear him of the locks of beauty and the attributes of heaven. . . .

2. The second defect of the traditionary and limited way of using the mind of Christ, is a consequence of the first; this, namely; that the Moral Nature, that Law of laws whose revelations introduce greatness,—yea, God himself,—into the open soul, is not explored as the fountain of the established teaching in society. Men have come to speak of the revelation as somewhat long ago given and done, as if God were dead. The injury to faith throttles the preacher; and the goodliest of institutions becomes an uncertain and inarticulate voice.

It is very certain that it is the effect of conversation with the beauty of the soul, to beget a desire and need to impart to others the same knowledge and love. If utterance is denied, the thought lies like a burden on the man. Always the seer is a sayer. Somehow his dream is told; somehow he publishes it with solemn joy: sometimes with pencil on canvas, sometimes with chisel on stone, sometimes in towers and aisles of granite, his soul's worship is builded; sometimes in anthems of indefinite music; but clearest and most permanent, in words.

The man enamored of this excellency becomes its priest or poet. The office is coeval with the world. But observe the condition, the spiritual limitation of the office. The spirit only can teach. Not any profane man, not any sensual, not any liar, not any slave can teach, but only he can give, who has; he only can create, who is. The man on whom the soul

194

descends, through whom the soul speaks, alone can teach. Courage, piety, love, wisdom, can teach; and every man can open his door to these angels, and they shall bring him the gift of tongues. But the man who aims to speak as books enable, as synods use, as the fashion guides, and as interest commands, babbles. Let him hush.

To this holy office you propose to devote yourselves. I wish you may feel your call in throbs of desire and hope. The office is the first in the world. It is of that reality that it cannot suffer the deduction of any falsehood. And it is my duty to say to you that the need was never greater of new revelation than now. From the views I have already expressed, you will infer the sad conviction, which I share, I believe, with numbers, of the universal decay and now almost death of faith in society. The soul is not preached. The Church seems to totter to its fall, almost all life extinct. On this occasion, any complaisance would be criminal which told you, whose hope and commission it is to preach the faith of Christ, that the faith of Christ is preached.

It is time that this ill-suppressed murmur of all thoughtful men against the famine of our churches;—this moaning of the heart because it is bereaved of the consolation, the hope, the grandeur that come alone out of the culture of the moral nature,—should be heard through the sleep of indolence, and over the din of routine. This great and perpetual office of the preacher is not discharged. Preaching is the expression of the moral sentiment in application to the duties of life. In how many churches, by how many prophets, tell me, is man made sensible that he is an infinite Soul; that the earth and heavens are passing into his mind; that he is drinking forever the soul of God? Where now sounds the persuasion, that by its very melody imparadises my heart, and so affirms its own origin in heaven? Where shall I hear words such as in elder ages drew men to leave all and follow,—father and mother, house and land, wife and child? Where shall I hear these august laws of moral being so pronounced as to fill my ear, and I feel ennobled by the offer of my uttermost action and passion? The test of the true faith, certainly, should be its power to charm and command the soul, as the laws of nature control the activity of the hands,—so commanding that we find pleasure and honor in obeying. The faith should blend with the light of rising and of setting suns, with the flying cloud, the singing bird, and the breath of flowers. But now the priest's Sabbath has lost the splendor of nature; it is unlovely; we are glad when it is done; we can make, we do make, even sitting in our pews, a far better, holier, sweeter, for ourselves.

Whenever the pulpit is usurped by a formalist, then is the worshipper defrauded and disconsolate. We shrink as soon as the prayers begin, which do not uplift, but smite and offend us. We are fain to wrap our cloaks about us, and secure, as best we can, a solitude that hears not. I once heard a preacher who sorely tempted me to say I would go to church no more. Men go, thought I, where they are wont to go, else had no soul entered the temple in the afternoon. A snow-storm was falling around us. The snow-storm was real, the preacher merely spectral, and the eye felt the sad contrast in looking at him, and then out of the window behind him into the beautiful meteor of the snow. He had lived in vain. He had no one word intimating that he had laughed or wept, was married or in love, had been commended, or cheated, or chagrined. If he had ever lived and acted, we were none the wiser for it. The capital secret of his profession, namely, to convert life into truth, he had not learned. Not one fact in all his experience had he yet imported into his doctrine. This man had ploughed and planted and talked and bought and sold; he had read books; he had eaten and drunken; his head aches, his heart throbs; he smiles and suffers; yet was there not a surmise, a hint, in all the discourse, that he had ever lived at all. Not a line did he draw out of real history. The true preacher can be known by this, that he deals out to the people his life,—life passed through the fire of thought. But of the bad preacher, it could not be told from his sermon what age of the world he fell in; whether he had a father or a child; whether he was a freeholder or a pauper; whether he was a citizen or a countryman; or any other fact of his biography. It seemed strange that the people should come to church. It seemed as if their houses were very unentertaining, that they should prefer this thoughtless clamor. It shows that there is a commanding attraction in the moral sentiment, that can lend a faint tint of light to dulness and ignorance coming in its name and place. The good hearer is sure he has been touched sometimes; is sure there is somewhat to be reached, and some word that can reach it. When he listens to these vain words, he comforts himself by their relation to his remembrance of better hours, and so they clatter and echo unchallenged.

I am not ignorant that when we preach unworthily, it is not always quite in vain. There is a good ear, in some men, that draws supplies to virtue out of very indifferent nutriment. There is poetic truth concealed in all the common-places of prayer and of sermons, and though foolishly spoken, they may be wisely heard; for each is some select expression that broke out in a moment of piety from some stricken or jubilant soul, and its excellency made it remembered. . . . Alas for the unhappy man that is called to stand in the pulpit, and *not* give bread of life. Everything that befalls, accuses him. Would he ask contributions for the missions, foreign or domestic? Instantly his face is suffused with shame, to propose to his parish that they should send money a hundred or a thousand miles, to furnish such poor fare as they have at home and would do well to go the hundred or the thousand miles to escape. Would he urge people to a godly way of living;—and can he ask a fellow-creature to come to Sabbath meetings, when he and they all know what is the poor uttermost they can hope for therein? Will he invite them privately to the Lord's Supper? He dares not. If no heart warm this rite, the hollow, dry, creaking formality is too plain than that he can face a man of wit and energy and put the invitation without terror. In the street, what has he to say to the bold village blasphemer? The village blasphemer sees fear in the face, form, and gait of the minister.

Let me not taint the sincerity of this plea by any oversight of the claims of good men. I know and honor the purity and strict conscience of numbers of the clergy. What life the public worship retains, it owes to the scattered company of pious men, who minister here and there in the churches, and who, sometimes accepting with too great tenderness the tenet of the elders, have not accepted from others, but from their own heart, the genuine impulses of virtue, and so still command our love and awe, to the sanctity of character. Moreover, the exceptions are not so much to be found in a few eminent preachers, as in the better hours, the truer inspirations of all,—nay, in the sincere moments of every man. But, with whatever exception, it is still true that tradition characterizes the preaching of this country; that it comes out of the memory, and not out of the soul; that it aims at what is usual, and not at what is necessary and eternal; that thus historical Christianity destroys the power of preaching, by withdrawing it from the exploration of the moral nature of man; where the sublime is, where are the resources of astonishment and power. What a cruel injustice it is to that Law, the joy of the whole earth, which alone can make thought dear and rich; that Law whose fatal sureness the astronomical orbits poorly emulate;—that it is travestied and depreciated, that it is behooted and behowled, and not a trait, not a word of it articulated. The pulpit in losing sight of this Law, loses its reason, and gropes after it knows not what. And for want of this culture the soul of the community is sick and faithless. It wants nothing so much as a stern, high, stoical, Christian discipline, to make it know itself and the divinity that speaks through it. Now man is ashamed of himself; he skulks and sneaks through the world, to be tolerated, to be pitied, and scarcely in a thousand years does any man dare to be wise and good, and so draw after him the tears and blessings of his kind.

Certainly there have been periods when, from the inactivity of the intellect on certain truths, a greater faith was possible in names and persons. The Puritans in England and America found in the Christ of the Catholic Church and in the dogmas inherited from Rome, scope for their austere piety and their longings for civil freedom. But their creed is passing away, and none arises in its room. I think no man can go with his thoughts about him into one of our churches, without feeling that what hold the public worship had on men is gone, or going. It has lost its grasp on the affection of the good and the fear of the bad. In the country, neighborhoods, half parishes are *signing off,* to use the local term. It is already beginning to indicate character and religion to withdraw from the religious meetings. . . .

My friends, in these two errors, I think, I find the causes of a decaying church and a wasting unbelief. And what greater calamity can fall upon a nation than the loss of worship? Then all things go to decay. Genius leaves the temple to haunt the senate or the market. Literature becomes frivolous. Science is cold. The eye of youth is not lighted by the hope of other worlds, and age is without honor. Society lives to trifles, and when men die we do not mention them.

And now, my brothers, you will ask, What in these desponding days can be done by us? The remedy is already declared in the ground of our complaint of the Church. We have contrasted the Church with the Soul. In the soul then let the redemption be sought. Wherever a man comes, there comes revolution. The old is for slaves. When a man comes, all books are legible, all things transparent, all religions are forms. He is religious. Man is the wonderworker. He is seen amid miracles. All men bless and curse. He saith yea and nay, only. The stationariness of religion; the assumption that the age of inspiration is past, that the Bible is closed; the fear of degrading the character of Jesus by representing him as a man;—indicate with sufficient clearness the falsehood of our theology. It is the office of a true teacher to show us that God is, not was; that He speaketh, nor spake. The true Christianity,—a faith like Christ's in the infinitude of man,—is lost. None believeth in the soul of man, but only in some man or person old and departed. Ah me! no man goeth alone. All men go in flocks to this saint or that poet, avoiding the God who seeth in secret. They cannot see in secret; they love to be blind in public. They think society wiser than their soul, and know not that one soul, and their soul, is wiser than the whole world. . . . Once leave your own knowledge of God, your own sentiment, and take secondary knowledge, as St. Paul's, or George Fox's, or Swedenborg's, and you get wide from God with every year this secondary form lasts, and if, as now, for centuries,—the chasm yawns to that breadth, that men can scarcely be convinced there is in them anything divine.

Let me admonish you, first of all, to go alone; to refuse the good models, even those which are sacred in the imagination of men, and dare to love God without mediator or veil. Friends enough you shall find who will hold up to your emulation Wesleys and Oberlins, Saints and Prophets. Thank God for these good men, but say, "I also am a man." Imitation cannot go above its model. The imitator dooms himself to hopeless mediocrity. The inventor did it because it was natural to him, and so in him it has a charm. In the imitator something else is natural, and he bereaves himself of his own beauty, to come short of another man's.

Yourself a newborn bard of the Holy Ghost, cast behind you all conformity, and acquaint men at first hand with Deity. Look to it first and only, that fashion, custom, authority, pleasure, and money, are nothing to you,—are not bandages over your eyes, that you cannot see,—but live with the privilege of the immeasurable mind. Not too anxious to visit periodically all families and each family in your parish connection,—when you meet one of these men or women, be to them a divine man; be to them thought and virtue; let their timid aspirations find in you a friend; let their trampled instincts be genially tempted out in your atmosphere; let their doubts know that you have doubted, and their wonder feel that you have wondered. By trusting your own heart, you shall gain more confidence in other men. For all our penny-wisdom, for all our soul-destroying slavery to habit, it is not to be doubted that all men have sublime thoughts; that all men value the few real hours of life; they love to be heard; they love to be caught up into the vision of principles. We mark with light in the memory the few interviews we have had, in the dreary years of routine and of sin, with souls that made our souls wiser; that spoke what we thought; that told us what we knew; that gave us leave to be what we inly were. Discharge to men the priestly office, and, present or absent, you shall be followed with their love as by an angel.

. . .

. . . O my friends, there are resources in us on which we have not drawn. There are men who rise refreshed on hearing a threat; men to whom a crisis which intimidates and paralyzes the majority,—demanding not the faculties of prudence and thrift, but comprehension, immovableness, the readiness of sacrifice,—comes graceful and beloved as a bride. Napoleon said of Massena, that he was not himself until the battle began to go against him; then, when the dead began to fall in ranks around him, awoke his powers of combination, and he put on terror and victory as a robe. So it is in rugged crises, in unweariable endurance, and in aims which put sympathy out of question, that the angel is shown. But these are heights that we can scarce remember and look up to without contrition and shame. Let us thank God that such things exist.

And now let us do what we can to rekindle the smouldering, nigh quenched fire on the altar. The evils of the church that now is are manifest. The question returns, What shall we do? I confess, all attempts to project and establish a Cultus with new rites and forms, seem to me vain. Faith makes us, and not we it, and faith makes its own forms. All attempts to contrive a system are as cold as the new worship introduced by the French to the goddess of Reason,—to-day, pasteboard and filigree, and ending to-morrow in madness and murder. Rather let the breath of new life be breathed by you through the forms already existing. For if once you are alive, you shall find they shall become plastic and new. The remedy to their deformity is first, soul, and second, soul, and evermore, soul. A whole popedom of forms one pulsation of virtue can uplift and vivify. Two inestimable advantages Christianity has given us; first the Sabbath, the jubilee of the whole world, whose light dawns welcome alike into the closet of the philosopher, into the garret of toil, and into prison-cells, and everywhere suggests, even to the vile, the dignity of spiritual being. Let it stand forevermore, a temple, which new love, new faith, new sight shall restore to more than its first splendor to mankind. And secondly, the institution of preaching,—the speech of man to men,— essentially the most flexible of all organs, of all forms. What hinders that now, everywhere, in pulpits, in lecture-rooms, in houses, in fields, wherever the invitation of men or your own occasions lead you, you speak the very truth, as your life and conscience teach it, and cheer the waiting, fainting hearts of men with new hope and new revelation?

. . . I look for the new Teacher that shall follow so far those shining laws that he shall see them come full circle; shall see their rounding complete grace; shall see the world to be the mirror of the soul; shall see the identity of the law of gravitation with purity of heart; and shall show that the Ought, that Duty, is one thing with Science, with Beauty, and with Joy.

### Note

1. In *The Complete Works of Ralph Waldo Emerson: Nature, Addresses and Lectures,* University Edition (New York: Sully and Kleinteich, 1883), pp. 120-48.

# Margaret Fuller

*Fuller (1810–1850), raised a Unitarian in Massachusetts, was among the most early, close, and independent-minded associates of Ralph Waldo Emerson and the circle of thinkers involved in the development of the Transcendentalist movement. Transcendentalism involved rethinking the relationship between human reason and divine revelation along post-Kantian and Romantic lines as well as devising a form of expression fit for the movement's "higher" sensibilities. She was cofounder, coeditor, and a major contributor to* The Dial *(1840-1844), the literary, philosophical, and religious organ of the new train of thought. Then in New York she pursued a career as journalist and literary and social commentator. While in Italy (1846–1850), she associated with Mazzini and other leaders of the revolution for national independence. She—along with her Italian husband and young son—perished in a shipwreck on America's North Atlantic seacoast.*

*Her most famous work,* Woman in the Nineteenth Century *(1845), was a revised, expanded version of "The Great Lawsuit: Man Versus Men, Woman Versus Women," a lengthy article published in* The Dial *(1843) in the form of a civil rights brief for woman's God-given equality, dignity, and rights before the tribunal of eternal judgment and human history. The book, a portion of which is excerpted, argued the same point in an even more panoramic view of human culture(s). In linking the "feminine" with "sentiment" Fuller was quintessentially Romantic, as she was in setting both the intelligibility and validity of Christianity's message in the context of possibilities for human attainment beyond those realized within the limits of historical circumstances to date. She wrote as prophet or seer of a theology of the future, sweeping traditional Christian themes—along with others—into a polyphonic chorus of voices.*

# WOMAN IN THE NINETEENTH CENTURY[1]

. . .

Man, in the order of time, was developed first; as energy comes before harmony; power before beauty.

Woman was therefore under his care as an elder. He might have been her guardian and teacher.

But, as human nature goes not straight forward, but by excessive action and then reaction in an undulated course, he misunderstood and abused his advantages, and became her temporal master instead of her spiritual sire.

On himself came the punishment. He educated Woman more as a servant than a daughter, and found himself a king without a queen.

The children of this unequal union showed unequal natures, and, more and more, men seemed sons of the handmaid, rather than princess.

At last, there were so many Ishmaelites that the rest grew frightened and indignant. They laid the blame on Hagar, and drove her forth into the wilderness.

But there were none the fewer Ishmaelites for that.

At last men became a little wiser, and saw that the infant Moses was, in every case, saved by the pure instincts of Woman's breast. For, as too much adversity is better for the moral nature than too much prosperity, Woman, in this respect, dwindled less than Man, though in other respects still a child in leading-strings.

So Man did her more and more justice, and grew more and more kind.

But yet—his habits and his will corrupted by the past—he did not clearly see that Woman was half himself; that her interests were identical with his; and that, by the law of their common being, he could never reach his true proportions while she remained in any wise shorn of hers.

And so it has gone on to our day; both ideas developing, but more slowly than they would under a clearer recognition of truth and justice, which would have permitted the sexes their due influence on one another, and mutual improvement from more dignified relations.

Wherever there was pure love, the natural influences were, for the time, restored.

Wherever the poet or artist gave free course to his genius, he saw the truth, and expressed it in worthy forms, for these men especially share and need the feminine principle. The divine birds need to be brooded into life and song by mothers.

Wherever religion (I mean the thirst for truth and good, not the love of sect and dogma) had its course, the original design was apprehended in its simplicity, and the dove presaged sweetly from Dodona's oak.

I have aimed to show that no age was left entirely without a witness of the equality of the sexes in function, duty and hope.

Also that, when there was unwillingness or ignorance, which prevented this being acted upon, women had not the less power for their want of light and noble freedom. But it was power which hurt alike them and those against whom they made use of the arms of the servile,—cunning, blandishment, and unreasonable emotion.

That now the time has come when a clearer vision and better action are possible—when Man and Woman may regard one another as brother and sister, the pillars of one porch, the priests of one worship.

I have believed and intimated that this hope would receive an ampler fruition, than ever before, in our own land.

And it will do so if this land carry out the principles from which sprang our national life.

I believe that, at present, women are the best helpers of one another.

Let them think; let them act; till they know what they need.

We only ask of men to remove arbitrary barriers. Some would like to do more. But I believe it needs that Woman show herself in her native dignity, to teach them how to aid her; their minds are so encumbered by tradition.

. . .

I think women need, especially at this juncture, a much greater range of occupation than they have, to rouse their latent powers. A party of travelers lately visited a lonely hut on a mountain. There they found an old woman, who told them she and her husband had lived there forty years. "Why," they said, "did you choose so barren a spot?" She "did not know; *it was the man's notion.*"

And during forty years, she had been content to act, without knowing why, upon "the man's notion." I would not have it so.

In families that I know, some little girls like to saw wood, others to use carpenters' tools. Where these tastes are indulged, cheerfulness and good-humor are promoted. Where they are forbidden, because "such things are not proper for girls," they grow sullen and mischievous.

Fourier had observed these wants of women, as no one can fail to do who watches the desires of little girls, or knows the ennui that haunts grown women, except where they make to themselves a serene little world by art of some kind. He, therefore, in proposing a great variety of employments, in manufactures or the care of plants and animals, allows for one third of women as likely to have a taste for masculine pursuits, one third of men for feminine.

Who does not observe the immediate glow and serenity that is diffused over the life of women, before restless or fretful, by engaging in gardening, building, or the lowest department of art? Here is something that is not routine, something that draws forth life towards the infinite.

I have no doubt, however, that a large proportion of women would give themselves to the same employments as now, because there are circumstances that must lead them. Mothers will delight to make the nest soft and warm. Nature would take care of that; no need to clip the wings of any bird that wants to soar and sing, or finds in itself the strength of pinion for a migratory flight unusual to its kind. The difference would be that *all* need not be constrained to employments for which *some* are unfit.

I have urged upon the sex self-subsistence in its two forms of self-reliance and self-impulse, because I believe them to be the needed means of the present juncture.

I have urged on Woman independence of Man, not that I do not think the sexes mutually needed by one another, but because in Woman this fact has led to an excessive devotion, which has cooled love, degraded marriage, and prevented either sex from being what it should be to itself or the other.

I wish Woman to live, *first* for God's sake. Then she will not make an imperfect man her god, and thus sink to idolatry. Then she will not take what is not fit for her from a sense of weakness and poverty. Then, if she finds what she needs in Man embodied, she will know how to love, and be worthy of being loved.

By being more a soul, she will not be less Woman, for nature is perfected through spirit.

Now there is no woman, only an overgrown child.

That her hand may be given with dignity, she must be able to stand alone. I wish to see men and women capable of such relations as are depicted by Landor in his *Pericles and Aspasia,* where grace is the natural garb of strength, and the affections are calm, because deep. The softness is that of a firm tissue, as when

> "The gods approve
> The depth, but not the tumult of the soul,
> A fervent, not ungovernable love."

A profound thinker has said, "No married woman can represent the female world, for she belongs to her husband. The idea of Woman must be represented by a virgin."

But that is the very fault of marriage, and of the present relation between the sexes, that the woman *does* belong to the man, instead of forming a whole with him. Were it otherwise, there would be no such limitation to the thought.

Woman, self-centred, would never be absorbed by any relation; it would be only an experience to her as to man. It is a vulgar error that love, *a* love, to Woman is her whole existence; she also is born for Truth and Love in their universal energy. Would she but assume her inheritance, Mary would not be the only virgin mother. Not Manzoni alone would celebrate in his wife the virgin mind with the maternal wisdom and conjugal affections. The soul is ever young, ever virgin.

And will not she soon appear?—the woman who shall vindicate their birthright for all women; who shall teach them what to claim, and how to use what they obtain? Shall not her name be for her era Victoria, for her country and life Virginia? Yet predictions are rash; she herself must teach us to give her the fitting name.

An idea not unknown to ancient times has of late been revived, that, in the metamorphoses of life, the soul assumes the form, first of Man, then of Woman, and takes the chances, and reaps the benefits of either lot. Why then, say some, lay such emphasis on the rights or needs of Woman? What she wins not as Woman will come to her as Man.

That makes no difference. It is not Woman, but the law of right, the law of growth, that speaks in us, and demands the perfection of each being in its kind—apple as apple, Woman as Woman. Without adopting your theory, I know that I, a daughter, live through the life of Man; but what concerns me now is, that my life be a beautiful, powerful, in a word, a complete life in its kind. Had I but one more moment to live I must wish the same.

Suppose, at the end of your cycle, your great world-year, all will be completed, whether I exert myself or not (and the supposition is *false*,— but suppose it true), am I to be indifferent about it? Not so! I must beat my own pulse true in the heart of the world; for *that* is virtue, excellence, health.

Thou, Lord of Day! didst leave us to-night so calmly glorious, not dismayed that cold winter is coming, not postponing thy beneficence to the fruitful summer! Thou didst smile on thy day's work when it was done,

and adorn thy down-going as thy up-rising, for thou art loyal, and it is thy nature to give life, if thou canst, and shine at all events!
. . .

### Note

1. In *Woman in the Nineteenth Century, and Kindred Papers Relating to the Sphere, Condition, and Duties of Woman,* ed. Arthur Fuller (Boston: Roberts Brothers, 1893), pp. 170-72, 174-78.

# Frederick A. Douglass

*Raised in slavery, Douglass (1818–1895) seized his freedom and self-education to become one of the foremost advocates of abolitionism, equality, and racial justice. The fugitive slave's gifts for oratory and writing emerged in the 1840s during his speaking tours and other activities with the American Anti-Slavery Society. He worked tirelessly thereafter as a leader in the moral crusades of the day, calling whites to their religious and moral duties and encouraging African Americans to uphold their God-given inalienable rights. He served for a time in later years as a federal marshal and United States consul in Haiti.*

*The themes lifted up in his writings grew out of his life experience, above all his experience of what might be called an infinite qualitative difference between Christianity's message of liberty and righteousness and the hypocritical Christians whose lives distort and defame it. His fiery denunciations of the churches prompted many stung by his words to question his belief in Christianity itself. He did in fact have little concern and no patience for the preoccupation with doctrine, liturgy, and polity that distracted Christians from actually doing the will of God on earth. This excerpt from his famous autobiography (written in 1845) records the flash point of his sense of calling.*

## MY BONDAGE AND MY FREEDOM[1]

. . .

Among my first concerns on reaching New Bedford, was to become united with the church, for I had never given up, in reality, my religious faith. I had become lukewarm and in a backslidden state, but I was still convinced that it was my duty to join the Methodist church. I was not then aware of the powerful influence of that religious body in favor of the enslavement of my race, nor did I see how the northern churches could be responsible for the conduct of southern churches; neither did I fully understand how it could be my duty to remain separate from the

207

church, because bad men were connected with it. The slaveholding church, with its Coveys, Weedens, Aulds, and Hopkins, I could see through at once, but I could not see how Elm Street church, in New Bedford, could be regarded as sanctioning the christianity of these characters in the church at St. Michael's. I therefore resolved to join the Methodist church in New Bedford, and to enjoy the spiritual advantage of public worship. The minister of the Elm Street Methodist church, was the Rev. Mr. Bonney; and although I was not allowed a seat in the body of the house, and was proscribed on account of my color, regarding this proscription simply as an accommodation of the unconverted congregation who had not yet been won to Christ and his brotherhood, I was willing thus to be proscribed, lest sinners should be driven away from the saving power of the gospel. Once converted, I thought they would be sure to treat me as a man and a brother. "Surely," thought I, "these christian people have none of this feeling against color. They, at least, have renounced this unholy feeling." Judge, then, dear reader, of my astonishment and mortification, when I found, as soon I did find, all my charitable assumptions at fault.

An opportunity was soon afforded me for ascertaining the exact position of Elm Street church on that subject. I had a chance of seeing the religious part of the congregation by themselves; and although they disowned, in affect, their black brothers and sisters, before the world, I did think that where none but the saints were assembled, and no offense could be given to the wicked, and the gospel could not be "blamed," they would certainly recognize us as children of the same Father, and heirs of the same salvation, on equal terms with themselves.

The occasion to which I refer, was the sacrament of the Lord's Supper, that most sacred and most solemn of all the ordinances of the christian church. Mr. Bonney had preached a very solemn and searching discourse, which really proved him to be acquainted with the inmost secrets of the human heart. At the close of his discourse, the congregation was dismissed, and the church remained to partake of the sacrament. I remained to see, as I thought, this holy sacrament celebrated in the spirit of its great Founder.

There were only about a half dozen colored members attached to the Elm Street church, at this time. After the congregation was dismissed, these descended from the gallery, and took a seat against the wall most distant from the altar. Brother Bonney was very animated, and sung very sweetly, "Salvation 'tis a joyful sound," and soon began to administer the sacrament. I was anxious to observe the bearing of the colored members, and the result was most humiliating. During the whole ceremony, they looked like sheep without a shepherd. The white members went forward to the altar by the bench full; and when it was evident that all the whites had been served with the bread and wine, Brother Bonney—pious Brother Bonney—after a long pause, as if inquiring whether all the white members had been served, and fully assuring himself on that important point, then raised his voice to an unnatural pitch, and looking to the corner where his black sheep seemed penned, beckoned with his hand, exclaiming, "Come forward, colored friends!—come forward! You, too, have an interest in the blood of Christ. God is no respecter of persons. Come forward, and take this holy sacrament to your comfort." The colored members—poor, slavish souls—went forward, as invited. I went *out*, and have never been in that church since, although I honestly went there with a view to joining that body. I found it impossible to respect the religious profession of any who were under the dominion of this wicked prejudice, and I could not, therefore, feel that in joining them, I was joining a christian church, at all. I tried other churches in New Bedford, with the same result, and, finally, I attached myself to a small body of colored Methodists, known as the Zion Methodists. Favored with the affection and confidence of the members of this humble communion, I was soon made a class-leader and a local preacher among them. Many seasons of peace and joy I experienced among them, the remembrance of which is still precious, although I could not see it to be my duty to remain with that body, when I found that it consented to the same spirit which held my brethren in chains.

In four or five months after reaching New Bedford, there came a young man to me, with a copy of the "Liberator," the paper edited by WILLIAM LLOYD GARRISON, and published by ISAAC KNAPP, and asked me to subscribe for it. I told him I had but just escaped from slavery, and was of course very poor, and remarked further, that I was unable to pay for it then; the agent, however, very willingly took me as a subscriber, and appeared to be much pleased with securing my name to his list. From this time I was brought in contact with the mind of William Lloyd Garrison. His paper took its place with me next to the bible.

The Liberator was a paper after my own heart. It detested slavery—exposed hypocrisy and wickedness in high places—made no truce with the traffickers in the bodies and souls of men; it preached human brotherhood, denounced oppression, and, with all the solemnity of God's word, demanded the complete emancipation of my race. I not only liked—I *loved* this paper, and its editor. He seemed a match for all the opponents of emancipation, whether they spoke in the name of the law, or the gospel. His words were few, full of holy fire, and straight to the point. Learning to love him, through his paper, I was prepared to be pleased with his presence. Something of a hero worshiper, by nature, here was one, on first sight, to excite my love and reverence. . . .

I had not long been a reader of the Liberator, and listener to its editor, before I got a clear apprehension of the principles of the anti-slavery movement. I had already the spirit of the movement, and only needed to understand its principles and measures. These I got from the Liberator, and from those who believed in that paper. My acquaintance with the movement increased my hope for the ultimate freedom of my race, and I united with it from a sense of delight, as well as duty.

Every week the Liberator came, and every week I made myself master of its contents. All the anti-slavery meetings held in New Bedford I promptly attended, my heart burning at every true utterance against the slave system, and every rebuke of its friends and supporters. Thus passed the first three years of my residence in New Bedford. I had not then dreamed of the possibility of my becoming a public advocate of the cause so deeply imbedded in my heart. It was enough for me to listen— to receive and applaud the great words of others, and only whisper in private, among the white laborers on the wharves, and elsewhere, the truths which burned in my breast.

### Note

1. In *The Oxford Frederick Douglass Reader*, ed. William L. Andrews (New York: Oxford University Press, 1996; original essay published in 1855), pp. 208-11.

# Orestes Augustus Brownson

*B*rownson *(1803–1876), first "converted" by Methodists, was a restless intellect and spiritual seeker whose journey took him to Congregationalism, Universalism, free-thinking, Unitarianism, and Transcendentalism before, in 1844, reaching its destination in the Roman Catholic Church. His literary, philosophical, and theological talents were already much in evidence during the late 1830s, when he with other younger Unitarian intellectuals abandoned rational supernaturalism and Common-Sense principles for the Romantic way blazed by Europe's avant-garde thinkers and artists. As a Catholic layperson, he continued to keep abreast of the lastest developments in philosophy and theology, importing them into the American scene and contributing to them in his own constructive writings.*

*During the period in which this selection was written, Brownson found himself greatly influenced by Pierre Leroux's doctrine of life by communion. This doctrine formed the theological foundation that led Brownson into the Roman Catholic Church. As he adapted it, Brownson emphasized that for one to live truly, one must live in communion with something other than oneself, namely the object. Since God is the only true self-existent being, only God is truly object. But human beings cannot commune directly with God; therefore, humanity needs a mediator, Jesus Christ, the only one who brings human and divine together. He explains the significance of this understanding to another great influence in his earlier life, William Ellery Channing, in the document that follows.*

## THE MEDIATORIAL LIFE OF JESUS: A LETTER TO WILLIAM ELLERY CHANNING, D.D.[1]

. . . I have sir, finally attained to a view of the plan of a world's salvation through a Mediator, which I think reconciles all conflicting theories, discloses new wisdom in that plan, and enables us to take, in its most obvious and literal sense, without any subtlety or refinement, what the scriptures say of Jesus, and of salvation through his life. The Gospel becomes to me now a reality, and the teachings of the New Testament throughout realities, having their corresponding facts in the positive world. The views to which I have attained appear to me to be new, grand, and of the greatest importance. . . .

. . .

In the doctrines I am about to present, I claim no originality. I merely claim originality for the process by which I demonstrate their philosophical truth. The doctrines have been taught ever since the time of Jesus; they have never, before this attempt of mine, so far as my knowledge extends, been demonstrated. What I have to offer on the main subject of this Letter, I shall take the liberty to arrange under three general heads.

*First.*—Whence comes the Mediator? *Second.*—What is his work? *Third.*—What is the method by which he performs it?

. . .

*First.*—Whence comes the Mediator? I should not detain you a moment with this inquiry, were it not that there is a tendency in some minds among us, to rank Jesus in the category of ordinary men. . . .

. . .

It seem to me, sir, that this tendency, which neither you nor I have wholly escaped, is a tendency to resolve God into the laws of nature,— the laws of the moral world, and those of the natural world. Now what is this but a tendency to sink God in nature, to lose him entirely, that is, to become atheists? . . .

. . .

When we resolve God into the laws of nature, whether as called the laws of the moral world or of the natural world, we have nothing remaining but nature. Nature, when there is no God seen behind it, to control it, to do with it as he will, in fact, that wills to overrule its seeming evil for real good, is a mere fate, an inexorable destiny, a dark, inscrutable, resistless necessity. It has no freedom, no justice. It sweeps on regardless of what it crushes or carries away before it; now with its lightnings striking down the old man in his sins, and now the infant in its innocence. Where is the ground for religious emotion—religious exercise? All is fixed, irrevocable. What shall we do? or wherefore attempt to do any thing? We may fear and tremble at the darkness before and behind us, but wherefore love, or be grateful? We may be anxious about the future, but wherefore pray? We may wish to be for-

given our sins, but who can forgive them? What is the ground of peni-
tence and pardon?

. . .

. . . It is God's grace, not human effort or human genius, that provides
the Mediator. It is impossible then to press Jesus into the category of
ordinary men. He stands out alone, distinct, peculiar. This much, I must
be permitted to assume in regard to Jesus, if I am to concern myself with
Christianity at all. In answer then to the question, Whence comes the
Mediator? I reply, from God, "who so loved the world that he gave his
only begotten Son to die, that whosoever should believe on him might
not perish, but have everlasting life."

*Second.*—But, assuming that God sent the Mediator, what did he send
him to do? What was the work to be done for human redemption and
sanctification? In other words, what is the condition in which the Gospel
assumes the human race to be *without Christ,* and from which God,
through the mediation of Christ, is represented as saving it? A great
question this, and one on which I feel that I cannot so fully sympathize
with your views as I once did. You say, in the sermon to which I have
already alluded, that "In ourselves are the elements of the Divinity. God,
then, does not sustain a figurative resemblance to man. It is the resemblance of a parent to a child, the likeness of a kindred nature."[2] I am not
sure that I catch your precise meaning in these sentences, but from these
and from your writings generally, I infer that you hold man to be created with a *nature* akin to that of the Divinity. In other words, man is
created with a divine nature, and therefore the human and divine must
be at bottom identical. This is the doctrine I have been accustomed to
draw from your writings, and which is termed, amongst your admirers,
the doctrine of the divinity of humanity.

This doctrine, which you have set forth on so many occasions, with
all the power of your rich and fervid eloquence, I must needs believe is
the real parent of that deification and worship of the human soul, which
has within a few years past manifested itself among our transcendentalists. Men more ardent but less discriminating than yourself, have seized
upon this expression, "in ourselves are the elements of the Divinity,"
and have inferred that God is nothing but the possibility of man. . . .

. . . I know well that while you have wished to defend the freedom of
those who have drawn it, and to do justice to the moral purity of their
characters, you have shrunk from the conclusion itself. Yet, you must
allow me to say that I feel that you have in some measure warranted this
deification and worship of the human soul. Assuming the divinity of

human nature as the starting point, as you do, I see not well how a logical mind, not restrained by an abundant stock of good sense, can avoid coming to this conclusion. I must confess that I cannot see how one can avoid it, save at the expense of his consistency.

. . .

Allow me to say, that I think it is an error to assume that Christianity takes the divinity of humanity as its point of departure. Christianity seems to me to assume throughout as its point of departure, man's sinfulness, depravity, alienation from God and heaven. It treats man everywhere as a sinner, as morally diseased, morally dead, and its work is always to restore him to moral life and health; not to a consciousness of the greatness and divinity of his soul, but to righteousness, to a spiritual communion and union with God. And after all, is not this view the true one? Is not man a sinner? Who is there of us, however exalted or however low our estate, cultivated or uncultivated our minds, however pure and blameless may be our lives, that does not bear on his heart the damning stain of sin? Who has not exclaimed, nay, who does not perpetually exclaim, "I am a sinner; the good I would I do not, and the evil that I would not that I do. O wretched man that I am, who shall deliver me from the body of this death?" The universal conscience of the race bears witness to the fact that all men sin, and come short of the glory of God. All religions are so many additional witnesses to this fact, for they are all so many methods dictated to man, or devised by him, for getting rid of sin, and placing himself at one with God.

This much you, I know, will admit, however it may or may not be reconcilable with what you say of man's divinity. But I think Christianity goes further than this. It assumes not only that all men are actual sinners, but also that human nature itself has been corrupted, is depraved, so that men by nature are prone to do evil. This is the doctrine which I know you have opposed; but I think I can present it in a light in which you will not refuse to accept it; because I see how I can accept it, and find also a place for the doctrine which you yourself have so much at heart.

This doctrine of the depravity of human nature is, you will admit, a doctrine of universal tradition. With me tradition is always good evidence when its subject-matter is not intrinsically improbable. This is, I am aware, a broad principle, but I am able to demonstrate its soundness. The pure reason is always incompetent to decide on questions which go out of the department of mathematics. In what concerns the race, tradition is the criterion of certainty, only we must not forget that the individual man must be free to sit in judgment on the question, what is or is not tradition. The doctrine of human depravity is admitted on all hands to be a doctrine of universal tradition. . . . Men cannot even by your rich and kindling eloquence, which is seldom surpassed, be made to believe, to any great extent, in your doctrine of the divinity of humanity. Even those of us the most anxious to embrace it, find ourselves unable to do so. We are too conscious of our own weakness and unworthiness. . . .

Moreover, the Scriptures seem to me to teach very clearly, that the actual sins of mankind, are not all the difficulties in the way of our salvation, that are to be overcome. I will say nothing now of Genesis; I confine myself to the New Testament. Paul teaches, beyond all question, that all men died in Adam, that through Adam sin entered into the world, and by sin a corruption of human nature. It was through the disobedience of one man that many, the many, that is, all men, were made sinners. Thus John, when he points to Jesus, says, "Behold the Lamb of God which taketh away the *sin* of the world." He does not say *sins*, but *sin*, that is, the original depravity of human nature.

Experience also, I think, indicates at least that there is in all men, even now, an under-current of depravity, by virtue of which men, if left to themselves, delight in sin rather than in holiness. Children are not always the sweet innocents we sometimes pretend. The little rogues not unfrequently show animation, spirit, intelligence, only when doing some mischief. Moreover, if human nature were not depraved, if it were what you represent it, and if there were no sin but actual sin, how could there be even actual sin? How comes it to pass that men, pure by nature, and possessing in themselves the very elements of God, do no sooner begin to develop their pure and godlike nature than they sin? What is it that works in us, and manifests itself in our acts? Is it not human nature? Since then the workings of this nature are unquestionably sinful, must not the nature itself be depraved?

I am willing to admit that the doctrine of human depravity, has assumed a form which is somewhat objectionable. Not indeed because it has been said to be total, that is, extending to and over all the faculties of the human soul. For the human soul is not many, but one, and acts ever as a unity. It would be grossly absurd then to assume that one phasis of it could remain undepraved while another was depraved. Sin also blunts the intellect as well as corrupts the heart. They who have pleasure in unrighteousness are easily deluded. They are the pure in heart who see God. But the error has been in assuming perfection as the point of departure for man and nature, and therefore in considering the imperfection we now see in man and nature to be the result of a fall from a perfect state. A fall from such a state is inconceivable. But man being originally created imperfect, as he must have been, naturally, if not inevitably, sinned, and this sin necessarily corrupted human nature.

I say *necessarily*. Grant me what you will not deny, that the first man, whether called Adam or not, sinned, and the doctrine of the inherent, hereditary depravity of human nature follows inevitably, necessarily. This may seem to be a strong statement, but I can justify it.

The old doctrine on this subject, is that God made a covenant with Adam, by virtue of which Adam became the federal head of humanity, so that all his posterity should be implicated in his transgression. I do not like the term *covenant*. Say that God so created man, and subjected him to such a law of life, that the first man could not sin without involving all his posterity in his sin, and you will say what I believe to be the strict truth. But how can this be? Shall the innocent be involved in the fate of the guilty? They are so in nature, and in this life, to some extent, in providence. This world does not realize our conceptions of justice. Hence the promise and the hope of another. But this is not the point.

Philosophy has succeeded in demonstrating,—what everybody has always believed without perceiving its full significance,—that we are dependent beings, and are in no case and in no sense able to live by and in ourselves alone. Man can no more *live* by himself alone, than he can *exist* alone. Cut him off from all communion with nature, and could he live? Cut him off from all communication with other men, with his race, would he not die? Does not man die in solitude? In perfect solitude could he ever be said to live, that is to live a human life? Could any of his affections, moral, religious, social, or domestic, be ever developed? Certainly not. Here then is a fact of immense importance.

Let us begin by distinguishing *life* from *being*. To be is not necessarily to live. Inorganic matter *is*, but we can hardly say that it *lives*. To live is to manifest. But no being except God the self-existent, and the self-living being, is able to manifest itself by itself alone. There is no act, no function that man can perform in a state of perfect isolation. He cannot think without thinking himself as the subject of the thought, and thinking something not himself as its object. He has the capacity to love, but he cannot manifest it, that is live it, without loving; and he cannot love without loving something, some object. This which I say of love I may say of all of man's capacities, whether physical, intellectual, sentient, or sentimental. To deny this, and to assume that man can in any case be his own object, were to assume that man is capable of living in himself alone; which would imply that he, like the infinite God is self-existent and self-living.

If to live is to manifest ourselves, and if we cannot manifest ourselves without communion with an object which we are not, it follows that our life is at once subjective and objective. A man's life is not all in himself. It is in himself and in his object—the object by means of which he lives. This, if we say man is a dependent being, insufficient for himself, is what we necessarily affirm.

Now man's object, by communion with which he lives, is other men, God, and nature. With God and nature he communes only indirectly. His direct, immediate object is other men. His life, then, is in himself and in other men. All men are brought by this into the indissoluble unity of one and the same life. All become members of one and the same body, and members one of another. The object of each man is all other men. Thus do the race live *in solido,* if I may use a legal term, the objective portion of each man's life being indissolubly in all other men, and, therefore, that of all men in each man.

It follows necessarily from this oneness of the life of all men, that no one member can be affected for good or evil, but the whole body, all humanity in space, time, and eternity must actually or virtually be affected with it.

Assume now, that the first man sinned, and it is a fair presumption that he did sin, to say the least. This man must have been the object by virtue of communion with which his children were enabled to live. They could not live without an object, and he must be that object. Life is indissolubly subjective and objective. He must furnish the objective portion of their life. This portion of their life must partake of his moral character. He had polluted himself by sin. This pollution is necessarily transmitted by virtue of the fact that he is their object, to them, who corrupted in the objective portion of their life, must needs be corrupted in the subjective portion.

Adam's sin must necessarily have been transmitted to his children, not solely by natural generation, as some have contended, but by moral generation. Nor could it stop there. His children must have been the object of their children, and thus have transmitted it to them. These again must have transmitted it to a later generation; and thus, since the preceding generation furnishes always the objective portion of the life of the succeeding generation, it must necessarily be transmitted from generation to generation forever, or till the race should cease to exist; unless the current were arrested and rolled back by a foreign power.

Bearing in mind this law of life, which philosophy has succeeded in demonstrating without once suspecting its application, and I think you will agree with me in accepting the doctrine in question, in believing that Paul meant what he said, that all die in Adam, and that through the disobedience of one man all were made sinners, and that, therefore, death hath passed upon all men. I think, also, that you will agree that the church generally, with which we have both warred on this point, has been right in asserting original sin, and the innate, hereditary depravity of human nature. The church seems to me to have erred only in considering this depravity, hereditary by virtue of a covenant or imputation, on the one hand, or by natural generation on the other. It is hereditary by virtue of the fact stated, that the preceding generation always furnishes the objective portion of the life of the succeeding generation, and without the objective portion the subjective portion would be as if it were not.

This principle of life which I have set forth is one of an immense reach. It shows at a glance the terrible nature of sin. In sin this principle is reversed, but is not destroyed. It operates for evil as, when in its normal condition, it does for good. By virtue of this principle, sin, whatever its degree, however great or however slight, by whomsoever committed, necessarily propagates itself, and must continue to propagate itself eternally, if not arrested by the sovereign grace of God. Humanity has originally in itself no more inherent power to overcome it than a body once set in motion has to arrest itself. How little then do they know of the true philosophy of life, who treat sin as if it were a light affair!

I am now prepared to answer the question, what is the work to be done? It is to redeem human nature from its inherent depravity, communicate to it a new and divine life, through which individuals may be saved from actual transgression, and raised to fellowship with the Father, by which they shall become really sons of God, and joint-heirs of a heavenly inheritance.

*Third.*—Having now determined the work there was for a Mediator to perform, I pass in the third and last place to consider the method by which he performs it; and I think I shall succeed in demonstrating the truth of the four following positions which are held by the church generally.

1. Man naturally does not and cannot commune directly with God, and therefore can come into fellowship with him only through a Mediator.

2. This Mediator must be at once and indissolubly, in the plain literal

218

sense of the terms, very God of very God, and very man of very man; and so being very God of very God, and very man of very man, he can literally and truly mediate between God and men.

3. Jesus saves man, redeems him from sin, and enables him to have fellowship, as John says, with the Father, by giving his life literally not only for him but to him.

4. Men have eternal life, that is, live a true normal life, only so far forth as they live the identical life of Jesus. "He that hath the Son hath life;" "he that hath not the Son hath not life;" "except ye eat the flesh and drink the blood of the Son of Man ye have no life in you."

These are strong positions, and such as we Unitarians have not generally embraced in a very literal sense; but I think I can show them to be not only tenable, but positions that we may accept without giving up any thing we now have, that we really value. They may require us to enlarge our faith, but not to alter or abandon it. Nay, they are virtually implied in what we are every day preaching.

Jesus says, in answer to a question put to him by Thomas, "I am the way, the truth, and the life." These words have a profound significance, and a literal truth, which I confess I for one have been but slow to comprehend. I confess, sir, that I have honestly believed, that we might have a very sufficient Christianity without including the historical person we call Jesus; not indeed that I have ever failed, in my own view of Christianity, to include him. But I have taught from the pulpit, and from the press, that Christianity did not necessarily and could not be made to stand or fall with the fact whether there ever was or was not such a person as Jesus. This I now see was a grave error. Christ, the literal person we call Christ, *is* Christianity. All begins and ends with him. To reject him historically is to reject Christianity. This is the truth which they have had who have accused some of us of advocating the "latest form of infidelity," though under other aspects we who have been so accused, have been much further from infidelity than our accusers.

. . .

I begin by assuming that the finite cannot commune directly with the infinite. Like does not and cannot commune with unlike. Moreover, the finite when regarded as depraved, all will agree, cannot commune, hold fellowship with infinite holiness. Man then could not commune directly with God; both because finite and because sinful. Then he must remain ever alienated from God, or a medium of communion, that is, a Mediator, must be provided. And this Mediator must of course be provided by the infinite, and not by the finite. It would be absurd to say that man, unable to commune with God, can nevertheless provide a medium of communion with him. God must provide it. That is, he must condescend, come down to the finite, down to man, and by so doing, take man up to himself.

The Mediator, or medium of communion must needs be both human and divine. For if it do not touch man on the one hand, and God on the other, it cannot bring the two together, and make them one. Moreover, it must be really, literally, and indissolubly human and divine, God-man; not figuratively, symbolically, or mythically, for the Gospel deals only with realities. Types and shadows disappeared with the Mosaic dispensation.

Now, if you will recall what I have said of life, and the law of life, you will see at once how truly, and how literally Jesus was this Mediator between God and men. To live is to manifest one's self, and no being, except the self-living being, God, can manifest itself save by communion with some object. Life, then, in all beings, but the Unbegotten, is at once subjective and objective. This is the principle of life, which philosophy has demonstrated beyond the possibility of cavil.

. . .

It is the life that mediates. Jesus, I have said, so has said the church, saves the world by communicating to it his life, not as a life for them to look at, to contemplate as an example, and to seek to copy, to imitate, but for them literally to live, to be *their* life. This is now quite explicable. Jesus was placed in the world in the midst of men. Men communed with him while he was in the flesh. Then by the very principle of life already stated, he must have become the objective portion of their life. Then his life literally enters into and becomes an inseparable portion of the life of those human beings, say his disciples, who lived in and by communion with him. He was the object to his disciples; then, the objective portion of their life, by virtue of which their subjective life was developed.

But the human race lives, as we have seen, *in solido;* all are members of one and the same body, and members one of another. There is a oneness of life which runs through them all, making them so strictly one, that the whole must feel whatever affects any one. The slightest vibrations in the heart of the least significant member are felt through the mighty heart of the whole. Consequently, the very moment that this new life of Jesus was communicated to the disciples, it was communicated virtually to the race. The disciples became objects with which others communed, and by means of their communion with others, necessarily

220

imparted this life to others, by virtue of that very principle of life by which they had received it, and by virtue of which, when reversed, we have seen the sin of Adam necessarily extended to all his posterity. By the fact that one generation overlaps another, and thus becomes its objective life, the generation in which Christ appeared must necessarily transmit it to its successor, and that successor to its successor, and thus generation carry it on to generation, so long as the succession of generations should last.

This doctrine of the transmission of the Life from generation to generation, is denied by no sect, to my knowledge, except the Baptists, who seem to me to mistake more fundamentally the real character of Christianity, than any other sect to which the Protestant reformation has given birth. In all other churches it is borne witness to by the doctrine of infant baptism. Children are baptized because it is felt that there is a sense in which the children of elect or believing parents are born into the kingdom. Infant baptism, then, has an important meaning. It is the symbol of a vital doctrine of Christianity, which is, to my understanding, rejected by all those who admit only baptism of adults, on voluntary profession of faith. . . .
. . .

This intimate relation of all men in the unity of one and the same life, explains the Eucharist or Communion. That rite of the church is not merely commemorative of the last supper of Jesus with his disciples. All Christianity clusters around it, centres in it: for all Christianity is in this one word *communion*. Jesus was the living bread which came down from heaven to give life to the world. This Life, the new Life, Eternal Life, the Life by living which we are redeemed from sin and united to God, could be communicated to the world, only by virtue of a communion between Jesus and his disciples, and to the rest of mankind in time and space only by communion with them. The great fact here affirmed is that the life of Jesus is communicated to the world, and spread from man to man according to the very principle of human life itself. . . .

We may now understand and accept what is said of the dignity of human nature. Taken as we find it to-day, in the bosom of Christian civilization, it unquestionably has a recuperative energy, even, if you will, a divine worth. My objection to what you have alleged of human nature, is that you affirm it of human nature originally and universally. You and the church in some respects agree. Both speak of human nature to-day, without intimating that the mission of Christ has in the least affected it. If human nature were always what you say, I cannot conceive what need

221

there was of a Redeemer; if it be now what the church generally affirms, that is, inherently and totally depraved, I am equally unable to conceive what the Redeemer has done. If there be any truth in the doctrine of life as I have set it forth; if there be any truth in the alleged fact that the Life of Jesus was a new life, a life *above the human life of the age in which he came;* then assuredly has the coming of Jesus redeemed human nature, and communicated to it higher and diviner elements. Human nature is not to-day what it was before the coming of Jesus. In speaking of human nature, meaning thereby the powers and capacities of man, we must have regard to chronology. It is false, what we say, that human nature is the same in all ages. The law of human life is the same in all ages; but that life is never the same for two successive generations, or else where were the idea of progress, without which the whole plan of Providence would be inexplicable? To assert that human nature is the same to-day that it was before the coming of Christ, is to "deny the Lord that bought us"; because it either denies that Jesus has come at all, or that he has come to any effect.

The coming of Jesus has communicated a new life to the race, which by means of *communion* of man with man shall extend to all individuals. This new life has not as yet, we all know, wholly overcome and effaced the death which was by Adam; but it is in the heart of humanity, an incorruptible seed, I had almost said, a seminal principle of divinity. The humanity of to-day has in its life, which is the indwelling Christ, the Christ that was to be with us unto the end of the world, a redeeming power, a recuperative energy, by virtue of which it is able to come into fellowship with the Father, and thus work out its own salvation. The possession of this principle, this energy, this life, literally, as I have endeavored to prove, the Christ, is that wherein human nature differs now from what it was before Jesus came. Then it had in its life no redeeming principle, now it has. This divinity is not *it,* but Christ formed within it, the hope of glory. Human nature in some sense then I own possesses to-day the divine worth you claim for it; not by virtue of its own inherent right, but by virtue of its union through the law of life to Christ, who is our head, and who is one with God. This union virtually complete, is actually incomplete. To complete it, and therefore to make all men one in Christ, and through him one with the Father, thus fulfilling his prayer, as recorded in the seventeenth chapter of John's Gospel, is the work to be done, towards which Christian civilization is tending, and to which all true Christians direct all their efforts, individual and social. We may be even far from this glorious result as yet, and we may even be in ourselves weak and inefficient; but the Life is in the world; Christ has entered into the life of humanity; the Word has become Flesh, and dwells among us; and as individuals and as a race we may do all things through Christ strengthening us. We can effect this, because God works in us both to will and to do. By communion with Jesus, we derive life, as I have said, from God himself; we are led by the Spirit of God, are sons of God; clothed upon with a life, majesty, and power, before which the empire of darkness and sin must be as chaff before the wind. We are placed at one with God. All things then are for us. The winds are our messengers, and flames of fire our ministers. Even the spirits shall obey us. Who can set bounds to our power, since our strength is not ours, but God's; since our life is hid in God, in whom we dwell, and who through his Son dwells in us. O, sir, I believe it will prove to be literally true, what Jesus said, "he that believeth on me, greater works than these shall he do." We know little of the power, of the moral force with which to overcome the world, true fellowship of man with man in the life and spirit of Jesus will give us. God is for us, who can be against us? Here, sir, is my hope. The world lieth in wickedness; man preys upon man; discordant sounds of wrongs, outrages and grief and death strike my ear on every hand; but I despair not; Christ is our life, because he lives we shall live also; Christ is our life, a true life, and I fear not but life will finally swallow up death in victory, and the new heavens and the new earth, wherein dwelleth righteousness, become a glorious reality, an everlasting inheritance for the generations of men.

. . .

## Notes

1. In *Orestes A. Brownson: Selected Writings*, ed. Patrick W. Carey, (New York and Mahwah: Paulist Press, 1991), pp. 205-27.
2. William Ellery Channing's *Likeness to God* (1828), reprinted in this volume; see p. 182.

# Isaac Thomas Hecker

*The son of German immigrants, Hecker (1819–1888) converted to Roman Catholicism in 1844 from what might be called a non-confessional, nondenominational Transcendentalist faith. Baptized Lutheran and familiar with his mother's Methodist perfectionism, a mystical experience led him at age 22 to Brook Farm, a Transcendentalist utopian community and for a while into association with Transcendentalists like Orestes Brownson. The two friends turned Catholic in the same year. Ordained a priest in 1849, Hecker went on to found the Paulist Order (1858), edit the* Catholic World, *direct the Catholic Publication Society, and serve as a theological adviser to Archbishop John Spalding.*

*His writings and other activities attested to a conviction that a new age of the Spirit was at hand: a renewed, wise, and righteous American Catholicism would inspire and guide all American Christians toward a spiritual unity and the fulfillment of the highest religious and moral ideals, which was the destiny God planned for them. The use of Hecker's name and the development of his themes after his death led, in the controversies over church authority at the end of the nineteenth century, to a papal condemnation that targeted "Heckerism" under the code name "Americanism."*

## AN EXPOSITION OF THE CHURCH IN VIEW OF RECENT DIFFICULTIES AND CONTROVERSIES AND THE PRESENT NEEDS OF THE AGE[1]

"These are not the times to sit with folded arms, while all the enemies of God are occupied in overthrowing every thing worthy of respect."—Pius IX., Jan. 13, 1873.

"Yes, this change, this triumph, will come. I know not whether it will come during my life, during the life of this poor Vicar of Jesus Christ; but that it must come, I know. The resurrection will take place and we

224

shall see the end of all impiety."—Pius IX., Anniversary of the Roman Plebiscite, 1872.

. . .

## VI. *The Way Out*

All things are to be viewed and valued as they bear on the destiny of man. Religion is the solution of the problem of man's destiny. Religion, therefore, lies at the root of everything which concerns man's true interest.

Religion means Christianity, to all men, or to nearly all, who hold to any religion among European nations. Christianity, intelligibly understood, signifies the church, the Catholic Church. The church is God acting through a visible organization directly on men, and, through men, on society.

The church is the sum of all problems, and the most potent fact in the whole wide universe. It is therefore illogical to look elsewhere for the radical remedy of all our evils. It is equally unworthy of a Catholic to look elsewhere for the renewal of religion.

The meditation of these great truths is the source from which the inspiration must come, if society is to be regenerated and the human race directed to its true destination. He who looks to any other quarter for a radical and adequate remedy and for true guidance is doomed to failure and disappointment.

## VII. *Mission of the Holy Spirit*

It cannot be too deeply and firmly impressed on the mind that the church is actuated by the instinct of the Holy Spirit; and to discern clearly its action, and to co-operate with it effectually, is the highest employment of our faculties, and at the same time the primary source of the greatest good to society.

Did we clearly see and understand the divine action of the Holy Spirit in the successive steps of the history of the church we would fully comprehend the law of all true progress. If in this later period more stress was laid on the necessity of obedience to the external authority of the church than in former days, it was, as has been shown, owing to the peculiar dangers to which the faithful were exposed. It would be an inexcusable mistake to suppose for a moment that the holy church, at any period of her existence, was ignorant or forgetful of the mission and office of the Holy Spirit. The Holy Spirit established the church, and can

225

he forget his own mission? It is true that he has to guide and govern through men, but he is the Sovereign of men, and especially of those whom he has chosen as his immediate instruments.

. . .

No one who reads the Holy Scriptures can fail to be struck with the repeated injunctions to turn our eyes inward, to walk in the divine presence, to see and taste and listen to God in the soul. These exhortations run all through the inspired books, beginning with that of Genesis, and ending with the Revelations of S. John. "I am the Almighty God, walk before me, and be perfect" (Gen 17:1 DV) was the lesson which God gave to the patriarch Abraham. "Be still and see that I am God." (Ps 45:11 DV [46:10])[2] "O taste, and see that the Lord is sweet; blessed is the man that hopeth in him." (Ps 33:9 DV [34:8]) God is the guide, the light of the living, and our strength. "God's kingdom is within you," said the divine Master. "Know you not that you are the temple of God, and that the Spirit of God dwelleth in you?" (1 Cor 3:16 DV) "For it is God who worketh in you both to will and to accomplish, according to his will." (Phil 2:13 DV) The object of divine revelation was to make known and to establish within the souls of men, and through them upon the earth, the kingdom of God.

In accordance with the Sacred Scriptures, the Catholic Church teaches that the Holy Spirit is infused, with all his gifts, into our souls by the sacrament of baptism, and that, without his actual prompting or inspiration and aid, no thought or act, or even wish, tending directly towards our true destiny, is possible.

The whole aim of the science of Christian perfection is to instruct men how to remove the hindrances in the way of the action of the Holy Spirit, and how to cultivate those virtues which are most favorable to his solicitations and inspirations. Thus the sum of Spiritual life consists in observing and fortifying the ways and movements of the Spirit of God in our soul, employing for this purpose all the exercises of prayer, spiritual reading, sacraments, the practice of virtues, and good works.

That divine action which is the immediate and principal cause of the salvation and perfection of the soul claims by right its direct and main attention. From this source within the soul there will gradually come to birth the consciousness of the indwelling presence of the Holy Spirit, out of which will spring a force surpassing all human strength, a courage higher than all human heroism, a sense of dignity excelling all human greatness. The light the age requires for its renewal can come only from the same source. The renewal of the age depends on the renewal of religion. The renewal of religion depends upon a greater effusion of the creative and renewing power of the Holy Spirit. The greater effusion of the Holy Spirit depends on the giving of increased attention to his movements and inspirations in the soul. The radical and adequate remedy for all the evils of our age, and the source of all true progress, consist in increased attention and fidelity to the action of the Holy Spirit in the Soul. "Thou shalt send forth thy Spirit, and they shall be created: and thou shalt renew the face of the earth." (Ps. 103:30 DV [104:30])

## VIII. The Men the Age Demands

This truth will be better seen by looking at the matter a little more in detail. The age, we are told, calls for men worthy of that name. Who are those worthy to be called men? Men, assuredly, whose intelligences and wills are divinely illuminated and fortified. This is precisely what is produced by the gifts of the Holy Spirit; they enlarge all the faculties of the soul at once.

The age is superficial; it needs the gift of wisdom, which enables the soul to contemplate the truth in its ultimate causes. The age is materialistic; it needs the gift of intelligence, by the light of which the intellect penetrates into the essence of things. The age is captivated by a false and one-sided science; it needs the gift of science, by the light of which is seen each order of truth in its true relations to other orders and in a divine unity. The age is in disorder; and is ignorant of the way to true progress; it needs the gift of counsel, which teaches how to choose the proper means to attain an object. The age is impious; it needs the gift of piety, which leads the soul to look up to God as the Heavenly Father, and to adore him with feelings of filial affection and love. The age is sensual and effeminate; it needs the gift of force, which imparts to the will the strength to endure the greatest burdens and to prosecute the greatest enterprises with ease and heroism. The age has lost and almost forgotten God; it needs the gift of fear, to bring the soul again to God, and make it feel conscious of its great responsibility and of its destiny.

Men endowed with these gifts are the men for whom—if it but knew it—the age calls: men whose minds are enlightened and whose wills are strengthened by an increased action of the Holy Spirit; men whose souls are actuated by the gifts of the Holy Spirit; men whose countenances are lit up with a heavenly joy, who breathe an air of inward peace, and act with a holy liberty and an unaccountable energy. One such soul does more to advance the kingdom of God than tens of thousands without such gifts. These are the men and this is the way—if the age could only be made to see and believe it—to universal restoration, universal reconciliation, and universal progress.

## IX. *The Church Has Entered on This Way*

The men the age and its needs demand depend on a greater infusion of the Holy Spirit in the souls of the faithful; and the church has been already prepared for this event.

Can one suppose for a moment that so long, so severe, a contest, as that of the three centuries just passed, which, moreover, has cost so dearly, has not been fraught with the greatest utility to the church? Does God ever allow his church to suffer loss in the struggle to accomplish her divine mission?

It is true that the powerful and persistent assaults of the errors of the XVIth century against the church forced her, so to speak, out of the usual orbit of her movement; but having completed her defence from all danger on that side, she is returning to her normal course with increased agencies—thanks to that contest—and is entering upon a new and fresh phase of life, and upon a more vigorous action in every sphere of her existence. The chiefest of these agencies, and the highest in importance, was that of the definition concerning the nature of papal authority. For the definition of the Vatican Council, having rendered the supreme authority of the church, which is the unerring interpreter and criterion of divinely-revealed truth, more explicit and complete, has prepared the way for the faithful to follow, with greater safety and liberty, the inspirations of the Holy Spirit. The dogmatic papal definition of the Vatican Council is, therefore, the axis on which turn the new course of the church, the renewal of religion, and the entire restoration of society.
. . .

### Notes

1. In *American Catholic Religious Thought,* ed. Patrick Carey (New York and Mahwah: Paulist Press, 1987), pp. 126, 132-36. Source: *Catholic World* 21 (April-September, 1875): 117-38.
2. The Douay-Rheims Version follows the Vulgate in referencing chapters and verses. Because its division of the book of Psalms differs from that of the Masoretic text, which is used by most English translations, citations of the latter are included in brackets.

# John Williamson Nevin

$N$*evin (1803–1886), working in conjunction with Philip Schaff, a young Swiss church historian schooled in Germany, helped transform the small seminary of Mercersburg, Pennsylvania, into a theological center of the German Reformed Church in America. Nevin was a Presbyterian, well trained at Princeton in that school's blend of Calvinist confessionalism and Common Sense. He taught from 1830 to 1840 at his church's Western Theological Seminary. There he began his readings in the new scholarship of Germany, the results of which emerged in full force during the Mercersburg years that followed. The Anxious Bench (1843) set forth his theological critique of revivalist religion generally and New Haven theology specifically. The book was preceded and followed by a series of writings designed to revivify the substance of historic Reformed doctrine and renew a sense of the corporate character of the church, its worship, and its sacraments. Nevin resigned his Mercersburg post in 1851 and ended his active career (1866–1876) as President of Franklin and Marshall College.*

*In its day, Mercersburg Theology was controversial and its influence limited. It represented, nonetheless, theological scholarship of exceptionally high quality in both learning and insight and had an impact on numerous later theologians as well as twentieth-century ecumenism. Two samples of Nevin's constructive historical-theological work follow: the first, an exposition of the nature of the church; the second, his account of the meaning of the Lord's Supper.*

## THE CHURCH[1]

Ephesians 1:23. Which is his body, the fullness of him that filleth all in all.

I propose, in connection with this passage, to consider, without further introduction, the nature of the *Christian Church*, for the purpose of ascertaining and determining, in a more general way, by the light of

God's most holy revelation, the privileges on the one hand and the duties on the other, which are comprehended in our common Christian profession.

## 1. What is the Church?

To answer this question intelligently, we must make a distinction. The Church exhibits itself to us under two aspects, which are in many respects very different, and yet both alike necessary to complete its proper conception. In one view it is the *Ideal Church,* in another it is the *Actual Church.*

### 1. Idea of the Church

. . .

The Ideal Church is the power of a new supernatural creation, which has been introduced into the actual history of the world by the Incarnation of Jesus Christ; and which is destined to go on, causing "old things to pass away and all things to become new" [Rev. 21:4, 5, adapted], till it shall triumph fully in the end over all sin and death, and the whole world shall appear transformed into its image and resplendent with its light. As such a power, it is actually at work in the world already, and has been so since the time of Christ. Very much is still wanting to the complete triumph of the gospel. But the force by which this full triumph is to be accomplished is not to be expected now, as by the Jews under the old dispensation, in the form of some new order of life supernaturally descending from the heavens to the earth. The new creation is already at hand, not developed, indeed, to its last necessary results, but as an active force, all sufficient for its own ends, and really comprehended in the order of the world's history as it now stands. It is exhibited to us in the Church.

The principle of this new creation is the Lord Jesus Christ. In him the Word became flesh, the divine nature was associated with the human as never before, and life and immortality were brought to light in our fallen world. The fact thus accomplished in his person was at the same time a fact for all time. It included in itself all the resources of life and salvation that were needed for the full redemption of humanity, onward to the grand millennial triumph in which it is destined to have its end. The Church, through all ages, is the depository of these resources. The life with which she is filled, the powers that are lodged in her constitution, were all comprehended originally in the person of Jesus Christ, and are all still the revelation only of the grace and truth which came by him in the beginning. He is the alpha and omega, the beginning and the end, of the Church, which is denominated on this account his body, the fullness of him that filleth all in all.

The general attributes of the Ideal Church, as thus described, are not difficult to determine. It is a living system, organically bound together in all its parts, springing from a common ground, and pervaded throughout with the force of a common nature. In its very conception, therefore, it is catholic, that is, one and universal. The kingdom of God, or the new creation in Christ Jesus, must be regarded in the nature of the case as the highest possible form of humanity itself; and in this view it cannot be less single or less comprehensive than the Idea of the human race as a whole. As a single life, moreover, flowing perpetually from the same fountain, it must ever remain in union with itself, always one and everywhere the same, in the midst of all possible extension and multiplication. There may be many states in the world, but there can be only one Church. Such is the doctrine of the New Testament throughout. Such has been the deep feeling of all Christendom from the beginning, as expressed in that ancient article of the Creed: "I believe in the holy, catholic Church." The Church is one, in all ages and through all lands.

In her Ideal character again, as the article of the Creed implies, the Church is absolutely holy and infallible, free from error and free from sin. Her constitution is derived wholly from Christ, who is the truth itself, and in whom the whole righteousness of the law is completely and forever fulfilled. Hence the Church is represented to be the organ and medium by which the world is reclaimed from the power of error, and transformed into a holy life. Her members are called to be saints [1 Cor. 1:2]. She is the pillar and ground of the truth [1 Tim. 3:15]. The gates of hell shall not prevail against her [Mt. 16:18]. In the end, she will be found holy and without blemish, a glorious Church, not having spot or wrinkle, or any such thing [Eph. 5:27].

. . .

Lastly, the Church under its Ideal character includes in itself the necessity of a visible externalization in the world. Without this necessity, it could not be real in any of the respects that have been already mentioned. For it is a fixed law in life, that every spiritual force which it comprehends must take some outward form in order to become complete. Pent up within itself as mere spirit, it must remain always an abstraction only, with no power whatever. The outward must ever be joined to the inward, to give it either reality or strength. And the more intensely spiritual any force may be, the more urgent and irresistible will

231

be found the operation of this law, requiring it to put on a body suitable to its own nature, and to appear thus under a visible form. The Church, then, as comprehending in itself the inmost, deepest life of humanity, cannot possibly exist in the character of a simply inward and invisible constitution. Of all forms of existence known among men, this is the very last of which any such imagination might reasonably be entertained. An invisible state, or invisible family, or invisible man, is not so great an absurdity and contradiction as an absolutely invisible Church. Christianity starts, indeed, as something spiritual and inward, as it is said, "The kingdom of God is within you" [Lk. 17: 21]; but it is only that it may reveal itself immediately in the way of external life, both in the single Christian and in the Church as a whole. The Idea of the Church includes visibility, just as the Idea of man supposes a body. And this visibility is demanded for all the attributes, too, under which the Church is properly known. It is not the visibility of single Christians, simply as such, that is required, but the visibility of the Church as an organic body, in whose presence alone all individual Christianity becomes real. The Church is required to be visible as a Church—that is, in the whole character which is comprehended in this idea. Its catholicity, unity, sanctity, all call for externalization. The article, *I believe in one, holy, catholic Church,* contemplates in this view no mere intellectual abstraction. It expresses faith in the Church as one, holy, and catholic, under an outward visible form, and those who give it a different sense, put violence upon the Creed in doing so, and wrong the idea of the Church at the same time. For an invisible unity, catholicity, and holiness can never satisfy the requisitions of the case. The Church, in its very nature, seeks visibility, and to be complete at all, this visibility must extend to all its qualities and attributes.

. . .

## 2. The Actual Church

This is exhibited to us in history, as it reaches from the Incarnation of Christ to the present time, and is destined to run forward still to the end of the world as it now stands. It is the kingdom of heaven, as it is found revealing itself in the way of actual life among men. It may be contemplated without reference to the past or future, under the form simply that belongs to it at a given time. Thus we have the Church of the present age, comprehending in itself the whole extent of the Christian life as it now exists in the world. And in the same way we may speak of the Church of the first century, the Church of the fourth century, the Church of the sixteenth century, or the Church of any other age, as something

232

separate and complete within itself. But the true and proper conception of the actual Church is not reached in this way. This includes always the past along with the present, as well as a reference also to the future. Through all periods the Church remains the same, and from beginning to end, her history is but the power of a single fact. The actual Church is a process, not only covering a large field in space, but reaching over a long tract in time; and to be understood at all, it must be apprehended and viewed in this way. . . .

The actual Church, as now described, must be expected, of course, to fall short, in every stage of its historical development, of the perfection which it is destined to reach in the end. This lies in its very conception. The Church is a new creation for the world, complete from the first in Christ, but requiring a process of historical evolution, according to the law of all life, to actualize itself with final, universal triumph in the world as a whole. This process supposes imperfection and defect at every point of its progress, on to the last; for when all defect shall have been surmounted, it will itself, of course, have come to an end. It implies opposition, contradiction, and conflict, disturbing forces, foreign elements, corruptions, distortions, aberrations. The historical Church is always the true Church, but never a pure or perfect Church. It is by no means free either from error or sin. The Church of Rome, in claiming to be infallible, claims to be in fact the Ideal Church itself, as though this had already actualized itself in full in her communion. But this claim is contradicted by palpable and acknowledged signs of imperfection under other forms. It belongs to the Idea of the Church to be holy as well as infallible. To be consistent, then, the Church of Rome should lay claim to sinless perfection, or absolute impeccability, along with her pretension to infallibility. But this she does not venture to do. She acknowledges that she is not free from sin. We will not allow, therefore, that she is free from error. There is no reason to say the actual Church may not err, any more than there is to say that she may not fall into sin. On the contrary, the very nature of the process in which she is involved, and in which her character at present consists, might lead us to presume confidently that she would be liable to error and sin both, more or less, in all ages.

In the same way, we cannot allow that a visible unity of organization and worship is indispensable to the truth of the Church, in the view now under consideration. That all this is required by the Idea of the Church, and that the Church can never become complete without it, has been already admitted. It belongs to the nature of the Church to be one and

233

universal, catholic as well as holy, in an outward visible way no less than in its unseen constitution. Our whole sect system (this testimony we may never cease to reiterate) is something wrong, an abomination in the temple of God that must pass away before it can be clean and fit for the coming of the Lord. But still it does not follow at once from all this that the actual Church can exist only in the form of such visible unity as is contended for by Romanists and high-church Episcopalians. Allow our divisions to be a great and sore defect, they are still not necessarily such a defect as is inconsistent with the conception of the actual Church, whose very nature it is to be involved in a perpetual communication, more or less intimate, with what is wrong, and which always includes in its constitution much that is to be expelled from it in the end. The unchurching dogma of the high-toned Episcopalian falls here into the same difficulty with the doctrine of infallibility as asserted by the Church of Rome. It transfers at once to the state of the actual Church what is true only of the Ideal Church, and identifies this last at the same time with its own particular communion. But to be consistent here, again, the claim should extend to *all* the attributes of the Ideal Church. If division be contrary to the Idea of the Church, the same thing is true also of all error and sin. If separation from a particular communion, the Episcopal Church for instance, be supposed to work a forfeiture of all interest in God's covenant, because visible unity is required by the Idea of the Church, it is hard to see why the want of any other attribute of a perfect Church should not do the same thing. Let us beware of this confusion of things which we are bound to keep separate and distinct. The actual Church is still very far from being a perfect Church. It is not, therefore, necessarily free from either heresy or schism. Its visible unity may be greatly marred by its distribution, more or less, into denominations and sects. This we are bound to lament, but we have no right to resort to the violence of unchurching all beyond some favorite communion in order to remedy the evil. As it now stands, especially, the Church with its divine life powers is not confined to any one organization exclusively, as Romanists and Tractarians believe, but extends its presence, with different measures of power, over different and divided communions. It has no sympathy, indeed, with the spirit of division and sect; but still it allows the evil to be comprehended for a time in the evolution of its own life (just as the abuses of the papacy were comprehended in it before the Reformation), in order that all may be the more gloriously surmounted in the end.

With all their difference, however, the actual Church and the Ideal

234

Church, it must always be borne in mind, are in the end the same. The Ideal Church, as before said, is no abstraction but a living divine constitution, which includes in itself from the beginning all that it is destined to become by development in the end, and whose very nature requires it to show itself real in this way. The history of the actual Church, then, is but the presence and life of the Ideal Church itself, struggling through a process of centuries to come to its last, full manifestation. In the end the process will be complete, and then, though not sooner, the actual will be found commensurate in all respects with the Ideal. Meanwhile, however, they are bound, in the process itself, inseparably together. The Ideal Church can have no reality save under the form of the historical, and the actual or historical Church can have no truth except through the presence of the Ideal. The historical Church may be involved in error or sunk in corruption, filled with heterogeneous elements, overloaded with all forms of perversion and abuse. But still it is always the bearer of the Ideal Church, and the form under which it has its manifestation in the world. However defective and abnormal, in the midst of all excrescences and disproportions it represents always notwithstanding the life and power of the Ideal Church, in the stage of development it has reached at the time. We may not look for this last in any other connection; we may not think of it as something independent wholly of the outward organization and action which constitute the presence of the other. The two can never fall asunder, nor is their conjunction accidental simply and external. The relation that joins them is inward and vital, like that which holds between soul and body. The invisible Church, as it is sometimes called, dwells in the visible, as its only possible home among men; and although it includes in itself much more than is actually revealed in this last at any given period, it is still here and nowhere else that all such hidden power is deposited, always ripening for actual life, and ready to show itself in its own time. The actual is the body of the Ideal in *growth,* the process, constantly changing and flowing, by which it is externalized and so made complete, as the great world-fact of redemption.

. . .

## THE MYSTICAL PRESENCE[2]

SECTION II. Systems Contrasted

1. In the old Reformed view, the communion of the believer with Christ in the Supper is taken to be *specific* in its nature, and *different* from all that has place in the common exercises of worship. The sacra-

ment—not the elements, of course, separately considered, but the ordinance as the union of element and Word—is held to be such an exhibition of saving grace as is presented to the faith of the Church under no other form. It is not simply the Word brought to mind in its ordinary force. The outward is not merely the occasion by which the inward, in the case, is made present to the soul as a separate existence; but inward and outward, by the energy of the Spirit, are made to flow together in the way of a common life, and come thus to exert a peculiar and altogether extraordinary power, in this form, to the benefit of the believer. "There is a peculiar communion with Christ," says Dr. Owen, "which we have in no other ordinance"; and this, he adds, has been the faith of the whole Church in all ages. "A way of receiving Christ by eating and drinking, something peculiar that is not in prayer, that is not in the hearing of the Word, nor in any other part of divine worship whatsoever; a peculiar participation of Christ, a peculiar acting of faith towards Christ." In the modern Puritan view, on the contrary, this specific peculiar virtue of the sacraments is not recognized. Christ is present, we are told by Dr. Dick, in all ordinances, "and he is present in the same manner in them all, namely, by his Spirit, who renders them effectual means of salvation." So with Dr. Dwight the entire force of the institution is made to consist in the occasion it affords for the affections and exercises of common religious worship. The idea of a peculiar sacramental power, belonging to this form of worship as such, seems to have no place at all in his system.

2. In the old Reformed view the sacramental transaction is a *mystery,* nay, in some sense an actual *miracle.* The Spirit works here in a way that transcends not only the human understanding, but the ordinary course of the world also in every other view. There is a form of action in the sacraments which now belongs, indeed, to the regular order of the life that is comprehended in the Church, but which as thus established still involves a character that may be denominated *supernatural,* as compared with the ordinary constitution not only of nature, but even of the Christian life itself. "Not without reason," says Calvin, "is the communication which makes us flesh of Christ's flesh and bone of his bones, denominated by Paul *a great mystery.* In the sacred Supper, therefore, we acknowledge it a *miracle,* transcending both nature and our own understanding, that Christ's life is made common to us with himself and his flesh given to us as aliment." "This *mystery* of our coalition with Christ," says the Gallic Confession, "is so sublime that it transcends all our senses and also the whole course of nature." "The mode is such,"

236

according to the Belgic Confession, "as to surpass the apprehension of our mind, and cannot be understood by any." "The *mysteriousness,*" we are told by Dr. Owen, "is beyond expression, the *mysterious* reception of Christ in this peculiar way of exhibition."

Contrast with this now the style in which the ordinance is represented, from the proper Puritan standpoint, in the extracts already quoted. We find it spoken of, it is true, with great respect, as full of interest, significance, and power. But it is no mystery, much less a miracle—as little so, it would seem, in the view of Dr. Dwight, as a common Fourth of July celebration. The ends contemplated in the one case are religious, in the other patriotic, but the institutions as related to these ends are in all material respects of one and the same order. The ends proposed in the Supper [are] "the enlargement and rectification of our *views* . . . the purification of our *affections* . . . the amendment of our *lives.* The means . . . are . . . efficacious and desirable, at the same time simple, *intelligible to the humblest capacity,* in no respect burdensome, lying within the reach of all men, incapable of being misconstrued without violence, and therefore not easily susceptible of *mystical* or superstitious perversion. In their own proper, undisguised nature, they appeal powerfully to the *senses,* the *imagination,* and the *heart,* and at the same time enlighten in the happiest manner, the *understanding.*" All this is said to show "the *wisdom* of this institution." "There seems to have been a disposition in that age," says Dr. Dick, with reference to the sixteenth century, "to believe that there was a presence of Christ in the Eucharist *different* from his presence in the other ordinances of the gospel; an undefined something, which corresponded to the strong language used at the institution of the Supper: *This is my body—this is my blood.* Acknowledging it to be figurative, many still thought that a *mystery* was couched under it." Dr. Dick himself, of course, finds no mystery in the case. Calvin's doctrine accordingly is rejected as *incomprehensible,* not understood by himself (as the great theologian indeed humbly admits), and beyond the understanding also of his readers. "Plain, literal language is best, especially on spiritual subjects, and should have been employed by Protestant churches with the utmost care, as the figurative terms of Scripture have been so grossly mistaken." To this we may add that the very reason why *such* plain, simple language as might have suited Dr. Dick has *not* been employed by the Protestant churches in their symbolical books, is to be found in the fact that these Protestant churches believed and intended to assert the presence of a mystery in the sacrament, for the idea of which no place is allowed in *his* creed, and that could not be properly represented therefore by any language which this creed might supply.

3. The old Reformed doctrine includes always the idea of an *objective force* in the sacraments. The sacramental union between the sign and the thing signified is real, and holds in virtue of the constitution of the ordinance itself, not in the faith simply or inward frame of the communicant. Without faith, indeed, this force which belongs to the sacrament cannot avail to the benefit of the communicant; faith forms the indispensable condition, by whose presence only the potential in this case can become actual, the life that is present be brought to take effect in the interior man. But the condition here, as in all other cases, is something different from the thing itself, for which it makes room. The grace of the sacrament comes from God; but it comes as such under the sacrament as its true and proper form, not inhering in the elements, indeed, outwardly considered, but still mysteriously lodged, by the power of the Holy Ghost, in the sacramental transaction as a whole. The grace is truly present, according to Calvin, even where it is excluded from the soul by unbelief, as much so as the fertilizing qualities of the rain that falls fruitless on the barren rock. Unbelief may make it of no effect, but the intrinsic virtue of the sacrament itself still remains the same. The bread and wine are the sure pledge still of the presence of what they represent, and "a true exhibition of it on the part of God." . . . The sacrament, in this view, not only signifies, but *seals* to believers, the grace it carries in its constitution. It is not simply a pledge that the blessings it represents are sure to them, in a general way, apart from this particular engagement itself; as when a man by some outward stipulation binds himself to fulfill the terms of a contract in another place and at another time. The sacramental transaction certifies and makes good the grace it represents, as actually communicated at the time. So it is said to *exhibit* also the thing signified. The thing is *there,* not the name of the thing only, and not its sign or shadow, but the actual substance itself. "The sacrament is no picture," says Calvin, "but the true, veritable pledge of our union with Christ." To say that the body of Christ is adumbrated by the symbol of bread, only as a dead statue is made to represent Hercules or Mercury, he pronounces profane. The signs, Owen tells us, "*exhibit* that which they do not contain. . . ." It is no "empty, painted feast. . . . Here is something really exhibited by Jesus Christ unto us, to receive, besides the outward pledges of bread and wine."

How different from all this, again, the light in which the subject is presented in our modern Puritan theology. Here, too, the sacraments are indeed said to seal, and also to exhibit, the grace they represent. But plainly the old, proper sense of these terms in the case is changed. The *seal* ratifies simply a covenant in virtue of which certain blessings are made sure to the believer, on certain conditions, under a wholly different form. Two parties in the transaction, Christ and his people, stipulate to be faithful to each other in fulfilling the engagements of a mutual contract, and in doing so, they both affix their seal to the sacramental bond. Such is the view presented very distinctly by Edwards, Hopkins, and Bellamy. The contract of salvation according to this last, is in the Lord's Supper, "externally and visibly sealed, ratified, and confirmed, on both sides, with as much formality as any 'written instrument' is mutually sealed by the parties in any covenant among men. And now if both parties are sincere in the covenant thus sealed, and if both abide by and act according to it, the communicant will be saved." So the sacrament is allowed to be exhibitional, not, however, of any actual present substance, as the old doctrine always held, but only in the way of figure, shadow, or sign. A picture or statue may be said to exhibit their original to the same extent. The sacramental elements are Christ's *proxy.* "Or the matter may be more fitly represented by *this* similitude: it is as if a prince should send an ambassador to a woman in a foreign land, proposing marriage, and by his ambassador should send her his *picture,* &c." With Dr. Dwight the sacrament is reduced fully to the character of a mere occasion by which religious affections are excited and supported in the breast of the worshipper. He seems to have no idea at all of an objective force belonging to the institution in its own nature. All is subjective and subjective only. All turns on the adaptation of the rite to instruct and affect. He measures its wisdom and power wholly by this standard. It is admirably *contrived* to work upon "the senses, the imagination, and the heart," as well as to "enlighten the understanding." Its whole force, when all is done, is the amount simply of the good thoughts, good feelings, and good purposes, that are brought to it, and made to go along with it, on the part of the worshippers themselves.

4. According to the old Reformed doctrine the invisible grace of the sacrament includes a real participation in his *person.* That which is made present to the believer is the very life of Christ himself in its true power and substance. The doctrine proceeds on the assumption that the Christian salvation stands in an actual union between Christ and his people, mystical but in the highest sense real, in virtue of which they are as closely joined to him as the limbs are to the head in the natural body. They are in him, and he is in them, not figuratively but truly, in the way

of a growing process that will become complete finally in the resurrection. The power of this fact is mysteriously concentrated in the Holy Supper. Here Christ communicates *himself* to his Church, not simply a right to the grace that resides in his person, or an interest by outward grant in the benefits of his life and death, but his person itself, as the ground and fountain from which all these other blessings may be expected to flow. This idea is exhibited under all forms in which it could well be presented, and in terms the most clear and explicit. Christ first, and *then* his benefits. Calvin will hear of no other order but this. The same view runs through all the Calvinistic symbols. Not a title to Christ *in* his benefits, the efficacy of his atonement, the work of his Spirit, but a true property in his life itself, out of which only that other title can legitimately spring. "We are quickened by a real participation of him, which he designates by the terms *eating* and *drinking* that no person might suppose the life which we receive from him to consist in simple knowledge." We communicate with Christ's *substance*. . . .

As the modern Puritan theory eviscerates the institution of all objective force, under any view, it must, of course, still more decidedly refuse to admit the idea of any such virtue belonging to it as that now mentioned. The union of the believer with Christ it makes to be moral only, or at least a figurative incorporation with his Spirit! The sacred Supper forms an occasion by which the graces of the pious communicant are called into favorable exercise, and his faith in particular is assisted in apprehending and appropriating the precious contents of the Christian salvation, as wrought out by the Redeemer's life and death! He participates in this way in the fruits of Christ's love, the benefits of his mediatorial work, his imputed righteousness, his heavenly intercession, the influences of his Spirit, &c., but in the substantial life of Christ himself he has no part whatever. "A mutual solemn profession of the two parties transacting the covenant of grace, and visibly united in that covenant."—Edwards. So also Hopkins and Bellamy. "Sensible impressions are much more powerful than those which are made on the understanding, &c."—Dwight. "The ends proposed in the institution of the Lord's Supper are, the enlargement and rectification of our views concerning the noblest of all subjects, the purification of our affections and the amendment of our lives." "Stript of all metaphorical terms, the action must mean that in the believing and grateful commemoration of his death, we enjoy the blessings which were purchased by it, in the same manner in which we enjoy them when we exercise faith in hearing the gospel."—Dick. "No man who admits that the bread and wine are only

signs and figures can consistently suppose the words, 1 Corinthians
10:16, to have any other meaning than that we have communion with
Christ in the fruits of his sufferings and death; or that receiving the symbols we receive by faith the benefits procured by the pains of his body
and the effusion of his blood." Christ's "*doctrine* is truly that which will
give life to the soul."—Barnes. "To dwell or abide in him, is to remain
in the belief of his doctrine and in the participation of all the benefits of
his death." "The whole design of the sacramental bread is by a striking
emblem to call to *remembrance,* in a vivid manner, the dying sufferings
of our Lord."

5. In the old Reformed view of the Lord's Supper, the communion of
the believer in the true person of Christ, in the form now stated, is supposed to hold with him especially as the Word made flesh. His humanity forms the medium of his union with the Church. The life of which he
is the fountain flows forth from him only as he is the Son of Man. To
have part in it at all, we must have part in it as a real human life; we
must eat his flesh and drink his blood, take into us the substance of what
he was as man, so as to become flesh of his flesh and bone of his bones.
"The very flesh in which he dwells is made to be vivific for us, that we
may be nourished by it to immortality."—Calvin. "This sacred communication of his flesh and blood, in which Christ transfuses his life into
us, just as if he penetrated our bones and marrow, he testifies and seals
also in the Holy Supper." "I do not teach that Christ dwells in us simply
by his Spirit, but that he so raises us to himself as to transfuse into us
the vivific vigor of his flesh." "The very substance itself of the Son of
Man."—Beza and Farel. "That same substance which he took in the
womb of the Virgin, and which he carried up into heaven."—Beza and
Peter Martyr. "As the eternal deity has imparted life and immortality to
the flesh of Jesus Christ, so likewise his flesh and blood, when eaten and
drunk by us, confer upon us the same prerogatives."—Old Scotch Confession. "That which is eaten is the very, natural body of Christ, and
what is drunk is his true blood."—Belgic Confession. "Flesh of his flesh
and bone of his bone. . . . We are as *really* partakers of his true body and
blood . . . as we receive these holy Signs."—Heidelberg Catechism. "We
are . . . in such sort coupled, knit, and incorporated into his true, essential human body, by his Spirit dwelling both in him and us, that we are
flesh of his flesh and bone of his bones."—Ursinus. "They that worthily
communicate in the sacrament of the Lord's Supper, do therein feed
upon the body and blood of Christ . . . truly and really."—Westminster
Catechism.

All this the modern Puritan view utterly repudiates as semi-popish mysticism. It will allow no real participation of Christ's person in the Lord's Supper, under any form, but least of all under the form of his humanity. Such communion as it is willing to admit, it limits to the presence of Christ in his divine nature, or to the energy he puts forth by his Spirit. As for all that is said about his body and blood, it is taken to be mere figure, intended to express the value of his sufferings and death. With his body in the strict sense, his life as incarnate, formerly on earth and now in heaven, we can have no communion at all, except in the way of remembering what was endured in it for our salvation. The *flesh* in any other view profiteth nothing; it is only the Spirit that quickeneth. The language of the Calvinistic confessions on this subject is resolved into bold, violent metaphor, that comes in the end to mean almost nothing. "If he (Calvin) meant that there is some mysterious communication with his human nature, we must be permitted to say the notion was as incomprehensible to himself as it is to his readers."—Dick. "There is an absurdity in the notion that there is any communion with the body and blood of Christ, considered in themselves." . . . "This broken bread shows the manner in which my body will be broken; or this will serve to call my dying sufferings to your *remembrance.*"—Barnes.

Let this suffice in the way of comparison. The two theories, it is clear, are different throughout. Nor is the difference such as may be considered of small account. It is not simply formal or accidental. The modern Puritan view evidently involves a material falling away, not merely from the form of the old Calvinistic doctrine, but from its inward life and force. It makes a great difference, surely, whether the union of the believer with Christ be regarded as the power of one and the same life, or as holding only in a correspondence of thought and feeling; whether the Lord's Supper be a sign and seal only of God's grace in general, or the pledge also of a special invisible grace present in the transaction itself; and whether we are united by means of it to the person of Christ, or only to his merits; and whether, finally, we communicate in the ordinance with the whole Christ, in a real way, or only with his divinity. Such, however, is the difference that stares us in the face, from the comparison now made. All must see and feel that it exists, and that it is serious. . . .

### Notes

1. In *The Mercersburg Theology,* ed. James Hastings Nichols (New York: Oxford University Press, 1966; original sermon delivered in 1846, published in 1847), pp. 57-65.
2. In ibid. (original essay published in 1846), pp. 207-16.

# Horace Bushnell

*B*ushnell (1802–1876), schooled in New Haven thought by
*Nathaniel Taylor and company, was led from the rational supernatural-*
*ist model of revelation and a Lockean–Common-Sense conception of*
*religious language to currents of post-Kantian, Romantic thinking in*
*large part by his reading of Samuel Taylor Coleridge's* Aids to Reflections. *During his career-long pastorate at North Church (Congregation-*
*alist) in Hartford, Connecticut, he first gained public "notoriety" by his*
*defense of Christian nurture over against revivalist religion: Christian*
*commitment and character arise from spiritual influences conveyed*
*gradually and invisibly by sharing in the life, education, and ordinary*
*means of grace within the church community and require no conversion*
*experience by an unmediated, instantaneous stroke of the Spirit on the*
*soul.*

*His attempts to reconcile theological differences between Unitarians*
*and Trinitarians and to promote "Christian comprehensiveness," which*
*encompassed nature and the supernatural as two parts of one interre-*
*lated whole by taking the language of scripture and theology as*
*metaphoric and symbolic expressions of truths that transcend the literal,*
*systematic grasp, earned him acclaim and controversy. The selection*
*here, a digest of his sermon "The Gospel a Gift to the Imagination," is*
*neither the most nor the least "scholarly" of his many writings. It is,*
*however, an expansive, populist, creative, and polished presentation of*
*the core elements of his theology and his approach to theological issues.*

## OUR GOSPEL A GIFT TO THE IMAGINATION[1]

. . .

I shall endeavor to exhibit, as far as I can in the restricted limits of
this article, the fact that our Christian Gospel is a Gift more especially
to the Human Imagination. It offers itself first of all and principally to
the interpretative imaginings and discernings of faith, never, save in that

manner, to the constructive processes of logic and speculative opinion. It is, in one sense, pictorial; its every line or lineament is traced in some image or metaphor, and by no possible ingenuity can it be gotten away from metaphor; for as certainly as one metaphoric image is escaped by a definition, another will be taken up, and must be, to fill its place in the definition itself. Mathematical language is a scheme of exact notation. All words that are names of mere physical acts and objects are literal, and even animals can, so far, learn their own names and the meaning of many acts done or commanded. But no animal ever understood a metaphor: that belongs to intelligence, and to man as a creature of intelligence; being a power to see, in all images, the faces of truth, and take their sense, or read [intus lego] their meaning, when thrown up in language before the imagination.

Every word is a figure called in to serve a metaphoric use, in virtue of the fact that it has a physical base naturally significant of the spiritual truth or meaning it is used metaphorically to express. Physical bases are the timber, in this manner, of all mental language, and are generally traced in the etymologies of the dictionaries; though sometimes they are lost and cannot be traced. And it is not merely the verbs, nouns, adjectives, that carry these metaphoric uses, but their very grammar of relationship, as they are found originally in space themselves, is also framed in terms of space by the little words called prepositions, which show their spatial images in their faces, *up, down, by, through, to, under, from, beyond* and the like. The whole web of speech is curiously woven metaphor, and we are able to talk out our thoughts in it,—never one of them visible,—by throwing out metaphoric images in metaphoric grammar so as to give them expression.

. . .

But we must look into language itself and see how the great revelation of God is coming and to come. First of all, it is impossible, as we have seen already, that any terms of language for mental notions, things of the spirit, unseen worlds, beings invisible, should ever exist, save as there are physical images found to serve as metaphoric bases of the necessary words; for we cannot show them to the eye and then name them, as we do acts or objects visible; we can only hint them by figures, or objects metaphorically significant of them. And so we see beforehand, that all the truths of religion are going to be given to men by images; so that all God's truth will come as to the imagination. Hence the necessity of the old physical religion to prepare draperies and figures for the new. Hence also, when we come to the new, we are constantly met, we per-

244

haps know not why or how, by images taken from the old, in a way that seems half fanciful and curiously mystical. Adam is the figure of him that was to come, the second Adam, because he, Christ, was to be the head, correspondently, of a spiritual generation. Christ is David, Melchizedek, high priest, the spiritual Rock, a prophet like unto Moses and I know not what beside. John the Baptist is Elias that was to come. In the same manner, heaven is a paradise or garden, or a new Jerusalem, or a state of glorious city life in God; the new society of grace is to be the kingdom of God, or the kingdom of heaven; and Christ himself is Messiah, that is, king. All the past is taken up as metaphor for all the future. All these things, we are to say, "happened unto them for ensamples," that is, types for the expression of our higher truth.

. . .

We shall get further insight into this matter by just considering the state of mind a prophet is in when he writes. He is lifted by his inspiration into a state of high beholding, as regards some matter which is to be the particular subject of his testimony; and the divine perceptiveness thus quickened in him,—so far the particular matter he sees,—will be the specially God-given import of his message. Then he is to conceive, express, set forth in words for himself what is in his beholding. But he cannot testify any thing unknown, we see at once, save by images taken from the known. Suppose him to be set in some high *pose* of seership that really relates, if he could say it, to our new western world and the new day some time here to be seen. He cannot say "America," for that is a name not known as Grecia was. If he says, "beyond the sea," it would only mean outside the pillars of Hercules or Gibraltar Rock. He cannot seize on images in the Gulf Stream, or the Mammoth Cave, or Niagara, or the great lakes, or the forests, or the prairies, or the rivers, or the fierce, wild warriors of the woods. He has not an image distinctly American in his whole stock. What then can he say? Manifestly nothing; because he has nothing in which to say it. Possibly some of Isaiah's pictures of the "Isles waiting for God," and "the ships of Tarshish bringing sons from far, their silver and their gold with them," may have a look this way, taking old Tarshish for a figure, but we can never know. Under this same law, we have the fact of creation, as given in the first chapter of Genesis, beautifully illustrated. No human spectator saw the creation, and the only way in which it could ever be reported was by a kind of prophecy backward. Some great prophet soul, we may imagine, coasting round the work of God in a power of holy insight, or divine beholding, framed, as it were, his own divine conception of the fact as

245

progressive, drawing itself on by irregular, indefinite stages—no matter how long or short, or even how many,—and to set the stages forth, he caught up the natural time-spacing symbol of days, and made up a chapter of progressions that took a week of days before it was finished. To conceive anything more pitiful than the grubbing literalism that cannot think of days going thus into metaphor because they are in the Almanac would, I think, be difficult. Was there ever a case for metaphor more easily discernible beforehand?

We perceive in these illustrations how every revelator and teacher of things spiritual or things future, gets and must get his power to express the unknown by drawing images and figures from the known. As he must portray the new world by some old image of a Tarshish in the sea, or by some other like symbol, if he does at all, or the creation by the spacing figure of days, or heaven by the image of a paradise, or a great city Jerusalem, so it must be with everything.

Thus if God is to be himself revealed, he has already thrown out symbols for it, filling the creation full of them, and these will all be played into metaphor. The day will be his image, the sea, the great rock's shadow, the earthquake, the dew, the fatherhood care of the child, and the raven and the feeble folk of the conies,—all that the creation is and contains, in all depths and heights and latitudes and longitudes of space,—everything expresses God by some image that is fit, as far as it goes. "Day unto day uttereth speech, and night unto night showeth knowledge." Metaphor on metaphor crowds the earth and the skies, bearing each a face that envisages the Eternal Mind, whose word or wording forth it is to be. Again he takes a particular people into covenant specially with himself, just in order to make their public history the Providential metaphor, so to speak, of his rulership and redeeming teachership, leading them on and about by his discipline, and raising light and shade as between them and the world-kingdoms of the false gods about them, to set himself in relief as the true Lord of all. And then, following still the same law of expression by outward fact and image, he crowns the revelation process by the incarnate life and life-story of his Son, erecting on earth a supernatural kingdom to govern the world in the interest of his supernatural redemption. And if we do not take the word in some light, frivolous, merely rhetorician way, we can say nothing of Christ so comprehensively adequate as to call him the metaphor of God; God's last metaphor! And when we have gotten all the metaphoric meanings of his life and death, all that is expressed and bodied in his person of God's saving help and new-creating, sin-forgiving, reconciling love, the sooner we dismiss all speculations on the literalities of his incarnate miracles, his derivation, the composition of his person, his suffering,—plainly transcendent as regards our possible understanding,—the wiser shall we be in our discipleship. We shall have him as the express image of God's person. We shall have "the light of the knowledge of the glory of God, in the face of Jesus Christ." Beholding in him as in a glass the glory of the Lord, we shall be changed into the same image. The metaphoric contents are ours, and beyond that nothing is given.

Going on then to matters of spiritual use and experience in what we call the doctrine of his gospel, we have these given also to the imagination in terms of metaphor. As far back as the days of Abraham and Moses, words and images for this kind of use were very scantily provided. Even prayer was best described as a wrestling match. The prophets found images more nearly sufficient. And when Christ came, great images were evoked that never had been used before. He was called a door to be entered, a bread from heaven to be fed upon, a water of life to quench the thirst, life, way, shepherd, healer, teacher, master, king, and rock. And when the very point of a new life begun is to be explained or expounded, he draws on the well-known fact of proselyte baptism and calls it regeneration: "Art thou a master in Israel and knowest not these things?" Have you not seen the Gentile proselyte, before unclean, washed by a baptism and so regenerated, born over, naturalized, as we say, in Israel? So the unclean soul of sin, born of water and the Spirit, is entered, as a spiritually new man, into the kingdom of God. The great experience wrought is imaged thus, how beautifully and comprehensively, as a change from the unclean to the clean; and so the soul that was alien from God is inducted into citizenship in God's everlasting kingdom. No finest words of analysis and psychologic statement could describe the great mystery of the Spirit half as effectively. . . .

The same again was true of the great reconciliation or atonement, in Christ's life and death. Plainly there was here no lamb, no fire, no altar, no literal sacrifice. There was a blood of murder, but no rite in blood, no sprinkling, no kind of lustral ceremony. And yet all these things are here as in metaphor, and are meant to be. One great object of the old ritual was to prepare these images and get them ready as a higher language for the supernatural truth. The people of the law were put in training under these patterns of the heavenly things, till the very mind of their nation should be stocked with images and metaphors thence derived for the heavenly things themselves. Who could ever have conceived the ministry and death of Jesus in these words of atonement, sacrifice, and cleansing, whose mind had not first been Judaized in the stock images of its thinking? Suppose, for example, that some gifted Greek, having a soul configured to Plato's methods and ideas, had been with Christ, as Peter was, all through his life, and then, after his death, had written his epistle to expound him and his religion to the world. What could he have said of him more adequate than to set him forth as a beautiful and wise character doing wonders by his power; a friend of the poor, a healer of the sick, patient of contradiction, submissive to enemies, meek, true, the ever good, the perfect fair? That he has done any thing which can be called his sacrifice, any thing to recompose the breach of sin or to reconcile the world to God, will not occur to him, and he has no words to speak of any such thing. Not one matter most distinctively prominent in Christ's work, as expounded by his apostles, filling out in metaphoric glory all the terms of the altar, could have been given, or even thought by him. All the better, many will now say; we shall gladly be rid of all such altar figures; for it is too late in the day to be making Hebrews of us now. But suppose it should happen to be true that the all-wise God made Hebrews partly for this very thing, to bring figures into speech that Greeks and Saxons had not; that so he might give to the world the perfectly transcendent, supernatural matter of a grace that reaches high enough to cover and compose the relations of men to his government, a grace of reconciliation. Call the words "old clothes" then of the Hebrews, putting what contempt we may upon them, still they are such types and metaphors of God's mercy as he has been able to prepare, and Christ is in them as in "glorious apparel!" Why to say: "Behold the Lamb of God, that taketh away the sin of the world," signifies, in the heart's uses, more than whole volumes of palaver in any possible words of natural language. No living disciple, having once gotten the sense of these types of the altar, will ever try to get his gospel out of them and preach it in the common terms of language. Quite as certainly will he never try, having once gotten their meaning, to hold them literally,—Christ made literally sin for us, a literal Lamb, literal sacrifice, bleeding literally for the uses of his blood. But he will want them as the dear interpreters and equivalents of God's mercy in the cross, putting himself before them to read and read again, and drink and drink again their full divine meanings into his soul. Beholding more truths in their faces than all the contrived theories and speculated propositions of schools, he will stay fast by them, or in them, wanting never to get clear of them, or away from the dear and still more dear impression of their power.

So far on our way in discovering the close relationship of God's revelations and the inlet function of imagination to which they are given, I cannot do more, in this part of the subject, than simply to generalize the argument by just calling attention to the fact that so great a part of our Bible is made up of compositions that are essentially poetic,—nearly all of it, except the parts rigidly historic or didactic, and even these have their prose largely sprinkled with poetry. History itself, in fact, is but a kind of figure, having its greatest value, not in what it is, but in what it signifies. Besides, the scripture books most nearly theologic are handling truths every moment, as we see at a glance, by their images. How didactic are the parables, and yet they are only metaphors drawn out! In the same way the disciples are God's living epistles, temples of the Holy Ghost, cities on hills, working as servants, running as in races, beholding as in glasses,—every single point of instruction comes out in some metaphor, so that we may safely challenge the specification of one that does not. . . . So strikingly is it shown us, everywhere on the face of scripture, that it is a gift in metaphor to the world's imagination.

Only God forbid that, when we draw ourselves out on this conclusion, we be understood to mean by the imagination what the rhetoricians teach, in the girlish definitions of their criticism. They describe it as a kind of ornamental, mind's-milliner faculty, that excels in the tricking out of subjects in high-wrought metaphoric draperies, and such they call "imaginative writing." As I am speaking here, the imagination has nothing to do with ornament. It is that which dawns in beauty like the day because the day is in it; that power in human bosoms which reads the types of the creation, beholding the stamps of God's meanings in their faces; the power that distinguishes truths in their images, and seizes hold of images for the expression of truths. So that a free, great soul, when it is charged with thoughts so high, and fresh beholdings in such vigor of life, that it cannot find how to express itself otherwise, does it by images and metaphors in flame that somehow body the meaning to imaginative apprehension.

Holding now this view of truth as presenting itself always by images metaphorically significant, never by any other possible means or media, it is very clear that all our modes of use and processes of interpretation must be powerfully affected by such a discovery.

First of all it must follow, as a principal consequence, that truth is to be gotten by a right beholding of the forms or images by which it is expressed. Ingenuity will miss it by overdoing; mere industry will do scarcely more than muddle it; only candor, a graciously open, clean candor will find it. We can take the sense of its images, only by offering a perfectly receptive imagination to them, a plate to fall upon that is flavored by no partisanship, corrugated by no bigotry, blotched by no prejudice or passion, warped by no self-will. There is nothing we cannot make out of them, by a very little abuse, or perversity. They are innocent people who can never vindicate themselves when wronged, further than to simply stand and wait for a more ingenuous beholding. And it is to be a very great part of our honor and advantage in the truth, that we have it by the clean docility and noble reverence that make us capable of it. We shall not be afraid of worshiping its images; for they are not graven images, but faces that express the truth because they are faces of God. We want, in fact, as a first condition, a mind so given to truth that our love and reverence shall open all our sympathies to it and quite indispose us to any violent practice on its terms.

All mere logically constructive practice on them, twisting meanings into them, or out of them, that are only deducible from their forms and are no part of their real significance, must be jealously restrained. Nicodemus was falling straightway into this kind of mischief, when the words "born again" put him on asking, whether a man can be born of his mother a second time? It was in the form of the words, but how far off from their meaning! So, when it is declared that God is a rock and that God is a river, what follows, since things that are equal to the same things are, in strict logic, equal to one another, but that a rock is a river? Meantime God was not declared to be either rock or river, except in a very partial, metaphoric way. . . . Nothing is to be gotten ever, by spinning conclusions out of the mere forms or images of truth, but mischief and delusion. And the record of religion is full of just this kind of delusion. . . .

But we must have a theology, some will say; how can religion or religious truth get body, or any firm hold of the world, without a theology? And what is theology? It is very commonly supposed to be a speculated system of doctrine, drawn out in propositions that are clear of all metaphor and are stated in terms that have finally obtained a literal and exact sense. But no such system is possible, for the very plain reason that we have no such terms. We have a great many words that have lost their roots or have come to be so far staled by use that the figures in their bases do not obtrude themselves on our notice. But if we suppose, as we very commonly do in all the logical uses of speculation, that they have become exact coins, or algebraic notations for the ideas represented by them, we are in a great mistake. When they are framed into propositions there is always some element of figure in the other words conjoined, or in the grammar of their prepositions, which makes a figure of the sentences constructed. . . .

Some years ago one of our most brilliant, most esteemed teachers of theology published a discourse on "The Theology of the Intellect and the Feeling," meaning, it will be seen, by the Feeling, that which feels, or takes the poetic sense of figures and images; the same that I am calling here the Imagination. But the Intellect, he conceives, comes in, after all such vague presences or presentations to the feeling, gathers up the varieties, eliminates the contrarieties, and puts down in the terms of an exact language the real Christian doctrine. Taking, for example, the manifold various terms and figures employed in the metaphoric draperies of scripture language relating to the beginning of a new life,—"repent," "believe," "make you a new heart," "be converted," "born again,"— "the intellect," he says, "educes light from the collision of these repugnant phrases, and then modifies and reconciles them into the doctrine,"—literal now, exact, full-made theology,—*that the character of our race needs an essential transformation by an interposed influence from God.*" It does not appear to be observed, that this very sentence, which affirms the great, inevitable, scientific truth of regeneration, is itself packed full of figures and images, and is, in fact, interpretable only with more difficulty and more ambiguity than any and all the figures proposed to be resolved by it. Thus, for a first metaphor, we have *"character:"* and what is character? Literally it is *mark* or *distinction.* Then naturally it is one thing, morally another, spiritually another. Is it external? Is it internal? Is it made up of acts and habits? Is it the general purpose of the man? Or is it a birth into good affections by the Spirit of God? Or is it both? There is almost nothing we conceive so variously, and unsteadily, and advance upon by so many rectifications, even to the end of life, as this matter of character. *"Needs:"* and by what kind of necessity? Is it in the sense that we have full capacity, which, in our perversity, we will not use? Or in the sense that we have no capacity? Or that we have a receptive, or a partly receptive and partly active capacity? Do we need the change before believing, or after believing, or by and through believing? *"Essential transformation."* Here we have two figures dead enough to be packed together, and which yet, if they were less dead, could hardly be joined at all. One relates to what is inmost, viz., to what is in the *essence* of a thing, and the other to what is outmost, the *form* of a thing. In what sense then essential? In what a transformation? In how many senses lighter and deeper can the words be

251

taken? *"Interposed influence:"* first a word of *pose* or position; secondly, a word of motion, or *flow*. And what is the inflow or influence, and what is it posited between? The Gospel revelation by Christ's life and death is one mode of influence; the power of the Spirit is another; the power of sacraments another; the human example of Jesus another. The influence may be summed up in truth, or it may be God's direct agency one side of truth. Could we but settle this one word *influence* alone, about all the great church controversies of eighteen centuries would be settled. *"From"*: in what sense from? Is it *by* God from without? Or *by* God within? Is it *by* God directly, or *by* God medially, as in the Gospel? Or is it only *from* God as the source in whatever manner? Now I do not mean that, knowing who the author of this general proposition is, we have so many doubts about his meaning in it, but that, bringing to it all the beliefs and misbeliefs of the world and the age, we have all these and a full thousand other questions raised by it. In one view it may be true that it "educes light;" at any rate there may be uses in a proposition thus generalized; and yet it was possible to be made, only because the words were staled in so many ambiguities. And all the terms of theology are under the same conditions. We think we are coming down, perhaps, on exact statements, because we are coming down upon words that forget their figures, and yet the propositions are all woven up in figures, and cover ambiguities only the more subtle that we do not see them.

But we must have science, some will remember; is there any hope for theologic science left? None at all, I answer most unequivocally. Human language is a gift to the imagination so essentially metaphoric, warp and woof, that it has no exact blocks of meaning to build a science of. . . . Words give up their deepest, truest meaning, only when they are read as images of the same.

But we must have definitions, it will be urged, else we cannot be sure what we mean by our words, and when we have the definitions, why can we not have science? But if we mean by definitions an exact literal measurement of ideas, no such thing is possible. In what we call our definitions, whether in theology, or moral philosophy, we only put one set of metaphors in place of another, and, if we understand ourselves, there may be a certain use in doing it, even as there is in shifting our weight upon the other leg; perhaps we make ourselves more intelligible by doing it. And yet there is a very great imposture lurking almost always in these definitions. . . . And probably another and still worse result will appear; for the generous broad natures that were going to be captivated by truth's free images, having them now defined and set in propositional statements, will, how often, be offended by their narrow theologic look and reject them utterly. Nothing makes infidels more surely than the spinning, splitting, nerveless refinements of theology. . . .

. . . And yet many cannot conceive that the gospel is a faith, only in that way to be received, and so the bond of unity. They are going still to think out a gospel, assuming that the Church has no other hope as regards this matter but in the completing of a scientific theology; which will probably be accomplished about the same time that words are substituted by algebraic notations, and poetry reduced to the methods of the calculus or the logarithmic tables. There was never a hope wider of reason. The solar system will die before either that or the hope of a complete philosophy is accomplished. No, we must go back to words, and compose our differences in them as they are, exploring them more by our faith and less by our speculative thinking. Having them as a gift to the imagination, we must stay in them as such, and feel out our agreement there in a common trust, and love, and worship.

See how it is with our two great schools or sects called Calvinism and Arminianism. The points at issue in the propositional methods of their theology are forever unreconcilable. They stand over against each other like Gerizim and Ebal. And yet they have a perfect understanding when they pray together, because they pray their faith out through their imaginative forms, and drop the word-logic forms of the Babel they before were building.

Again, we have a grand fundamental and most practical truth that we call trinity; Father, Son, and Holy Ghost, one God. These three images are God as delivered to the imagination, and the grammatic threeness in which they stand is a truth in metaphor, even as the grammatic personalities are metaphoric and not literal persons; and the God-idea, figured under these relativities, obtains, in the resulting mystery, the largest, freshest, liveliest impression possible. In what manner, at what point, the unity and plurality meet, we may never know. We only know that the unity is absolute and eternal; and the threeness, either a necessary incident of God's revelations, or of his own self-conscious activities considered as the revelation of himself to himself; in either case eternal. We also know that using the three freely as the mind's necessary instrumentations, all speculation apart, we have God as he is, and coalesce in him as in perfect unity. But we cannot rest in this, we must be wiser; so we begin to speculate and make up a theology. Have we not three persons here represented by the personal pronouns of grammar? And what are persons but self-conscious, free-will beings, such as we know them to be

253

and are in fact ourselves? Now we have gotten our three persons out of the metaphor-world into strict literality, and are landed of course in absolute tritheism; such as permits no unity at all. We have no unity even if we say we have, but only a three as absolutely plural as John, James, and Peter. Over opposite, seeing now the very evident absurdity we are in, comes out the Unitarian, using our same false method over again, so to make up another conclusion just as wide of the truth. Is not a person a person? If then God is declared to be one person, and again to be three persons in the same sense, how are we going to believe it? So rejecting the three that were three transcendently, as in metaphoric type and grammar, he falls back on the one, the Father: he alone is God, and reason is no more offended. In that one personality he is thus a person thought, a dogmatic one person, having, of course, the exact type of the human person. The disciple of the new speculation is greatly relieved and with much self-gratulation. But let him not be surprised to find, as he goes on to assert the Father, always the Father, under the type of a finite personality, that his God is gradually losing dimensions and growing smaller and smaller, even to worship itself. The three metaphoric persons were going, at once, to save God's personality and his magnitudes, by the maze and mystery created, but now they are gone, and the one finite personality left sinks everything with it to the ground; so that one, and another, and another of the great authors in this key begin, spontaneously, to make up size for their deity, by speaking of the gods, and what is due the gods. How plain is it now that, if we all could take the scripture one and three, as given to the imagination, pouring in at that free gate to get our broadest possible knowledge of God, we should neither starve in the one, nor be distracted in the three, nor worried by controversy with each other as regards either one or three.

So when we come to the person of Christ; what he is to the imagination, as the express image of God, God thus manifest in the flesh, is everything; what he is in his merely human personality, and how that personality is related to and unified with the divine nature, is nothing. All is easy when we take him for what of God is expressed in him; but when we raise our psychologic problem in his person, insisting on finding exactly what and how much is in it, and how it is compacted, we are out of our limit, and our speculation is only profane jangling.

Exactly the same thing is true in respect to the metaphors of the altar, when applied to signify Christ's saving work and sacrifice. Take them as they rise in the apostolic teachings, God's figures for the men of old, in the time then present, and for us in the time now present; then as facts of atoning, now as metaphors of the same; and they will be full of God's mean-ing, we shall know ourselves atoned once for all by their power. But if we undertake to make a science out of them, and speculate them into a ratio-nal theory, it will be no gospel that we make, but a poor dry jargon rather; a righteousness that makes nobody righteous, a justice satisfied by injus-tice, a mercy on the basis of pay, a penal deliverance that keeps on foot all the penal liabilities. All attempts to think out the cross and have it in dog-matic statement have resulted only in disagreement and distraction. And yet there is a remarkable consent of utterance, we plainly discover, when the cross is preached, as for salvation's sake, in the simple use of the scrip-ture symbols taken all as figures for the time then present.

. . .

Here then is the point on which all sects and divisions may be gravi-tating and coming into settled unity. What is wanted, above all things, for this end is not that we carefully compose our scientific theology, but that we properly observe, and are principally concerned to know God in his own appointed images and symbols. We must get our light by perusing the faces of his truth; we must behold him with reverent desire in the mir-rors that reveal him, caring more to have our insight purged than to spin deductions and frame propositions that are in the modes of science or of system. We shall of course have opinions concerning it. A considerable activity in opinions is even desirable, because it will sharpen our percep-tiveness of the symbols and draw us on, in that manner, towards a more general and perfect agreement. Only our opinions must be opinions, not laws, either to us or to anybody; perhaps they will change color some-what even by to-morrow. We must also understand that our opinions or propositional statements are just as truly in metaphor as the scripture itself, only metaphor probably which is a good deal more covert and often as much more ambiguous. We may draw as many creeds as we please, the more the better, if we duly understand that they are standards only as being in metaphor, and not in terms of exact notation. . . .

And yet there will be many who can see no possibility, taking this view of the Christian truth, of any thing solid left. We set every thing afloat, they will say; nothing definite and fixed remains to be the base-work of a firm-set, stanchly effective gospel. What is the Christian truth but a dissolving view of something to be known only by its shadows? But we are easily imposed upon here by what has no such value as we think. We commence our thinking process at some point, we analyze, we deduce, we define, we construct, and when we have gotten the given truth out of its scripture images into our own, and made an opinion or definited thing of it, we think we have touched bottom in it and feel a certain confidence of having so much now established. But the reason is, not that we have made the truth more true, but that we have entered our own self-assertion into it in making an opinion or dogma of it, and have so far given a positivity to it that is from ourselves. And yet, the real fact is exactly contrary; viz., that there is just as much less of solidity in it as there is more that is from ourselves. We take up, for example, the doctrine so-called of repentance, and we find a certain word representing it which means thinking over, changing the mind, and then we lay it down as the positive doctrine that repentance is forming a new governing purpose. That sounds very definite, quite scientific; something we have now found that is clear and determinate. But it turns out, after a few years of preaching in this strain, that the truth we thought so solid is so inadequately true after all as not to have the value we supposed. As a merely one-figure doctrine it is of the lean-kine order, and we get no sense of breadth and body in the change defined, till we bring in all the other figures, the "godly sorrow," the "carefulness," the "self-clearing," the "indignation," the "fear," the "vehement desire," the "zeal," the "revenge," conceiving all these fruits to be from God's inward cogency working thus in us to will and to do. Now we take broad hold; these are the solidities of a completely, roundly adequate conception.

We never so utterly mistake as when we attempt to build up in terms of opinion something more solid and decisively controlling, than what comes to us in the terms of the imagination; that is, by metaphor. . . . Again there is nothing, as we all are wont to feel, that is more solid than our heavenly state, and we call it, in that view, the city that hath foundations. And yet we have no formula that defines it, and no single word of description for it that is not confessedly a figure. It is a garden, a tabernacle, a bosom of Abraham, a new Jerusalem, a city of God cubically built on stones that are gems. If then, nothing is solid, as some will be ready to judge, that is representable only in terms of the imagination, our hopes are all afloat in the sky, or on the air, and our heaven is but a phantom-state which, determinately speaking, is just nowhere and nothing. And yet we do not think so. No Christian man or woman has any such misgiving. . . .

### Note

1. In *Building Eras in Religion*, Centenary Edition (New York: Charles Scribner's Sons, 1910; originally published in 1869), pp. 252-83.

# Henry B. Smith

*Though historians of theology routinely accord "earlier" theologians credit or blame for "the rise of liberalism" in America, the "mediating" thought of Smith (1815–1877) might well be considered the leading indicator of the transition from old to new Protestantism within the larger churches of "Calvinist" heritage. Schooled in New Divinity theology at Andover and Bangor, Smith was one of America's first "evangelical Protestants" to undertake graduate studies in Germany. He joined the New School (pro-revival) Presbyterians in 1850 and taught for the remainder of his career at Union Theological Seminary in New York.*

*As a translator of German works, scholarly editor and reviewer, influential teacher, ecumenist, and conciliatory church politician, he promoted a christocentric, historical-critical, and organic developmental approach to scripture and tradition without "radical" challenges to the inspiration and authority of the Bible or the theological convictions basic to Reformed Christianity. His major historical and constructive studies, formulated for his teaching, were posthumously published in the years after his death. The portions of his early essay featured here, "Faith and Philosophy," lay out the position he had come to before the Civil War and hint at others he would arrive at during the last three decades of the nineteenth century and extend thereafter.*

## THE RELATIONS OF FAITH AND PHILOSOPHY[1]

. . . By making Christ and his redemption the centre of Christian theology, we are fully persuaded that he [Schleiermacher] rendered an invaluable service to the Christian science of his native land, in the time of its greatest need.[2]

Permit me to say that on this point I am the more ready to bear my unambitious yet grateful testimony to the merits of Schleiermacher and of the theological science of that land of intellect, because in the present state of our popular criticism upon German theology and philosophy, I believe it to be an act of simple justice, due to them and to the truth. In the name of the republic of letters, in the name of all generous scholarship, in the very name of Christian charity, I dare not refrain from testifying, that the indiscriminate censure of all that is German, or that may so be called, is a sign rather of the power of prejudice than of a rational love for all truth. A criticism which describes a circumference of which one's ignorance is the generating radius can only stretch far beyond the confines of justice and of wisdom. A criticism which begins by saying that a system is absolutely unintelligible; which, secondly, asserts that this unintelligible system teaches the most frightful dogmas, definitely drawn out; and which concludes by holding it responsible for all the consequences that a perverse ingenuity can deduce from these definite dogmas of the unintelligible system; is indeed a source of unintelligent and anxious wonder to the ignorant, but it is a profounder wonder to every thoughtful mind. A criticism which includes the Christian Neander and the pantheistic Strauss in one and the same condemnation is truly deplorable. Let us at least learn to adopt the humane rules of civilized warfare, and not, like the brutal soldiery of a ruder age, involve friends and foes in one indiscriminate massacre. Germany cannot give us faith; and he who goes there to have his doubts resolved, goes into the very thick of the conflict in a fruitless search for its results; but even Germany may teach us what is the real "state of the controversy" in our age; what are the principles now at work more unconsciously among ourselves. And can we, in our inglorious intellectual ease, find it in our hearts only to condemn the men who have overcome trials and doubts to which our simple or iron faith has never been exposed; who have stood in the very front rank of the fiercest battle that Christianity has ever fought, and there contended hand to hand with its most inveterate and wary foes; and who are leading on our faith—as we trust in Christ so will we believe it! to the sublimest triumph it has ever celebrated?

When, Oh! when, will scholars and Christian men learn that orthodoxy can afford to be just, to be generous; and that in this age it cannot afford to be otherwise; since it thus loses its hold over the minds which are open to truth and foes chiefly to bigotry. When shall we learn that it is quality and not quantity which gives its value to all criticism; that to stigmatize whole classes by opprobrious epithets, by names "of uncertain meaning yet of certain disparagement," is the impulse of an unlettered zeal, which inflames the worst passions of our foes and arouses only the spurious ardor of our friends. When shall we learn the high les-

258

son, that in our present conflicts, it is not nations, or men, or even parties that are to be conquered, but only error and sin; and that the victory belongs not alone to us, but to truth, to righteousness, and to God.

We have said, that the German Christianity, by the urgency of the pressure of the unbelieving systems of the times upon it, has been driven to the position, that all Christian theology centres in the doctrine respecting Christ, as to its very citadel. This principle, we have claimed, lies at the heart of all true Christian theology and Christian experience. We add, that it is eminently adapted, when brought out in its fulness and fitness to counteract some of the extreme tendencies among ourselves, as also to present Christianity in its rightful attitude towards an unbelieving world.

No one moderately acquainted with our theological and philosophical discussions, can have failed to note the influence of one strong tendency, bringing our speculations and doctrines to concentrate upon a single point, upon man's internal state. Everything is judged by its reference to man's soul and its powers. We may call it the vast, subjective process of modern theology and philosophy. This tendency has its rights and necessity; it is perhaps a mark of Protestantism; it is more fully seen in Calvinism than in Lutheranism; it is a very distinct trait of many New England movements. And if most noticeable in those who have carried our systems to their extremes, or who have become aliens to the orthodox faith, we ought not to avoid feeling a deep interest in it, as a sign of the times; and we are bound to see how the general mind is working, whether it be centrifugal or centripetal in respect to ourselves. In this tendency, too, may be something of our strength; but here also is much of our danger.

We can only rapidly indicate some of its signs. Christianity is viewed rather as a system intended to cultivate certain states of feeling, than as a revelation to build us up in the knowledge of God and of Christ. The nature of man's affections is more fully discussed than the nature of Christ. Faith is defined, not as once by its objects, but by its internal traits; and if it be called, trust in God, the emphasis is laid on the trust rather than on God. The efficacy of prayer is sometimes restricted to the believer's heart. The whole process of regeneration has been explained without reference to divine agency. Sin is viewed chiefly as a matter of individual consciousness, and less in its connections with the race and with the Divine purposes. The atonement is regarded as a life and not as a sacrifice; it is defined by its relations to us and not by its relations to God; and many who call it a declaration of the divine justice explain no further. Justification is pardon; and pardon is known by a change in our feelings. Nor with these doctrines does the process end. The Incarnation is a vehicle for the communication of a vague spiritual life; the Trinity is resolved into a mere series of manifestations, which do not teach us anything of the real nature of the Godhead; it is like a dramatic spectacle, and when the drama has been played out, the persons retire, and leave us not a higher knowledge of God, but stronger and warmer feelings; as in a parable, the moral lesson is the great end.

Some of our philosophical tendencies are in the same line. Mental philosophy is studied, as if all philosophy were in knowing the powers of the mind; it is made the basis of theology. Self-determination is the great fact about mind and morals. Personal well-being is the great end, even when we act in view of the universal good; the sum of ethics is happiness, and this happiness in its last analysis is viewed as subjective and not as objective. Man becomes the measure of all things; not the glory of God, but the happiness of man is the chief end. God is for man, rather than man for God; and, as in the infancy of science, the sun again revolves around the earth.

Thus the grand, objective force of truth and of Christianity, and of Christian doctrines, their reality in themselves and as a revelation of God, are in danger of being merged in the inquiry after their value as a means of moving us. . . .

. . .

Now, that this subjective tendency has its rights, as well as its force, that without internal experience all else is vain, that the letter kills if the spirit be not there, no one can rationally deny. That our chief dangers lie in the extremes of this tendency, is equally undeniable. That there must be a reaction from this extreme is manifest from all history, from the very laws of the mind, from the very signs of the times.

The question for us to weigh, then, is this: how shall we both encourage and restrain this mighty current?

Some would bid us back to the rites and forms and alleged succession of a visible church; but let the dead bury their dead; let us rather arise and follow our Lord. We have outgrown the power and the necessity of the beggarly elements. . . .

Shall we insist with new tenacity upon our old formulas? But words and formulas alone have but slight force against such an in-wrought and potent tendency. And they are no effectual guards against heresy, since, as has been well observed, heresy can as readily enter, and does as often couch itself under the guise of old terms as of new. Let us rather seek to know the real sense of the formulas; let us come to have a deeper sense of the grand realities of our faith.

To come to these is our safety, our defence. To see and feel and know what Christianity really is in its inward and distinctive character; to study those central truths which lie at its foundation; here is our strength. Let us come unto Jesus. When Christ is to us more than a doctrine, and the atonement more than a plan; when the Incarnation assumes as high a place in revealed, as creation does in natural theology; when the Trinity is viewed not as a formula, but as a vital truth, underlying and interwoven with the whole Christian system; when from this foundation the whole edifice rises up majestically, grand in its proportions, sublime in its aims, filled with God in all its parts; when we feel its inherent force streaming out from its living centres; then, then are we saved from those extreme tendencies which are the most significant and alarming sign of our times; then, then are we elevated above those lesser controversies which have narrowed our minds and divided our hearts. Here also we have a real inward experience as well as an objective reality; for the best and fullest inward experience is that which centres in Christ; and the centre of the experience is then identical with the centre of the divine revelation.

Never are we so far from having any abstract ethical or metaphysical principles exercise an undue influence; never are we so far from a too fond reliance on self and never is self so full and satisfied; never are we in a better position for judging all our controversies with a righteous judgment, or nearer to the highest Christian union; never do the divine decrees shine in so mild a lustre, so benignant with grace, so solemn and severe in justice; never can we be more wisely delivered from the material attractions of an outward rite, or from the ideal seductions of a pantheistic system; never is doctrine so full of life, and life so richly expressed in doctrine; never does systematic theology so perfectly present the full substance of the Christian faith in a truly scientific form; and never are philosophy and faith so joined in hymeneal bonds, where they may "exult in over-measure," as when Christ is set forth as the living centre of all faith and of all theology, in whom the whole body is fitly joined together, compacted by that which every joint supplieth. . . .
. . .
. . . We have spoken of the characteristics, the opposition, the reconciliation, and the respective rights of Faith and Philosophy. We have, then, maintained the positions, that their full reconciliation is the true aim of systematic theology, whose office it is to present the substance of

the Christian faith in a scientific form, and in harmony with all other truth; that the central principle of the system, as of the revelation and of the believer's consciousness, is to be found in the Person of Christ; and that such a view of Christianity will encourage whatever is healthful, and restrain what is noxious in the prevailing tendencies of our times.

And now, in conclusion, we say, the Christian system, thus viewed, gives us all that philosophy aims after, and in a more perfect form; that it also gives us more than philosophy can give; and this more than it gives is what man most needs and what reason alone never could divine. And, therefore, we conclude that it is not within the scope of the human mind to conceive a system more complete, richer in all blessings.

It gives us all that philosophy aims after, and in a more perfect form. For, in a harmonious system of Christian truth, nature, with all its laws and processes, is not denied or annulled; it is only made subservient to higher, to moral ends; its course is interrupted for a nobler purpose than a fixed order could ensure; and thus a higher dignity is imparted to it than when we consider it as only a mere succession of material changes. And its very order and harmony are best explained when regarded as the product of infinite wisdom and benevolence, acting with the wisest and most benevolent intent. All ethical truth and all great moral ends, human rights and human happiness and a perfect social state, are included in the Christian system as truly as in philosophy; and a new glory is cast around them when they are made integral parts of a divine kingdom, established in justice and animated by love, which is not only to be realized here upon the earth, but is to reach forward even to eternity. Moral principles and ends thus retain all their meaning and value; but they are made more effective and permanent when contemplated as inherent in the nature and government of a wise and holy God, and as the basis and aim of an eternal kingdom. We thus have not merely a perfect social state here, but a holy state, animated with the very presence and power of God, forevermore. All that natural religion can prove or claim is retained, all that an internal revelation and inspiration ever boasted itself to have is allowed by the Christian system; but the truths of natural religion are fortified by a higher authority; and the inward revelation is illumined by a clearer light, when it is seen in the brightness of that express manifestation of God in the person of his Son, whose teachings have both chastened and elevated all our views of God and of religion.

Thus may Christianity give us all that philosophy can give, and in a more perfect form. But it also gives us more; and this more that it gives is what man most needs, and, unaided, never could attain. God is infinite, man is finite; how, then, can man come unto and know his Creator and sovereign? Man is sinful and God is holy; how can a sinful man be reconciled to a holy God? how can a sinful nature become regenerate? Man is mortal, as well as sinful; how can he obtain certainty, entire certainty, as to a future life and his eternal destiny? Here are the real and vital problems of human destiny; before them reason is abashed, and conscience can only warn, and man can only fear. The urgency, the intense interest of these questions no thinking mind can doubt; the uncertainty and timidity of human reason, when it meets them, are almost proverbial. If these questions are not answered, if these problems are not solved in Christianity they are absolutely answered nowhere. And precisely here it is that we contend that the Christian system has a permanent power, and a perfect fitness to man's condition; for you cannot name a vital problem of our moral destiny which it does not profess to solve, and to solve in a way beyond which human thought can conceive of nothing greater, and the human heart can ask for nothing more; in a way which is to the simplest heart most simple, and to the highest intellect most profound. The highest ideas and ends which reason can propound are really embraced, the deepest wants which man can know are truly satisfied, the sharpest antagonisms which the mind can propose, are declared to be reconciled, in the ideas, the means, and the ends which are contained in that revelation which centres in the Person of Jesus Christ our Lord.

For, the highest idea which man can frame is that of a union of divinity with humanity; this is the very verge of a possible conception for the human intellect; and in the Person of our Saviour we have this idea realized in its fulness, and with such a marvellous adaptation to human sympathies that they are made the very means of drawing us within the hallowed sphere of the glories of divinity. Through Jesus Christ, and Him alone, does finite man come to the Infinite I am.

. . .

## Notes

1. In *Faith and Philosophy: Discourses and Essays By Henry B. Smith, D.D., LL.D*, ed. George L. Prentiss (New York: Charles Scribner's Sons, 1886), pp. 37-46. An address before the Porter Rhetorical Society of Andover Theological Seminary, at its anniversary, Sept. 4, 1849.
2. These characteristics of Schleiermacher's system which have given to it its really beneficent influence, are only obscurely brought out in Mr. Morrell's unsound Philosophy of Religion.

# POST–CIVIL WAR AND NEW INTELLECTUAL FRONTIER

(1866–1918)

# William Newton Clarke

*A Baptist, Clarke (1841–1912) gained his early schooling amid an interdenominational mix of evangelical religion, graduating from Hamilton Theological Seminary in 1863. His career was spent as professor of systematic theology at Colgate University (1890 on). His basic textbook on systematic theology,* The Christian Doctrine of God *(first published in 1898), found widespread classroom use in seminaries. It, along with numerous other books and many lectures, made him one of the best known theologians of christocentric or evangelical liberalism, and hence a prime exemplar of that movement. Clarke's scholarship was not that of a "theologian's theologian." His arguments and idiom shift—better, slide—between traditionalism and reconstruction. In both respects his work is illustrative of turn-of-the-century churchly liberals.*

*This excerpt focuses on the developing tendency to focus on the personal and practical aspects of theology, as well as the individual and communal results of God's activity in the world. How does God work in human life? Clarke's answer is that there is a dynamic spiritual force in the lives of individuals and communities. This view of divine activity unites individualistic conversion with social ethics, a point often expressed by the phrase "one serves God by serving others." It also affirms biblical inspiration, understood as God's self-disclosure to the original authors of scripture amid their life circumstances rather than as a feature of the biblical texts themselves.*

## GOD IN HUMAN LIFE[1]

Our view of God in relations with men must not close without mention of God as he is manifested in actual human life, inner and outer, personal and collective. We must show how men have to do with him in whatever life they live.

. . .

. . . In that which God has given a man, God speaks to him as long as he possesses the gift, and appeals to him to use it worthily. The demand for right and worthy use, which comes with every occasion for using a power or principle, is an appeal of God himself. Men may not know it, but it is so, and the learning of this constitutes a great part of learning the significance of life. For example, it was God, creating him in his own likeness, that made man a rational being and made his rational nature the key to his destiny. Therefore it is right to say that all genuine and worthy suggestions of this destiny-making rationality are from God. The man may hear them without discerning the voice of God, but that is where he misunderstands himself. Every rational suggestion comes not only from our own nature, but from God who gave it.

There are as many illustrations here as there are aspects of human nature. A man is a social being also, and God made him so. A thousand relations with others press upon him; and in them all he is receiving God's perpetual suggestion that he act as a social being ought, suppressing lower motives, and raising conscience and unselfishness to the supreme place. A man is a being of aesthetic endowments: he loves beauty, he has imitative and constructive ability, he has a true creative power, within limits, to produce the beautiful. He has poetic insight. All the fine arts are outgrowths of his nature, and by them he strikes into a wonderful harmony with the order of nature about him, and acts upon the very principles whereby God made the beauty of the universe. God made him thus, and gave him his æsthetic faculties as a part of his own likeness. In these faculties God speaks to him still, appealing to him to prize the gift, to train it normally, and to use it in harmony with the highest good. A man loves pleasure, and God made him so. In all pleasure, and in all appeals of pleasure, God addresses him, urging him to enjoy the pleasure in purity and worthiness, to judge its worth correctly, to keep it in its right place, and make it servant to his higher powers. A man is an active being, with capacities for work, and a nature that cannot prosper without it. He is an aspiring being, with ambitions that reach out for better things, constitutionally discontented with his lot and seeking an upward way. He is a truth-lover, all too unworthily and yet really and forever, perpetually inquiring, longing to see things as they are, clamouring at the gates of mystery beyond which he is sure that reality may be found. He is a worshipper, with eyes turned upward to superior powers, seeking for his soul a fellowship above the human. God made him thus active, aspiring, truth-loving, adoring, and through the possession of these qualities God is constantly in communication with him. In this manner God is in communication with the inner life of every man, no matter where or in what human period, always suggesting through the power the normal use of the power, and calling upon the man to be himself. And when temptations come, urging the man to destroy the balance of his nature, to put pleasure first, to trample down his fellows, to be ambitious for himself alone, to forget God, to enthrone the brute and not the soul, with these also he may hear the voice of God, warning him not thus to defeat his own being, and bidding him rise upon this opportunity of evil to a new assertion, encouragement and strengthening of his better part.

By such means God is in the inner life of men—not of a few men specially privileged, but of all whom he has created human. A God who has placed within a race a growing soul is always in communication with that race through the presence of that soul. With the growth of the soul the moral element in life becomes larger and the religious element more full of meaning, and through conscience and religious aspiration God becomes yet more deeply and closely present in the inner life. Men have known it, too—dimly and gropingly indeed, and without knowing how much it means, and yet so well as to be aware that all their life has moral meaning, and to retain the impression that it has to do with God.

. . .

To God the Spirit, operative within, is attributed the awakening of that new life which consists in spiritual fellowship with himself. The Spirit regenerates. He bears inward witness to the sonship of the man to God, confirming from the divine side the certainty of the human that such sonship is a fact. As a Spirit of adoption he evokes the cry, "Father," from the child: that is, he develops the free and joyful filial life, and establishes it as the conscious life of the man. He suggests prayer so great and deep as to be beyond expression: that is, he awakens the longings of the soul after the highest good and keeps them stretching forth with untold eagerness, not merely as desires, but as prayers to the Father's love. He thus helps the weakness of those in whom he dwells, stirring the noblest in them to lofty flights of aspiration (Rom. viii. 15-27). He has all sweet and holy traits of character and works of life for the results of his presence, so that "the fruit of the Spirit" includes (Gal. v.22) all the worthiest things that are known to men. He is the comforter in trouble, the sustainer in reproach, the author of fraternal grace and forgiveness, the inspirer of brotherly love and usefulness. He makes divine realities known to the soul that can discern them, revealing the very deeps of God. He makes Christ ever better known and more richly appreciated. He brings in deep and strong convictions concerning sin and righteousness and God's eternal judgment of the difference between them. He reminds the soul of forgotten truth, and guides on toward ever fuller understanding of what God reveals. He is the very Spirit of truth, who makes truth dear to all who know him. He makes the soul wise with a heavenly wisdom, such as this world untaught by him can never master. He is the inspirer of holy and spiritual hope, both for this life and the life that is to come, and his presence with the soul is the pledge of an inheritance in life eternal. He opposes and defeats the inferior being, sets the soul at liberty, and is the inspiration of the victorious life, wherein hope is fulfilled and the will of God is done.

. . .

From considering God in the inner life, we turn to think of God in the open life, and especially in the common life of mankind. It is an old misunderstanding of Christianity to suppose it a religion of the individual alone. There is a passage in Augustine, in which an inquirer for truth is asked what it is that he desires and prays to know; and he declares that it is "God and the soul." "Nothing more?" his companion asks, and "Nothing whatever" is the answer. That religion is a matter between God and the soul alone has never been a doctrine of Christianity, but it has been a frequent impression among Christians, fostered by much true but partial teaching. But if one wishes to see God in the light of Jesus, it is not enough to look above and within: one must look also without and around. God, the soul, and the men with whom we live form a triad not to be diminished if we desire to know any one of the three aright. So the doctrine of God in relations with men is not completed by viewing it as doctrine of God in the inner life. God must be found and recognized in the common life, or the life of men together, no less than in the interior life of the soul.

The starting-point for this part of the doctrine is not a new one, but has been already indicated. That nature of man through which God is always speaking to him includes his social nature. As we have seen, man is not himself, and would never have come to be himself, but for the social relations in which he is placed. If we say that God permanently appeals to man through the nature that he has given him, of course it is implied that the appeals of his social nature are appeals of God. The word of God is in the life of man. The opportunity to live according to righteousness with his fellows is a word of God to him, bringing counsel, illumination and appeal. So is the opportunity to live according to love and in the spirit of helpful fellowship. The language of natural affection utters in the heart a word of God. The cry of misery and want brings the sound of two voices, the voice of the wretched and the voice of God. All appeals of sudden occasion or of steady need, to which a man may make answer with help both warm and wise, are God's appeals. All suggestions arising in the course of history, when common wrong has brought forth misery and human beings are losing their value through the common fault, are God's authoritative suggestions for promotion of a better social righteousness. Not only is God speaking through all awakenings of the public conscience and agitations for better conduct: he is speaking through all the crises in public affairs that bring such awakening of conscience, and through those that ought to bring it but do not. In all the burning evils of the common life God is speaking, often with a voice of thunder, calling men to better things. In all the moral aspects of the life of men together, God is giving voice to his own moral nature, that men may learn; and all the life of men together is moral, so that God is working through it at every point, perpetually revealing himself, and giving counsel, reproof and higher instruction. As in the inner life, so in the common life, men may not know that God is there, and may miss his call or misinterpret his counsel; but none the less is God there, with his living word for them to hear.

These statements are not to be understood as applying to Christian lands and times alone. This work of God comes to pass by no special revelation; it comes in the course of nature. That we have not discerned it does not destroy it. God has made men so that this instruction from him comes to them by their very nature. Through the moral nature of their social life, as well as of their inner life, God keeps in administrative communication, so to speak, with all human beings. His authority is upon them in their social duties. . . . There has never been a human being who did not have to do with God in the duties that he owed to the men who lived about him. There is no proud structure of social order that does not stand approved or condemned in God's own presence, according as it does right or wrong toward the human beings whose destinies are committed to its care. Through the relations and attendant duties that he has constituted throughout humanity, God stands in authority over all men, and their relations to one another form an element in their relation to him.

This is the same as to say that no man and no society can fulfil duty toward God by considering God alone. Human relations enter into religion. Duty toward men is part of duty toward God, and the two can never be separated. It is in the very constitution of nature that God must be served by serving men. Not by this alone is he to be served, but without this never to the full; and God, being the God that he is, could not have appointed it to be otherwise.

When we come to that clearer manifestation of God which is made in Jesus Christ, we find this provision of nature reaffirmed with perfect distinctness. From Jesus we hear that the supreme requirements in religion are two, not one. They are alike, he says, but they are two. "Thou shalt love the Lord thy God with all thy heart" is one, and "Thou shalt love thy neighbour as thyself" is the other (Mt. xxii. 37-39). They are alike, in that both are calls for love. Each requires the placing of self where self belongs but does not always wish to go, and the choosing and honouring of another object. Here is the triad that was mentioned a little while ago—God, the self and the neighbour—and all three are included in the scope of religion. . . .

. . .

In the very centre of Christianity this law is again expressed in supreme power and beauty. Jesus is the finest illustration that we know of love to God. All the signs of love—the confidence, the devotion, the delight—appear in him. To God he was absolutely loyal, and in his love he performed God's will with an understanding of it most profoundly true. When we ask how he showed this most loyal and intelligent love to God, and how he satisfied his own heart in doing the Father's will, the answer is ready. He showed his love to God in the service that he performed for men. He loved his neighbour as himself, and better, as our hearts cry when we behold his cross, and it was in such love that he expressed his love and wrought out his loyalty to God. In life and death, Jesus is the supreme illustration of the truth that God is served in serving men.

. . .

This truth offers itself to the Christian doctrine of God as a descriptive statement. God is a Being who can be served by serving men. More—he is a God who must be served by serving men, if service to him is to be of the kind that will please him best. Service to him consists in contributing to the accomplishment of his purpose; and his purpose, which we call his will, includes worthy and successful life, both for the person who serves and for the common humanity to which he belongs. So a man may serve God by seeking to fulfil his own true destiny, and by helping others to fulfil theirs. Service that is not gathered under one of these two heads is mere formality or court-service. It may take some approved and acceptable form, but it accomplishes nothing beyond itself, and contributes nothing to the doing of the will of God.

Here we meet again the ancient conception of the Kingdom of God,

272

and here we can best understand it in relation to the present time. Whatever else the kingdom of God was expected to be, it was to include a multitude of men, who would have to do with one another and with God. It was not to be a fact in the field of individualism, but an institution of the common life, a social fact.

. . .

. . . Bringing the biblical idea to present application, by the kingdom of God we mean God's moral government of social life on Christian principles. The kingdom of God is a very different thing from a body of people, to be enumerated in a census, and from a visible institution with its organization and official corps. No man has ever seen it. It is not the Church, as has often been supposed. The Church is one of its agencies, but the kingdom itself is that which the Church is intended to promote. It is not a domain but a dominion. It is a divine pervasion of human facts. It is an influence, a searching and controlling Christian force, taking effect upon the life that men live together. We cannot put it into an exhaustive definition; but when the kingdom has come, the eternal goodness loving in wisdom will have human goodness loving in wisdom for its counterpart on earth. When the kingdom has come, the relations of man with man, of man with woman, of parent with child, of neighbour with neighbour, of individual with society, of class with class, of trade with trade, of citizen with state, of strong with weak, of nation with nation, of race with race, will be determined and pervaded by the mind of Christ, which is the will of God. In so far as these relations are thus determined and God does have his way, the kingdom of God has come, and his will is done on earth as it is in heaven. In so far as this is not yet true, the kingdom has yet to come, and may be promoted by any man's endeavour.

. . . The extension of the mind of Christ is his means of answering the prayer, "Thy will be done." Any church that would represent him worthily must devote itself alike to the saving of individuals and the promotion of the social kingdom. To neglect either object is to fall out of his fellowship. This quick and powerful conception of the God of universal morality is just as essential to the Christian doctrine as any view of him that may be accounted more doctrinal or more technically religious, for in this manner God is in human life, seeking actually to become the Lord of all men and all their doings.

### Note

1. In *The Christian Doctrine of God*, International Theological Library (New York: Charles Scribner's Sons, 1909), 249-64.

# William P. DuBose

*The theology of DuBose (1836–1918) developed over the course of long service at the University of the South in Sewanee, Tennessee. He was educated at the Citadel, the University of Virginia (M.A., 1859), and the theological seminary of the Episcopal Church in South Carolina. Military chaplaincy during the Civil War and then priestly ordination (1866) followed. He was appointed chaplain of the newly founded school at Sewanee in 1871, and remained there, until his death, as teacher of the arts and sciences; founder of the theological department; professor of Divinity, Old Testament, and New Testament; and, for a time (1895–1908), dean.*

*Primarily a New Testament scholar, DuBose's major works, beginning with* Soteriology of the New Testament *(1892), addressed breaking issues of scholarship related to a historical approach to Christian theology. His adoption of historical-critical method on behalf of "catholic" church doctrine marked two developments of wide, national and international, significance at one and the same time: an Episcopalian-Anglican accord with Protestant evangelical liberalism without sacrificing emphasis on the Trinity and incarnation as divine mysteries, and an Anglo American strand of biblical study finding continuities of church tradition to be of equal or superior weight to discontinuities in any critical historical-theological judgment. This selection, from* The Gospel in the Gospels *(1906), sets forth DuBose's account of the historic doctrine of the Trinity in light of critical reflection.*

## THE TRINITY[1]

The truth takes its own forms and expresses itself in its own ways. Our efforts at defining, proving, or establishing it are all acts after the event. It is what it is, and not what we make it. Christianity prevails in the world in a fact which we have called Trinity, and which *is* Trinity, however inadequate and unsatisfactory our explanations of the term or our analyses of the thing may be. I would describe Christianity in its largest sense to be the fulfilment of God in the world through the fulfilment of the world in God. This assumes that the world is completed in man, in whom also God is completed in the world. And so, God, the world, and man are at once completed in Jesus Christ—who, as He was the *logos* or thought of all in the divine foreknowledge of the past, so also is He the *telos* or end of all in the predestination of the future. That is to say, the perfect psychical, moral, and spiritual manhood of which Jesus Christ is to us the realization and the expression is the end of God in creation, or in evolution. I hold that neither science, philosophy, nor religion can come to any higher or other, either conjecture or conclusion, than that. But now, when we come to the actual terms or elements of God's self-realization in us and ours in Him, we cannot think or express the process otherwise than in the threefold form of the divine love, the divine grace, and the divine fellowship, in operation or action. Putting it into scriptural phrase, we speak as exactly as popularly in defining the matter of the Gospel to be, The love of the Father, the grace of the Son, and the fellowship of the Spirit. As our spiritual life is dependent upon each and all of these three constituents, so we can know God at all only as we know Him in the actual threefold relation to us of Father, Son, and Spirit.

The first element in the essential constitution of the Gospel is the fact in itself that God is love. That God is love means that He is so not only in Himself but in every activity that proceeds from Him. The very phrase The love of the Father expresses the whole principle of the universe. That God is Father means that it is His nature, or His essential activity, to reproduce Himself, to produce in all other that which He Himself is. That God in Himself is love carries with it the truth that from the beginning all things else mean, and are destined to come to, love in the end. The mystery on the way that somehow light must come out of darkness, that love must needs conquer hate, and that in everything good seems to be only the final and far off goal of ill, may puzzle us but it does not disturb the principle itself. When we come to enter fairly upon the evolution of the future, the higher not merely psychical or social or moral but spiritual life and destiny of man, all the truth gradually dawns upon us in the following discoveries, which are already established facts of spiritual experience: The truth of all spirit is love; the matter of all law is goodness; God is not creator or cause only, nor lord or lawgiver only, but Father of all things, since all things through man are destined to share His spirit, to be partakers of His nature, and to reproduce Himself

275

as Father in themselves as children. In order to be sons of God through actual participation in the divine nature there stands in the way indeed the need of a mighty redemption from sin and an as yet far off completion in holiness; but no matter how unredeemed or incomplete, we know beyond further question that all our salvation lies in redemption and completion, and that we shall be ourselves and the world will come to its meaning only when the self-realization of God as Father shall have accomplished itself in our self-realization as His children. If we knew the fact only that God in Himself is love, it would be to us a gospel indeed of great joy, because it would carry in it the assurance of the highest good, whatever that might be. But it would be but a partial gospel, and in fact only a gospel at all through its certainty of proceeding further.

The phrase Grace of the Son expresses that which perfectly complements and completes all that is meant by the Love of the Father. What is Fatherhood without a correlative Sonship? And what is all love even in God as its subject apart from its actuality and activity as grace in man as its object? The divine propriety of the terms Father and Son as applied to God cannot be too much magnified. The distinction between God as He is in Himself and God as He is in all possible expressions of Himself is one that we cannot think Him at all without making. The most perfect expression of love is contained in the statement, that Love loves love. Its nature is to produce, to reproduce, to multiply itself. Itself is forever the true object of itself, at the same time that it is ever a going forth from itself into that which is not itself. This essential principle of love or self-reproduction is what makes God eternally Father. But the eternal Fatherhood is actualized only in an eternal Sonship. Nothing proceeds from the Father which is not reproduction of the Father, and is not therefore Son. Man sees himself now in nature and destinature son of God. He feels his call and obligation to fulfil God in him as Father by realizing himself in God as son. His spiritual end and impulse is to know as also he is known, to love in return as he is first loved, to apprehend that for which he is apprehended of God in Christ. In proportion as he finds the meaning and truth of his own being in the reproduction of God, in being son of God, he finds the meaning and truth of the whole creation realized and expressed in his own sonship as heir of all and end of all. And in proportion again as he thus finds all things meaning and ending in sonship, he comes at last to see God Himself as realized in the universal sonship—Himself therein realized as Eternal Father. So it is that in Jesus Christ we see everything expressed, because everything realized or fulfilled. He is all truth, because He is the truth of all things—

God, Creation, Man. And because He is thus truth and expression of all, He is *Logos* of all. What else could the *Logos* of all be but Son, or the Son but *Logos*? What could perfectly express God but that which is the perfect reproduction of Himself, or what is perfect sonship but perfect likeness?

The Grace of the Son is the divine gift of sonship. How could we have known God only in Himself? How could God have been actually our Father without the actuality of our sonship to Him? And could we have known, could we have wanted, could we have willed, could we have accomplished or attained our sonship without the gift or grace of sonship in Jesus Christ? God, we are told, predestinated us unto sonship through Jesus Christ unto himself. He predestinated us to be conformed to the image of His Son, that He might be the first born among many brethren. In bringing many sons to glory, He gave to us a Captain of our salvation, an Author and Finisher of the faith of sonship and so of the sonship of faith, who was Himself perfected as Son through the sufferings that are necessary to the perfecting of sonship in us. We see in Jesus Christ all that is meant, involved, or implied, in the fact that He is the divine Fatherhood realized and expressed in human sonship.

If that fact, viewed in its totality, signifies not only a human act, nor only a divine act, but a divine-human act, an act of God in man which is equally an act of man in God,—then we say that Jesus Christ is not only as well the humanity as the divinity in that act, but He is the divinity as well as the humanity. He is not only the *gratia gratiata* in it but the *gratia gratians*—not only the manhood infinitely graced but the Godhead infinitely gracing.

Jesus Christ is therefore to us no mere sample or example of divine sonship. He is no mere one man who more successfully than others has grasped and expressed the ideal of a divine sonship. Neither is He a single individual of our race whom God has elected from among equally possible others, in whom as mere revelation or example to all others to manifest the truth of God in man and man in God. On the contrary, Jesus Christ is Himself the reality of all that is manifested or expressed in Him. He is as God the grace communicating and as man the grace communicated. He is both Generator and generated with reference to the life incarnate in Him—both the sonship eternally in God to be begotten and the sonship actually begotten in man. As He was in the beginning with God and was God, so is He universally with man and is universal man.

When we have thus adequately conceived Christ as the universal truth

277

and reality of ourselves, and in ourselves of all creation, and in creation and ourselves of God, then we are prepared for the conclusion that we know God at all, or are sons to Him as our Father, or are capable in that relation of partaking of His nature or entering into His Spirit or living His life, only in and through Jesus Christ; because Jesus Christ is the incarnation or human expression to us of the whole *Logos* of God—that is to say, of God Himself as in any way whatever knowable or communicable. We cannot get at God to know or possess Him otherwise than as He reveals and imparts Himself; and He reveals Himself through His own Word and imparts Himself in His own Son. There and there alone is He to be known, and there He is all our own. The *Logos* who is the eternal Self-revelation of God manifests Himself as ideal principle, first and final cause, meaning and end, of creation; and the end of the whole creation which manifests God is realized through spiritual humanity in the imparted sonship of the Everlasting Son of the Father.

There is yet one other condition of truly knowing or really possessing God as wholly our God. As God is unknowable and incommunicable but through Christ, so is Christ, however perfectly He is in Himself the self-revelation and self-communication of God, not so to us but through the coequal action of the Holy Ghost. There is no knowledge of God in Himself only, there is no knowledge of God in creation only, or in others, or even in Christ only, without the answering knowledge of God in ourselves also. It is only like that answers to like. The deep that answers to deep must be the same deep. Jesus Christ expected in every son of man not only the answer of the man in him to Himself as eternal and universal Son of man, but the answer of the God in him to the perfect Godhead in Himself. Ye cannot see God in me, He says, because ye have not God in you. No man cometh unto me except the Father draw Him. I do not wish to urge the mere conventional language of Christianity, true as I believe it and helpful as I may find it to myself. I would if possible speak in the common language of common experience. When we speak of knowing God, and having God, it must mean knowing Him where He is to be known and having Him as He is to be had. Now, whatever God is in Himself, He is knowable to us only in Jesus Christ, and He can be *our* God only as He is conceived in us by the operation of the Spirit of God and born of the want which He implants and the faith which He generates.

The doctrine of the Trinity is ordinarily thought of as the very extreme of speculative reasoning upon the nature of God. But let us remember that practical faith in the Trinity antedated any speculative thought or doctrine of the Trinity. And behind that faith the fact itself of the Trinity is all that makes God knowable by us or us capable of knowing God. Before there was the word Trinity, the new world of Christianity had come to know God in Christ, and to know Christ in itself. The entire doctrine developed out of that actual experience was nothing but a positive affirmation and a determined defence of the fulness of the truth of God in Christ and Christ in us. . . .

. . .

It has not been my object to add to the solution of the speculative problem of the Trinity. I have only aimed to show practically and spiritually that if at all we are to know and worship God in reality as our God, we must do so as Christianity has always done—in Trinity. We must worship God in the Father, and the Son, and the Holy Ghost. Because God is, and is operative for us, not alone in one but in all these. We cannot but distinguish the Three; it is only in the completeness of their threefold operation that we can perfectly know the One.

### Note

1. In *The Gospel in the Gospels*, 2nd ed. (New York: Longmans, Green, and Co., 1906), pp. 274-81, 289. This selection illustrates well the dominance of male imagery in the traditional theological expressions about God in the early twentieth century.

279

# Newman Smyth

$N$ewman Smyth (1843–1925) was educated at Andover
Theological Seminary (class of 1867). Dissatisfied with orthodoxy, he
sought to reconcile science and religion. He continued his education in
Berlin and Halle, working with August Tholuck and Isaak Dorner. In
many respects, Smyth's life represents the transition from New England
Calvinism to the "new theology" of liberalism that took place at
Andover during the 1880s. In 1881, Andover chose Smyth to replace the
retiring Edwards A. Park. The Board of Visitors, established at the seminary's founding to protect the orthodoxy of the faculty, refused to
approve Smyth's appointment. Though the charge against him was that
he lacked teaching skills, lack of support most likely stemmed from his
open attack on the old forms of Calvinism and his endorsement of the
doctrine of probation for those who died before they heard the gospel.
In spite of the Visitors' victory in blocking the Smyth appointment, they
lost the overall battle to keep the liberals out. By 1892, the new theology freely dominated at the school.[1] For his part, Smyth served content-
edly as a pastor-scholar for over forty years.

Smyth's work represents an "evangelical liberal" approach to scripture,
one that readily embraced the developing historical-critical methods he
encountered in Germany. In general, Newman took seriously the belief
that all religious ideas are subject to the conditioning brought to bear
upon them by both history and culture. Therefore he refused to understand revelation as a deposit of static or changeless truth. This particular
selection argues that scripture illustrates a "progressive revelation."

### THE COURSE OF MORAL EDUCATION
### AND PROGRESS OF REVELATION[2]

. . .
    . . . The Bible is a living book. There is movement and life in it. Ideas
grow in it. Truths blossom out, and come to their maturity in it. The

purpose of love ripens, and bears at last its perfect fruit, in this sacred history. The Bible is not a mere repository of the words of God, a receptacle of doctrines, like an apothecary's shop stored with the essences and abstractions of the products of nature; all labeled and ready for use, according to some favorite prescription. Tbe Bible is not an abstract of useful doctrines to be administered by rule; it is rather, like nature, full of mystery, and full of life. We can follow, as it were, the whole course of the seasons through it—the springtime, the early days of promise, the time of sowing, and the times of waiting; the days when the growth seems checked, when the tares an enemy hath sown multiply; the dark days and the stormy, the hours of hurricane and desolation, as well as the days of blossoming and song;—and through all its changes, through the long succession of its ages, are to be discovered the steady advance and working out of one purpose, and the sure coming of the harvest. And, like the growth of nature, this progressive course of revelation, the gradual unfolding of its seed-truths, and the final and glorious fulfillment of its promise, are phenomena which imply the operation of higher laws, and greater forces, than the acts or the thoughts of the laborers who ploughed in hope, and scattered the seed, and looked forward, with prophetic expectation, to the harvest at the end of time.

The view which we have gained of the process of revelation lifts us at once out of many other moral difficulties which are often popularly urged against the authority of revelation, and which sometimes vex the hearts of believers. We need hardly follow them here farther into their details. The faults of the Old Testament are, as Herder said, the faults of the pupil, not of the teacher. They are the necessary incidents of a course of moral education; they are the unavoidable limitations of a partial and progressive revelation. If God chooses to enter upon a historic course of revelation, then that revelation must be accommodated to the necessities, and limited by the capacities, mental and moral, of each successive age. Otherwise, revelation would be a wild, destructive power—a flood sweeping everything away, and not the river of life. We cannot suppose that the Almighty can pour the Mississippi River into the banks of a mountain-brook. He can begin, however, with the springs and the brooks, and make in time the broad Mississippi River. We cannot expect God to pour the full Christian era into the limited moral experience of the patriarchal age. He may begin, however, with the first welling up of truth in far-off times, to prepare for the Christian era. He will not, by a too early flood, wash away the very possibility of an enlarging revelation. His stream keeps within its banks; his revelation never breaks through the appointed limits of a great historical influence. But this patience of the divine Teacher with man's slowly maturing capacity for instruction, this self-restraint of revelation, is itself the sign of a higher wisdom. It would have been like us to have hurried an Elijah on into a John the Baptist; to have spoiled Moses by making him into a Paul; we should have had no place or patience for the conservative life and the partial truth of an apostle like James, between Judaism and a full-grown Christianity. But with the Divine Instructor a thousand years are as one day. His unit of time is not the short axis of a revolving world, and his good providence puts no blessing in peril by unseemly haste. These very limitations, imperfections, and moral deficiencies of particular stages of revelation, so often alleged against the Bible, are among the signs which cannot be counterfeited of God's handwriting in it. The same powers of development, the same law of evolution, seem to have been followed, alike, in nature and in the Bible. The Koran is like a world made all at once, in the six literal days of some theologians. The Bible resembles a world that has been long in growing, and which may well be pronounced good when it is done.

In general, then, it may be remarked of many moral difficulties accompanying a progressive revelation, which our limits will not permit us to consider more specifically, that an earnest, true, moral purpose must use, at one stage of history, at some points in its progress, a certain roughness of procedure, a severity, at least, of judgment, which would neither be necessary nor allowable at another time, or in a more advanced era. Into the great mass of human ignorance and idolatry, God causes, in the call of Abraham, the sharp edge of his good purpose to enter; hard blows must be dealt to drive that thickening wedge in; and providence is too divinely in earnest, in its work of driving that wedge of Hebrew history into the tough resistance of mankind, to spare, when needed, strong, sharp, decisive strokes. Many vigorous providences were necessary and right in the divine order of history, as were the blows of the pioneer's axe and the smoke of his fires, when the forests were to be cleared and the wilderness made habitable. Moses and the judges, and the prophets, even, were God's chosen pioneers; and theirs was the rough, hard work of history. How much suffering and hardship does not nature relentlessly compel in the pioneer age! The necessities of the times determine the rights and the truths which must be made paramount and commanding. Thus, the right of the individual to life is an undeniable principle of morality; but, at times, the right of a race to its redemption may be more sacred. The rights of every individual Ammonite and Canaanite, slain by the children of Israel in execution of a divine mission, a just God cannot in the final judgment despise; but the right of the world to the coming of the kingdom of righteousness and peace may, at any particular crisis of history, outweigh all consideration of individuals in the scale of a just providence. Moreover, it should not be forgotten that the individual, who for the moment may be sacrificed for the good of the whole, has himself an immortality, in which the very good for which he was destroyed may return upon him in blessing. The stern, temporal measures sanctioned in the earlier stages of the Bible cannot be fairly judged except in the light of immortality thrown upon all the inequalities of human life by the finished Bible. Indeed, the very conception of a divine education of the race requires for its completion the thought of a future in which the final blessing shall be imparted to all who have passed away before its coming. All who at any stage of the process contributed to the result, or who have been, under temporal exigencies, severely used by the course of Providence, have their recompense in the final issue. Hence, we are never envious of the future, of coming days of greater good, because the future, too, as well as the past, is for all who fulfil aright their present part. The end of the world-age is for all the generations of man.[3]

Thus the revelator sees the kings of the earth bringing the honor and glory of the nations into the gate of the celestial city. The end of time is the blessing of that Messianic kingdom of which all the ages are the heirs. One would need, therefore, a view comprehensive both of the past and its exigencies, and the future and the final good, before one would be qualified to sit in judgment upon the public justice of Jehovah. The fact of history which does lie within our comprehension, is the fact that through it, and especially by means of the chosen people, a great moral purpose of human redemption has been pushed steadily forward, and with the stern mercy, at times, of nature's own laws of development.

We have thus far taken no notice of the significant fact that it is to the Bible itself we owe our own power of judging the Bible. The hard places in the Old Testament are revealed by the increasing light of the Bible itself. The Bible is its own commentary and corrective. When that which is perfect is come, that which is in part of itself falls away from the divine law. This very fact that we are able to judge the imperfections of the Old Dispensation by a more advanced standard, shows how effectually through all those ages of patient education the Spirit of Truth has pursued its work. The conclusive logic of facts shows that the divine policy of revelation has been successful. The real morality of the Bible is its final morality, the morality in the intention of the Lawgiver from the beginning.[4] The divineness of the whole process is evident from the very fact that it has taken place. Other nations "ended as they began;" no other ancient system of law and religion had in itself a principle of development, a constructive force, the power of passing on to perfection. In its very *evolution* we have a sign of the supernatural life in the religion of Israel. There is the continuity of a divine purpose here.

One other remarkable feature of the Bible, throughout, which indicates the continuous purpose and wisdom of a Divine Teacher in it, remains to be more distinctly noticed. Our view of the educational worth, and the pedagogical purport of Scripture, would be incomplete, did we not at least point out this characteristic in passing. We refer to the limits of the extent of revelation. The silence of Scripture is often one of the most superhuman characteristics of it. Not only, as we have shown, was the Bible, in the process of its formation from age to age, adapted to the receptive capacity of those to whom the word of God came—the commandment, as Augustine finely said, being in accordance with the heart of him to whom it was given—but also the Bible as a whole, in what it reveals and in what it does not reveal, is adjusted to the limits of the powers, and the moral necessities, of mankind. The light of revelation seems adapted to the eye of the human understanding in a manner so remarkable as to indicate a higher wisdom as the author of both. False prophets never know where to stop. Mahomet and Swedenborg know too much. But something seems to have laid a restraint upon prophets and apostles, and to have sobered them even in the midst of supernal revelations. There is a more than human wisdom in the silence of the Bible. It is divine as the silence of nature. Of the being and purposes of God, of the unseen world and its retributions, enough is revealed to us for the motives and duties of the present life; but little or nothing to gratify curiosity. There is enough of both Heaven and Hell revealed for all practical purposes now, but nothing for merely imaginative or speculative uses. Revelation is limited by the moral ends of a system of education and trial; and in that adaptation of it appears again the thoughtful provision of the schoolmaster. Everything here seems to be fitted up to make this world a scene of discipline and moral education for us. Life is a school, we say, and from it only the suicide can play truant. A genuine message, then, from the author of nature might be expected to conform to the disciplinary or pedagogical purport of the present system of things. Precisely such a revelation we find the Bible as a whole to be. It is fitted wisely to the purpose of forming *character.* It is a revelation clear enough to render faith possible, and obscure enough to leave unbelief possible. It affords thus a

284

trial or test of character. It searches the heart. Too bright as well as too dark a revelation might defeat the very end of revelation. It would bring the educational and probationary period of life to a close; it would bring on the day of judgment. The very difficulties and limitations of revelation are adapted, also, to the conditions of moral growth. It requires, and it repays, toil. It tasks, and tries, and puzzles, and strengthens faith. It is like man to make everything regular, easy, and plain; but that is not like the God of nature, of history, or of the Bible. A revelation in which the way never could be missed; a revelation made level and smooth to our feet, would be like the work of man, but not like the builder of the mountains. Were there no Alps for men to climb; no ocean depths beneath the plummet's reach; no stars still unresolved; no Scylla and Charybdis waiting to catch up the unskilful voyager; no burdens of toil and sorrow laid upon our manhood; if this life were only the play of children, and all the days were sunshine: then, indeed, might we expect to find a Bible without difficulties; a Gospel without parables; a kingdom of truth without tasks for the athlete, and without rewards for the victor. But the God of nature, of history, and of the Bible, surely does not intend to people his heaven with a race of moral imbeciles. "To him that overcometh," is the promise—seven times repeated—of the crown of life.

Our whole discussion, then, of the morality of the Bible, is summed up in the conclusion that the development of the Bible has followed a beneficent moral purpose. We have given reasons for the belief, that in its growth, its historical influence, its unfolding of truth, and its limitations, the Bible follows the moral order of the God of history; flows with his purpose, and works out his design of redemption. The whole moral development of revelation, often against nature, across the grain of Israel, and in spite of all opposing forces, is to us an evidence of a higher than a merely natural revelation; it bears witness of a supernatural course of history.

### Notes

1. See the story of Andover Theological Seminary, and Smyth's role in it, found in Daniel Day Williams, *The Andover Liberals: A Study in American Theology* (New York: Octagon Books, 1970).
2. In *Old Faiths in New Light,* 2nd ed. (New York: Charles Scribner's Sons, 1879), pp. 116-27.
3. See Lotze: *Mikrokosmus,* iii., pp. 50-53. The difference between this philosophy of history as a real working out of good—a process of human education whose fruits shall be at last for all generations—and the emptiness of the Hegelian thought-process, or any purely idealistic conception, is at once apparent.
4. See Mozley's fine lecture on "The End the Test of a Progressive Revelation."

# Antoinette Brown Blackwell

*Contesting the strictures the religious establishment placed on women, Blackwell (1825–1921) became both a minister and a scholar, and as such addressed a wide range of issues concerning theology's relationship to society, philosophy, and science. A Congregationalist, she was one of the first women to receive a formal college education, at Oberlin, and then continued ministerial studies in that school's theological department, despite restrictions imposed on her and the denial of an "official" degree at the end. Active in the reform movements of the time, especially Women's Rights, she was ordained in 1853 and spent a brief, difficult church ministry in New York state. In 1878 she received Unitarian ordination, preaching often but devoting her time mainly to studies for lectures and publications.*

*Of chief concern in her scholarly works was the reconciliation of religion, philosophy, and science—a special problem for thoughtful Christians after the Civil War, who faced challenges to Common-Sense philosophy, advances in the natural sciences, and developmental approaches (including Darwinian evolution) in studies of the physical world and human history. This selection from the final chapter of the* Social Side of Mind and Action *highlights affirmations of religious faith that she holds to be warranted by reason, given the limits of human comprehension. Accepting evolutionary theory, Blackwell has a liberal confidence in progress, while reminding readers that despite improvements, human views of nature's law still evidence "the trail of the serpent over them all."*

## Some Fundamental Conclusions[1]

It is now frankly admitted by those who have given the most earnest and careful attention to the subject that there has not been a specially revealed,—a divinely authorized code of morals. Like the laws of matter, the laws of mind, of ethics, of esthetics, and of art, have had a gradual unfolding, in correspondence with the growing and recognizing human comprehension.

Nature and Nature's Creator have never commanded, "thou shalt," nor, "thou shalt not!" The principles of things are ingrained in the things themselves. Mankind is as thoroughly part and parcel of Nature as are the rocks and the trees.

Mind, to be mind, must initiate its own purposes, make its own choices, and reach its own decisions; it must see for itself and act for itself. To be finite mind it must see things in their true relationships, and it must act in strict correlation with other existences,—material, mental, or mento-material.

To act for oneself in any capacity, one must be individual. Action is inherently individual. Action is the all-comprehensive function,—the exclusive function,—of all real things; the one reality in their relations and processes.

No one mind does,—no one mind can acquire all truth; but to the collective human mind truth has been slowly but progressively acquired. In general it has not been an individual jump from a lower outlook to a higher and broader prospect. On the whole, numbers are found to be slowly walking up along different lines of an inclined plane, each advancing observer taking some outlook individual in its details. When the higher plane is reached the details when fitted together reveal the larger truth that includes the many less complete truths. This has been the history of human knowledge, and this type of history is still in process. Finite process can never be divided from individuality. Though a hundred,—though a universe of finite units are associated in one process, yet each acts literally for itself at its own option, even when helping a feebler worker and taking a share of action in excess of its own individual requirements.

Action being as generically on-going as its substance is static, undiminishable action perpetually increases, and one's activities, if wisely associated, may be continuously increased.

The values of perceived truth, wisely applied in corresponding achievements, are the highest and best of all possible performances. Truth is the reality in all self-revealing, it is discovered in its own authentic setting of co-operating truths. All truth is one, but with many varieties.

All finite truth is true because God created it true, and infinite truth is true because it is the innate expression of His own infinite, everexisting, self-existing unity of Being.

Here I must return once more to essential self-existence, because the proof of it is unquestionably more than equivalent to any other possible demonstration; if only such words be used as will be understood and recognized as having definite meanings.

If one can see that substance in itself, of itself, must be uncreatable,—because of its innate nature,—then that claim is its own proof.

If in finite Being everything that begins to be is process,—correlating new modes of force and structure while essential substance remains intact, static, and in and of infinity of substance,—can there be the shadow of a doubt that substance is uncreatable, eternally self-existent? Since nothing can be either found or imagined that could produce it,—and since no process of production can be conceived in self-consistent thought, or can be put into words that have any dependent, connected meanings,—it is unjust to say that the theory that asserts: "No substance, as essential being, ever could have been created," is a mere speculation. If it is, then nothing ever was proved, nothing ever will be proved. Every act of creation is itself a process.

Then, too, if the claim that the processes of the universe that are derived from self-existing substance, and its eternal property force, could not be made interdependent by adding two opposed units of substance equal in their dimensions, united by the process that blended them into one individualized unit, is a mere speculation, then what is reasoning? And what is reasonable?

But admitting those groundwork claims, we must admit the intelligence of the Author of the universe,—an intelligence equal to the conception of the stupendous thought scheme, with force and skill equal, putting it and keeping it in continuous, harmonious, co-operative activity.

As to the question of the goodness, the loving-kindness of the Creator who gave of His own Being to each unit,—directly, by Himself, of Himself,—the individual use of its own individual endowment, I shall only claim that every part and feature of the universal whole has achieved immensely more good than harm; that it has proved to be the very acme of good, supreme economy, and that no one has as yet suggested a real, an internally consistent improvement.

Then, if Divine Wisdom has not directly told us what is right and true, are we all afloat and without a rudder?

Assuredly not! God has embodied in His universe the entire system of universal truth. There it is, offering its entire record to whomever can and will read and interpret any or every phase of it. What is more historically certain than that no class of truth ever has been discovered that

288

was not found within the very substance, and in the special type of substance that includes that particular class of structure?

Relative co-operation cannot transform itself into independent action. Authority cannot guarantee truth; but all that is true is self-revealing. In its own light and in that of its relationships near and remote truth waits to be recognized.

Automatic Nature is called unmoral. As mindless, so it must be, but as representative of the mind that created its actual unit of process it is the embodiment of pure, active truth, whether in a human, normal machine or in Nature. The strength of associated movements is consummate beauty. Art indicates what it aims to represent, but at its best it excludes the faults of to-day in its model, and includes the higher values of to-morrow. Vegetation does exactly the same thing when it transforms the angles of minerals into the curves of plant beauty, and provides for the still softer roundness of the higher organisms. Nature is truth and beauty is its incorporated goodness. Nature and beauty then are truth's message to humanity. Classifications are a human contribution in the interest of humanity. Nature deals only with the individual. The individual is designed and constructed to do the work, and to reap the harvest; mankind finds it convenient to gather the reapers and products into groups and bundles.

The like efficient binding together process has made time the symbol for all change: the measured periods of duration, the measured periods of local action and reaction, arranging them as nearly as possible by their normal successions. Space, after the same fashion, has been made the symbol of extensive relations. Ambitious finite mind is trying,—has tried, as history teaches, ever since thought began—to extend space outside and beyond Infinity. It has never, however, really succeeded in stretching its conceptions more than a fraction of the distance in the directions of real extensions, in which presumably each least individuality is the constructed center of its own rounded universe of extensiveness.

Time, space, and force are the great representative names for three of the united phases of represented process. Law is the fourth representing symbol of the mighty quartet. Law represents structural on-going modifications, and also Nature's corresponding force modifications.

Nature's laws are the inherent properties of universal Nature. To take away the laws of things is to take the heart out of the body, or to remove all of the organs from the organism, leaving perhaps the skin-covered skeleton, with maybe a few intervening strands of living flesh.

Undisputedly that would be bad enough, but there is worse still to follow. Just as primitive mankind created deities resembling themselves,—but larger and more powerful,—so they created natural laws like human laws of that era, though larger and more powerful. With the progress of events human laws have improved; so have interpretations of Nature's laws. Still "the trail of the serpent is over them all." "Precedent" is yet probably the most used of all legal terms and the most influential in blocking the road to improvement.

It is only fair to admit that precedent is neither the blocking theory, nor the habit of science; and that, so far from hanging upon the breaking string that dangles from old authority, science is gladly discovering new truth,—truth that is large enough to discredit the main bulk of self-assertive ancient authority. But science has not yet freed itself from some of the worst human law conceptions, such as the practical relationships between law and conduct, and the province of natural law as an active agent.

Nature's laws maintain their own unchanging, constitutional integrity as does also their substance. They hold all operations with which they are concerned within their assigned bounds, but they are not arbitrary properties of Being; nor are they independent arbitrary promoters of activities. They do not initiate the modes of human conduct nor those of automatic activities, nor are natural laws responsible for any kind of results. In other words, they are the dependents, the representatives in the scheme of things. Laws promote activities, they are not themselves activities.

Laws promote actions of kinds special to each law, for itself, only. Force promotes activities of all kinds; but all the special modes of force action are immediately determined by prior acting conditions, while the laws of Nature remain, as effectually as does the substance of Nature, of which they are specialized but inseparable constituents.

Added to these constitutional diversities is the appalling certainty that to exalt law and force into independent entities means to annihilate both matter and finite minds. Even though Infinite Mind might perhaps survive, finite individuality would be annihilated.

In all action, as we see it, force is not visible. We see moving objects. We do not see the force that moves them. Is it probable that for centuries of centuries force, still invisible, has been masquerading as the total of all visible existences, and still continues to do so? Is Nature so incorrigible a make-believe? Is force both visible and invisible, or is this modern phase of crippled idealism to subside like its scientific predecessors? Force has no self direction, it cannot be an abstract.

So far as has been tested, all substances may be transformed into gases, their least units may be distributed as invisible vapors, beyond the recognition of present-day human science, but that does not prove the destruction of the vapors as material substance. We can now, thanks to finite inventiveness, see multitudes of vast starry masses and other multitudes of infinitesimal masses, both formerly invisible.

The ambitious tendency of finite thought to do more than the Creator did when He devised the universe,—create a new finite-thought universe from either half of the present universe,—is a curious illustration of mental resourcefulness. If all this castle building kept to the same half of Nature for building materials, the result might be more impressive and less confusing.

Here now is a double-sided theory, which is ready for individual verification,—or disproof. This theory claims that each finite, indivisible least unit, either actually or potentially, is a constitutionally constructed, correlated unity. These facts are offered in proof, and appeal is made to the consciousness of each reader to prove or disprove the alleged facts. Human experience of each one must testify for itself.

In all physical work, where mind and organism do the work together, the mind orders the work to be done by physical process,—as for example, chopping wood, lifting a weight, pushing any object out of the way, drawing a sled, picking up and tossing a stone—in brief, any and every process where the mind initiates the process, which then is to become distinctly a physical process. In all such processes the mental sensation becomes a definite physical sensation, the amount of the sensation and the variety of it is in exact correspondence with the amount of work and the kind being done.

The feeling is not a thought, not an emotion like any other mental experience. Of course it is in consciousness, yet it is not of the usual mind-consciousness. However, it proves that one's individuality is larger than the mind, is more than mind, is different in kind from the mind. Lifting a heavy weight calls out a marked sense of physical exertion quite unlike that of chopping into a log of wood, or of tasting a lump of sugar, or the feeling of hot water, or of cold water.

In general the mental phases of a sensation and the material are united, yet they are clearly distinguishable. One can tell in the dark whether a blow received is hard or light, was given by a bare hand, a gloved hand, or by a metal or a wooden ruler. To send a stone skipping over the surface of the lake requires more mental action and more physical skill than to toss the stone out of the road, though both have a real purpose. To

291

read a page in a printed book calls out many phases of action,—both mental and material. The two types are always associated, in some way, whenever mind takes its share in the operation. There is a marked,—a very obvious, difference between when the mind is taking its part in the process, and when it is only an observer of a process, as in watching a game in which others are the actors, watching from day to day the rapid spring growth of the young green foliage. In these, and their kindred, there is no sense of personal action beyond that of looking on. Riding in a steam car has its own bundle of sensations, but there is no feeling of personal exertion in the progress made. One's own weight is only so much opposing inertia, a passive, more than active, existence.

Reaction has its specialized responses, differentiated from one another, and generically separated from all initiative action. With normal open eyes, looking at an apple tree we must see the tree, the leaves, the apples, the surrounding landscape. By shutting the eyes we shall see none of these things. By shutting the mind, to mental insight, we may keep out of action almost any type of relationships, so far as we are personally concerned; we do not, however, interfere with Nature's constructive relationships.

Every possible correlation must remain structurally provided for, and intact. Every mental-material co-operation must remain as perfectly balanced, and differentiated as to its kinds, and their varieties, as are the purely physical partnerships. Moreover, mind and its correlate matter work in perfect correspondence. If the personal consciousness cannot readily separate the physical sensibility by its acquired special energizing practice in analyzing the sensations as they arise, comparing them with their physical causes will soon enable one to do so with readiness.

Nature's completed units, mature in mind, in normal co-operation with the organic environment, can assuredly prove to its own satisfaction that it is a real, personal unity of mind and its own atomic matter, able to work and to recognize its own mental-material processes as exact, actional correlations. Each mind must solve that problem for itself. It is a problem of personal experience.

If we no longer may accept truth solely on the authority of another, some long, dearly cherished beliefs must be retested in the light of modern knowledge. It has been an almost unquestioned hope that after the earthly death, by some comforting help (widely different in different minds) we shall find conditions better than they are here. Different unquestionably they must be; better, if we have helped make them better, while God's provisions are always just and helpful.

But suppose one has wasted opportunities and life here, been meanly cruel to oneself, been meanly cruel and harmful to others; what then must be the new life? If wrong motives and wrong conduct trail their own results into the future life, Heaven, then, must be still far away.

The effort to find some way out of personal responsibility for personal sin was a sore temptation. It is now proving itself to be a failure, a moral impossibility; but with it has gone the brooding horror of reprobation and eternal suffering.

All humanity now stands upon the one broad platform of personal and social conduct. On the one side of all activities are motives and deeds. On the other side their natural, unfailing, innately correlated consequences. Nothing arbitrary is found, no injustice, cruelty nor ill will, nothing but the fairness dreamed of in the whole complex constitution of Divine provision!

What we know of life,—as it is and as it has been,—makes it certain that there must still be long and deep repentance, with its beginnings of a better life, and still plenty of need for social service, for forgiveness,—not guilt blotted out.

If each one of us really is a mental-material individual, we may be still structurally allied to this earth, with Heaven not far remote; as the traditions of the ages, as the floating fragments of testimony have insisted. It is certain that with the open door for all, wherever the future world may be located, its domain must be immense, with room for the patriarchs of all tribes and of all nations as well as for their descendants up to date, and even in the future. True democracy must become a practical issue. God is the Father of us all.

It may be desirable just here to take some account of our main stock of correlated opinions. No individual creed can be obligatory for all, yet since truth is one in all its varieties, there will, as knowledge increases, be increasing tolerance of others' opinions, with increasing unity of thought.

The following thesis sums up the main religious tenets of this Essay:

1—God, self-existent, total of Being; Force and Duration His infinite properties.

2—Universal Nature and its innate constitutional laws,—the embodiment of supreme good will, and infinite wisdom.

3—Nature's primary or least units, individualized by internal correlations.

4—Mankind endowed with liberty to obey or not to obey Nature's laws, accepting the legitimate results of obedience or disobedience.

5—Personal immorality our direct inheritance God. [*sic*]

Life has two strictly different types of values. In the one class are the really good, pleasant, enjoyable present interests,—our rightful possessions. They are the supplies for our present needs in our life's present conditions. We have the full right to appreciate and enjoy them,—subject to social justice and benevolence; but they are ever perishable. In the other class are to be found the deathless gifts of mankind.

The millionaire may step into the future life with no more wealth to his credit than the laborer who each day worked for the daily bread of himself and his motherless children,—possibly with much less current values.

The wealth that counts everywhere cannot be given away. Another may be helped to acquire its like, but it remains in one's own keeping. To teach a truth, to quicken a thought or purpose in another is not to lose these imperishable gifts oneself. Every good example, even when unconscious to its possessor, is caught up and followed, perhaps almost as unconsciously, by the observers. Like light, it illuminates its neighborhood, yet remains itself here and everywhere in God's many mansions,—or vast domain! Generous love is as pervasive as the air we breathe.

All humanity needs to be sustained, strengthened by help from one another, and by helping one another we help ourselves.

These higher, and better,—or debasing yet gainful,—acquirements either strengthen, mold, sweeten, and elevate character in all its many ever-varying and increasing potentialities, or the entire character becomes pitifully degraded, exactly in accord with, and to the extent of, the misuse. There is no known, no authentic nor credible way of evading this exclusively personal responsibility.

Neither does the responsibility end with ourselves and for ourselves. One's bad example, like malaria, taints the moral atmosphere and is contagious. Even unconscious influence is either like darkness,—a cause of stumbling to others,—or like light,—a helpful illumination to others. Example, either conscious or unconscious, is one of the most effective of all influences. Fortunately the good, the thoroughly good, example is even more a source of emulation than a bad example. "The laurels of Miltiades will not let me rest."

Catching as all mental values are, they cannot be given to another as we can give the objective good things; they remain subjective possessions. We may give knowledge, truth of any variety, may cultivate in others a sense of the beautiful and of the good,—that only renews and increases the love of the same treasure within ourselves. We cannot give away our own knowledge.

To cultivate the imperishable values that will be ours through all eternity is evidence of life's truest and yet most unselfish wisdom as well as of the highest self-endowment.

If we can get a conception of God sufficiently comprehensive to enable us to believe in His ever-existent goodness and wisdom,—that will give us rest and peace.

If we can admit that the internal correlation of equal but opposite forces of Infinite Being would produce finite beings, created mutually dependent in all copartnerships constitutionally enforced in order to increase both personal and social values,—that will give us courage and hope.

If we can recognize the innate necessity of ever-lasting, conscious existence for all humanity,—that will give us undoubting faith in God, in ourselves, and in our opportunities, both individual and social. All life will then be glorified. Sin itself will slowly but surely die.

### Note

1. In the *Social Side of Mind and Action* (New York: The Neale Publishing Company, 1915), pp. 125-40.

# Walter Rauschenbusch

*Among the most theologically creative and scholarly lead-*
*ers of the social gospel, Rauschenbusch (1861–1918) stands out as the*
*movement's prime exemplar because he helped define, early on, its bases*
*and aims and then, later on, reevaluated the theological adequacy of his*
*initial thoughts. Born into a well-educated, pietistic German Baptist*
*family (his father taught in the "German Department" of Rochester*
*Theological Seminary in New York), he was educated in Germany,*
*where he learned of the scholarship and social concerns of German lib-*
*eralism, finishing studies for ministry in Rochester. Eleven years of first-*
*hand experience with urban problems as a pastor in New York City,*
*near "Hell's Kitchen," crystallized his resolve to find a "theology for*
*social gospel"—the title of the last book (1917) he published before his*
*death. From 1897 on he taught at the Rochester Theological Seminary.*
*His writings and activities were marked, throughout, by the interweav-*
*ing of a biblical piety, social analysis, and doctrinal liberalism.*

*Two selections here record significant contents and the temper of his*
*thought. The first, from* Christianity and the Social Crisis *(1907) reveals*
*his confidence that fresh readings of scripture, employing the new his-*
*torical-critical methods, could disclose the "revolutionary" personality*
*of Jesus. The second, from* A Theology for the Social Gospel *(1917),*
*deals with his key theme, the kingdom of God, which he understood to*
*be the most essential in Christian life. The kingdom of God, initiated by*
*Christ, was, he declared, divine in origin, progress, and consummation,*
*and revealed the true purpose of the church in human history.*

## THE SOCIAL AIMS OF JESUS[1]

. . .

Jesus proceeded from the common people. He had worked as a car-
penter for years, and there was nothing in his thinking to neutralize the
sense of class solidarity which grows up under such circumstances. The

common people heard him gladly[2] because he said what was in their hearts. His triumphal entry into Jerusalem was a poor man's procession; the coats from their backs were his tapestry, their throats his brass band, and a donkey was his steed. During the last days in Jerusalem he was constantly walking into the lion's cage and brushing the sleeve of death. It was the fear of the people which protected him while he bearded the powers that be. His midnight arrest, his hasty trial, the anxious efforts to work on the feelings of the crowd against him, were all a tribute to his standing with the common people.

Dr. W. M. Thomson, in his "Land and the Book,"[3] beautifully says: "With uncontrolled power to possess all, he owned nothing. He had no place to be born in but another man's stable, no closet to pray in but the wilderness, no place to die but on the cross of an enemy, and no grave but one lent by a friend." That, perhaps, overstates his poverty. But it is fair to say that by birth and training, by moral insight and conviction, by his sympathy for those who were down, and by his success in winning them to his side, Jesus was a man of the common people, and he never deserted their cause as so many others have done. Whenever the people have caught a glimpse of him as he really was, their hearts have hailed Jesus of Nazareth as one of them.

There was a revolutionary consciousness in Jesus; not, of course, in the common use of the word "revolutionary," which connects it with violence and bloodshed. But Jesus knew that he had come to kindle a fire on earth. Much as he loved peace, he knew that the actual result of his work would be not peace but the sword. His mother in her song had recognized in her own experience the settled custom of God to "put down the proud and exalt them of low degree," to "fill the hungry with good things and to send the rich empty away."[4] King Robert of Sicily recognized the revolutionary ring in those phrases, and thought it well that the Magnificat was sung only in Latin. The son of Mary expected a great reversal of values. The first would be last and the last would be first.[5] He saw that what was exalted among man was an abomination before God,[6] and therefore these exalted things had no glamour for his eye. This revolutionary note runs even through the beatitudes where we should least expect it. The point of them is that henceforth those were to be blessed whom the world had not blessed, for the kingdom of God would reverse their relative standing. Now the poor and the hungry and sad were to be satisfied and comforted; the meek who had been shouldered aside by the ruthless would get their chance to inherit the earth, and conflict and persecution would be inevitable in the process.[7]

We are apt to forget that his attack on the religious leaders and authorities of his day was of revolutionary boldness and thoroughness. He called the ecclesiastical leaders hypocrites, blind leaders who fumbled in their casuistry, and everywhere missed the decisive facts in teaching right and wrong. Their piety was no piety; their law was inadequate; they harmed the men whom they wanted to convert.[8] Even the publicans and harlots had a truer piety than theirs.[9] If we remember that religion was still the foundation of the Jewish State, and that the religious authorities were the pillars of existing society, much as in medieval Catholic Europe, we shall realize how revolutionary were his invectives. It was like Luther anathematizing the Catholic hierarchy.

His mind was similarly liberated from spiritual subjection to the existing civil powers. He called Herod, his own liege sovereign, "that fox."[10] When the mother of James and John tried to steal a march on the others and secure for her sons a pledge of the highest places in the Messianic kingdom,[11] Jesus felt that this was a backsliding into the scrambling methods of the present social order, in which each tries to make the others serve him, and he is greatest who can compel service from most. In the new social order, which was expressed in his own life, each must seek to give the maximum of service, and he would be greatest who would serve utterly. In that connection he sketched with a few strokes the pseudo-greatness of the present aristocracy: "Ye know that they which are supposed to rule over the nations lord it over them, and their great ones tyrannize over them. Thus shall it not be among you."[12] The monarchies and aristocracies have always lived on the fiction that they exist for the good of the people, and yet it is an appalling fact how few kings have loved their people and have lived to serve. Usually the great ones have regarded the people as their oyster. In a similar saying reported by Luke, Jesus wittily adds that these selfish exploiters of the people graciously allow themselves to be called "Benefactors."[13] His eyes were open to the unintentional irony of the titles in which the "majesties," "excellencies," and "holinesses" of the world have always decked themselves. Every time the inbred instinct to seek precedence cropped up among his disciples he sternly suppressed it. They must not allow themselves to be called Rabbi or Father or Master, "for all ye are brothers."[14] Christ's ideal of society involved the abolition of rank and the extinction of those badges of rank in which former inequality was incrusted. The only title to greatness was to be distinguished service at cost to self.[15] All this shows the keenest insight into the masked selfishness of those who hold power, and involves a revolutionary consciousness, emancipated from reverence for things as they are.

The text, "Give to Caesar what is Caesar's,"[16] seems to mark off a definite sphere of power for the emperor, coördinate with God's sphere. It implies passive obedience to constituted authority and above all guarantees Caesar's right to levy taxes. Consequently it has been very dear to all who were anxious to secure the sanctions of religion for the existing political order. During the Middle Ages that text was one of the spiritual pillars that supported the Holy Roman Empire.[17] But in fact we misread it if we take it as a solemn decision, fixing two coördinate spheres of life, the religious and the political. His opponents were trying to corner Jesus. If he said "pay the Roman tax," he disgusted the people. If he said "do not pay," Rome would seize him, for its patience was short when its taxes were touched. Jesus wittily cut the Gordian knot by calling for one of the coins. It bore the hated Roman face and stamp on it—clear evidence whence it issued and to whom it belonged. If they filled their pockets with Caesar's money, let them pay Caesar's tax. The significant fact to us is that Jesus spoke from an inward plane which rose superior to the entire question. It was a vital question for Jewish religion; it did not even touch the religion of Jesus. Moreover, it was not purely a religious question with them; matters that concern money somehow never are purely religious. In paying tribute to Caesar, they seemed to deny the sovereignty of Jehovah, Israel's only king; that was, indeed, one point for grief. But another point was that they had to pay, pay, pay; and money is such a dear thing! Jesus felt none of their fond reverence for cash. Hence he could say, Give to Caesar the stuff that belongs to him, and give to God what he claims.

We have another incident in which his inward attitude to taxation comes out.[18] The Jews annually paid a poll-tax of half a shekel for the support of the temple worship, which sufficed to maintain it in splendor. The collector met Peter and asked if his master did not intend to pay. Peter, probably knowing his custom hitherto, said, "Certainly." When he came into the house, Jesus, who seems to have overheard the conversation, asked him from whom the kings of the earth usually exacted taxes, from their subjects or their sons. Peter rightly judged that the subjects usually did the paying, and the members of the royal family were exempt. "Then," said Jesus, "as we are sons of God and princes of the blood-royal, we are exempt from God's temple-tax. But lest we give offence, go catch a fish and pay the tax." We all know by experience that the expression of the face and eye are often quite essential for understanding the spirit of a conversation. We must think of Jesus with a smile on his lips during this conversation with his friend Peter. Yet

299

something of his most fundamental attitude to existing institutions found expression in this gentle raillery. He was inwardly free. He paid because he wanted to, and not because he had to.

Camille Desmoulins, one of the spiritual leaders of the French Revolution, called Jesus "le bon sansculotte." Emile de Laveleye, the eminent Belgian economist, who had the deepest reverence for Christianity as a social force, said, "If Christianity were taught and understood conformably to the spirit of its Founder, the existing social organism could not last a day."[19] James Russell Lowell said, "There is dynamite enough in the New Testament, if illegitimately applied, to blow all our existing institutions to atoms."[20]

These men have not seen amiss. Jesus was not a child of this world. He did not revere the men it called great; he did not accept its customs and social usages as final; his moral conceptions did not run along the grooves marked out by it. He nourished within his soul the ideal of a common life so radically different from the present that it involved a reversal of values, a revolutionary displacement of existing relations. This ideal was not merely a beautiful dream to solace his soul. He lived it out in his own daily life. He urged others to live that way. He held that it was the only true life, and that the ordinary way was misery and folly. He dared to believe that it would triumph. When he saw that the people were turning from him, and that his nation had chosen the evil way and was drifting toward the rocks that would destroy it, unutterable sadness filled his soul, but he never abandoned his faith in the final triumph of that kingdom of God for which he had lived. For the present, the cross; but beyond the cross, the kingdom of God. If he was not to achieve it now, he would return and do it then.

That was the faith of Jesus. Have his followers shared it? We shall see later what changes and limitations the original purpose and spirit of Christianity suffered in the course of history. But the Church has never been able to get entirely away from the revolutionary spirit of Jesus. It is an essential doctrine of Christianity that the world is fundamentally good and practically bad, for it was made by God, but is now controlled by sin. If a man wants to be a Christian, he must stand over against things as they are and condemn them in the name of that higher conception of life which Jesus revealed. If a man is satisfied with things as they are, he belongs to the other side. For many centuries the Church felt so deeply that the Christian conception of life and the actual social life are incompatible, that any one who wanted to live the genuine Christian life, had to leave the world and live in a monastic community.

Protestantism has abandoned the monastic life and settled down to live in the world. If that implies that it accepts the present condition as good and final, it means a silencing of its Christian protest and its surrender to "the world." There is another alternative. Ascetic Christianity called the world evil and left it. Humanity is waiting for a revolutionary Christianity which will call the world evil and change it. We do not want "to blow all our existing institutions to atoms," but we do want to remould every one of them. A tank of gasolene can blow a car sky-high in a single explosion, or push it to the top of a hill in a perpetual succession of little explosions. We need a combination between the faith of Jesus in the need and the possibility of the kingdom of God, and the modern comprehension of the organic development of human society.

We saw at the outset of our discussion that Jesus was not a mere social reformer. Religion was the heart of his life, and all that he said on social relations was said from the religious point of view. He has been called the first socialist. He was more; he was the first real man, the inaugurator of a new humanity. But as such he bore within him the germs of a new social and political order. He was too great to be the Saviour of a fractional part of human life. His redemption extends to all human needs and powers and relations. Theologians have felt no hesitation in founding a system of speculative thought on the teachings of Jesus, and yet Jesus was never an inhabitant of the realm of speculative thought. He has been made the founder and organizer of a great ecclesiastical machine, which derives authority for its offices and institutions from him, and yet "hardly any problem of exegesis is more difficult than to discover in the gospels an administrative or organizing or ecclesiastical Christ."[21] There is at least as much justification in invoking his name to-day as the champion of a great movement for a more righteous social life. He was neither a theologian, nor an ecclesiastic, nor a socialist. But if we were forced to classify him either with the great theologians who elaborated the fine distinctions of scholasticism; or with the mighty popes and princes of the Church who built up their power in his name; or with the men who are giving their heart and life to the propaganda of a new social system—where should we place him?

## THE KINGDOM OF GOD[22]

If theology is to offer an adequate doctrinal basis for the social gospel, it must not only make room for the doctrine of the Kingdom of God, but give it a central place and revise all other doctrines so that they will articulate organically with it.

This doctrine is itself the social gospel. Without it, the idea of redeeming the social order will be but an annex to the orthodox conception of the scheme of salvation. It will live like a negro servant family in a detached cabin back of the white man's house in the South. If this doctrine gets the place which has always been its legitimate right, the practical proclamation and application of social morality will have a firm footing.

To those whose minds live in the social gospel, the Kingdom of God is a dear truth, the marrow of the gospel, just as the incarnation was to Athanasius, justification by faith alone to Luther, and the sovereignty of God to Jonathan Edwards. It was just as dear to Jesus. He too lived in it, and from it looked out on the world and the work he had to do.

Jesus always spoke of the Kingdom of God. Only two of his reported sayings contain the word "Church," and both passages are of questionable authenticity. It is safe to say that he never thought of founding the kind of institution which afterward claimed to be acting for him.

Yet immediately after his death, groups of disciples joined and consolidated by inward necessity. Each local group knew that it was part of a divinely founded fellowship mysteriously spreading through humanity, and awaiting the return of the Lord and the establishing of his Kingdom. This universal Church was loved with the same religious faith and reverence with which Jesus had loved the Kingdom of God. It was the partial and earthly realization of the divine Society, and at the Parousia the Church and the Kingdom would merge.

But the Kingdom was merely a hope, the Church a present reality. The chief interest and affection flowed toward the Church. Soon, through a combination of causes, the name and idea of "the Kingdom" began to be displaced by the name and idea of "the Church" in the preaching, literature, and theological thought of the Church. Augustine completed this process in his *De Civitate Dei*. The Kingdom of God which has, throughout human history, opposed the Kingdom of Sin, is today embodied in the Church. The millennium began when the Church was founded. This practically substituted the actual, not the ideal Church for the Kingdom of God. The beloved ideal of Jesus became a vague phrase which kept intruding from the New Testament. Like Cinderella in the kitchen, it saw the other great dogmas furbished up for the ball, but no

302

prince of theology restored it to its rightful place. The Reformation, too, brought no renascence of the doctrine of the Kingdom; it had only eschatological value, or was defined in blurred phrases borrowed from the Church. The present revival of the Kingdom idea is due to the combined influence of the historical study of the Bible and of the social gospel.

When the doctrine of the Kingdom of God shriveled to an undeveloped and pathetic remnant in Christian thought, this loss was bound to have far-reaching consequences. We are told that the loss of a single tooth from the arch of the mouth in childhood may spoil the symmetrical development of the skull and produce malformations affecting the mind and character. The atrophy of that idea which had occupied the chief place in the mind of Jesus, necessarily affected the conception of Christianity, the life of the Church, the progress of humanity, and the structure of theology. I shall briefly enumerate some of the consequences affecting theology. This list, however, is by no means complete.

1. Theology lost its contact with the synoptic thought of Jesus. Its problems were not at all the same which had occupied his mind. It lost his point of view and became to some extent incapable of understanding him. His ideas had to be rediscovered in our time. Traditional theology and the mind of Jesus Christ became incommensurable quantities. It claimed to regard his revelation and the substance of his thought as divine, and yet did not learn to think like him. The loss of the Kingdom idea is one key to this situation.

2. The distinctive ethical principles of Jesus were the direct outgrowth of his conception of the Kingdom of God. When the latter disappeared from theology, the former disappeared from ethics. Only persons having the substance of the Kingdom ideal in their minds, seem to be able to get relish out of the ethics of Jesus. Only those church bodies which have been in opposition to organized society and have looked for a better city with its foundations in heaven, have taken the Sermon on the Mount seriously.

3. The Church is primarily a fellowship for worship; the Kingdom is a fellowship of righteousness. When the latter was neglected in theology, the ethical force of Christianity was weakened; when the former was emphasized in theology, the importance of worship was exaggerated. The prophets and Jesus had cried down sacrifices and ceremonial performances, and cried up righteousness, mercy, solidarity. Theology now reversed this, and by its theoretical discussions did its best to stimulate sacramental actions and priestly importance. Thus the religious energy

and enthusiasm which might have saved mankind from its great sins, were used up in hearing and endowing masses, or in maintaining competitive church organizations, while mankind is still stuck in the mud. There are nations in which the ethical condition of the masses is the reverse of the frequency of the masses in the churches.

4. When the Kingdom ceased to be the dominating religious reality, the Church moved up into the position of the supreme good. To promote the power of the Church and its control over all rival political forces was equivalent to promoting the supreme ends of Christianity. This increased the arrogance of churchmen and took the moral check off their policies. For the Kingdom of God can never be promoted by lies, craft, crime or war, but the wealth and power of the Church have often been promoted by these means. The medieval ideal of the supremacy of the Church over the State was the logical consequence of making the Church the highest good with no superior ethical standard by which to test it. The medieval doctrines concerning the Church and the Papacy were the direct theological outcome of the struggles for Church supremacy, and were meant to be weapons in that struggle.

5. The Kingdom ideal is the test and corrective of the influence of the Church. When the Kingdom ideal disappeared, the conscience of the Church was muffled. It became possible for the missionary expansion of Christianity to halt for centuries without creating any sense of shortcoming. It became possible for the most unjust social conditions to fasten themselves on Christian nations without awakening any consciousness that the purpose of Christ was being defied and beaten back. The practical undertakings of the Church remained within narrow lines, and the theological thought of the Church was necessarily confined in a similar way. The claims of the Church were allowed to stand in theology with no conditions and obligations to test and balance them. If the Kingdom had stood as the purpose for which the Church exists, the Church could not have fallen into such corruption and sloth. Theology bears part of the guilt for the pride, the greed, and the ambition of the Church.

6. The Kingdom ideal contains the revolutionary force of Christianity. When this ideal faded out of the systematic thought of the Church, it became a conservative social influence and increased the weight of the other stationary forces in society. If the Kingdom of God had remained part of the theological and Christian consciousness, the Church could not, down to our times, have been salaried by autocratic class governments to keep the democratic and economic impulses of the people under check.

7. Reversely, the movements for democracy and social justice were left without a religious backing for lack of the Kingdom idea. The Kingdom of God as the fellowship of righteousness, would be advanced by the abolition of industrial slavery and the disappearance of the slums of civilization; the Church would only indirectly gain through such social changes. Even today many Christians cannot see any religious importance in social justice and fraternity because it does not increase the number of conversions nor fill the churches. Thus the practical conception of salvation, which is the effective theology of the common man and minister, has been cut back and crippled for lack of the Kingdom ideal.

8. Secular life is belittled as compared with church life. Services rendered to the Church get a higher religious rating than services rendered to the community.[23] Thus the religious value is taken out of the activities of the common man and the prophetic services to society. Wherever the Kingdom of God is a living reality in Christian thought, any advance of social righteousness is seen as a part of redemption and arouses inward joy and the triumphant sense of salvation. When the Church absorbs interest, a subtle asceticism creeps back into our theology and the world looks different.

9. When the doctrine of the Kingdom of God is lacking in theology, the salvation of the individual is seen in its relation to the Church and to the future life, but not in its relation to the task of saving the social order. Theology has left this important point in a condition so hazy and muddled that it has taken us almost a generation to see that the salvation of the individual and the redemption of the social order are closely related, and how.

10. Finally, theology has been deprived of the inspiration of great ideas contained in the idea of the Kingdom and in labor for it. The Kingdom of God breeds prophets; the Church breeds priests and theologians. The Church runs to tradition and dogma; the Kingdom of God rejoices in forecasts and boundless horizons. The men who have contributed the most fruitful impulses to Christian thought have been men of prophetic vision, and their theology has proved most effective for future times where it has been most concerned with past history, with present social problems, and with the future of human society. The Kingdom of God is to theology what outdoor colour and light are to art. It is impossible to estimate what inspirational impulses have been lost to theology and to the Church, because it did not develop the doctrine of the Kingdom of God and see the world and its redemption from that point of view.

These are some of the historical effects which the loss of the doctrine

305

of the Kingdom of God has inflicted on systematic theology. The chief contribution which the social gospel has made and will make to theology is to give new vitality and importance to that doctrine. In doing so it will be a reformatory force of the highest importance in the field of doctrinal theology, for any systematic conception of Christianity must be not only defective but incorrect if the idea of the Kingdom of God does not govern it.

The restoration of the doctrine of the Kingdom has already made progress. Some of the ablest and most voluminous works of the old theology in their thousands of pages gave the Kingdom of God but a scanty mention, usually in connection with eschatology, and saw no connection between it and the Calvinistic doctrines of personal redemption. The newer manuals not only make constant reference to it in connection with various doctrines, but they arrange their entire subject matter so that the Kingdom of God becomes the governing idea.[24]

In the following brief propositions I should like to offer a few suggestions, on behalf of the social gospel, for the theological formulation of the doctrine of the Kingdom. Something like this is needed to give us "a theology for the social gospel."

1. The Kingdom of God is divine in its origin, progress and consummation. It was initiated by Jesus Christ, in whom the prophetic spirit came to its consummation, it is sustained by the Holy Spirit, and it will be brought to its fulfilment by the power of God in his own time. The passive and active resistance of the Kingdom of Evil at every stage of its advance is so great, and the human resources of the Kingdom of God so slender, that no explanation can satisfy a religious mind which does not see the power of God in its movements. The Kingdom of God, therefore, is miraculous all the way, and is the continuous revelation of the power, the righteousness, and the love of God. The establishment of a community of righteousness in mankind is just as much a saving act of God as the salvation of an individual from his natural selfishness and moral inability. The Kingdom of God, therefore, is not merely ethical, but has a rightful place in theology. This doctrine is absolutely necessary to establish that organic union between religion and morality, between theology and ethics, which is one of the characteristics of the Christian religion. When our moral actions are consciously related to the Kingdom of God they gain religious quality. Without this doctrine we shall have expositions of schemes of redemption and we shall have systems of ethics, but we shall not have a true exposition of Christianity. The first step to the reform of the Churches is the restoration of the doctrine of the Kingdom of God.

2. The Kingdom of God contains the teleology of the Christian religion. It translates theology from the static to the dynamic. It sees, not doctrines or rites to be conserved and perpetuated, but resistance to be overcome and great ends to be achieved. Since the Kingdom of God is the supreme purpose of God, we shall understand the Kingdom so far as we understand God, and we shall understand God so far as we understand his Kingdom. As long as organized sin is in the world, the Kingdom of God is characterized by conflict with evil. But if there were no evil, or after evil has been overcome, the Kingdom of God will still be the end to which God is lifting the race. It is realized not only by redemption, but also by the education of mankind and the revelation of his life within it.

3. Since God is in it, the Kingdom of God is always both present and future. Like God it is in all tenses, eternal in the midst of time. It is the energy of God realizing itself in human life. Its future lies among the mysteries of God. It invites and justifies prophecy, but all prophecy is fallible; it is valuable in so far as it grows out of action for the Kingdom and impels action. No theories about the future of the Kingdom of God are likely to be valuable or true which paralyze or postpone redemptive action on our part. To those who postpone, it is a theory and not a reality. It is for us to see the Kingdom of God as always coming, always pressing in on the present, always big with possibility, and always inviting immediate action. We walk by faith. Every human life is so placed that it can share with God in the creation of the Kingdom, or can resist and retard its progress. The Kingdom is for each of us the supreme task and the supreme gift of God. By accepting it as a task, we experience it as a gift. By labouring for it we enter into the joy and peace of the Kingdom as our divine fatherland and habitation.

4. Even before Christ, men of God saw the Kingdom of God as the great end to which all divine leadings were pointing. Every idealistic interpretation of the world, religious or philosophical, needs some such conception. Within the Christian religion the idea of the Kingdom gets its distinctive interpretation from Christ. (a) Jesus emancipated the idea of the Kingdom from previous nationalistic limitations and from the debasement of lower religious tendencies, and made it world-wide and spiritual. (b) He made the purpose of salvation essential in it. (c) He imposed his own mind, his personality, his love and holy will on the idea of the Kingdom. (d) He not only foretold it but initiated it by his life and work. As humanity more and more develops a racial consciousness in

307

modern life, idealistic interpretations of the destiny of humanity will become more influential and important. Unless theology has a solidaristic vision higher and fuller than any other, it cannot maintain the spiritual leadership of mankind, but will be outdistanced. Its business is to infuse the distinctive qualities of Jesus Christ into its teachings about the Kingdom, and this will be a fresh competitive test of his continued headship of humanity.

5. The Kingdom of God is humanity organized according to the will of God. Interpreting it through the consciousness of Jesus we may affirm these convictions about the ethical relations within the Kingdom: (a) Since Christ revealed the divine worth of life and personality, and since his salvation seeks the restoration and fulfilment of even the least, it follows that the Kingdom of God, at every stage of human development, tends toward a social order which will best guarantee to all personalities their freest and highest development. This involves the redemption of social life from the cramping influence of religious bigotry, from the repression of self-assertion in the relation of upper and lower classes, and from all forms of slavery in which human beings are treated as mere means to serve the ends of others. (b) Since love is the supreme law of Christ, the Kingdom of God implies a progressive reign of love in human affairs. We can see its advance wherever the free will of love supersedes the use of force and legal coercion as a regulative of the social order. This involves the redemption of society from political autocracies and economic oligarchies; the substitution of redemptive for vindictive penology; the abolition of constraint through hunger as part of the industrial system; and the abolition of war as the supreme expression of hate and the completest cessation of freedom. (c) The highest expression of love is the free surrender of what is truly our own, life, property, and rights. A much lower but perhaps more decisive expression of love is the surrender of any opportunity to exploit men. No social group or organization can claim to be clearly within the Kingdom of God which drains others for its own ease, and resists the effort to abate this fundamental evil. This involves the redemption of society from private property in the natural resources of the earth, and from any condition in industry which makes monopoly profits possible. (d) The reign of love tends toward the progressive unity of mankind, but with the maintenance of individual liberty and the opportunity of nations to work out their own national peculiarities and ideals.

6. Since the Kingdom is the supreme end of God, it must be the purpose for which the Church exists. The measure in which it fulfils this

purpose is also the measure of its spiritual authority and honour. The institutions of the Church, its activities, its worship, and its theology must in the long run be tested by its effectiveness in creating the Kingdom of God. For the Church to see itself apart from the Kingdom, and to find its aims in itself, is the same sin of selfish detachment as when an individual selfishly separates himself from the common good. The Church has the power to save in so far as the Kingdom of God is present in it. If the Church is not living for the Kingdom, its institutions are part of the "world." In that case it is not the power of redemption but its object. It may even become an anti-Christian power. If any form of church organization which formerly aided the Kingdom now impedes it, the reason for its existence is gone.

7. Since the Kingdom is the supreme end, all problems of personal salvation must be reconsidered from the point of view of the Kingdom. It is not sufficient to set the two aims of Christianity side by side. There must be a synthesis, and theology must explain how the two react on each other. The entire redemptive work of Christ must also be reconsidered under this orientation. Early Greek theology saw salvation chiefly as the redemption from ignorance by the revelation of God and from earthliness by the impartation of immortality. It interpreted the work of Christ accordingly, and laid stress on his incarnation and resurrection. Western theology saw salvation mainly as forgiveness of guilt and freedom from punishment. It interpreted the work of Christ accordingly, and laid stress on the death and atonement. If the Kingdom of God was the guiding idea and chief end of Jesus—as we now know it was—we may be sure that every step in His life, including His death, was related to that aim and its realization, and when the idea of the Kingdom of God takes its due place in theology, the work of Christ will have to be interpreted afresh.

8. The Kingdom of God is not confined within the limits of the Church and its activities. It embraces the whole of human life. It is the Christian transfiguration of the social order. The Church is one social institution alongside of the family, the industrial organization of society, and the State. The Kingdom of God is in all these, and realizes itself through them all. During the Middle Ages all society was ruled and guided by the Church. Few of us would want modern life to return to such a condition. Functions which the Church used to perform, have now far outgrown its capacities. The Church is indispensable to the religious education of humanity and to the conservation of religion, but the greatest future awaits religion in the public life of humanity.

309

## Notes

1. In *Christianity and the Social Crisis*. (1907; reprint, New York and Evanston: Harper & Row, 1964), pp. 84-92.
2. Mark 12:37.
3. P. 407.
4. Luke 1:52-53. [Throughout this essay Rauschenbusch seems to be paraphrasing, rather than directly quoting, the King James Version of the Bible.]
5. Mark 10:31.
6. Luke 16:15.
7. Matthew 5:1-12.
8. See the whole of Matthew 23.
9. Matthew 21:23-32.
10. Luke 13:32.
11. Matthew 20:20-28.
12. The English translation, "exercise authority over them," is far too weak to do justice to the preposition in (κατεξουσιάζουσιν). Weizsaecker tranlates it *vergewaltigen*; the Twentieth Century New Testament, "oppress." It carries the meaning both of injustice and coercion.
13. Luke 22:25.
14. Matthew 23:1-12.
15. Matthew 20:26-28.
16. Matthew 22:15-22.
17. See Bryce, "Holy Roman Empire," 112-13.
18. Matthew 17:24-27.
19. "Primitive Property," xxxi.
20. In his essay on "The Progress of the World."
21. Frances G. Peabody, "Jesus Christ and the Social Question," 89.
22. In *A Theology for the Social Gospel* (1917; reprint, Nashville: Abingdon Press, 1978), pp. 131-45.
23. After the death of Susan B. Anthony a minister commented on her life, regretting that she was not orthodox in her beliefs. In the same address he spoke glowingly about a new linoleum laid in the church kitchen.
24. William Adams Brown, "Christian Theology in Outline," p. 192: "We are witnessing to-day a reaction against this exaggerated individualism (of Reformation theology). It has become an axiom of modern thought that the government of God has social as well as individual significance, and the conception of the Kingdom of God—obscured in the earlier Protestantism—is coming again into the forefront of theological thought." . . .

    Albrecht Ritschl, in his great monograph on Justification and Reconciliation, begins the discussion of his own views in Volume III (§2) by insisting that personal salvation must be organically connected with the Kingdom of God. He says ("Rechtfertigung und Versöhnung," III, p. 111): "Theology has taken a very unequal interest in the two chief characteristics of Christianity. Everything pertaining to its character as the redemption of men has been made the subject of the most minute consideration; consequently redemption by Christ has been taken as the centre of all Christian knowledge and life, whereas the ethical conception of Christianity contained in the idea of the Kingdom of God has been slighted. . . . It has been fatal for Protestantism that the Reformers did not cleanse the idea of the ethical Kingdom of God or Christ from its hierarchical corruption (i.e. the idea that the visible Church is identical with the Kingdom), but worked out the idea only in an academic and unpractical form." Kant first recognized the importance of the Kingdom of God for ethics. Schleiermacher first applied the teleological quality of Christianity to the definition of its nature, but he still treated now of personal redemption and now of the Kingdom of God, without adequately working out their connection. Ritschl has done more than any one else to put the idea to the front in German theology, but he does not get beyond a few great general ideas. He was born too early to get sociological ideas.

# Frances E. Willard

W*illard (1839–1898) is duly noted in church historical
studies as a founder and energetic leader of the Woman's Christian Temperance Union and an activist as well for women's rights and other
moral reforms. Her commitments to such causes came, as it were, naturally. Her first five years were spent in the midst of the extension of New
Haven Protestantism that Charles G. Finney established at Oberlin,
Ohio, a hotbed of revivalism and social reform. With her family she
moved to the upper Midwest and to strict Methodism oriented toward
sanctification and holiness. She completed her education at Methodist
schools, graduating from the North Western Female College (1859) in
Evanston, Illinois, and thereafter, until 1874, held posts as school
teacher and college instructor and president. Leadership in the W.C.T.U.
followed.*

*In terms of the history of theology, Willard points out and toward
developments in process that are often too hastily passed over. This
selection is from her best-known writing,* Woman in the Pulpit. *It is "of
course" an early, sustained argument for the ordination of women. It is
also a fateful work in posing precisely that issue as a theological question, requiring a theological answer rooted in faith's most basic convictions, not mere proof-texting or expediency. Plus, in pointing to where
that answer is to be found, Willard the Methodist-holiness crusader
uplifts a "Christ, not Paul" motif that shows her solidarity with the
christocentrism of the era, giving it an incipient "feminist" turn.*

## THE SPIRIT GIVETH LIFE[1]

Christ, not Paul, is the source of all churchly authority and power.
What do we find him saying? How did he deal with women? In the presence of the multitude, he drew from Martha the same testimony that he
required of his Apostles, and she publicly replied, almost in Peter's very
words, "Yea, Lord, I believe that thou art the Christ, the Son of God,

which should come into the world." He declared his commission to the woman at the well of Samaria, with an emphasis and a particularity hardly equalled in any of his public addresses, and her embassy was abundantly rewarded. What pastor would not rejoice to hear such words as these: "Now we believe, not because of thy saying, for we have heard him ourselves, and know that this is indeed the Christ, the Saviour of the world."

It is objected that he called no woman to be an apostle. Granted, but he himself said that he chose one man who had a devil; is this a precedent? One is half inclined to think so, when one reads the long record of priestly intolerance, its culmination being the ostracism of Christ's most faithful followers from their right to proclaim the risen Lord, who gave to Mary the first commission to declare his resurrection. True, he did not designate women as his followers; they came without a call; from their sex he had his human origin; with the immeasurable dignities of his incarnation and his birth, only God and woman were concerned; no utterance of his marks woman as ineligible to any position in the church he came to found; but his gracious words and deeds, his impartation of his purposes and plans to women, his stern reproofs to men who did them wrong, his chosen companionships, and the tenor of his whole life and teaching, all point out precisely the opposite conclusion. Indeed, Luke explicitly declares (viii. 1, 2, 3) that, as "he went throughout every city and village, preaching and showing the glad tidings of the Kingdom of God," "the twelve were with him, *and certain women*," among whom were " Joanna, the wife of Chuza, Herod's steward, and Susanna, and many others, which ministered unto him of their substance."

What a spectacle must that have been for the "Scribes and Pharisees, hypocrites." What loss of caste came to those fearless women, who, breaking away from the customs of society and traditions of religion, dared to follow the greatest of Iconoclasts from city to village with a publicity and a persistence nothing less than outrageous to the conservatives of that day.

Verily, Devotion, thy name is Woman!

> "Not she with trait'rous kiss her Saviour stung;
> Not she denied him with unholy tongue;
> She, while apostles shrank, could danger brave,
> Last at his cross, and earliest at his grave."

Christ's commission only is authoritative. To whom did he give it after his resurrection, until which time the new dispensation was not fairly ushered in? If we are to accept specific statements, rather than the drift and spirit of the inspired book, as conclusive of a question involving half the human race, let us, then, here take our stand on our Lord's final words and deeds. It is stated (Luke xxiv. 33) that the two disciples to whom Christ appeared on the way to Emmaus "returned to Jerusalem, and found the eleven gathered together, and *them that were with them*, saying, 'The Lord is risen, indeed, and hath appeared to Simon.' " Be it understood that women used this language, the women "which came with him from Galilee." It was "them that were with them" (*i.e.*, with the eleven), who were saying, "The Lord is risen indeed."

While they were thus assembled and talking of the wonderful experience of that day, Jesus appeared again, saying, "Peace be unto you." Let us turn to John xx. 19-23, where we have an account of this same appearance of Christ to his disciples for it says explicitly (after stating that Mary Magdalene came and told the disciples that she had seen the Lord), "Then the same day at evening . . . Jesus stood in the midst and saith unto them, Peace be unto you; as my Father hath sent me even so send I you. And when he had said this, he breathed on them and saith unto them, Receive ye the Holy Ghost; whosesoever sins ye remit they are remitted unto them, and whosesoever sins ye retain they are retained." These, then, are his words spoken to the eleven and "*them that were with them*." He then "opened their understanding that they might understand the Scriptures," and declared that "repentance and remission of sins should be preached in his name among all nations, beginning at Jerusalem," and declared, "*ye are witnesses* of these things. And behold, I send the promise of my Father upon you, but tarry ye in Jerusalem until ye be endued with power from on high. And he led them out as far as to Bethany, and he lifted up his hands, and blessed them. And it came to pass, while he blessed them, he was parted from them, and carried up into heaven. And they worshipped him, and returned to Jerusalem with great joy."

Does any reasonable person suppose that His mother was not there, or that the other Marys were not? or the great company of women that had ministered to Him? But we are not left in doubt. Turn to Acts i. 13-14. After stating Christ's command that they should not depart from Jerusalem, but wait for the promise of the Father, "For ye shall be baptized with the Holy Ghost not many days hence," after which "Ye shall be witnesses unto me unto the uttermost parts of the earth;" and after giving a brief account of the Resurrection, this passage occurs[:] "Then

314

returned they unto Jerusalem, and when they were come in, they went up into an upper room where abode both Peter and James and John . . . these all continued with one accord in prayer and supplication *with the women,* and Mary, the mother of Jesus, and with his brethren. And when the day of Pentecost was fully come, they were *all* with one accord in one place. . . . And they were *all* filled with the Holy Ghost and began to speak with other tongues as the Spirit gave them utterance." Then Peter said: "This is that which was spoken by the prophet Joel, I will pour out my Spirit upon *all* flesh, and your sons and *your daughters* shall prophesy, and on my servants and on my *handmaids* I will pour out my Spirit, and *they shall prophesy.*" Paul proves that prophesying may be preaching when he says (1 Cor. xiv. 3): "But he that prophesieth speaketh unto men to edification and exhortation and comfort." Well said Gamaliel of this new dispensation: "If this counsel or this work be of men, it will come to naught; but if it be of God, ye cannot overthrow it, lest haply ye be found to fight against God."

Let not conservative ecclesiastical leaders try to steady the Lord's ark; let them not bind what God hath loosed; let them not retain the bondage he hath remitted, lest haply they be found to fight against God!

"We want the earth," is the world-old motto of men. They have had their desire, and we behold the white male dynasty reigning undisputed until our own day; lording it over every heritage, and constituting the only unquestioned "apostolic succession." Only one thing can end the dire enchantment we are under, and that is to know the truth, for truth alone makes free. And the truth of God, a thousand times repeated by the voice of history, science, and every-day experience, resounds louder to-day than in all preceding ages: "It is not good for man to be alone!" Suppose it be admitted that the dual-natured founder of Christianity, in whose character the force that smote the money-changers of the temple was commingled with the love that yearned to gather Jerusalem as a hen gathers "her chickens under her wings," chose as his apostles the only ones who in that barbarous age would be tolerated in preaching it. Be it remembered that Protestantism recognizes the apostles as having had no successors. Hence, any argument built on man's primacy as related to them and the manner of their choosing falls to the ground. It is curious, considering certain exegetical literalism, that their method of choosing by lot should not have been insisted upon as a part of the divine order!

In the revolt from Roman license, the clergy early declared woman a delusion and a snare, banished her from the company of men who aspired to holiness, and, by introducing the denaturalizing heresy of a

315

celibate clergy, made it impossible for the doctrine of God's eternal fatherhood to be so understood by the preacher that it should become vital in the hearer's heart. It is *men* who have defrauded manhood and womanhood, in the persons of priest and monk and nun, of the right to the sanctities of home; men who have invented hierarchies, enthroned a fisherman as God's vicegerent, lighted inquisitorial fires, and made the Prince of peace a mighty man of war. It is men who have taken the simple, loving, tender Gospel of the New Testament, so suited to be the proclamation of a woman's lips, and translated it in terms of sacerdotalism, dogma, and martyrdom. It is men who have given us the dead letter rather than the living Gospel. The mother-heart of God will never be known to the world until translated into terms of speech by mother-hearted women. Law and love will never balance in the realm of grace until a woman's hand shall hold the scales.

Men preach a creed; women will declare a life. Men deal in formulas, women in facts. Men have always tithed mint and rue and cummin in their exegesis and their ecclesiasticism, while the world's heart has cried out for compassion, forgiveness, and sympathy. Men's preaching has left heads committed to a catechism, and left hearts hard as nether millstones. The Greek bishop who said, "My creed is faultless, with my life you have nothing to do," condensed into a sentence two thousand years of priestly dogma. Men reason in the abstract, women in the concrete. A syllogism symbolizes one, a rule of life the other. In saying this I wish distinctly to disclaim any attack upon the clergy, any slighting allusion to the highest and holiest of callings; I am speaking only of the intolerant sacerdotal element that has handicapped the church from the earliest ages even until now, and which has been more severely criticised by the best element in the church than by any words that I have penned.

Religion is an affair of the heart. The world is hungry for the comfort of Christ's Gospel, and thirsty for its every-day beatitudes of that holiness which alone constitutes happiness. Men have lost faith in themselves and each other. Boodlerism and "corners" on the market, greed of gain, passion for power, desire for drink, impurity of life, the complicity of the church, Protestant as well as Papal, with the liquor traffic, the preference of a partisan to a conscientious ballot, have combined to make the men of this generation faithless toward one another. The masses of the people have forsaken God's house, and solace themselves in the saloons or with the Sunday newspaper. But the masses will go to hear women when they speak, and every woman who leads a life of weekday holiness, and has the Gospel in her looks, however plain her face and dress may be, has round her head the sweet Madonna's halo, in the eyes of every man who sees her, and she speaks to him with the sacred cadence of his own mother's voice. The devil knew what he was doing when he exhausted sophistry to keep woman down and silent. He knew that "the only consecrated place on earth is where God's Spirit is," and that a Christian woman's heart enshrines that holy Guest more surely than many a "consecrated" pulpit.

Men have been preaching well-nigh two thousand years, and the large majority of the converts have been women. Suppose now that women should share the preaching power, might it not be reasonably expected that a majority of the converts under their administration would be men? Indeed, how else are the latter to have a fair chance at the Gospel? The question is asked in all seriousness, and if its practical answer shall be the equipping of women for the pulpit, it may be reasonably claimed that men's hopes of heaven will be immeasurably increased. Hence, one who urges the taking-off of the arbitrary ruling which now excludes woman from a choice portion of her kingdom may well claim to have manifested especial considerateness toward the interests of men.

The entrance of woman upon the ministerial vocation will give to humanity just twice the probability of strengthening and comforting speech, for women have at least as much sympathy, reverence, and spirituality as men, and they have at least equal felicity of manner and of utterance. Why, then, should the pulpit be shorn of half its power?

To the exegesis of the cloister we oppose that of common life. To the Orientalism that is passing off the stage, we oppose modern Christianity. In our day, the ministers of a great church[2] have struck the word "obey" out of the marriage service, have made women eligible to nearly every rank except the ecclesiastic, and are withheld from raising her to the ministerial office only by the influence of a few leaders, who are insecurely seated on the safety-valve of that mighty engine, Progress. In our day, all churches, except the hierarchical Presbyterian, Episcopal, and Roman Catholic, have made women eligible as members of their councils, leaders in their Sunday-school systems, in several cases have set them apart to the ministry, and in almost all have opened their pulpits to them; even the slow-moving Presbyterian having done this quite generally in later years, and the Episcopal, in several instances, granting women "where to stand" in its chapels, outside the charmed arc of its chancel-rail.

Whoever quotes to the intelligent and devout women of the American church to-day the specific instructions given by Paul to the illiterate and immoral women of Corinth does so at the expense of sound judgment, not to say scholarship. An exegesis so strained and so outworn is on a par with that which would pronounce the Saviour of the world "a glutton and a wine-bibber," because the Pharisees, when he came eating and drinking, declared him to be such.

The lifeless prayer-meetings, from which women's voices are excluded, are largely given over to perfunctory, official prayers, and the churches that still quote "He shall rule over thee" as a Gospel precept are deserted by the great humanity that beats its life along the stony streets. "Behold, your house is left unto you desolate" is the requiem of empty pews that would be full if men and women stood side by side at the church, as they are now fast learning to do at the home altars. For the "man of the house" to do all the praying is to deprive the children of one of life's most sacred ministries—that of their mother's voice in prayer and in the giving of thanks for daily food. Observation in a great variety of homes convinces me that this joint leadership in household worship is being largely introduced. Probably the extreme of masculine prerogative in this regard was illustrated in an Eastern town some years ago, when a boy of twelve was called in from his play to say grace over the lunch prepared between meals for his young lady cousin, a guest newly arrived. The incident is perfectly authentic, and the act was entirely consistent and devout, upon the theory of man's divinely constituted primacy in matters spiritual.

"Behold, I make all things new" was the joyful declaration of woman's great Deliverer. "He hath sent me to heal the broken-hearted, to preach deliverance to the captives, and recovering of sight to the blind, to set at liberty them that are bruised." Above all other beings these words must refer to woman, who, without Christ, lies prostrate under society's pitiless and crushing pyramid. Whether they perceive it or not, it is chiefly ecclesiasticism and not Christianity that Robert Ingersoll and Elizabeth Cady Stanton have been fighting; it is the burdens grievous to be borne that men have laid upon weak shoulders, but which they themselves would not touch with one of their fingers. Christ knew that this would be; he had to place the treasure of his Gospel in the earthen vessels of selfish human hearts. But that treasure is like the leaven that a woman took and hid in three measures of meal until the whole was leavened.

"Behold, I make all things new;" "the letter killeth, the spirit giveth life." These are his words, who spake not as man speaketh; and how the letter killeth to-day, let the sectarianism, the sacerdotalism, and the woman-silencing of the church bear witness. The time has come when those men in high places, "dressed in a little brief authority" within the church of Christ, who seek to shut women out of the pastorate, cannot do so with impunity. . . .

. . .

Let me, as a loyal daughter of the church, urge upon younger women who feel a call, as I once did, to preach the unsearchable riches of Christ, their duty to seek admission to the doors that would hardly close against them now, in any theological seminary, save those of the Roman, Episcopal, and Presbyterian churches; and let me pleadingly beseech all Christian people who grieve over the world's great heartache, to encourage every true and capable woman, whose heart God has touched, in her wistful purpose of entering upon that blessed Gospel ministry, through which her strong yet gentle words and work may help to heal that heartache, and to comfort the sinful and the sad "as one whom his mother comforteth."

### Notes

1. In *Woman in the Pulpit* (Washington, D.C.: Zenger Publishing, 1978; originally published in 1889), pp. 40-52, 62.
2. The Methodist Episcopal, with two millions of members.

# Alexander Crummell

*Crummell (1819–1898) was an early "theological liberal" voice in the Episcopal church as well as a prominent spokesperson for the concerns and well-being of African Americans during and after the Reconstruction era. Born a free black in New York state, he overcame prejudice in the North, receiving Episcopal ordination and a B.A. from Queen's College, Cambridge (1853). He lived for nearly twenty years thereafter in Liberia, as a citizen, an Episcopal leader urging an independent black church, an educator, and an advocate of the return of blacks to Africa as colonists to lead native Africans to English civilization.*

*After 1872, having changed his views on "colonization," he served as an Episcopal priest in Washington, D.C., founding and ministering to a black parish. The year before his death he started the American Negro Academy, designed to foster separate, self-help efforts among African Americans led by an elite corps of the educated. The sermon that follows reflects his confidence in the benefits of English civilization, as well as his christocentric liberal beliefs in the progressive nature of Christ's influence upon history and the value of the development of character.*

## THE GREATNESS OF CHRIST[1]

*(Christmas.)*
*And when they were come into the house, they saw the young child with Mary, his mother, and fell down, and worshipped him; and when they had opened their treasures, they presented unto him gifts; gold, and frankincense, and myrrh.—Matthew 2:11*

It was a little child, nay, a feeble, helpless infant, to Whom all this reverence and devotion were given. And it is, by imagination, the same little babe that all Christendom to-day turns back to and approaches with joy, and salutations, and profoundest worship. The point of interest in this little child is not simply that its body was small and weak, but that

320

His person, diminutive as it was, was the germ of wondrous power, was the fountain-head of a world-wide ocean, was the root of prodigious reality which reaches from time over into deepest eternity.

It is one of the wide, general facts of nature, that the things of magnitude throughout the universe spring from small and minute causes. It is so with plants, and trees, and forests: tiny seeds are the parents of vast and formidable wildernesses; so with beasts, and birds, and fishes; so with the stars of heaven, whose brilliant bodies derive from the impalpable nebulae of the spheres; so with the nations of the earth, with families and individuals. All the great things, all the great men we see, hear, or read of, passed from littleness up to magnitude and importance. It is, then, strictly in accordance with the analogy of all the things of God, that He, whose Advent we celebrate to-day, began His wondrous life in the feebleness of infancy. But our joy springs from the miracle of His life, which was divine, and the majesty of His mission, which was princely, beneficent, and godlike in all the minutiae of His work.

. . .

I wish to speak to-day of the greatness of Christ. It is a greatness which has constantly manifested itself through the ages by a gracious but irresistible revolution, which has never, at any time, known a moment of cessation. We talk of the influence of Christianity; and men ofttimes seem happy when they can thus drop or deny a personality and make a catch-word of a system. But it is best, at all times, to speak the real facts of a case. No system, of itself, produces results. It is, in its results, the work of either devils, or of angels, or of men, or of God. There is a personality behind every organized institution, behind every bank, behind every insurance company, every mercantile house, every manufactory. So, too, of Christianity. It does not work itself. It is not the work of men and ministers. It is a result, in all nations, societies, families, and persons,—a result that is produced by Jesus Christ, present in this world by the power and energy of the Holy Ghost.

Let me point out a few things which the Lord Jesus has done, and which never would have been done if He had not come into this world, and which He alone, of all the intelligences, had the power to do.

First, see the great change our blessed Lord has made in the domain of thought. I refer to this special point at the first, not because I would exaggerate the intellect, as superior to the moral nature; for I do not. I speak first of our Lord's work in the realm of thought because the life of man and the life of society is determined chiefly by the convictions which are reached by the intellect. As a man "thinketh in his heart, so he is." According to the ruling ideas of an age or a nation, so is it.

Now the power of every being, in the sphere of mind, may be seen in three special respects, viz.: (1) In the ability to stimulate thought; (2) in the specific weight or quality of the thought expressed; (3) in the practical or active nature of the thought put into human souls. In these several respects, you can see how unique, and how exalted, has been the force of the Lord Jesus, in all human history.

You will remember that always and everywhere the mind of man has been active; for activity is a native quality of mind. It was active at the period of our Lord's Nativity; active in its show of greed; active in philosophy; active in war and conquest; active in the ambitions and dominancy of great men and great nations. It was an era of great luxury; it was an age of prying and abstruse philosophies; it was a period of subjugation of provinces and empires. The mind of men, at the time of the Saviour's birth, was seething, burning, with large and important problems and gigantic undertakings.

But previous to the time of Christ, notwithstanding all the activity of the human mind, there was a whole class of subjects, subjects of vast importance to the human soul, from which the mind of man was universally divorced. Religion was the possession and the practice of all peoples. But those noble features of religion which flow in lofty truths and sacred precepts from the lips of Jesus had never before circled the brains, nor agitated the hearts, nor stimulated the sensibilities. I read the histories of men, pick out the annals of the noblest Pagan nations, select the writings of the most elevated of their sages, but search in vain, in the most abstruse and most elaborate of their treatises, for the grand divine conceptions which Jesus of Nazareth has put into the minds of men and of nations, and which have awakened them to life and energy.

I turn to the Scriptures, and find there the grandest ideas and principles which ever entered the mind of man; which did not come from the human mind, and which could only be of divine origin. The grand thought of Christ may be analyzed and presented somewhat under these three aspects: (a) That of His sovereignty and rule. He tells us of a divine and eternal government set up in this world, founded upon righteousness, sustained by heavenly affections, generated in our sinful nature by divine influences. "I establish a kingdom," says our Lord; and the Church, "the Kingdom of Heaven" on earth, the "Body of Christ," springs into existence; higher in authority than all the kingdoms of this world, mastering governments and dominions; and never has it failed;

"and the gates of hell shall not prevail against it." (b) Another phase of this truth of Christ is that of a reconstructed and spiritualized humanity, produced by the operations of the Holy Ghost in the kingdom of Christ. Our Lord promises a righteousness put into our being, of which man had never before conceived. He guarantees us the reality of a regenerated humanity. He shows us, in His own life and excellence, the possibility of disinterested virtue as the possession of exalted men here on earth. He encourages us with the idea of a benignity and brotherhood among men, which shall destroy everywhere the spirit of revenge, national enmity, and fiery war, and usher in the reign of universal peace. And (c) He crowns these teachings and instructions with a phase of His truth which is at once celestial and transporting. He holds up to view a future state, where the everlasting craving of the soul shall be for the treasures which are incorruptible, and the riches which are eternal. That state is a state of eternal well-being in another sphere, in which men shall company forever with angels and archangels, and eternally enjoy the presence and glory of God!

These are the grand thoughts, yet only partially presented, which Christ has put into the minds of men: earthly in one aspect, working out philanthropies and enterprise in human society; heavenly in another and higher view, because reaching onward to eternal issues. See the wonderful revolutions they have produced among men! See the grand impulses they have started in all the lines of human action! See the great mastery they have given to select peoples, whom they have elevated and invigorated! Note, above all, how, that, having once entered the soul of man, they have taken to themselves the law of heredity, and come down not only in the polity, in the governments, in the liberties, in the letters and literature, and in the laws, but actually in the blood of mighty nations, from age to age! Generations come and go, but these great thoughts of our Lord abide and reproduce themselves. Aye, and they are destined to stay here till the crack of doom! Persecutions like those of the Caesars could not destroy them! Revolutions like that of France in 1792 could not crush them out! These thoughts are thoroughly vitalized with the life of God Himself. They are the thoughts of eternity, and have become so incorporated with our humanity in its very best conditions that they will work, quicken, and animate the masses of men, until, by and by, they get the ascendency over all the thought, reasoning, and reflection of mankind.

. . .

Second, I turn to another evidence of the greatness of Christ. I refer to that broad transformation of man's civilization which He has wrought. We have only to go back into the past histories of nations, and we shall see the nature of this achievement.

We all know somewhat the cultivation of Egypt, Babylonia, Phoenicia, Greece, and Rome. We know how various were the forms of this cultivation in these several peoples; but we find one broad generalization that may be made of them all, that is, that they were saturated with the spirit of brutality, lust, and murder. When one goes into the museums of Paris or London, and looks at the monuments of ancient art, dug up after centuries of dark repose from the ruins and debris of Nineveh, or Cyprus, or Greece, or Rome, it is difficult to say which form of astonishment is the greater, the astonishment at the exquisite perfection of the art, or the astonishment at the moral debasement they discover. The same contrast and disparity constantly come to mind, in reading the poetry and the histories of pagan writers. The paintings and the sculpture are too often vile and infamous. The condition of woman among them was degrading. Their family-life was barbarous, and not seldom shameless. Their social state presented the varied aspect of great luxury, dazzling splendor, allied to gross license and unrestrained indulgence.
. . .

See now the great work which has been done by our Lord in changing the moral complexion of human civilization. This revolution began in the family. It destroyed, first of all, the pagan status of womanly life. The Gospel law was a proclamation of equality to woman. In the Church of God she found at once, and for the first time, her place as man's equal and his companion. The elevation of woman in the Church was, at the same time, the reconstruction of the family. The household, thus sanctified and elevated, was a "Church in the House"; and it became an organic unit for wider, nobler uses beyond itself. As Christian households increased, the whole structure of social and domestic life became changed and purified. The saints, in heathen communities, carried the divine principle into their traffic, business, trades, professions, civil relations, and service; and so, gradually, the old, impure, pagan elements of society were everywhere antagonized by the Cross, and beaten down from supremacy. The leaven of Christianity spread into every section of society; it seized upon every occupation; it entered every relation of life; it penetrated the army, the civil courts, the senate; and at last it reached the seat of Imperial Caesar. "We are a people of yesterday," says Tertullian in his Apology; "and yet we have filled every place belonging to you,—cities, islands, castles, towns, assemblies, your very camp, your tribes, companies, palace, senate, forum! We leave you your temples only. We can count your armies; our numbers in a single province will be greater." . . .

When the Gospel had done its work in the Roman Empire, it stretched out for new conquests in the other states of Europe. Nay, the Roman Empire was God's instrument and agency for the spread of this newly-created Christian civilization. The empire conquered tribe after tribe, province after province, one barbarous nation after another, and subjected them to Roman law and authority. And then the Church seized, in Christ's Name, upon the Empire, and made it her agent, whereby a chastened Christian civilization was spread throughout Europe. And this day every one sees the grand outcome of the whole process. Christianity, at this moment, is the masterful power in every European state, and through their laws, colonies, and commerce, wields the sceptre of the globe.

Let us pause, just here, for a moment, and make a reckoning of our Master's great work this nineteen hundred years, in the renovation of the world's civilization. You will recall what I suggested as the elements of civilization—the family, the status of woman, dress, culture, manners, social life, art. Art, however, may be taken as the crowning point, the criterion of civilization. See, then, herein, the wonderful change Christ has made in this regard. . . .

. . .

Third, your notice is called to one other striking evidence of the greatness of Christ,—the humanizing influence He has put into, and diffused throughout the world.

We mourn, day by day, at the brutal acts which are chronicled in our newspapers. We are horror-struck at the fearful murders which are constantly committed. Our souls sink when we read or think of the ravages and slaughter of the battlefield, which still disgrace this Christian era.

. . .

My contention, be it noticed, is not that Christianity has abolished war. Christianity, in its best results, is not an extemporaneous affair. God, in His providence, moves with majesty, and not in a flash. To use the words of Guizot, "He hurries not himself to display to-day the consequences of the principle that He yesterday laid down; He will draw it out in the lapse of ages, when the hour is come." Christianity has not yet entirely abolished war. But the greatness of Christ is seen in the fact that He *has been abolishing war* all the centuries through, by the humanization which He has introduced into the policy of nations. All along the Christian era His faith has been lessening the frequency of wars; diminishing the cruel, pagan slaughter of war; extinguishing the brutish, heathen love of war; and, above all, counteracting and extirpating the *idea* of war as a motive of national and personal action. So that now, in the nineteenth century, we have reached this state of the case, namely: that nations are hesitant about entering upon war; *when* war does take place, it is under the most urgent, absolute necessity; *while* it is carrying on, everything possible is done to alleviate its horrors; and especially that, when a Minister of State, in any land, proclaims in any way to the world that the trade of war is a prime policy of his country, the Christian world rises up in indignation, and by the voice of a Burke, or a Channing, or a Gladstone, blasts that statesman to utter ruin, and drives him to disgrace and confusion. Added to all this is the notable fact that, in our own day the principle of arbitration has become a part of international law, as a preventive of the slaughter of men, and for the promotion of national peace, equity, and justice!

See, too, the humanizing influence of Christianity in the suppression of the slave trade, in the destruction of piracy, in the abolition of slavery, in the reformation of prisons, in the progress of the temperance cause, in the improvement of tenement houses, in the increase of hospitals and infirmaries; in the care of the blind, the deaf, and the dumb; in the godly efforts to prevent the ravages of licentiousness; and in the merciful endeavours to save the victims of prostitution! In all these generous, gracious ventures which one sees throughout all Christendom, we recognize the working of that quality of mercy, the special attribute of Christ,

> It droppeth as the gentle rain from heaven
> Upon the place beneath.

This spirit has been working its way nigh two thousand years, against the deep depravity of mankind; but only in this age has it succeeded, to any large degree, in the exercise of its fullest power. We have now, at last, reached the age of missions and noblest charities. In these times we are permitted to see, not only in Christian lands, but in the pagan quarters of the globe, whither the Church of God is speeding, all the fair humanities, the large philanthropies, the saving appliances which are fitted to restore, uplift, and regenerate the most degraded of the human species. Never before in the history of man has the thoughtful mind been so alert and active as now, in ingenious effort for human good. The beneficence of man is instinct with curiosity. The spirit of benevolence, and even of evangelization, is no longer confined to the Church of God. It is the spirit of the age. Our Lord Christ has put this spirit into insurance companies, and mercantile ventures. It stimulates adventure. It prompts geographical research. It vitalizes science. It gives coloring and tone to literature. Just take this single, simple fact, and ponder on it. . . .

I have thus given you a few tokens of the greatness of Christ, in words that may seem somewhat as though a man should take a single ray from the burning lustre of the midday sky, and hold it up as a specimen of sunlight. The evidences of our Lord's greatness and majesty crowd the eye, and overcome both mind and memory. It seems impossible but that they should impress us all with the deepest sensibility and the greatest reverence. Here is a Being who comes into the world in precisely the same manner as every one of us has entered it. He was born of woman. His infancy was helpless and feeble. But all His after-life was unique, separate in its influence and power, from every other being that ever lived on earth. He lived some thirty-three years, a life of blessedness, labor, suffering, and insult, and at last died an ignominious death! And yet His divine face, the odor of His sanctity, the glories of His nature, and the mystical power of His resurrection come streaming down the centuries, neutralizing the might, majesty, and splendor of kings, states-men, and warriors, and, casting them all in the shade, attracting to Him-self the homage of the centuries! Mine is not the task to-day to produce evidences of the truth of Christianity. It is no purpose of mine to vindi-cate the Deity of my Master; but I submit, that this singular fact in human history, the greatness of Christ, is unaccountable, if it be not divine! . . .

### Note

1. In *The Greatness of Christ and Other Sermons* (New York: Thomas Whittaker, 1882), pp. 1-18.

# Henry M. Turner

*The career of Turner (1834–1915) spanned the years of Civil War, Reconstruction, and its aftermath. His services as a minister of the African Methodist Church in the South included striking works in all three periods: as a black chaplain in the Union Army, a state legislator of South Carolina following the war, and a Bishop of his church who took an active interest not only in its growth but also in its wider social and ecumenical responsibilities. He was also, early on, a leading advocate of African American emigration to Africa and, later, a vigorous opponent of assimilationist views that urged blacks to forget Africa, slavery, and "blackness" and pursue self-help conformity to white culture, white Christianity—and white theology.*

*Prophetic theology in one sense for its times and in yet another for the last half of the twentieth century, Turner's brief, to-the-point defense of his remark "God is a Negro" brings into focus an entire complex of themes, concerns, and issues important for the history of Christian theology in America. Turner fixes his sights right away on connections and discrepancies between biblical references to "the image of God" and symbolic, anthropomorphic, projectionist personifications of God's nature on the one hand and human self-image, self-respect, and justice in this world on the other.*

## GOD IS A NEGRO[1]

We have as much right biblically and otherwise to believe that God is a Negro, as you buckra, or white, people have to believe that God is a fine looking, symmetrical and ornamented white man. For the bulk of you, and all the fool Negroes of the country, believe that God is white-skinned, blue-eyed, straight-haired, projecting-nosed, compressed-lipped and finely-robed *white* gentleman, sitting upon a throne somewhere in the heavens. Every race of people since time began who have attempted to describe their God by words, or by paintings, or by carvings, or by any other form or figure, have conveyed the idea that the God who

328

made them and shaped their destinies was symbolized in themselves, and why should not the Negro believe that he resembles God as much so as other people? We do not believe that there is any hope for a race of people who do not believe that they look like God.

Demented though we be, whenever we reach the conclusion that God or even that Jesus Christ, while in the flesh, was a white man, we shall hang our gospel trumpet upon the willow and cease to preach.

We had rather be an atheist and believe in no God, or a pantheist and believe that all nature is God, than to believe in the personality of a God and not to believe that He is a Negro. Blackness is much older than whiteness, for black was here before white, if the Hebrew word, coshach, or chasack, has *any* meaning. We do not believe in the eternity of matter, but we do believe that chaos floated in infinite darkness or blackness, millions, billions, quintillions and eons of years before God said; "Let there be light," and that during that time God had no material light Himself and was shrouded in darkness, so far as *human* comprehension is able to grasp the situation.

Yet we are no stickler as to God's color, anyway, but if He has any we would prefer to believe that it is nearer symbolized in the blue sky above us and the blue water of the seas and oceans; but we certainly protest against God being a white man or against God being white *at all;* abstract as this theme must forever remain while we are in the flesh. This is one of the reasons we favor African emigration, or Negro nationalization, wherever we can find a domain, for as long as we remain among the whites, the Negro will believe that the devil is black and that he (the Negro) favors the devil, and that God is white and that he (the Negro) bears no resemblance to Him, and the effect of such a sentiment is contemptuous and degrading, and one-half of the Negro race will be trying to get white and the other half will spend their days trying to be white men's scullions in order to please the whites; and the time they should be giving to the study of such things as will dignify and make our race great will be devoted to studying about how unfortunate they are in not being white.

We conclude these remarks by repeating for the information of the *Observer* what it adjudged us demented for—*God is a Negro.*

### Note

1. In *Respect Black: The Writings and Speeches of Henry McNeal Turner,* compiled and edited by Edwin S. Redkey (New York: Arno Press and The New York Times, 1971), pp. 176-77. Turner wrote this editorial for *The Voice of Missions* (February 1898) in response to press coverage by white journalists critical of his public comment that "God is a Negro."

329

# Benjamin B. Warfield and Archibald A. Hodge

*A. A. Hodge (1823–1886) was the son of Charles Hodge and, after 1878, his successor as professor of "didactic and polemic theology" at Princeton Theological Seminary. His college and seminary training too was Princetonian. Warfield (1851–1921) was graduated from the Seminary in 1876, having studied with Charles Hodge during the period A. A. Hodge served as his aging father's assistant, and was appointed to his teachers' chair of theology in 1887. The Princeton School's unbroken line of theological succession, extending for more than a century—Archibald Alexander, Charles Hodge, A. A. Hodge, and Warfield—is a marvel in the history of American theological education. Fidelity to tradition, Princeton's strength during the era, was not without irony. The linkage between Reformed confessional orthodoxy and Lockean–Common-Sense rationality had shifted over the course of the nineteenth century, without itself moving, from an innovative to a "conservative" theological position.*

*In 1881 Hodge and Warfield collaborated on the article "Biblical Inspiration." The extended argument regarding the inspiration and inerrancy of the "original autographs" of the Bible became a touchstone of evangelical conservativism, prominent in church conflicts over liberal "heresy" in the late nineteenth century, the fundamental-modernist controversies of the 1920s, and segments of Protestant conservatism thereafter. This excerpt reveals the thrust as well as the learning and tenor of the argument.*

## INSPIRATION[1]

. . .

### Statement of the Doctrine

During the entire history of Christian theology the word "Inspiration" has been used to express either some or all of the activities of God

330

co-operating with its human authors in the genesis of Holy Scripture. We prefer to use it in the single sense of God's continued work of super-intendence, by which, his providential, gracious and supernatural con-tributions having been presupposed, he presided over the sacred writers in their entire work of writing, with the design and effect of rendering that writing an errorless record of the matters he designed them to com-municate, and hence constituting the entire volume in all its parts the word of God to us.

While we have restricted the word "Inspiration" to a narrower sphere than that in which it has been used by many in the past, nevertheless we are certain that the above statement of the divine origin and infallibility of Scripture accurately expresses the faith of the Christian Church from the first. Still, several points remain to be more particularly considered, concerning which some difference of opinion at present prevails.

*First.* Is it proper to call this inspiration "plenary"? This word, which has often been made the occasion of strife, is in itself indefinite, and its use contributes nothing either to the precision or the emphasis of the definition. The word means simply "full," "complete," perfectly ade-quate for the attainment of the end designed, whatever that might have been. There ought not to be on any side any hesitancy to affirm this of the books of the Bible.

*Second.* Can this inspiration be properly said to be "verbal"? The objection to the application of this predicate to inspiration is urged upon three distinct grounds:

(1.) We believe that the great majority of those who object to the affir-mation that inspiration is verbal are impelled thereto by a feeling, more or less definite, that the phrase implies that inspiration is, in its essence, a process of verbal dictation, or that, at least in some way, the revelation of the thought or the inspiration of the writer was by means of the con-trol which God exercised over his words. And there is the more excuse for this misapprehension because of the extremely mechanical concep-tions of inspiration maintained by many former advocates of the use of this term "verbal." This view, however, we repudiate as earnestly as any of those who object to the language in question. At the present time the advocates of the strictest doctrine of inspiration in insisting that it is ver-bal do not mean that in any way the thoughts were inspired by means of the words, but simply that the divine superintendence, which we call inspiration, extended to the verbal expression of the thoughts of the sacred writers, as well as to the thoughts themselves, and that hence the Bible, considered as a record, an utterance in words of a divine revela-

331

tion, is the word of God to us. Hence, in all the affirmations of Scripture of every kind there is no more error in the words of the original autographs than in the thoughts they were chosen to express. The thoughts and words are both alike human, and therefore subject to human limitations, but the divine superintendence and guarantee extend to the one as much as the other.

(2.) There are others who, while insisting as strongly as any upon the presence of the divine element in Scripture, developed through special providences and gracious dealings, religious experiences and mental processes, in the very manner we have just set forth under the head of the "Genesis of Scripture," yet substantially deny what we have here called "inspiration." They retain the word "inspiration," but signify by it the divine element in the revelation, or providential or gracious dealing aforesaid, and they believe that the sacred writers, having been divinely helped to certain knowledge, were left to the natural limitations and fallibility incidental to their human and personal characters, alike in their thinking out their several narrations and expositions of divine truth, and in their reduction of them to writing. This view gives up the whole matter of the immediate divine authorship of the Bible as the word of God, and its infallibility and authority as a rule of faith and practice. We have only the several versions of God's revelations as rendered mentally and verbally, more or less adequately, yet always imperfectly, by the different sacred writers. This class of objectors are, of course, self-consistent in rejecting verbal inspiration in any sense. But this view is not consistent either with the claims of Scripture, the consciousness of Christians or the historic doctrine of the Church.

(3.) There are others who maintain that the Scriptures have been certainly inspired so far forth as to constitute them in all their parts, and as a whole, an infallible and divinely-authoritative rule of faith and practice, and yet hold that, while the thoughts of the sacred writers concerning doctrine and duty were inspired and errorless, their language was of purely human suggestion, and more or less accurate. The question as to whether the elements of Scripture relating to the course of Nature and to the events of history are without error will be considered below: it is sufficient to say under the present head that it is self-evident that, just as far as the thoughts of Scripture relating to any element or topic whatsoever are inspired, the words in which those thoughts are expressed must be inspired also. Every element of Scripture, whether doctrine or history, of which God has guaranteed the infallibility, must be infallible in its verbal expression. No matter how in other respects generated, the Scriptures are a product of human thought, and every process of human thought involves language. "The slightest consideration will show that words are as essential to intellectual processes as they are to mutual intercourse. . . . Thoughts are wedded to words as necessarily as soul to body. Without it the mysteries unveiled before the eyes of the seer would be confused shadows; with it, they are made clear lessons for human life."[2]

Besides this, the Scriptures are a *record* of divine revelations, and as such consist of words; and as far as the record is inspired at all, and as far as it is in any element infallible, its inspiration must reach to its words. Infallible thought must be definite thought, and definite thought implies words. But if God could have rendered the thoughts of the apostles regarding doctrine and duty infallibly correct without words, and then left them to convey it to us in their own language, we should be left to precisely that amount of certainty for the foundation of our faith as is guaranteed by the natural competency of the human authors, and neither more nor less. There would be no divine guarantee whatever. The human medium would everywhere interpose its fallibility between God and us. Besides, most believers admit that some of the prophetical parts of Scripture were verbally dictated. It was, moreover, promised that the apostles should speak as the Spirit gave them utterance. "The word of God came unto the prophet." The Church has always held, as expressed by the Helvetic Confession, II., "that the canonical Scriptures *are the word of God*." Paul claims that the Holy Spirit superintended and guaranteed his words as well as his thoughts (1 Cor. ii.13). The things of the Spirit we teach "not in the words which man's wisdom teacheth, but which the Holy Ghost teacheth" (συγχρίνοντες), combining spiritual things with spiritual—*i.e.* spiritual thoughts with spiritual words.

It is evident, therefore, that it is not clearness of thought which inclines any of the advocates of a real inspiration of the Holy Scriptures to deny that it extends to the words. Whatever discrepancies or other human limitations may attach to the sacred record, *the line* (of inspired or not inspired, of infallible or fallible) *can never rationally be drawn between the thoughts and the words of Scripture.*

*Third.* It is asked again: In what way, and to what extent, is the doctrine of inspiration dependent upon the supposed results of modern criticism as to the dates, authors, sources and modes of composition of the several books? To us the following answer appears to be well founded, and to set the limits within which the Church doctrine of inspiration is in equilibrium with the results of modern criticism fairly and certainly:

The doctrine of inspiration, in its essence—and, consequently, in all its forms—presupposes a supernatural revelation and a supernatural providential guidance entering into and determining the genesis of Scripture from the beginning. Every naturalistic theory, therefore, of the evolution of Scripture, however disguised, is necessarily opposed to any true version of the catholic doctrine of inspiration. It is also a well-known matter of fact that Christ himself is the ultimate witness on whose testimony the Scriptures, as well as their doctrinal contents, rest. We receive the Old Testament just as Christ handed it to us, and on his authority. And we receive as belonging to the New Testament all, and only those, books which an apostolically-instructed age testifies to have been produced by the apostles or their companions—*i.e.* by the men whom Christ commissioned, and to whom he promised infallibility in teaching. It is evident, therefore, that every supposed conclusion of critical investigation which denies the apostolical origin of a New-Testament book or the truth of any part of Christ's testimony in relation to the Old Testament and its contents, or which is inconsistent with the absolute truthfulness of any affirmation of any book so authenticated, must be inconsistent with the true doctrine of inspiration. On the other hand, the defenders of the strictest doctrine of inspiration should cheerfully acknowledge that theories as to the authors, dates, sources and modes of composition of the several books which are not plainly inconsistent with the testimony of Christ or his apostles as to the Old Testament, or with the apostolic origin of the books of the New Testament, or with the absolute truthfulness of any of the affirmations of these books so authenticated, cannot in the least invalidate the evidence or pervert the meaning of the historical doctrine of inspiration.

*Fourth.* The real point at issue between the more strict and the more lax views of inspiration maintained by believing scholars remains to be stated. It is claimed, and admitted equally on both sides, that the great design and effect of inspiration is to render the Sacred Scriptures in all their parts a divinely infallible and authoritative rule of faith and practice, and hence that in all their elements of thought and expression, concerned in the great purpose of conveying to men a revelation of spiritual doctrine or duty, the Scriptures are absolutely infallible. But if this be so, it is argued by the more liberal school of Christian scholars that this admitted fact is not inconsistent with other facts which they claim are matters of their personal observation: to wit, that in certain elements of Scripture which are purely incidental to their great end of teaching spiritual truth, such as history, natural history, ethnology, archaeology,

334

geography, natural science and philosophy, they, like all the best human writings of their age, are, while for the most part reliable, yet limited by inaccuracies and discrepancies. While this is maintained, it is generally at the same time affirmed that when compared with other books of the same antiquity these inaccuracies and discrepancies of the Bible are inconsiderable in number, and always of secondary importance, in no degree invalidating the great attribute of Scripture—its absolute infallibility and its divine authority as a rule of faith and practice.

The writers of this article are sincerely convinced of the perfect soundness of the great catholic doctrine of biblical inspiration—*i.e.* that the Scriptures not only contain, but ARE, THE WORD OF GOD, and hence that all their elements and all their affirmations are absolutely errorless, and binding the faith and obedience of men. Nevertheless, we admit that the question between ourselves and the advocates of the view just stated is one of fact, to be decided only by an exhaustive and impartial examination of all the sources of evidence.—*i.e.* the claims and the phenomena of the Scriptures themselves. There will undoubtedly be found upon the surface many apparent affirmations presumably inconsistent with the present teachings of science, with facts of history or with other statements of the sacred books themselves. Such apparent inconsistencies and collisions with other sources of information are to be expected in imperfect copies of ancient writings, from the fact that the original reading may have been lost, or that we may fail to realize the point of view of the author, or that we are destitute of the circumstantial knowledge which would fill up and harmonize the record. Besides, the human forms of knowledge by which the critics test the accuracy of Scripture are themselves subject to error. In view of all the facts known to us, we affirm that a candid inspection of all the ascertained phenomena of the original text of Scripture will leave unmodified the ancient faith of the Church. In all their real affirmations these books are without error.

It must be remembered that it is not claimed that the Scriptures, any more than their authors, are omniscient. The information they convey is in the forms of human thought, and limited on all sides. They were not designed to teach philosophy, science or human history as such. They were not designed to furnish an infallible system of speculative theology. They are written in human languages, whose words, inflections, constructions and idioms bear everywhere indelible traces of human error. The record itself furnishes evidence that the writers were in large measure dependent for their knowledge upon sources and methods in themselves fallible, and that their personal knowledge and judgments were in many matters hesitating and defective, or even wrong. Nevertheless, the historical faith of the Church has always been that all the affirmations of Scripture of all kinds, whether of spiritual doctrine or duty, or of physical or historical fact, or of psychological or philosophical principle, are without any error when the *ipsissima verba* of the original autographs are ascertained and interpreted in their natural and intended sense. There is a vast difference between exactness of statement, which includes an exhaustive rendering of details, an absolute literalness, which the Scriptures never profess, and accuracy, on the other hand, which secures a correct statement of facts or principles intended to be affirmed. It is this accuracy, and this alone, as distinct from exactness, which the Church doctrine maintains of every affirmation in the original text of Scripture without exception. Every statement accurately corresponds to truth just as far forth as affirmed.

. . .

### Legitimate Presumptions

In testing this question by a critical investigation of the phenomena of Scripture, it is evident that the stricter view, which denies the existence of errors, discrepancies or inaccurate statements in Scripture, has the presumption in its favor, and that the *onus probandi* rests upon the advocates of the other view. The latter may fairly be required to furnish positive and conclusive evidence in each alleged instance of error until the presumption has been turned over to the other side. The *primâ facie* evidence of the claims of Scripture is assuredly all in favor of an errorless infallibility of all scriptural affirmations. This has been from the first the general faith of the historical Church and of the Bible-loving, spiritual people of God. The very letter of the Word has been proved from ancient times to be a tremendous power in human life.

It is a question also of infinite importance. If the new views are untrue, they threaten not only to shake the confidence of men in the Scriptures, but the very Scriptures themselves as an objective ground of faith. We have seen that the Holy Spirit has, as a matter of fact, preserved the sacred writers to a degree unparalleled elsewhere in literature from error in the departments of philosophy and science. Who then shall determine the limit of that preserving influence? We have seen that in God's plan doctrine grows out of history, and that redemption itself was wrought out in human history. If, then, the inspiration of the sacred writers did not embrace the department of history, or only of sacred and not of profane history, who shall set the limit and define what is of the essence of faith and what the uncertain accident? It would assuredly appear that, as no organism can be stronger than its weakest part, if error be found in any one element or in any class of statements, certainty as to any portion could rise no higher than belongs to that exercise of human reason to which it will be left to discriminate the infallible from the fallible.

The critical investigation must be made, and we must abide by the result when it is unquestionably reached. But surely it must be carried on with infinite humility and teachableness, and with prayer for the constant guidance of the gracious Spirit. The signs of success will never be presumption, an evident sense of intellectual superiority, or a want of sympathy with the spiritual Church of all ages or with the painful confusion of God's humble people of the present.

With these presumptions and in this spirit let it (1) be proved that each alleged discrepant statement certainly occurred in the original autograph of the sacred book in which it is said to be found. (2) Let it be proved that the interpretation which occasions the apparent discrepancy is the one which the passage was evidently intended to bear. It is not sufficient to show a difficulty, which may spring out of our defective knowledge of the circumstances. The true meaning must be definitely and certainly ascertained, and then shown to be irreconcilable with other known truth. (3) Let it be proved that the true sense or some part of the original autograph is directly and necessarily inconsistent with some certainly-known fact of history or truth of science, or some other statement of Scripture certainly ascertained and interpreted. We believe that it can be shown that this has never yet been successfully done in the case of one single alleged instance of error in the WORD OF GOD.

### Notes

1. In *Inspiration* (Grand Rapids: Baker Book House, 1979; originally published in 1881), pp. 17-29, 34-36.
2. Canon Westcott's *Introduction to the Study of the Gospels,* 5th ed.: Introduction, pp. 14, 15.

# Lydia Maria Child

*H*istorians *of American Christianity rightly place Child
(1802–1880) among the number of talented women activists engaged in
causes of moral, social, and political reform during the middle third of
the nineteenth century. She was one of the first such crusaders famed for
her literary achievement, using novels, short stories, and other forms of
"secular" writing to expose injustice and stimulate moral reform. Advocacy of the immediate emancipation of slaves during the 1830s vaulted
her to posts of leadership among Protestant abolitionists. Though she
did not join the public campaign for women's rights, her two-volume
study* History of the Condition of Women, in Various Ages and Nations
*(1835) was an early and influential contribution to that cause.*

*Raised in a New England Calvinist household, she (like many other
New England intellectuals), sought paths other than those "tradition"
had set. Hers proved to be an ongoing spiritual quest for religious truth,
never settling with evangelical Protestantism, Unitarianism, Swedenbor-
gianism, or any other one "way." Her 1855 study* Progress of Religious
Ideas, Through Successive Ideas *was a pioneering American effort in the
study of the historical development of religious thought. Selected here is
an article from late in her career, illustrating her continuing study of the
diversity of religions among diverse cultures—an interest by this time
shared by scholars of the emergent field of comparative religion and
growing among informed Christian leaders. Her reflections on syncreti-
cism within historic Christianity prompt further thought on an "eclectic" faith.*

## THE INTERMINGLING OF RELIGIONS[1]

In the November number of the Atlantic for 1870 some striking
resemblances were pointed out between the Buddhist and Roman
Catholic religions. This similarity, which has long been recognized, can
be accounted for only in two ways: either Roman Catholics must have

borrowed from Buddhists or Buddhists must have borrowed from them. The latter supposition has been generally adopted; the coincidences being traced to the teaching of Nestorian missionaries in India. Some say the Apostle Thomas carried Christianity into India, and that the resemblances are the fruits of his preaching. But there are many reasons why both these conclusions seem improbable.

. . .

If the Apostle Thomas ever travelled into India, it is difficult to imagine what could have induced him to teach the people to prostrate themselves before images, to establish monasteries, to say their prayers on rosaries, and believe in miracle-working relics. The Jews, among whom Thomas was educated, were accustomed to none of these things. They formed no part of the teaching of Jesus, in which we find none of the characteristic features of Oriental asceticism. His enemies reproached him that he "came eating and drinking," and that he did not impose frequent fasts upon his disciples. He sanctioned a wedding with his presence, and said nothing to indicate that celibacy was essential to holiness. We have no means of knowing whether his disciples were generally married men; but that Peter had a wife is implied by the Scripture, which informs us that her mother "lay sick of a fever."

It also seems unlikely that Nestorians, of any sect, should have introduced monasteries, rosaries, etc., into India, for they were separated from the Christian Church early in the fifth century, and the first monastery in Christendom was established by Saint Benedict full a hundred years later; and this was followed by the introduction of rosaries to facilitate the recitation of prayers. In brief, these and many other customs of the Catholic Church cannot be historically traced to the Jews, or to Jesus, or to the Apostles, or to the Christian churches in the first centuries, or to Nestorius, who was cut off from the Christian Church because he objected to the worship of the Virgin.

But in ancient Hindostan, ages before the birth of Jesus, we do find models for these things. Their earliest Sacred Books teach that the soul of man, by entering a mortal body, had become separated from the Supreme Soul of the Universe, and that the only way to become one with God again was to mortify and abuse the body, and keep the soul constantly occupied with the contemplation of divine things. Some of the Hindoo devotees stood for years on one foot; others lived sunk up to their chins in deep narrow holes of the ground, dependent upon charity for the food that kept them alive. Simeon Stylites, the Christian devotee, made his body about as uncomfortable, by living thirty-seven years on the top of a high pillar that afforded merely room enough to stand upon. Long before our era there were communities of Hindoo hermits who took vows of celibacy, fasted to extremity, and spent their lives repeating prayers on strings of beads. Some of them were vowed to perpetual silence, and kept skulls constantly before them, to remind them of the emancipation of the soul by the dissolution of the body. They had very close imitators in the Catholic monks of La Trappe, who daily dug their own graves, and never spoke, except to salute each other, as they passed, with the words, "We must die."

An historical glance backward will help to explain many things that might otherwise seem unaccountable. At the time that Christianity began to assume the form of a distinct religion the world was in an unprecedented state of activity, intercommunication, and change. The conquests of Julius Caesar and Alexander the Great had brought remote nations into contact. The pathway of commerce was immensely extended, and philosophers and devotees from all points of the compass followed in her train. Two new forces were beginning to agitate the world, both of them animated by the zeal which characterizes reformers before their ideas become established. Buddha had striven to teach his countrymen that their religious ideas were too narrow and exclusive; that the road to holiness was open to all classes and conditions; to women as well as men, to foreign nations as well as to Hindoos. Expelled from Hindostan by reason of these doctrines, his disciples had spread over various Asiatic countries, and eighty thousand of their missionaries were perambulating the world. Among the Jews, who considered themselves the chosen people of Jehovah, in whose sight all other nations were unclean, had arisen a great reformer, who held communication with despised Samaritans and publicans, and taught that all men were brethren. His disciples were also driven from their native land, and spread into the neighboring kingdoms of Asia, among the Grecians in Europe, and throughout the Roman Empire, where their countrymen were already more numerous than in Palestine. And wherever these missionaries went they proclaimed the doctrine that God was equally the Father of all; that in his sight there was "neither Jew nor Gentile, bond or free, men or women; but all were one in Christ Jesus." To those who look upon all mankind as brethren, there is something beautiful in both these great tides of reform, enlarging the scope of human sympathies, and sweeping away the ancient barriers that had separated classes and peoples.

Antioch, where the first church of Christians was gathered in Gentile lands, was on the high road between Europe and Asia. Ephesus, one of

340

the earliest head-quarters of the Christians, was always swarming with foreigners, especially with Orientals. Rome, where a Christian church was very early gathered, was full of the spoils of many conquered nations, and of their theories also. Alexander the Great had built the new Egyptian city of Alexandria, to which he was very desirous to attract the learning and commerce of the world. For that purpose he encouraged the greatest freedom of discussion, and unbounded toleration of opinions. Thither flocked zealots and philosophers from all quarters, eager for controversy. Such a seething caldron of doctrines the world had never witnessed. Dion Chrysostom, who wrote in the beginning of the second century, informs us that Greeks and Romans, Syrians, Ethiopians, Arabians, Persians, and travellers from India were always to be found in that cosmopolitan city. In this focus of diverse ideas the Christians early planted a church. Jewish converts to Christianity were for a long time extremely tenacious of their old Hebrew traditions and customs; while Gentile converts, from various nations, manifested a great tendency to amalgamate the teaching of Jesus with the old ideas and ceremonies in which they had been educated. In the conflict of sects arising from this state of things it was almost inevitable that the teaching of Jesus and his Apostles should become more or less largely interfused with ideas from various religions; especially with those from Hindostan and Persia, which prevailed so extensively at that period.

These Oriental ideas have had such a very important influence, not only on the faith, but on the social conditions of men, that it is worth while to trace them briefly to their abstract source. Orientals conceived of the Supreme as the Central Source of Being, dwelling in passionless repose in regions of resplendent light. He did not create anything; but all spirits radiated from him, in successive series of emanations, from the highest seraphs down to the souls of men. Coeternal with him was an antagonistic principle called Matter; a dark, inert mass, which gave birth to the Devil and all forms of evil. When some of the lower series of Spirits of Light approached the region of Matter, the Spirits of Darkness were attracted by their splendor and sought to draw them down among themselves. They succeeded; and thus mankind came into existence, with ethereal souls derived from God and material bodies derived from the Devil. The only way for these Spirits of Light, imprisoned in Matter, to get back to the Divine Source whence they emanated was to subdue the body by all sorts of abstinence and tormenting penance, while the soul was kept in steadfast contemplation on spiritual things.

The Jews had quite a different theory of creation. They conceived of

God as an active Being, who made the body of man with his own hands and then breathed a soul into it. Thus regarding the body as divine workmanship, they had no contempt for it and did not consider its senses sinful.

When these different ideas, coming from afar, met front to front in the Christian churches, they gave rise to a motley amalgamation of doctrines. The most conspicuous specimen of this is to be found in the numerous sects classed under the general denomination of Gnostics. The name is derived from the Greek word "Gnosis," signifying wisdom; and it was besowed on them because, however they might differ on other points, they all believed that by subjugation of the senses human souls might be restored to their original oneness with God, and thus become recipients of intuitive wisdom directly emanating from him. With few exceptions, all these Gnostics were of Gentile origin, and their doctrines bear the obvious stamp of Hindostan and Persia; though it is likely that they derived them from various intermediate sources. Many of their leaders were men of uncommon talent and learning, wedded to ancient theories, but sincerely attracted by the teaching of Jesus. They troubled the Christian churches as early as the time of Paul, who alludes to them as "seducing spirits, forbidding to marry and commanding to abstain from meats." Their theories proved very attractive, especially to scholars prone to abstract speculations. The celebrated Saint Augustine was for several years a Gnostic, and Christian converts were not unfrequently drawn aside into their erratic paths. They increased with such rapidity, that at one time their flood of Oriental ideas threatened to sweep away the Jewish foundations of Christianity. In the middle of the fifth century, the Bishop of Cyprus records that he found a million of them in his diocese, and succeeded in bringing them all within the fold of his church. How much it was necessary to compromise with their ideas in order to accomplish that object he does not inform us.

The different elements that were jostled into contact during this transition state of the world gave rise to much controversy that sounds odd enough to modern ears. The Jews were such an exclusive people, that Gentile nations had very little opportunity to become acquainted with their religious views, till they met together on the common ground of reverence for Jesus. Jehovah was to them an altogether foreign God; and having no traditional reverence for his name, they discussed his character as freely as we do that of Jupiter. It was a revolting idea to them that the Supreme Being could have formed anything out of Matter, which in their minds was associated with everything evil and unclean. And believing that all Spirits were evolved, without effort, from the Central Source, by the mere necessity of outflowing, they ridiculed the idea that God worked six days to make the world, and then had to rest from his labors. They declared that if Jehovah confined his care to one people, and was jealous when they gave glory to other gods, if his anger waxed hot when they disobeyed him, if he commanded them to slaughter their enemies, and promised them mere earthly rewards for obedience to his laws, he could not possibly be the Supreme Being, for he was altogether free from passion. Some of the Gnostics admitted that Jehovah might belong to one of the inferior orders of Spirits, evolved from the Source of Light; others maintained that he must be an Evil Spirit, and that the Scriptures said to be inspired by him were obviously the work of the Devil. They all believed Jesus to be one of the Spirits of Light; but their ideas concerning the inherent wickedness of Matter led them to reject the idea that he could be born of a woman. They said he merely appeared to have a body, for the purpose of performing on earth the benevolent mission of helping Spirits out of the prison-house of Matter, and restoring them to their original oneness with God. Paul probably aimed a shaft at this doctrine, when he said, "Every spirit that confesseth not that Jesus is Christ come in the *flesh* is not of God." Asceticism, in a greater or less degree, characterized all the Gnostic sects. They despised all luxuries, ornaments, shows, and amusements; everything, in fact, which contributed to the pleasure of the senses. They abstained from wine and animal food, and ate merely sufficient to sustain life. They all regarded matrimony as incompatible with holiness; and some thought it a great sin, inasmuch as the reproduction of human bodies was entering into a league with Spirits of Darkness to help them to incarcerate Spirits of Light in the prison-house of Matter.

These ascetic ideas, so conspicuous in very ancient Hindoo writings, were, in one form or another, afloat almost everywhere at the time the Christian Church was in the process of formation out of a great variety of nations. By early emigration, or otherwise, they had come to prevail extensively in Egypt, where the deserts swarmed with hermits vowed to celibacy and severe mortification of the senses. In Grecian mythology, copied by the Romans, there was no antagonism between Spirit and Matter. Those nations had never been taught that their bodies came from the Devil, and consequently they had no contempt for the senses. They revelled in physical enjoyment, and ascribed the same tendencies to their gods. Bacchus was their jovial companion, and Venus adored as the beautifier of life. But though the people were on such gay and

343

sociable terms with their deities, philosophers had introduced from Egypt the sombre ideas of the Orient. Plato taught that Matter was the original Source of Evil, antagonistic to the Principle of Good. Plotinus, the most celebrated of his later followers, was ashamed of his body, though it is said to have been a remarkably beautiful one. He blushed for his parents that they had given birth to it, and any allusion to physical instincts or necessities was deeply mortifying to him. While Egyptian zealots and Grecian philosophers were strewing abroad the seed of ancient asceticism, Buddhist missionaries were also industriously propagating it. We are told that travellers from India were always in Alexandria, which was the great focus of Gnostic sects. Bardesanes, one of the leaders of the Gnostics in the second century, wrote an account of religious communities in India, the members of which merely endured life as an inevitable bondage, and sought, by devout contemplation and severe mortification of the senses, to rise above the prison-house of the body. Mani, who lived in the third century, and was perhaps the most remarkable of all the Gnostics, studied a book called "The Treasury of Mysteries, by Buddha, said to have been born of a Virgin." And it was a common doctrine with these sects that Zoroaster, Buddha, and Jesus were the same Spirit of Light appearing on earth in different places and forms, for the benevolent purpose of bringing back to oneness with God those stray Spirits which had become separated from him by being shut up in material bodies. These sects, standing between the old religions and the new, were hotly persecuted by both. They finally vanished from the scene; but for several centuries their theories, under various modifications, reappeared to trouble the churches.

Every one knows that the Roman Catholic Church abounds in ceremonies and traditions of which no trace can be found in the Old Testament or the New. The teachers of that church say they are derived from the Christian Fathers, whose authority they deem sacred. The prominent preachers of Christianity during the first three centuries, called Fathers of the Church, were, almost without exception, converts from the Gentile religions, mostly Greek and Roman. The rejection of foreign customs had been religiously inculcated upon Jews; and those of them who accepted Jesus as their promised Messiah retained that extreme aversion to innovation which characterized them as a people. But Gentile converts, who were far more numerous, had received quite a different training. Grecians easily adopted the festivals and the gods of other nations; and Romans manifested still greater facility in that respect. They never attempted to convert the numerous nations they conquered. If they

344

found among them religious festivals which seemed useful or agreeable, they adopted them; and if they took a liking to any of their deities, they placed their images in the Pantheon with their own gods.

These elastic habits of mind may have had considerable influence in producing that system of politic adaptation to circumstances observable in the Christian Church, especially after Constantine had made Christianity the established religion of the state. I believe it is Mosheim, who, in allusion to this process of adaptation to the customs of converted nations, says: "It is difficult to determine whether the heathen were most Christianized, or Christians most heathenized."

The Emperor Constantine was for forty years a worshipper of Apollo, God of the Sun, whom he regarded as his tutelary deity, his own especial guardian and benefactor. Many things show that this long habit of trust and reverence was never quite obliterated from his mind. One of the earliest acts of his reign was to require the universal observance of the Sun's Day; for which purpose he issued a proclamation: "Let all the people rest on the venerated Day of the Sun." Saturday, the seventh day of the week, was the Sabbath of the Jews, and converts from Judaism to Christianity long continued to observe that as their holy day; but Christians were accustomed to meet together on the first day of the week, in memory of the resurrection of Jesus; and as that harmonized with the proclamation of the Emperor, and with an old custom in Grecian and Roman worship, the Sabbath of the Apostles was superseded by Sun-Day.

Festivals that were universally observed, and endeared to the populace by long habit and as occasions for social gatherings, were generally retained by the Christian Church, though the old forms were consecrated to new ideas. Almost all the ancient nations hailed the return of the sun from the winter solstice by a great festival on the 25th of December, during which they performed religious ceremonies in honor of the sun, feasted each other, and interchanged gifts. To have abolished this day would have been as unpopular among the masses of Gentile proselytes as the abolition of Thanksgiving day would be in New England. It was accordingly retained as the birthday of the "Sun of Righteousness," concerning whose real birthday history leaves us entirely in the dark.

The ancient Germans observed in the early spring a festival in honor of Ostera, who was probably their Goddess of Nature, or of the Earth. Scholars derive her name from Oster, which signifies rising. The festival was to hail the rising of Nature from her winter sleep. Oster-fires were kindled in honor of the returning warmth, and Oster-eggs were

345

exchanged; the egg being an ancient and very common symbol of fecundity, or germinating life. Teutonic converts to Christianity were allowed to keep up their old festival, but they were taught to do it in honor of the rising of Jesus, instead of the rising of Nature. Easter-fires are still kindled, and Easter-eggs, variously ornamented, are still exchanged in several Catholic countries. Almost all ancient nations had a great festival in the spring. The Jewish Passover occurred at that season. Converts from all nations were well satisfied to keep up their old holiday and accept its new significance.

. . .

Mortals, finding themselves surrounded by solemn mysteries, feeling the need of constant protection, and unable to comprehend the Infinite Being from whom existence is derived, have always manifested a strong tendency to bring God nearer to themselves by means of intermediate spiritual agents. Almost every ancient nation had some Mother Goddess, whose favor they sought to propitiate by prayers and offerings. . . .

When Christianity superseded the old religions, the ancient ideas and forms took new names. By a gradual process of substitution, the Saints of the Catholic Church glided into the place of the old guardian deities. Nations that had been accustomed to worship the Goddess of Nature as a Mother Goddess easily transferred their offerings and prayers to the Virgin Mary, their Spiritual Mother. . . .

. . .

The numerous deities of Greece and Rome were distinguished by symbols, signifying their characters or achievements. Jupiter was represented with a thunderbolt, Neptune with a trident, Minerva with an owl, Apollo with a lyre, and Mercury with a rod twined with serpents. The host of Christian Saints are also distinguished by emblems indicating well-known traditions. Saint Peter is represented with two keys, Saint Agnes with a lamb, Saint John with a sacramental cup, Saint Catherine with a wheel, Saint Lucia with a lamp. Some of these Saints are of universal popularity, others are local favorites. In various subordinate degrees they share the honors paid to the Virgin. Churches and chapels are dedicated to them, adorned with their pictures and symbols, and with their images in marble or ivory, clay or chalk. The walls are hung with votive tablets, written or printed, describing their miraculous intervention to avert dangers or cure diseases. . . .

Thus is human life in all its phases presented to the notice and protection of tutelary saints, as it formerly was to tutelary deities. It is curious to trace the manner in which the multifarious traditions of these saints have grown up.

Professor Max Müller, in one of his lectures, describes a singular migration from the records of Eastern Saints into those of the Western. Johannes Damascenus, who was a famous Christian theologian a thousand years ago, had passed his youth in the court of the Caliph Almanzor, where his father held a position of trust. There he stored his mind with Asiatic lore, and the Life of Buddha was among the books he read. His imagination was captivated by the account of that prince, whose tenderness of heart had led him to renounce his rank and devote himself to prayers for his fellow-creatures and to the alleviation of their misery. Damascenus wove the main points of the story into a religious novel entitled "Balaam and Josaphat." A later age accepted it as the veritable history of a Christian Saint; and thus Buddha became regularly canonized under the name of Saint Josaphat, whose festival is observed by the Greek Church on the 16th of August, and by the Roman Catholic Church on the 27th of November.

Whether there was the same facility in adopting widely extended and deeply rooted doctrines, that was manifested in the adoption of old customs and legends, is an open question. In ambitious minds, a desire to extend the power and increase the wealth of the Church would prove a very strong temptation to compromise with the preconceived ideas of influential converts; and even devout, unselfish men might be drawn into it by a benevolent wish to bring peoples into a better form of religion by such processes as were readiest at hand. Paul, whose life was spent in Gentile lands, seems to have lost much of Jewish exclusiveness, and to have acquired something of Grecian and Roman facility of adaptation to circumstances. To the church at Corinth he wrote: "Unto the Jews I became as a Jew, that I might gain the Jews; to them that are without the Law [of Moses] as without the Law, that I might gain them that are without the Law. To the weak became I as weak, that I might gain the weak: I am made all things to all men, that I might by all means save some."

Such intermingling of various elements is by no means peculiar to the Christian Church. It is according to the laws of human nature. The same mosaic of patterns and colors can be found throughout the world's history, in all changes of Church or State, by whomsoever seeks the separate stones that form the picture. The modern theory that nothing is created entirely new, but that every form of being is the development of some antecedent form, may or may not be true in natural science, but it is certainly true of all spiritual progress.

When mortals find a kernel of truth, they seek to appropriate it as

347

exclusively their own; and whatsoever kernel is picked up by others is declared to be a stone, from which no bread of life can ever be produced. But the great harvest-field of the world is managed on different principles by the Father of All. While men are planting in narrow enclosures, he sends forth seed upon the winds; he scatters them on great floods, whose waters subside and leave them in rich alluvial soil; and birds of the air, unconscious of anything but their own subsistence, are his agents to scatter them abroad all over the earth. And when we think we have the harvest all to ourselves, lo! we find the same grain waving in far-off fields.

Undeniably there *is* a strong resemblance between the Buddhist and Roman Catholic churches; and whether India is the borrower or the lender does not affect the assertion that John Chinaman and Patrick O'Dublin have an equal right to the free exercise of their religion under our impartial laws. All we have to do, in either case, is to spread abroad as much light as possible, that all men may have a chance to distinguish between the true and the spurious. Having done this duty, we must leave the result to time.

Enlightened travellers would doubtless find in Buddhist countries a vast deal that seemed like very puerile and absurd superstitions and gross immorality under the garb of religion; but a similar impression would be produced on their minds by a sojourn in Italy or Spain. The Catholic Church abounds in holy sayings and examples, and because it is a Christian church they do not excite our surprise; but when we find similar things among the Buddhists, we ask with astonishment whence they could possibly have come; forgetful that "God is the Father of *all*," and that "*every* good gift cometh from him." The Commandments of the Buddhists are very similar to our own. There are commands not to kill, not to steal, not to lie, not to be licentious, and not to utter slanders; and to these are added, "Thou shalt not drink wine, nor any intoxicating liquors." "Thou shalt not excite quarrels by repeating the words of others." "Thou shalt not speak of injuries." The following are among the maxims of Buddhist Saints: "Glory not in thyself, but rather in thy neighbor." "Be lowly in thy heart, that thou mayest be lowly in thy acts." "Judge not thy neighbor." "Be equally kind to all men." "Use no perfumes but the sweetness of thy thoughts." In some respects Buddhism can show a cleaner record than Christianity. It has had no such institution as the Inquisition, and has never put men to death for heretical opinions. They treat with reverence whatsoever is deemed holy by other men. . . .

Though the Founder of Christianity preached a Gospel of Peace, the religion that took his name was far from being peaceful in its progress, after the first three centuries. Into Armenia, Norway, and Germany Christianity was introduced at the point of the sword. Conquered armies had no alternative but baptism or slaughter. And the number of Jews, Romans, and heretics who were slain to bring about the unity of the Christian Church is too large for calculation. Though Buddhism spread through many countries, I have found no record that it was in a single instance established by force.

The fact is, the more we know of our brethren in the East, the more the conviction grows upon us that Buddha was a great reformer and a benevolent, holy man. The present state of the world is in some respects similar to its condition at the commencement of our era. Electricity and steam bring remote countries into acquaintance with each other. Old traditions are everywhere relaxing their hold upon the minds of men. From all parts of the world come increasing manifestations of a tendency toward eclecticism. Men find there are gems hidden among all sorts of rubbish. These will be selected and combined in that Church of the Future now in the process of formation. We shall not live to see it; but we may be certain that, according to the laws of spiritual growth, it will retain a likeness to all the present, as the present does to all the past. But it will stand on a higher plane, be larger in its proportions, and more harmonious in its beauty. Milan Cathedral, lifting its thousand snow-white images of saints into the clear blue of heaven, is typical of that Eclectic Church, which shall gather forms of holy aspiration from all ages and nations, and set them on high in their immortal beauty, with the sunlight of heaven to glorify them all.

### Note

1. In *A Lydia Maria Child Reader,* ed. Carolyn L. Karcher (Durham: Duke University Press, 1997), pp. 419-34. Originally published in *Atlantic Monthly* 28 (October 1871): 385-95.

# Borden Parker Bowne

*From 1876 on, Bowne (1847–1910) served as professor of philosophy at Boston University. A lifelong Methodist, he developed from Neo-Kantianism, idealism, pragmatic thought, and the emergent social sciences a philosophical theology he finally called transcendental idealism, but which is most widely known as Personalism. His turn to philosophy was, for some Methodists, a sign of the maturing of the Wesleyan heritage and, for others, a lapse due to his studies in Germany, his liberalism, or accommodation to modern culture. In what is sometimes called Methodism's "last heresy trial," he survived the effort of opponents to condemn him in 1904. The case is not to be retried, but it can be noted that since Wesley's religion of the heart was linked to Lockean reason and that of his nineteenth-century heirs to Common-Sense thought, Bowne was "traditional" in seeking a new philosophy to replace the Scottish School, which by late–nineteenth-century norms was widely judged antiquated.*

*This excerpt from* Personalism *reflects his view of God as cosmic Intellect, distinct as "person" from the world but immanent within the order of creation and the course of history. Personalist themes are most evident in his emphasis on the human experience of God and his belief that the best religion is to be judged on the basis of its ideals and attitudes and how it contributes to human life. Also displayed is the growing appreciation among Christian intellectuals for the non-Christian religions, as Bowne affirms that "traces of divine guidance and inspiration" have been manifest in other than Christian lands.*

## The Personal World[1]

. . .

In general, the question of religion has a much better standing in the intellectual world than it had years ago. The sensational philosophy long held that religion, as a late growth, is to be understood through its psychological antecedents as a product of evolution. Thus it was largely regarded as an adventitious excrescence upon human nature and without any real significance for human life, and many held that it would be a decided gain for humanity, and especially for the treasury, if religion could be finally exorcised. In all this the essential ambiguity of empirical and evolution doctrine was completely overlooked, and it was assumed as a matter of course that that which was temporally first in psychological development was the truly real, or the material out of which all later developments were made. Accordingly, as the earlier phases of religion, like the earlier phases of all things human, were pretty crude, it was supposed that these were the true originals and essential meaning of religion. Now all this has passed away. We have come to see that this historical study at best could give only the order of temporal development, without deciding whether there was not some immanent law underlying the unfolding. We have equally come to see that no development is possible without assuming such a law, and that the true nature of a developing thing can be learned, not by looking at the crude beginnings, but only by studying the full unfolding of the finished product. If we would know what intelligence is, we must consider it in its mighty works and not in its first, blind gropings. So if we would know what religion is, we must consider it in its great historical manifestations, rather than in the dim imaginings of undeveloped men.

On all these accounts religion has come to be recognized as a great human fact. It is not an invention of priests or politicians, nor an unimportant annex of life, but it is deep rooted in humanity itself. Neither is it something that has significance only for the future life; for religion is clearly seen to have profound significance for this life, either for good or evil. There are religions that debase and defile; there are religions that industrially cripple and politically paralyze the people. The forces that make for evil or for obstruction have in many cases incarnated themselves in the people's religion, and there can be little industrial progress, or social development, or political improvement, until the grip of these religions has been broken. And, on the other hand, religion may be a great source of progress, of illumination, of inspiration, both for the individual and for the people. This changed point of view is everywhere apparent to one acquainted with the course of thought in the last twenty-five years. I never so fully realized it before as I did at the World's Fair in St. Louis. I attended there an International Congress of Arts and Sciences, the members of which were scholars from all over the civilized world, and I was greatly impressed by the fact that whenever religion

351

was mentioned, or whenever any question arose that directly or indirectly bore upon it, the references to religion were all of a friendly kind. It was taken for granted as a great human fact, as a fact in which human nature culminates, and as a fact having the same warrant as all other human facts. It is to be studied sympathetically, therefore, and with an open mind. This is indeed progress.

It is equally gratifying to note that the Christian attitude also toward the non-Christian religions has greatly changed in recent years. Christians themselves have been slow in understanding the truth and glory of the Gospel, the good news of God. For a long time it was held that God was good only to those to whom the Christian revelation had come, and that all others were unconditionally lost. But at last we have learned that God is not made good by the Christian revelation, but only declared and shown to be good; he has always been good; he has always been the Father Almighty, and has always had purposes of grace concerning his children, whether they knew him or not. The insufferable blasphemy that condemned the whole non-Christian world indiscriminately has utterly disappeared among intelligent Christians. The God who has been dealing with all past generations is the God of grace whom our Lord has revealed, and they are still in his hands, whether in this world or in any other.

Similarly, Christian thought has changed concerning the great outlying non-Christian systems. These also were thought at one time to be evil and only evil, and without any value whatever for their adherents. Accordingly, it was the fashion to deride and decry these religions, to emphasize their shortcomings and failures, and to oppose to them Christianity in its ideal form. But further study has revealed how unjust all this was, and now we have come to believe that the great non-Christian systems also had their place in God's providential plan for men. We find it possible to think of Confucius, Mencius, and Buddha, and many another as veritable prophets of the Most High, and as having done an important work among the people for whom they wrought; not indeed making anything perfect, but preparing the way and contributing much to the organization and development of the people. And this, too, should not surprise, still less offend, any Christian, for we are told that "a portion of the Spirit is given to every man," that "there is a light which lighteth every man that cometh into the world;" that "God is no respecter of persons, but that in every nation he that feareth God and worketh righteousness is accepted of him." With this faith and our conviction that the world always has been in the hands of God, we are not surprised but rather delighted to find traces of divine guidance and inspiration in other than Christian lands; and when we read the Sacred Books of the East we rejoice to find indications of the Holy Spirit's presence. This does not mean, of course, that these systems are perfect or final; on the contrary, criticism shows how far from perfect they are, and that they never could build humanity into its best estate; but it does mean that God has not been absent from the religious history of the race, and has never left himself anywhere without a witness. The sun does not envy the stars, yet they disappear in the brightness of its shining; so Christianity does not envy any of these lesser lights, but gathers up into itself all their illumination so that they, too, disappear in the brightness of its shining. And if one should point to the aberrations of these other religions in disproof of this view, the obvious remark is that Christianity itself has gone astray in not a few times and places, sinking now and then to as utter superstition as could be found in sorcery or incantation.

Any one inclined to emphasize as decisive the failure of the non-Christian religions to reach their ideal might profitably reflect on the history of the Christian churches of western Asia and northeastern Africa, or on the religious rabble that gather and fight, except as restrained by Turkish soldiery, about the church of the Holy Sepulchre.

So, then, religion also is a fact of human experience, and must receive its recognition and interpretation as belonging to reality. This fact preëminently leads to a personal conception of existence. Pantheism, as said, is a philosophy rather than a religion, and whenever it is held as a philosophy the need of personality soon vindicates itself by some form of polytheism. We must now consider the direction the normal development of religion must take.

Religion can begin with almost nothing, but it can have a normal unfolding only under appropriate conditions. Religion is no simple and changeless thing, but it is a function of our whole nature and varies with our development. Intellect, heart, conscience, and will alike contribute to our religious conceptions. Hence when there is little mental or moral development the religious instinct can cling to a stick or a stone or some low and hideous animal. But as life unfolds and intellect is clarified and conscience becomes regnant in our religious thinking, it then appears that there are certain conditions that must be met by any religion that is to command the assent of developed humanity. First of all, the object worshiped must be something which satisfies the intellect. As I have just said, when intellect is asleep almost anything can be made a religious object, but when intellect is awake and alert and thought has done its work, it then becomes impossible for the intellect to worship any being

353

lower than the Highest. Religion in idea aims at the perfect, and will have the perfect or nothing. When our insight is scanty we may content ourselves with very imperfect notions; but when once the larger vision comes, the older conception must either be abandoned or must be enlarged to meet the newer insight. This fact does away with all low superstitions; they flourish only in the darkness of ignorance. But when the mind has been nourished on the great truths of science, the great revelations of world study and historical and philosophical study, it becomes simply impossible for that mind to rest in any of the forms of polytheism and idolatry. Such a mind may make the motions of religion for selfish or other reasons, but it never really worships in any temple where the god is lower than the Highest. And if it be said that these images, etc., are but symbols, the answer is the same. No developed mind can find any worthy symbol of the Highest in animal forms and idolatrous rites and practices. The intellect stands in such a temple either silent or scoffing, and this is equally true whether the temple be Christian or non-Christian. Intellect has its inalienable rights in religion; and when they are not regarded, religion is sure, sooner or later, to grovel in abject and paralyzing superstition. The history of the Christian religion furnishes abundant illustration.

And equally religious development must take the direction of affirming not only a supreme reason but also a supreme righteousness. As a matter of fact, humanity has been distressingly slow in uniting the ethical and religious ideal, and historically there has been a great deal of religion that was either non-ethical or immoral, the two factors, the religious and the ethical, being brought into no vital union. We see this in both the ethnic religions and the non-Christian universal religions, and we see it also even in Christian lands. A great many people who are nominally Christians and who verily believe themselves to be really such, seem to have little thought that their religion makes any demands upon their conscience and that it should root and result in righteousness. Mechanical devices of ritual and the repetition of verbal forms appear to be the sum of their religion. They differ from other idolaters, not in the spirit of their worship, but in the accident of its form. But there can be as genuine idolatry with words and phrases as with wood or stone images. "God is a spirit, and they that worship him must worship him in spirit and in truth." "He hath showed thee, O man, what is good; and what doth the Lord require of thee, but to do justly, and to love kindness, and to walk humbly with thy God?" These great words strike with doom all superstitions and all immoral and mechanical religion. It is manifest that nothing can claim to be the perfect religion in which the religious and ethical factors are not indissolubly blended. The failure to unite these two factors is the great source of the hideous and destructive aberrations that have defiled religious history and made many religions the enemies of humanity. All these must wither away under the rebuking gaze of the developed intellect and conscience.

And not only must the object of worship be supreme reason and supreme righteousness, it must also be supreme goodness. This is a continuation of the somewhat negative conception of righteousness into the positive conception of ethical love. It is at this point that religious thinking has oftenest come short. If God is to be of any religious value to us and an object of real and adoring worship, he must be supremely good. This demand has by no means always been understood, and in consequence we find a kind of subconscious effort in religious development to think a truly ethical thought about God in connection with a world like this. The outlying religions have largely conceived God as indifferent and selfish. The gods of Epicurus were deaf or indifferent to human sorrow. The God of philosophy has largely been of the same sort, a kind of absolute metaphysical being, with no active moral quality, or if moral at all, in an abstract and unreal way. Likewise the God of theology for a long time hardly attained to any real active goodness, such as the thought of ethical love implies. This God, too, was rather metaphysically conceived, and his holiness consisted mainly in making rules for men and in punishing their transgression. He was conceived largely after the fashion of the medieval despot, and the conception of any obligation on his part to his creatures would have been looked upon almost as blasphemy. But now we have begun to think more clearly and profoundly as to what ethical love demands, and with this thought the immoral, selfish, and indifferent gods have disappeared, and the God of theology, also, has been greatly modified. We see that the law of love applies to power as well as to weakness, that the strong ought to bear the burdens of the weak and not to please themselves; that the greatest of all must be the servant of all, and the chief of burden bearers. This insight has already wrought a great change in our traditional theology, and the end is not yet. We are no longer content with an absolute being selfishly enjoying himself, or with a simply benevolent being who gives gifts to men at no cost to himself. Such a being falls below the moral heroes of our race, and even below the ordinary man and woman who live lives of devotion and sacrifice. We cannot worship any being who falls below our human ideals of love and goodness.

It is but an extension of the same thought to add that the final religion must be one that has a worthy thought of man, and provides a task for him which will furnish the will with an adequate object and a supreme inspiration. We might conceivably get along without any religion, but when thought is once awake we see that a religion which is to command our lives must be one which brings man also to his highest estate. We cannot believe in man without believing in God, and we cannot believe in God without believing in man. God's goodness itself would disappear if the religion did not mean our highest life and blessing; and if our life is to end with the visible scene and we are to be cast aside like the worn-out straw sandals of the coolies, then religion itself collapses; the universe is a failure, and God is a failure, too. It is not a selfish interest on our part which dictates thoughts like this. It is rather the desire to think worthily of God and of his work, and that is impossible so long as we fail to think worthily of man and of his destiny in God's plan.

Here again the non-Christian religions have largely come short: they have not been able to think consistently, and in such a way as to carry conviction, of the destiny of man. They have wavered between annihilation and a dreary round of undesirable existence, with no power to awe or attract. And here again Christianity is a revelation of supreme significance and magnificent audacity. Looked at from the outside we are animals like the other animals, having the human form, indeed, and yet subject to the same general laws as the animal world,—birth and death, hunger and pain, labor and weariness. But our Christian faith holds that this is only the outward appearance, not the inward spiritual fact. We are now the children of God, and it doth not yet appear what we shall be, but we know that when he shall appear we shall be like him, for we shall see him as he is. And thus our life is transformed. We are not simply the highest in the animal world, we are also and more essentially children of the Highest, made in his image likewise, and to go on forevermore with him; made, as the old catechism had it, to glorify God and to enjoy him forever, growing evermore into his likeness and into ever deepening sympathy and fellowship with the eternal as we go on through the unending years, until we are "filled with all the fullness of God." This is the true evolution. Man is making, he is not yet made.

"All about him shadow still, but, while the races flower and fade,
Prophet eyes may catch a glory slowly gaining on the shade."

There is darkness enough in the valleys, no doubt, but there is also a gleam upon the hills and a glow in the upper air.

These are great dreams. They are not dreams that speculation can justify, neither are they dreams that speculation can discredit. They are rooted in the spiritual nature and historical life of our race. If criticism denies knowledge it equally overthrows unbelief, and leaves all room for belief if life and its unfolding needs point that way. This is no small service. This is not a machine and dead world, but a world of life and personality and morals and religion; and in such a world it is permitted to see visions and dream dreams, to form ideals and live in their inspiration, and to venture beyond knowledge in obedience to those "high instincts" which have always been, and still remain, the "fountain light" of all our spiritual day.

### Note

1. In *Personalism* (Boston and New York: Houghton, Mifflin and Company, 1908), pp. 285-302.

# William James

*Although he neither sought to be nor became a "Christian church theologian," James (1842–1910) was a product of New England Calvinism's stormy passage through Enlightenment, post-Kantian, and Transcendentalist eras to new frontiers of philosophy and science. His thinking has also had profound influence on theology and the church in America. Trained in medicine, he began his career as a teacher in that field at Harvard in 1873 and shifted to academic posts there in psychology and philosophy. His research, teaching, and publications established his reputation as a pioneer in psychological science, the psychology and philosophy of religion, and pragmatic and radical empirical thought.*

*Of his contributions to theology in particular, as distinct from those he made to the psychology of religion and from there to pastoral care and counseling, his seminal essay "The Will to Believe" (1897) appears here, in condensed form. It reflected and addressed—in its own distinctive way—questions regarding the bases, intelligibility, and validity of beliefs that church theologians often pursued and often skirted. James, arguing against William Clifford, an English agnostic thinker attacking the "credibility" of religious belief, shifts the defense of religious belief from theory to the roots, roles, and outcomes of religious affirmations in human living.*

## THE WILL TO BELIEVE[1]

In the recently published Life by Leslie Stephen of his brother, Fitz-James, there is an account of a school to which the latter went when he was a boy. The teacher, a certain Mr. Guest, used to converse with his pupils in this wise: "Gurney, what is the difference between justification and sanctification?—Stephen, prove the omnipotence of God!" etc. In the midst of our Harvard freethinking and indifference we are prone to imagine that here at your good old orthodox College conversation continues to be somewhat upon this order; and to show you that we at Harvard have not lost all interest in these vital subjects, I have brought with me to-night something like a sermon on justification by faith to read to you,—I mean, an essay in justification *of* faith, a defense of our right to adopt a believing attitude in religious matters, in spite of the fact that our merely logical intellect may not have been coerced. "The Will to Believe," accordingly, is the title of my paper.

. . .

*I.*

Let us give the name of *hypothesis* to anything that may be proposed to our belief; and just as the electricians speak of live and dead wires, let us speak of any hypothesis as either *live* or *dead*. A live hypothesis is one which appeals as a real possibility to him to whom it is proposed. If I ask you to believe in the Mahdi, the notion makes no electric connection with your nature,—it refuses to scintillate with any credibility at all. As an hypothesis it is completely dead. To an Arab, however (even if he be not one of the Mahdi's followers), the hypothesis is among the mind's possibilities: it is alive. This shows that deadness and liveness in an hypothesis are not intrinsic properties, but relations to the individual thinker. They are measured by his willingness to act. The maximum of liveness in an hypothesis means willingness to act irrevocably. Practically, that means belief; but there is some believing tendency wherever there is willingness to act at all.

Next, let us call the decision between two hypotheses an *option*. Options may be of several kinds. They may be—1, *living* or *dead*; 2, *forced* or *avoidable*; 3, *momentous* or *trivial*; and for our purposes we may call an option a *genuine* option when it is of the forced, living, and momentous kind.

1. A living option is one in which both hypotheses are live ones. If I say to you: "Be a theosophist or be a Mohammedan," it is probably a dead option, because for you neither hypothesis is likely to be alive. But if I say: "Be an agnostic or be a Christian," it is otherwise: trained as you are, each hypothesis makes some appeal, however small, to your belief.

2. Next, if I say to you: "Choose between going out with your umbrella or without it," I do not offer you a genuine option, for it is not forced. You can easily avoid it by not going out at all. Similarly, if I say, "Either love me or hate me," "Either call my theory true or call it false," your option is avoidable. You may remain indifferent to me, neither loving nor hating, and you may decline to offer any judgment as to my theory. But if I say, "Either accept this truth or go without it," I put on you

a forced option, for there is no standing place outside of the alternative. Every dilemma based on a complete logical disjunction, with no possibility of not choosing, is an option of this forced kind.

3. Finally, if I were Dr. Nansen and proposed to you to join my North Pole expedition, your option would be momentous; for this would probably be your only similar opportunity, and your choice now would either exclude you from the North Pole sort of immortality altogether or put at least the chance of it into your hands. He who refuses to embrace a unique opportunity loses the prize as surely as if he tried and failed. *Per contra,* the option is trivial when the opportunity is not unique, when the stake is insignificant, or when the decision is reversible if it later prove unwise. Such trivial options abound in the scientific life. A chemist finds an hypothesis live enough to spend a year in its verification: he believes in it to that extent. But if his experiments prove inconclusive either way, he is quit for his loss of time, no vital harm being done.

It will facilitate our discussion if we keep all these distinctions well in mind.

*II.*

The next matter to consider is the actual psychology of human opinion. When we look at certain facts, it seems as if our passional and volitional nature lay at the root of all our convictions. When we look at others, it seems as if they could do nothing when the intellect had once said its say. Let us take the latter facts up first.

Does it not seem preposterous on the very face of it to talk of our opinions being modifiable at will? Can our will either help or hinder our intellect in its perceptions of truth? Can we, by just willing it, believe that Abraham Lincoln's existence is a myth, and that the portraits of him in McClure's Magazine are all of some one else? Can we, by any effort of our will, or by any strength of wish that it were true, believe ourselves well and about when we are roaring with rheumatism in bed, or feel certain that the sum of the two one-dollar bills in our pocket must be a hundred dollars? We can *say* any of these things, but we are absolutely impotent to believe them; and of just such things is the whole fabric of the truths that we do believe in made up,—matters of fact, immediate or remote, as Hume said, and relations between ideas, which are either there or not there for us if we see them so, and which if not there cannot be put there by any action of our own.

In Pascal's Thoughts there is a celebrated passage known in literature

360

as Pascal's wager. In it he tries to force us into Christianity by reasoning as if our concern with truth resembled our concern with the stakes in a game of chance. Translated freely his words are these: You must either believe or not believe that God is—which will you do? Your human reason cannot say. A game is going on between you and the nature of things which at the day of judgment will bring out either heads or tails. Weigh what your gains and your losses would be if you should stake all you have on heads, or God's existence: if you win in such case, you gain eternal beatitude; if you lose, you lose nothing at all. If there were an infinity of chances, and only one for God in this wager, still you ought to stake your all on God; for though you surely risk a finite loss by this procedure, any finite loss is reasonable, even a certain one is reasonable, if there is but the possibility of infinite gain. Go, then, and take holy water, and have masses said; belief will come and stupefy your scruples,—*Cela vous fera croire et vous abêtira*. Why should you not? At bottom, what have you to lose?

You probably feel that when religious faith expresses itself thus, in the language of the gaming-table, it is put to its last trumps. Surely Pascal's own personal belief in masses and holy water had far other springs; and this celebrated page of his is but an argument for others, a last desperate snatch at a weapon against the hardness of the unbelieving heart. We feel that a faith in masses and holy water adopted wilfully after such a mechanical calculation would lack the inner soul of faith's reality; and if we were ourselves in the place of the Deity, we should probably take particular pleasure in cutting off believers of this pattern from their infinite reward. It is evident that unless there be some pre-existing tendency to believe in masses and holy water, the option offered to the will by Pascal is not a living option. Certainly no Turk ever took to masses and holy water on its account; and even to us Protestants these means of salvation seem such foregone impossibilities that Pascal's logic, invoked for them specifically, leaves us unmoved. As well might the Mahdi write to us, saying, "I am the Expected One whom God has created in his effulgence. You shall be infinitely happy if you confess me; otherwise you shall be cut off from the light of the sun. Weigh, then, your infinite gain if I am genuine against your finite sacrifice if I am not!" His logic would be that of Pascal; but he would vainly use it on us, for the hypothesis he offers us is dead. No tendency to act on it exists in us to any degree.

. . .

. . . And that delicious *enfant terrible* Clifford writes: "Belief is desecrated when given to unproved and unquestioned statements for the

361

solace and private pleasure of the believer. . . . Whoso would deserve well of his fellows in this matter will guard the purity of his belief with a very fanaticism of jealous care, lest at any time it should rest on an unworthy object, and catch a stain which can never be wiped away. . . . If [a] belief has been accepted on insufficient evidence [even though the belief be true, as Clifford on the same page explains] the pleasure is a stolen one. . . . It is sinful because it is stolen in defiance of our duty to mankind. That duty is to guard ourselves from such beliefs as from a pestilence which may shortly master our own body and then spread to the rest of the town. . . . It is wrong always, everywhere, and for every one, to believe anything upon insufficient evidence."

*III.*

All this strikes one as healthy, even when expressed, as by Clifford, with somewhat too much of robustious pathos in the voice. Free-will and simple wishing do seem, in the matter of our credences, to be only fifth wheels to the coach. Yet if any one should thereupon assume that intellectual insight is what remains after wish and will and sentimental preference have taken wing, or that pure reason is what then settles our opinions, he would fly quite as directly in the teeth of the facts.
. . .

As a rule we disbelieve all facts and theories for which we have no use. Clifford's cosmic emotions find no use for Christian feelings. Huxley belabors the bishops because there is no use for sacerdotalism in his scheme of life. Newman, on the contrary, goes over to Romanism, and finds all sorts of reasons good for staying there, because a priestly system is for him an organic need and delight. Why do so few 'scientists' even look at the evidence for telepathy, so called? Because they think, as a leading biologist, now dead, once said to me, that even if such a thing were true, scientists ought to band together to keep it suppressed and concealed. It would undo the uniformity of Nature and all sorts of other things without which scientists cannot carry on their pursuits. But if this very man had been shown something which as a scientist he might *do* with telepathy, he might not only have examined the evidence, but even have found it good enough. This very law which the logicians would impose upon us—if I may give the name of logicians to those who would rule out our willing nature here—is based on nothing but their own natural wish to exclude all elements for which they, in their professional quality of logicians, can find no use.

Evidently, then, our non-intellectual nature does influence our convictions. There are passional tendencies and volitions which run before and others which come after belief, and it is only the latter that are too late for the fair; and they are not too late when the previous passional work has been already in their own direction. Pascal's argument, instead of being powerless, then seems a regular clincher, and is the last stroke needed to make our faith in masses and holy water complete. The state of things is evidently far from simple; and pure insight and logic, whatever they might do ideally, are not the only things that really do produce our creeds.

*IV.*

. . . The thesis I defend is, briefly stated, this: *Our passional nature not only lawfully may, but must, decide an option between propositions, whenever it is a genuine option that cannot by its nature be decided on intellectual grounds; for to say, under such circumstances, "Do not decide, but leave the question open," is itself a passional decision,—just like deciding yes or no,—and is attended with the same risk of losing the truth.* The thesis thus abstractly expressed will, I trust, soon become quite clear. But I must first indulge in a bit more of preliminary work. . . .

*VII.*

One more point, small but important, and our preliminaries are done. There are two ways of looking at our duty in the matter of opinion,— ways entirely different, and yet ways about whose difference the theory of knowledge seems hitherto to have shown very little concern. *We must know the truth*; and *we must avoid error*,—these are our first and great commandments as would-be knowers; but they are not two ways of stating an identical commandment, they are two separable laws. . . .

Believe truth! Shun error!—these, we see, are two materially different laws; and by choosing between them we may end by coloring differently our whole intellectual life. We may regard the chase for truth as paramount, and the avoidance of error as secondary; or we may, on the other hand, treat the avoidance of error as more imperative, and let truth take its chance. Clifford, in the instructive passage which I have quoted, exhorts us to the latter course. Believe nothing, he tells us, keep your mind in suspense forever, rather than by closing it on insufficient evidence incur the awful risk of believing lies. You, on the other hand, may think that the risk of being in error is a very small matter when com-

363

pared with the blessings of real knowledge, and be ready to be duped many times in your investigation rather than postpone indefinitely the chance of guessing true. I myself find it impossible to go with Clifford. We must remember that these feelings of our duty about either truth or error are in any case only expressions of our passional life. Biologically considered, our minds are as ready to grind out falsehood as veracity, and he who says, "Better go without belief forever than believe a lie!" merely shows his own preponderant private horror of becoming a dupe. He may be critical of many of his desires and fears, but this fear he slav-ishly obeys. He cannot imagine any one questioning its binding force. For my own part, I have also a horror of being duped; but I can believe that worse things than being duped may happen to a man in this world: so Clifford's exhortation has to my ears a thoroughly fantastic sound. It is like a general informing his soldiers that it is better to keep out of bat-tle forever than to risk a single wound. Not so are victories either over enemies or over nature gained. Our errors are surely not such awfully solemn things. In a world where we are so certain to incur them in spite of all our caution, a certain lightness of heart seems healthier than this excessive nervousness on their behalf. At any rate, it seems the fittest thing for the empiricist philosopher.

*VIII.*

And now, after all this introduction, let us go straight at our question. I have said, and now repeat it, that not only as a matter of fact do we find our passional nature influencing us in our opinions, but that there are some options between opinions in which this influence must be regarded both as an inevitable and as a lawful determinant of our choice.

I fear here that some of you my hearers will begin to scent danger, and lend an inhospitable ear. Two first steps of passion you have indeed had to admit as necessary,—we must think so as to avoid dupery, and we must think so as to gain truth; but the surest path to those ideal con-summations, you will probably consider, is from now onwards to take no further passional step.

Well, of course, I agree as far as the facts will allow. Wherever the option between losing truth and gaining it is not momentous, we can throw the chance of *gaining truth* away, and at any rate save ourselves from any chance of *believing falsehood,* by not making up our minds at all till objective evidence has come. In scientific questions, this is almost always the case; and even in human affairs in general, the need of acting is seldom so urgent that a false belief to act on is better than no belief at all. Law courts, indeed, have to decide on the best evidence attainable for the moment, because a judge's duty is to make law as well as to ascertain it, and (as a learned judge once said to me) few cases are worth spending much time over: the great thing is to have them decided on *any* acceptable principle, and got out of the way. But in our dealings with objective nature we obviously are recorders, not makers, of the truth; and decisions for the mere sake of deciding promptly and getting on to the next business would be wholly out of place. Throughout the breadth of physical nature facts are what they are quite independently of us, and seldom is there any such hurry about them that the risks of being duped by believing a premature theory need be faced. The questions here are always trivial options, the hypotheses are hardly living (at any rate not living for us spectators), the choice between believing truth or falsehood is seldom forced. The attitude of sceptical balance is therefore the absolutely wise one if we would escape mistakes. What difference, indeed, does it make to most of us whether we have or have not a theory of the Röntgen rays, whether we believe or not in mind-stuff, or have a conviction about the causality of conscious states? It makes no difference. Such options are not forced on us. On every account it is better not to make them, but still keep weighing reasons *pro et contra* with an indifferent hand.

I speak, of course, here of the purely judging mind. For purposes of discovery such indifference is to be less highly recommended, and science would be far less advanced than she is if the passionate desires of individuals to get their own faiths confirmed had been kept out of the game. See for example the sagacity which Spencer and Weismann now display. On the other hand, if you want an absolute duffer in an investigation, you must, after all, take the man who has no interest whatever in its results: he is the warranted incapable, the positive fool. The most useful investigator, because the most sensitive observer, is always he whose eager interest in one side of the question is balanced by an equally keen nervousness lest he become deceived.[2] Science has organized this nervousness into a regular *technique,* her so-called method of verification; and she has fallen so deeply in love with the method that one may even say she has ceased to care for truth by itself at all. It is only truth as technically verified that interests her. The truth of truths might come in merely affirmative form, and she would decline to touch it. Such truth as that, she might repeat with Clifford, would be stolen in defiance of her duty to mankind. Human passions, however, are stronger than technical rules. "Le coeur a ses raisons," as Pascal says, "que la raison ne connaît pas;" and however indifferent to all but the bare rules of the game the umpire, the abstract intellect, may be, the concrete players who furnish him the materials to judge of are usually, each one of them, in love with some pet "live hypothesis" of his own. Let us agree, however, that wherever there is no forced option, the dispassionately judicial intellect with no pet hypothesis, saving us, as it does, from dupery at any rate, ought to be our ideal.

The question next arises: Are there not somewhere forced options in our speculative questions, and can we (as men who may be interested at least as much in positively gaining truth as in merely escaping dupery) always wait with impunity till the coercive evidence shall have arrived? It seems *a priori* improbable that the truth should be so nicely adjusted to our needs and powers as that. In the great boarding-house of nature, the cakes and the butter and the syrup seldom come out so even and leave the plates so clean. Indeed, we should view them with scientific suspicion if they did.

## IX.

*Moral questions* immediately present themselves as questions whose solution cannot wait for sensible proof. A moral question is a question not of what sensibly exists, but of what is good, or would be good if it did exist. Science can tell us what exists; but to compare the *worths*, both of what exists and of what does not exist, we must consult not science, but what Pascal calls our heart. Science herself consults her heart when she lays it down that the infinite ascertainment of fact and correction of false belief are the supreme goods for man. Challenge the statement, and science can only repeat it oracularly, or else prove it by showing that such ascertainment and correction bring man all sorts of other goods which man's heart in turn declares. The question of having moral beliefs at all or not having them is decided by our will. Are our moral preferences true or false, or are they only odd biological phenomena, making things good or bad for *us*, but in themselves indifferent? How can your pure intellect decide? If your heart does not *want* a world of moral reality, your head will assuredly never make you believe in one. Mephistophelian scepticism, indeed, will satisfy the head's play-instincts much better than any rigorous idealism can. Some men (even at the student age) are so naturally cool-hearted that the moralistic hypothesis never has for them any pungent life, and in their supercilious presence the hot young moralist always feels strangely ill at ease. The appearance of knowingness is on their side, of *naïveté* and gullibility on his. Yet, in the inarticulate heart of him, he clings to it that he is not a dupe, and that there is a realm in which (as Emerson says) all their wit and intellectual superiority is no better than the cunning of a fox. Moral scepticism can no more be refuted or proved by logic than intellectual scepticism can. When we stick to it that there *is* truth (be it of either kind), we do so with our whole nature, and resolve to stand or fall by the results. The sceptic with his whole nature adopts the doubting attitude; but which of us is the wiser, Omniscience only knows.

Turn now from these wide questions of good to a certain class of questions of fact, questions concerning personal relations, states of mind between one man and another. *Do you like me or not?*—for example. Whether you do or not depends, in countless instances, on whether I meet you half-way, am willing to assume that you must like me, and show you trust and expectation. The previous faith on my part in your liking's existence is in such cases what makes your liking come. But if I stand aloof, and refuse to budge an inch until I have objective evidence, until you shall have done something apt, as the absolutists say, *ad extorquendum assensum meum,* ten to one your liking never comes. How many women's hearts are vanquished by the mere sanguine insistence of some man that they *must* love him! He will not consent to the hypothesis that they cannot. The desire for a certain kind of truth here brings about that special truth's existence; and so it is in innumerable cases of other sorts. Who gains promotions, boons, appointments, but the man in whose life they are seen to play the part of live hypotheses, who discounts them, sacrifices other things for their sake before they have come, and takes risks for them in advance? His faith acts on the powers above him as a claim, and creates its own verification.

A social organism of any sort whatever, large or small, is what it is because each member proceeds to his own duty with a trust that the other members will simultaneously do theirs. Wherever a desired result is achieved by the co-operation of many independent persons, its existence as a fact is a pure consequence of the precursive faith in one another of those immediately concerned. A government, an army, a commercial system, a ship, a college, an athletic team, all exist on this condition, without which not only is nothing achieved, but nothing is even attempted. A whole train of passengers (individually brave enough) will be looted by a few highwaymen, simply because the latter can count on one another, while each passenger fears that if he makes a movement of resistance, he will be shot before any one else backs him up. If we believed that the whole car-full would rise at once with us, we should each severally rise, and train-robbing would never even be attempted. There are, then, cases where a fact cannot come at all unless a preliminary faith exists in its coming. *And where faith in a fact can help create the fact*, that would be an insane logic which should say that faith running ahead of scientific evidence is the 'lowest kind of immorality' into which a thinking being can fall. Yet such is the logic by which our scientific absolutists pretend to regulate our lives!

## X.

In truths dependent on our personal action, then, faith based on desire is certainly a lawful and possibly an indispensable thing.

But now, it will be said, these are all childish human cases, and have nothing to do with great cosmical matters, like the question of religious faith. Let us then pass on to that. Religions differ so much in their accidents that in discussing the religious question we must make it very generic and broad. What then do we now mean by the religious hypothesis? Science says things are; morality says some things are better than other things; and religion says essentially two things.

First, she says that the best things are the more eternal things, the overlapping things, the things in the universe that throw the last stone, so to speak, and say the final word. "Perfection is eternal,"—this phrase of Charles Secrétan seems a good way of putting this first affirmation of religion, an affirmation which obviously cannot yet be verified scientifically at all.

The second affirmation of religion is that we are better off even now if we believe her first affirmation to be true.

Now, let us consider what the logical elements of this situation are *in case the religious hypothesis in both its branches be really true*. (Of course, we must admit that possibility at the outset. If we are to discuss the question at all, it must involve a living option. If for any of you religion be a hypothesis that cannot, by any living possibility be true, then you need go no farther. I speak to the 'saving remnant' alone.) So proceeding, we see, first, that religion offers itself as a *momentous* option. We are supposed to gain, even now, by our belief, and to lose by our non-belief, a certain vital good. Secondly, religion is a *forced* option, so far as that good goes. We cannot escape the issue by remaining sceptical and waiting for more light, because, although we do avoid error in that way *if religion be untrue*, we lose the good, *if it be true*, just as certainly as if we positively chose to disbelieve. It is as if a man should hesitate indefinitely to ask a certain woman to marry him because he was not perfectly sure that she would prove an angel after he brought her home. Would he not cut himself off from that particular angel-possibility as decisively as if he went and married some one else? Scepticism, then, is not avoidance of option; it is option of a certain particular kind of risk. *Better risk loss of truth than chance of error,*—that is your faith-vetoer's exact position. He is actively playing his stake as much as the believer is; he is backing the field against the religious hypothesis, just as the believer is backing the religious hypothesis against the field. To preach scepticism to us as a duty until 'sufficient evidence' for religion be found, is tantamount therefore to telling us, when in presence of the religious hypothesis, that to yield to our fear of its being error is wiser and better than to yield to our hope that it may be true. It is not intellect against all passions, then; it is only intellect with one passion laying down its law. And by what, forsooth, is the supreme wisdom of this passion warranted? Dupery for dupery, what proof is there that dupery through hope is so much worse than dupery through fear? I, for one, can see no proof; and I simply refuse obedience to the scientist's command to imitate his kind of option, in a case where my own stake is important enough to give me the right to choose my own form of risk. If religion be true and the evidence for it be still insufficient, I do not wish, by putting your extinguisher upon my nature (which feels to me as if it had after all some business in this matter), to forfeit my sole chance in life of getting upon the winning side,—that chance depending, of course, on my willingness to run the risk of acting as if my passional need of taking the world religiously might be prophetic and right.

All this is on the supposition that it really may be prophetic and right, and that, even to us who are discussing the matter, religion is a live hypothesis which may be true. Now, to most of us religion comes in a still further way that makes a veto on our active faith even more illogical. The more perfect and more eternal aspect of the universe is represented in our religions as having personal form. The universe is no longer a mere *It* to us, but a *Thou,* if we are religious; and any relation that may be possible from person to person might be possible here. For instance, although in one sense we are passive portions of the universe, in another we show a curious autonomy, as if we were small active centres on our own account. We feel, too, as if the appeal of religion to us were made to our own active good-will, as if evidence might be forever withheld from us unless we met the hypothesis half-way. To take a trivial illustration: just as a man who in a company of gentlemen made no advances, asked a warrant for every concession, and believed no one's word without proof, would cut himself off by such churlishness from all the social rewards that a more trusting spirit would earn,—so here, one who should shut himself up in snarling logicality and try to make the gods extort his recognition willy-nilly, or not get it at all, might cut himself off forever from his only opportunity of making the gods' acquaintance. This feeling, forced on us we know not whence, that by obstinately believing that there are gods (although not to do so would be so easy both for our logic and our life) we are doing the universe the deepest service we can, seems part of the living essence of the religious hypothesis. If the hypothesis *were* true in all its parts, including this one, then pure intellectualism, with its veto on our making willing advances, would be an absurdity; and some participation of our sympathetic nature would be logically required. I, therefore, for one, cannot see my way to accepting the agnostic rules for truth-seeking, or wilfully agree to keep my willing nature out of the game. I cannot do so for this plain reason, that *a rule of thinking which would absolutely prevent me from acknowledging certain kinds of truth if those kinds of truth were really there, would be an irrational rule.* That for me is the long and short of the formal logic of the situation, no matter what the kinds of truth might materially be.

I confess I do not see how this logic can be escaped. But sad experience makes me fear that some of you may still shrink from radically saying with me, *in abstracto,* that we have the right to believe at our own risk any hypothesis that is live enough to tempt our will. I suspect, however, that if this is so, it is because you have got away from the abstract logical point of view altogether, and are thinking (perhaps without realizing it) of some particular religious hypothesis which for you is dead. The freedom to "believe what we will" you apply to the case of some patent superstition; and the faith you think of is the faith defined by the schoolboy when he said, "Faith is when you believe something that you know ain't true." I can only repeat that this is misapprehension. *In concreto,* the freedom to believe can only cover living options which the intellect of the individual cannot by itself resolve; and living options never seem absurdities to him who has them to consider. When I look at the religious question as it really puts itself to concrete men, and when I think of all the possibilities which both practically and theoretically it involves, then this command that we shall put a stopper on our heart, instincts, and courage, and *wait*—acting of course meanwhile more or less as if religion were *not* true[3]—till doomsday, or till such time as our intellect and senses working together may have raked in evidence enough,—this command, I say, seems to me the queerest idol ever manufactured in the philosophic cave. Were we scholastic absolutists, there might be more excuse. If we had an infallible intellect with its objective certitudes, we might feel ourselves disloyal to such a perfect organ of knowledge in not trusting to it exclusively, in not waiting for its releasing word. But if we are empiricists, if we believe that no bell in us tolls to let us know for certain when truth is in our grasp, then it seems a piece of idle fantasticality to preach so solemnly our duty of waiting for the bell. Indeed we *may* wait if we will,—I hope you do not think that I am denying that,—but if we do so, we do so at our peril as much as if we believed. In either case we *act,* taking our life in our hands. No one of us ought to issue vetoes to the other, nor should we bandy words of abuse. We ought, on the contrary, delicately and profoundly to respect one another's mental freedom: then only shall we bring about the intellectual republic; then only shall we have that spirit of inner tolerance without which all our outer tolerance is soulless, and which is empiricism's glory; then only shall we live and let live, in speculative as well as in practical things.

I began by a reference to Fitz James Stephen; let me end by a quotation from him. "What do you think of yourself? What do you think of the world? . . . These are questions with which all must deal as it seems good to them. They are riddles of the Sphinx, and in some way or other we must deal with them. . . . In all important transactions of life we have to take a leap in the dark. . . . If we decide to leave the riddles unanswered, that is a choice; if we waver in our answer, that, too, is a choice: but whatever choice we make, we make it at our peril. If a man chooses to turn his back altogether on God and the future, no one can prevent him; no one can show beyond reasonable doubt that he is mistaken. If a man thinks otherwise and acts as he thinks, I do not see that any one can prove that *he* is mistaken. Each must act as he thinks best; and if he is wrong, so much the worse for him. We stand on a mountain pass in the midst of whirling snow and blinding mist, through which we get glimpses now and then of paths which may be deceptive. If we stand still we shall be frozen to death. If we take the wrong road we shall be dashed to pieces. We do not certainly know whether there is any right one. What must we do? 'Be strong and of a good courage.' Act for the best, hope for the best, and take what comes. . . . If death ends all, we cannot meet death better."[4]

## Notes

1. In *The Will to Believe and Other Essays in Popular Philosophy* (New York: Longmans, Green, and Co., 1897), pp. 1-31. Original was an address to the Philosophical Clubs of Yale and Brown Universities. Published in the *New World* (June 1896).
2. Compare Wilfrid Ward's Essay, "The Wish to Believe," in his *Witnesses to the Unseen,* Macmillan & Co., 1893.
3. Since belief is measured by action, he who forbids us to believe religion to be true, necessarily also forbids us to act as we should if we did believe it to be true. The whole defence of religious faith hinges upon action. If the action required or inspired by the religious hypothesis is in no way different from that dictated by the naturalistic hypothesis, then religious faith is a pure superfluity, better pruned away, and controversy about its legitimacy is a piece of idle trifling, unworthy of serious minds. I myself believe, of course, that the religious hypothesis gives to the world an expression which specifically determines our reactions, and makes them in a large part unlike what they might be on a purely naturalistic scheme of belief.
4. *Liberty, Equality, Fraternity,* p. 353, 2d edition. London, 1874.

# Josiah Royce

*After studies at the University of California and in Germany, where he made contact with neo-Kantian and idealist thought, Royce (1855–1916) completed his Ph.D. at Johns Hopkins. An 1882 call from Harvard to leave his teaching at the University of California for a year, while William James took sabbatical leave, led to a permanent appointment. His first important book,* The Religious Aspect of Philosophy *(1885), set him along his career path as a specialist in the philosophy of religion, and he wrote several other books significant to that field in due course. He characterized his metaphysical system as an "absolute idealism." The system itself was one of many produced by idealist thinkers in Germany, England, and the United States following Kant's Copernican Revolution. More distinctive and challenging were Royce's analyses of the human condition.*

*One focus of attention was human values, which Royce—in line with neo-Kantianism generally—explored because they could not be accounted for, or judged, in terms of pure fact or pure theory. The "religious" factor at play in human valuing was of central concern to Royce, and study of the Christian religion in this regard was more than an arbitrarily chosen, philosophical test case to him. The essential and inescapable relationality of human beings was an idea basic to his thought; loyalty and community were two themes he returned to again and again. All three appear in the selection that follows, from his last major work,* The Problem of Christianity *(1913), where they are treated in the context of Christianity's idea of universal community as the "realm of grace."*

## THE REALM OF GRACE[1]

The Christian world has been still more deeply influenced by the apostle Paul's teaching concerning the divine grace that saves, than by his account of the moral burden of the individual. The traditional lore of salvation is more winning, and, in many respects, less technical, than is the Christian teaching regarding our lost state.

The present lecture is to be devoted to a study of some aspects of the doctrine of grace. Yet, since our moral burden, and our escape from that burden, are matters intimately connected, we shall find that both topics belong to the exposition of the same essential Christian idea, and that, at the same time, they throw new light upon the first of the three essential Christian ideas, the idea of the universal community. Our present task will therefore enable us to reach a new stage in our survey of the larger connections of the Christian doctrine of life.

*I*

Christianity is most familiarly known as a religion of love, and this view, as far as it extends, is a true view of Christianity. Our second lecture has shown us, however, that this characterization is inadequate, because it does not render justly clear the nature of the objects to which, in our human world, Christian love is most deeply and essentially devoted. A man is known by the company that he keeps. In its human relations, and apart from an explicit account of its faith concerning the realm of the gods, or concerning God, a religion can be justly estimated only when you understand what kinds and grades of human beings it bids you recognize, as well as what it counsels you to do in presence of the beings of each grade. Now, as our second lecture endeavoured to point out, there are in the human world two profoundly different grades, or levels, of mental beings,—namely, the beings that we usually call human individuals, and the beings that we call communities. . . .

Any highly organized community—so in our second lecture we argued—is as truly a human being as you and I are individually human. Only a community is not what we usually call an individual human being; because it has no one separate and internally well-knit physical organism of its own; and because its mind, if you attribute to it any one mind, is therefore not manifested through the expressive moments of such a single separate human organism.

Yet there are reasons for attributing to a community a mind of its own. Some of these reasons were briefly indicated in our second lecture; and they will call for further scrutiny hereafter. Just here it concerns my purpose simply to call attention to the former argument, and to say, that the difference between the individual human beings of our ordinary social intercourse, and the communities, is a difference justly characterized, in my opinion, by speaking of these two as *grades* or *levels* of human life.

The communities are vastly more complex, and, in many ways, are also immeasurably more potent and enduring than are the individuals. Their mental life possesses, as Wundt has pointed out, a psychology of its own, which can be systematically studied. Their mental existence is no mere creation of abstract thinking or of metaphor; and is no more a topic for mystical insight, or for fantastic speculation, than is the mental existence of an individual man. As empirical facts, communities are known to us by their deeds, by their workings, by their intelligent and coherent behavior, just as the minds of our individual neighbors are known to us through their expressions.

Considered as merely natural existences, communities, like individuals, may be either good or evil, beneficent or mischievous. The level of mental existence which belongs to communities insures their complexity; and renders them, in general, far more potent and, for certain purposes and in certain of their activities, much more intelligent than are the human individuals whose separate physical organisms we ordinarily regard as signs of so many separate minds.

But a community,—in so far like a fallen angel,—may be as base and depraved as any individual man can become, and may be far worse than a man. Communities may make unjust war, may enslave mankind, may deceive and betray and torment as basely as do individuals, only more dangerously. The question whether communities are or are not real human beings, with their own level of mental existence, is therefore quite distinct from the question as to what worth this or that community possesses in the spiritual world. And, in our study of the doctrine of grace, we shall find how intimately the Christian teaching concerning the salvation of the individual man is bound up with the Christian definition, both of the saving community and of the power which, according to the Christian tradition, has redeemed that community, and has infused divine life into the level of human existence which this community, and not any merely human individual, occupies.

*II*

To the two levels of human mental existence correspond two possible forms of love: love for human individuals; love for communities. In our second lecture we spoke of the natural fact that communities can be the object of love; and that this love may lead to the complete practical devotion of an individual to the community which he loves. Such vital and effective love of an individual for a community constitutes what we called, in that lecture, Loyalty. And when, in our second lecture, the conception of loyalty as the love of an individual for a being that is on the level of a community first entered our argument, we approached this conception by using, as illustrations, what might be called either the more natural or the more primitive types of loyalty,—types such as grow out of family life, and tribal solidarity, and war. As we pointed out in the second lecture, Christianity is essentially a religion of loyalty. We have learned in our third lecture that, for Christianity, the problem of loyalty is enriched, and meanwhile made more difficult, by the nature of that ideal or universal community to which Paul first invited his converts to be loyal.

Paul and his apostolic Christians were not content with family loyalty, or with clan loyalty, or with a love for any community that they conceived as merely natural in its origin. A miracle, as they held, had created the body of Christ. To this new spiritual being, whose level was that of a community, and whose membership was human, but whose origin was, in their opinion, divine, their love and their life were due. Christianity was the religion of loyalty to this new creation. The idea involved has since remained, with all its problems and tragedies, essential to Christianity.

Our study of the moral burden of the individual has now prepared us for a new insight into the special problem which, ever since Paul's time, Christian loyalty has had to solve. This is no longer anywhere nearly as free from complications as are the problems which family loyalty and clan loyalty present, manifold as those problems of natural loyalty actually are. Even the idea of the rational brotherhood of mankind, of the universal community as the Stoics conceived it, presents no problems nearly as complex as is the problem which the Pauline concept of charity, and of Christian loyalty, has to meet.

For Paul, as you now know, finds that the individual man has to be won over, not to a loyalty which at first seems, to the fleshly mind, natural, but to an essentially new life. The natural man has to be delivered from a doom to which "the law" only binds him faster, the more he seeks to escape. And this escape involves finding, for the individual man, a community to which, when the new life comes, he is to be thenceforth loyal as no natural clan loyalty or family loyalty could make him.

The power that gives to the Christian convert the new loyalty is what Paul calls Grace. And the community to which, when grace saves him, the convert is thenceforth to be loyal, we may here venture to call by a name which we have not hitherto used. Let this name be "The Beloved

Community." This is another name for what we before called the Universal Community. Only now the universal community will appear to us in a new light, in view of its relations to the doctrine of grace. And the realm of this Beloved Community, whose relations Christianity conceives, for the most part, in supernatural terms, will constitute what, in our discussion, shall be meant by the term "The Realm of Grace."

. . .

## IV

Let us next summarily review the original and distinctively Pauline doctrine, both of our fallen state and of the grace which saves.

The last lecture furnished the materials for such a review. The pith of the matter can be expressed, in terms of purely human psychology, thus: Man's fallen state is due to his nature as a social animal. This nature is such that you can train his conscience only by awakening his self-will. By self-will, I here mean, as Paul meant, man's conscious and active assertion of his own individual desires, worth, and undertakings, over against the social will. Another name for this sort of conscious self-will is the modern term "individualism," when it is used to mean the tendency to prefer what the individual man demands to what the collective will requires. In general, and upon high levels of human intelligence, when you train individualism, you also train collectivism; that is, you train in the individual a respect for the collective will. And it belongs to Paul's very deep and searching insight to assert that these two tendencies—the tendency towards individualism, and that towards collectivism—do not exclude, but intensify and inflame each other.

Training, if formally successful in producing the skilful member of human society, breeds respect, although not love, for "the law," that is, for the expression of the collective will. But training also makes the individual conscious of the "other law" in "his members," which "wars against" the law of the social will. The result may be, for his outward conduct, whatever the individual's wits and powers make it. But so far as this result is due to cultivation in intelligent conduct, it inevitably leads to an inner division of the self, a disease of self-consciousness, which Paul finds to be the curse of all merely natural human civilization.

This curse is rooted in the primal constitution which makes man social, and which adapts him to win his intelligence through social conflicts with his neighbors. Hence the curse belongs to the whole "flesh" of man; for by "flesh" Paul means whatever first expresses itself in our instincts and thus lies at the basis of our training, and so of our natural life. The curse afflicts equally the race and the individual. Man is by inheritance adapted for this training to self-will and to inner division.

The social order, in training individuals, therefore breeds conscious sinners; and sins both in them and against them. The natural community is, in its united collective will, a community of sin. Its state is made, by its vast powers, worse than that of the individual. But it trains the individual to be as great a sinner as his powers permit.

If you need illustrations, Paul teaches you to look for them in the whole social order, both of Jews and of Gentiles. But vices and crimes, frequent as they are, merely illustrate the principle. The disease lies much deeper than the outward conduct can show; and respectability of behavior brings no relief. All are under the curse. Cultivation increases the curse. The individual is helpless to escape by any will or deed of his own.

The only escape lies in Loyalty. Loyalty, in the individual, is his love for an united community, expressed in a life of devotion to that community. For such love can be true love only if the unified community both exists and is lovable. For training makes self-will fastidious, and abiding love for a community difficult.

In fact, no social training that a community can give to its members can train such love in those who have it not, or who do not win it through other aid than their training supplies. And no social will that men can intelligently devise, apart from previously active and effective loyalty, can make a community loveable. The creation of the truly lovable community, and the awakening of the highly trained individual to a true love for that community, are, to Paul's mind, spiritual triumphs beyond the wit of man to devise, and beyond the power of man to accomplish. That which actually accomplishes these triumphs is what Paul means by the divine grace.

. . .

## VIII

We now may see how the characterization of Christianity as not only a religion of love, but as also, in essence, a religion of loyalty, tends to throw light upon some of the otherwise most difficult aspects of the problem of Christianity. We can already predict how great this light, if it grows, promises to become.

Christianity is not the only religion in whose conceptions and experiences a community has been central. Loyalty has not left itself without a witness in many ages of human life, and in many peoples. And all the higher forms of loyalty are, in their spirit, religious; for they rest upon the discovery, or upon the faith, that, in all the darkness of our earthly existence, we individual human beings, separate as our organisms seem in their physical weakness, and sundered as our souls appear by their narrowness, and by their diverse loves and fortunes, are not as much alone, and not as helpless, in our chaos of divided will, as we seem.

For we are members one of another, and members, too, of a real life that, although human, is nevertheless, when it is lovable, also above the level upon which we, the separate individuals, live our existence. By our organisms and by our individual divisions of knowledge and of purpose, we are chained to an order of nature. By our loyalty, and by the real communities to which we are worthily loyal, we are linked with a level of mental existence such that, when compared with our individual existence, this higher level lies in the direction of the divine. Whatever the origin of men's ideals of their gods, there should be no doubt that these gods have often been conceived, by their worshippers, as the representatives of some human community, and as in some sense identical with that community.

But loyalty exists in countless forms and gradations. Christianity is characterized not only by the universality of the ideal community to which, in its greatest deeds and ages, it has, according to its intent, been loyal; but also by the depth and by the practical intensity and the efficacy of the love towards this community which has inspired its most representative leaders and reformers; and, finally, by the profoundly significant doctrines and customs to which it has been led in the course of its efforts to identify the being of its ideal community with the being of God.

Other religions have been inspired by loyalty. Other religions have identified a community with a divine being. And, occasionally,—yes, as the world has grown wiser and more united, increasingly,—non-Christian thinking and non-Christian religion have conceived an ideal community as inclusive as mankind, or as inclusive as the whole of beings with minds, however vast that realm may be.

But, historically speaking, Christianity has been distinguished by the concreteness and intensity with which, in the early stages of its growth, it grasped, loved, and served its own ideal of the visible community, supposed to be universal, which it called its Church. It has further been contrasted with other religions by the skill with which it gradually revised its views of the divine nature, in order to be able to identify the spirit that, as it believed, guided, inspired, and ruled this Church, with the spirit of the one whom it had come to worship as its risen Lord.

379

*IX*

If we bear these facts in mind, there is much in the otherwise so difficult history of Christian dogma which we can easily see in a new light. I myself am far from being a technical theologian, and, in coming to the few fragments of an understanding of the meaning of the history of dogma which I possess, I owe much to views such as, in England, Professor Percy Gardner has set forth, both in his earlier discussions, and notably in his recent book on "The Religious Experience of the Apostle Paul." I also owe new light to the remarkable conclusions which Professor Troeltsch of Heidelberg states, at the close of his recently published volume on "The Social Doctrines of the Christian Churches." I shall make no endeavor in this place to deal with those technical aspects of the history of dogma which lie beyond my province as a philosophical student of the Christian doctrine of life. But if I attempt to restate a very few of the results of others in terms of that view of the essence of Christian loyalty which does concern me, my word, at this stage of our discussion, must be as follows:—

Jesus unquestionably taught, in the best-attested, and in the best-known, of his sayings, love for all individual human beings. But he taught this as an organic part of his doctrine of the Kingdom of Heaven. The individual whom you are bidden to love as your brother and your neighbor is, even while Jesus depicts him, transformed before your eyes. For, first, he is no longer the separate organism with a separate mind and a detached being and destiny, whom you ordinarily loathe if he is your enemy, and resist if he endangers or oppresses you. No,—when he asks your aid,—though he be "the least of these my brethren"—he speaks with the voice of the judge of all men, with the voice that you hope to hear saying: "Come ye blessed of my Father, for I was hungered and ye gave me meat." In other words, the real man, whom your eyes only seem to see, but whom on the level of ordinary human intercourse you simply ignore, actually belongs to another level of spiritual existence, above the level of our present life of divisions. The mystery of the real being of this man is open only to the divine Love.

If you view your neighbor as your Father would have you view him, you view him not only as God's image, but also as God's will and God's love. If one asks for further light as to how the divine love views this man, the answer of Jesus, in the parables is, in substance, that this man is a member of the Kingdom of Heaven.

The Kingdom of Heaven is obviously a community. But this community is itself a mystery,—soon to be revealed,—but so far in the visible world, of which Jesus speaks, not yet to be discovered. This Kingdom is a treasure hid in a field. Its Master has gone into a far country. Watch and be ready. The Lord will soon return. The doctrine of Christian love, as thus taught by Jesus, so far as the records guide us, implies loyalty to the Kingdom; but it expresses itself in forms which demand further interpretation, and which the Master intended to have further interpreted.

Now the apostolic churches held that those visions of the risen Lord, upon the memory and report of which their life as communities was so largely based, had begun for them this further interpretation. For them Christian loyalty soon became explicit; because their community became visible. And they believed their community to be the realization of the Kingdom; because they were sure that their risen Lord, whom the reported and recorded visions had shown, was henceforth in their midst as the spirit of this community.

This realm of grace, thus present to the Christian consciousness, needed to be further explored. The explorers were those who helped to define dogmas. The later development of the principal dogmas of the post-apostolic Church was due to a process in which, as Professor Troeltsch persuasively insists, speculation and the use of the results of ancient philosophy (however skilful and learned such processes might be), were in all the great crises of the history of doctrine wholly subordinate to practical religious motives.

To use the phraseology that I myself am obliged to prefer: The common sense of the Christian Church had three problems to solve. First: It was loyal to the universal spiritual community; and upon this loyalty, according to its view, salvation depended. But this universal community must be something concrete and practically efficacious. Hence the visible Church had to be organized as the appearance on earth of God's Kingdom. For what the parables had left mysterious about the object and the life of love, an authoritative interpretation, valid for the believers of those times, must be found, and was found in the visible Church.

Secondly, The life, the unity, the spirit of the Church had meanwhile to be identified with the person and with the spirit of the risen and ascended Lord, whom the visions of the first disciples had made henceforth a central fact in the belief of the Church.

The supernatural being whose body was now the Church, whose spirit was thus identified with the will and with the mind of a community, had once, as man, walked the earth, had really suffered and died. But since he had risen and ascended, henceforth—precisely because he was as the spirit whose body was this community, the Church—he was divine. Such was the essential article of the new faith.

Paul had already taught this. This very doctrine, in its further development, must be kept by the Church as concrete as the recorded life of the Master had been, as close to real life as the work of the visible Church was, and as true to the faith in the divine unity and destiny of the universal community, as Christian loyalty in all those formative centuries remained.

And yet all this must be held in touch with that doctrine of the unity, the personality, and the ineffable transcendence of God,—that doctrine which was the heritage of the Church, both from the religion of Israel and from the wisdom of Greece. Speaking in a purely historical and human sense, the dogma of the Trinity was the psychologically inevitable effort at a solution of this complex but intensely practical problem.

Loyalty to the community inspired this solution. The problem of the two natures of Christ, divine and human, was also psychologically forced upon Christianity by the very problem of the two levels of our human existence which I have just sketched.

I speak still, not of the truth, but of the psychological motives of the dogma. The problem of the two levels of human existence is concrete, is practical, and exists for all of us. Every man who learns what the true goal of life is must live this twofold existence,—as separate individual, limited by the flesh of this maladjusted and dying organism,—yet also as member of a spiritual community which, if loyal, he loves, and in which, in so far as he is loyal, he knows that his only true life is hidden, and is lived.

But for Christianity this problem of the two levels was vital, not only for the individual Christian, but also for the interpretation of the person of Christ, and for the life of the Church. Since, for historical and psychological reasons, the solution of this problem could not be, for Christianity, either polytheistic or disloyal in its spirit, the only humanly natural course was, first, to distinguish the transcendent divine being from the concretely active spirit whose daily work was that of the Church, and then also to distinguish both of these from the human individuality of the Master who had taught the mystery of the Kingdom, and who had then suffered and died, and, as was believed, had risen to create his Church. One had, I say, clearly to distinguish all these; to declare them all to be perfectly real facts. And then one had to unite and, in form, to identify them all, by means of dogmas which were much less merely ingenious speculations than earnest resolutions to act and to believe whatever the loyal Christian life and the work of the Church demanded for the unity of humanity and for the salvation of the world.

382

The result may be estimated philosophically, as one may judge to be reasonable. I have said nothing about the metaphysical truth of these dogmas. But the result should not be judged as due to merely speculative subtleties, or as a practical degeneration of the spirit of the early Church.

The common sense of the Church was simply doing its best to express the meaning of its loyalty. This loyalty had its spiritual community and its human master. And its problems were the problems of all loyalty. And it was as a religion of loyalty, with a community, a Lord, and a Spirit to interpret, that Christianity was led to the doctrine of the two natures of Christ, and to the dogma of the Trinity.

## X

The psychological motives and the historical background of the capital dogmas of the Church are therefore best to be understood in the light of the conception of the universal community, if only one recognizes the historical fact that the Christian consciousness was by purely human motives obliged to define its community as due to the work of the Master who once walked the earth.

It is not surprising, then, that the Fourth Gospel, wherein the Pauline conception of the Church as the body of Christ, and of Christ as the spirit of the Church, is perfectly united with the idea of the divine Word made flesh, is, of all the Gospels, the one which, although much the farthest from the literal history of the human Master's earthly words and deeds, has been, in its wholeness, the nearest to the heart of the Christian world during many centuries.

The Synoptic Gospels stir the spirits of men by the single word or saying of Jesus, by the recorded parable, or by the impressive incident, be this incident a legend, or a fragment of literally true portrayal (we often know not which).

But the Fourth Gospel impresses us most in its wholeness. This Gospel faces the central practical problem of Christianity,—the problem of grace, the transformation of the very essence of the individual man. This transformation is to save him by making him a dweller in the realm which is at once inaccessibly above his merely natural level as an individual, and yet daily near to whatever gives to his otherwise ruined natural existence its entire value. This realm is the realm of the level of the united and lovable community.

From this realm comes all saving grace. Wherever two or three are gathered together in a genuine unity of spirit,—this realm does indeed begin to display itself. Other religions besides Christianity have illustrated that fact. And whatever, apart from legend on the one hand, and speculative interpretation on the other, we human beings can appreciate, in a vital sense, concerning the meaning of what we call divine, we learn through such love for communities as arises from the companionships of those who are thus joined.

This truth humanity at large has long since possessed in countless expressions and disguises. But the fortune of Christianity led the Church to owe its foundation to teachings, to events, to visions, and, above all, to a practical devotion, which, from the first, required the faithful to identify a human individual with the saving spirit of a community, and with the spirit of a community which was also conceived as wholly divine.

The union of the concrete and the ineffable which hereupon resulted,—the union of what touches the human heart and stirs the soul as only the voice of a living individual leader can touch it,—the complete union of this with the greatest and most inspiring of human mysteries,— the mystery of loving membership in a community whose meaning seems divine,—this union became the central interest of Christianity.

Apart from what is specifically Christian in belief, such union of the two levels has its place in our daily lives wherever the loyalty of an individual leader shows to other men the way that leads them to the realm of the spirit. And whenever that union takes place, the divine and the human seem to come into touch with each other as elsewhere they never do.

The mystery of loyalty, as Paul well knew, is the typical mystery of grace. It is, in another guise, the mystery of the incarnation. According to the mind of the early Christian Church, one individual had solved that mystery for all men.

He had risen from the shameful death that, for Christianity, as for its greatest rival Buddhism, is not only the inevitable but the just doom of whoever is born on the natural level of the human individual;—he had ascended to the level of the Spirit, and had become, in the belief of the faithful, the spirit of a community whose boundaries were coextensive with the world, and of whose dominion there was to be no end.

. . .

### Note

1. From *The Problem of Christianity,* in *The Religious Philosophy of Josiah Royce,* ed. Stuart Gerry Brown (Syracuse: Syracuse University Press, 1952; original essay published in 1913), pp. 178-84, 190-96.

# Daniel D. Whedon

*The most noted Methodist theologian of his time, Whedon (1808–1885) developed from his church's historic English resources a distinctly American form of Methodist theology, one quite compatible with an American democratic ethos that stressed the freedom and responsibility of the individual. His theological viewpoint also matched well the philosophic ideals of the age, with its appeal to the authority of scripture, reason, and human religious experience. He knew service as a church pastor and university teacher, but his influence on church theology derived from his twenty-eight-year term (1856–1884) as editor of the* Methodist Quarterly Review, *along with his addresses, biblical commentaries, and other publications.*

*His monograph or treatise* Freedom of the Will *(1864) addressed anew the one—perhaps for all intents and purposes, the only—doctrinally substantive point at issue between the "Arminianism" of Methodists and the "Calvinism" of their main competitors on the revival field. Excerpted here is Whedon's rejoinder to the standard but cutting objection of Calvinists that Arminianism glorifies human nature and humanity rather than God.*

## FREEDOM EXALTS MAN AND DISHONORS GOD?[1]

. . . It is not the power to do evil which is an imperfection; if it were, a statue would be in this respect superior to the first angels before they fell; but it is the evil exercise of that power which is the deficiency and the deformity. He who is right from incapacity is safely, but not nobly, nor meritoriously, right. It is the height of virtue to be in full possession of the mastery of both good and of evil, and yet to do good alone. Such a mastery and supremacy belong in the highest degree to God. For it is *eternally* that he possesses full power for choice of right or wrong; and it is eternally that he chooses solely right.

"To exalt man's will," . . . is to exalt man in that respect in which he is in "the image of God," and in which to depreciate him below his measure is to dishonor his Original. But when we so exalt man's Will it is not merely to assert his dignity of nature, which in its place is a just procedure, but to show him responsible for his deeds, and to justify God in his judgments. It is indeed an exalted prerogative to be a responsible subject of the Government of God; and it is but honoring that government to place in its full relief that faculty in which does mainly lie the qualification for that high citizenship. It is a foolish way, worthy the narrowness of a bigot, for the sake of humbling human pride to depreciate man's intellect and make him a brute, or to nullify his free agency and make him a block or a clock. The freedom of the Will in the moral agent does thus furnish the true condition for the moral government of God.

As living being is superior to insensate matter, and intellectual is superior to living animal being, so of intellectual the highest is free moral being. So far as we know, the highest declarative glory of God consists in the existence of his retributive moral government. But the very existence of such a government requires of God the concession to his creature of a power which in its course of action he will neither annihilate nor violate; leaving the capability, but not the necessity, of freedom to guilt, which is judicable, or freedom to good desert, which is rewardable, and of a free holiness, worship, honor, and glorification of God, which are the highest result of a moral kingdom.

The denying the freedom of man does not honor but degrade God's sovereignty, sinking him from the position of a Ruler of free subjects to a manipulator of mechanisms. It takes from him the possibility of justice by making him propel the act he is to punish. Nor is there any ascription of meanness to God more mean than that which makes him attempt to inaugurate a glorious free probationary system, and yet *to fail*, purely from a penurious grudging of the necessary bestowment of power to constitute a true responsible agent, and from a fear that the possession of an alternative power of Will by the finite agent might disturb the stability of the throne of the Omnipotent. The former is a parsimony, and the latter a cowardice, which it is discreditable to any man to ascribe to the God of the universe.

If the maintenance of freedom of the Will "exalts man's Will," and the denial of it degrades the dignity of man's Will, the same denial must degrade the dignity of the Divine Will. The assertion, therefore, of the necessitation of the divine Will, so strenuously maintained by Edwards and other necessitarians, does bring degradation and dishonor upon the divine Will. While, on the other hand, to maintain the freedom of the divine Will from any such causative determination of volitions is to maintain its dignity and honor.

Another argument against this view of divine sovereignty maintains that it is a supposition *unworthy the divine dignity* that any of his decrees or actions should be DEPENDENT upon the action or non-action of insignificant man. The assumption, we reply, that the action of God cannot be conditioned on the *action* or *other matter* of a finite being, (for it cannot be limited to the *action,* but must extend to every finite attribute of the creature,) renders creation, preservation, government, retribution all alike impossible. In such case God cannot create a finite being, for the act of creation must be modified by, and conditioned upon the nature of the finite to be created. If he is to be one sort of a creature, one sort of creation must be performed; if another, another. Preservation also must depend upon the actual existence, nature, and purpose of the creature to be preserved. Government requires laws which must depend upon the nature of the being or thing to be governed. No regard must be paid by God to prayer; nothing must take place in consequence of the prayers of the holiest finite being; for that would be making God's action dependent upon the action of a finite being, obliging him to wait until man performs before he can act. Nor can men be rewarded according to their works, blessed with heaven upon a life of faith and holiness, or cursed with hell on account of a life of wickedness. Such a doctrine shuts the Deity up in a dignified reserve from all the concerns of his creatures, making his sovereignty too exalted to be any sovereign at all. Nay, it deprives him of the power of producing any creatures, rendering a finite universe impossible.

*Freedom is* also held by necessitarians as *attributing to man* MERIT in exercising the act of *faith* and performing the conditions of salvation, so that heaven is attained *not by* GRACE *but by* WORKS. We reply,

1. By their own maxim of desert necessitarians are as truly obliged to attribute merit to faith and works as freedomists. By that maxim *it matters not how we come by our right volitions;* whether by necessitation, causation, predestination, or creation, they are equally deserving of reward or condemnation. No matter, then, if our faith and works be foreordained, necessitated, created by the resistless influences of the Spirit, they are still *volitions;* are *free* with the highest degree of freedom conceivable, and are to be credited with all the merit, good desert, and rewardableness that the loftiest Arminian can conceive. So that all the glory that Calvinism claims to itself for overthrowing human merit is thus by itself overthrown. *It teaches by its fundamental maxim of merit*

387

*the meritoriousness of human faith and works, and the attainment of salvation by our own good desert.*

2. Faith *is* excellent and well-deserving. It would be derogatory to God to suppose that he would not choose a good and excellent act as an antecedent to our justification. As between good and bad, faith is good and not bad; it is ethically right and not wrong. Unbelief [and] infidelity are wrong; faith and obedience are right. The very reason why faith is a meet condition for salvation, and a right initiation of a holy life, is that it is in itself a self-surrender and self-consecration to God and to all goodness. Performed in the use of a previous gracious aid, it is ethically meritorious; and there is a just and right sense in which we may be said to be justified for the merit of our faith and to be saved by a good work. And yet,

3. Such is not the merit of our faith that we thereby intrinsically *deserve justification*; nor such the merit of our good works as that we thereby earn eternal life. Notwithstanding our faith, God, apart from his gracious promises, is under no obligation to forgive our past sins; nor do our works form any purchase of so great a gift as heaven and endless glory. Absolutely at the moment of an act of complete faith God needs us not, and he might justly drop us into non-existence. So that after all we are his workmanship, and all our salvation is from the free and abundant grace of God.

If man's act of accepting faith be not free and alternative, able to be withheld as to be put forth, possessing the freedom *from* as well as the freedom *to*, then there is possible no divine government, but only an automatism. If man's will, in the given case, accept divine grace, either by an intrinsic automatic spring of the Will, or by an omnipotent securative touch of the spring of the Will by the divine finger, then the very conditions of a free probationary system are destroyed. Men are the mechanically moving figures of a great panorama, and God himself is but a mechanical counterpart—both forming one stupendous reciprocal interactive automatism. Herein, Dr. Chalmers[2] assures us, lies the vital point of difference between Calvinism and Arminianism; and herein, we reply, lies the difference between a divine government and an automatism.

### Notes

1. In *The Freedom of the Will as a Basis of Human Responsibility and a Divine Government* (New York: Phillips & Hunt; Cincinnati: Hitchcock & Walden, 1864), pp. 322-27.
2. Notes of Hill's Lectures, Book iv, chap. viii.

# THE MODERN ERA

(Since 1918)

# Shailer Mathews

$M$*athews (1863–1941), a Baptist, studied theology at the Newton Theological Institute and in Berlin, Germany, following his graduation from Colby College in his home state of Maine. His first major work,* The Social Teaching of Jesus *(1897), established him as a notable exponent of liberalism and social-gospel concerns. What appeared there, and even more conspicuously in works to follow, was a new, sharper critical edge that distinguished his liberalism from that typical of the "Evangelicals." The distinction was due in part to rigorous use of empirical-historical and social-scientific thought in his biblical studies and theology, both notable for emphasis on functionalist interpretations of religion. But it was due also to a sense that the challenges of modern living and thought required, in addition to ideals, a tougher, harder-hitting, no-nonsense reappraisal and reconstruction of traditional Christian ideas.*

*This "new" approach, widely shared among the talented group of scholars at Chicago's Divinity School, especially during Mathews' term as Dean (1908–1933), gave rise to the name "the Chicago School of Theology" and its identification as "Modernist." Surveys of major theologians of the era would record a number of Matthew's associates. Here Mathews alone represents the School as a whole, as he often did. And of his works that vie for inclusion in a reader, his clear and programmatic answer to the question "What Is Modernism?" (1924) is especially telling.*

## WHAT IS MODERNISM?[1]

Modernism is a projection of the Christian movement into modern conditions. It proceeds within the religious limits set by an ongoing Christian group; it distinguishes permanent Christian convictions from their doctrinal expression; it uses these convictions in meeting the actual needs of our modern world.

The term Modernism itself is somewhat unfortunate. Despite all protestation to the contrary it gives the impression of self-satisfaction, as if only those who hold certain views are intellectually abreast of the times. Yet the terms "Modernism" and "Modernists" have come into such common use that they cannot be avoided. This much, at least, can be said in their favor: they indicate a real tendency in our religious life. This tendency is to be seen when one compares the intellectual habits of Christians as they expound Christianity. Some rely on scientific method; others, on church authority. The former may be said in general to be those indicated when Modernists are mentioned. But strictly speaking, "Modernism" and "Modernist" imply no new theology or organized denominational movement. The habits of mind and tendencies of thought which the terms have come loosely to represent are to be found in all Christian groups in all parts of the world. Until Modernism is distinguished from fundamentally theological interests, it will be misunderstood. Modernists are not members of a group which prescribes doctrinal views, but Christians who use certain methods of thought are described as Modernists. These methods, with their points of view, must be considered in detail.

. . .

*III.*

What then is Modernism? A heresy? An infidelity? A denial of truth? A new religion? So its ecclesiastical opponents have called it. But it is none of these. To describe it is like describing that science which has made our modern intellectual world so creative. It is not a denomination or a theology. *It is the use of the methods of modern science to find, state and use the permanent and central values of inherited orthodoxy in meeting the needs of a modern world.* The needs themselves point the way to formulas. Modernists endeavor to reach beliefs and their application in the same way that chemists or historians reach and apply their conclusions. They do not vote in conventions and do not enforce beliefs by discipline. Modernism has no Confession. Its theological affirmations are the formulation of results of investigation both of human needs and the Christian religion. The Dogmatist starts with doctrines, the Modernist with the religion that gave rise to doctrines. The Dogmatist relies on conformity through group authority; the Modernist, upon inductive method and action in accord with group loyalty.

An examination of the Modernist movement will disclose distinct aspects of these characteristics.

1. The Modernist movement is a phase of the scientific struggle for freedom in thought and belief.

The dogmatic mind found its natural and most effective expression in the Roman Catholic Church and in the Protestantism of the sixteenth and seventeenth centuries. Because it developed under the influences of Roman law, its possessors were trained in the methods of the lawyer and the schoolman, and dominated by deductive logic. It regarded doctrine as of the nature of law and church-membership as an obedience to theological statutes passed by church authorities. Its range of interest in philosophy was practically limited to Aristotle, and its theological method was to organize texts of the Bible and bring about the adoption of the resulting formulas or dogmas as authoritative statements comparable with a legal code. Protestantism preserved most of these dogmas while setting up new authority for accepting them. It was not interested in the church as an historical movement, but in the literature of the first stages of that movement. It detached the Bible from history and declared it to be the sole and divinely given basis of revealed truth. Yet the Bible it accepted was determined by authority, and biblical truth was authoritatively said to be expressed in creeds and catechisms and Confessions adopted and enforced by authority. The dogmatic mind has always sought to express its beliefs sharply and clearly and with condemnatory clauses. Its century-long anathematizing of heretics shows that it is quite as truly interested in keeping non-conformists out of the church as in expressing truth held by the church. Naturally it has never been primarily interested in science, international peace, or social justice. It has often attacked scientists; it has never thought of abolishing war; and it has preferred charity and heaven to economic readjustment. One of its most bitter controversies has been over the relation of "works" to faith.

We must in justice distinguish between the dogmatic mind relying upon authority and Christians who approve of dogma. One has only to read the biographies and the histories of the sixteenth and seventeenth centuries to see how many Christians responded to deeply religious and social motives and rose superior to the intensely theological atmosphere in which they lived. Such men were Melancthon, Thomas Moore and Grotius—many of whom suffered persecution. The persons who wrote the Confessions of the sixteenth and seventeenth centuries, which are now said to be final, were the same people who made themselves secure by executing, imprisoning, or banishing their opponents and confiscating their property. It was they who carried on the Wars of Religion in France, the Thirty Years' War in Germany, the Civil War in England, and the wars between the Spaniards and Dutch in Holland. Loyalty to a church was identical with loyalty to a nation. To break with dogma was like a break with a law. In the nature of the case, if Christianity as thus conceived is the only Christianity, the treatment of dogmas as law will continue.

Theological controversy has seldom if ever tended toward Christian love. If one party won, the other party lost. The winner disciplined the loser. Whether Roman Catholic or Protestant, Calvinist or Arminian, the ecclesiastic has never insisted that salvation involved the acceptance of some formulas essentially moral. Neither the Apostles', the Nicene, the Chalcedonian, nor the Athanasian creed makes any reference to morality beyond the mere statement of the belief in the forgiveness of sin. So far as each is concerned, the teaching of Jesus contained in the Sermon on the Mount might as well never have existed. The same is not equally true of the great Protestant Confessions, but the chief interest in all those Confessions is theological rather than ethical. According to them faith is not merely an attitude of loyalty to Christ, trust in God and an application of truth to life, but an acceptance of some doctrinal formula.

This is not to say that the church has been indifferent to morality. Any such assertion would be scandalously untrue, but the "fundamentals" of salvation have not been seen by the dogmatic mind in the field of morals or religious experience but in that of authoritative theology. To hold heretical doctrine was to be assured of hell fire; not to believe in some theological tenet was and still is in the minds of some Christians to make entrance of Heaven impossible. The dogmatic mind has never been as severe with sinners as it has been with heretics.

Such a position is easily understood. Dogmas and confessions like oaths of loyalty and constitutions make easy tests. It was natural that conviction of the finality of such tests should become permanent in groups which originated in theological controversy and which were either prosecuted, or persecuted, or both. Confessions adopted for political as well as religious purposes are still used as a test. That is to say, the habit of making dogmas a test of Christianity is a survival of an age when men looked upon Christianity as identical with its doctrines and upon its doctrines as law and upon coercion as warranted by the danger of heresy.

But Christianity is more than dogma. It is and always has been a way of ordering life and its institutions. The insufficiency of dogmatic Christianity to express fully the religion of Jesus Christ has always been felt. Especially of late since the days of Moody, evangelical Christianity has been developing a layman's theology which has placed increased emphasis on practical religion, the love of God and His readiness to receive those who seek Him. Thus many doctrines once judged invaluable for Christian living have been tacitly outgrown. It would, for instance, perplex the majority of Presbyterians to give the Five Points of Calvinism, yet three hundred years ago these were vehemently asserted and enforced by the Reformed churches. One might go on indefinitely showing how doctrines are not repudiated, but cease to function in the life of earnest Christians whose attention has shifted from technical theology to practical religious interests.

The simple fact is that the center of interest in religion is passing from theology to life. This tendency is bound to demand intellectual justification other than inherited authority can give. Men seek to answer questions of practical living suggested to their religious faith by methods successful in other fields of inquiry.

There are thousands of persons both within and without the churches who distrust the ability of the dogmatic mind to meet such questions. To them the conception of Christianity as a legal system is untenable. They will not be coerced into religious conformity. They demand freedom in belief. They prefer no theology to what seems to them an irrational and ineffective theology. It is these men and women threatened by new temptations, possessed of new powers, new knowledge, new discontent, facing new problems and new tasks, determined upon intellectual freedom, whom the Modernist would serve. The Dogmatists may, if they can, serve others.

The habits of medieval Catholicism and national churches, the appeal to some supernaturally authoritative church or Bible, arguments based neither upon a study of the nature and history of either Bible or church, but upon usage or ecclesiastical action, do not satisfy free minds. There is an indubitable struggle between ecclesiastical authority and free scientific method. The two have never been compatible. The Modernist, conscious of his loyalty to Jesus Christ, recognizes the value of all theologies, but with him scientific method has replaced the philosophy and the patterns with which the church fathers defended and organized Christian truth as well as the church authority with which their formulas have been enforced. He, too, has propositions for which he would die, but the freedom he asks for himself he would grant to his opponents. If he had the power to enforce his own beliefs on the church he would not use it. Truth can be trusted to find its own defense in efficiency.

The new movement in evangelical Christianity is, therefore, not to be understood by emphasizing its points of difference with systems of theology. It can be appreciated only as one recognizes that it is the outcome and expression of the Christian life of those who rely upon the inductive method as a way to reality and upon freedom as imperative in religious thought.

*IV.*

2. Modernists are Christians who accept the results of scientific research as data with which to think religiously.

It would, of course, be unsafe to accept every scientific theory as material for theological thinking. But the Modernist starts with the assumption that scientists know more about nature and man than did the theologians who drew up the Creeds and Confessions. He is open-minded in regard to scientific discovery. Believing that all facts, whether they be those of religious experience or those of the laboratory, can fit into the general scheme of things, he welcomes new facts as rapidly as they can be discovered.

When, therefore, he finds experts in all fields of scientific investigation accepting the general principle of evolution, he makes it a part of his intellectual apparatus. He does this not because he has a theology to be supported, but because he accepts modern science. He has no illusions as to the finality of this or that theory, which, like Darwinism, attempts, though imperfectly, to describe an evolutionary process, but he is convinced that scientists have discovered that there is continuity of development in the physical world, and that, therefore, such continuity must be recognized by religious thinkers. He is cautious about appropriating philosophies, but he is frankly and hopefully an evolutionist because of facts furnished by experts. In this attitude he is reproducing that of earlier religious thinkers when they abandoned the Ptolemaic system of the universe and adopted the Copernican. When he wants to estimate the worth of dogmatic hostility to such attitudes he recalls the attack upon the views of Copernicus by those who had identified Ptolemaic science with religion, and waits for good people to show good sense.

Furthermore, in the light of sociological and historical facts, the Modernist uses the methods of science in his quest for religious assurance. He knows that the Christian religion develops as a group-possession when men's experience and knowledge grow. He is not content simply to accept a doctrine. He seeks to understand its real purpose and service.

He therefore seeks to discover why it arose. He searches for its origins and estimates its efficiency in the light of its conformity with social forces and its capacity to nerve men and women for more courageous living. The beliefs of Christians are less extensive than the loyalties of Christians. A religion is a way of living and the Modernist refuses to think of it as an accumulation of decrees. Attitudes and convictions, he discovers from a study of the Christian movement, are not identical with the language and concepts in which they are expressed.

3. Modernists are Christians who adopt the methods of historical and literary science in the study of the Bible and religion.

From some points of view, this, although not the most fundamental, is their most obvious characteristic. It was the critical study of the Scriptures with which the movement started in the Roman Catholic Church and it has laid the foundation for theological discussion in Protestantism. The Modernist is a critic and an historian before he is a theologian. His interest in method precedes his interest in results. The details of his attitude as to the Bible will appear in a later chapter, but in general the Modernist may be said to be first of all a Christian who implicitly trusts the historical method of an approach to Christian truth.

Modernists believe themselves true to the spirit and purpose of Jesus Christ when they emphasize his teachings and the inner faith of a century-long movement rather than the formulas in which aspects of this faith were authoritatively expressed. In this Modernists are doing for Christianity what Americans did for Americanism when they changed their Constitution in order to give truer application to the principles the Constitution itself expressed. Men who abolished slavery and gave the suffrage to women were more consistently expressing the principle of liberty than the framers of the Constitution themselves, for they limited suffrage to men and permitted the existence of slavery.

4. The Modernist Christian believes the Christian religion will help men meet social as well as individual needs.

Any acquaintance with social facts makes plain how responsive the individual is to social influences. Any intelligent religious program must take such facts into account. But programs differ. Some emphasize rescue and others emphasize salvation. The dogmatic mind has always preferred rescue. In practice it has varied from the asceticism of the monk to the rejection of social idealism. In theology it has limited salvation to elect individuals. On the other hand, students of society know that the relation of the individual to the social order involves him in responsibility for social actions as well as liability to social influences. Therefore,

397

they undertake to transform social forces for the benefit of the individual. Such a policy is furthest possible from a belief that humanity needs only better physical conditions. It is a solemn affirmation that the Christian cannot hold himself guiltless if he permits the existence of economic, political and recreational evils, and that he will be the victim of such evils if he does not undertake to correct or destroy them.

Modernists believe that the Gospel is as significant for social forces as for individuals. They find little hope in rescue of brands from burning; they want to put out the fire. They believe that the same God who so loved the world as to give his only begotten Son that those individuals who believe in him might not perish, also sent his Son into the world that the world might be saved.

But when the Modernist speaks of saving society he does not believe that society will save itself. He believes that the constant need of God's gracious help is to be understood as clearly through the laws given him by the sociologist as by the psychologist. He, therefore, hopefully undertakes to apply the Golden Rule to group-action as truly as to individuals. He would carry Christian attitudes and convictions into our entire life. He urges the duty of sacrifice on the part of nations and of classes, whether they be employers or employees, as truly as on that of individuals. For Jesus Christ to him is more than the savior of isolated individuals. He is the savior of men in society.

This is one reason why the Modernist is an object of suspicion. The dogmatic mind is almost always to be found among social reactionaries. To no small degree Modernism in theology is opposed because Modernists urge reform in economic matters. In the struggle over economic privilege the Modernist is properly feared as one who takes Jesus seriously and believes implicitly that his Gospel applies to wages and war as truly as to oaths, charity and respectability.

5. The Modernist is a Christian who believes that the spiritual and moral needs of the world can be met because he is intellectually convinced that Christian attitudes and faiths are consistent with other realities.

In so far as by trustworthy methods he reaches intellectual conclusions not in accord with those reached by deduction or by major premises given by authority, the Modernist knows himself an emancipator. Christianity is under suspicion in so far as it refuses to submit any tenet to impartial scrutiny. Each intellectual epoch has made that scrutiny. Modernism as a scientific method is for to-day what scholasticism and legal methods were to the past. It is no more negative than is chemistry. If all its conclusions are not the same as those previously held, it is because some things are established beyond question and the perspective of the importance of beliefs has been determined. A scientific method cannot start with authority because it cannot assume conclusions at the beginning of its investigation.

6. Modernists as a class are evangelical Christians. That is, they accept Jesus Christ as the revelation of a Savior God.

The Modernist movement is, therefore, not identical with Liberalism. With all due respect for the influence of Liberalism in clarifying religious thought, its origin and interest tend toward the emphasis of intellectual belief and the criticism and repudiation of doctrines *per se*. The Modernist like any other investigator has a presumption in favor of the reality of that which he is studying. Both historically and by preference his religious starting point is the inherited orthodoxy of a continuing community of Christians. To this group he belongs. The place of evangelical Christianity in social and ethical life, the aid it gives to millions of human hearts, the moral impetus it has given social reforms, forbid treating Christianity as an unborn child of human thought. But if it is to carry conviction as a way of organizing life it must be studied and applied according to methods judged effective by those to whom it is recommended. As the early church fathers were Christians who utilized their Hellenistic training to expound the Christianity brought them by Jews; as the Schoolmen were Christians who followed Aristotle; so the Modernists are Christians who use scientific method to estimate and apply the values of that evangelical inheritance in which they share. One might as well expect a student of politics to deny the existence of the State as to expect a Modernist to be disloyal to the Christian church; to expect a student of medicine to be indifferent to human ills and skeptical as to the use of medicine, as to expect that investigators within the Christian church should be indifferent or skeptical as to faith.

In brief, then, *the use of scientific, historical, social method in understanding and applying evangelical Christianity to the needs of living persons, is Modernism.* Its interests are not those of theological controversy or appeal to authority. They do not involve the rejection of the supernatural when rightly defined. Modernists believe that they can discover the ideals and directions needed for Christian living by the application of critical and historical methods to the study of the Bible; that they can discover by similar methods the permanent attitudes and convictions of Christians constituting a continuous and developing group; and that these permanent elements will help and inspire the intelligent and sympathetic organization of life under modern conditions. Modernists are thus evangelical Christians who use modern methods to meet modern needs. Confessionalism is the evangelicalism of the dogmatic mind. Modernism is the evangelicalism of the scientific mind.

### Note

1. In *The Faith of Modernism* (New York: Macmillan, 1924), pp. 15-16, 22-36. This book was also reprinted by AMS Press in 1969.

# Douglas C. Macintosh

*B*orn in Canada, Macintosh (1877–1948) studied at *McMaster University, gained a Ph.D. from the University of Chicago, and, from 1909, taught at Yale Divinity School. Issues of religious epistemology were his chief concern. That concern was timely as well as critical early in the twentieth century, as the nineteenth-century framework of Common-Sense Thought versus German-born post-Kantian idealism buckled under the pressures of the "hard sciences," attention to contextual and evolutionary variations, and social-scientific, pragmatic, and diverse neoempirical trends of thought. Macintosh's handling of the problem of religious knowledge was formulated in his first major book of 1915 and amplified but consistently upheld in its basics up to his last publication in 1940. His thinking, which he called a "critical monistic realism," was too independent to be classified as, or formative of, a broader "school."*

*His position was empirically oriented. Religious experiencing is the matrix within which the object(s) and values of religious faith become known as realities other than merely subjective ideas or ideals. Empirical studies of that matrix, attentive to what is disclosed there, prompt and warrant theological reconstructions of the essential ideas of faith.*

## REVELATION[1]

The problem of divine providence in face of the facts of evil is one of the two chief problems suggested by the essentially Christian idea of God which moral optimism involves. The second problem, not entirely separable from the former, is that of revelation. Moral optimism implies the existence of God, a dependable higher Power, great enough and favorable enough to man to do for man what he imperatively needs to have done for him, if he is to be logically justified in his moral optimism. This adequate and friendly higher power is, as we have seen, reasonably believed to be essentially personal, social, moral, acting consciously,

401

intelligently, and in holy love with reference to the true welfare of human beings.

All this being reasonable belief on the basis of moral optimism, the question is sure to arise, Is it not reasonable to expect that this personal, moral, social God will reveal Himself to man? Must not the divine love express itself in communication of some sort with human persons? Is it not reasonable to expect God to take the initiative in such communication and revelation? And, more especially, if man were whole-heartedly to seek after God, would it not be incredible that a God adequate to man's needs in wisdom, love, and power, should persistently refuse to reveal himself in response to man's appeal?

The movement of our thought here is similar to that of the older apologetics. There it was maintained that it was reasonable to expect a moral personal God to reveal himself to man. But it was assumed that that revelation would necessarily involve a miraculous intrusion of the supernatural, and that its content would be found in the sacred book of some religious faith. The next step was to compare the sacred books of the great world religions, with the result that to the Christian apologist it was very evident that the Christian Scriptures were vastly superior to the sacred writings of any other religion. Accepting the Bible, then, as divine revelation, it was concluded that it must be perfect in every respect, inerrant, and infallible, since God, who gave it, was himself perfect in wisdom, in goodness, and in power. Naturally the miracle-stories were taken as at once evidence of the supernaturalness and divine authority of the record and themselves proved authentic by their being recorded in that infallible divine Book.

This procedure of the older apologetics was notoriously an illustration of the false and vicious "rationalization" to which reference has already been made. What really actuated the older apologists was the wish to dispense with reason as a guide as soon as possible—for it was a guide of which they were secretly afraid—to take refuge in some absolute external authority. One can understand the motive of the older apologists, but their argument is unsound in at least three particulars. It is indeed reasonable to expect revelation from a friendly Being of adequate wisdom and power, but it does not follow, and it is dogmatic to assume, that the revelation will turn out to be an infallible Book—or, for that matter, the *ex cathedra* utterances of an infallible church. A particular book, authorized by a particular church, might conceivably contain a human record of divine revelation, but it would not follow that it was itself that revelation. In fact, it cannot even be assumed that revelation will be primarily in the realm of doctrine, propositions addressed to the intellect. It is quite conceivable that it should be in experience, in the deeper realms of the spiritual life.

Again, the supposed book-revelation and church-revelation are easily seen by the critically-minded to be very far from inerrant and infallible. To refer to a specific instance, can we accept as inerrant the statement, made in the supposedly infallible Book and endorsed by the supposedly infallible Church, that in the time of David it was a sin to take a census of the population, but that God commanded David to number the people and then punished the people for what David did at God's command? And if we can accept this, can we also accept as inerrant the statement made in another part of the Bible with regard to the same incident that it was Satan who led David to number the people?

In the third place and finally, the older apologists were dogmatic in assuming that revelation necessarily involves miracle in the ordinary sense of that word. On the contrary, we have seen good reason why the world should be an orderly and dependable world, and there is the same reason why revelation should not make it cease to be thus orderly and dependable. In fact, if there is to be revelation, there are the best of reasons why it, too, should be orderly and dependable, not arbitrary or exclusive, but equally accessible to all who fulfil the same conditions.

Turning, then, from criticism to construction, we assume not only that revelation is to be expected, but that the to-be-expected revelation will itself be orderly and dependable. Next, let us return to the thought that in the general constitution of the world as a world of natural law, of the orderly evolution of sensation, thought, and human freedom, of educative discipline through consequences and opportunity for the religious experience of moral salvation, we have confirmation of that adequate providential control of the universe which moral optimism logically involves. Then let us bring these two lines of thought together and find, in the processes to which we have just referred, the true and universally accessible revelation of the God of our morally optimistic and essentially Christian faith. On the one hand, there is natural law and the orderly evolution of life, leading through sensation to thought and creative human freedom, with capacity for aspiration toward the spiritual ideal. All this, confirming belief in the general providence of God, as we have seen, may be interpreted as constituting at the same time God's *general revelation,* accessible to all who are capable of normal human experience. The philosophical conception suggested is that of a constant and progressive immanence of God in the world of nature and of man.

On the other hand, in the special religious experience of moral salvation, of spiritual achievement through a definite religious adjustment, an experience accessible to all who will fulfil the necessary conditions, there is what may be regarded not only as special providence but at the same time as *special revelation*. This normal religious experience of spiritual uplift through the right religious adjustment is the true answer to prayer. It is the dependable response of Reality to the faith and self-devotion of man, and that Reality which responds in dependable fashion to religious faith and self-devotion is what religion must regard as God.

By this experience of special revelation is not meant, at least primarily, the mystical experience, though there is a place in true religion for mysticism, so long as it remains under rational and moral control. In the more mystical phase of normal experimental religion the individual gains a highly dynamic and wholly desirable subjective assurance of the most essential truths of religion. Moreover, in mystical religion hypotheses are suggested which may be tested in reflection and in the experiences of practical life in general and in those of the practical religious life in particular. But the special revelation of God in religious experience to which we have been referring has nothing necessarily esoteric about it. It is not primarily an emotional experience, but an experience in the realm of the will. It is simply the difference which persistence in a certain practical religious attitude, which we may call the right religious adjustment, makes in the spiritual and particularly in the moral achievement of normal human beings.

In this idea of special divine revelation in special religious experience we have the vital essence of the old miracle-faith. It is what we may call *the new Christian supernaturalism*. The revelation is found in the dependable response of Reality to man's right religious adjustment. But there is room, also, for recognition of the divine initiative in leading man into the right religious adjustment. This divine initiative may be partly a matter of what we have called general providence and general revelation, and partly a matter of what we have called special providence and special revelation. There are events within the field of human experience, in the present as well as in the past, which have special significance, objectively as well as subjectively, as furnishing evidence of the reality, presence, and activity of God as a living, responding Factor in the lives of human beings. This is all that is essential in supernaturalism.

And yet, while this view, that special revelation is to be found in the dependable experience of spiritual and particularly moral salvation through the right religious adjustment, is the permanently valid essence of Christian supernaturalism, it would be equally true to say that it overcomes the old antithesis between natural and revealed religion. Revelation of the reality of God in the religious experience of moral salvation is as normal and natural as any other process of cognition. It is the discovery of reality through experience.

A dependable religious experience is what we ought to expect of a dependable religious Reality, when we discover and practice the right religious adjustment. And whatever else that responding Reality may be, it is at once an existent factor and the God of experimental religion. It seems to be what Christianity has meant, essentially, by the "Holy Spirit." The existence and revelation of this God may not be universally verified; but the claim is made with a challenge to investigation, that it is universally verifiable. And the verifiable fact, it should be noted, is not simply a fact of subjective religious experience, a fact of the psychology of religion; it is a fact statable in terms of what a real Factor can be depended upon for, and as such it is a verifiable fact of religious knowledge, of theology. Even if everything else in our thought of God were to remain mere postulate and theory, this at least would be scientific fact and enough to make empirical theology, in germ at least, truly scientific.

In this use of the religious experience of moral salvation to establish as fact the existence of the God of experimental religion, we have the complement to the moral argument in one of its possible forms. On the basis of sinful man's need of moral salvation, the existence of God, the moral Saviour, may be postulated as humanly imperative. What this argument postulates as necessary (and it is what moral optimism would find it reasonable to believe), this the religious experience of moral salvation reveals as truth and Reality, namely, a Power, not identifiable with ourselves, that makes for righteousness in and through us, when we persist in the right religious adjustment.

As a matter of fact, the only adequate proof of the existence of the God of religion is to be found in experience, and in religious experience particularly. It is always through experience that existence is demonstrated, whether the particular existent in question be a physical thing, one's own personal self, another human person, or God. Mere deduction can establish no more than logical possibility. As is being seen more clearly in our day than formerly, the ontological argument—proceeding from an analysis of the idea to an affirmation of existence—is valid only when experience can be appealed to as establishing the idea. One phase of this empirical ontological argument is virtually present, as we have already seen, in Schleiermacher's substitution of the universality of the feeling of absolute dependence for the supposedly universal classic arguments. In our inescapable experience of absolute dependence we are aware of a Reality upon which we are dependent, and this reality, ill-defined as it may be at first, is God. But in moral experimental religion, as we now see, we can carry this empirical argument further. In the dependable experience of moral salvation through a certain religious adjustment we are aware of the existence of a Factor in Reality which delivers from evil and makes higher spiritual achievement possible; and that Factor is the God of moral experimental religion, or, to use the historic Christian term, the "Holy Spirit."

We see, then, that in its true form, as Professor Hocking has well said, the ontological argument is a report of experience. But it is an argument which, even in its empirical form, is not without its difficulties. While it is readily seen that the existence of God, defined in some very general way, can be proved from dependably successful religious adjustment, it seems more difficult to establish in this way the existence of the highly defined moral personal God of Christian faith. We may surmise, indeed, that the ontological argument in its finally satisfactory form is an ideal which has never yet been completely realized. To prove the existence of God by experience, the idea of God must be correct and experience adequate, and most modern religion is defective in both respects.

In this connection it is interesting to place in juxtaposition a typical philosophical statement and a declaration which has been common among mystics. A well-known philosopher (the late Professor Simmel, of Berlin) has made the assertion that there is nothing more certain than what God is—as Object of spiritual worship He can be no less than ideal personality—but, it is added, there is nothing more uncertain than *that* God is. The mystic, on the other hand, says he is immediately certain that God is, but confesses inability to say just what God is. The ideal for religion would be to bring together these two complementary assurances. This would mean being assured through religious experience of the existence of a Being in whom the true ideal of personality is embodied. (Is it not significant that, according to tradition, the historic Jesus was assured of the existence of ideal Personality—one who is at once "Your Father" and "perfect"?)

Acknowledging, then, that the ontological argument in its full and final form may very well be, as far as we are concerned, an unrealized ideal, we may ask how far in the direction of that ideal we are in a position to go. The answer is to be found in large part, we should say, in bringing together the universal religious consciousness of a Reality upon which we are absolutely dependent and the results of our analysis of the belief in God involved in moral optimism—this on the one hand, and, on the other hand, the proof, in the dependable experience of moral salvation through a certain religious adjustment, of the existence of a dependable morally saving and uplifting Factor in Reality. The Object of our ultimate dependence undoubtedly exists, and if moral optimism is valid, there must exist, as the Factor upon which we are ultimately dependent, a Being great enough and good enough for our absolute trust, and thus essentially identical with "God the Father Almighty, Maker of heaven and earth." On the other hand, the God of ultimately successful religious dependence, the dependable Factor making for moral salvation and spiritual achievement, especially on condition of the right religious adjustment, whose existence is proved in experimental religion at its best, is essentially identical with "the Holy Spirit" of Christian faith. Nor does it seem unreasonable to surmise that these two, God the Father and God the Holy Spirit, are in reality one and the same God, differently conceived and experienced because differently approached. At any rate, according to the principle of parsimony, the burden of proof would seem to be on those who would assert that there are two Gods, rather than one.

In showing, as we have done, the reasonableness, on the basis of moral optimism and religious experience, of believing in the existence of an Object of absolute human dependence, an essentially personal, rational, and moral Being, sufficient in power to conserve all absolute values, and a Factor dependable, on condition of a certain religious adjustment, for the experience of moral salvation; and finding nothing fatal to the natural religious surmise that these are one and the same religious Object, we may consider ourselves to have vindicated sufficiently for practical religious purposes the reasonableness of an essentially Christian idea of God. In view, too, of our earlier discussions, we may now claim to have shown the reasonableness of essential Christianity, both as morality and as religion. What we have done has made for the supplying of the missing link in modern apologetic argument between the valid elements in the Ritschlian and in the Hegelian apologetics, between the proposition that essential Christianity is what is most valuable in historic Christianity and the proposition that what is reasonable is true. In other words, we have gathered evidence which goes to show that what is most valuable in historic Christianity is reasonable, thereby indicating the logical conclusion that essential Christianity is true.

Our argument has thus avoided the characteristic weakness of most recent apologetics, the resting, first and last, in subjective feeling. It has been addressed to the outsider quite as much as to those already committed to the Christian faith. It has thus led to reasons—not purely speculative but deeply grounded in life, and yet universally valid and objective—for accepting essentially Christian views of freedom, immortality, God, providence, and revelation. It only remains to inquire into the reasonableness of the Christian faith in the divine person and saving work of Jesus, who is called Christ.

### Note

1. In *The Reasonableness of Christianity* (New York: Charles Scribner's Sons, 1925), pp. 120-33.

# Henry Nelson Wieman

*First known as "liberal" and then "modernist," the University of Chicago's Divinity School underwent transfiguration without death during the middle third of the twentieth century. There is no consensus label for the result—the "new" or "second" or "empirical" Chicago School of Theology. It was, broadly speaking, "more" empirical than before (and now philosophically as well as social-scientifically) and more "daring" in reformulating Christian doctrines, but at the same time more "theocentric" and critical of the "idealism" of liberalism's values. The work of Wieman (1884–1975) is an index of as well as a factor in these shifts.*

*Wieman joined the Chicago faculty in 1927, with a doctorate from Harvard (1917) and ten years teaching experience at Occidental College. A decade, 1956–1966, of active "retirement" with Southern Illinois University followed. At Chicago he developed his conceptions of God as the creative process that was source of human good and faith as commitment to God amid the ongoing creative interchanges of living experience. His interpretations of this and other Christian themes were naturalistic, and hence an alternative to neoorthodox thought, and yet emphatic with regard to the reality of faith's objects, as opposed to altogether pragmatic, humanist liberalisms. The selection here comes from his essay "A Workable Idea of God," a popularized statement of his views.*

## A Workable Idea of God[1]

We want a workable idea of God, just as we want a workable idea of the sunshine or the next door neighbor. A workable idea of the sunshine is one which will enable a man to get from it the life-giving, health-conserving, energy-producing powers that are in it. Some people have lovely ideas about the sunshine which have no practical value. They can write poetry about it and sing songs about it but they do not know how

409

to get the health and vigor and vitality which the sunshine has to give. Many a man has a delightful idea of his next door neighbor. He can dream about that neighbor and make beautiful speeches and possibly even songs and poems about him; but he does not know how to enter into friendly cooperation and mutual understanding with him in such a way that the two of them can live a richer and more satisfying life of common support and shared experience. To do this last, one must have a workable idea of his neighbor. The same is often true of our idea of home and native land or anything else you want to mention. Is our idea about any such thing workable? That is the important question.

*Workable Idea Needed*

A workable idea enables us to join ourselves with the activities of sunshine or neighbor or native land so that we promote these activities and they enrich and strengthen us. A workable idea of God is one which enables us to join ourselves with his working in such a way as to promote it and to be sustained and strengthened and enriched by it.

A great many people want an enjoyable rather than a workable idea of God. What they want is an inner experience which will make them feel happy when things go wrong, but will not enable them to draw upon the power which makes things go right. Ideas of God which give pleasant inner experiences but have no other practical value are dangerous because they either soothe us to negligent passivity or else divert our energies into unprofitable channels.

There is a play now running in Chicago called "In Abraham's Bosom," which shows the evil that comes into human life when people use their conscious minds merely to cultivate pleasant inner experiences without practical consequences. It shows how the Negroes of North Carolina, at the time and in the place represented by this play, were unable to escape from their miserable state of existence because they refused to seek and entertain workable ideas. All they wanted was to dream and dance and sing and laugh and talk and have pleasant inner experiences despite the wretched conditions under which they lived. Instead of seeking out the means and resources to change these conditions, they were content to put themselves in a state of mind which was oblivious to the evil round about them and hanging over them. Their religion was a device for producing such a comfortable oblivion. Such religion has been called the opiate of the people. That is the right name for it.

*That Which Lifts*

Over against such a religion, we say we need a working religion; and that requires above all a workable idea of God. The first requirement of such an idea of God is this: It must identify God with whatever actual operating process in the universe is capable of producing the greatest good. If we find something going on which will lift human life to the highest when right connections are made with it, then our idea must identify God with that, no matter what it is and no matter how different it may be from what we had thought God must be. We must make our idea fit the facts, and not ignore them for the sake of a cherished idea which warms the heart but otherwise gives no practical guidance. If the processes which actually do sustain and magnify the goods of life should be found to be electrons, or the organic chemistry of the living cell, or the autonomic nervous system or the sun or anything else, then the workable idea of God would say: Lo, this is God. This is what we must work with and connect with, in order to attain the greatest goods.

In order to develop a workable idea of God, six questions must be asked and answered. We shall discuss these six in order.

First, is there a value-making process at work in the universe? We do not see how anyone can doubt it, since men actually do experience values. Human hunger actually is sometimes satisfied, no matter how many starve to death. Human friendships actually are occasionally consummated, however frequently hearts are broken. A fair degree of health does actually come within the scope of human experience, no matter how widespread disease may be. Beauty is sometimes perceived in sky and sea, woodland and meadow and human form, even though wide reaches of space and time are dismal and disgusting. Since values are experienced in the actual existing world, we cannot escape the conclusion that there is a value-making process at work in the universe, even though other contrary processes may also be at work.

*Apples and Values*

Our second question is: What constitutes value? Apples, for instance, are of value. Apples serve to nourish us and gives us pleasure; and we serve to cultivate apples and conserve them, until the world has in it millions of apples which would never be there if we did not plant and cultivate and protect them. The same is true of every case of value. Wherever we find anything which can be called a value or a good, we find two or more activities or factors working together to sustain and

411

enhance one another. If it is not man and apple, then it is man and man in the relation of friendship in which each works to sustain and magnify the other. Or it is man and beautiful objects between which there occurs this interaction of mutual support and enrichment. Or it is the productive interaction of many men in an industrial plant. Or it is the farmer and his land, or the student and his sources of information. Always wherever we find value we find some organic whole in which the several parts work together to sustain and enhance one another. And wherever we find a human value, a human being must be at least one member in the organic whole of mutually sustaining parts.

Value then consists of organic unity, wholeness, integration. Whenever a man experiences an organic unity in which he himself is one of the mutually sustaining factors, he experiences something which satisfies him and which is therefore a value. All value is of this sort, whether it be bodily value such as good health, or esthetic value, or intellectual or moral or political or the value of friendly intercourse. Value is integration.

### Members One of Another

Now we can turn to our third question. How does this process work which sustains and magnifies the values of the world? It works by progressive integration. The value-making process of the universe is that process by which activities are brought together in such a way as to sustain one another. It is that process by which various factors are so organized as to become members one of another. Value is increased by increasing the degree to which factors support one another and also by increasing the number of different factors which enter into mutual support. At its highest level in human life it works by increasing peace, good will and love among men.

The fourth question which we set out to answer is this: Where does this value-making process work—in nature as a part of nature, or beyond nature and above it? Our answer is: This value-making process is in nature. It is a part of nature. It is not all of nature, for there is much in nature which destroys organic unity. There is much that disintegrates and produces mutual destruction of parts. But we also see in nature the development of organic unities. We see flowers grow, and friendships grow, and health appear, and knowledge increase, and whole cultural systems develop to maturity, and works of beauty come into existence and win admirers. All this production of value we see in nature. It is nature generating organic unity. It is the value-making process going on in nature, despite the fact that there is much in nature which tears down and destroys the organizations which constitute value.

Is this value-making process which goes on in nature purely human? Is it wholly the work of man? Or is it more than human?

All the works of man are also the works of nature, not only because man himself is a part of nature, but also because he is always dependent upon the rest of nature and must cooperate with it in bringing forth any good thing. A grain field ready for the harvest is the work of man; but it is even more the work of extra-human processes. It is the work of sunshine and rain and soil. Furthermore, it is the work of many centuries of cultural development which no man or group of men ever planned and guided. It is the work of psychological and social processes which far exceed the control of any human intelligence. The same is true of machinery. A steam engine, an aeroplane or automobile reveal the working of nature as truly as a volcano. And the working of the machinery, as well as its invention and manufacture, is a process which involves activities and resources which are cosmic in their scope.

### What Does the Artist Do?

Even works of art, such as poems, songs, musical compositions, are produced only in part by human effort and intelligence, the greater part being the work of something far vaster than human effort. How did "Thanatopsis" come into existence? Or the musical composition "The Messiah," or that work of architectural beauty, the chapel of the University of Chicago, or any other beautiful creation? What does the artist do? He simply gets into right relations with other works of beauty, other artists, with nature and society and other conditions. Then, when the circuit is closed, the connections made, the work of beauty springs into being, or grows slowly, like a growing tree. But however it comes, it is due in part to organic chemistry, in part to physiological and subconscious processes, in part to mere physical elements, in part to historical and social movements, over which the individual has no control. It is, we say, the creation of the integrative process of nature, using the artist as one, but only one, of the many factors which go to make the beautiful object.

This applies also to industry and economic wealth, to good will and cooperation among men, scientific invention and to science itself. These and all other creations of value arise out of the interaction between climate and soil, diverse cultures and peoples, individuals and groups and innumerable other factors, many of which no doubt have never yet come

413

within the bounds of human knowledge. This vast process of nature generating new and richer organic wholes through developing mutual support between diverse activities, is the value-making process. Man plays a noble part in it, but his part is puny compared to the vast working of the process as a whole. In its vastness and its wholeness it is God.

### Humanity in the Universe

We have already suggested an answer to the sixth and last question: What place has humanity and the individual human personality in the value-making process of the universe?

Suppose a plant grew to maturity and entered into mutually sustaining relations with other plants, with insects and animals and climatic conditions in such a way as to give rise to a tropical jungle which choked out the life of man or threw him back into savagery. Would that be the work of the value-making process? Our answer is: It would be value-making in so far as richer integrations had been achieved. But it would not yield human value. It would be value-making in which man had failed to make right connections and missed his own opportunity. But that is not all. The failure would be much more serious than that. So far as our evidence can guide us, it would be a cosmic failure. To understand that is to understand the place of humanity in the progressive integration of the universe.

### Supreme Values

No tropical jungle can display the richness of integration which is found in human life. It is in the human personality and in that interaction of human personalities called human culture with all the arts and sciences that the most intimate and subtle and complicated mutual support and enhancement of activities arise. In so far as we have explored this universe it displays its greatest value in human life, if we accept our definition of value as richness of organic unity or integration. To be sure, the greatest evils are also to be found in human life because evil is the destruction of good, and in human life we have the greatest goods to be destroyed. But that is only further support to our claim that in human life the greatest actual achievement of value is to be found.

The great problem of human life is to provide those connections—social, psychological, zoological, physical, chemical—through which the integrative process of nature can fulfil itself to the attainment of the richest possible integrations. So far as we can now see, that requires the continued preservation and development of individual human persons and human society. It is conceivable that greater values than those of human life might develop, but that is merely a matter of speculation and we have no empirical evidence to support it. Therefore, we must hold that the way of progressive integration lies through the increase of *human* good. The value-making process of the universe must operate through human personalities and groups if the greatest values are to be achieved.

### The Integrative Working Called God

Certain connections must be made, certain circuits closed, before the integrative working called God can fulfil itself. Seed and soil must be rightly connected, and plant and animal, and all these with men; and groups of men must be brought into right relations with one another. When these connections are made and the circuit closed, something begins to work which is far vaster than humanity but which fulfils itself most abundantly in human life. It thrills through all the universe but comes to fullest flower in human friendliness and mutual understanding, in esthetic and logical organization of shared experience, in all the arts and sciences and in a planet transfigured with creations of beauty.

Let us now make our final statement of the workable idea of God. God is not the all. God is not identical with the universe. He is not the whole of nature. But he is one constitutional tendency of the universe. He is the constitutional tendency of the universe toward progressive integration. We say he is constitutional because he enters into the constitution of things in such a way that there could be no universe without this integration and mutual support of activities. Without this tendency the universe would fall to pieces and become a multiverse or chaos. Hence the tendency toward progressive integration is inescapable and indestructible so long as the universe lasts. That does not mean that the universe will inevitably develop richer integrations and higher values, because there are other tendencies which work against it. But it does mean that the tendency which is God, no matter how obstructed, will always operate as long as there is any universe at all. To destroy God it would be necessary to destroy the universe, for without integration there can be no universe.

### God as Tendency

Man can alienate himself from this constitutional tendency of the universe toward progressive integration. He can work against it. He can

415

become a promoter of disintegration. When he does this he sins and is playing traitor to something more holy and more cosmic than social welfare. But man can also work with God and God can work with him and in him.

It is man's chief business and high destiny to establish connections between himself and other factors in nature, and above all connections between human individuals and groups, so that the constitutional tendency of the universe toward progressive integration can fulfil itself in the greatest possible values. A workable idea of God is one which enables man to do this intelligently.

### Note

1. In *The Christian Century* 46, 7 (14 February 1929): 226-28.

# Edward J. Carnell

$C$*arnell (1919–1967) was a notable intellectual leader of the "new evangelical" movement which took shape after the Second World War. A Baptist, he studied at Wheaton College, Illinois, and Westminster Theological Seminary, schools associated with the evangelical conservatism and Reformed confessionalism that were component elements of the Fundamentalist movement. After his degree from Westminster (1944), he entered the strongholds of liberalism, completing in 1948 both a Harvard Th.D. and a Ph.D. in philosophy at Boston University. The result of his studies,* Christian Apologetics *(1948), brought him acclaim among Evangelicals for its critique of modern liberalism and its reasoned defense of historic doctrine.*

*As teacher and president at Fuller Theological Seminary (1954–1959), he promoted on behalf of evangelical theology a school of thinking equal in academic quality to the educational institutions of liberalism. His publications aimed at demonstrating the credibility and superiority of "orthodox" Christian views of God, humanity, and the universe on the basis of their rational, systemic consistency and explanatory power. His last book,* The Case for Orthodox Theology *(1959), written just before the breakdown of health that led to his death, set his views alongside those of liberal and neoorthodox scholarship—and also contrasted the "orthodoxy" he upheld from Fundamentalism. A selection from that work follows.*

## AUTHORITY[1]

. . .

### 1. The Living and Written Word of God

We have defined orthodoxy as "that branch of Christendom which limits the ground of religious authority to the Bible." The important element

417

in this definition is the term "limits." All branches of Christendom, whatever their stripe, salute the Bible as a general source of religious information. Apart from Scripture we would have no access to the redemptive events. Orthodoxy is unique in that it argues for the *plenary* inspiration of Scripture. The Bible, and the Bible alone, is the Word of God written.

Unless the claims of orthodoxy are spelled out with care, however, they may connote an odious Biblicism. For example, critics sometimes say, "We believe the Bible on the authority of Jesus Christ, and not the other way around." This is supposed to be a more precise way of stating things. But orthodoxy has *always* insisted that the written Word does not commend itself unless the heart is confronted by the living Word. Paul did not see Christ in Scripture until he met Christ on the Damascus road. The Bible is the Word of God "out there," whether or not anyone is confronted by it; but it does not address the heart as the Word of God until Christ is met in personal fellowship. The living Word is the soul of the written Word.

. . .

. . . The Word of God commands as well as charms; it communicates as well as affects. "If you love me," says Jesus Christ, "you will keep my commandments." (John 14:15 RSV) To say we are confronted by Christ, when we do not obey him—what is this but to offend the work of love? Love is fettered by the will of the beloved. "He who does not love me does not keep my words." (V. 24 RSV)

Therefore, in the one act of reading Scripture, we meet Christ in two complementary ways. *First,* we confront Christ's person. "By this we know that we abide in him and he in us, because he has given us of his own Spirit." (1 John 4:13 RSV.) *Secondly,* we receive a propositional revelation of Christ's will. "In many and various ways God spoke of old to our fathers by the prophets; but in these last days he has spoken to us by a Son." (Heb. 1:1-2 RSV.) These two elements cannot be separated without offending the unity of revelation.

The written Word is the locus of confrontation with the living Word. If we extend this locus, we have no criterion by which to test for error. And when the church cannot test for error, it cannot claim truth; for its claim may be one expression of an error for which there is no test. The church's sole message is the gospel, and the gospel is the substance of the written Word. God made a covenant with Abraham, and Jesus Christ is the blessing of this covenant. Everything in Scripture either looks forward to Christ or flows from him. "Do not think that I shall accuse you to the Father; it is Moses who accuses you, on whom you set your hope. If you believed

Moses, you would believe me, for he wrote of me. But if you do not believe his writings, how will you believe my words?" (John 5:45-46 RSV.)

## 2. Jesus Christ and the Old Testament

When orthodoxy is asked why it accepts the Old Testament as the inspired Word of God, it answers, Because Jesus Christ, the Lord of the church, did. The orthodox apologist rests his case on this single datum. "For him who has been brought to the Christ, and who on his knees worships him as his Lord and his God, the end of all contradiction is hereby reached. When the Christ, whose Spirit witnessed beforehand in the prophets, attributes such authority to the Scripture of the Old Covenant, and by his apostles indicates the ground for that authority in the theopneusty, there is no power that can prevent the recognition of that authority by him who believes in Jesus. Not to recognize it would avenge itself in the representation that in the very holiest things Christ had wholly mistaken himself. This would imply *the loss of his Savior*."[2]

Jesus entered a society that was already bound by a canon of sacred writings. Malachi was the last of the written prophets. An interval of some four hundred years separated Malachi from the birth of Christ. Jerusalem was restored; the Maccabees performed their heroic deeds; the Temple was rebuilt by Herod; and Israel was overtaken first by Greece, then by Rome. When Jesus began his public ministry, he in no way contradicted the prevailing Jewish attitude toward the authority of the Law and the Prophets. On the contrary, he appealed to this corpus of revelation when validating his own Messianic claims. "We observe that our Lord, throughout the entire duration of his ministry, represents himself as fulfilling, in person, the scheme of the former covenant; we know, too, that he has made the Old Testament the basis of his teaching; continually employing it, as it was received in his time by the Jews, without letting fall the slightest hint that any portion of it was done away. So far from stating anything to this effect, he has expressed himself in a manner which proves the very reverse; making use of language by which he has not only defined the permanent authority of the Old Testament, but also indicated its true place in the new dispensation."[3]

Certainly the Jews would never have defended and preserved a canon of documents that condemned their own practices, and that placed them under oppressive judicial burdens, unless they believed they were in possession of divine oracles. Jesus shared this conviction.

Even radical critics acknowledge that Jesus believed in the divine authority of the Old Testament. Such critics merely reject the Lordship of Christ. Orthodoxy does not. *When Christ speaks of the Scriptures, he means the Old Testament; and when he says that the Scriptures cannot be broken, he means they have the force of law and are to be received in the church on divine authority.*

. . .

### 6. The Union of Christ and the Father

Some say that Jesus was *mistaken* in his view of Scripture. The assumption is that if Jesus had enjoyed the benefits of modern criticism, he would have entertained a different attitude toward the Old Testament. Orthodoxy rejects this because it destroys our faith in God the Father. Let us establish this by setting down a series of propositions.

*Proposition One:* Jesus is Emmanuel, "God with us." When the eternal Son became incarnate, he did not forfeit his divine attributes. Continuing what he was, he took on what he was not. Jesus merely emptied himself of the right to express unveiled deity. This was the true kenosis. The Son subordinated himself to the will of the Father for the sake of redeeming the world.

*Proposition Two:* All that Jesus did or said transpired in the human nature. It is an unfortunate formula, one quite foreign to Scripture, that Jesus "hungered in his human nature" but "performed miracles in his divine nature." The *entire Messianic office* was confined to the divine person in human nature. Jesus was the last Adam; he was the federal head of a new and holy race.

*Proposition Three:* The human nature of Jesus was so perfectly united with the divine person, and the divine person was so perfectly united with the will of the Father, that all that Jesus did or said derived from the Father. "Jesus said to them, 'Truly, truly, I say to you, the Son can do nothing of his own accord, but only what he sees the Father doing; for whatever he does, that the Son does likewise.' " (John 5:19 RSV.) "I can do nothing on my own authority; as I hear, I judge; and my judgment is just, because I seek not my own will but the will of him who sent me." (V. 30 RSV.)

Since Christ was so intimately united with the Father, we cannot impugn the judgment of Christ without inpugning the judgment of the Father. Jesus and the Father were one in teaching as well as essence. "For I have not spoken on my own authority; the Father who sent me has himself given me commandment what to say and what to speak." (Ch. 12:49 RSV.) "Do you not believe that I am in the Father and the Father in me? The words that I say to you I do not speak on my own authority; but the Father who dwells in me does his works." (Ch. 14:10 RSV.)

420

"The word which you hear is not mine but the Father's who sent me."
(V. 24 RSV.)

There is only one consistent position for the church. *Since Jesus received
his doctrine from the Father, everything that Jesus says is true on divine
authority.* Any other position leads to skepticism. "Can he have been—
mistaken, mistaken—with respect to holiest things, in what must be to us
the ground and source of our faith! Mistaken also, therefore, in assigning,
on the basis of the Scripture, a high Messianic character to himself! But
the very idea is incompatible with the confession of Jesus' divine nature.
Erring in what is holy is no mere failure in intellect, but betrays a state of
ruin of one's whole inner being. In the sinner, therefore, a mistake is natural, but not in one who is holy. . . . The conflict, which is begun in order
to rob us of the Scripture as Holy Scripture, can have no other tendency
than to rob us of the Christ. If the Holy Scripture . . . falls, then Jesus was
a man and nothing more, who was mistaken in the centrum of what was
holy, and who consequently can neither escape from the fellowship of sin,
nor yet in what is holiest and tenderest be your absolute guide."[4]

### 7. The View of the Apostles

Christ appointed an apostolate to bear witness to all that he did and
said. Even as Christ was sent to declare the will of the Father, so the
apostles were sent to declare the will of Christ.

Whoever reads the New Testament with an eye to fairness will perceive
that the apostles defended the same view of Scripture that Jesus did.
Scripture has the force of law; the Word of God cannot be broken. "This
appears clearly in Acts ii.24, 25, where Peter says, 'It was not possible
that he should be holden of death.' And why does he deem this impossible? Because Jesus was the Son of God? Undoubtedly for this also; of
this, however, Peter makes no mention, but states as the only reason that
it was thus written in Ps. xvi.: 'Neither wilt thou give thy Holy One to
see corruption.' Hence the 'impossibility' rests upon the fact that the
opposite to this was written in the Old Testament; an argument which
suits only with the supposition that the Old Testament furnishes us with
the program of what *must* happen according to God's counsel and will."[5]
. . .

To trace this sort of evidence through the entire apostolic testimony
would be to dwell on the obvious. "The uniform manner of speaking of
the Old Testament which we trace in the sayings and writings of Christ
and his apostles in the New—is such as to be wholly incompatible with
any other idea than that of its full and verbal inspiration: and cannot but

convey to a simple reader the impression that they regarded every word of that Testament as divine."[6]

. . .

## 8. The Canon of the Old Testament

Authenticity is ordinarily distinct from credibility. It might be proved, for example, that a copy of Lewis Carroll's *Alice's Adventures in Wonderland* is authentic. But this would not make the book credible. In the case of the Biblical canon, however, authenticity ensures credibility; for canonicity respects the *extent*, not the *fact*, of an inspired text.

The question of the canon is settled by historical evidences, not by personal confrontation with Christ. "The teaching of the Holy Ghost, while indispensable to a saving apprehension of Biblical truth, is not available at this point. The Holy Spirit teaches in regard to the credibility, but not in regard to the canonicity of Scripture."[7]

Orthodoxy settles the authenticity of the Old Testament in the only way that it can or should he settled, namely, by an appeal to Christ and the apostles. "The question of the canon of the Old Testament being by the principles clearly deducible from the statements of Christ and his apostles limited to this, what were the books which composed the received Jewish canon at that time? There is no material difficulty in determining that point. We have sufficient materials for ascertaining what books were then generally received by the Jews as canonical. We have these materials to a large extent in the New Testament itself, in the testimony of the contemporary Jewish authors, Josephus and Philo; in the universal and unwavering belief of the Jews from that period to the present day; and in the testimonies of some of the early Christian fathers, particularly that of Melito (preserved by Eusebius), who lived in the second century, and who made the investigating of the canon of the Old Testament an object of peculiar attention and of diligent inquiry. The books which compose the Protestant canon of the Old Testament alone were received as of divine authority by the Jews of our Savior's days, and therefore these alone received his sanction."[8] Christ and the apostles accepted the prevailing threefold division of the Jewish canon: the Law, the Prophets, and the Writings. This decided the matter for the early church, and it decides it for orthodoxy in any age.

## 9. The Canon of the New Testament

Although the New Testament canon is established in the same manner as that of the Old Testament, the steps in the argument are a bit more involved. Let us establish this by a series of propositions.

*Proposition One:* Christ defended the divine authority of the Old Testament canon. And he received this judgment from the Father.

*Proposition Two:* Christ did *not* invest the Old Testament with authority. The Old Testament anteceded his Messianic office. A process of revelation was already at work in history.

*Proposition Three:* The Old Testament, on divine authority, bears witness to its own incompleteness; it looks to a revelation yet to come. Thus, the "same *necessity of the scripture,* which existed for the manifestation of the prophetic dispensation, was here repeated."[9]

*Proposition Four:* The apostles were commissioned to take the gospel to all nations, and there was only one way in which this could be done. That was by the medium of inspired documents. Hence, the apostles address the church with the authority of *prophets.* The New Testament writers "do not for an instant imagine themselves, as ministers of a new covenant, less in possession of the Spirit of God than the ministers of the old covenant: they freely recognize, indeed, that they have no sufficiency of themselves, but they know that God has made them sufficient (2 Cor. iii.5.6). They prosecute their work of proclaiming the gospel, therefore, in full confidence that they speak 'by the Holy Spirit' (1 Pet. i.12), to whom they attribute both the matter and form of their teaching (1 Cor. ii.13). They, therefore, speak with the utmost assurance of their teaching (Gal. i.7.8); and they issue commands with the completest authority (1 Thess. iv.2.14; 2 Thess. iii.6.12), making it, indeed, the test of whether one has the Spirit that he should recognize what they demand as commandments of God (1 Cor. xiv.37)."[10] "I adjure you by the Lord that this letter be read to all the brethren." (1 Thess. 5:27 RSV.)

*Proposition Five:* The canon of the New Testament was decided by the apostles themselves, for they alone knew what documents were inspired, and thus were normative for the church. "All doubt is dispelled when we observe the New Testament writers placing the writings of one another in the same category of 'Scripture' with the books of the Old Testament. The same Paul who, in 2 Tim. iii.16, declared that 'every' or 'all scripture is God-breathed' had already written in 1 Tim. v.18: 'For the scripture saith, Thou shalt not muzzle the ox when he treadeth out the corn. And, The laborer is worthy of his hire.' The first clause here is derived from Deuteronomy and the second from the Gospel of Luke, though both are cited as together constituting, or better, forming part of the 'Scripture' which Paul adduces as so authoritative as by its mere citation to end all strife. . . . And the same Peter who declared that every 'prophecy of scripture' was the product of men who spoke 'from God,' being 'borne' by the Holy Ghost (2 Pet. i.21), in this same epistle (iii.16), places Paul's Epistles in the category of Scripture along with whatever other books deserve that name. For Paul, says he, wrote these epistles, not out of his own wisdom, but 'according to the wisdom given to him,' and though there are some things in them hard to be understood, yet it is only 'the ignorant and unstedfast' who wrest these difficult passages—as what else could be expected of men who wrest 'also the other Scriptures' (obviously the Old Testament is meant)—'unto their own destruction'?"[11]

The church merely had to determine whether a particular book bore the marks of apostolic authority. This judgment involved a sifting of historical evidences. The debate was over authenticity, not credibility. And the doubts about authenticity were not resolved until at least the fourth century. "The point to which the doubts that were entertained attached was this, and this only, *whether or not these books were really written by the men whose names they bore, and to whom they were generally ascribed.* Now, considering the condition of the world and the state of the churches, the means of intercourse, etc., there is no difficulty whatever in conceiving that writings published in one part of the world might be long in becoming known in another, and that even after they were in some measure known, it might not be very easy for some time to ascertain precisely their history, and to procure satisfactory evidence as to the matters of fact alleged concerning them. . . . There were many apocryphal books in circulation pretending to be written by apostles, and the churches were on their guard against being deceived by any false pretenses on this subject. Paul encouraged the churches to jealousy upon this point, by virtually telling them . . . that they were to receive no epistles of his as genuine unless the salutation was written with his own hand. And this salutary caution and jealousy they seem to have faithfully practiced—a fact which at once accounts for the doubts entertained for a time in some quarters of the church, about some books in regard to which they had not for the present access to any satisfactory evidence that they were the productions of apostles or inspired men, and gives great weight to their testimony in favor of those in regard to which no doubt was ever entertained, and also to the ultimate testimony of the church in general in favor of the others likewise, after the doubts which had once attached to them had been removed, i.e., after satisfactory and conclusive evidence had been diffused over the whole extent of the Christian church that they were the production of the men whose names they bore, and to whom they were generally ascribed."[12]

Let us linger with this question a bit longer, for the issue is very critical. The church did *not* invest the canon with authority; nor was the gift of inspiration required to decide which books bore apostolic marks and which did not. *"The evidence by which the canonical authority of the books of the New Testament is proved, is the same in kind as that by which we establish their genuineness. The books are proved to be genuine when it is shown that they were the productions of the men whose names they bear.* . . . Now there really never was any such thing as what seems to be conceived of under the designation of establishing or settling the canon of the New Testament. The canonical authority of the books, their right to be regarded as an authoritative communication of the will of God, depends entirely upon the actual matter of fact of their having been composed by divinely inspired authors; and the settlement of the canon properly means nothing else than the establishment of this as a matter of fact by the appropriate evidence with respect to those books on whose behalf a claim to canonical authority has been put forth. . . . The question as to when the books which compose the canon of the New Testament were first collected into one volume is a mere matter of historical curiosity, and has really nothing to do with settling their canonical authority, though these two questions have been commonly confounded by those who have labored to involve this whole matter in obscurity and uncertainty. Their canonical authority depends upon their authorship, and we estimate the testimonies, whether of individuals or churches or councils, the whole mass of quotations, references, and other materials derived from the works of ancient writers, *upon the ordinary recognized principles applicable to the historical evidence of a matter of fact."*[13] We submit to the judgment of the early church because we have no reason to question the ground on which the sufficiency of evidences was established. If God ordained the church to *hear* the Word of the Son, the means to this end were also ordained.

## 10. The Problem of Mark and Luke

But if only *apostles* were authorized to give a normative interpretation of Christ's life, death, and resurrection, why are Mark and Luke in the canon? The answer is, Mark and Luke belonged to the "circle of revelation." The apostles validated the work of Mark and Luke; and it is apostolic *validation,* not apostolic *authorship,* which entitles a book to a place in the canon. . . .

. . .

## 11. Conclusion

Since orthodoxy defends the plenary inspiration of Scripture, it is always tempted to make propositional revelation an end in itself. Whenever it yields to this temptation, it offends its own presuppositions. Propositional revelation is an instrumental value; it is designed to bring us into fellowship with Jesus Christ. "These are written that you may believe that Jesus is the Christ, the Son of God, and that believing you may have life in his name." (John 20:31 RSV.) "Inspiration is no isolated fact, which stands by itself. He who takes it in this sense arrives at some sort of Koran, but not at the Holy Scripture. In that case the principal of knowing *(cognoscendi)* is taken entirely apart from the principium of being *(essendi)*, and causes the appearance of an exclusively intellectual product which is outside of reality. We then would have an inspiration which dictated intellectually, and could not communicate to us anything but a doctrine and a law."[14]

The gospel is the good news that God entered history and did something that man could not do for himself. The redemptive events are the foundation of the normative interpretation, and not the other way around. To conceive of the Bible as the primary revelation is heresy. If there had been no redemptive events, there would be no theology.

### Notes

1. In *The Case For Orthodox Theology* (Philadelphia: The Westminster Press, 1959), pp. 33-36, 39-49.
2. Abraham Kuyper, *Principles of Sacred Theology,* p. 551. Wm. B. Eerdmans Publishing Company, 1954.
3. William Lee, *The Inspiration of Holy Scripture* (3rd ed.), p. 102. Hodges, Smith & Company, Dublin, 1864.
4. Kuyper, *Principles of Sacred Theology,* pp. 455-57.
5. *Ibid.,* p. 446.
6. Robert C. Candlish, *Reason and Revelation,* p. 36. Thomas Nelson and Sons, Ltd., London, 1859.
7. William G. T. Shedd, *Dogmatic Theology,* Vol. I, p. 143, Zondervan Publishing House, n.d.
8. William Cunningham, *Theological Lectures,* pp. 414-15. Robert Carter & Brothers, 1878.
9. Kuyper, *Principles of Sacred Theology,* p. 465.
10. B. B. Warfield, *The Inspiration and Authority of the Bible,* p. 163. The Presbyterian and Reformed Publishing Company, 1948.
11. *Ibid.,* pp. 164-65.
12. Cunningham, *Theological Lectures,* pp. 442-43 (italics mine).
13. *Ibid.,* pp. 425-28 (Italics mine).
14. Kuyper, *Principles of Sacred Theology,* pp. 413-14.

# Paul Tillich

*Tillich (1886–1965), the son of a Lutheran pastor, gained his doctorate at the University of Breslau. He served as a military chaplain during World War I and rose to prominence early on in Weimar Germany while teaching at Dresden, Marburg, Leipzig, and Frankfurt and immersing himself in the arts, literature, philosophy, and politics of the times, as well as its theology. Denied permission to teach when Hitler came to power in 1933 because of his commitments to religious socialism, he accepted the invitation of Union Theological Seminary and Columbia University to relocate in the United States. He taught at Union for twenty-two years (1933–1955), and thereafter at Harvard (1955–1962). The last three years of his life were spent at the University of Chicago's Divinity School.*

*His magnum opus was a three-volume* Systematic Theology *(1951–1963), following in the "grand" tradition of* summa theologica *and Protestant dogmatics but employing a dialectical "method of correlation" between analyses of the human condition and Christian symbols and themes. This approach was developed in the course of lifelong work in the "theology of culture," which led to major contributions in the psychology of religion and religion and the arts and other fields in addition to doctrine per se. The range and influence of Tillich's thinking are too vast for a text or two to cover the whole. Basic to both, however, were his reflections on a correlative theological method, and it is this that is set forth in the text that follows.*

## THE PROBLEM OF THEOLOGICAL METHOD[1]

### 1. Method and Reality

Method is the systematic way of doing something, especially of gaining knowledge. No method can be found in separation from its actual exercise; methodological considerations are abstractions from methods actually used. Descartes's *Discours de la méthode* followed Galileo's application of the method of mathematical physics and brought it to general consciousness and philosophical definiteness. Schleiermacher's method, as used in the *Glaubenslehre,* followed the mystical-romantic reinterpretation of religion and established methodology of inner experience. The methodological remarks made in this paper describe the method actually used in my attempts to elaborate a theology of "self-transcending Realism" *(gläubiger Realismus),* which is supposed to overcome supra-naturalism as well as its naturalistic counterpart.

It is not a sound procedure to borrow a method for a special realm of inquiry from another realm in which this method has been successfully used. It seems that the emphasis on the so-called "empirical" method in theology has not grown out of actual theological demands but has been imposed on theology under the pressure of a "methodological imperialism," exercised by the pattern of natural sciences. This subjection of theology to a strange pattern has resulted in an undue extension of the concept "empirical" and the lack of a clear distinction between the different meanings of "experience" in the theological enterprise. For some it is the general human experience on the basis of which they try to approach inferentially the religious objects; for others it is the religious experience of mankind, empathically interpreted. Sometimes it is the religious experience of the theologian and the group to which he belongs that gives the material for an "empirical" theology. Sometimes an ontological intuition is called "experience." Certainly, every concrete reality is open to many methods, according to its different "levels" or "functional potentialities." And each of the ways mentioned (besides some others) can contribute something to the investigation of a phenomenon as complex as religion. But the confusing term "empirical" should not be imposed on all of them; nor should the attempt be made to establish a methodological monism which includes chemistry as well as theology. Reality itself makes demands, and the method must follow; reality offers itself in different ways, and our cognitive intellect must receive it in different ways. An exclusive method applied to everything closes many ways of approach and impoverishes our vision of reality. A world construed according to the model of classical mechanics or Hegelian dialectics or behavioristic protocols is not the cognitive fulfillment of the potentialities of reality. In this respect a genuine pragmatism which refuses to close any door is much more realistic than a dogmatic empiricism with which it is sometimes confused—even by its own followers.

We encounter reality—or reality imposes itself upon us—sometimes in a more complex way, sometimes in definite and distinguishable elements and functions. Whenever we encounter reality in the one or the other way, it challenges our cognitive power and brings it into action. The way in which the cognitive power works is dependent on three factors: its own structure, the structure of the reality it encounters, and the relation of the two structures. In a methodical approach these three factors are noticed, analyzed, and evaluated. But the *prius* of all this is the encounter itself; and nothing is more destructive for knowledge than the establishment of methods which, by their very nature, prevent the actual encounter or prejudice its interpretation. (It is my opinion that the term "encounter" is more adequate for our pretheoretical relation to reality than the term "experience," which has lost so much of its specific meaning that it needs to be "saved," namely, restricted to a theoretically interpreted encounter.)

The presupposition of theology is that there is a special encounter with reality—or a special way in which reality imposes itself on us—which is ordinarily called "religious." And it is the presupposition of this paper that "having a religious encounter with reality" means "being ultimately concerned about reality."

## 2. Theology and Philosophy of Religion

The ultimate concern or the religious encounter with reality can be considered in two ways. It can be looked at as an event beside other events, to be observed and described in theoretical detachment; or it can be understood as an event in which he who considers it is "existentially" involved. In the first case the philosopher of religion is at work, in the second the theologian speaks. The philosopher of religion notices the ultimate concern, which he cannot help finding in the history of religion as a quality of practically all representative personalities, symbols, and activities that are called "religious." But in his dealing with this characteristic of religion he himself is only theoretically, but not existentially, concerned. The religious concern is not his concern in so far as he is a philosopher of religion. He points to it, he explains it, but his work is not an expression of the religious encounter with reality. This is different in the theologian. He applies his ultimate concern to everything, as an *ultimate* concern demands—even to his theoretical interpretation of the religious encounter. For the theologian the interpretation of the ultimate concern is itself a matter of ultimate concern, a *religious* work.

But this distinction is not unambiguous. There is an element in every philosophy (not only in every philosopher) which is "existential," i.e.,

429

which has the character of an ultimate decision about the meaning of reality. The less technical and the more creative a philosophy is, the more it shows, at least implicitly, an ultimate concern. No creative philosophy can escape its religious background. This is the reason for the tremendous influence that philosophy has had not only on theology but also on the history of religion and vice versa; for, as the philosopher cannot escape his theological background, so the theologian cannot escape his philosophical tool. Those who try to do so deceive themselves: their language, which is shaped through philosophy, betrays them (as even Barth has admitted).

Nevertheless, the distinction between theology and philosophy of religion is valid and cannot be obliterated without dangerous consequences. It is very unfortunate that the so-called "Continental" theology has brought into disregard the function of an independent philosophy of religion, thus creating an intolerable theological absolutism; and it is equally unfortunate that American (nonfundamentalistic) theology was not able to protect itself from being dissolved into a general philosophy of religion, thus producing a self-destructive relativism.

Theology is the existential and, at the same time, methodical interpretation of an ultimate concern. The interpretation of an ultimate concern is "existential" if it is done in the situation of concern. The interpretation of an ultimate concern is methodical if it relates the concern rationally to the whole of experience. Theology, literally and historically, unites these two elements. Theological propositions, therefore, are propositions which deal with an object in so far as it is related to an ultimate concern. No object is excluded from theology if this criterion is applied, not even a piece of stone; and no object is in itself a matter of theology, not even God as an object of inference. This makes theology absolutely universal, on the one hand, and absolutely definite, on the other hand. Theology has to deal with everything, but only under the theological criterion, the ultimate concern.

The concept "ultimate concern" is itself the result of a theological procedure. It expresses two sides of the religious experience: (1) The one side is the absolute or unconditional or ultimate element in religious experience. Every religious relation, attitude, symbol, and action is unconditionally *serious; decisive* in an absolute sense; *transcending* any preliminary, transitory, and dependent value. The whole history of religion confirms this side of religious experience. Where there is a living religion, it makes an absolute claim; it claims the "whole heart"; it does not admit anything ultimate besides itself. (2) The other side is the dynamic presence of the "ultimate" as a continuous, never ceasing, concrete, and universal concern, always demanding and giving, always threatening and promising. As an actual concern it expresses itself in the actualities of life, qualifying every section of existence and using every section of existence for its own embodiment in symbols and actions; for the religious or ultimate concern refers to the ultimate foundation of our being and the ultimate meaning of our existence. Therefore, we can formulate the abstract criterion of every theological work in this way: Those propositions are theological which deal with a subject in so far as it belongs to the foundation of our being and in so far as the meaning of our existence depends on it.

### 3. The Positive Element in the Theological Method

The ultimate concern is a concrete concern; otherwise it could not be a concern at all. Even mysticism lives in concrete traditions and symbols in order to express, in action and thought, that which transcends everything concrete. Theology, therefore, must interpret the totality of symbols, institutions, and ideas in which an ultimate concern has embodied itself; theology is, first of all, *positive*. It works on the basis, in the material, and for the purpose of an actual religion. The participation in a religious reality is a presupposition of all theology. You have to be within the circle of a concrete religion in order to interpret it existentially. This is the "theological circle" which theology cannot (and never should try to) escape. This circle is not vicious, but its denial is dishonest, for it could be denied only in the name of an assumedly higher ultimate, which immediately would establish the same circle.

Traditionally, the theological circle has been expressed in the assertion that faith is the precondition of theology. (*Pistis* precedes *gnosis,* as the Alexandrians said; *credo ut intelligam,* as Anselm, following Augustine, formulated it.) Faith, in this context, means a convinced and active participation in the life of a religious group, its traditions, its tensions, its activities. It is not the individual belief of the theologian to which they refer (as we are inclined to misinterpret the *credo ut intelligam*); but it is the spiritual substance out of which a theologian must create, even if he is aware of the weakness of his personal faith (otherwise there would be no honest theologian).

The ultimate concern out of which *we* are working as theologians is embodied in Christianity. If a Christian theologian says that for him Christianity is one among other elements in the religion he intends to interpret, this can mean two things—either that he is not a theologian but a philosopher of religion or that he belongs to a new religious synthesis which is, like everything concrete, inclusive and exclusive at the same time and which therefore establishes a theological circle, just as Christianity does. Since such a concrete synthesis has not yet appeared within my own theological circle and since I am convinced that Christianity is able to take all possible elements of religious truth into itself without ceasing to be Christianity, I am going to speak now about Christian theology, as the only one which is within my essential reach.

Christian theology is a work of the Christian church. The theological function is one of its essential functions, which never can be lost so long as there is the church. Christian theology, moreover, cannot be carried on except by the church. The positive character of the ultimate concern makes "individual theology" impossible. The individual theologian can and should find more adequate methods of interpretation. But he cannot find that which he is asked to interpret. Concretely speaking: Christian theology is the interpretation of the message that Jesus is the Christ, and of the symbols and institutions based on this message. Theology is the methodical self-interpretation of the Christian church (1) in the direction of its foundation, the "new reality" which has become manifest in Jesus as the Christ, and (2) in the direction of the life, past and present, which is determined by this new reality. The original document of the new reality is the Bible; the expression of the life determined by this new reality is the Tradition.

### 4. The Theological Method with Respect to Bible and Tradition

Bible and Tradition give the material in which the theologian works. The Bible implies three elements which have different impacts on the theological method. First, and basically, it contains the decisive manifestation of what concerns us ultimately, in the picture of Jesus as the Christ. This is the criterion of all Christian theology, the criterion also of the theological use of the Bible, for the Bible contains, second, the reception of this manifestation in the original church. Every biblical writer is, at the same time, a witness to the new reality in Jesus as the Christ and a witness of the way in which he and the group to which he belongs have received the new reality. In the latter sense they have started the Tradition. In the first sense they point to that which judges the Tradition, including their own contribution to it. (This is the meaning of Luther's statement that the Bible is the "Word of God" in so far as it *Christum treibet;* in the power of this criterion he himself judged the canon.) From this it follows that not the Bible as such, as a part of the history of religion, is the norm of Christian theology but the Bible in so far as it is the genuine witness to the new reality. It is the permanent task of Christian theology (in unity with the developing religious and historical understanding of the Bible) to elaborate the norm of Christian theology out of the whole of the biblical material and to apply the norm equally to Bible and Tradition. The third element in the biblical literature that is important for theological method is the preparation for the decisive manifestation of the new reality and for its reception by the church. In the Old as well as in the New Testament we find in language, rites, and ideas a large element of general revelation as it has occurred and continuously occurs within human religion generally. Our eyes have been opened to this element by the work of the *religionsgeschichtliche Schule* in historical theology. So far as method goes, this means that in every theological statement we must take into consideration the religious substance which is transformed and purified in the prophetic and apostolic message. Only in this sense, but in this sense definitely, the *history of religion* belongs to the positive element in Christian theology. The universality of the Christian claim implies that there is no religion, not even the most primitive, which has not contributed or will not contribute to the preparation and reception of the new reality in history. In this sense the theologian always must be a "pagan" and a "Jew" and a "Greek" (humanist) and bring their spiritual substance under the criterion of the theological norm. For instance, the terms "Son of Man," "Messiah," "Son of God," "Kyrios," "Logos," appear in the history of religion; and, if they are used for the interpretation of the new reality, they contribute to it with their previous connotations, but in such a way that their meaning is judged and saved at the same time. This method of *judging and saving the history of a religion* is exercised by all the biblical writers. It must be done methodically and creatively by the theologian.

Methodologically, the Tradition (the beginning of which is the biblical literature) is not normative but *guiding*. This is a rejection of the Roman Catholic point of view; just as the subordination of the biblical literature to the theological norm implied in it is a rejection of orthodox Protestantism. Tradition cannot be normative in Christian theology because there is always an element in Tradition which must be judged and cannot be the judge itself. But Tradition can and must be guiding for the theologian, because it is the expression of the continuous reception of the new reality in history and because, without tradition, no theological existence is possible. It is rather a naïve illusion of some Protestants

433

to believe that by jumping over two thousand years of Christian tradition they can come into a direct and existential (more than philological) relation to the biblical texts. The guiding function of the Tradition has a positive and a negative side. Positively, the Tradition shows the questions implied in the Christian message, the main possibilities of answers, and the points in which Christians have agreed and have disagreed. Negatively, the Tradition shows answers which have generally been avoided and, above all, answers which have been characterized by the church as "heretical." He who takes the Tradition seriously must take heresies seriously. He knows that a heresy is supposed to be, not a deviating opinion, but an existential attack on, or a distortion of, the theological norm in the name of theology. He will not easily—not without the consciousness that he risks his participation in the new reality—promote a view which has been characterized as heretical by the church as a whole. This, of course, should not prevent anyone from following his theological conscience (as Luther did in Worms); but it should sharpen that conscience.

The positive element in theological method is historically given. But nothing is more ambiguous than the concept "historical." When the Anglican church accepted the apostolic succession as one of its basic doctrines, it meant to emphasize the historical continuity of the manifestation of the new reality in history. In this sense the doctrine emphasized the historical element in church and theology. But when Anglican theologians, answering Roman attacks, tried to justify the apostolic character of their episcopate by an 8,000 to 1 documentary probability that there was a real apostolic succession, they introduced another meaning of "historical," namely, the probabilities (which never can become religious certainties) of historical research. In that moment their religious position was scientifically undermined because they confused the two meanings of "historical." The same is true of biblical criticism. If the Christian faith is based even on a 100,000 to 1 probability that Jesus has said or done or suffered this or that; if Christianity is based on possible birth-registers of Nazareth or crime-registers of Pontius Pilate, then it has lost its foundation completely. Then the historical event, that a new reality has appeared in mankind and the world (a reality which is reflected in the picture of Jesus as the Christ), has become a matter of empirical verification, ideally through a competent reporter, armed with a camera, phonograph, and psychograph. Since such a reporter, unfortunately, was not available in the year A.D. 30, we have to replace him by more or less probable conjectures. But this is not the historical character of Jesus as the Christ. It is regrettable that one of the greatest events in the history of religion—the radical criticism of the holy legend of Christianity by Christian theologians, which destroyed a whole system of pious superstition—has been abused for the purpose of giving a pseudo-scientific foundation to the Christian faith. The historical foundation of theological method does not mean that the theologian has to wait, with fear and trembling, for the next mail which may bring him a new, more critical, or more conservative statement about some important facts of the "life of Jesus" according to which he has to change his faith and his theology. But it does mean that his theology is determined by the event of the appearance of the new reality in history, as reflected in the *full* biblical picture of Jesus as the Christ and as witnessed by all biblical writers and by the whole tradition of Christianity.

### 5. The Element of Immediacy in the Theological Method

The positive element in theology, as discussed above, gives the *content* of theological work; the rational element, to be discussed later, gives the *form* of theological work; and the element of immediacy, to be discussed now, gives the *medium* of theological work. Without participation in the reality within which theology speaks, no theology is possible; it is the air in which theology breathes. We call this participation "experience" in the larger sense of the word, in which it covers the mere encounter as well as the cognitively conscious encounter. "Experience" in both senses is the medium, the element in which theology lives. But the religious experience of the theologian is not a positive source and not a norm of systematic theology. Everybody's religious experience is shaped by the denominational group to which he belongs. The education in his own church opened the door to religious reality for every theologian. Later he has personal experiences which confirm or transform his earlier ones. But his intention should never be to make his earlier or later experiences the content of his theology; they certainly will enter into it, but this is an event, not an intention. It is the function of the medium to mediate, not to hold fast. It was the danger of Schleiermacher's theology that his concept of "religious consciousness" became confused with "experience." But it contradicts the basic principle of the Reformation to look at one's self instead of looking beyond one's self at the new reality which liberates man from himself. Our experience is changing and fragmentary; it is not the source of truth, although without it no truth can become *our* truth.

It might be said that the whole history of religion, including the bib-

435

lical religion and the development of Christianity, is the reservoir of man's religious experience and that the positive element of theology is identical with the contents of this experience. Such a statement is correct, but ambiguous. A content, e.g., of the experience of the prophet Isaiah, is the paradoxical acting of God in history. This divine acting transcends every immediate experience. It has become manifest to the prophet in a situation which we should call "revelation." Of course, the prophet is aware of this situation, and to that extent it is an "experience." Not the experiential side, however, is significant for the prophet and for the theologian, but the revelatory side. The word "revelation" has been distorted into "supra-natural communication of knowledge"; it is hard to save the word (and many others) from this state of corruption into which it has been brought by both supra-naturalism and naturalism. Nevertheless, "revelation" points to something for which no other adequate word is available—certainly not "religious experience." Revelation is the manifestation of the ultimate ground and meaning of human existence (and implicitly of all existence). It is not a matter of objective knowledge, of empirical research or rational inference. It is a matter of ultimate concern; it grasps the total personality and is effective through a set of symbols. Revelation is not restricted to a special period of history, to special personalities or writings. It occurs whenever it "wills." But we can speak of it only if it has become revelation *for us,* if we have experienced it existentially. Not experience, but revelation received *in* experience, gives the content of every theology.

There is, however, one point (which is only a point, without length or breadth) in which medium and content are identical, because in this point subject and object are identical: It is the awareness of the ultimate itself, the *esse ipsum,* which transcends the difference between subject and object and lies, as the presupposition of all doubts, beyond doubt; it is the *veritas ipsa,* as Augustine has called it. It is wrong to call this point "God" (as the ontological argument does), but it is necessary to call it "that in us which makes it impossible for us to escape God." It is the presence of the element of "ultimacy" in the structure of our existence, the basis of religious experience. It has been called "religious *a priori*"; but if we use this phrase (in the sense of *anima naturaliter religiosa*), we must remove every content from it and reduce it to the pure potentiality of having experiences with the character of "ultimate concern." Every content of such an experience is dependent on revelation, namely, on the special way, form, and situation in which this potentiality is actualized by a concern which is concrete and ultimate at the same time. While the certainty of the pure ultimacy is ultimate, conditioned by nothing, its concrete embodiment in symbols and acts is a matter of destiny and venturing faith. Whenever we speak of religious experience, it is important to distinguish these (inseparable) elements: (1) the "point" of immediate awareness of the unconditional which *is* empty but unconditionally certain; and (2) the "breadth" of a concrete concern which is full of content but has the conditional certainty of venturing faith. Theology deals with the second element, while presupposing the first and measuring every theological statement by the standard of the ultimacy of the ultimate concern.

### 6. *The Element of Rationality in the Theological Method*

Theology is the rational "word" about God; it is the methodical interpretation of our ultimate concern. The rational element is not a source of theology. It does not give the content. But it gives the form; and the relation between form and content is extremely complex and demands careful analysis.

Theology is often identified with systematic theology. Although this terminology is bad, because it excludes historical and practical theology from their full part in the whole world of theology, it indicates that theology is essentially systematic. The word "system" has a narrower and a larger meaning. In its narrower sense the word points to the ideal of a deductive method in which a whole of interdependent presuppositions is derived from highest principles. Attempts have been made to develop such a system in the history of Christian thought. But the positive element in theology utterly resists a "system" in this sense; it includes openness and undermines a closed system. But "system" has also a larger sense. It designates a whole of propositions which are consistent, interdependent, and developed according to a definite method. In this sense all classical theology was systematic, and no theology, however fragmentary its actual work may be, can surrender the systematic idea. Every meaningful fragment is an implicit system, as every system is an explicit fragment; for man, and especially the theologian, lives in fragments, in reality as well as in thought.

It is obvious that the positive character of theology excludes a rational or natural theology, if these terms mean that, without existential participation in an ultimate concern, a detached analysis of reality can produce theological propositions. Even the rational substructure on which, according to scholasticism, the revealed superstructure is built, has convincing power only in the situation of faith. Even if (with

437

Thomas and against Duns Scotus) the logical necessity and correctness of the arguments of natural theology are acknowledged, their existential significance without revelation is not asserted.

The terms "natural religion" or "natural revelation" or "natural theology" are extremely misleading. If religion is the state of being grasped by an ultimate concern, "natural religion" can only mean that the ultimate concern is experienced in an encounter with nature. This, of course, is not only possible and real, but it is a necessary part of every ultimate concern; but it cannot be separated from other elements which also belong to every ultimate concern, such as personal and social elements. The concepts "natural revelation" and "natural theology" are often used for a knowledge of God which is inferentially derived from the structure of reality. But, whether such conclusions are valid or not, in neither case have they the character of "revelation," and they should not be called "theological," for there is no meaningful speaking of God if he is taken as an object which is not, at the same time, the ground of the speaking about him. There is no meaningful speaking of God except in an existential attitude or in the situation of revelation. In any other attitude the religious word "God" is used after it has been deprived of its genuine, namely, its religious, meaning. So we can say: There *is* revelation through nature; but there is no natural (rational) revelation. And there *is* theology dealing with nature; but there is no natural theology. Reason elaborates but does not produce theological propositions.

But the question arises as to whether the "elaboration" of the positive element in theology does not introduce a rational element into the substance itself. The urgency of this question is obvious when we look at the large number of philosophical concepts which have been used for theological purposes throughout the whole history of Christian thought.

It is possible to make a distinction between two types of theology, the *kerygmatic* and the *apologetic* type. In the kerygmatic type the kerygma—the message—is reproduced, interpreted, and organized either in predominantly biblical terms or in terms taken from the classical tradition. In the apologetic type the kerygma is related to the prephilosophical and the philosophical interpretations of reality. An apology "makes answer"—answers the questions asked of, and the criticisms directed against, a concrete religion. But an answer is possible only if there is a common ground between the one who asks and the one who answers. Apologetic theology presupposes the idea of a universal revelation, to which reference can be made because it is acknowledged by both sides. Here the rational element in theological method becomes most important and most intimately connected with the positive element. The way in which this connection has been and should be carried through can be called the "method of correlation."

## 7. The Method of Correlation

Wherever theology is understood in "existential" terms, all theological statements have the character of "correlation." Luther has expressed this principle very often and very strongly: "As you believe, so you have." This does not mean that the belief produces its contents; such an idea would have been utterly blasphemous for Luther. But it does mean that the objective and the subjective side of faith are interrelated, for faith is the expression of the impact of an ultimate concern on the human personality; it is the expression of an "existential situation" and not the acceptance of an objective assertion. Therefore, it is always subjective and objective in a strict interdependence. It is the beginning of a process of disintegration in theology if the objective side is isolated as a quasi-scientific assertion and the subjective side as an emotional "will to believe" in spite of a lack of evidence. The problem of truth in theology cannot be solved in terms of objective evidence. It can be solved only in terms of existential criteria. In the prophetic, as well as in the mystical, literature one criterion always appears: the unconditional character of the unconditional. Symbolically, it is called the "majesty of God"; or his exclusiveness against all finite claims (idols) or the unconditional dependence of every power on the divine power; or the "justification by grace alone." Every genuine heresy is an attack on the divinity of the divine. It gives to something finite infinite validity. It conditions the unconditional, for instance, by human morality or rationality. The "truth" of the Reformation theology against the canons of the Council of Trent is its emphasis on the ultimacy of the ultimate concern; it is not a "scientific" superiority of the Protestant over the Catholic propositions. It is an "existential," not an "objective," truth. This is the reason why the struggle of theologians is significant. They discuss, at least in principle, questions of "to be or not to be."

The method of correlation is especially the method of apologetic theology. Question and answer must be correlated in such a way that the religious symbol is interpreted as the adequate answer to a question, implied in man's existence, and asked in primitive, prephilosophical, or elaborated philosophical terms. For instance, the question implied in human finitude is answered in the symbols which constitute the idea of God; or the symbol of revelation answers the questions which drive reason to its own boundary; or the question implied in man's existential disruption and despair is answered in the symbol of the Christ and his appearance under the conditions of existence; or the idea of the divine Spirit is interpreted as the answer to the question implied in the tragic ambiguities of life, especially man's spiritual life; or the problems of the meaning of history are answered in the symbol of the Kingdom of God. In all these cases the method of correlation establishes a mutual interdependence between questions and answers. The questions implied in human existence determine the meaning and the theological interpretation of the answers as they appear in the classical religious concepts. The form of the questions, whether primitive or philosophical, is decisive for the theological form in which the answer is given. And, conversely, the substance of the question is determined by the substance of the answer. Nobody is able to ask questions concerning God, revelation, Christ, etc., who has not already received some answer. So we can say: With respect to man's ultimate concern the questions contain the substance of the answers, and the answers are shaped by the form of the questions. Here the rational element in theological method has a determining influence on theological propositions—not on their substance but on their form. But there is no way of saying a priori how much substance is hidden in the form. This can be said only in the process of theological work, and never fully. The reception of the "new reality" is always conditioned by the "old reality," which is conquered and fulfilled by it. This is the reason why early Christianity formulated the doctrine of the Logos, who has appeared in a unique way in Jesus as the Christ and is, at the same time, the universal principle of revelation in religion and culture. In this way the old reality can be considered as preparation for the new one; and the philosophical form is ultimately related to the substance of the theological answer instead of being alien to it. It seems to me that, without some form of a Logos doctrine (even if the term "Logos" is not used), no theology—certainly no apologetic theology—is possible.

A few examples may suffice to give a concrete impression of the method of correlation. If the question implied in human finitude is the question of God and the idea of God is the answer to this question, then modern existential analysis of human finitude becomes extremely valuable for the theological treatment of the idea of God. God becomes the correlate to human anxiety and contingency. He becomes the symbol of a "transcendent courage," in which the characteristics of finitude, as essential insecurity, loneliness, having to die, etc., are overcome. In this way the idea of God receives existential significance. The meaningless and self-contradictory question about the "existence of God" is replaced by an intensely meaningful question concerning our participation in an infinite communion, security, power, and meaning in the divine life.

In the same way the question implied in the self-destructive trends of man's personal and social life is to be understood as the question to which the central Christian statement that Jesus is the Christ gives the answer. If Christology is treated on the basis of this correlation, it interprets the picture of Jesus Christ as the ultimate manifestation of saving power in life and history, as the appearance of a "new reality," a power of wholeness and reconciliation conquering the "demonic" mechanisms in personal and social existence. Then our recent rediscovery of the contradictory structures in soul and community determines the form of our christological answer and makes this answer existential for our time. The method of correlation liberates Christology from a historism which tries to base the Christian faith in the new reality on doubtful historical probabilities, and it also liberates Christology from the "alchemy" of the doctrine of two natures, interpreting its meaning as a statement of the paradox of the victorious maintenance of the divine-human unity in a personal life against all the disruptive attacks of man's existential situation.

The method of correlation, as these examples show, is at no point forced into the vicious debate between naturalism and supra-naturalism. It describes things as they show themselves to the religious consciousness in the light of the human situation, the questions implied in it, and the answers given to it by the Christian message. Theology has rediscovered its correlative and existential character. It has overcome a theology of objective statements and subjective emotions. It has become again a way of giving answers to the questions which are our ultimate concern.

### Note

1. In *Paul Tillich: Theologian of the Boundaries*, ed. Mark Kline Taylor, The Making of Modern Theology: Nineteenth- and Twentieth-Century Texts, John W. de Gruchy, general editor (Minneapolis: Fortress Press, 1991), pp. 127-41.

# Reinhold Niebuhr

Niebuhr (1892–1971) was arguably the most prominent of the group of native-born Americans, including his brother H. Richard, who revised the heritage of classic liberalism in response both to the criticism and resources of emergent "dialectical" or "neoorthodox" thought in Europe and the challenges of national and international affairs. The son of a German immigrant pastor of the North America's (German) Evangelical Synod, Niebuhr studied first at church-related schools (Elmhurst College and Eden Theological Seminary) and then at Yale Divinity School (1914–1915). As a pastor in Detroit, Michigan, from 1915 to 1928, facing the conflicts of labor and management in industrialized society, he became a leading advocate of social-gospel ideals. He was appointed in 1928 to teach "applied Christianity" at Union Theological Seminary in New York. Association with that school was to continue until his death, eleven years after his formal retirement.

Niebuhr emerged as a major theologian during the 1930s. In Moral Man and Immoral Society (1932) and An Interpretation of Christian Ethics (1935), he criticized the liberalism of the times as naive in its optimistic, idealistic views of human goodness and moral progress. His interest in a more sober appraisal of the human situation, one in keeping with the biblical witness and the course of history, developed into a position known as "Christian realism," more aptly regarded as a distinct American parallel to than as an imitation of European neoorthodox thought. One difference was Niebuhr's ongoing social-political activism, from socialism and pacifism in the 1920s to New Deal politics, support of war against Hitler and the containment of communism, defense of nonviolent protest in the civil rights movement, and opposition to the Vietnam War thereafter. Though his counsel of practical "realism" in ethics remains influential and controversial long after his death, The Nature and Destiny of Man (2 vols., 1941–1943), his Gifford Lectures of 1939, represent his theological testament. Selected here is a key section of his exposition of the Christian doctrine of sin.

## MAN AS SINNER[1]

*III: The Sin of Pride*

Biblical and Christian thought has maintained with a fair degree of consistency that pride is more basic than sensuality and that the latter is, in some way, derived from the former. We have previously considered the Biblical definition of basic sin as pride and have suggested that the Pauline exposition of man's self-glorification ("they changed the glory of the incorruptible God into an image made like unto corruptible man") is really an admirable summary of the whole Biblical doctrine of sin.[2]

This Biblical definition is strictly adhered to in that strain of Christian theology which manages to maintain the Biblical viewpoint against the influence of the rationalist-classical view of man, in which sin tends to be identified with ignorance or the passions of the body. The Biblical view colours the definitions of Christian rationalists so that when they define sin primarily as sensuality, they recognize, at least, that this sensuality is not merely the expression of physical impulse but represents an inordinate quality made possible by the freedom of the spirit.[3] We are not at present concerned with the emphasis of Christian theology upon the inexcusable character of this pride and the insistence that sin is rooted in an evil will and not in some antecedent weakness of man.[4] Our present interest is to relate the Biblical and distinctively Christian conception of sin as pride and self-love to the observable behaviour of men. It will be convenient in this analysis to distinguish between three types of pride, which are, however, never completely distinct in actual life: pride of power, pride of knowledge and pride of virtue.[5] The third type, the pride of self-righteousness, rises to a form of spiritual pride, which is at once a fourth type and yet not a specific form of pride at all but pride and self-glorification in its inclusive and quintessential form.

*(a)* "Of the infinite desires of man," declares Bertrand Russell, "the chief are the desires for power and glory. They are not identical though closely allied."[6] Mr. Russell is not quite clear about the relation of the two to each other, and the relation is, as a matter of fact, rather complex. There is a pride of power in which the human ego assumes its self-sufficiency and self-mastery and imagines itself secure against all vicissitudes. It does not recognize the contingent and dependent character of its life and believes itself to be the author of its own existence, the judge of its own values and the master of its own destiny. This proud pretension is present in an inchoate form in all human life but

443

it rises to greater heights among those individuals and classes who have a more than ordinary degree of social power.[7] Closely related to the pride which seems to rest upon the possession of either the ordinary or some extraordinary measure of human freedom and self-mastery, is the lust for power which has pride as its end. The ego does not feel secure and therefore grasps for more power in order to make itself secure. It does not regard itself as sufficiently significant or respected or feared and therefore seeks to enhance its position in nature and in society.

In the one case the ego seems unconscious of the finite and determinate character of its existence. In the other case the lust for power is prompted by a darkly conscious realization of its insecurity.[8] The first form of the pride of power is particularly characteristic of individuals and groups whose position in society is, or seems to be, secure. In Biblical prophecy this security is declared to be bogus and those who rest in it are warned against an impending doom. Thus the second Isaiah describes the pride of Babylon in the words: "Thou saidst, I shall be a lady forever; so that thou dost not lay these things to thy heart." The impending doom is defined as a revelation of the weakness and insecurity of Babylon: "Thy nakedness shall be uncovered; yea, thy shame shall be seen."[9] In the same way the first Isaiah warns the rulers of Israel who are described as "the crown of pride" that their "glorious beauty is a fading flower." He declares that in the day of judgment the "Lord of hosts" will be vindicated and will be "for a crown of glory and for a diadem of beauty" (Is. 28:1-5). In other words history invariably shatters the illusions of those who overestimate the power of human life and in the day of judgment God is revealed as the true source and end of life as the "crown of glory." In Ezekiel's prophecies of doom upon the nations of the earth, they are constantly accused of having foolishly overestimated their security, independence and self-mastery. Egypt, for instance, is accused of imagining herself the creator of the river Nile and saying, "My river is my own, I have made it for myself." In the doom which overtakes this pride the real source and end of life will be revealed: "They shall know that I am the Lord" (Ez. 30:8).

The second form of the pride of power is more obviously prompted by the sense of insecurity. It is the sin of those, who knowing themselves to be insecure, seek sufficient power to guarantee their security, inevitably of course at the expense of other life. It is particularly the sin of the advancing forces of human society in distinction to the established forces. Among those who are less obviously secure, either in terms of

444

social recognition, or economic stability or even physical health, the temptation arises to overcome or to obscure insecurity by arrogating a greater degree of power to the self. Sometimes this lust for power expresses itself in terms of man's conquest of nature, in which the legitimate freedom and mastery of man in the world of nature[10] is corrupted into a mere exploitation of nature. Man's sense of dependence upon nature and his reverent gratitude toward the miracle of nature's perennial abundance is destroyed by his arrogant sense of independence and his greedy effort to overcome the insecurity of nature's rhythms and seasons by garnering her stores with excessive zeal and beyond natural requirements. Greed is in short the expression of man's inordinate ambition to hide his insecurity in nature. It is perfectly described in Jesus' parable of the rich fool who assures himself: "Soul, thou hast much goods laid up for many years; take thine ease, eat, drink, and be merry." Significantly this false security is shattered by the prospect of death, a vicissitude of nature which greed cannot master. God said to the rich fool, "This night thy soul shall be required of thee" (Luke 12:19-20).

Greed as a form of the will-to-power has been a particularly flagrant sin in the modern era because modern technology has tempted contemporary man to overestimate the possibility and the value of eliminating his insecurity in nature. Greed has thus become the besetting sin of a bourgeois culture. This culture is constantly tempted to regard physical comfort and security as life's final good and to hope for its attainment to a degree which is beyond human possibilities. "Modern man," said a cynical doctor, "has forgotten that nature intends to kill man and will succeed in the end."[11]

Since man's insecurity arises not merely from the vicissitudes of nature but from the uncertainties of society and history, it is natural that the ego should seek to overcome social as well as natural insecurity and should express the impulse of "power over men" as well as "power over matter." The peril of a competing human will is overcome by subordinating that will to the ego and by using the power of many subordinated wills to ward off the enmity which such subordination creates. The will-to-power is thus inevitably involved in the vicious circle of accentuating the insecurity which it intends to eliminate. "Woe to thee," declares the prophet Isaiah, "that spoilest, and thou wast not spoiled; and dealest treacherously, and they dealt not treacherously with thee! when thou shalt cease to spoil, thou shalt be spoiled" (Is. 33:1). The will-to-power in short involves the ego in injustice. It seeks a security beyond the limits of human finiteness and this inordinate ambition arouses fears and

445

enmities which the world of pure nature, with its competing impulses of survival, does not know.

The school of modern psychology which regards the will-to-power as the most dominant of human motives has not yet recognized how basically it is related to insecurity. Adler attributes it to specific forms of the sense of inferiority and therefore believes that a correct therapy can eliminate it. Karen Horney relates the will-to-power to a broader anxiety than the specific cases of the sense of inferiority which Adler enumerates. But she thinks that the will-to-power springs from the general insecurities of a competitive civilization and therefore holds out hope for its elimination in a co-operative society.[12] This is still far short of the real truth. The truth is that man is tempted by the basic insecurity of human existence to make himself doubly secure and by the insignificance of his place in the total scheme of life to prove his significance. The will-to-power is in short both a direct form and an indirect instrument of the pride which Christianity regards as sin in its quintessential form.

We have provisionally distinguished between the pride which does not recognize human weakness and the pride which seeks power in order to overcome or obscure a recognized weakness; and we have sought to attribute the former to the more established and traditionally respected individuals and groups, while attributing the latter to the less secure, that is, to the advancing rather than established groups in society. This distinction is justified only if regarded as strictly provisional. The fact is that the proudest monarch and the most secure oligarch is driven to assert himself beyond measure partly by a sense of insecurity. This is partly due to the fact that the greater his power and glory, the more the common mortality of humankind appears to him in the guise of an incongruous fate. Thus the greatest monarchs of the ancient world, the Pharaohs of Egypt, exhausted the resources of their realm to build pyramids, which were intended to establish or to prove their immortality. A common mortal's fear of death is thus one prompting motive of the pretensions and ambitions of the greatest lords.[13]

But furthermore, the more man establishes himself in power and glory, the greater is the fear of tumbling from his eminence, or losing his treasure, or being discovered in his pretension. Poverty is a peril to the wealthy but not to the poor. Obscurity is feared, not by those who are habituated to its twilight but by those who have become accustomed to public acclaim. Nor is this sense of insecurity of the powerful and the great to be wholly discounted as being concerned with mere vanities. Life's basic securities are involved in the secondary securities of power and glory. The tyrant fears not only the loss of his power but the possible loss of his life. The powerful nation, secure against its individual foes, must fear the possibility that its power may challenge its various foes to make common cause against it. The person accustomed to luxury and ease actually meets a greater danger to life and mere existence in the hardships of poverty than those who have been hardened by its rigours. The will-to-power is thus an expression of insecurity even when it has achieved ends which, from the perspective of an ordinary mortal, would seem to guarantee complete security. The fact that human ambitions know no limits must therefore be attributed not merely to the infinite capacities of the human imagination but to an uneasy recognition of man's finiteness, weakness and dependence, which become the more apparent the more we seek to obscure them, and which generate ultimate perils, the more immediate insecurities are eliminated. Thus man seeks to make himself God because he is betrayed by both his greatness and his weakness; and there is no level of greatness and power in which the lash of fear is not at least one strand in the whip of ambition.

*(b)* The intellectual pride of man is of course a more spiritual sublimation of his pride of power. Sometimes it is so deeply involved in the more brutal and obvious pride of power that the two cannot be distinguished. Every ruling oligarchy of history has found ideological pretensions as important a bulwark of authority as its police power. But intellectual pride is confined neither to the political oligarchs nor to the savants of society. All human knowledge is tainted with an "ideological" taint. It pretends to be more true than it is. It is finite knowledge, gained from a particular perspective; but it pretends to be final and ultimate knowledge. Exactly analogous to the cruder pride of power, the pride of intellect is derived on the one hand from ignorance of the finiteness of the human mind and on the other hand from an attempt to obscure the known conditioned character of human knowledge and the taint of self-interest in human truth.

The philosopher who imagines himself capable of stating a final truth merely because he has sufficient perspective upon past history to be able to detect previous philosophical errors is clearly the victim of the ignorance of his ignorance. Standing on a high pinnacle of history he forgets that this pinnacle also has a particular locus and that his perspective will seem as partial to posterity as the pathetic parochialism of previous thinkers. This is a very obvious fact but no philosophical system has been great enough to take full account of it. Each great thinker makes the same mistake, in turn, of imagining himself the final thinker.

447

Descartes, Hegel, Kant, and Comte, to mention only a few moderns, were so certain of the finality of their thought that they have become fair sport for any wayfaring cynic. Not the least pathetic is the certainty of a naturalistic age that its philosophy is a final philosophy because it rests upon science, a certainty which betrays ignorance of its own prejudices and failure to recognize the limits of scientific knowledge.

Intellectual pride is thus the pride of reason which forgets that it is involved in a temporal process and imagines itself in complete transcendence over history. "It is this appearance of independent history of state constitutions, systems of law, of ideologies in every special field which above all has blinded so many people," declares Friederich Engels.[14] Yet intellectual pride is something more than the mere ignorance of ignorance. It always involves, besides, a conscious or subconscious effort to obscure a known or partly known taint of interest. Despite the tremendous contribution of Marxist thought in the discovery of the ideological taint in all culture, it is precisely the element of pretense which it fails to understand. Its too simple theory of human consciousness betrays it here. Thus Engels declares: "The real driving force which moves it [ideology] remains unconscious otherwise it would not be an ideological process."[15] But the real fact is that all pretensions of final knowledge and ultimate truth are partly prompted by the uneasy feeling that the truth is not final and also by an uneasy conscience which realizes that the interests of the ego are compounded with this truth.

Sometimes this root of insecurity in intellectual pride is revealed in the pathetic pretense of an individual thinker; sometimes the thinker hides and exposes not his own insecurity but that of an age, a class or a nation. Descartes' intellectual pride was something more than the ignorance of his ignorance. That was disclosed when he resented the reminder of a friend that his "*Cogito, ergo sum,*" the keystone of his philosophical arch, was derived from Augustinian thought.[16] Schopenhauer's pride was more than the consequence of his inability to measure the limits of his system. It was compensation for his lack of recognition in competition with more widely acclaimed idealistic thinkers. In the case of such men as Hegel and Comte, individual and representative pride is curiously mingled. Hegel not only proclaimed the finality of his own thought but regarded his contemporary Prussian military state as the culmination of human history. Comte believed his philosophy to be final not only as a philosophy but as a religion; and with pathetic national pride he predicted that Paris would be the centre of the new universal culture which he would found.[17]

448

A particular significant aspect of intellectual pride is the inability of the agent to recognize the same or similar limitations of perspective in himself which he has detected in others. The Marxist detection of ideological taint in the thought of all bourgeois culture is significantly unembarrassed by any scruples about the conditioned character of its own viewpoints. "Socialist thought," declares Karl Mannheim, "which hitherto has unmasked all its adversaries' utopias as ideologies, never raised the problem of determinateness about its own position. It never applied this method to itself and checked its own desire to be absolute."[18] The fanaticism which springs from this blindness becomes particularly tragic and revealing when it is expressed in conflict between various schools of Marxist thought as for instance between the Stalinists and Trotskyites. Each is forced to prove and to believe that the opponent is really a covert capitalist or fascist, since ideological taint in genuine proletarian thought is inconceivable. The proud achievement of Marxism in discovering the intellectual pride and pretension of previous cultures therefore ends in a pitiful display of the same sin. It has no inkling of the truth of the Pauline observation: "For wherein thou judgest another, thou condemnest thyself; for thou that judgest doest the same things" (Romans 2:1).

The Marxist pride may, as in other instances of similar pride, be regarded as merely the fruit of the ignorance of ignorance. The Marxist has mistakenly confined ideological taint to economic life and therefore erroneously hopes for a universal rational perspective when economic privileges would be equalized. But one has the right to suspect that something more than ignorance is involved. The vehemence with which the foe is accused of errors of which the self regards itself free betrays the usual desperation with which the self seeks to hide the finiteness and determinateness of its own position from itself.

There is in short no manifestation of intellectual pride in which the temptations of both human freedom and human insecurity are not apparent. If man were not a free spirit who transcends every situation in which he is involved he would have no concern for unconditioned truth and he would not be tempted to claim absolute validity for his partial perspectives. If he were completely immersed in the contingencies and necessities of nature he would have only his own truth and would not be tempted to confuse his truth with *the* truth. But in that case he would have no truth at all, for no particular event or value could be related meaningfully to the whole. If on the other hand man were wholly transcendent he would not be tempted to insinuate the necessities of the moment and the vagaries of the hour into the truth and thus corrupt it. Nor would he be prompted to deny the finiteness of his knowledge in order to escape the despair of scepticism which threatens him upon the admission of such ignorance. Yet the ignorance of ignorance which underlies every attempt at knowledge can never be described as a mere ignorance. The ignorance presupposes pride, for there is always an ideal possibility that man should recognize his own limits. This implicit pride becomes explicit in the conscious efforts to obscure the partiality of the perspective from which the truth is apprehended. The explicit character of this pride is fully revealed in all cases in which the universalistic note in human knowledge becomes the basis of an imperial desire for domination over life which does not conform to it. The modern religious nationalist thus declares in one moment that his culture is not an export article but is valid for his nation alone. In the next moment he declares that he will save the world by destroying inferior forms of culture.

The insecurity which hides behind this pride is not quite as patent as the pride, yet it is also apparent. In the relations of majority and minority racial groups for instance, for which the negro-white relation is a convenient example, the majority group justifies the disabilities which it imposes upon the minority group on the ground that the subject group is not capable of enjoying or profiting from the privileges of culture or civilization. Yet it can never completely hide, and it sometimes frankly expresses the fear that the grant of such privileges would eliminate the inequalities of endowment which supposedly justify the inequalities of privilege.[19] The pretension of pride is thus a weapon against a feared competitor. Sometimes it is intended to save the self from the abyss of self-contempt which always yawns before it.[20]

*(c)* All elements of moral pride are involved in the intellectual pride which we have sought to analyse. In all but the most abstract philosophical debates the pretension of possessing an unconditioned truth is meant primarily to establish "my good" as unconditioned moral value. Moral pride is revealed in all "self-righteous" judgments in which the other is condemned because he fails to conform to the highly arbitrary standards of the self. Since the self judges itself by its own standards it finds itself good. It judges others by its own standards and finds them evil, when their standards fail to conform to its own. This is the secret of the relationship between cruelty and self-righteousness. When the self mistakes its standards for God's standards it is naturally inclined to attribute the very essence of evil to non-conformists. The character of moral pride is perfectly described in the words of St. Paul: "For I bear

450

them record that they have the zeal of God, but not according to knowledge. For they, being ignorant of God's righteousness and going about to establish their own righteousness, have not submitted themselves unto the righteousness of God" (Romans 10:2-3). Moral pride is the pretension of finite man that his highly conditioned virtue is the final righteousness and that his very relative moral standards are absolute. Moral pride thus makes virtue the very vehicle of sin, a fact which explains why the New Testament is so critical of the righteous in comparison with "publicans and sinners." This note in the Bible distinguishes Biblical moral theory from all simple moralism, including Christian moralism. It is the meaning of Jesus' struggle with the pharisees, of St. Paul's insistence that man is saved "not by works lest any man should boast," in fact of the whole Pauline polemic against the "righteousness of works"; and it is the primary issue in the Protestant Reformation. Luther rightly insisted that the unwillingness of the sinner to be regarded as a sinner was the final form of sin.[21] The final proof that man no longer knows God is that he does not know his own sin.[22] The sinner who justifies himself does not know God as judge and does not need God as Saviour. One might add that the sin of self-righteousness is not only the final sin in the subjective sense but also in the objective sense. It involves us in the greatest guilt. It is responsible for our most serious cruelties, injustices and defamations against our fellowmen. The whole history of racial, national, religious and other social struggles is a commentary on the objective wickedness and social miseries which result from self-righteousness.

(d) The sin of moral pride, when it has conceived, brings forth spiritual pride. The ultimate sin is the religious sin of making the self-deification implied in moral pride explicit. This is done when our partial standards and relative attainments are explicitly related to the unconditioned good, and claim divine sanction. For this reason religion is not simply as is generally supposed an inherently virtuous human quest for God. It is merely a final battleground between God and man's self-esteem. In that battle even the most pious practices may be instruments of human pride. The same man may in one moment regard Christ as his judge and in the next moment seek to prove that the figure, the standards and the righteousness of Christ bear a greater similarity to his own righteousness than to that of his enemy. The worst form of class domination is religious class domination in which, as for instance in the Indian caste system, a dominant priestly class not only subjects subordinate classes to social disabilities but finally excludes them from participation in any universe of meaning. The worst form of intolerance is religious intolerance, in which the particular interests of the contestants hide behind religious absolutes.[23] The worst form of self-assertion is religious self-assertion in which under the guise of contrition before God, He is claimed as the exclusive ally of our contingent self. "What goes by the name of 'religion' in the modern world," declares a modern missionary, "is to a great extent unbridled human self-assertion in religious disguise."[24]

Christianity rightly regards itself as a religion, not so much of man's search for God, in the process of which he may make himself God; but as a religion of revelation in which a holy and loving God is revealed to man as the source and end of all finite existence against whom the self-will of man is shattered and his pride abased. But as soon as the Christian assumes that he is, by virtue of possessing this revelation, more righteous, because more contrite, than other men, he increases the sin of self-righteousness and makes the forms of a religion of contrition the tool of his pride.

Protestantism is right in insisting that Catholicism identifies the church too simply with the Kingdom of God. This identification, which allows a religious institution, involved in all the relativities of history, to claim unconditioned truth for its doctrines and unconditioned moral authority for its standards, makes it just another tool of human pride. For this reason Luther's insistence that the pope is Anti-Christ was religiously correct. A vicar of Christ on earth is bound to be, in a sense, Anti-Christ. The whole contemporary political situation yields evidence of the perils of the Catholic doctrine of the church. Everywhere the church claims to be fighting the enemies of God without realizing to what degree these enemies are merely the rebels against a corrupt feudal civilization.

But as soon as the Protestant assumes that his more prophetic statement and interpretation of the Christian gospel guarantees him a superior virtue, he is also lost in the sin of self-righteousness. The fact is that the Protestant doctrine of the priesthood of all believers may result in an individual self-deification against which Catholic doctrine has more adequate checks. The modern revival of Reformation theology may be right in regarding the simple moralism of Christian liberalism as just another form of pharisaism. But the final mystery of human sin cannot be understood if it is not recognized that the greatest teachers of this Reformation doctrine of the sinfulness of all men used it on occasion as the instrument of an arrogant will-to-power against theological oppo-

452

nents.[25] There is no final guarantee against the spiritual pride of man. Even the recognition in the sight of God that he is a sinner can be used as a vehicle of that very sin.[26] If that final mystery of the sin of pride is not recognized the meaning of the Christian gospel cannot be understood.

It must be added that it is not necessary to be explicitly religious in order to raise moral pride to explicit religious proportions. Stalin can be as explicit in making unconditioned claims as the pope; and a French revolutionist of the eighteenth century can be as cruel in his religious fervour as the "God-ordained" feudal system which he seeks to destroy. We have previously dwelt upon the fallacious hope of modern culture, that the elimination of religion might result in the elimination of religious intolerance. Religion, by whatever name, is the inevitable fruit of the spiritual stature of man; and religious intolerance and pride is the final expression of his sinfulness. A religion of revelation is grounded in the faith that God speaks to man from beyond the highest pinnacle of the human spirit; and that this voice of God will discover man's highest not only to be short of the highest but involved in the dishonesty of claiming that it is the highest.

## Notes

1. In *The Nature and Destiny of Man: A Christian Interpretation*, vol. 1, *Human Nature* (New York: Charles Scribner's Sons, 1947), pp. 186-203.
2. Again it cannot be claimed that Christian thought is absolutely consistent in regarding pride as the basic sin. Wherever the classical view of man predominates, whether in early Greek theology, or medieval or modern liberal thought, the tendency is to equate sin with sensuality. The definition of sin as pride is consistently maintained in the strain of theology generally known as Augustinian. Augustine defines sin as follows: "What could begin this evil but pride, that is the beginning of all sin? And what is pride but a perverse desire of height, in forsaking Him to whom the soul ought solely to cleave, as the beginning thereof, to make the self seem the beginning. This is when it likes itself too well. . . ." *De civ. Dei*, Book XII, Ch. 13.

   Or again: "What is pride but undue exaltation? And this is undue exaltation, when the soul abandons Him to whom it ought to cleave as its end and becomes a kind of end in itself." *De civ. Dei*, Book XIV, Ch. 13.

   Pascal's definition is: "This I is hateful. . . . In one word it has two qualities: It is essentially unjust in that it makes self the centre of everything and it is troublesome to others in that it seeks to make them subservient; for each I is the enemy and would be the tyrant of all others." Faugère, Vol. I, p. 197.

   In Luther, pride and self-love are used synonymously *(Superbia et amor sui)*. Original sin is sometimes defined as the lust of the soul in general *(Universa concupiscentia)* (Weimer edition III. 215), which expresses itself in the turning of the soul from God to the creature. Luther's definition of concupiscence is not in opposition to or sharp distinction from sin as pride. Both have their source in *caro*, which for Luther has the exact connotation of the Pauline σαρξ. It is not the "body" as symbol of man's finiteness but "flesh" as symbol of his sinfulness. Stomph defines Luther's conception as follows: "With 'self as flesh' Luther means that the sinner desires himself just as he is, though he does not see himself just as he is and does not expressly will himself as such." M. A. H. Stomph, *Die Anthropologie Martin Luthers*, p. 73.

Thomas Aquinas derives sensuality from a more basic self-love: "The proper and direct cause of sin is to be considered on the part of the adherence to a mutable good, in which respect every sinful act proceeds from inordinate desire for some temporal good. Now the fact that some one desires a temporal good inordinately is due to the fact that he loves himself inordinately." *Summa*, Part I, Third Number, Question 77, Art. 4.

Calvin consistently holds to the Pauline definition of sin given in Romans 1. Sin is pride and not ignorance: "They worship not Him but figments of their own brains instead. This pravity Paul expressly remarks: 'Professing themselves wise they became fools.' He had before said 'they became vain in their imaginations.' But lest any should exculpate them, he adds that they were deservedly blinded, because, not content with the bounds of sobriety, but arrogating themselves more than was right they wilfully darkened and even infatuated themselves with pride, vanity and perverseness. Whence it follows that their folly is inexcusable, which originates not only in a vain curiosity but in false confidence and in immoderate desire to exceed the limits of human knowledge." *Institutes*, Book I, Ch. 4.

3. Gregory of Nyssa for instance analyses anger as follows: "Thus the arising of anger in us is indeed akin to the impulses of brutes; but it grows by the alliance of thought." *On the Making of Man*, XVIII, 4.

4. This aspect of the problem of sin will be considered in Ch. 9.

5. This is a traditional distinction in Christian thought. *Cf.* Mueller, *On the Christian Doctrine of Sin*, Vol. I, p. 177.

6. *Power, A New Social Analysis*, p. 11.

7. "Every man would like to be God," declares Mr. Russell, "if it were possible; some few find it difficult to admit the impossibility." *Ibid.*, p. 11.

8. In modern international life Great Britain with its too strong a sense of security, which prevented it from taking proper measures of defense in time, and Germany with its maniacal will-to-power, are perfect symbols of the different forms which pride takes among the established and the advancing social forces. The inner stability and external security of Great Britain has been of such long duration that she may be said to have committed the sin of Babylon and declared, "I shall be no widow and I shall never know sorrow." Germany on the other hand suffered from an accentuated form of inferiority long before her defeat in the World War. Her boundless contemporary self-assertion which literally transgresses all bounds previously known in religion, culture and law is a very accentuated form of the power impulse which betrays a marked inner insecurity.

9. Is. 47:3-7. See also Rev. 18:7; Zeph. 2:15.

10. A legitimate mastery is symbolically expressed in the words of Genesis 1:26: "Let us make man in our image, after our likeness: and let them have dominion over the fish of the sea, and over the fowl of the air, and over the cattle, and over all the earth, and over every creeping thing that creepeth upon the earth."

11. Bertrand Russell makes the mistake of assuming that economic desires are never inordinate unless they are the servants of social pride and power. He writes: "The desire for commodities, when separated from power and glory, is finite, and can be fully satisfied by a modest competence. . . . When a moderate degree of comfort is assured, both individuals and communities will pursue power and glory rather than wealth: they may seek wealth as a means to power, or they may forego an increase of wealth to secure an increase of power but in the former as in the latter case the fundamental motive is not economic." *Power*, p. 12.

454

Mr. Russell rightly criticizes the too simple Marxian interpretation of the primacy of economic motives. But his own interpretation is faulty because he regards the desire for "power and glory" in purely social terms. Greed may indeed be the servant of the desire for social power, since money is one form of "power over men." But the economic motive may be inordinate even when no power over men is sought after. The typical miser seeks absolute security and not social recognition. He wants power over his fate and not over his fellowmen.

12. *The Neurotic Personality of Our Time.*
13. Bertrand Russell doubts whether fear or anxiety could be regarded as the root of the will-to-power among the great leaders of mankind. He is inclined to believe that a "hereditary position of command" is a more plausible basis for it. He would, in other words, sharply separate the pride which does not know its own weakness and the pride which compensates for a recognized weakness. He cites Queen Elizabeth as one whose will-to-power was prompted by an hereditary position rather than by fear (*op. cit.*, p. 20). Yet a modern historian makes this interesting observation upon the fears which harassed Elizabeth: "Strong as was her sense of public duty, it failed her here [in dealing with the problem of her succession]. Her egotism blinded her to the dangers to which her failure to discuss the subject was likely to expose the state. The thought that her dignities must, by the efflux of time, pass to another seems only to have suggested to her the insecurity of her own tenure of them and the coming extinction of her own authority. Such a prospect she could not nerve herself to face." J. K. Laughton in *The Cambridge Modern History*, Vol. III, p. 359.
14. From a letter to F. Mehring, quoted by Sidney Hook, *Toward an Understanding of Karl Marx*, p. 341.
15. *Ibid.*, p. 341.
16. *Cf.* Etienne Gilson, *Unity of Philosophical Experience*, p. 157.
17. Auguste Comte, *Catechism of Positive Religion*, p. 211.
18. *Ideology and Utopia*, p. 225.
19. *Cf.* Paul Levinson, *Race, Class and Party*, for striking examples of this sense of insecurity in the dominant group.
20. An interesting example of pride as defense against self-contempt is offered by an historian of the French Directory. He writes: "These profiteers were also doctrinaires and they clung to their doctrines with the greater tenacity because only thus could they escape the self-contempt which otherwise they would have felt in their secret hearts. They were under no illusion as to the life they were leading, the system of government they had established or the persons they employed to maintain it. But sunk though they were in foulness they cling to the shadow of an ideal aim. . . . They asked nothing better than to be stigmatized as sectaries, illuminati and fanatics, for in that case people would forget to call them 'rotten.' " Pierre Gaxotte, *The French Revolution*, p. 390.
21. *Superbus primo est excusator sui ac defensor, justificator,* Weimar ed. of *Works,* Vol. 3, p. 288.
22. *Nescimus, quid Deus, quid justitia, denique quid ipsum peccatum sit.* ibid., Vol. 2, p. 106.
23. One example is worth quoting, the manifesto of Philip of Spain against William of Nassau: "Philip by the grace of God, King of Castile . . . whereas William of Nassau, a foreigner in our realm once honoured and promoted by the late emperor and ourselves, has by sinister practices and arts gained over malcontents, lawless men, insolvents, innovators, and especially those whose religion was suspected, and has instigated these heretics to rebel, to destroy sacred images and churches and to profane the sacraments of God . . . with a view of exterminating by impieties our Holy Catholic faith . . . whereas the country can

have no peace with this wretched hypocrite . . . we empower all and every to seize the person and property of this William of Nassau as an enemy of the human race and hereby on the word of a king and minister of God promise any one . . . who will deliver him dead or alive . . . the sum of 25,000 crowns in gold . . . and we will pardon him of any crime if he has been guilty and give him a patent of nobility."

24. Henrik Kraemer, *The Christian Message in the Non-Christian World,* p. 212.

25. Luther's attitude toward Schwenkfeld for instance and Calvin's against Castellio and Servetus. It may not be amiss to call attention to the fact that Karl Barth engaged in theological controversy with Emil Brunner some years ago on the theological issues raised in this chapter. He feared that Brunner's pamphlet on "Nature and Grace" conceded too much to the natural goodness of men. His own answer, entitled *Nein,* is informed by a peculiar quality of personal arrogance and disrespect for the opponent.

26. "Discourses on humility are a source of pride to the vain," declares Pascal, "and of humility in the humble." *Pensées,* 377.

# H. Richard Niebuhr

*H. Richard Niebuhr (1894–1962), like his brother Rein-hold, developed during the midsection of the twentieth century a dis-tinctive theological position that re-formed the liberal tradition of the nineteenth century along lines more sensitive to the thrust both of his-torical (biblical-theological) terminology and of contemporary under-standings of social life. He received his B.D. and Ph.D. (1924) degrees at Yale Divinity School after studies at Elmhurst College and Eden The-ological Seminary. After three years as President at Elmhurst and teacher at Eden and the publication of his first major book,* The Social Sources of Denominationalism *(1929), he joined Yale's Divinity School faculty in 1931, where he remained until his death.*

*His writings addressed timely topics and issues—the nature of faith, revelation, culture, historical relativity, the character and course of American Protestantism, theological education, the church, and ethics—and combined categories common to a "liberal" commitment to social-scientific and pragmatic analysis on the one hand and a "neoorthodox" recovery of such traditional themes as divine sovereignty, human sin-fulness, and grace on the other. Yet the creativity of his retooling and dialectical handling of those familiar categories, as well as conclusions frequently "ahead of the curve" of the times, made it hard to pin a "school" label on him during his lifetime and harder still for admirers to imitate with equal success. Excerpted here is a portion from* Radical Monotheism and Western Culture.

## FAITH IN GODS AND IN GOD[1]

There is nothing distinctive or peculiar about a Protestant's interest in the ultimate theological problem. We are concerned with the questions of God's nature and existence not as Protestants or Catholics, Christians or Jews, theologians or philosophers, laymen or clergy, but simply as human beings. Yet each of us raises these problems in a specific form, each asks his question in that special way which he has not only learned from his tradition, but which has been made necessary by his own personal wrestling with the question of life's meaning. Hence we often quarrel about the answers we get to our questions without realizing that they are answers to different questions. And sometimes we quarrel about our questions, maintaining that our way of asking is the only significant way; that our problem is the only meaningful one. So the philosopher of religion may begin with a certain definition of the term "God" and then ask, "Does a being having this nature exist?" This is a perfectly legitimate question. But it is wrong to think of it as the only proper way of raising the problem. Many different definitions of the nature of God may be framed, and hence many problems of existence may be raised; and the contention about the answers may simply be contention about the social meaning of a word, a matter on which we ought to be able to come to an agreement easily were it not for the emotional and sentimental attachment we have to certain words. The question about God may be raised in a wholly different way, in the manner of the metaphysician who asks, "What is the ultimate nature of reality, or what is the first cause, what the final end, what the nature of the primal energy, what are the attributes of substance?" Here we have a different series of questions, and the relation of the answers given to them to the answers given to the question whether "God" exists is not immediately apparent. If the term "God" is used in this latter, metaphysical type of inquiry, it is not to be taken for granted that the word has the same reference, the same meaning, which it has in the former type.

It is important, first of all, to recognize that each of us raises the question about "God" in a specific way, that it is necessary for us to phrase our question as sharply as we can, to seek an answer to that particular question and to avoid the defensiveness which makes us regard our question, just because it is ours, as more important than anyone else's. We need also, of course, to avoid the feeling that our question is unimportant because others have other questions. As a Protestant theologian or as a man who seeks to understand what he believes with the aid of Protestant theology, I do not raise the question of God in the way the philosopher of religion or the metaphysician does; while I cannot maintain that my way of asking is superior to theirs, neither can I be easily convinced that my question is illegitimate, that it is not a true, human, and important question.

It appears that the different methods we employ in religious inquiry are not wholly unlike the different methods used in science. Though all scientists are interested in truth they do not raise the question about truth in the abstract, but ask specific questions, such as those which psychologists on the one hand, physicists on the other, natural scientists on the one hand, social scientists on the other, raise and attempt to answer. Each scientist, doubtless, tends to think that his question and mode of inquiry is the most important, yet he learns eventually to live in a certain democracy of science, wherein he maintains his right to seek truth in a specific way without requiring all others to abandon their specific inquiries and to join him in his search. In some such fashion I conceive Protestant theology at work. It is well aware of other inquirers in the same general field and it profits greatly by counsel and debate with them. Yet it seeks to remain true to its own particular problem and to its own method of inquiry.

How, then, does Protestantism raise the question of God and how does it seek and find its answers to its problems? How does the problem of God present itself to us who work in this living tradition? It comes to us as an eminently practical problem, a problem of human existence and destiny, of the meaning of human life in general and of the life of self and its community in particular. It does not arise for us in the speculative form of such questions as "Does God exist?" or "What is the first cause, what the ultimate substance?" Our first question is "*How is faith in God possible?*" In other words, the problem of God arises for us in its subjective rather than objective, or, better, in personal rather than impersonal form. (That we are exposed to certain great dangers in consequence—to solipsism, for instance—is evident but every inquiry involves particular dangers and the possibility of particular errors.) This seems to be the way in which the great Protestant thinkers—Luther, Calvin, Edwards, Schleiermacher, Kierkegaard—and that philosopher who is most Protestant of all philosophers, Kant—raised the question about God primarily. It is also the way in which Protestantism as a religious movement has approached the religious problem of the ordinary man. It has not sought to convince a speculative, detached mind of the existence of God, but has begun with actual moral and religious experience, with the practical reasoning of the existing person rather than with the speculative interests of a detached mind.

## 1. What Is Faith?

The point at which such Protestants begin their analysis of the problem of God is that of practical human faith in deity. Such faith may be described in various ways, but it is never correctly described when it is initially defined in terms of intellectual belief. The belief that something exists is an experience of a wholly different order from the experience of reliance on it. The faith we speak of in Protestantism and of which, it seems to us, the classic book of Christianity, the Bible, speaks, is not intellectual assent to the truth of certain propositions, but a personal, practical trusting in, reliance on, counting upon something. So we have faith in democracy not insofar as we believe that democracy exists, but insofar as we rely upon the democratic idea or spirit to maintain itself and to influence the lives of people continuously. We have faith in the people not insofar as we believe in the existence of such a reality as "the people" but insofar as we count upon the character of what we call the people to manifest itself steadfastly in the maintenance of certain values. Faith, in other words, always refers primarily to character and power rather than to existence. Existence is implied and necessarily implied; but there is no direct road from assent to the intellectual proposition that something exists to the act of confidence and reliance upon it. Faith is an active thing, a committing of self to something, an anticipation. It is directed toward something that is also active, that has power or is power. It is distinguished from belief both on its subjective side and with respect to that to which it refers. For belief as assent to the truth of propositions does not necessarily involve reliance in action on that which is believed, and it refers to propositions rather than, as faith does, to agencies and powers.

Now it is evident, when we inquire into ourselves and into our common life, that without such active faith or such reliance and confidence on power we do not and cannot live. Not only the just but also the unjust, insofar as they live, live by faith. We live by knowledge also, it is true, but not by knowledge without faith. In order to know we must always rely on something we do not know; in order to walk by sight we need to rely on what we do not see. The most evident example of that truth is to be found in science, which conducts its massive campaign against obscurity and error on the basis of a great faith in the intelligibility of things; when it does not know and finds hindrances in the path of knowledge, it asserts with stubborn faith that knowledge nevertheless is possible, that there is pattern and intelligibility in the things which are not yet intelligible. Such faith is validated in practice, yet it evermore outruns practice. Our social life, also, proceeds from moment to moment on the ground of a confidence we have in each other which is distinct from our belief in each other's existence and distinct also from our knowledge of each other's character, though such belief and such knowledge do form the background and the foreground of our faith. How much we live by faith in this area becomes apparent to us when we are deceived or betrayed by those on whom we have relied. When treaties are broken, when bankers embezzle, when marriage partners become disloyal, when friends betray, then doubt of all things invades our minds and we understand how much we have lived by reliance on our fellow men. But we also discover that without some confidence which goes beyond our knowledge we cannot exist at all since we are social persons who cannot live in isolation, and that we are ignorant persons who must in all their living go far beyond their knowledge of each other if they would live at all.

When we inquire into this element of faith or confidence in our life as human beings we become aware of one aspect of it which may above all else be called religious, because it is related to our existence as worshiping beings, even as our faith in the intelligibility of nature is related to our existence as knowing beings and our confidence in each other is related to our moral life. This is the faith that life is worth living, or better, the reliance on certain centers of value as able to bestow significance and worth on our existence. It is a curious and inescapable fact about our lives, of which I think we all become aware at some time or another, that we cannot live without a cause, without some object of devotion, some center of worth, something on which we rely for our meaning. In this sense all men have faith because they are men and cannot help themselves, just as they must and do have some knowledge of their world, though their knowledge be erroneous.

The universality of such religious faith is obscured for us. For one thing, we tend in highly institutionalized societies, such as our own, to confuse the reality of human processes with their institutional organization and expression. So we have a tendency to think of schools, laboratories, books, and teachers when we speak of education. Doubtless this institutional education is very important but we need again and again to be made aware of the fact that the actual process of conditioning human minds, of equipping them with the instruments of words and ideas, of giving them an orientation in the world, of transmitting a tradition and developing latent possibilities, goes far beyond the schools and can go on even without the aid of official education. The political process, also, whereby men are governed and govern each other, whereby power is balanced against power, goes on in our community even when the official agencies of politics, the institutionalized forms, are not present. It is so with religion and religious faith and worship. We tend to confuse these with the official organizations and habits, with observance of special rites, with the functioning of a special leadership, and with the expression of a specific faith. But religion is a much more various thing. And it is inescapable as institutions of religion are not. As the faith that life is worth living, as the reference of life to a source of meaning and value, as the practice of adoration and worship, it is common to all men. For no man lives without living for some purpose, for the glorification of some god, for the advancement of some cause. If we do not wish to call this faith religion, there is no need to contend about the word. Let us say then that our problem is the problem of faith rather than of religion.

Now to have faith and to have a god is one and the same thing, as it is one and the same thing to have knowledge and an object of knowledge. When we believe that life is worth living by the same act we refer to some being which makes our life worth living. We never merely believe that life is worth living, but always think of it as made worth living by something on which we rely. And this being, whatever it be, is properly termed our god.

## 2. Who Is God?

We arrive, then, at the problem of deity by setting out from the universal human experience of faith, of reliance or trust in something. Luther expressed this idea long ago when he asked, "What does it mean to have a god, or what is God?" and answered his question by saying, "Trust and faith of the heart alone make both God and idol. . . . For the two, faith and God, hold close together. Whatever then thy heart clings to . . . and relies upon, that is properly thy God."

Now if this be true, that the word "god" means the object of human faith in life's worthwhileness, it is evident that men have many gods, that our natural religion is polytheistic. (It is also evident that there can be no such thing as an actual atheist though there may be many who profess atheism.) Whatever be our relation to the official monotheism of our religious institutions, the private faith by which we live is likely to be a multifarious thing with many objects of devotion and worship. The most common object of devotion on which we depend for our meaning and value is the self. We tend in human life to a kind of religious Narcissism whereby we make ourselves the most admired of all beings and seek to interpret the meaning of all experiences by reference to their meaning for the central self. The self becomes the center of value and at the same time the being which is to guarantee its own life against meaninglessness, worthlessness, and the threat of frustration.

But this self is never an adequate god for a self. We are forced to recognize that many things bring satisfaction into our lives from the outside, as it were, and we are so interdependent on all the beings about us that we inevitably admire, adore, and look to others as sources of value and meaning to ourselves. Hence we live not only for our own sakes but for the sake of other persons. It is not a figure of speech but a truth that mothers make gods out of their sons and daughters, that the home is the god of all men to a certain extent, since they live for the sake of that home, labor for it and adore it in many an hour of private devotion. One of the most powerful gods of all times, of primitive, as of civilized periods, is sex which is represented by many symbols, for the sake of which, and for the enjoyment of which men live. Beyond the dark powers, the Chthonian deities of the physical life of man, there are our Olympian gods—our country, our ideologies, our democracies, civilizations, churches, our art which we practice for art's sake, our truth which we pursue for truth's sake, our moral values, our ideas and the social forces which we personalize, adore, and on which we depend for deliverance from sheer nothingness and the utter inconsequence of existence.

One does not need to draw too sharp a line between personal and institutional religion at this point, as though personal religion were by and large polytheistic while institutional religion is monotheistic. It would be difficult to make out a strong case for the actual montheism of institutional faith. For instance, one of the beings on which institutionalized faith relies for deliverance from meaninglessness is religion itself.

We note that these centers of value, these objects of adoration, have many different forms of existence. Some are visible and tangible objects of whose reality our senses give us assurance. Some are essences, ideas, concepts, or images which are accessible only to abstract thought, but which exercise a certain compulsion over the mind. Some are movements known only by a kind of empathy or by an intuition that outruns sense; some have the peculiar and hard-to-define reality of selves or persons. But in some sense they all exist.

Yet this is true—and this constitutes the tragedy of our religious life— that none of these values or centers of value exists universally, or can be object of a universal faith. None of them can guarantee meaning to our life in the world save for a time. They are all finite in time as in space and make finite claims upon us. Hence we become aware of two characteristics of our faith and its gods: that we are divided within ourselves and socially by our religion, and that our gods are unable to save us from the ultimate frustration of meaningless existence.

Sometimes we speak of our internal division as though it were caused by the incompleteness of reason's domination over the more primitive desires which are rooted in our physical constitution. But then we realize that we do not desire as primitives or as animals do, but with a passion that indicates how great an investment we have made in the objects of desire. We note also that the life of reason is not without its desire and devotion. We become aware of the truth that our internal divisions are due to a diversity of religious attachments. We look to the objects of the mind for meaning, but we cannot make our physical existence meaningful by our attention and devotion to truth. Our inner conflicts seem due to the fact that we have many sources of value, and that these cannot all be served. Our social conflicts also always have religious character. We cannot and do not fight our wars simply for the sake of maintaining our physical existence. We always appeal to values for the sake of which we live and without which we think that life would not be worth living. We battle for America and England and Germany, which give worth to our lives, and not simply for ourselves. We fight for liberty or solidarity, for equality or for order, for fraternity in a large or in a narrow sense. But none of these gods is universal, and therefore devotion to one always implies exclusion of another. So the gods are divisive socially as well as within the person.

In this situation we dream of integration, of a great pantheon in which all the gods will be duly served, each in its proper sphere. So we speak sometimes of establishing a new synthesis of civilization, of the integration of personality, of the recognition of a great hierarchy of values. But the synthesis is never achieved, the integration never worked out. For each god in turn requires a certain absolute devotion and the denial of the claims of the other gods. So long as country seems an absolute source of value to us, so long devotion to one country will make us deny the claims of every other. So long as we pursue art for art's sake, so long art will be the enemy of morality and of truth. The best we can achieve in this realm is a sort of compromise among many absolute claims. We remain beings, therefore, with many faiths held in succession. We practice a kind of successive polygamy, being married now to this and now to that object of devotion.

The tragedy of our religious life is not only that it divides us within ourselves and from each other. There is a greater tragedy—the twilight of the gods. None of these beings on which we rely to give content and meaning to our lives is able to supply continuous meaning and value. The causes for which we live all die. The great social movements pass and are supplanted by others. The ideals we fashion are revealed by time to be relative. The empires and cities to which we are devoted all decay. At the end nothing is left to defend us against the void of meaninglessness. We try to evade this knowledge, but it is ever in the background of our minds. The apocalyptic vision of the end of all things assails us, whether we see that end as the prophets of the pre-Christian era did or as the pessimists of our time do. We know that "on us and all our race the slow, sure doom falls pitiless and dark." All our causes, all our ideas, all the beings on which we relied to save us from worthlessness are doomed to pass.

### 3. *God*

What is it that is responsible for this passing, that dooms our human faith to frustration? We may call it the nature of things, we may call it fate, we may call it reality. But by whatever name we call it, this law of things, this reality, this way things are, is something with which we all must reckon. We may not be able to give a name to it, calling it only the "void" out of which everything comes and to which everything returns, though that is also a name. But it is there—the last shadowy and vague reality, the secret of existence by virtue of which things come into being, are what they are, and pass away. Against it there is no defense. This reality, this nature of things, abides when all else passes. It is the source of all things and the end of all. It surrounds our life as the great abyss into which all things plunge and as the great source whence they all come. What it is we do not know save that it is and that it is the supreme reality with which we must reckon.

Now a strange thing has happened in our history and in our personal life; our faith has been attached to that great void, to that enemy of all our causes, to that opponent of all our gods. The strange thing has happened that we have been enabled to say of this reality, this last power in which we live and move and have our being, "Though it slay us yet will we trust it." We have been allowed to attach our confidence to it, and put our reliance in it which is the one reality beyond all the many, which is the last power, the infinite source of all particular beings as well as their end. And insofar as our faith, our reliance for meaning and worth, has been attached to this source and enemy of all our gods, we have been enabled to call this reality God.

Let us raise three questions about this fact that faith has become attached to the void and to the enemy which surrounds our life. The first one is, What does it mean to attach faith to this power? The second,

How does such faith come about? And the third, What are the consequences of such faith?

First, to have faith in this reality means that, having been driven away from our reliance on all the lesser causes, we have learned to conceive of and to rely upon this last power, this nature of things, as itself the greatest of all causes, the undefeatable cause. We have learned to say, "For this cause was I born and therefore I came into the world that I might make glorious the name and exhibit the power of this last cause." And we have been enabled to say it with satisfaction, with love and hope and confidence; for to have faith in something as able to give value to our lives is to love it. Without such love there is no faith. And to have faith is also to live in hope, in constant anticipation of new unfoldings of worth and meaning.

To attach faith, hope, and love to this last being, this source of all things and this slayer of all, is to have confidence which is not subject to time, for this is the eternal reality, this is the last power. It is to have a love for that which is not exclusive but inclusive, since this reality, this great X, is the source of all things and the end of all. It is, therefore, to be put into the position of those who can love all things in him or in it, and who deny all things in it. "It is a consoling idea," wrote Kierkegaard, "that before God we are always in the wrong." All the relative judgments of worth are equalized in the presence of this One who loves all and hates all, but whose love like whose hatred is without emotion, without favoritism. To have hope of this One is to have hope that is eternal. This being cannot pass away. And to hope for the manifestations of his judgments and his love is to hope to eternity.

When we conceive faith in this one, our foundations have indeed been laid in despair, not in the grandiloquent despair of *A Free Man's Worship*, but in the sober despair which has faced the reality of the death of all things and the endlessness of the creative process.

Another way of describing this faith is one which I have learned from Professor Whitehead's little book on religion. Religion, he says, "is transition from God the void to God the enemy, and from God the enemy to God the companion."[2] When we say that we conceive faith in the great void and the great enemy we mean that we have learned to count on it as friend. We have learned to rely on it as a cause to which we may devote our lives, as that which will make all our lives and the lives of all things valuable even though it bring them to death.

Second, how is such a faith possible? How does it happen that this void, this enemy, is recognized as friend, that faith attaches itself to the last power, to the great hidden mystery, and calls it God, that man can lose himself in adoration of this being, saying with the Psalmist, "Whom have I in heaven but thee? and there is none upon earth that I desire beside thee?" or with Job, "Though he slay me, yet will I trust in him"?

It has happened in our human history and it does happen in personal histories. Men may dispute endlessly about the worth of that happening, though when they do they always do so on the basis of another faith than faith in this God. But there can be no doubt of the fact that it has happened and that it does happen.

How does it happen to the individual? It does not happen without the struggle of his reason. For by reason he discovers the inadequacy of all his gods and is driven to despair in life's meaning. It does not happen without experience, without the experience of frustration, of noting the death of all things, the experience of the internal division in which his various worship involves him, the experience of the great social catastrophes which show the weakness of the great causes and beings in which he trusted as saviors of life. It does not happen without the operation of something we must call spiritual, something which is like the intuition of the thinker, like the creative insight of the artist, like the flash of recognition of truth. All these elements are involved. Furthermore, this transfer of faith to the ultimate being does not take place without moral struggle, without recognition of the unworthiness both of our transgressions and our obediences to our moral laws.

But for most men another element is involved—the concrete meeting with other men who have received this faith, and the concrete meeting with Jesus Christ. There may be other ways, but this is the usual way for us, that we confront in the event of Jesus Christ the presence of that last power which brings to apparent nothingness the life of the most loyal man. Here we confront the slayer, and here we become aware that this slayer is the life-giver. He does not put to shame those who trust in him. In the presence of Jesus Christ we most often conceive, or are given that faith. We may try to understand how we might have received the faith without Jesus Christ; but the fact remains that when this faith was given Jesus Christ was there.

So it is in history. This faith in the One has had its occasional manifestations elsewhere. But it has happened in history that it has been conceived and received where a people who regarded themselves as chosen suffered the most cruel fate, and where a Son of man who was obedient to death actually suffered death. Here the great reconciliation with the

467

divine enemy has occurred. And since it has occurred, there is no way of getting rid of it. It is in our human history.

We do not say that this faith in the last power is something men ought to have. We say only this, that it is the end of the road of faith, that it is unassailable, and that when men receive it they receive a great gift. We say that it is given, that it has been given, that it is being given, and that when it is received very profound consequences follow.

Third, the consequences of faith in the one, final, and only God are not automatic, for faith involves the whole person, and the gift of faith is not a possession which we can hold in our power. It is something that lives in man and by which man lives. It is not a possession which can be held fast in the form of a creed. It is a basis for all thinking, but though it may he expressed in the form of a thought, it is not itself a thought; it is the reliance of a person on a person. Beginning with that faith life is involved intellectually and morally in a continuous revolution.

This faith opens the way to knowledge. It removes the taboos which surround our intellectual life, making some subjects too holy to be inquired into and some too dangerous for us to venture into. Yet it grants reverence to the mind for which now no being is too low to be worthy of a loving curiosity. All knowledge becomes reverent and all being is open to inquiry. So long as we try to maintain faith in the gods, we fear to examine them too closely lest their relativity in goodness and in power become evident, as when Bible worshipers fear Biblical criticism, or democracy worshipers fear objective examination of democracy. But when man's faith is attached to the One, all relative beings may be received at his hands for nurture and for understanding. Understanding is not automatically given with faith; faith makes possible and demands the labor of the intellect that it may understand.

The moral consequences of this faith is that it makes relative all those values which polytheism makes absolute, and so puts an end to the strife of the gods. But it does not relativize them as self-love does. A new sacredness attaches to the relative goods. Whatever is, is now known to be good, to have value, though its value be still hidden to us. The moral consequences of faith in God is the universal love of all being in him. It is not an automatic consequence. Faith is never so complete that it is not accompanied by self-defensiveness. But this is its requirement: that all beings, not only our friends but also our enemies, not only men but also animals and the inanimate, be met with reverence, for all are friends in the friendship of the one to whom we are reconciled in faith.

So faith in God involves us in a permanent revolution of the mind and of the heart, a continuous life which opens out infinitely into ever new possibilities. It does not, therefore, afford grounds for boasting but only for simple thankfulness. It is a gift of God.

### Notes

1. In *Radical Monotheism and Western Culture: With Supplementary Essays* (Louisville: Westminster/John Knox Press, 1960), pp. 114-26. Essay originally entitled "The Nature and Existence of God," from *Motive,* December 1943.
2. A. N. Whitehead, *Religion in the Making,* 1926, pp. 16f.

# Georgia E. Harkness

$G$*eorgia E. Harkness (1891–1974), a Methodist, was the first American woman to hold a mainline seminary position in the area of theology. A graduate of Cornell and Boston University, Harkness found herself attracted to the activism of the social gospel and, during her doctoral work, to the personalism of her teachers Albert Knudson and Edgar Brightman. Later she came to emphasize less the philosophical elements of religious understanding and shifted more toward theological themes, like redemption, sin, holiness, justice, and mission. Most of her written work emerged during the years she taught at Garrett Biblical Institute (1939–1950) and the Pacific School of Religion (1950–1961).*

*Harkness wrote theology more for the church than for the academy. She struggled in her work to narrow the gaps emerging during the twentieth century between professional theologians and lay theologians. Because of her interests in the twin concerns of human justice and human personality, most of her writing had some connection with what it means to be human in a context defined by both God's creative intentions and the realities of human sin. In this excerpt, Harkness deals with these two themes as she takes up the question of salvation, what it means and how one comes "to be saved."*

## SALVATION[1]

The word "salvation" has largely gone out of fashion in our time. This does not mean that the desire to be saved has vanished; for, apart from any religious meaning, the hope of salvation is as wide as the sweep of human desire. Every advertisement appeals to it. This new kitchen equipment will save you from drudgery, this brand of fruit juice from vitamin deficiency, this deodorant from social embarrassment and a lonely spinsterhood! Ranging all the way from "success" books to tell how to be saved from unpopularity to books on the present world situ-

470

ation, our literature is full of attempts to point the way to salvation. Why, then, are we so squeamish about it in religion?

Even among many people otherwise favorable to religion, the idea of salvation is in poor standing. This is chiefly for two reasons. First, the term is not well understood. From revival sermons of an earlier day it has come to mean a sharp separation of the saved from the damned, with the saved going to the bliss of heaven while sinners forever burn in hell. This seems so inconsistent with the God of love revealed in Christ that this idea of salvation has been widely given up, but with nothing to put in its place. In the second place, those who see a more appropriate meaning in terms of the peace, joy, and spiritual victory of the Christian are often still at a loss to know how to lay hold upon it for themselves.

We shall, therefore, attempt in this chapter first to say what Christian salvation is, and then to suggest how it may be found.

## 1. The Meaning of Salvation

In its most elementary meaning, "to be saved" means to be rescued, delivered, made safe from something we ought to be rid of. As we saw in the last chapter, the most persistent evil we need to be freed from is sin; hence, salvation from sin has always been at the center of Christian faith and life. But we need also to be delivered from frustration, inadequacy, destructive inner conflict, despair. There is no full salvation or spiritual victory unless there is a lifting of the chains, not only of sin, but of futility. The saved person feels himself "more than conqueror," through a power not his own, over the forces within and without that assail and crush the spirit.

This suggests that salvation is not merely a negative process. It is more than getting rid of something—whether sin or frustration; it is positive, joyous spiritual health. As the German word for it, *Heil*, suggests, it means health, healing, wholeness of living. We are saved *from* whatever separates us from God and our best living; we are saved *to* the kind of life in which we can work with God victoriously and zestfully to do his will.

This does not mean that we are saved to complete sinlessness or entire efficiency in our attempts to serve God. As long as we live, we are human, and both our good intentions and our accomplishments have human limits. But there is a vast difference between a life that is halting, stumbling, warped by its own selfishness, and a life that is free and strong in the power of God. It is to this fullness of life, with a new center of loyalty, a new strength, and a new sense of direction, that we are saved.

What, then, are we saved *by?* This can be said in a sentence but requires a lifetime for its understanding. We are saved by the grace of God—by the free, gracious, outpouring of God's love upon us and his forgiveness when we repent of our sin and turn to him for cleansing and strength. We do not save ourselves; it is God that saves us. But this does not mean that it costs nothing on our part. God can save us only as we meet his conditions and open our lives to receive his power.

Salvation, according to Christian faith, is for both this life and the next. Both are important. However, we shall leave the discussion of salvation in the next life to a later chapter, when we take up the belief in immortality, for it belongs in that field. Also, since salvation for the next world has often bulked so large as to obscure its meaning for this one, it may be useful to shift the emphasis. If salvation now is real, its continuance to the next life is probable; if salvation made no difference here, no amount of speculation about heaven or hell could possibly ring true.

## 2. Terms, Old and New

The meaning of salvation may become clearer if we look at some of the terms connected with it. Many of the older ones have been given up because they were so encrusted with tradition. Rather than discard them, we had better rub off the dust and see what permanent truth lies hidden in them.

First, what is a "lost soul"? To be lost means simply to be out of right relations, as a lost book is one not in its proper place on the library shelf, a lost coin is one that has fallen out of the purse where it belongs, a lost child is one that has strayed from its home and does not know the way back. In a religious sense, to be "lost" is to be out of right relations with God—separated from fellowship with him through our own indifference and self-will, cut off from our own best living because we have cut ourselves off from its sources in God. Jesus told some immortal parables that illustrate this—about a lost sheep, a lost piece of silver, a lost boy that we call the prodigal son.[2] Only as these were eagerly and lovingly sought after and restored to where they belonged were they saved. This is the basic Christian meaning of God's love that yearns always to save the lost.

But the term "lost soul" has another meaning that fits most of us. To be "lost" when confronted by any situation is to be confused, bewildered, unable to decide what to do next or which way to turn. From this kind of lostness also we need salvation. George Matheson in his hymn "Make Me a Captive, Lord," describes it perfectly:

> My heart is weak and poor
> Until it master find;
> It has no spring of action sure—
> It varies with the wind.

Only as we let God direct and master us can we find freedom to go forward with assurance. As was suggested earlier, salvation from the lostness of inadequacy and futility must accompany salvation from sin if life is to be made whole.

Next, what do we mean by "conversion"? "To be converted," as its derivation suggests, means to "turn around," to turn about from a self-centered to a God-centered life. This turning may be a very gradual process, involving many decisions and growth by almost imperceptible stages. Or the turning may be sudden, dramatic, and overwhelming in emotional power. Though the term "evangelism" has sometimes been used for conversion of the second type only, it ought not to be thus limited. A person is as truly converted if the process takes place with relatively little emotional fireworks and over a considerable period as he is if it happens all at once. In both types there is preparation, for sudden conversion is the rapid crystallization of factors previously imbedded in the subconscious mind—as Paul on the Damascus road had been "kicking against the pricks" ever since he witnessed the stoning of Stephen. In both types there is decision, for there is no real conversion until one decides for himself to try to obey God and to open his life to the power of God. When this happens and one resolves earnestly by the help of God to live henceforth, not for oneself alone, but for God and for other people, a change takes place that is the greatest thing that can happen to any soul.[3]

"Regeneration" is another word that is no longer heard very often. It means to be "born again," to come to new life through the power of God in Christ. This may seem to us too mysterious to grasp, as it did to Nicodemus, who came to Jesus by night. When Jesus said to him, "Except one be born anew, he cannot see the kingdom of God," Nicodemus—literalist like ourselves—cried out, "How can a man be born when he is old?"[4] Yet through the centuries millions of Christians have demonstrated by their lives that it is possible in maturity to "come alive," and in the midst of a humdrum existence to find a fresh vitality born of the Spirit of God, which makes life meaningful and good.

"Redemption" is another great word for Christian salvation, the meaning of which was explained in chapter five. As we saw, this was taken in the Bible originally from the metaphor of redeeming, or buying

473

back, a slave in the market place. However, it means to us now the whole great process of the salvation of the world through the yearning, merciful love of God—a process in which he calls us to work with him in love, as followers of Christ, to bring individuals and nations to his way. Redemption is God's supreme gift. As the prayer of general thanksgiving in *The Book of Common Prayer* puts it: "We bless thee for our creation, preservation, and all the blessings of this life; but above all, for thine inestimable love in the redemption of the world by our Lord Jesus Christ."

"Justification" has its setting in a court of law. We are "justified by faith," as Paul put it, to "have peace with God through our Lord Jesus Christ"[5] when in repentance and humble trust we accept the mercy and forgiveness of God and know that he holds nothing against us in spite of our sin. Justification is meaningless apart from God's condemnation of sin; but if God's judgment is as real as both the Bible and the events of history show, justification is the other side of it. Knowing ourselves to be sinners, we find our peace in spite of guilt, not by evasion or by frantically doing good works, but by repentance. Seeing our sin as evil as it is and knowing that the God whose infinite mercy we see in Christ does not charge it up against us, we can go forward. A better analogy than the law court by which to understand this is the human parent who suffers in love because a child has done wrong, yet in love forgives and goes on trusting.

Forgiveness does, and does not, cancel sin. Every sin leaves its scars of evil consequences, and forgiveness does not change these effects. They are there to spur us on to make whatever amends we can. But, no longer weighed down with a sense of guilt, with a new vitality born of gratitude the forgiven sinner can make a fresh start toward the doing of God's will.

"Sanctification" does not mean, as is often supposed, that one ever gets to the point where he no longer sins. To assert such a view is very dangerous, for it leads to self-righteousness and a false sense of moral security. Even the best Christians must fight moral battles which they sometimes lose and must repeatedly ask for forgiveness. The term may well be avoided for this reason. But if one wants to use it, it should mean the dedication of oneself to God and the hallowing of all life through the power of the Holy Spirit. To the mature Christian, as he seeks to live and work in fellowship with God, there is a sanctity and holiness about everything he does which seems not to come from his own effort but to be the gift of God. If he has a conscience sensitive to God's demands to keep him humble, such a sense of the abiding presence of God is a source of great joy and strength.

We have been looking at some old terms; it may be best to take a glance at some more modern ones. "Integration of personality" means wholeness of personality—the bringing together of life's disjointed fragments into a unity. In this unity the conflicts that were tearing one's life apart and keeping it weak and ineffective are replaced by inner security and strength. This is probably what Jesus did in his miracles of healing, particularly those in which he cast out demons, and he describes it perfectly in the words he spoke repeatedly, "Thy faith hath made thee whole." It is a tragedy of our time that psychologists and educators who have so much to say about the integration of personality have often so small a place for life's greatest integrating force—Christian faith.

"Commitment" and "dedication" are fairly common terms to indicate the giving of oneself to a new center of loyalty. They ought not to be regarded as in contrast with conversion, but as a part of it. It is immaterial whether one speaks of dedication to God or to Christ, provided he means by it the commitment of life to the God revealed and brought to us in Christ.

"Religious awakening" implies that one has been asleep and is now awake to the beauty and power of the Christian gospel. "Orientation," like "conversion," means that a life askew and off center needs to he turned around and set right.

All of these terms, requiring less definition than the older ones, have their place. It is better to use them than to confuse or close people's minds by words against which emotional barriers have been set up. Yet it is to be doubted whether any one of these terms has the depth of meaning to be found in those that have come from the Bible and have been used through the centuries. There is danger, also, that in using the more modern terms the emphasis may be put too much on what we do and not enough on what God does. Yet in our time, as in Paul's, we must be "all things to all men" if we would by all means save some.

## 3. What Must We Do to Be Saved?

There is no more searching question that anyone can ask than the one which the Philippian jailer put to Paul, "What must I do to be saved?" Paul's answer, "Believe on the Lord Jesus Christ," is bedrock for Christian faith and experience, and in chapter five we tried to discover something as to what this means. But even when one knows that he ought to be a follower of Christ and sees that through Christ others find a power

475

that transforms their living, the question still remains as to how to enter into this experience.

The purpose of this section is to try to trace the steps one must take who would appropriate for himself the power and grace of God channeled to us through Christ. There is no exact technique for entering into this new fellowship with God any more than there is for falling in love with another human person. Yet there are some things required of us—some things to do and some not to do. Understanding the process will not cause it to happen in us, but misunderstanding may block the way.

The first step is awareness of need. In the story of the prodigal son it was when the boy saw that he lacked something and said, "I will arise and go to my Father," that his redemption began. As long as a person thinks that he is good enough or has enough, not even God himself can break down this wall of indifference. We must open the door before God can help us. "Behold, I stand at the door and knock." This requirement has been vividly portrayed in Holman Hunt's great picture of Christ knocking at a door which can be opened only from the inside.

The awareness of need which is essential to the finding of God comes most often, if not always, through a human agency. This is true in two senses. God to save us came to earth in the human form of Jesus, and the more we live with the personality of Jesus as we find the record in the Bible, the more we see our own littleness and are challenged to want to be something better. This is why there is no substitute for acquaintance with Jesus through the New Testament. But in a second sense God uses human agencies, as we see what Christ means in the lives and words of his followers, past and present. The stimulus that awakens us to our own need may be a book, a sermon, a service of worship and prayer, a conversation or discussion, the lift that comes from a group of Christians united in a common task, the story of Christian courage and sacrifice under testing, or, most potent of all, the influence of the daily living and personal friendship of a great Christian. In short, the thing that wakes us up can be anything that shows the difference Christ makes in the lives of persons who place him at the center of their faith and loyalty.

This awareness of need can come at any time, during the smoothest existence or the most stormy. We are especially open to this discovery when something occurs to upset our familiar pattern of life—a great new responsibility, such as marriage, parenthood, or a new vocation; an emergency, such as failure, illness, separation by physical absence or death from someone that is loved. Even our hardest experiences and darkest hours, as many found during the strains of war, can be avenues to the discovery of our own need and the availability of God's limitless power.

The second step, growing out of the first without clear separation, is *surrender of will*. The term "surrender" sounds strange to modern ears, for it reflects a mood at variance with the prevailing mental climate. We want to be masters of our fate and captains of our souls—that is, if we still believe there is a soul of which to be captain. The idea of surrendering to anybody or anything suggests servility, and we do not want to be servile.

Until we can shake ourselves out of this mood, no very widespread revival of religion is likely to take place. What makes religion *religion* is willingness to worship, to bow in humility before an utterly holy deity, and to subordinate self to the service of that deity. As long as religion is used as a means to an end—even though a very worthy end—it eludes us. "Using" religion means trying to make God do what men want done, which is not religion at all, but magic. "Being religious" means subjecting man's will to the will of God.

How to know what God wills is less simple than is sometimes supposed. We cannot safely trust tradition or intuition by itself. The will of God is a matter to be discerned in the light of our most sensitive insights and most reasoned judgments. Prayer is needed; so is weighing of the probable consequences of any proposed act. Neither is a substitute for the other, and the attempt to make one do duty for the other is neither good sense nor good religion.

To decide what to do is important; to be willing to do it is indispensable. Without such surrender of will there can be no conversion, no turning from a self-centered to a God-centered life. With it self-will does not wholly disappear, but the self is enlarged and enriched by the inclusion of many interests hitherto rejected. Persons and causes to be served move from the outer circle to the center of attention; and with these and God in the center, life gains a new stability and strength.

This richness and stability are acquired only at the cost of repentance. God "delivers us from evil," but deliverance and forgiveness come only when we have done all that we can to open the way. Repentance means facing our sins squarely, without morbidness and without self-delusion. It means confession of our sins to God, and often also to trusted human persons, but it does not mean a public advertising of them. It means earnest self-searching, sincere contrition, and so far as possible making amends for the harm one has done to others. Whoever is unwilling to pay this price can get no farther.

477

The third step has already been suggested. This is *deliverance*. No magical perfection ensues, but an increase in poise and power. There is a paradoxical freedom here, for by the surrender of self-will one gains a higher freedom. This third step, like all the others, is one in which openness of spirit must be joined with active effort. God delivers, but delivers only those who will accept what is offered. God saves the person who is "lost," but only him who is willing to find the way.

Such deliverance means far more than a comfortable emotional glow. When it is only this, it soon cools and disappears. It means reorganization of life from the inside out, and from the bottom up. Failure to recognize this fact has led to the gruesome practice of counting the number of souls saved in meetings, and it has helped to fill church rosters with people whom the rest of the world call hypocrites.

Acceptance of deliverance means earnest, persistent grappling with the habitual sins that hold us in their grip—not always flagrant offenses against the moral code, but the more insidious and therefore more dangerous sins of a bad temper, faultfinding, jealousy, arrogance, irresponsibility, laziness, self-delusion, petty-mindedness. To overcome these is both to take up one's cross daily and to rejoice thankfully in victory.

The fourth step, therefore, is *spiritual growth*. This does not mean either a sudden or a final sinlessness. It does mean in the dedicated Christian the progressive achievement of moral victory and the abundant life. It means increasing spiritual insight and increasing moral earnestness, fed by the life of worship and empowered by, as well as for, the doing of constructive tasks of human service. Without such expression in life there is no religious vitality.

The person who achieves most fully the experience which has been described will be the last to boast of being a Christian. But others will call him this and will see in him a living witness to the power of Christ, who is "the author and perfecter of our faith."

Putting from us spiritual arrogance and indifference, we must sense our need, surrender our wills in repentance, accept God's deliverance, and live the life of victory over sin and chaos. There need be nothing dramatic or spectacular about this. But it does not happen by accident. These steps suggest the route which the great religious spirits have always followed. These are the steps which need to be taken today if we are to find power in God to grapple with the problems of our time.

## Notes

1. In *Understanding the Christian Faith* (New York and Nashville: Abingdon-Cokesbury Press, 1947), pp. 106-20.
2. Luke 15.
3. The question is often raised as to whether religious education should eliminate the need for conversion. It can make the sudden type unnecessary, but, even with the best of Christian nurture, personal decision is still necessary.
4. John 3.
5. Romans 5:1.

# Martin Luther King, Jr.

*Martin Luther King, Jr., (1929–1968) grew up surrounded by the strong Baptist ministerial tradition provided by two strong Baptist preachers in his family, his father Martin Luther King, Sr., and his mother's father, Alfred Daniel Williams. The only American theologian or religious leader to have a national holiday named after him, King, through the articulate witness of both his passionate voice and his powerful life, taught a nation filled with reluctant students the meaning of racial justice. Educated at Morehouse, Crozer Theological Seminary, and Boston University School of Theology, King combined his doctoral interest in personalism with the black church's emphasis on the human worth of every person in the eyes of God. His involvement with the civil rights movement caused him to theologize about the relationship between God's justice and the racial struggles of the African American people.*

*In 1958, The Christian Century, one of mainline Protestantism's most important voices during the tumultuous 1960s, announced King's appointment as an editor-at-large. Within those pages, the first nationally published version of King's "Letter From Birmingham Jail" appeared. The first of the selections found here (published in February 1957) represents King's initial written contribution to the* Century, *coming nearly a year and a half before his formal affiliation with the magazine. In it, he addressed the theological foundations for his nonviolent approach to racial justice. The second selection appeared in the* Century's *pages in April 1960. Somewhat autobiographical, this second essay reflects upon King's theological journey during the 1950s, particularly his encounters with both theological liberalism and neoorthodoxy. A growing interest in existentialism, the social gospel movement, and Gandhi's philosophy of nonviolence combined with the practical lessons learned in Montgomery to produce a synthesis of all these streams. King's resultant theology tended to emphasize three key themes: justice, love, and hope.*

# Nonviolence and Racial Justice[1]

It is commonly observed that the crisis in race relations dominates the arena of American life. This crisis has been precipitated by two factors: the determined resistance of reactionary elements in the south to the Supreme Court's momentous decision outlawing segregation in the public schools, and the radical change in the Negro's evaluation of himself. While southern legislative halls ring with open defiance through "interposition" and "nullification," while a modern version of the Ku Klux Klan has arisen in the form of "respectable" white citizens' councils, a revolutionary change has taken place in the Negro's conception of his own nature and destiny. Once he thought of himself as an inferior and patiently accepted injustice and exploitation. Those days are gone.

The first Negroes landed on the shores of this nation in 1619, one year ahead of the Pilgrim Fathers. They were brought here from Africa and, unlike the Pilgrims, they were brought against their will, as slaves. Throughout the era of slavery the Negro was treated in inhuman fashion. He was considered a thing to be used, not a person to be respected. He was merely a depersonalized cog in a vast plantation machine. The famous Dred Scott decision of 1857 well illustrates his status during slavery. In this decision the Supreme Court of the United States said, in substance, that the Negro is not a citizen of the United States; he is merely property subject to the dictates of his owner.

After his emancipation in 1863, the Negro still confronted oppression and inequality. It is true that for a time, while the army of occupation remained in the south and Reconstruction ruled, he had a brief period of eminence and political power. But he was quickly overwhelmed by the white majority. Then in 1896, through the Plessy v. Ferguson decision, a new kind of slavery came into being. In this decision the Supreme Court of the nation established the doctrine of "separate but equal" as the law of the land. Very soon it was discovered that the concrete result of this doctrine was strict enforcement of the "separate," without the slightest intention to abide by the "equal." So the Plessy doctrine ended up plunging the Negro into the abyss of exploitation where he experienced the bleakness of nagging injustice.

## A Peace That Was No Peace

Living under these conditions, many Negroes lost faith in themselves. They came to feel that perhaps they were less than human. So long as the Negro maintained this subservient attitude and accepted the "place"

481

assigned him, a sort of racial peace existed. But it was an uneasy peace in which the Negro was forced patiently to submit to insult, injustice and exploitation. It was a negative peace. True peace is not merely the absence of some negative force—tension, confusion or war; it is the presence of some positive force—justice, good will and brotherhood.

Then circumstances made it necessary for the Negro to travel more. From the rural plantation he migrated to the urban industrial community. His economic life began gradually to rise, his crippling illiteracy gradually to decline. A myriad of factors came together to cause the Negro to take a new look at himself. Individually and as a group, he began to re-evaluate himself. And so he came to feel that he was somebody. His religion revealed to him that God loves all his children and that the important thing about a man is "not his specificity but his fundamentum," not the texture of his hair or the color of his skin but the quality of his soul.

This new self-respect and sense of dignity on the part of the Negro undermined the south's negative peace, since the white man refused to accept the change. The tension we are witnessing in race relations today can be explained in part by this revolutionary change in the Negro's evaluation of himself and his determination to struggle and sacrifice until the walls of segregation have been finally crushed by the battering rams of justice.

## Quest for Freedom Everywhere

The determination of Negro Americans to win freedom from every form of oppression springs from the same profound longing for freedom that motivates oppressed peoples all over the world. The rhythmic beat of deep discontent in Africa and Asia is at bottom a quest for freedom and human dignity on the part of people who have long been victims of colonialism. The struggle for freedom on the part of oppressed people in general and of the American Negro in particular has developed slowly and is not going to end suddenly. Privileged groups rarely give up their privileges without strong resistance. But when oppressed people rise up against oppression there is no stopping point short of full freedom. Realism compels us to admit that the struggle will continue until freedom is a reality for all the oppressed peoples of the world.

Hence the basic question which confronts the world's oppressed is: How is the struggle against the forces of injustice to be waged? There are two possible answers. One is resort to the all too prevalent method of physical violence and corroding hatred. The danger of this method is its futility. Violence solves no social problems; it merely creates new and more complicated ones. Through the vistas of time a voice still cries to every potential Peter, "Put up your sword!" The shores of history are white with the bleached bones of nations and communities that failed to follow this command. If the American Negro and other victims of oppression succumb to the temptation of using violence in the struggle for justice, unborn generations will live in a desolate night of bitterness, and their chief legacy will be an endless reign of chaos.

### Alternative to Violence

The alternative to violence is nonviolent resistance. This method was made famous in our generation by Mohandas K. Gandhi, who used it to free India from the domination of the British empire. Five points can be made concerning nonviolence as a method in bringing about better racial conditions.

First, this is not a method for cowards; it *does* resist. The nonviolent resister is just as strongly opposed to the evil against which he protests as is the person who uses violence. His method is passive or nonaggressive in the sense that he is not physically aggressive toward his opponent. But his mind and emotions are always active, constantly seeking to persuade the opponent that he is mistaken. This method is passive physically but strongly active spiritually; it is nonaggressive physically but dynamically aggressive spiritually.

A second point is that nonviolent resistance does not seek to defeat or humiliate the opponent, but to win his friendship and understanding. The nonviolent resister must often express his protest through noncooperation or boycotts, but he realizes that noncooperation and boycotts are not ends themselves; they are merely means to awaken a sense of moral shame in the opponent. The end is redemption and reconciliation. The aftermath of nonviolence is the creation of the beloved community, while the aftermath of violence is tragic bitterness.

A third characteristic of this method is that the attack is directed against forces of evil rather than against persons who are caught in those forces. It is evil we are seeking to defeat, not the persons victimized by evil. Those of us who struggle against racial injustice must come to see that the basic tension is not between races. As I like to say to the people in Montgomery, Alabama: "The tension in this city is not between white people and Negro people. The tension is at bottom between justice and injustice, between the forces of light and the forces of darkness. And if there is a victory it will be a victory not merely for 50,000 Negroes, but a victory for justice and the forces of light. We are out to defeat injustice and not white persons who may happen to be unjust."

A fourth point that must be brought out concerning nonviolent resistance is that it avoids not only external physical violence but also internal violence of spirit. At the center of nonviolence stands the principle of love. In struggling for human dignity the oppressed people of the world must not allow themselves to become bitter or indulge in hate campaigns. To retaliate with hate and bitterness would do nothing but intensify the hate in the world. Along the way of life, someone must have sense enough and morality enough to cut off the chain of hate. This can be done only by projecting the ethics of love to the center of our lives.

*The Meaning of 'Love'*

In speaking of love at this point, we are not referring to some sentimental emotion. It would be nonsense to urge men to love their oppressors in an affectionate sense. "Love" in this connection means understanding good will. There are three words for love in the Greek New Testament. First, there is *eros*. In Platonic philosophy *eros* meant the yearning of the soul for the realm of the divine. It has come now to mean a sort of aesthetic or romantic love. Second, there is *philia*. It meant intimate affectionateness between friends. *Philia* denotes a sort of reciprocal love: the person loves because he is loved. When we speak of loving those who oppose us we refer to neither *eros* nor *philia*; we speak of a love which is expressed in the Greek word *agape*. *Agape* means nothing sentimental or basically affectionate; it means understanding, redeeming good will for all men, an overflowing love which seeks nothing in return. It is the love of God working in the lives of men. When we love on the *agape* level we love men not because we like them, not because their attitudes and ways appeal to us, but because God loves them. Here we rise to the position of loving the person who does the evil deed while hating the deed he does.

Finally, the method of nonviolence is based on the conviction that the universe is on the side of justice. It is this deep faith in the future that causes the nonviolent resister to accept suffering without retaliation. He knows that in his struggle for justice he has cosmic companionship. This belief that God is on the side of truth and justice comes down to us from the long tradition of our Christian faith. There is something at the very center of our faith which reminds us that Good Friday may reign for a day, but ultimately it must give way to the triumphant beat of the Easter drums. Evil may so shape events that Caesar will occupy a palace and Christ a cross, but one day that same Christ will rise up and split history into A.D. and B.C., so that even the life of Caesar must be dated by his name. So in Montgomery we can walk and never get weary, because we know that there will be a great camp meeting in the promised land of freedom and justice.

This, in brief, is the method of nonviolent resistance. It is a method that challenges all people struggling for justice and freedom. God grant that we wage the struggle with dignity and discipline. May all who suffer oppression in this world reject the self-defeating method of retaliatory violence and choose the method that seeks to redeem. Through using this method wisely and courageously we will emerge from the bleak and desolate midnight of man's inhumanity to man into the bright daybreak of freedom and justice.

## PILGRIMAGE TO NONVIOLENCE[2]

Ten years ago I was just entering my senior year in theological seminary. Like most theological students I was engaged in the exciting job of studying various theological theories. Having been raised in a rather strict fundamentalistic tradition, I was occasionally shocked as my intellectual journey carried me through new and sometimes complex doctrinal lands. But despite the shock the pilgrimage was always stimulating, and it gave me a new appreciation for objective appraisal and critical analysis. My early theological training did the same for me as the reading of Hume did for Kant: it knocked me out of my dogmatic slumber.

At this stage of my development I was a thoroughgoing liberal. Liberalism provided me with an intellectual satisfaction that I could never find in fundamentalism. I became so enamored of the insights of liberalism that I almost fell into the trap of accepting uncritically everything that came under its name. I was absolutely convinced of the natural goodness of man and the natural power of human reason.

*I*

The basic change in my thinking came when I began to question some of the theories that had been associated with so-called liberal theology. Of course there is one phase of liberalism that I hope to cherish always: its devotion to the search for truth, its insistence on an open and analytical mind, its refusal to abandon the best light of reason. Liberalism's contribution to the philological-historical criticism of biblical literature

485

has been of immeasurable value and should be defended with religious and scientific passion.

It was mainly the liberal doctrine of man that I began to question. The more I observed the tragedies of history and man's shameful inclination to choose the low road, the more I came to see the depths and strength of sin. My reading of the works of Reinhold Niebuhr made me aware of the complexity of human motives and the reality of sin on every level of man's existence. Moreover, I came to recognize the complexity of man's social involvement and the glaring reality of collective evil. I came to feel that liberalism had been all too sentimental concerning human nature and that it leaned toward a false idealism.

I also came to see that liberalism's superficial optimism concerning human nature caused it to overlook the fact that reason is darkened by sin. The more I thought about human nature the more I saw how our tragic inclination for sin causes us to use our minds to rationalize our actions. Liberalism failed to see that reason by itself is little more than an instrument to justify man's defensive ways of thinking. Reason, devoid of the purifying power of faith, can never free itself from distortions and rationalizations.

In spite of the fact that I had to reject some aspects of liberalism, I never came to an all-out acceptance of neo-orthodoxy. While I saw neo-orthodoxy as a helpful corrective for a liberalism that had become all too sentimental, I never felt that it provided an adequate answer to the basic questions. If liberalism was too optimistic concerning human nature, neo-orthodoxy was too pessimistic. Not only on the question of man but also on other vital issues neo-orthodoxy went too far in its revolt. In its attempt to preserve the transcendence of God, which had been neglected by liberalism's overstress of his immanence, neo-orthodoxy went to the extreme of stressing a God who was hidden, unknown and "wholly other." In its revolt against liberalism's overemphasis on the power of reason, neo-orthodoxy fell into a mood of anti-rationalism and semifundamentalism, stressing a narrow, uncritical biblicism. This approach, I felt, was inadequate both for the church and for personal life.

So although liberalism left me unsatisfied on the question of the nature of man, I found no refuge in neo-orthodoxy. I am now convinced that the truth about man is found neither in liberalism nor in neo-orthodoxy. Each represents a partial truth. A large segment of Protestant liberalism defined man only in terms of his essential nature, his capacity for good. Neo-orthodoxy tended to define man only in terms of his existential nature, his capacity for evil. An adequate understanding of man is found neither in the thesis of liberalism nor in the antithesis of neo-orthodoxy, but in a synthesis which reconciles the truths of both.

During the past decade I also gained a new appreciation for the philosophy of existentialism. My first contact with this philosophy came through my reading of Kierkegaard and Nietzsche. Later I turned to a study of Jaspers, Heidegger and Sartre. All of these thinkers stimulated my thinking; while finding things to question in each, I nevertheless learned a great deal from study of them. When I finally turned to a serious study of the works of Paul Tillich I became convinced that existentialism, in spite of the fact that it had become all too fashionable, had grasped certain basic truths about man and his condition that could not be permanently overlooked.

Its understanding of the "finite freedom" of man is one of existentialism's most lasting contributions, and its perception of the anxiety and conflict produced in man's personal and social life as a result of the perilous and ambiguous structure of existence is especially meaningful for our time. The common point in all existentialism, whether it is atheistic or theistic, is that man's existential situation is a state of estrangement from his essential nature. In their revolt against Hegel's essentialism, all existentialists contend that the world is fragmented. History is a series of unreconciled conflicts and man's existence is filled with anxiety and threatened with meaninglessness. While the ultimate Christian answer is not found in any of these existential assertions, there is much here that the theologian can use to describe the true state of man's existence.

Although most of my formal study during this decade has been in systematic theology and philosophy, I have become more and more interested in social ethics. Of course my concern for social problems was already substantial before the beginning of this decade. From my early teens in Atlanta I was deeply concerned about the problem of racial injustice. I grew up abhorring segregation, considering it both rationally inexplicable and morally unjustifiable. I could never accept the fact of having to go to the back of a bus or sit in the segregated section of a train. The first time that I was seated behind a curtain in a dining car I felt as if the curtain had been dropped on my selfhood. I had also learned that the inseparable twin of racial injustice is economic injustice. I saw how the systems of segregation ended up in the exploitation of the Negro as well as the poor whites. Through these early experiences I grew up deeply conscious of the varieties of injustice in our society.

*II*

Not until I entered theological seminary, however, did I begin a serious intellectual quest for a method to eliminate social evil. I was immediately influenced by the social gospel. In the early '50s I read Rauschenbusch's *Christianity and the Social Crisis,* a book which left an indelible imprint on my thinking. Of course there were points at which I differed with Rauschenbusch. I felt that he had fallen victim to the 19th-century "cult of inevitable progress," which led him to an unwarranted optimism concerning human nature. Moreover, he came perilously close to identifying the kingdom of God with a particular social and economic system—a temptation which the church should never give in to. But in spite of these shortcomings Rauschenbusch gave to American Protestantism a sense of social responsibility that it should never lose. The gospel at its best deals with the whole man, not only his soul but his body, not only his spiritual well-being, but his material well-being. Any religion that professes to be concerned about the souls of men and is not concerned about the slums that damn them, the economic conditions that strangle them and the social conditions that cripple them is a spiritually moribund religion awaiting burial.

After reading Rauschenbusch I turned to a serious study of the social and ethical theories of the great philosophers. During this period I had almost despaired of the power of love in solving social problems. The "turn the other cheek" philosophy and the "love your enemies" philosophy are only valid, I felt, when individuals are in conflict with other individuals; when racial groups and nations are in conflict a more realistic approach is necessary. Then I came upon the life and teachings of Mahatma Gandhi. As I read his works I became deeply fascinated by his campaigns of nonviolent resistance. The whole Gandhian concept of *satyagraha* (*satya* is truth which equals love, and *graha* is force; *satyagraha* thus means truth-force or love-force) was profoundly significant to me. As I delved deeper into the philosophy of Gandhi my skepticism concerning the power of love gradually diminished, and I came to see for the first time that the Christian doctrine of love operating through the Gandhian method of nonviolence was one of the most potent weapons available to oppressed people in their struggle for freedom. At this time, however, I had a merely intellectual understanding and appreciation of the position, with no firm determination to organize it in a socially effective situation.

When I went to Montgomery, Alabama, as a pastor in 1954, I had not the slightest idea that I would later become involved in a crisis in which nonviolent resistance would be applicable. After I had lived in the community about a year, the bus boycott began. The Negro people of Montgomery, exhausted by the humiliating experiences that they had constantly faced on the buses, expressed in a massive act of noncooperation their determination to be free. They came to see that it was ultimately more honorable to walk the streets in dignity than to ride the buses in humiliation. At the beginning of the protest the people called on me to serve as their spokesman. In accepting this responsibility my mind, consciously or unconsciously, was driven back to the Sermon on the Mount and the Gandhian method of nonviolent resistance. This principle became the guiding light of our movement. Christ furnished the spirit and motivation while Gandhi furnished the method.

The experience in Montgomery did more to clarify my thinking on the question of nonviolence than all of the books that I had read. As the days unfolded I became more and more convinced of the power of nonviolence. Living through the actual experience of the protest, nonviolence became more than a method to which I gave intellectual assent; it became a commitment to a way of life. Many issues I had not cleared up intellectually concerning nonviolence were now solved in the sphere of practical action.

A few months ago I had the privilege of traveling to India. The trip had a great impact on me personally and left me even more convinced of the power of nonviolence. It was a marvelous thing to see the amazing results of a nonviolent struggle. India won her independence, but without violence on the part of Indians. The aftermath of hatred and bitterness that usually follows a violent campaign is found nowhere in India. Today a mutual friendship based on complete equality exists between the Indian and British people within the commonwealth.

I do not want to give the impression that nonviolence will work miracles overnight. Men are not easily moved from their mental ruts or purged of their prejudiced and irrational feelings. When the underprivileged demand freedom, the privileged first react with bitterness and resistance. Even when the demands are couched in nonviolent terms, the initial response is the same. I am sure that many of our white brothers in Montgomery and across the south are still bitter toward Negro leaders, even though these leaders have sought to follow a way of love and nonviolence. So the nonviolent approach does not immediately change the heart of the oppressor. It first does something to the hearts and souls of those committed to it. It gives them new self-respect; it calls up resources of strength and courage that they did not know they had.

Finally, it reaches the opponent and so stirs his conscience that reconciliation becomes a reality.

*III*

During recent months I have come to see more and more the need for the method of nonviolence in international relations. While I was convinced during my student days of the power of nonviolence in group conflicts within nations, I was not yet convinced of its efficacy in conflicts between nations. I felt that while war could never be a positive or absolute good, it could serve as a negative good in the sense of preventing the spread and growth of an evil force. War, I felt, horrible as it is, might be preferable to surrender to a totalitarian system. But more and more I have come to the conclusion that the potential destructiveness of modern weapons of war totally rules out the possibility of war ever serving again as a negative good. If we assume that mankind has a right to survive then we must find an alternative to war and destruction. In a day when sputniks dash through outer space and guided ballistic missiles are carving highways of death through the stratosphere, nobody can win a war. The choice today is no longer between violence and nonviolence. It is either nonviolence or nonexistence.

I am no doctrinaire pacifist. I have tried to embrace a realistic pacifism. Moreover, I see the pacifist position not as sinless but as the lesser evil in the circumstances. Therefore I do not claim to be free from the moral dilemmas that the Christian nonpacifist confronts. But I am convinced that the church cannot remain silent while mankind faces the threat of being plunged into the abyss of nuclear annihilation. If the church is true to its mission it must call for an end to the arms race.

In recent months I have also become more and more convinced of the reality of a personal God. True, I have always believed in the personality of God. But in past years the idea of a personal God was little more than a metaphysical category which I found theologically and philosophically satisfying. Now it is a living reality that has been validated in the experiences of everyday life. Perhaps the suffering, frustration and agonizing moments which I have had to undergo occasionally as a result of my involvement in a difficult struggle have drawn me closer to God. Whatever the cause, God has been profoundly real to me in recent months. In the midst of outer dangers I have felt an inner calm and known resources of strength that only God could give. In many instances I have felt the power of God transforming the fatigue of despair into the buoyancy of hope. I am convinced that the universe is under the control of a loving purpose and that in the struggle for righteousness man has cosmic companionship. Behind the harsh appearances of the world there is a benign power. To say God is personal is not to make him an object among other objects or attribute to him the finiteness and limitations of human personality; it is to take what is finest and noblest in our consciousness and affirm its perfect existence in him. It is certainly true that human personality is limited, but personality as such involves no necessary limitations. It simply means self-consciousness and self-direction. So in the truest sense of the word, God is a living God. In him there is feeling and will, responsive to the deepest yearnings of the human heart: this God both evokes and answers prayers.

The past decade has been a most exciting one. In spite of the tensions and uncertainties of our age something profoundly meaningful has begun. Old systems of exploitation and oppression are passing away and new systems of justice and equality are being born. In a real sense ours is a great time in which to be alive. Therefore I am not yet discouraged about the future. Granted that the easygoing optimism of yesterday is impossible. Granted that we face a world crisis which often leaves us standing amid the surging murmur of life's restless sea. But every crisis has both its dangers and its opportunities. Each can spell either salvation or doom. In a dark, confused world the spirit of God may yet reign supreme.

### Notes

1. In *The Christian Century* (6 February 1957): 165-67.
2. In *The Christian Century* (13 April 1960): 439-41.

# Marcus Garvey

*B*orn in Jamaica, Marcus Garvey (1887–1940) had no confidence in the work or theology of the churches he had known. Their
content was much too otherworldly for his liking. Garvey promoted a
theology built upon self-reliance and black nationalism. He understood
the importance of the link between how one thought about God and
how one understood the self. Therefore, Garvey believed, Africans
should think of God as black. In essence, Garvey sought a redefinition
of all theology in order to support the need for African liberation. A very
early form, therefore, of liberation theology, his work brought hope to
many of the poor who heard it.

Garvey put his theology into action through the Universal Negro
Improvement Association (UNIA), founded in Harlem, New York, in
1917. It would not be too far off the mark to claim that the UNIA
served as Garvey's church, since the organization worked to achieve
the purposes defined by his theology: justice for Africans worldwide,
the importance of African unity, and the "resurrection of the Negro"
to a place of equality with all other races. This latter theme is
addressed in our Garvey selection, an Easter sermon preached in
1922.

## THE RESURRECTION OF THE NEGRO[1]

Easter Sunday Sermon Delivered at Liberty Hall, New York City, N. Y.
April 16th, 1922.

The Lord is risen! A little over nineteen hundred years ago a man
came to this world called JESUS. He was sent here for the propagation
of a cause—that of saving fallen humanity. When He came the world
refused to hear Him; the world rejected Him; the world persecuted Him;
men crucified Him. A couple days ago He was nailed to the cross of Cal-
vary; He died; He was buried. To-day He is risen; risen the spiritual
leader of creation; risen as the first fruit of them that slept. To-day that

492

crucified Lord, that crucified Christ sees the affairs of man from His own spiritual throne on high.

After hundreds of years have rolled by, the doctrine He taught has become the accepted religion of hundreds of millions of human beings. He in His resurrection triumphed over death and the grave; He by His resurrection convinced humanity that His cause was spiritual. The world felt the truth about Jesus too late to have accepted His doctrine in His lifetime. But what was done to Jesus in His lifetime is just what is done to all reformers and reform movements. He came to change the spiritual attitude of man toward his brother. That was regarded in His day as an irregularity, even as it is regarded to-day. The one who attempts to bring about changes in the order of human society becomes a dangerous imposter upon society, and to those who control the systems of the day.

## The Desire to Enslave Others

It has been an historic attitude of man to keep his brother in slavery—in subjection for the purpose of exploitation. When Jesus came the privileged few were taking advantage of the unfortunate masses. Because the teaching of Jesus sought to equalize the spiritual and even the temporal rights of man, those who held authority, sway and dominion sought His liberty by prosecution, sought His life by death. He was called to yield up that life for the cause He loved—because He was indeed a true reformer.

## The Example Set by Christ

The example set by our Lord and Master nineteen hundred years ago is but the example that every reformer must make up his mind to follow if we are indeed to serve those to whom we minister. Service to humanity means sacrifice. That has been demonstrated by our blessed Lord and Redeemer whose resurrection we commemorate this day. As Christ triumphed nearly two thousand years ago over death and the grave, as He was risen from the dead, so do I hope that 400,000,000 Negroes of to-day will triumph over the slavishness of the past, intellectually, physically, morally and even religiously; that on this anniversary of our risen Lord, we ourselves will be risen from the slumber of the ages; risen in thought to higher ideals, to a loftier purpose, to a truer conception of life.

## The Hope of the U.N.I.A.

It is the hope of the Universal Negro Improvement Association that the 400,000,000 Negroes of the world will get to realize that we are about to live a new life—a risen life—a life of knowing ourselves.

493

How many of us know ourselves? How many of us understand our-selves? The major number of us for ages have failed to recognize in our-selves the absolute masters of our own destiny—the absolute directors and creators of our own fate.

To-day as we think of our risen Lord may we not also think of the life He gave to us—the life that made us His instruments, His children—The life that He gave to us to make us possessors of the land that He himself created through His Father? How many of us can reach out to that higher life; that higher purpose; that creative world that says to you you are a man, a sovereign, a lord—lord of the creation? On this beautiful spring day, may we not realize that God made Nature for us; God has given it to us as our province, our dominion? May we not realize that God has created no superior being to us in this world, but Himself? May we not know that we are the true lords and creators of our own fate and of our own physical destiny?

The work of the Universal Negro Improvement Association for the past four and a half years has been that of guiding us to realize that there should be a resurrection in us, and if at no other time I trust that at this Easter-tide we will realize that there is a great need for a resurrection—a resurrection from the lethargy of the past—the sleep of the past—from that feeling that made us accept the idea and opinion that God intended that we should occupy an inferior place in the world.

### No Superiority or Inferiority

Men and women of Liberty Hall, men and women of my race, do you know that the God we love, the God we adore, the God who sent His Son to this world nearly two thousand years ago never created an inferior man? That God we love, that God we worship and adore has created man in His own image, equal in every respect, wheresoever he may be; let him be white; let him be yellow; let him be red; let him be black; God has cre-ated him the equal of his brother. He is such a loving God. He is such a merciful God. He is such a God that He is no respecter of persons, that He would not in His great love create a superior race and an inferior one. The God that you worship is a God that expects you to be the equal of other men. The God that I adore is such a God and He could be no other.

Some of us seem to accept the fatalist position, the fatalist attitude, that God accorded to us a certain position and condition, and therefore there is no need trying to be otherwise. The moment you accept such an attitude, the moment you accept such an opinion, the moment you har-bor such an idea, you hurl an insult at the great God who created you,

494

because you question Him for His love, you question Him for His mercy. God has created man, and has placed him in this world as the lord of the creation, as the sovereign of everything that you see, let it be land, let it be sea, let it be the lakes, rivers and everything therein. All that you see in creation, all that you see in the world, was created by God for the use of man, and you four hundred million black souls have as much right to your possession in this world as any other race.

Created in the image of the same God we have the same common rights, and to-day I trust that there will be a spiritual and material resurrection among Negroes everywhere; that you will lift yourselves from the doubts of the past; that you will lift yourselves from the slumbers of the past, that you will lift yourselves from the lethargy of the past, and strike out in this new life—in this resurrected life—to see things as they are.

## See Life as Others See It

The Universal Negro Improvement Association desires that the four hundred million members of our race see life as the other races see it. The great white race sees life in an attitude of sovereignity; the great yellow race sees life in a similar way, that is to say that man, let him be white or yellow, sees that he is master and owner and possessor of everything that God has created in this world, and given to us in Nature; and that is why by knowing himself, by understanding himself, and by understanding his God, man has gone, throughout the length and breadth of this world, conquering the very elements, harnessing nature and making a servant of everything that God placed within his reach.

As he has done that for thousands of years pleasing God and justifying his existence, so we are appealing to the members of our race to do that now in this risen life, and if you have never made up your minds before I trust on this Easter Sunday you will do so.

## Masters of Your Own Destiny

I repeat that God created you masters of your own destiny, masters of your own fate, and you can pay no higher tribute to your Divine Master than function as man, as He created you.

The highest compliment we can pay to our Creator; the highest respect we can pay to our risen Lord and Savior, is that of feeling that He has created us as His masterpiece; His perfect instruments of His own existence, because in us is reflected the very being of God. When it is said that we are created in His own image, we ourselves reflect His

495

greatness, we ourselves reflect the part of God the Father, God the Son, and God the Holy Ghost, and when we allow ourselves to be subjected and create others as our superior, we hurl an insult at our Creator who made us in the fullness of ourselves.

I trust that you will so live to-day as to realize that you are masters of your own destiny, masters of your fate; if there is anything you want in this world it is for you to strike out with confidence and faith in self and reach for it, because God has created it for your happiness wheresoever you may find it in nature. Nature is bountiful; nature is resourceful, and nature is willing to obey the command of man—Man the sovereign lord; man who is supposed to hold dominion and take possession of this great world of ours.

## The Difference Between Strong and Weak Races

The difference between the strong and weak races is that the strong races seem to know themselves; seem to discover themselves; seem to realize and know fully that there is but a link between them and the Creator; that above them there is no other but God and anything that bears human form is but their equal in standing and to that form there should be no obeisance; there should be no regard for superiority. Because of that feeling they have been able to hold their own in this world; they have been able to take care of the situation as it confronts them in nature; but because of our lack of faith and confidence in ourselves we have caused others created in a like image to ourselves, to take advantage of us for hundreds of years.

For hundreds of years we have been the footstool of other races and nations of the earth simply because we have failed to realize to recognize and know ourselves as other men have known themselves and felt that there is nothing in the world that is above them except the influence of God.

The understanding that others have gotten out of life is the same understanding that 400,000,000 Negroes must get out of this existence of ours. I pray that a new inspiration will come to us as a race; that we will think of nature as our servant; that we will think of man as our partner through life, and go through the length and breadth of this world achieving and doing as other men, as other nations and other races.

### Note

1. In *Philosophy and Opinions of Marcus Garvey,* ed. Amy Jacques-Garvey, Studies in American Negro Life, August Meier, general editor (New York: Atheneum, 1968; originally published in 1923), pp. 87-92.

# John Courtney Murray

$O$*ne of the most important Catholic public theologians in the twentieth century, John Courtney Murray (1904–1967) helped to teach many American Catholics how they could be both good Americans and good Catholics. A Jesuit, Murray was educated in philosophy at Weston College and in theological work at Woodstock College and the Gregorianum in Rome. He served for thirty years as a member of the pontifical faculty of theology at Woodstock. Murray is well known for the work he did near the end of his life on* Dignitatis Humanae *(The Declaration on Religious Freedom) at Vatican II. Yet the content of this important document of the modern Catholic Church merely reflected his lifelong commitment to religious liberty and the importance of public and ecumenical dialogue. Murray's work constituted a reconstruction of Catholic thinking about the natural-law tradition that utilized many of the principles found in the works of Locke and early Americans like Thomas Jefferson and James Madison. His theological reflection upon the meaning of religious freedom brought Catholic theology into the public arena in America in new and significant ways.*

*The excerpt published here is from* We Hold These Truths. *In this particular essay, Murray raises important questions about the relationship between history and the work of the Church. Within Christianity one finds two seemingly incompatible strands: contempt for the world (eschatological humanism) and the affirmation of the worldly (incarnational humanism). How are these views to be reconciled? "Does the cultivation of human values by human energies . . . contribute to the coming of the Kingdom of God? Or is it fundamentally irrelevant—a form of basket weaving?"*

# IS IT BASKET WEAVING?

## The Question of Christianity and Human Values[1]

. . .

An observer may therefore say that there are discernible in the United States certain signs of the two orientations that Catholic thought has taken, as it has faced the problem of a Christian humanism. But neither of the orientations—participation vs. withdrawal—is clearly defined or fully reasoned. Each of them ought to be, and it might help in this direction to look briefly at these two orientations. One looks towards what may be called an eschatological humanism; the other, towards an incarnational humanism.

### Contempt of the World

The first orientation makes its dominant appeal to Scripture, and its emphases coincide with certain scriptural emphases upon fundamental aspects of the *res christiana*. The first emphasis is upon the fact that in the present order the end of man is transcendent to any end that man himself might envisage. The human purpose, as set by grace, not only extends beyond time and earth; it also looks to fulfillment in a manner of perfection that, properly speaking, is not worked out but received as a gift. This perfection will lie in seeing God as He is in Himself, in knowing and loving Him by grace as He knows and loves Himself by nature. This perfection will be indeed a perfection of the human, but it is discontinuous with all purely human effort. By the same token, heaven, the state of this perfection, is radically discontinuous with history, the arena of human effort and achievement. And even history has a Master who causes all things within it to work together towards a good that is not of this world and that lies beyond human desire and striving. The meaning of history lies in the Pauline "mystery," the hidden divine action, the ever-renewed act of divine power whereby the Kingdom of God comes. The Kingdom is not built from below, nor does it repose upon any cornerstone laid by human hands. It is a divine act; it is an irruption from above.

And this City of God is the proper city of man. Within the earthly City man is an alien; it is not his home, he does not find his family there, he is no longer even native to it, he has been reborn. At best, he is a pilgrim in its streets, a man in passage, restless to be on the way toward the Holy City that is his goal. While he lingers, almost literally overnight, his attitude is one of waiting and expectancy. He can strike no roots; for the soil is not such as could nourish the life he cherishes. Ever before his eyes is the *dies Domini,* the day of the Great Catastrophe, when all the laborious magnificence of this man-built City will suddenly vanish, as the ground beneath its seemingly solid substance is withdrawn. Abruptly, there will be an end; this City will no longer be. And that which is will be only He Who Is, with those who are in Him. In these perspectives, only those human values are worth affirming which grace itself evokes; all others will end in insubstantial ashes. All true humanism is therefore eschatological; the only true human values are those which are supernatural and eternal.

The works of earth, the objects upon which human energies may be poured out, the multiplicity of tasks which make up the whole human cultural enterprise—upon these the judgment of the early hermits is still fundamentally valid. They are the works of time, only valuable because they fill in the time of waiting. The old monk wove a basket one day; the next day he unwove it. The basket itself did not matter; but the weaving and unweaving of it served as a means of spending an interval, necessary to the frail human spirit, between periods of performance of the only task that did matter, the contemplation of heavenly things. Only the making of a soul was the true human value. For the rest, what did it matter whether one wove baskets or wrought whole civilizations?

Again, the eschatological view lays emphasis upon sin as a permanent human fact that casts a shadow over all human achievements, whatever the purity of their conception. If sin be not overcome by grace, and a new principle of life imparted to man by God, even the highest human virtues are but *splendida vitia.* . . .

. . .

Finally, the eschatological view lays emphasis on the central truth that Christianity is the Cross. And the Cross represents the inversion of all human values. The human is put to death; and out of death comes life. Darkness overtakes the light; and in that moment the light disperses the darkness. The truth goes down to defeat; and that is its hour of victory. The Kingdom is refused; and thus it comes. Earthly hopes find their definitive disappointment; and out of their wreckage there rises by the sole power of God a new hope, glorious, immortal, the creation of the Spirit.

. . .

These, briefly, are the dominant accents in the doctrine of eschatological humanism. Pushed to the extreme, the conclusion would be that man not only may in fact neglect, but even should by right neglect, what is called the cultural enterprise—the cultivation of science and the arts, the pursuit of human values by human energies, the work of civilization—in order to give undivided energies to the invisible things of the spirit. No Christian of course draws this extreme conclusion and makes it a law for humanity, though individuals may hear it, in one or other form, as the word of God to them, and hearken to it, and be God's witnesses to the oneness of the one thing necessary, by the completeness of their contempt for the world.

### Affirmation of the Worldly

The tendency towards an incarnational humanism is founded on accents laid on other, and no less Christian, principles. The end of man, it asserts, is indeed transcendent, supernatural; but it is an end of *man* and in its achievement man truly finds the perfection of his nature. Grace perfects nature, does not destroy it—this is the central point of emphasis. There is indeed a radical discontinuity between nature and grace, but nature does not therefore become irrelevant to grace. There must be no Lutheranism, which would fix a great gulf of separation between orders that are only distinct. Again, the perfect man of St. Paul will achieve the fullness of his age and stature only in heaven and not in history; nonetheless he grows in history. The Body of Christ is really a-building here in time. And its growth is that of a Body, not simply of a soul. There must be no Platonism, which would make man only a soul. The *res sacra* which grace would achieve is likewise a *res humana* in the full sense.

. . .

The Church then is catholic in her redemptive scope; all men are to be saved, all that is human is to be saved. There is indeed to be a war upon the flesh, but in order that the body may be dignified. The Christian heart must cultivate a contempt for the world, but diligently cherish its reverence for the work of the Creator, who is Creator not only of heaven but of the earth, of the visible as well as the invisible. . . .

Therefore in the perspectives of an incarnational humanism there is a place for all that is natural, human, terrestrial. The heavens and the earth are not destined for an eternal dust-heap, but for a transformation. There will be a new heaven and a new earth; and those who knew them once will recognize them, for all their newness.

. . .

Furthermore, this incarnational humanism stresses the fact that He who entered the stream of history as its Redeemer is the Logos, Eternal

Reason. Through His Spirit He is still immanent in history, there to do a work of reason—that work of reason which is justice, and that work of pacification which is in turn the work of justice. Hence all efforts, by whomsoever put forth, toward the rationalization of human society, its "justification" and its pacification, are put forth in the line of action of the Logos Himself. . . .

. . .

History shows that the whole cultural enterprise was not unrelated to Christianity in its origins. And history proves too that it was not unrelated to Christianity in its finality. The faith was once supported by a civilization. It does not, if you will, absolutely need this support—at least the individual Christian does not. He can live the Christian life amid the barren horror of a concentration camp. But the Church, the community of the faithful, not all of whom are heroes, does need this manner of support. And therefore the creation of a temporal order of justice and civic fraternity has been a humanistic aspiration connatural to the Christian heart. The aspiration is never Utopian. The Christian knows how intertwined are the human and the sinful; how "the Christian world" is not "the Church" and cannot be. Achievements in this order are never ideal; but they are human achievements. Their value is real, if limited, and is not to be undermined by any exaggerations of the Christian contempt for the world. In their humanism they are Christian achievements.

### Prudence and Confidence

Here then, in very brief compass, are the two general orientations which Christian thought has taken as it has meditated on the problem of a Christian humanism. It is obvious that the doctrines upon which the tendencies respectively rest are not mutually exclusive; these doctrines are integral to the Gospel and complementary to each other. However, the emphases made in the eschatological view are exclusive of those made in the incarnational view; and each set of emphases, when really lived, results in a distinct style of life. The choice of emphasis is one of the privileges of Christian freedom. . . .

Finally, there are risks inherent in each tendency. An eschatological humanism runs the risk of entrusting the fortunes of this world and the forms of all its institutions to the dubious wisdom of the unregenerate. And this would condemn the faithful to live in conditions of barbarism—perhaps the highly civilized barbarism which the wisdom of the flesh, making use of the instrumentalities of science, is capable of creat-

501

ing. The Egyptians can indeed accumulate great spoils; but as long as they remain only in Egyptian hands they can only help make Egypt a land of bondage. On the other hand, he who would seek to make his way toward the Kingdom of God and His grace through a search for the common good of the earthly City and an affirmation of the goods of nature is taking a long and difficult road. The effort to despoil the Egyptians can result in inner self-despoilment.

All this and much more must be borne in mind when one approaches the problem of Christian humanism in its American position. Actually, there are two problems. First, is there a place in good theology for the human values which America has historically emphasized? More practically, is a terrestrial, incarnational humanism possible within the conditions of society which the American emphasis tends to create? More important, can this manner of humanism be useful to the Christian in his specially Christian quest, the quest for sanctity? Are conditions of freedom and great material prosperity valuable only because they enlarge the opportunities for Christian renunciation? Or are they simply analogous to that Ciceronian period in which the patrons of "devout humanism" preached? They preached in these cadences not because they are particularly "good in themselves," but merely in order to be heard and heeded in an age whose ear was attuned to the Ciceronian period. In application, have these conditions of freedom and prosperity simply an "apostolic value," such that one should simply "use" them as means to an end no more related to them than a Ciceronian period is related to the Gospel message? On this hypothesis these social conditions, institutions, and ideals might well have only the character of a necessary evil.

Or is this whole American situation and the humanism to which it tends and the style of life to which it leads capable of being affirmed as a human good, an end-in-itself—an intermediate end indeed, but not solely a means? (The question here obviously concerns only what is good and of human value in the total dynamism which creates what is called "the American situation.") Concretely, is the ideal of a "free people" and a "prosperous nation" a genuine value, a legitimate end to be striven for as good in itself? Or is it simply a means to an entirely disproportionate end, in the sense that a free people can protect the freedom of the Church and a wealthy nation can support her institutions?

The second problem is analogous but wider. What is the relation between terrestrial and eschatological humanism? In other words, does the cultivation of human values by human energies deployed in a effort that is not directly aroused by grace but is open to its direction, once aroused—does this manner of humanism contribute to the coming of the Kingdom of God? Or is it fundamentally irrelevant—a form of basket weaving? To ask this, of course, is to raise the question of the relation between history and the Church—the relation between the great human effort at unification, which is the basic cultural enterprise, and the divine effort of the Spirit, which is to "gather into one the scattered children of God." This is indeed a mighty question. And to raise it is to invite to a journey down avenues of mystery, which, for all that, are legitimate avenues of reverent Christian inquiry.

It remains only to indicate the spirit of the inquiry, as set by the Church herself. In her doctrinal affirmations the Church is confident, even optimistic. True religion and profound humaneness, she says, are not rivals but sisters, who have nothing to fear from each other but everything to gain. This is a very firm assertion. On the other hand, the Church is prudent, even cautious, in the area of practice. Her concrete counsels to her children have not the same confidence as her doctrinal statements; they are touched with an accent of warning, even of fear. She boldly urges the truth; she carefully guides action.

The reason for this difference in attitude is clear. The wound of nature, which is our heritage from the original sin, makes itself felt in two lines—in the line of intelligence in its relation to the true, and in the line of the will in its relation to the good. But in the latter line the wound is more profound, mysterious, crippling. The will deviates from the good more easily and radically than the intelligence deviates from the true. Hence the Church stoutly defends reason and its powers of knowing and of harmonizing its knowledge with its Christian beliefs. She is less certain of man himself in his total being and less confident of his power to harmonize his whole human effort with his Christian faith, in that ever precarious synthesis known as a Christian humanism. It is in this same spirit of both confidence and prudence that the problem is to be approached.

### Note

1. In *We Hold These Truths: Catholic Reflections on the American Proposition* (New York: Sheed and Ward, 1960), pp. 185-96.

# Georges Florovsky

*The scholarly-spiritual traditions of the Russian Orthodox Church entered with force into the discussion of theology in America upon the appointment of Florovsky (1893–1979) as dean and professor of dogmatics and patristics of the newly founded St. Vladimir's Theological Seminary in 1948. Born in Russia, Florovsky was educated at Odessa University, where he taught until 1920, when he fled the Russian Revolution. Settling in France, he joined (1926) the faculty of the new St. Sergius Theological Academy, a center of the Russian religious renaissance of the early twentieth century. During the 1930s he became increasingly involved in ecumenical affairs, playing notable roles in the Faith and Order movement and the World Council of Churches. Posts at Harvard Divinity School (1954–1964) and then Princeton University followed his years at St. Vladimir's.*

*Florovsky's scholarship had at its core a concern for what he called a "neo-patristic synthesis." Specialized church historical studies as well as ecumenical and other reflections on the heritage of Orthodoxy were, in his view, essential means by which to recover and renew the church's living tradition in modern times.*

## CONFESSIONAL LOYALTY IN THE ECUMENICAL MOVEMENT[1]

It has been recently suggested that what we need most urgently in the ecumenical movement is a "theology of the abnormal." Christian theology strictly speaking is basically concerned with the abnormal, with the most radical deviation from the divine norm of existence, with fall and sin. Even in the redeemed world we are faced with an appalling impact of sin. Sin is indeed already forgiven and a new humanity has been inaugurated in and by the Second Man. The fatherly embrace of God is again charitably extended to the repentant. Yet, repentance is still a task for man to perform, and it proves to be an exceedingly difficult one for frail man to accomplish. The prodigal son is still very slow in going back

504

home. And therefore, in Christian theology, we find ourselves again and again in a paradoxical situation. Christian disruption, utter disunity in Christendom, is nothing but an antinomy and a paradox. The fold of Christ ought not to be disrupted. Theological intelligence fails completely to comprehend the predicament of disunity, created by human unfaithfulness and aberration.

The ecumenical movement, an endeavour to overcome and to heal the Christian schism, is inescapably a paradoxical venture. The final goal is, indeed, a reunited Christendom. Yet, the nature and scope of this prospective unity and reunion is variously described and interpreted by Christians of different backgrounds and traditions. The method of *re*-union depends ultimately upon the conception one holds of the existing *dis*-union. And these conceptions utterly differ. Prescription always depends upon diagnosis. And, in our case, it is precisely the diagnosis that is uncertain and controversial. That is why it is so difficult to agree on the prescription. Several solutions have been suggested. Roughly speaking, one group of solutions can be described as a "theory of a common denominator" and the other as "the true Church and the secessions." Let us examine them in turn.

### A Common Denominator

The theory of "a common denominator" amounts, in practice, to a recommendation to act *as if* there was no real schism, no true disruption, but rather only a sad misunderstanding, which could possibly be settled by some agreement. Christians are divided and mutually estranged indeed; nobody can deny this grim fact. Yet, in spite of all their unhappy divisions and separations, they are at one on many basic points. They are united in their common allegiance to the same Lord. One might have added, they are, above all, united in His redeeming will and love. He came precisely to recover the lost sheep and the scattered. In this perspective, it seems but reasonable to disregard the existing dissensions and disagreements, and to act accordingly, *as if* all Christians were really at one. Are not all these disagreements utterly human—human misconceptions—and unity, a divine gift, that has been already given free in Jesus Christ, the Lord of all flesh. It is precisely at this point that the problem of what is usually described as an "open communion" arises and the predicament of the schism is felt most grievously and painfully. It seems to be a shameful scandal that those who proclaim their common allegiance to Jesus the Christ, the Son of the living God and the Saviour of the world, the only sure hope in ages past and to come, are still unable

505

to join together at His table. Much worse than that, a large part of them emphatically refuses to do so. The champions of an easy solution are utterly depressed by what seems to them to be obstinacy, lack of charity and brotherly understanding. It seems to them that the whole ecumenical endeavour is compromised by this obstinate resistance.

Now, from another point of view, it is not the ecumenical endeavour, but only a particular interpretation of it that is wrecked on the proposal of an "open communion." In fact, the whole theory of a common denominator comes into a blind alley, since it fails to carry a unanimous conviction. This fact in itself indicates that possibly the measure of existing unity or agreement has been somehow exaggerated and misunderstood. It suggests that the division probably goes much deeper than has been admitted by those who were ready to act together. It is indeed a dreadful thing that Christians cannot join together at one and the same altar. But it is exactly what should have been expected. For they are *really* divided. Several and separate communion services at an ecumenical gathering are but a spectacular projection of the very fact of the schism. And the schism cannot be overcome simply by agreements on our human level. One has to be courageous enough to bear the pain, and those who are compelled by their conscience to abstain from any "open communion" suffer, no less, but probably much more, than those who are prepared to go together.

## The Marks of a Church

It is usually suggested that this obstinate refusal to join at the common Table is inspired by exaggerated "confessional loyalty" and by a lack of true ecumenical comprehension. Now, the phrase "confessional loyalty" is ambiguous and misleading. Surely, nobody would pledge his loyalty simply to a denomination, but only to the Church of Christ. The trouble is that this loyalty to the Church is variously conceived and interpreted. All "confessions" identify themselves, in one sense or another, with the Church of Christ, "protestants" no less than "catholics." In our present state of Christian confusion and chaos, one simply cannot escape some sort of discrimination between a "true" and an "untrue" church. It is no good pretending that the whole guilt of intransigeancy is on one side. Moreover, it is no good bringing forward the charge of intransigeancy at all. For, in fact, the word is but another and depreciatory name for conviction. We have to recognise, boldly and humbly, that our deep convictions differ. Yet, in spite of that, we have to stay together. The whole burden of the ecumenical endeavour is tied precisely to this small phrase: "in spite."

Obviously, "protestants" would suggest that all empirical churches should become churches in very truth, and in order to accomplish this purpose should go through a certain kind of reform and purification, more or less identical with the European Reformation of the sixteenth and seventeenth centuries. They are committed, by the very logic of their belief, to an emphatic claim that the churches of the Reformation are representative of a true kind of church and that, consequently, no church can ever be true unless it has gone through a process of reformation. Un-reformed means in this connection exactly un-true.

On the other hand, a "catholic" will never regard the Catholic Church as one particular denomination among many others. He will identify her with the Church of Christ. The claim may seem arrogant, it may easily be dismissed as a proof of spiritual pride or intransigeant hypocrisy. Yet, it is to be understood that a "catholic" is committed to this claim by the very logic of his belief and conviction. Again, it is to be understood that this claim does not unchurch those who do not belong to the Catholic Church of history. The most rigid "catholic" will regard all faithful Christians as related, in some sense to be defined, or even as belonging, to the Church of Christ. There is implied in the "catholic" claim no anticipation of the ultimate eschatological judgment. The claim is laid down on the level of history, i.e. on the level of Christian practice and action. The true composition of the Church is known to the Lord of the Church only—no "catholic" has ever doubted that, and St. Augustine has stated it most frankly and emphatically.

Perhaps the real point is this: was the Reformation a gain or a loss— a step forward or a step astray? Of course, this is only a rough way of putting it, and both the question and the answers must be carefully defined (which is, unfortunately, quite beyond the scope and the competence of the present paper). It may be very painful for a "protestant" to read this, it is very painful indeed for a "catholic" to write it. But it is not written to pain or offend anybody. Conviction is bound to be outspoken. And we have to share our respective pains, to bear each other's burdens, and to prove thereby our mutual confidence and our true brotherly affection. Both "protestants" and "catholics" are concerned with the marks of a true church. The tragedy is that they identify these marks differently, or even in opposite senses.

### Open Communion and Intercommunion

One may seriously doubt whether what is called an "open communion" is open in the strict sense. The case seems to be rather obscure.

There are two possible interpretations. Either it is presumed that all doctrinal convictions are at this point irrelevant, and that doctrinal conformity should not be regarded as a term of admission to Holy Communion; obviously, this assumption is itself a kind of doctrinal conviction, which is unacceptable for many Christians. Or, and this seems to be the case, an "open communion" is open only to those who satisfy certain requirements, of an obviously doctrinal character, and such an "open" table is still fenced. It is really irrelevant, whether a fencing formula is actually said or omitted: in any case it is implied.

In either case, the practice of an "open" communion is justified by a certain particular conception of the Holy Communion, which is not acceptable to those who refuse to join. The opposition of an "open" communion and a "confessional" communion is wrong. Strictly speaking, an "open" communion is also meant for a particular confession, i.e. for people of a particular persuasion, even if this persuasion is so wide as to ignore all doctrinal dissensions. An un-baptised member of the Salvation Army would usually be admitted, although he disbelieves the divine institution of the sacrament. A member of the Society of Friends would also be admitted if he so wished, although it has been made clear that any Friend who finds himself in need of habitual participation is to be reminded that his place is probably not with the Society. The door seems to be ajar in the direction of vagueness and indifference.

But surely those who hold a "catholic" view of the sacrament cannot conscientiously be admitted, since their belief in the sacrifice of the mass is to be styled a "corruption" and an "erroneous doctrine" along with many of their other superstitions. A "catholic" therefore finds himself excluded from the "open" communion by the implied terms of admission and by the conception of the rite therein implied. It is no good talking of his obstinate resistance. His participation would be a non-sensical betrayal on his side, and a concealed insincerity on the other. And, in the end, it would not promote the ecumenical fellowship at all. A sentimental gesture cannot solve the conflict of deep convictions. Unity of brotherly feeling is not yet unity of faith. Are we permitted in the Church to be satisfied with anything less than this unity of faith?

Briefly, there are three main objections which constitute a radical impediment to an all-inclusive and "ecumenical" fellowship in the Holy Communion. *First*, utter divergence in the sacramental doctrine itself—possibly the conception of a sacramental sacrifice is the very point of demarcation. There can be no communion, because there is no *common* belief. *Secondly*, and this is but the wider context in which the first is to be seen, there are deep divergences in doctrine in general, although these divergences, in our own age at least, definitely cut across the historical confessions. And communion presupposes "one mind," no less than "one heart." *Thirdly*—and this is probably the crucial point, at least in the practical field—there is utter disagreement on the doctrine of Christian ministry. A "catholic" cannot divorce order from faith, a very definite Church order is for him an article of his integral Christian faith or dogma.

This fact has been partially recognised in recent times, in so far as many recent schemes of reunion included the restoration of a "historical episcopate." This restoration was, however, compromised and rendered meaningless (from the "catholic" point of view), since this order was emphatically excluded from faith or doctrine. For the "catholics," the point is not merely the restoration of an episcopal order, but the recognition of the sacramental character of the priesthood; but this still seems to many to be nothing but detestable "sacerdotalism." For a "catholic" an all-inclusive communion will be possible only after the integrity of the faith and the fullness of the sacramental fabric of the Church has been restored in the whole of Christendom. It will then be not simply a manifestation, by a human arrangement, of Christian charity and mutual recognition—and, in catholic conviction, the sacrament of the Eucharist was not instituted or meant for that purpose—but a true revelation of the Holy Church of God, in all her power and glory.

The whole ecumenical situation is certainly complicated and obscured by the fact that those who claim for themselves the name of "catholics" (not merely in a vague and general, but in a concrete and specific historical sense) are also divided and are not in communion with each other. And at this point another serious and painful problem arises, that of intercommunion. The difficulty in this case is of a different, though similar, character. Again, what is required for intercommunion is obviously unity of faith and the integrity of the sacramental structure. Unless this is secured and avowed, no action should be taken. The practice of an occasional intercommunion (or even of an occasional open communion) adopted in certain episcopal churches only confuses the issue. A true intercommunion can only be a corporate and catholic action. In a case in which the sacramental integrity of two churches which are not in communion with each other is mutually recognised, the unity of faith has still to be identified and emphasised by a corporate action of the churches concerned, and not simply by a personal conviction of some advanced individuals. In the whole process there is no question of confessional loyalty, but solely of the catholic truth.

509

*A Fellowship in Search*

The tragedy of Christendom is precisely that the truth of God is still divergently apprehended. What is a sacred treasury for some, is a deplorable superstition for others. What is an advance in the eyes of one part of Christendom is a step astray in the conviction of the other. Yet, *in spite* of all that, all Christians within the ecumenical movement and beyond its actual boundaries should pledge themselves to stay together and to profess their common allegiance to the same Lord and Master. It is a paradoxical situation, certainly. Yet it is exactly that paradox that makes the pledge so valuable and promising. They should stay together, exactly because they are divided. The pledge is valuable because it implies pain and tension. We are given the cross of patience to bear; let us glory in that cross. Our Christian pain is a token of recovery, a recovery which is to come from the Lord.

The ecumenical movement is primarily a fellowship in search. It is a venture or an adventure, not an achievement. It is a way, not the goal. And therefore an open communion would compromise the whole endeavour. It would be to pretend falsely that Christendom has already been reunited. We know only too well that it has not. Tension remains, compelling us to move on. For that reason we still have only an ecumenical movement and not a reunited Christendom. It is true, some unexpected agreements have been discovered and achieved recently, exactly in the process of a common search. Let them not be disavowed by any premature and unwarranted action, in which some of the partners in the discourse will never conscientiously participate. There is still a long and dangerous journey ahead.

It has been recently suggested that in the ecumenical conversation there has been a certain tendency to postpone agreements, even when they were possible; once an agreement on some particular point seemed to be at hand and rather imposing, the subject has been deliberately changed and another highly controversial topic brought into the discussion. Possibly this is an exaggeration. What is true, however, is that in the ecumenical discourse we do not trust our most compelling agreements. We behave once more in a most paradoxical manner. We mistrust ourselves because we have a deeper insight into the mystery under discussion, and we are aware of an ultimate disagreement which we are unable or perhaps too shy even to mention or to describe.

Possibly it is the reverse tendency that is more prevalent. There is a tendency to invite or even to compel one's opponents to think in categories unfamiliar or alien to them. A "protestant" theologian will write his books and make his statements in his particular idiom and primarily for his own edification and will expect the "catholics" to follow his argument. Usually he will be misunderstood, simply because his partner in conversation fails completely to follow his peculiar manner of speech. A "catholic" will habitually do just the same, and each will accuse the other of misconception and misunderstanding. The guilt obviously is on both sides. We have to learn each other's idioms or rather we have to create a true ecumenical and common language in theology and possibly to un-learn our party idioms. It is an enormous task; yet we can hardly escape it. We have to identify ourselves mentally with those partners in the discourse who do not share our own convictions, if we are going to arrive anywhere. Let us try to state the "catholic" conviction in the idiom of the "protestants" and let us invite them to talk to us in our own idiom. What is often taken to be confessional loyalty may prove to be inadequate phrasing of a commonly accepted truth.

### The True Church

This paper is an attempt to write in a new and ecumenical language. Probably the attempt has not been successful. Probably some would detect in it a heavy confessional flavour, and others would complain of vagueness. And so it will not be out of place to summarise briefly my main contentions in a language familiar to myself. As a member and priest of the Orthodox Church I believe that the church in which I was baptised and brought up *is* in very truth *the Church,* i. e. *the true* Church and the *only* true Church. I believe that for many reasons: by personal conviction and by the inner testimony of the Spirit which breathes in the sacraments of the Church and by all that I could learn from Scripture and from the universal tradition of the Church. I am compelled therefore to regard all other Christian churches as deficient, and in many cases I can identify these deficiencies accurately enough. Therefore, for me, Christian reunion is just universal conversion to Orthodoxy. I have no confessional loyalty; my loyalty belongs solely to the *Una Sancta.*

I know well that my claim will be disavowed by many Christians. It will seem to be an arrogant and futile claim. I know well that many things I believe with full and uttermost conviction are disbelieved by others. Now, I do not see any reason whatever to doubt them or disbelieve them myself. All I can reasonably do is this, to proclaim my faith and to try to phrase it in such a way and in such a manner that my poor idiom may not obscure the truth. Because, I am sure, the truth of God carries conviction. It does not mean that everything in the past or present state of the Orthodox Church is to be equated with the truth of God. Many things are obviously changeable; indeed many things need improvement. The *true* Church is not yet the *perfect* Church.

The Church of Christ has to grow and be built up in history. Yet the whole and the full truth has been already given and entrusted to the Church. Revision and re-statement is always possible, sometimes imperative. The whole history of the Ecumenical Councils in the past is evidence of that. The holy Fathers of the Church were engaged in this task. Yet, on the whole, the deposit was faithfully kept and the testimony of faith was gaining accuracy and precision. Above all, the sacramental structure of the Body has been kept integral and intact. Here again, I know, this conviction of mine may be rejected as an illusion. For me it is a matter of evidence. If this is obstinacy, it is the obstinacy of evidence. I can only see what I actually do see. I cannot help it. But in no way am I going to "un-church" anybody at all. The judgment has been given to the Son. Nobody is entitled to anticipate His judgment. Yet the Church has her own authority in history. It is, first of all, an authority to teach and to keep faithfully the word of truth. There is a certain rule of faith and order that is to be regarded as normal. What is beyond is just abnormal. But the abnormal should be cured, and not simply condemned. This is a justification for the participation of an Orthodox in the ecumenical discourse, in the hope that through his witness the Truth of God may win human hearts and minds.

### Note

1. In *Student World* 43, 1 (1950), pp. 59-70.

# John Meyendorff

$M$eyendorff (1926–1992) was born in France of Russian
emigré parents and completed his studies of theology at the Orthodox
Theological Institute of St. Sergius in Paris (1949) and received his doctorate from the Sorbonne in 1958. Upon ordination as priest in the
Russian Orthodox Church in France, he joined the faculty of St.
Valdimir's Orthodox Theological Seminary. A year later (1959) he was
vaulted to fame for his patristic and Byzantine scholarship and relocated
with his family to New York as a faculty member of St. Vladimir's
Orthodox Theological Seminary. His teaching and writings there and in
association with Harvard University's Byzantine research center, Ford-
ham University, and the World Council of Churches had a profound
influence not only on his own church but far beyond. At the time of his
death he was serving (since 1984) as St. Vladimir's Dean and was vitally
active in diverse scholarly and ecumenical affairs.

Critical to his work was his conviction that the apostolic faith of
Christianity and its continuity in the Orthodox church—though not
there exclusively or exclusivistically—was a living tradition of benefit to
the whole church and the whole world. Fidelity to historic doctrine, for
example, was rightly understood not solely in terms of human efforts to
conceptualize mysteries of divine revelation transcending adequate conceptualization but also in terms of the church's abiding dependence on
sacramental and personal life in communion with God.

## ORTHODOX THEOLOGY TODAY[1]

II

The doctrine of the Holy Spirit loses much when it is treated *in
abstracto*. This is probably one of the reasons why so little good theological writing is done about the Holy Spirit, and why even the Fathers
treat Him almost exclusively either in occasional polemical writings or
in writings on spirituality. However, neither patristic christology, nor the

ecclesiology of the early centuries, nor the very notion of salvation is understandable without a fundamentally pneumatological context.

I will try to illustrate this point with five examples, which also appear to me as the very issues which make the Orthodox witness relevant to the contemporary theological situation. These five examples are fundamental affirmations of patristic and Orthodox theology.

1. The world is not divine and it needs salvation.
2. Man is a theocentric being.
3. Christian theology is christocentric.
4. True ecclesiology is personalistic.
5. The true conception of God is trinitarian.

### 1. The World is not Divine.

In the New Testament, and not only in the Johannine writings, there is a constant opposition between the "Spirit who proceeds from the Father" (John 15:26 RSV), "whom the world cannot receive, because it neither sees Him nor knows Him" (John 14:17 RSV), and the "spirits" which must be "tested to see whether they are of God" (I John 4:1 RSV). In Colossians the entire cosmos is described as controlled by the powers and principalities, "the elemental spirits of the universe" opposed to Christ, although "created through Him and for Him" (Col. 1:16; 2:8 RSV). One of the most characteristic novelties of Christianity was what it demystified or, if you wish, secularized the cosmos. The idea that God abides in the elements, in water, in springs, in stars, in the emperor, was totally and from the beginning rejected by the Apostolic Church. At the same time, this same Church condemned every Manicheism, every dualism. The world is not evil in itself; the elements must proclaim the glory of God; water can be sanctified; the cosmos can be controlled; the emperor can become God's servant. All these elements of the world are not goals in themselves, for to consider them as such was precisely what was meant when the ancient pre-Christian world deified them, but they are defined at the very bottom of their existence by their relation to their Creator and also to man, the Creator's image in the world.

This is why all the rites of sanctification, of which the Orthodox Byzantine liturgy (as well as all the other ancient Christian liturgies) are so fond, all include:

[a] elements of exorcism: "Thou didst crush the heads of the serpents which lurked there" (from the Great Blessing of Water on Epiphany day);

[b] an invocation of the Spirit "who proceeds *from the Father,*" i.e. not "from the world"; and

[c] the affirmation that in its new sanctified existence matter will be reoriented to God and replaced in its original relation to the Creator, and will now serve *man,* whom God established as master of the universe.

An act of blessing and sanctification of any element of the world thus *liberates* man from dependence on it and puts it at man's service.

Ancient Christianity thus demystified the elements of the physical world. The task of theology today is to demystify "Society," "Sex," "the State," "Revolution," and other modern idols. Our modern prophets of secularization are not all wrong about the secularizing responsibility of Christians—secularization of the cosmos has been a Christian idea since the beginning—but the problem is that they secularize the Church and replace it with new idolatry, an idolatry of the world whereby man renounces again the freedom which was given to him in the Holy Spirit and submits himself anew to the determinism of history or sociology, of Freudian psychology or utopian progressivism.

## 2. Man is a Theocentric Being.

In order to understand what the "freedom in the Holy Spirit" is, let us first recall a quite paradoxical statement of St. Irenaeus of Lyons: "The perfect man consists in the commingling and the union of the soul receiving the Spirit of the Father, and the mixture of that fleshly nature which also was molded after the image of God" (*Adversus haereses* V, 6, 1). This passage of Irenaeus, as well as its several parallels, is to be evaluated not according to the precisions of post-Nicene theology, for according to that criterion it does present many problems, but in its positive content which will also be expressed, in different terms, by the entire consensus of the patristic tradition. What makes man truly man is the presence of this Spirit of God. Man is not an autonomous and self-sufficient being; his humanity consists firstly in an openness to the Absolute, to immortality, to creativity in the image of the Creator, and secondly in the fact that God met this openness when He created man and that, therefore, communion and participation in divine life and glory is man's *natural* element.

Later patristic tradition has consistently developed Irenaeus' idea (not necessarily his terminology), and this development is especially important in relation to the doctrine of human freedom.

For Gregory of Nyssa, the fall of man consisted precisely in the fact that man fell under the control of cosmic determinism, whereas originally, when he participated in divine life, when he preserved in himself

515

the image and likeness of God, he was *truly free*. Freedom, therefore, is not opposed to grace and grace, i.e. divine life itself, is neither a way through which God forces us to obey Him, nor an additional element superimposed upon human nature to obtain greater credit for human good works. Grace is the *milieu* in which man is wholly free. "When a man turns to the Lord the veil is removed. Now the Lord is the Spirit, and where the Spirit of the Lord is, there is freedom. And we all, with unveiled face, beholding the glory of the Lord, are being changed into His likeness from one degree of glory to another" (II Cor. 3:16-18).

One of the most fundamental presuppositions of this passage from St. Paul, as well as the anthropologies of St. Irenaeus and St. Gregory of Nyssa, is that nature and grace, man and God, the human mind and Holy Spirit, human freedom and divine presence, *do not exclude each other*. On the contrary, true humanity, in its authentic creativity, in its true freedom, in its original beauty and harmony, appears exactly when it participates in God or when, as both St. Paul and St. Gregory of Nyssa proclaim, it progresses from glory to glory without ever exhausting either the riches of God or the potentialities of man.

It is common today to affirm that theology should become anthropology. An Orthodox theologian can, and even should, accept a dialogue on this basis, provided he adopts at the very start an *open* view [of] man. The modern dogmas of secularism, of man's autonomy, of cosmo-centricity, or sociomagnetism, must first be rejected as dogmas. Many of these modern dogmas have, as we have already said, very deep roots in Western Christianity's ancient fear of the idea of "participation" (which it generally identifies with emotional mysticism) and in its predisposition to view man as an autonomous being. But these dogmas are fundamentally false.

Even today the prophets of "Godless Christianity" are, first of all, misinterpreting *man*. Our younger generation is not "secularistic," it desperately tries to satisfy its natural thirst for the "Other," for the Transcendent, for the True One, in such ambiguous escapes as Oriental religions, drugs, or psychedelic devices. Our age is not only the age of secularism, but also an age of emerging new religions, or substitutes for religion. This is unavoidable because man is a theocentric being; when he is denied the true God, he creates false ones.

### 3. Christocentric Theology.

If the view of man held by the Fathers is a true one, every Christian theology must necessarily be christocentric. A christocentric theology which is based, as it often has been, upon the idea of extrinsic redemption, of "satisfaction," of the grace of justification being externally added to an otherwise autonomous human existence, is often opposed to pneumatology, for indeed there is no place in it for the action of the Spirit. But if our God-centered anthropology is true, if the presence of the Spirit is what makes man truly man, if human destiny is in restoring *communion* with God, then Jesus, the New Adam, the one man in whom true humanity was manifested because He was born, in history "from the Holy Spirit and the Virgin Mary," is necessarily in the center of theology; and this centrality does not in any way limit the role of the Holy Spirit.

Christocentrism in theology is under heavy attack today on the part of Bultmannian hermeneutics. If every event is a myth unless it follows the laws of empirical science and experience, the "Christ-event" loses its absolute uniqueness, for its uniqueness is, in fact, subjectivized. Nevertheless, christocentrism is still strongly affirmed not only among the remnants of Barthian Neo-Orthodoxy, but also by Tillich. It coexists in the works of theologians who, like John Macquarrie, attempt to reconcile demythologizing of such events as the Resurrection and the Ascension[2] with a generally classical exposition of theological themes.

However, even in those comparatively traditional or semitraditional authors one can observe a very explicit taste for Nestorian or adoptionist christology.

Tillich, for example, formally expresses this when he writes that without the concept of adoption Christ "would be deprived of his finite freedom; for a transmuted being does not have the freedom to be other than divine."[3] What is evident in this position is the old Western idea that God and man, grace and freedom, are mutually exclusive. It is a remnant in Tillich's thought of a "closed" anthropology which excludes Orthodox christology.

The rehabilitation of Nestorius and his teacher, Theodore of Mopsuestia, has been undertaken by both historians and theologians since the last century in the name of the autonomy of man. This rehabilitation has even made some prominent Orthodox converts, who also show a marked preference for this "historicity" of the school of Antioch, postulating that history can be only "human" history. To be an *historical* being, Jesus must have been not only fully, but somehow *independently* a man. The central affirmations of Cyril of Alexandria about the Logos Himself becoming son of Mary—who is therefore Theotokos—or the theopaschite formulae officially proclaimed as criteria of Orthodoxy by

517

the Fifth Council in 553, appear to them as being at best terminological abuses or "baroque" theology. How can the Logos, i.e. God Himself, *die* on the cross, according to the flesh, since God is by definition immortal?

There is no need to enter here into a detailed discussion of theological concepts related to the doctrine of hypostatic union. I would like simply to affirm very strongly that the theopaschite formula of St. Cyril of Alexandria, "the Logos suffered in the flesh," is one of the greatest existing Christian affirmations of the *authenticity* of humanity. For if the Son of God Himself, in order to identify Himself with humanity, in order to become "similar to us in all things, including death"—human death—died on the cross, He testified in a manner greater than any human imagination could ever have conceived that humanity is indeed the most precious, the most vital, the most imperishable creation of God.

Of course Cyrillian christology presupposes the "open" anthropology of the early and later Fathers; the humanity of Jesus, by being "enhypostasized" in the Logos, was no less full humanity, because the presence of God does not destroy man. Moreover, one can even say that Jesus was more fully man than any of us. Here again, to quote Karl Rahner (who, among the contemporary Western theologians is on this point the closest to the mainstream of patristic tradition), "Human being is a reality absolutely open upwards; a reality which reaches its highest perfection, the realization of the highest possibility of man's being, when in it the Logos Himself becomes existent in the world."[4] One can also say that a christology which includes theopaschism presupposes *openness* in God's being as well.

It is therefore against the background of *this* christology that one can accept the idea that theology is also necessarily anthropology, and, vice versa that the only true Christian understanding of man—his creation, fall, salvation, and ultimate destiny—is revealed in Jesus Christ, the Logos of God, crucified and risen.

## 4. Personalistic Ecclesiology.

If the presence of the Holy Spirit in man *liberates* him, if grace means emancipation from slavery to the deterministic contingencies of the world, membership in the Body of Christ also means freedom. Finally, freedom means *personal* existence.

Our liturgy teaches us very clearly that membership in the Church is an eminently *personal* responsibility. Catechetical instruction, the pre-baptismal dialogue, the development of the penitential discipline, the evolution of communion practices, all illustrate the *personal* character of the Christian commitment. It is also well known that in the New Testament the term "member" (μέλος), when it designates the Christians as "members of Christ" (I Cor. 6:15) or as "members of each other" (Eph. 4:25), is applied only to individuals, and never to corporate entities such as local churches. The local church, a eucharistic community, is the *body,* while *membership* in it is an exclusively personal act.

To speak of "personal Christianity" and of "personal" faith is today highly unpopular, largely because religious personalism is immediately associated, in the West, with pietism and emotionalism. Here again we observe the same old incomprehension of the idea of real participation in divine life. When "grace" is either a thing bestowed by the institutional Church or a sort of general gratuitous act bestowed upon all of humanity by God's just and unequivocal omnipotence, the manifestations of personal experience of God become either pietism or emotional mysticism. Meanwhile, there is the tremendous urge of many Christians today to identify their Christian faith with social activism, with group dynamics, with political causes, of which [read as "or with"] utopian theories of historical development, precisely because they lack that which is the center of the New Testament message, a personal living experience of a personal God. When the latter is being preached by evangelistic revivalists or pentecostals, it indeed often takes the form of emotional superficiliality, but only because it has no basis in either theology or ecclesiology.

It is, therefore, the very particular responsibility of Orthodoxy to realize the tremendous importance of the scriptural and patristic experience of the Church as a body which is both a *sacrament,* i.e. implying an objective presence of God in a hierarchical structure independent of the individual worthiness of the members, and a *community of living free persons* with individual and direct responsibility to God, to the Church, and to each other. Personal experience receives both its reality and its authenticity from the sacrament, but the latter is given to the community in order to make the personal experience possible. The paradox which is implied here is best illustrated by the great St. Symeon the New Theologian, who is perhaps the most "sacramental" of the Byzantine spiritual writers, but who also describes as the greatest heresy ever confessed the opinion held by some of his contemporaries that a personal experience of God is impossible.[5] All saints, both ancient and modern, will confirm that this paradox stands at the very center of Christian existence in the present *aion.*

Obviously, it is through this antinomy between the "sacramental" and the "personal" that one finds the key for the understanding of authority in the Church. Here again, the responsibility of Orthodoxy is almost unique. It becomes increasingly clear today that the problem of authority is not simply a peripheral issue between East and West in the Middle Ages, expressed in the dispute between Constantinople and Rome, but that the tremendous drama of the entire Western Christianity is contained precisely in this issue. An authority, which wrongly considered itself for centuries as alone responsible for truth, has achieved a remarkable success in training the entire Church membership in the virtue of obedience, but meanwhile has liberated it from responsibility. It is being openly challenged today, mostly for the wrong reasons and for wrong causes, while it tries itself to give head-on-battles on untenable positions. In fact, salvation may come not from authority any more, for faith in authority is obviously lacking, but from a theological "restoration." Will Orthodox theology, with its justified claim to have preserved the balance between authority, freedom, and responsibility for truth, have anything to say? If not, the real tragedy will not be in our losing denominational pride, for self-righteousness is always a demonic feeling, but in the consequences which may well result for the Christian faith as such in the world today.

### 5. The True Conception of God Is Trinitarian.

A little earlier we mentioned the Cyrillian christological formula—"One of the Holy Trinity suffered in the flesh"—the formula sung at every liturgy as part of the hymn "Only-Begotten Son." We affirmed that it was firstly a recognition of *humanity* as a value sufficiently important for God Himself, important enough to bring Him to the cross; but this formula also implies a personal or "hypostatic" existence of God.

Objections against this formula are all based upon the identification of God's existence with his essence. God cannot die, said the Antiochian theologians, because He is immortal and changeless by nature or essence. For them, the concept of "death of God" was such a logical contradiction in terms that it could not be true, either religiously or philosophically. At best it was, just as the term *Theotokos* applied to the Virgin Mary, a pious periphrasis. Meanwhile, in Orthodox theology the Cyrillian formula has been not only accepted as true, both religiously and theologically, but made a criterion of Orthodoxy.

God is not bound by the philosophical necessities or attributes which our logics attribute to Him. The patristic notion of ὑπόστασις, which was unknown to Greek philosophy (it used the word ὑπόστασις in a different sense) and which is different, in God's being, from His unknown, unknowable, and therefore undefinable essence, implies an openness on the part of God that makes it possible for a divine person, or hypostasis, to *become* fully man. It meets the "openness upwards" which is characteristic of man. It makes possible the fact that God does not stay "up there," or "in heaven," but that He really comes all the way down to the human mortal condition, not in order to absorb it or to destroy it, but in order to save it and to restore its original communion with Himself.

In patristic theology this "condescension" of God occurs on the level of the personal or hypostatic existence of God. If it occurred in reference to God's nature or essence—as some so-called "kenotic" theories have asserted—then the Logos would, so to say, gradually become less and less God by approaching death, and cease finally to be God at the moment of death. The Cyrillian formula implies, on the contrary, that to the question, "Who died on the Cross?" there is no other answer than "God," because in Christ there was no other personal existence than that of the Logos and that death is necessarily a *personal* act. Only *somebody* can die, not *something*.

"You were in the tomb according to the flesh, in paradise with the thief, on the throne with the Father and the Spirit, O Indescribable One." This is what the Church proclaims in its paschal hymn: a union in one hypostasis of the essential characteristics of both the divine and the human natures, each remaining what it always is.

The human intellect cannot argue against this doctrine by referring to the qualities of divine essence, because this essence is totally unknown and indescribable and because, if we know God directly, it is precisely because the person of the Son assumed *another nature* than the divine, made an *inrush* into created existence and thus spoke with the human mouth of Jesus, died a human death, rose from a human grave, and established an eternal communion with humanity by sending the Holy Spirit. "No one has ever seen God; the only Son, who is in the bosom of the Father, He has made Him known" (John 1:18 RSV).

It would obviously be much too easy to establish a parallel between our modern "death of God" theologians and St. Cyril of Alexandria. The context and the purpose of theology there and here are radically different. But it is indeed possible, and for Orthodox theologians quite necessary, to affirm that God is not a philosophical notion, an "essence with characteristics," a concept, but that He is what Jesus Christ is, that knowledge of Him is primarily a personal encounter with the one in whom the Apostles recognized the Incarnate Logos, and also with the "Other One" who was sent afterwards as our advocate in our present expectation of the end, and that in Christ and through the Spirit we are led to the Father Himself.

Orthodox theology does not start with proofs of God's existence, with converting men to philosophical deism. It confronts them with the Gospel of Jesus Christ and expects their free response to this challenge.

It has been often said that the Eastern Fathers, when speaking of God, always start with the three persons, to prove later their "consubstantiality," while the West starts with God as one essence, tries later to suggest also the distinction into three persons. These two tendencies are at the origin of the *filioque* dispute, but they are also of great relevance for the present. God is, in Orthodox theology, the Father, the Son, and the Spirit, as persons. Their common divine essence is totally unknowable and transcendent, and its characteristics themselves are best described in negative terms. But the three act personally; they make their common divine Life (or "energy") participable. Through baptism "in the Name of the Father, of the Son, and of the Holy Spirit" new life and immortality is a living reality and experience, and becomes available to man.

### Notes

1. In *Living Tradition: Orthodox Witness in the Contemporary World* (Crestwood, NY: St. Vladimir's Seminary Press, 1978), pp. 173-84. Originally published in *St. Vladimir's Theological Quarterly* 13:1/2 (1969), pp. 77-92.
2. John Macquarrie, *Principles of Christian Theology* (New York: Charles Scribner's Sons, 1966), pp. 265-67.
3. Paul Tillich, *Systematic Theology,* II, p. 149. A good critique of Tillich's position is found in George H. Tavard, *Paul Tillich and the Christian Message* (London: Burns and Oats, 1962), pp. 129-32.
4. Karl Rahner, *Theological Investigations,* I, trans. C. Ernst (Baltimore: Helicon Press, 1961), p. 183.
5. *Catéchèse XXIX,* ed. Basile Krivochéine, in the collection "Sources Chrétiennes," 113 (Paris, 1968), pp. 177-79.

# John B. Cobb, Jr.

*T*he term process theology *emerged early in the middle third of the twentieth century as a creative and powerful force in discussions of "philosophical theology" and thereafter had a significant impact on a wide range of theological topics, including practical theology and the practice(s) of ministry. It arose from the "process philosophy" of Alfred North Whitehead and Charles Hartshorne, who undertook a recasting of classical metaphysics in terms of conceiving reality as a complex, ongoing process of interrelated events of experience. During the 1930s various applications of this revised metaphysics to views of God's reality and relations to the world immediately developed among a number of leading theologians, Henry Nelson Wieman among them, as well as in process philosophy per se.*

*Cobb (born 1925) represents, as it were, process theology's second generation, and David Ray Griffin (born 1939), his student, the third. Cobb, influenced by Hartshorne at the University of Chicago (Ph.D., 1952), revised and expanded the Whitehead-Hartshorne categorical schema for conceiving reality and God to the wider sphere of Christian doctrine, and throughout his teaching at Claremont Theological Seminary (1958-1990) and his writings, he was influential in the incorporation of process theology into "church theological" circles. Griffin's dissertation, written under Cobb, on process christology (revised for publication, 1973) further developed the "process tradition," as did his teaching at Claremont and his leadership with Cobb of the Center for Process Studies (after 1973) and his later reflections on evil, theodicy, and postmodernity.*

*Included here is a selection from* Process Theology: An Introductory Exposition *(1976), which Cobb and Griffin coauthored so that process categories might be understood and used by church people, not by philosophical theologians or philosophers alone.*

# GOD AS CREATIVE-RESPONSIVE LOVE[1]

## Divine Creative Love as Persuasive

. . . [T]raditional theism portrayed God as the Controlling Power. The doctrine of divine omnipotence finally meant that God controlled every detail of the world process. Some traditional theologians, such as Thomas Aquinas, muted this implication of their thought as much as possible (in order to protect the doctrine of human freedom). Others, such as Luther and Calvin, proclaimed the doctrine from the housetops (in order to guard against both pride and anxiety). But, in either case, the doctrine followed logically from other doctrines that were affirmed. The notion that God knows the world, and that this knowledge is unchanging, suggests that God must in fact determine every detail of the world, lest something happen which was not immutably known. The doctrine that God is completely independent of the world implies that the divine knowledge of it cannot be dependent upon it, and this can only be if the world does nothing which was not totally determined by God. The doctrine of divine simplicity involves the assertion that all the divine attributes are identical; hence God's knowing the world is identical with God's causing it. The Biblical record is quite ambivalent on the question of whether God is in complete control of the world. There is much in the Bible which implies that divine providence is not all-determining. But the interpretation of the Biblical God in terms of valuations about perfection derived from Greek philosophy ruled out this side of the Biblical witness, thereby making creaturely freedom vis-à-vis God merely apparent.

Process thought, with its different understanding of perfection, sees the divine creative activity as based upon responsiveness to the world. Since the very meaning of actuality involves internal relatedness, God as an actuality is essentially related to the world. Since actuality as such is partially self-creative, future events are not yet determinate, so that even perfect knowledge cannot know the future, and God does not wholly control the world. Any divine creative influence must be persuasive, not coercive.

Whitehead's fundamentally new conception of divine creativity in the world centers around the notion that God provides each worldly actuality with an "initial aim." This is an impulse, initially felt conformally by the occasion, to actualize the best possibility open to it, given its concrete situation. But this initial aim does not automatically become the subject's own aim. Rather, this "subjective aim" is a product of its own

524

decision. The subject may choose to actualize the initial aim; but it may also choose from among the other real possibilities open to it, given its context. In other words, God seeks to persuade each occasion toward that possibility for its own existence which would be best for it; but God cannot control the finite occasion's self-actualization. Accordingly, the divine creative activity involves risk. The obvious point is that, since God is not in complete control of the events of the world, the occurrence of genuine evil is not incompatible with God's beneficence toward all his creatures.

A less obvious but equally important consequence is that, since persuasion and not control is the divine way of doing things, this is the way we should seek to accomplish our ends. Much of the tragedy in the course of human affairs can be attributed to the feeling that to control others, and the course of events, is to share in divinity. Although traditional theism said that God was essentially love, the divine love was subordinated to the divine power. Although the result of Jesus' message, life, and death should have been to redefine divine power in terms of the divine love, this did not happen. Power, in the sense of controlling domination, remained the *essential* definition of deity. Accordingly, the control of things, events, and other persons, which is to some extent a "natural" human tendency, took on that added sense of satisfaction which comes from participating in an attribute understood (more or less consciously) to be divine.

Process theology's understanding of divine love is in harmony with the insight, which we can gain both from psychologists and from our own experience, that if we truly love others we do not seek to control them. We do not seek to pressure them with promises and threats involving extrinsic rewards and punishments. Instead we try to persuade them to actualize those possibilities which they themselves will find intrinsically rewarding. We do this by providing ourselves as an environment that helps open up new, intrinsically attractive possibilities.

Insofar as the notion that divine love is persuasive is accepted, the exercise of persuasive influence becomes intrinsically rewarding. It takes on that aura of extra importance that has too often been associated with the feeling of controlling others. This change has implications in all our relations, from one-to-one I-thou encounters to international relations. It does not mean that coercive control could be eliminated, but it does mean that such control is exercised as a last resort and with a sense of regret rather than with the thrill that comes from the sense of imitating deity.

## Divine Creative Love as Promoting Enjoyment

In traditional Christianity, God has been understood as a Cosmic Moralist, in the sense of being *primarily* concerned with the development of moral behavior and attitudes in human beings. Negatively, this meant that the promotion of creaturely enjoyment was not God's first concern. In fact, in most Christian circles enjoyment has been understood as something that God at best tolerated, and often as something that he opposed. Thus the pleasure of sexual relations is tolerated, as long as it is only a concomitant of the primary function of sex, which is the morally sound intention to have children. The use of contraceptives has been frowned upon, since their use would mean the explicit admission that sexual intercourse was being engaged in solely for the enjoyment it brings.

This attitude toward sex is only the extreme example of the church's traditional attitude toward enjoyment in general, which has been taken to be a reflection of God's attitude. The result has been a stern, lifeless Christianity, being in tension with rather than supportive of the natural drive to enjoy life. The man whom Christians have called the Christ was called by some a "glutton and a drunkard" (Matt. 11:19; Luke 7:34 RSV) and could be quoted by one of the Evangelists as saying, "I came that they may have life, and have it abundantly" (John 10:10 RSV). But the Christian church has been perceived, not as the community that encourages the enjoyment of the abundant life, but as the institution that discourages most forms of enjoyment in the name of "being good." To put it crudely, one does not attend church to have a good time, but to atone for the good time one had the night before! God has been understood as commanding us to suppress our desire for most of those experiences which we find *intrinsically* good in favor of being *morally* good. And moral goodness has primarily been understood negatively, that is, as involving the suppression of many of the natural forms of enjoyment.

This notion of God as Cosmic Moralist is not unrelated to the idea of God as Controlling Power. The problem of evil would too evidently disprove the existence of God, if God be understood not only as controlling all events but also as willing the maximum enjoyment of his creatures. If the primary focus is on the creatures' enjoyment of existence, the great amount and variety of suffering and the great inequalities involved would easily suggest that God was either malevolent or incompetent, if not both. Hence, the notion that God is competently in control of all things can be saved by saying that creaturely enjoyment is not a high priority. In fact, the sufferings of life, and even the inequalities in this regard, can be regarded as divinely intended means to promote the desired moral and religious attitudes.

Hence, the notion of God as Cosmic Moralist supports the notion of God as Controlling Power. A development in this regard in the history of Christian thought can be detected. In the earlier centuries, and especially in the thought of Augustine, there was a heavy stress on the intrinsic goodness of being actual. This stress was supported by the goodness of the creation as declared by God in Gen., ch. 1, and the Platonic equation of being and goodness. This position was maintained throughout the Middle Ages—it is still dominant in Thomas Aquinas, for example—in spite of the added difficulty it creates for the problem of evil. This was possible partly because the Biblical and rational proofs for the existence of God (as conceived by traditional theists) were thought to be so strong that the problem of evil could be dismissed. However, in modern times, especially in Protestant thought, the idea of the intrinsic goodness of existence has faded, and Christian theology has become increasingly moralistic. This is no doubt due to several factors. The ontological dualism of the modern age, especially in its Cartesian variety, made it difficult to think of existence as such as intrinsically good, since humans were the only created beings with any intrinsic (experiential) reality. Also, the loss of confidence in the rational and then the Biblical evidences for God's existence made the problem of evil more desperate. Accordingly, and especially in modern Protestant thought, the dominant trend in theodicy has been to explain the great sufferings of the world by declaring that God did not intend the world as a "hedonistic paradise," but as a "vale of soul-making."[2]

Process theology sees God's fundamental aim to be the promotion of the creatures' own enjoyment. God's creative influence upon them is loving, because it aims at promoting that which the creatures experience as intrinsically good. Since God is not in complete control, the divine love is not contradicted by the great amount of intrinsic evil, or "disenjoyment," in the world. The creatures in part create both themselves and their successors.

God's creative love extends to all the creatures, since all actualities, as experiential, have some degree of enjoyment. The promotion of enjoyment is God's primary concern throughout the whole process of creative evolution. The contrary doctrine, which sees God's primary concern to be the development of moral attitudes, is in the uncomfortable position of maintaining that over 99 percent of the history of our planet was spent in merely preparing the way for beings who are capable of the only kind of experience that really interests God.

527

Enjoyment is God's primary concern even with those beings who are capable of developing moral attitudes. But this is not in conflict with an emphasis on morality. God wants us to enjoy, true. But he wants us *all* to enjoy. Accordingly, he wants us to enjoy in ways that do not unnecessarily inhibit enjoyment on the part of others. That puts it negatively. Positively stated, God wants our enjoyment to be such as to increase the enjoyments of others. To be moral is to actualize oneself in such a way as to maximize the enjoyments of future actualities, insofar as these future enjoyments can be conditioned by one's present decision. Hence, although the development of moral attitudes is of extreme importance, it is a derivative concern, secondary to the primary value, which is enjoyment itself.

In traditional Christianity, morality and enjoyment were often seen as in fundamental opposition. In process thought, morality stands in the service of enjoyment. However, the question still arises of the possible tension between them. There is the possible tension between enjoying the present moment to the hilt, and forgoing some of this possible enjoyment in order to prepare for increased enjoyment in the future. Also there is the tension, in regard to the future, between my *own* future occasions of experience, and the future experiences of other enduring individuals. This tension, and its ideal resolution, will be discussed in Chapter 5. Suffice it here to say that the creative love of God is also relevant to this problem. The divine initial aim for our human experiences is such as to transform into immediate enjoyment the intention to contribute to future good.

### Divine Creative Love as Adventurous

One respect in which God's creative love is adventurous has already been discussed: since God's creative activity is persuasive, not controlling, it is a love that takes risks. Hence, each divine creative impulse into the world is adventurous, in that God does not know what the result will be.

However, there is another dimension to the divine adventurousness. Traditional theology tended to portray God as the Sanctioner of the Status Quo. The notions of "God" and "order" were closely associated. In the political realm, the connection between obedience to God and submission to the political status quo was supported by the notorious appeal to Rom., ch. 13, where Paul says that we should "be subject to the governing authorities" because they "have been instituted by God," so that "he who resists the authorities resists what God has appointed."

This notion of God is also closely connected with the notion of God as Controlling Power. Paul's statement is one of those Biblical statements which presuppose that God is in control at least of the major features of the world process. The development of traditional theism, in which God was more consistently said to be in complete control of every detail, further strengthened the conviction that the political status quo should be affirmed. For if God had not wanted those rulers in power, they would not be in power. It is largely due to this notion that those who have been in opposition to despotic rulers have also found themselves in opposition to the church, and have found it useful to espouse atheism.

In the realm of morality in general, belief in God has been closely associated with the idea of moral absolutes, especially of a negative nature. Certain kinds of actions have been said to be wrong in themselves, whether or not in a particular context they served to promote abundant life. This has focused moral attention on rules or fixed principles and distracted from consideration of what would increase the quality of life in the future. Hence the notion that Christian morality consists primarily in abstaining from certain kinds of acts that God has prohibited serves doubly to sanction the status quo. It does so directly, simply by virtue of the notion of immutable moral absolutes. It does so indirectly by diverting attention from the primary moral question of how we should act so as to increase enjoyment of life now and in the future.

The notion of God as Sanctioner of the Status Quo is closely connected with that of God as Cosmic Moralist. The focus on the development of moral attitudes, understood as being in opposition to the growth of enjoyment, distracted attention from the question of what kinds of conditions are needed in order to maximize the possibilities for enjoying existence. This question was not of ultimate importance, since moral attitudes can be developed in any situation. In fact, as some theologians have argued, the more difficult the circumstances, the greater the opportunity for developing moral qualities such as patience!

Process theology understands God precisely as the basic source of unrest in the universe. In Whitehead's words, "The pure conservative is fighting against the essence of the universe."[3] When he speaks of the essence of the universe, Whitehead primarily has in mind the notion that actuality is process, and that at the root of process there is the Primordial Nature of God, which he sometimes calls the Divine Eros. This is conceived as "the active entertainment of all ideals, with the urge to their finite realization, each in its due season."[4] Not all ideal possibilities can be realized simultaneously. This is why there is process.[5] But also no ideal can be repeated indefinitely without its freshness being lost. The Primordial Nature of God is the goad toward novelty in the universe,[6] stimulating us to realize new possibilities after the old ones no longer are sufficient to give zest to our enjoyment of being actual.

Order is an essential ingredient in the maximization of enjoyment. For example, the richness of human experience could emerge only on the basis of the order of the body. "It is by reason of the body, with its miracle of order, that the treasures of the past environment are poured into the living occasion."[7] On the other hand, excessive order can inhibit enjoyment. Hence, Whitehead speaks of "the contrast between order as the condition for excellence, and order as stifling the freshness of living."[8] Hence, order must not be lost, but it also must not be dominant. "The art of progress is to preserve order amid change, and to preserve change amid order."[9]

God is the source of order. But two important qualifications must be made. Order represents dominance of an ideal possibility which was at one time a novel element in the world. Hence God is the source of order by virtue of first being the source of novelty. Second, neither order nor novelty is understood as intrinsically good, but only as instrumental to the one intrinsic good, which is the enjoyment of intense experience. "God's purpose in the creative advance is the evocation of intensities. The evocation of societies is purely subsidiary to this absolute end."[10] " 'Order' and 'novelty' are but the instruments of his subjective aim which is the intensification of 'formal immediacy.' "[11] In brief, although God is the source of order, the order is derivative from novelty, and both order and novelty are good only insofar as they contribute to the enjoyment of experience. As Whitehead puts it elsewhere, the aim toward order, which is impersonal, is subservient to the love of individuals, which is personal. Therefore, types of order are to be rated "according to their success in magnifying the individual actualities, that is to say, in promoting strength of experience."[12]

Hence, no type of social order is to be maintained if it no longer tends to maximize the enjoyment of the members of the society. Also, it is impossible for any form of social order to continue indefinitely to be instrumentally good. God, far from being the Sanctioner of the Status Quo, is the source of some of the chaos in the world. "If there is to be progress beyond limited ideals, the course of history by way of escape must venture along the borders of chaos in its substitution of higher for lower types of order."[13] (God is said to be the source of only *some* of the chaos, since only some of it can in principle lead to a higher type of order and thereby a richer form of enjoyment.)

530

The connection between the notion of God as the source of adventure toward novel ideals and that of divine creative love as fostering enjoyment has already been made clear. The connection with God as persuasive power is also obvious. Since God does not control the details of any worldly process, the existence of a given state of affairs does not imply that God willed it. Further, since God encourages the actualization of novel possibilities as a means to maximizing creaturely enjoyment, continuation of a state of affairs that originally resulted from a high degree of conformity to God's aims may not express God's present will. As Henry Nelson Wieman has stressed, partly under the influence of Whitehead, we should worship the Creative Good, not the created good.

Besides the two senses already mentioned in which God's love is adventurous—that it takes risks and promotes adventure toward novelty in the world—there is a third sense. This results from combining this creative side of God's love (God as Divine Eros) with the responsive side. The result is, in Whitehead's words, "the concept of an Adventure in the Universe as One."[14] This is simply a way of describing God. "This Adventure embraces all particular occasions but as an actual fact stands beyond any one of them."[15] The point is that God's own life is an adventure, for the novel enjoyments that are promoted among the creatures are then the experiences providing the material for God's own enjoyment. "The Unity of Adventure includes the Eros which is the living urge towards all possibilities, claiming the goodness of their realization."[16] And God's life is also an adventure in the sense of being a risk, since God will feel the discord as well as the beautiful experiences involved in the finite actualizations: "The Adventure of the Universe starts with the dream and reaps tragic Beauty."[17]

### God as Creative-Responsive Love

The traditional concept of God is in many respects stereotypically masculine. God was conceived to be active, unresponsive, impassive, inflexible, impatient, and moralistic. This being had none of the stereotypically feminine traits—it was not at all passive, responsive, emotional, flexible, patient, and it did not balance moral concern with an appreciation of beauty. This has led to a one-sided and hence unhealthy Christianity.

An overreaction resulting in a concept of God devoid of the stereotypically masculine attributes would also be destructive of authentic Christian existence. Losing the active or creative side of the divine love would undercut much of the good that Biblical faiths have brought into

531

history, as we have already suggested. The same is true of the strong element of moral concern that has been attributed to God in the cultures decisively influenced by the Biblical faiths. Likewise, the loss of the notion of a divine purpose that at its most general level is inflexible would lead to a complete relativism. The positive aspects of these "masculine" attributes can be retained, without their destructive implications, if they are incorporated into a revolutionized concept of God into which the stereotypically feminine traits are integrated. For, in the integrated result, the former traits are changed qualitatively.

Unfortunately, in some passages Whitehead does not describe the two "natures" of God as if they were truly integrated. Sometimes the Primordial Nature is described as if it were static order of the eternal possibilities, and the "initial aim" for each worldly actuality is said to be derived from this Primordial Nature. This would mean that the creative input of God into the world in each moment would be based upon a completely inflexible vision; it would not be based upon a sympathetic response to the previous state of affairs. However, in other passages Whitehead makes it clear that the ideals toward which the world is called by God in one moment are based upon God's loving response to the facts of the previous moments.[18] The world does not really have to do with two "natures" or "poles" of God that stand externally related to each other, the one influencing the world and the other being influenced by it. Rather, the Primordial Nature is abstract, while the Consequent Nature is God as fully actual.[19] It is finally to God as a whole that we are related. The creative activity of God is based upon sympathetic responsiveness; and the responsiveness of God is an active receptiveness made in the light of an intended creative influence upon the future.

The process dipolar notion of deity has some affinity with the Taoist notion of the Tao, in which the "feminine" and "masculine" (yin and yang) dimensions of reality are perfectly integrated. The Tao is spoken of as a power that works slowly and undramatically, but is finally the most effective agency in reality. Whereas there are aspects of the notion of the Tao which have unfortunate implications, the Taoist vision of deity does contain an important element which should all along have been part of the Christian vision.

### Notes

1. In *Process Theology: An Introductory Exposition.* By John B. Cobb, Jr., and David Ray Griffin (Philadelphia: The Westminster Press, 1976), pp. 52-62.
2. Cf. John Hick, *Evil and the God of Love* (Harper & Row Publishers, Inc., 1966), pp. 291-97; and A. C. Knudson, *The Doctrine of Redemption*

(Abingdon Press, 1933), p. 215.
3. Alfred North Whitehead, *Adventures of Ideas* (New York: The Macmillan Company, 1933), p. 354.
4. Ibid., p. 357.
5. Alfred North Whitehead, *Modes of Thought* (New York: The Macmillan Company, 1938), p. 53.
6. Alfred North Whitehead, *Process and Reality* (New York: The Macmillan Company, 1929), p. 135.
7. Ibid., p. 516.
8. Ibid., p. 514.
9. Ibid., p. 515.
10. Ibid., p. 161.
11. Ibid., p. 135.
12. Whitehead, *Adventures of Ideas,* p. 376.
13. Whitehead, *Process and Reality,* p. 169.
14. Whitehead, *Adventures of Ideas,* p. 380.
15. Ibid.
16. Ibid., p. 381.
17. Ibid.
18. Alfred North Whitehead, *Religion in the Making* (New York: The Macmillan Company, 1926), pp. 148-49, 151, 152.
19. Whitehead, *Process and Reality,* pp. 524, 532.

# Rosemary Radford Ruether

$O$*f the early and leading pioneers of "feminist theology,"
Ruether (born 1936) has made, through her prolific work, critical and
constructive advances of notable impact across a wide front of concerns.
Her own upbringing in Roman Catholicism was anticipatory of reforms
only partially realized by Vatican II. She completed her theological
studies at Claremont School of Theology (Ph.D., 1965). She teaches at
Garrett-Evangelical Theological Seminary. The titles of her first three
important books,* To Change the World: Christology and Cultural Criticism *(1981),* Disputed Questions: On Being a Christian *(1982), and*
Sexism and God-Talk: Toward a Feminist Theology *(1983) are themselves signals of an ambitious agenda, rooted in historic and current theological ground but pressing in directions beyond the status quo. Later,
and still ongoing, reflection on sexuality and gender, ecofeminism, and
"Women-Church" as well as on theological method and doctrinal
reconstruction make her a singular, avowedly iconoclastic, "representative" of emergent feminist-liberationist thought.*

*Among the great strengths brought to the theological work of Rose-
mary Ruether are her indefatigable energy and her willingness to address
different types of audiences, including academic professionals, church
leadership, and laypeople. In this 1985 essay, which appeared in* Christianity & Crisis, *Ruether offers a readily accessible analysis of feminist
theology and its struggle to gain a hearing within the theological academy. In the midst of her analysis, she defines the three "moments" of
feminist theology.*

## FEMINIST THEOLOGY IN THE ACADEMY[1]

Feminist theology arises as a critique of the patriarchal bias of traditional theology. Indeed, the critique is as old as the patriarchal tradition
itself: It has surfaced, been suppressed, been recovered and then resup-
pressed, again and again. Today, thanks to the feminist scholarship of

534

the last 15 years, feminist theology has gained a foothold in the academy. It has emerged in the mainstream as a recognized alternative theological perspective. Already, however, it is clear that we can speak only tentatively about its future. For once again the forces that would deny its claim to a future, to defining what the "tradition" will be, are formidable.

To ask about the future of feminist theology in the academy, therefore, is not to ask whether the patriarchal tradition and feminism have a future together. Of course they don't. It is to ask whether feminist theology will sufficiently transform theology as it is taught in the seminaries and preached in the churches, so that we no longer have patriarchal theology but an inclusive theology, a theology that affirms the full humanity and interrelationship of women and men. Or will patriarchal theology succeed in confining feminist theology to the margins of the theological enterprise, so that the next generation of theological students will no longer be able to raise feminist questions because they will have been ruled out-of-bounds by the guardians of theological "orthodoxy"?

In thinking about this question, I need to acknowledge at the outset that I speak from a white Western Christian context. Theology should overcome patterns of thought within it that vilify or exclude persons by gender, race, or religion. But this does not mean that we seek a theology that is universalistic in the sense of encompassing all cultures and religions. Such universalism is, in fact, cultural imperialism—an attempt by one religious culture to monopolize not only theology but salvation, to claim that it alone has authentic access to the divine. Christian patriarchal theology has typically been imperialistic, claiming that white male Christian experience is equivalent to universal humanity.

Feminist theology, by contrast, must be consciously pluralistic. Despite similarities among patriarchal patterns, a Christian feminism will be different from a Jewish feminism or a Buddhist or Muslim feminism. Moreover, an Asian Christian feminist or an African Christian feminist or an American black Christian feminist will also have distinct problems and will come up with different syntheses. Pagan feminists, who seek to break with all patriarchal religious contexts and to rediscover an ancient female-centered religion or to create one today, pose yet a different problematic.

Despite these differences, however, there is one theme that is not at issue in feminist theology, in my view, and that is the legitimacy of encountering the divine as goddess.

Feminist theology, then, needs to be seen as a network of solidarity

535

that exists among many feminist communities engaged in the critique of patriarchalism in distinct cultural and religious contexts, rather than one dominant form of feminism that claims to speak for the whole of womankind.

### A Critical Engagement

Feminist theology is engaged in a critique of the androcentrism and misogyny of patriarchal theology. What does this mean? First of all it means that in patriarchal theology the male is taken to be the normative representative of the human species, the norm for imaging God and for defining anthropology, sin, redemption, and ministry. The female, in contrast, is seen as subordinate and auxiliary to the male. Women never appear in patriarchal theology as representatives of humanity as such. Their normative position is that of absence and silence. When patriarchal theology mentions women, it does so to reinforce its definition of their "place" in its system. When women challenge this definition— when they break the silence and assert their presence as subjects in their own right—patriarchal theology becomes not only androcentric, but overtly misogynist. Misogyny is male dominance engaged in self-defense of its right to define and control women and all other reality.

Androcentrism and misogyny are characteristic of Christian patriarchal theology. The attempt to exclude women as subjects of theology begins within the New Testament:

> I permit no woman to teach or to have authority over men; she is to keep
> silent.                                                  1 Timothy 2:12 RSV

This ban against women as teachers or preachers—that is to say, as creators and exponents of theology—is continued in the early church orders, such as the *Didascalia* (early third century) and the *Apostolic Constitutions* (late fourth century). (The *Constitutions* declare that Jesus chose to commission men and not women, that the male is the head of the woman and, therefore, a woman may not teach.) It continues in the Middle Ages and is renewed in the mainline Protestant traditions of the Reformation. It is echoed in 19th- and 20th-century arguments against women's right to preach. Although a few theological schools, such as Oberlin College, were open to women in the 19th century, most have been slower to open to women than other professional schools, such as law and medicine, whose record is bad enough.

Even those theological schools that did admit women at first required

536

them to be silent and even forbade their asking questions in class. The first female theological graduate and first woman to be ordained to a Christian denomination, Antoinette Brown, was valedictorian of her class. A male had to read her speech for her, however, since she was not allowed to speak. Major theological schools, such as Harvard Divinity School, were open to women only in the 1950s, and the right of women to attend some Catholic theological seminaries is still in dispute. In fact, it has only been in the past 10 to 15 years in the United States that women have begun to attend theological schools in significant numbers.

Thus, in one sense the question of feminist theology is very recent. While patriarchal theology reaches back more than 3,000 years into the roots of the Hebrew Bible, women have only very recently gained enough of a foothold in theological education even to begin to ask questions about the androcentric and misogynist bias of this tradition. It is not surprising, therefore, that women do not yet have all the answers, and indeed are only beginning to formulate the questions. What is surprising is the enormous amount of solid work in all fields that has been accomplished in these past 15 years—from biblical studies to history, to theology, to ethics, to pastoral psychology, to ministry. Today, it is no longer possible in any field of religious studies to claim that there are no good materials to incorporate into the curriculum. The problem, rather, is that most theological teachers refuse to read these materials and to redefine their teaching to incorporate them. As a result, they reproduce another generation of students socialized to identify theology with patriarchal theology and to pass on the patriarchal tradition as normative Christianity.

### Moments in Concurrent Development

One can speak of three stages in the development of feminist theology, although these stages do not simply succeed each other but are constantly developing in interaction with each other. During the first stage one begins to criticize the overt misogyny of the theological tradition and thereby to throw its authority into question. Only gradually does it become apparent that overt misogyny is but the tip of the iceberg and, indeed, probably occurs precisely at those moments when some women are challenging male dominance of the tradition.

Underneath the overt misogyny is the buried continent of unconscious androcentrism that has shaped all stages of the theological enterprise, from revelatory experience and its earliest statements to all its redactions and commentaries. As the endless debates about sexist language have

537

shown, this pervasive assumption that the male is the normative human subject is more difficult to unmask precisely because it is so unconscious and so taken-for-granted. The invisibility of women can never be seen by those for whom the generic "man" is simply assumed to include "women."

This first-stage work begins with surveys of the most blatant types of discrimination and misogyny and develops into more specialized discussions of particular thinkers or schools of theology and to more subtle analyses of methodologies of discernment. Gradually one begins to define the full impact of androcentrism on theology, not only as it runs through all periods and schools of theology but also as it has distorted every theological symbol.

Starting with the basic assumption that the male is the normative human person and, therefore, also the normative image of God, all symbols, from God-language and Christology to church and ministry, are shaped by the pervasive pattern of the male as center, the female as subordinate and auxiliary. This is true also where female symbols appear: The traditional feminine theological symbol of Wisdom as a mediating principle within God which communicates the divine to humanity is modeled after the wife or mother who mediates the "word" of the father of the household to its children or servants. Similarly the symbol of "Mother Church," as a feminine collective symbol for the Christian community, mediates as a mother between the divine father and the Christian as child or "son." The feminine image of the soul as the bride of Christ in mystical nuptials also sees the feminine as the creaturely passive and receptive principle *vis-a-vis* male divine power.

Most importantly, androcentrism biases the definition of sin, or the naming of evil, in the Christian tradition. By adopting the Hebrew folk story of the expulsion from paradise as its key paradigm for the origin and nature of evil, Christianity reinforces theologically a victim-blaming ideology of patriarchalism. The myth of female primacy in the origin of evil reinforces the patriarchal definition of woman as subordinate and auxiliary by claiming that woman caused evil to come into the world by speaking and acting *autonomously*. The subordination of women as "nature" is redoubled as punishment for sin.

Given the ideology of sin, "redemption" for women is not hard for patriarchy to define. Women are redeemed by voluntarily submitting to their gender roles: childbearing, sexual repression, and social subordination. They are thus asked to accept the guilt for their own victimization by patriarchy. This extends in patriarchal culture even to acts of violence by men against women. If a man rapes her, it is presumed that she "asked" for it. If her husband beats her, it is because she has provoked it by her complaints. That she must have "deserved it" defines the basic stance of patriarchy toward assaults on women.

Victim-blaming ideologies of sin prevent a culture from rightly naming evil and function to justify evil by describing it as nature, just punishment, and divine will. The essential core of feminist theology lies in the unmasking of this victim-blaming ideology of sin: Patriarchalism as a social system that legitimizes the dominating power of a male ruling class and reduces women and servants to subjection is named as evil. It is shown to be a system that both produces and justifies aggressive power over women and other subjugated people and denies a genuine reciprocal humanity. The quest for an authentic humanity begins at the point where patriarchy's claims to name the world are de-legitimized.

The second moment in feminist theology seeks alternative traditions that support the autonomous personhood of women. This quest takes many forms at the present time. It takes the form of feminist studies of Hebrew Scripture and the New Testament to discern alternative traditions that affirm women's personhood, her equality in the image of God, her equal redeemability, her participation in prophecy, teaching, and leadership. This does not mean a denial or cover-up of patriarchal bias, but rather a demonstration that, even amid this bias, there are glimpses of alternative realities. Patriarchal ideology did not succeed in defining what women actually were or did in past times. Woman is there in the biblical drama, not merely as object, but as subject, as seeker and questioner of God, and as agent of the divine Spirit.

The quest for alternative tradition also goes on in the various periods of Christian history, discovering and chronicling the church mothers who were there, but whose stories have been covered up or silenced. This historical quest makes the power of patriarchal control over the tradition all the more clear. Those women who have been lifted up as models have been selected by men and have functioned, by and large, to reinforce male ideologies about female roles. This means that their lives were censored by patriarchy, both within and after their lifetimes, so we know about them only those things that patriarchy wishes us to know. This meager procession of masochistic women is what patriarchy calls the female "saints." Sometimes by digging deeper, we can glimpse an alternative, more autonomous personality in these women, but such information has survived censorship by accident.

Occasionally a woman in the tradition stands out as so powerful and so central that she can neither be silenced nor sanitized. Here the patri-archal censor resorts to what might be called a "mud-slinging job." Thus, Miriam—named as co-equal leader of the exodus with Moses and Aaron—is besmirched in the book of Numbers by being turned by God into a leper in punishment for her criticism of Moses. God is said to be the father who has spit in her face, that is, has totally repudiated her as daughter.

Likewise, the Christian tradition marginalized Mary Magdalene by turning her into a repentant prostitute, thereby masking her position as leading female apostle and first witness of the resurrection, commis-sioned to bring the good news back to the male disciples who had fled the scene and were trembling in the upper room. The controversy stories between Peter and Mary Magdalene in the gnostic gospels have clarified that the controversy over the status of Mary Magdalene was indeed understood in early Christianity as a controversy over women's apos-tolic authority.

Many other women's stories have been pushed to the margins of the tradition. These women have been defined as heretics, witches, or lunatics, their writings have been destroyed and their memory survives only in the negative judgments made against them. Woman Studies seeks to read between the lines of these judgments and to gather the fragments of writings that have survived. Occasionally a lucky find—such as the Nag Hammadi library, buried by fourth-century Christian dissidents to prevent its destruction by the orthodox and disinterred in modern times—allows us to read the writings of banished traditions in their own voice. Only in more recent centuries have dissident writings survived, such as Margaret Fell's 17th-century defense of women's right to preach. Orthodox patriarchalism has marginalized these traditions by simply not incorporating them into what is read by students in the dominant theological traditions, but the documents are, at least, there to be dis-covered.

As this work of making women visible and audible progresses, it becomes apparent that ours is not the first feminist critique of patriar-chal theology. Again and again such a critique has begun, sometimes in what appears to be an isolated voice. Whether it is Christian de Pisan in the 14th century, Margaret Fell and other feminist writers of 17th-century English radical puritanism, or Elizabeth Cady Stanton in the 19th century, we discover again and again the same arguments against patriarchal ideology, the same refutations of its claims to define God, humanity, and reality.

Indeed, feminist theology has been endlessly reinventing the wheel and endlessly losing its inventions, precisely *because* it does not control the definition of the tradition. It has not been able to determine what will be read and remembered by the next generation of theological students. So it ever loses its own history and has to begin again as though its questions had never been asked and answered before. This reality is what raises the question for the future of feminist theology today. Despite all the impressive work of recovery and development of the last 15 years, will we once again lose our history because this work will not be reincorporated into the main curriculum and taught as part of what must now define our heritage and our identity?

*The Moment of Construction*

The third moment of feminist theology, then, takes the form of tentative efforts to restate the norms and methods of theology itself in the light of this critique and alternative tradition, to reenvision the basic categories of theology itself as a new center and norm. It is not enough merely to show that the myth of Eve is a victim-blaming ideology that mislabels evil. One needs to explain *our* understanding of good and evil, an understanding which can rightly name our authentic potential and that which corrupts it, which can lead us to a more mature and responsible humanity for women as well as men, and not simply to a reversal of patriarchal distortions.

It is here that the feminist theologian must operate not simply as a critic of the past or as a historian seeking to recover something of our lost story, but as a constructive theologian for a contemporary community of faith; for a contemporary understanding of church which seeks to live its faith as repentance of sexism, exodus from patriarchy, and entrance into a new humanity. Such an understanding will place this community in tension with the self-understanding of existing historical churches for whom patriarchy remains normative. As it becomes evident that feminist theology is not just a minor tinkering with the externals of dress, language, and personnel, but a major recentering of the meaning of the story itself, hostility will grow. To know and be prepared for this is not paranoia, but realism. As the counterassault on feminist theology begins, moreover, the maturity of feminist spirituality becomes all the more urgent. We need to love one another, and also to love our enemies in the sense of refusing to dehumanize them, without denying that their enmity is real, serious, and dehumanizing. We must be prepared to suffer, but also to grow in solidarity and self-knowledge.

541

The feminist theologian stands, not as an isolated academic, but as an "organic intellectual" (Gramsci) within a feminist community of faith that is engaged in exodus from patriarchy. It is the task of feminist theology to clarify the vision and make clear the criteria for testing what is authentic. The community of the good news against patriarchy needs the courage of its convictions, the confident trust that they are indeed in communion with the true divine ground of Being when they struggle against patriarchy, despite all the claims of its authority. This faith cannot lie first of all in the church, its tradition, or its Scripture, for the patriarchal distortion of all tradition throws feminist theology back upon the primary intuitions of religious experience itself: namely, the belief in a divine foundation of reality which is ultimately good, which does not wish evil or create evil, but affirms and upholds our autonomous personhood as women, in whose image we are made.

This means that feminist theology cannot rely on exegesis of past tradition, however ingeniously redefined to appear inclusive. It must be engaged in a primal re-encounter with divine reality, and in this re-encounter new stories will grow and be told as new foundations of our identity. Such an encounter is expressed in a recent account in my class on violence against women. One woman recounted her experience of being raped in a woods. During the rape she became convinced that she would be killed and resigned herself to her impending death. When the rapist finally fled, and she found herself still alive, she experienced a vision of Christ as a crucified woman. This vision filled her with relief and healing: "I would not have to explain to a male God that I had been raped. God knew what it was like to be a woman who had been raped."

Thus, feminist theology does not just rework past language and tradition. It allows the divine to be experienced in new places and in different ways. It must and will generate new stories, new accounts of religious experience, which will become the symbols of a new tradition. This may not be experienced as total discontinuity with the past; the story I have just recounted builds upon and re-envisions the old one of the Christian tradition, just as the Christian story built upon and re-envisioned the stories of the Hebrew tradition and Hebrew stories, in turn, built upon and re-envisioned Canaanite and Babylonian stories. One does not have to lose or repudiate one's past to claim the right to build a new future, in which the divine is experienced from women's perspective in a way not previously allowed or, at least, not remembered by a religious tradition biased by patriarchy.

Feminist theology, then, is not just engaged in a reformation to some original good moment in the past, some unblemished period of origins, because no such period can be discovered for women, either in the Judaeo-Christian tradition or before it. Even for those who claim some continuity with the Jewish or Christian traditions, feminist theology must stand as a new *midrash* or a third covenant, that does not merely repristinate a past revelation, but makes a new beginning, in which the personhood of woman is no longer at the margins but at the center, where woman is not defined as object, but defines herself as subject. . . .

### Note

1. In *Christianity and Crisis* 45, 3 (4 March 1985): 57-61.

# Sallie McFague

$W$*oven together in the thought of McFague (born 1933) are many and diverse issues of concern in theology during the last third of the twentieth century—some long suppressed or ignored, others left over from midcentury as unresolved or unraveling, and still others new indeed. She finished seminary and doctoral studies at Yale (Ph.D., 1964), following a B.A. from Smith College. Her academic career has been spent, since 1970, at Vanderbilt Divinity School and included service as Dean (1975–1979). She proceeded from early work on theology and literature to the pursuit of a theological program leading to a series of important books. These books have dealt with faith's language (parable, autobiography, metaphor, story, and models of God), liberationist and feminist themes, and ecology, both in the sense of care for the environment and its inhabitants (whether human or nonhuman) and in the sense of a paradigm for understanding the relationship between God and the world.*

*The scope of her interests, and her critical acumen and creativity in handling them, establish her as formative as well as representative of contemporary developments in theology. The selection included here highlights her mature reflection on the task of "metaphorical theology," a form and style of theological thinking that is intermediary between faith's immediate (and often creative but uncritical) testimonies and the formulation of conceptually precise but abstract and brittle ideas and theological systems.*

## THE CHRISTIAN PARADIGM[1]

The material norm of Christian faith involves a specification of what distinguishes this faith. It involves risking an interpretation of what, most basically, Christian faith is about. Such interpretation is, of course, not done in general or for all time; it is always a partial, limited account of the contours of the salvific power of God in a particular time in light

544

of the paradigmatic figure Jesus of Nazareth. To see the story of Jesus as paradigmatic means to see it as illuminative and illustrative of basic characteristics of the Christian understanding of the God-world relationship. These characteristics are not known solely from that story nor exemplified only in it, but that story is a classic instance, embodying critical dimensions of the relationship between God and the world. A metaphorical theology, as I have suggested, does not take the Christian constant, in either its formal or material mode, as the only source and resource for theology. The question as we approach the issue of the paradigmatic figure Jesus of Nazareth is not whether everything we need in order to do theology in our time can be generated from that figure but whether there are clues or hints here for an interpretation of salvation in our time. That is to say, are there distinguishing marks of the story of Jesus that are relevant to a holistic, nuclear age? If one understands the life and death of Jesus of Nazareth as a parable of God's relation to the world, and if to be a Christian means to be willing to look "God-wards" through his story, then one is constrained to say in what ways that story is significant now.[2]

This will involve understanding the story differently from in the past, but, I believe, in a way that has "demonstrable continuities" with the past. My perspective on that story is similar to that of the so-called liberation theologies. Each of these theologies, from the standpoint of race, gender, class, or another basic human distinction, claims that the Christian gospel is opposed to oppression of some by others, opposed to hierarchies and dualisms, opposed to the domination of the weak by the powerful. These theologies, however, unlike the short-lived death-of-God or play theologies, are not just another fad; like other major revisions of the Christian paradigm, they are a new way of understanding the relationship between God and the world, a new way of interpreting what salvation means. These theologies are not marginal, strange, or even particularly novel enterprises, relevant only to the groups from which they emerge. Rather, they are in the classical tradition of fundamental reformulations of Christian faith, just like the theologies of Augustine, Luther, and Schleiermacher. In the case of each of these writers, something about the writer's own experience did not fit with current understandings of Christianity: his experience presented an anomaly that could not be contained in the contemporary paradigm. A changed interpretation was imperative if the writer was to continue to identify himself as a Christian—and if Christian faith was to speak to the critical issues of the times. These theologians, however, believed they were interpreting Christianity not just for themselves or their own kind but for all. From a particular perspective came a universal claim.

These two notes of fundamental revisionist interpretation—experience and universality—are present also in the liberation theologies. The experience of being oppressed by gender, race, or poverty does not limit the theology that emerges to women, people of color, or the poor. Rather, the particular experiences of oppression serve as glasses bringing into sharper focus what one asserts the heart of the gospel truly to be for one's own time. There are important differences among the liberation theologies, but there are common notes as well, and they stand in significant contrast to some other readings of Christianity. But such theologies, and the material norm of Christianity that they suggest, should be judged in the same way and with the same criteria as other theologies. Here I am echoing Letty Russell's objection that feminist, black, and Third World theologies need to be qualified by an adjective, whereas white, male, Western theologies are called just theology.[3] These other theologies are also just theology. As with all theology, they emerge out of a concrete, social context; they identify what they believe the central vision of Christianity to be; they offer particular insights, insights that emerge in part because of special perspectives—insights that ought to be seen as illuminating to all people, if they are indeed in continuity with the Christianity paradigm and an appropriate rendering of it for our time. The crucial difference between these new theologies and classical theology is that for the first time they are coming from women, from people of color, and from the poor.

These theologies share a common reading of the material norm of Christianity in certain respects. First, Christian faith is seen as destabilizing conventional expectations and worldly standards. At the very least, it is a disorienting perspective that upsets usual divisions and dualisms. Second, Christian faith is inclusive, reaching out to the weak, to the outsider, to the stranger, to the outcast. Third, Christian faith is antihierarchical and antitriumphalist, epitomized in the metaphor of the king who became a servant, one who suffers for and alongside the oppressed. These points are general ones (and different liberation theologies would orient them differently—toward, especially, the oppressive situation of women, people of color, or the poor); nonetheless, they constitute a significantly different rendering of Christian faith from that found in other interpretations. It is not the traditional and still-popular message that Jesus Christ, fully God and fully man, died for the sins of all humanity and was resurrected to new life, as his followers shall be also. Nor is it the more recent so-called liberal interpretation that Jesus is the power by which the individual can overcome alienation, meaninglessness, and despair. In the first case, the issue to which the gospel speaks is death from sin; hence, the good news is eternal life. In the second case, the issue to which the gospel speaks is personal, existential anguish; hence, the answer is new meaning. Liberation theologies claim (in different ways) that the issue to which the gospel speaks is the destructive, oppressive domination of some over others; hence, the answer is a new way of being in the world free of all hierarchies. If one were to identify the heart of the gospel for these theologies—their material norm—it would be the surprising invitation to all, especially to the outcast and oppressed. It is a destabilizing, inclusive, nonhierarchical vision of Christian faith, the claim that the gospel of Christianity is a new creation for all of creation—a life of freedom and fulfillment for all.

But is this vision in continuity with the Christian paradigm? Is it a revision, a reseeing of that vision, or is it a substitution for it? Can a claim be advanced that it is one credible, strong candidate for interpreting salvation in our time within the Christian paradigm, or is it a marginal or even bogus view? To answer these questions, we will first look briefly at the story of Jesus as a destabilizing, inclusive, nonhierarchical vision. Second, we will go beyond most of the liberation theologies to extend this vision to the cosmos and our responsibility for it.[4] That is, we will look at the paradigmatic story of Jesus for clues and hints concerning the kind of metaphors most appropriate for modeling the relationship between God and the world, and hence between human beings and the world, in an ecological, nuclear era.

It is clear that the story of Jesus is a resource, but not the only source, for the material norm of the liberation theologies, that Christian faith gives a destabilizing, inclusive, nonhierarchical vision of fulfillment for all of creation.[5] For although that vision is compatible with and illuminated by the paradigmatic story of Jesus, it is generated as much by the social, economic, political, and ecological realities of the late twentieth century. Nonetheless, if the paradigmatic story is revelatory of God's "way with the world," then it will be relevant to our world and can, without misrepresentation or distortion, be shown to be. Does this mean that each age reads into the story what it needs to, what it must, in order to make it speak to the deepest crises of its own time? Perhaps. Still, each theology—and liberation theologies are no exception—claims that its interpretation is a truer, less distorted interpretation of the story. Interpretations can and must change from age to age, and often they change substantially in order to address radically new situations; nevertheless, the theologian is constrained to return to the paradigmatic story of Jesus for validation and illumination.[6]

What case can be made that the paradigmatic Christian story is a destabilizing, inclusive, nonhierarchical vision of fulfillment for all of creation? Can a portrait—though not necessarily the only portrait—be sketched along these lines? Nothing more than a "cartoon," in the sense of a preliminary draft, is possible here, but that is sufficient, for what we seek are the chief features or characteristics of that story, not its historical basis or subsequent interpretation. Three aspects that appear to be characteristic of the story of Jesus are his speaking in parables, his table fellowship with outcasts, and his death on a cross. Each is suggestive, and much has been made of each. The parables have been interpreted as moral imperatives; the table fellowship as a symbol of the eucharistic sacrifice; the death on the cross as God's triumph over sin, death, and the devil. But whatever the interpretations, few dispute that these three features are part of the story. A liberation theologian would interpret them differently: the parables illuminate the destabilizing aspect of the good news of Christianity; the table fellowship its inclusive character; and the death on the cross its nonhierarchical emphasis. As we look at each of these in more detail, what is being sought is not primarily validation of the story of Jesus as having these characteristics but illumination of our situation by that paradigmatic story.

The interpretation of the parables of Jesus in the last quarter century makes the case that they are a destabilizing, disorienting inversion of expectations and conventional standards.[7] The parables, brief stories told in the secular language of Jesus' time, are extended metaphors that say something about the unfamiliar, the "kingdom of God," in terms of the familiar, a narrative of ordinary people doing ordinary things. They work, however, on a pattern of orientation, disorientation, and reorientation: the parable begins in the ordinary world with its conventional standards and expectations, but in the course of the story a radically different perspective is introduced, often by means of a surrealistic extravagance, that disorients the listener, and finally, through the interaction of the two competing viewpoints tension is created that results in a reorientation, a redescription of life in the world.[8] A parable is, in this analysis, an assault on the accepted conventions, including the social, economic, and mythic structures that people build for their own comfort and security. A parable is a story meant to invert and subvert these structures and to suggest that the way of the kingdom is not the way of the world. In Jesus' parables we see an elder son who does not get what he deserves and a younger son who gets what he does not deserve; late workers being paid the same as those who have labored all day; a feast that is given for the poor and the outcasts when the prominent guests decline; a foreigner who comes to the aid of a Jew when his own religious leaders walk by on the other side. Throughout the parables two standards are in permanent tension with each other, and the effect of their interaction is disorientation for the listener. As John Dominic Crossan points out, not "liking" the parables is the appropriate reaction to them, for they undermine efforts at conventional security: "You have built a lovely home, myth assures us: but, whispers parable, you are right above an earthquake fault."[9]

At the very least the parables suggest that attempts at separating the "worthy" from the "unworthy," dualisms such as rich/poor, Jew/Gentile, elder/younger son, etc.—and by implication, male/female, white/colored, straight/gay, Christian/non-Christian—are without basis in the vision of existence alluded to by the phrase "the kingdom of God." What is suggested is a radically egalitarian, nondualistic way of being in the world. Liberation theologies make the case that Scripture is on the side of the poor and oppressed, but what is distinctive in the parables is not primarily a reversal that elevates the "unworthy" but a destabilization of *all* dualisms. Such destabilization is far more radical than an inversion, for it means refusing all categorizations of insider/outsider, though human beings appear naturally and deeply to desire such distinctions. But the parables, as one aspect of the portrait of our paradigmatic story, sketch a world in which such categorizations are disrupted and overturned.

Is it appropriate to extend this disruption beyond the human dualisms to those of spirit/flesh, mind/matter, soul/body, human/nonhuman, sky/earth? Flesh, matter, body, the nonhuman, and the earth are conventionally, perhaps even "naturally," considered inferior, and notably in the Christian tradition they have been so considered. But if the destabilization of the parables is to support the holistic sensibility needed in our time, then the oppression of flesh, matter, body, the nonhuman, and the earth must also be ended. If sin from the perspective of parabolic destabilization is the "natural" desire of human beings to separate themselves, in superior/inferior dualisms, from one another and from the earth, then salvation from this perspective would be an overturning of those patterns—a making whole or healing of the divisions. What is needed for a holistic sensibility to become a reality in our time is a change of consciousness in the way we see our world and ourselves in relation to the world. The destabilization of the parables is a necessary radical first step: when extended to the cosmos, it proclaims the end of the conventional, hierarchical, oppressive dualism of human/nonhuman.

What we see in Jesus' parables becomes more explicit in his table fellowship: the destabilization of the parables becomes an "enacted parable" as Jesus invites the outcasts of society to eat with him. Some scholars argue that Jesus' practice of eating with "tax collectors and sinners" was both the central feature of his ministry and its major scandal.[10] Like the parables, Jesus' table fellowship is destabilizing, but it goes further than the disruption of conventional dualisms, for as a friend of outcasts (Matt. 11:19), inviting them to eat with him, he epitomizes the scandal of inclusiveness for his time. What is proclaimed in Luke 4 as the heart of Jesus' ministry—good news to the poor, release to the captives, liberty for the oppressed—and what is manifested as well by his healings of the sick is pushed to an extreme in his invitation to the ritually unclean to eat with him. Jesus offended by inviting the outsiders to come in, to join with him not merely as needy outcasts but as his friends in joyful feasting. The central symbol of the new vision of life, the kingdom of God, is a community joined together in a festive meal where the bread that sustains life and the joy that sustains the spirit are shared with all.[11] The radical inclusiveness of this vision is eloquently summarized by Elisabeth Schüssler Fiorenza: "Since the reality of the *basileia* for Jesus spells not primarily holiness but wholeness, the salvation of God's *basileia* is present and experientially available whenever Jesus casts out demons (Luke 11:20), heals the sick and the ritually unclean, tells stories about the lost who are found, of the uninvited who are invited, of the last who will be first. . . . Not the holiness of the elect but the wholeness *of all* is the central vision of Jesus."[12]

The emphasis here is on inclusiveness: all are invited and what they are invited to is a feast, fulfillment, joy. The invitation is not to chosen individuals but to all. But unless we envision this feast as merely an allegory of a spiritual feast in another world—as solely an eschatological, mythological feast—it has implications for the holistic sensibility needed in our time. That is, the insistence of liberation theologies that salvation must be a social, political, economic reality in history, since oppression is precisely that kind of reality, means that in order for all to be invited, an ecological attitude must emerge. Without enough bread, some cannot be invited. An ecological sensibility that cares for the earth that "cares for us" must accompany a vision of social, political, economic justice if that vision is to become anything other than rhetoric.[13] Only a sensibility that accepts our intrinsic interdependence not only with all other people but also with the earth will be able to create the conditions necessary to help bring about the fulfillment of all as salvation for our time.

An ecological sensibility is not only an aesthetic appreciation for the intrinsic value of all forms of life—an attitude of "bending toward the mountain"—though it includes such appreciation; it is also a different way of thinking, a change to thinking the way nature itself works in terms of interdependence, relationality, reciprocity. As Rosemary Radford Ruether puts it, we must "convert our minds to the earth," turn away from linear, dichotomized, dualistic thinking that gives the human desire for short-term gains predominance over the long-term well-being of the earth and its ability to support us.[14] The aesthetic and utilitarian (in the sense of ecologically wise) attitudes are intrinsically related: we cannot be supported by an earth we do not support. Hence, political and economic liberation and the ecological, holistic sensibility are not two projects but one. The inclusiveness of the gospel—the invitation to fulfillment for all—must extend to the cosmos as well as to all peoples. The feast of joy, the invitation to share the bread and wine that symbolize both life itself and the good life, cannot be accepted unless we become caretakers of the earth. In our time, salvation must be understood to extend to all, or it will apply to none.

Nowhere is this fact more evident, of course, than in the threat of a nuclear holocaust. It stands as the ultimate challenge to accept the global village as our model of reality as we approach the twenty-first century. If political and economic liberation are intrinsically related to an ecological sensibility, so also is the acceptance of human responsibility for nuclear knowledge, for here also, and with chilling exactitude, salvation must be seen as extending to all people and to our earth: if we do not learn to live together, we will die together.

The parables, the table fellowship, and now the cross—they form a pattern in the sketch we are attempting of an interpretation of the story of Jesus for an ecological, nuclear age. The destabilization of the parables that is fleshed out in the invitation to all, especially to the "unworthy" and the outcast to share in the feast of life, is radicalized further in the cross. Here the way necessary to bring about this new mode of being is suggested. The way is radical identification with all others. In a world in which hierarchies and dualisms are fiercely defended, such identification will bring punishment, often swift and brutal punishment. The cross epitomizes the retribution that comes to those who give up con-

551

trolling and triumphalist postures in order to relate to others in mutual love.

As many have noted, there are ambiguous if not contradictory interpretations of the cross in Christianity, some seeing it as the critique of triumphalism epitomized in the king who becomes a servant, and others as but the prelude to the resurrection, when the king will reign in glory, as shall his loyal subjects.[15] The first interpretation is consonant with the parables and the table fellowship, for it continues and sharpens the distinction between two ways of being in the world, one of which is destabilizing, inclusive, and nonhierarchical and the other of which is conventional, exclusive, and triumphalist. That is to say, the first interpretation is a direct assault on the second; in fact, if one accepts it, one must criticize the second as a perversion of the gospel. If one accepts the interpretation of the parables and the table fellowship of Jesus advanced here, then a triumphalist christology and atonement must be rejected. The mythology in which the cross and especially the resurrection have been interpreted is not only anachronistic but harmful, for the destabilizing, inclusive, nonhierarchical vision of salvation needed in a holistic, nuclear age is undermined by it. For instance, if we see Jesus as "fully God and fully man," the substitutionary sacrifice who atoned for the sins of the world two thousand years ago and who now reigns triumphant along with all who loyally accept his kingly, gracious forgiveness of their sins, we not only accept a salvation we do not need but weaken if not destroy our ability to understand and accept the salvation we do need. The triumphalist mythology makes impossible the interpretation of the way to our salvation on several points.

First, it insists that salvation rests with one individual and in one past act. In first-century Palestine and throughout many centuries of Christian history, the notion of a representative human being in whose act and existence others, even centuries removed, could participate made sense in terms of Platonic and Aristotelian philosophies. It does not any longer. Both the individualism and the remoteness of this view, from our perspective, are contrary to the idea that salvation in our time must be the task of all human beings working in concert with the loving power of God as a present and future activity. It is not what one individual did two thousand years ago that is critical but what we, with God, do now.

Second, the classical mythology assumes that sin is against God—that it is traitorous or rebellious behavior against the King, Lord, or Father—whereas in the interpretation of the parables and table fellowship we have suggested, sin is against other people and the earth: it is exclusivistic, dualistic, hierarchical separation of insiders from outsiders. The classical mythology supports escapism of the worst sort: it is a misplaced religiosity that provides comfortable, personal assurance while undermining the will to work to overcome the oppression and domination of some by others—to overcome, that is, sin as it needs to be viewed in our time.

Third, the classical mythology supports metaphors and models of God contrary to those needed for imagining the God-world relationship in our time. It encourages us to think of God in triumphalist, royalist, highly individualistic, "distant" political imagery that is counterproductive to the kind of metaphors in which *we* need to think of God. In the classical imagery the King "empties" himself, becoming a servant only for the duration of Jesus' brief ministry and the sacrifice of the cross, but his true being is as almighty King, Lord, and Father, and he returns in the resurrection to his power and glory. If, however, one sees the cross not as the King's sacrifice, in the mode of his Son, for the sins of the world, but as a paradigm of God's way with the world always, other possibilities emerge. If one sees the cross as revealing God's distinctive way of being in and with the world, one will have a significantly different understanding both of God and of the way to speak to God—and an understanding more relevant to *our* salvation. In other words, if Jesus of Nazareth as paradigmatic of God is not just a "phase" of God but is genuinely revelatory of God, then the mode of the cross, the way of radical identification with all, which will inevitably bring punishment, sometimes to the point of death, becomes a permanent reality. It becomes the way of the destabilizing, inclusive, nonhierarchical vision.

Jesus of Nazareth, then, does not "do something on our behalf" but, far more important, manifests in his own life and death that the heart of the universe is unqualified love working to befriend the needy, the outcast, the oppressed. This we never would have guessed; it can scarcely be believed; and mostly, it is not. But if one takes clues from the parables, Jesus' table fellowship, and the cross, to believe in Jesus as a paradigm of God means that or something like that. It means that God is "like Jesus" and if Jesus is not a king but a servant, then God should be spoken of in "servant" language in relation to the world.

At this point, however, metaphorical theology should step in. That is to say, although the inclusive way of the cross and the triumphalist way of resurrection were in Jesus' time powerfully and appropriately contrasted by the metaphors of servant and king, they can be no longer. The language of servitude is no longer current, acceptable, or significant for

553

expressing the distinctive and unconventional kind of love epitomized in the cross. There are, I believe, other metaphors, such as those of mother, lover, and friend, that express dimensions of that love more fully and appropriately for our time. If one accepts that salvation in our time needs to be understood as a destabilizing, inclusive, nonhierarchical vision, these metaphors with their associations of caring, mutuality, attraction, nurturing, supporting, empathy, responsibility, service, self-sacrifice, forgiveness, and creativity are highly suggestive. They not only underscore self-sacrifice and radical self-giving to others, as does the servant metaphor, but also suggest dimensions of salvation for our time that the servant metaphor cannot: the interdependence of all life, including the life of God with the world, and reciprocity, including our responsibility to work with God for the fulfillment of all that lives. To see God's relationship to the world through the paradigm of the cross of Jesus is illuminating of salvation for our time if neither the servant nor the king is a major model but some other highly significant and very rich metaphors are investigated for their potential as expressions of the destabilizing, inclusive, nonhierarchical vision in an ecological, nuclear age. That is my thesis.

If, in other words, Jesus of Nazareth in his parables, table fellowship, and cross is a paradigm of God's relationship to the world, if he is a model or parable through which we can grasp something of God as well as discover a way to speak of God, then we have to ask how this can and should be expressed in different times and places. Metaphorical theology says it always has to be interpreted differently. We circle back, then, to an opening question of this chapter: What should we be doing for our time that would be comparable to what Paul and John did for theirs? One task is to conduct a thought experiment with new metaphors (and their accompanying concepts) that appear to have potential to express the trustworthiness and graciousness of the power of the universe *for our time*. . . .

### Notes

1. In *Models of God: Theology for an Ecological, Nuclear Age* (Philadelphia: Fortress Press, 1987), pp. 45-57.
2. For a treatment of Jesus of Nazareth as parable of God, see my *Metaphorical Theology*, chap. 2.
3. A frequent comment made in lectures and other public occasions, confirmed in conversation, July 21, 1986.
4. I agree basically with the perspective of Rosemary Radford Ruether on two critical points: (1) that a prophetic, critical principle can be seen, in spite of the androcentric bias, in both the Hebrew Scriptures and the story of Jesus of

Nazareth (but like her, I do not find these sources sufficient); (2) that the new vision of inclusive mutuality must be extended to the earth. I am especially indebted to her work on this latter point and recommend the excellent chapter "Woman, Body, and Nature: Sexism and the Theology of Creation," in her *Sexism and God-Talk: Toward a Feminist Theology* (Boston: Beacon Press, 1983).

5. The "hermeneutics of suspicion" presses most liberation theologies to insist that the destabilizing, inclusive, nonhierarchical vision is so embedded in texts distorted by ideologies of power that no "hermeneutics of retrieval" would be possible were the canonical texts (and the tradition built upon them) taken as the only source. Schüssler Fiorenza in her fine book *In Memory of Her* and in other writings makes this point eloquently and persuasively.

6. The theologian's life would be much easier if this were not the case, especially since it is increasingly difficult for theologians to know how to use Scripture responsibly and creatively. For a helpful treatment of the options, see David H. Kelsey, *The Uses of Scripture in Recent Theology* (Philadelphia: Fortress Press, 1975).

7. The literature on parable interpretation is extensive and growing. For a more complete treatment of my position, see my *Metaphorical Theology*, 42-54. I am indebted especially to the work of C. H. Dodd, Amos Wilder, Robert Funk, John Dominic Crossan, Leander Keck, Paul Ricoeur, and John Donahue.

8. See Ricoeur, "Biblical Hermeneutics," 122-28.

9. John Dominic Crossan, *The Dark Interval: Towards a Theology of Story* (Niles, Ill.: Argus Communications, 1975), 56-57.

10. See Joachim Jeremias, *New Testament Theology* (New York: Charles Scribner's Sons, 1971), 1:115-16; Günther Bornkamm, *Jesus of Nazareth*, trans. Irene and Fraser McLuskey with James Robinson (New York: Harper & Row, 1960), 80-81; Norman Perrin, *Rediscovering the Teaching of Jesus* (New York: Harper & Row, 1967), 102, 107; Schüssler Fiorenza, *In Memory of Her*, 121: "The power of God's *basileia* is realized in Jesus' table community with the poor, the sinners, the tax collectors and prostitutes—with all those who 'do not belong' to the 'holy people,' who are somehow deficient in the eyes of the righteous."

11. Jeremias, *New Testament Theology*, 115-16; Bornkamm, *Jesus of Nazareth*, 81; Perrin, *Rediscovering the Teaching of Jesus*, 107; Schüssler Fiorenza, *In Memory of Her*, 119.

12. Schüssler Fiorenza, *In Memory of Her*, 120-21.

13. Ruether makes the relationship between ecological and social justice clear: "There can be no ecological ethic simply as a new relation of 'man to nature.' Any ecological ethic must always take into account the structures of social domination and exploitation that mediate domination of nature and prevent concern for the welfare of the whole community in favor of the immediate advantage of the dominant class, race, and sex. An ecological ethic must always be an ethic of eco-justice that recognizes the interconnection of social domination and domination of nature" (*Sexism and God-Talk*, 91).

14. Ibid., 89-91.

15. See the excellent treatment of this point in Gordon D. Kaufman, *Theology for a Nuclear Age* (Philadelphia: Westminster Press, 1985), chap. 4, as well as in Ruether, *Sexism and God-Talk*: "Perhaps it is this very idea of God as a great king, ruling nations as His servants, that has been done away with by Jesus' death on the cross. With Jesus' death, God, the heavenly Ruler, has left the heavens and has been poured out upon the earth with his blood. A new God is being born in our hearts to teach us to level the heavens and exalt the earth and create a new world without masters and slaves, rulers and subjects" (pp. 10-11).

# Delores S. Williams

*W*illiams *(born 1943) was educated at the University of Louisville and then Union Theological Seminary and Columbia University (Ph.D., 1991) and taught at the School of Theology at Drew University before returning to Union as a faculty member. Through her writing and lecturing, she has been at the forefront of the "womanist" movement among African American women theologians. This movement takes its name from the word used by Alice Walker to describe the character and commitments of African American women in her book* In Search of Our Mothers' Gardens *(1983). Womanists have been concerned with rethinking and enriching Christian views—and practices— of freedom and justice in light of the long, ongoing history of multiple oppressions, encounters with scripture, and spiritual strength known in the experience of African American women.*

*This excerpt is a section of an essay entitled "A Womanist Perspective on Sin" (1993). In this selection, Williams concentrates on the womanist notion of sin and describes how it arises from the experience of black women and ways in which it is both similar to and different from the notion of sin found in spiritual songs, ex-slave autobiographies, and the theology of James Cone.*

## A WOMANIST NOTION OF SIN[1]

Hence we can claim that at least two social sources fed into this "unworthiness" felt by some Black women. One source was the elevation of white womanhood and the devaluation of Black womanhood which was, in actuality, a devaluation of Black women's humanity. The other source was the indifference of the U.S. legal system to the defilement of Black women's bodies—especially through overwork, lynching, and rape of Black women by white men.[2] Defilement here carries the dictionary meaning "to ravish, violate . . . to sully, dishonor."[3] The narratives of nineteenth-century Black women relate many incidents of the rape and violation of Black women's bodies by white male overseers and slaveholders. During slavery, many Black women were also violated through their work; their labor was thoroughly abused.[4] There are narratives in which the white slaveholding class refer to Black women and their progeny as filthy and dirty and therefore "proper" subjects for physical violation and destruction.[5] As early as 1565 John Hammond, in his tract about women's work written during that year, confirmed that servant women (i.e., poor white women) "were not put to work in the fields but in domestic employments." Then he adds: "some wenches that are nasty, and beastly [i.e., Black women] and not fit to be so employed are put into the ground [i.e., put in the fields to work]."[6]

In the construction of a womanist notion of sin informed by the Black community's and Black theology's belief in social sin, it is quite legitimate to identify devaluation of Black women's humanity and the "defilement" of their bodies as the social sin American patriarchy[7] and demonarchy[8] have committed against Black women and their children. Even among the gods of the ancients in Western culture, defilement of the body was considered a most grievous act for which one received severe punishment. In Homer's *Iliad,* the gods become angry with Achilles not because he kills his opponent Hector, but because he defiles Hector's body after he has killed him. Death is humility enough, but to defile a person after death deserves the punishment of being cut off from eternal life—which, of course, was the punishment Achilles received. He loses his invulnerability, and his heel becomes his vulnerable point which, if properly wounded, can lead to his death.

In the context of both the Hebrew Testament and the Christian Testament, defilement was a serious matter yielding grave consequences. Jacob's daughter Dinah (in the book of Genesis) is defiled (raped) by a prince. Her brothers murder the rapist, his father and all the men in the territory over which the prince's father rules. In the Christian Testament, the Pharisees accuse Jesus' disciples of not observing the Jewish laws concerning defilement (Mark 7:1-8). Jesus' message contradicted Jewish laws about defilement related to ritual cleanliness and helped lead to his death (Matt. 15:10-20). Jesus tried to change Jewish traditional association of defilement with physical realities like unclean hands before one eats and with foods designated as unclean. Thus Jesus says "whatever goes into the mouth passes into the stomach, and so passes on. . . . But what comes out of the mouth proceeds from the heart, and this defiles a man [*sic*]. For out of the heart come evil thoughts, murder, adultery. . . . These are what defile a man [*sic*]; but to eat with unwashed hands does not defile a man" (Matt. 15:17-20). In other words, it is atrocious actions against another person that constitute defilement. Inasmuch as womanist theology takes the Bible seriously as a validating tool, a womanist notion of sin claims that defilement of Black women's bodies and the resulting attack upon their spirits and self-esteem constitute the gravest kind of social sin of which American patriarchal and demonarchal society is guilty.

In our own time, this American way of defilement has also reached beyond Black women to nature itself. The powers that be in America have defiled the land with their rapid industrial and technological advancement. The waters are polluted by oil spills and debris from industrial plants. The air is unfit to breath because of industrial smog. The fruit and vegetables from the land are poisoned by the chemical spraying of the land. Certain animals that were once plentiful in the United States are now extinct or nearly extinct because of the male lust for "the hunt" or because of the greedy lust for money to be gained from animal fur. Hence womanist theology can claim a definite parallel between the defilement of Black women's bodies and the defilement of the health of earth's body (the land, air, and water) by the people who own the means of production. The spirit and self-esteem of the land are just as impaired by this defilement as are Black women's spirit and self-esteem injured by defilement of their bodies. All of this constitutes the sin of which our society is guilty.

Like theologian James Cone's way of identifying sin as a society's way of taking away people's humanity, womanist theologians can claim that society's way of devaluing Black womanhood is also sin. For Black women's womanhood is their humanity. To devalue Black women's womanhood is to take away their humanity. This can be illustrated by focusing upon some aspects of Alice Walker's understanding of Black womanhood suggested in her definition of a womanist.[9]

Walker identifies a womanist as Black or of other color. Cone has shown well enough how Black people's color has been the basis upon which many white Americans have judged Black people to be subhuman. Walker lifts up Black women involved in the single-parenting act of passing on advice to the female child. The relationship between mother and child in a single-parent household is not valued as the proper circumstance out of which "normal" and psychologically healthy children can come. These kinds of relationships and family life are devalued. Needless to say, American culture does not value the advice that women give. Walker, in her description of a womanist, challenges stereo-

558

typical ideas devaluating Black women. She describes a womanist as "Responsible . . . in charge . . . serious." This challenges the stigma of "childlike," "girlish," and "frivolous," which patriarchal and demonarchal social attitudes assign to Black women. According to Walker, a womanist loves men and women sexually or nonsexually. This challenges those who devalue the humanity of lesbian women. A womanist defines universality in terms of an array of skin colors. This gives intrinsic value to *all* skin color: "brown, pink and yellow" as well as "white, beige and black." Walker describes Black women's love in terms of dance, the moon, the spirit, love, food, roundness, struggle, the folks, and love of themselves as women. This affirms the cultural elements through which Black women express their humanity. To devalue any of this understanding of a womanist is to devalue Black women's womanhood, to devalue their humanity, to be guilty of sin—the sin that denies that Black women's humanity is in the image of God as is all humanity.[10]

In accord, then, with spiritual songs and the theology of James Cone, the womanist understanding of sin in this essay places guilt on the side of society at large. But unlike the spiritual songs, the narratives of ex-slaves and the theology of James Cone, this womanist notion of social sin also extends to the African-American community. There, Black woman's humanity is also devalued and their bodies are defiled by rape and domestic violence. Black lesbian women are the most devalued in the Black community where homophobia abounds. Hence Christian womanist women oppose sin when they make political alliances with liberated feminist forces and *enlightened* males acting to alleviate this kind of social sin in Black, white, and other cultural communities.

A question may be raised at this point. What constitutes individual sin according to womanist theology? And does this definition of sin as devaluation of Black womanhood and as defilement exempt Black women from being sinners? Individual sin has to do with participating in society's systems that devalue Black women's womanhood (humanity) through a process of invisibilization—that is, invisibilizing the womanist character of Black women's experience and emphasizing the stereotypical images of Black women that prevail and are perpetuated in the larger society. These stereotypes image Black women as having "childlike mentality," as being "girlish" in their actions and as being "frivolous and loose" in character. These stereotypical images reflect Black womanhood as unserious and not worthy of serious valuation. Participating in the perpetuation of this kind of understanding of Black womanhood and Black women's humanity constitutes individual sin. Black women also participate in sin when they do not challenge the patriarchal and demonarchal systems in society defiling Black women's bodies through physical violence, sexual abuse, and exploited labor.

There are, then, at least four distinctive features of this womanist notion of sin:

1) Unlike ideas about sin in spiritual songs, ex-slave autobiographies and in Cone's theology, this womanist notion of sin takes the human body and its sexual resources very seriously; the abuse and depletion of these resources amount to defilement which constitutes sin;

2) Black womanhood and humanity are synonymous and in the image of God; Black women's sexual being is also in the image of God; therefore to devalue the womanhood and sexuality of Black women is sin; to devalue the womanhood and sexuality of Black lesbian women is also sin;

3) Feelings of personal "unworthiness" expressed in the Black women's narratives used in this study indicate problems in women's self-esteem. Unlike the spiritual songs, autobiographies and Cone's ideas about sin, the womanist notion of sin in this essay takes seriously Black women's depleted self-esteem. Thus elevating and healing Black women's self-esteem figures into womanist notions of what constitutes salvation for the oppressed African-American community.

4) In the history of Black Christian thought, this womanist notion of sin is unique in its suggestion of parallels between the defilement of Black women's bodies and the defilement of nature.

The great hope of womanist theology is for Christians to come together and work in concert to alleviate the sin of devaluation and defilement threatening the lives and spirits of Black women as well as the life of the natural environment that sustains all life.

### Notes

1. In *A Troubling in My Soul: Womanist Perspectives on Evil and Suffering.* Edited by Emilie M. Townes (Maryknoll, New York: Orbis Books, 1993), pp. 143-47.

2. For an account of the lynching Black people, male and female, have experienced in the United States see Ralph Ginzburg, *One Hundred Years of Lynching* (Baltimore: Black Classic Press, 1962). Especially see page 38: "Negro Suspect Eludes Mob; Sister Lynched Instead." Also see this entry that appears on page 36: "HARVARD PROFESSOR FAVORS LEGALIZING LYNCHINGS." Reporting a 1900 newspaper account, the book printed this: "Professor Albert Bushnell Hart, of Harvard College, speaking before the American Historical Association in convention . . . said that if the people of certain States are determined to burn colored men at the stake, those States would better legalize the practice."

3. *Webster's Seventh New Collegiate Dictionary* (Springfield, MA: G. & C. Merriam Co., 1971), 216.
4. For an account of Black women's defilement through their work, see the reference to Hetty in Prince, "The History of Mary Prince, A West Indian Slave," in *Six Women's Slave Narratives.*
5. For instance, see the reference to the physical abuse of a Black woman and the destruction of her child by a white slave owner on page 135 above [Note refers to *A Troubling in My Soul,* p. 135—Ed.].
6. Winthrop D. Jordan, *White Over Black* (New York: Norton, 1968), 77.
7. For a discussion of the way in which Black women's experience challenges Christian notions of redemption on the basis of this sin of defilement see Delores S. Williams, "Black Women's Surrogacy Experience Challenges Christian Notions of Redemption," in Paula Cooley, William Eakin, and Jay McDaniel, eds., *After Patriarchy* (Maryknoll, NY: Orbis Books, 1991).
8. Delores Williams coined the term *demonarchy* to name the oppression that white American social institutions, directed by both white men and white women, exert upon the lives of Black women. Contrasting patriarchy and demonarchy, Williams identifies a positive side of patriarchy that white women enjoy but is not extended to Black women. This positive side has merit because it allows white women to get the education it takes to secure for themselves most of the jobs and benefits the American civil rights movement obtains for women. White-controlled social institutions, which feminists have characterized as patriarchal, also intend to preserve and save the lives of the children of white women as long as those children issue from the sexual relations of white men and women together. On the other hand, white-controlled American institutions do not intend to preserve and save the lives of the children of Black women. Rather, these institutions employ demonic government in relation to Black children and Black women which intends to destroy their lives. See Williams' treatment of demonarchy in her article, "The Color of Feminism: Or Speaking the Black Woman's Tongue," in the *Journal of Religious Thought* 43 (Spring-Summer, 1986).
9. See Alice Walker, *In Search of Our Mothers' Gardens: Womanist Prose* (New York: Harcourt Brace Jovanovich, 1983), xi-xii.
10. This womanist notion of social sin as devaluation of humanity also includes racism, sexism, and classism which cannot happen in a society unless one group devalues the humanity and equal worth of another group.

# James H. Cone

*The theological body of work produced by James H. Cone has shaped the development of black theology from the beginning. Born (1938) in a small community southwest of Little Rock, Arkansas, Cone made his way from Philander Smith College to the Garrett Biblical Institute and eventually to doctoral work in systematic theology at Garrett-Northwestern. Cone, through his personal encounters with racial prejudice and his involvement in the civil rights movement, became an advocate of "black power." By 1969, not too long after turning thirty, Cone had published a theological defense of black power (Black Theology and Black Power) that gave early expression to a new form of liberation theology in America. By the mid-1970s, his understanding of black theology expanded to express wider implications, especially in the form of his belief that all Christian theology, in order to be Christian, had to be primarily identified with the struggles of oppressed peoples. His most systematic expression of black theology appeared in his book* God of the Oppressed *(1975). As illustrated within that book, Cone increasingly has made good use of the cultural resources of the black community as he develops his theology. In* Malcolm & Martin & America *(1991), Cone turned his substantial critical skills toward offering a significant social analysis of the personal and historical contexts surrounding the lives of both Martin Luther King, Jr., and Malcolm X. Over the years, Cone has been willing to learn from his critics and to adjust his theological understanding in important ways, not the least of which has been demonstrated in his ability to take seriously the critiques of his work offered by feminist and womanist theologians.*

*For more than twenty-five years, Cone has served on the faculty of Union Theological Seminary, currently as the Charles A. Briggs Professor of Systematic Theology. Since his arrival at Union and his first attempts to address what Christian theology in America had long ignored, Cone's work has influenced an entire generation of black and white theologians. In this brief selection, first published in 1975, Cone describes the content and method of black theology. The essay reflects Cone's serious interest in speaking theologically about human liberation by drawing upon black experience, scripture, and Jesus Christ.*

## THE CONTENT AND METHOD OF BLACK THEOLOGY[1]

### Black Religion and Black Theology

Because Black Theology is a theology of and for black people, its primary task is to reflect upon God's story of his dealings with his people in North America and throughout the world. This task involves a critical analysis of the theological function of black religion as disclosed in sermon, song, prayer, and testimony. It is important for the black theologian to recognize that theology is not identical with these black expressions, although its reason for being is grounded in them. To do Black Theology, therefore, black theologians must know and experience the black story. The content and method of Black Theology must be derived from black religion's story of liberation. In sermon, prayer, song, and testimony are found the black theologians' sources for the development of a Black Theology. Our theological task is to uncover the structures and forms of the black religious experience, because the categories of interpretation must arise out of the thought forms of the black experience itself.

Although Black Theology arises out of and is dependent upon the black story, it is different from these primary expressions of black life. Black Theology is reflection that arises from participation in the black story. The black theologian performs the secondary but vital function of subjecting the story to critical scrutiny. For instance, in contrast to the black preacher, the theologian does not merely recite a story. He asks about the meaning of story for the lives of the people who have lived it. In what sense has our story been consistent with God's story for us, his will to take us to be with him in his own eschatological future? In what sense has our story been liberating and enslaving? Not all black sermons are liberating and neither are all black worship services an expression of the presence of the freedom of God's Spirit. Thus the black theologian's task is to sort out for the community those elements that are positive and negative so that the people will know what they are saying and doing and why. His role is to be a critic of the faith, because of his own commitment to it and also because of his love for the community that has made possible his existence as theologian.

563

What does it mean to do theology in the light of the black struggle for liberation? That is the central question for black theologians. I would like to suggest four points. (1) To do theology in the light of the black story means that our theological reflections must arise from our participation in and commitment to that story as it is lived by the people. We are not philosophers who are committed to a structure of logic independent of the faith of the people. Thus we do not ask whether the faith of the people is "true" independently of the people's struggle for truth. To be sure, as black theologians, we should be interested in the history of western philosophy, including its more recent concern about language and semantic logic. And we should be interested in assessing the validity of the claims of faith as compared with other human assertions. But our interest in western philosophy, ancient and modern, is not defined by western philosophy itself, but our struggle for freedom. Our faith cannot be tested by Descartes, Hume or Locke, for their philosophical reasoning did not arise from the social context of black slavery. As black theologians we can test the faith of black people as we become involved in their faith, thereby suffering with the people in the liberation struggle. What we say, negatively or positively, about the black story must arise from a commitment to the story. We cannot afford to be spectator-theologians, criticizing what the people believe because we happened to know a little about Sartre and Camus, neither of whom know much about our struggle. To claim to do theology of and for black Christian people and not respect the faith of the people is to ridicule the very community one claims to represent. Thus there is no Black Theology in the Christian sense that does not arise out of the theologian's commitment to faith in struggle. In this sense, black theological thought arises out of action, out of the actual lives of the people struggling for liberation.

(2) To do theology in the light of the black story means that its language is connected with passion, and thus reflects the rhythm and feelings that arise out of the struggle of freedom. It is the passionate character of black theological language that connects it with the sermon, song, prayer and testimony, although it is not identical with any of these. The language of black theology is not only based on the story but displays a passion similar to the mood in which the story is sung and preached. The storyteller's total involvement must be matched by the theologian's.

(3) To do theology on the basis of the black story also means taking the function of reason seriously. Black Theology must not reject reason, for without it there is no way to assess the validity of one claim over another. Without reason, theology cannot be critical and thus relate

what the people preach to what they do. As black theologians who reject much of the function of reason in western philosophy and theology, we must be careful not to allow our rejection of reason *per se* to be dependent on white people's misuse of it. Reason is an important tool of theological analysis, and without it the community is left exposed to fanatics and other self-appointed prophets of God. If what is preached and sung as a part of the black story cannot stand the test of reason and the structure of logic as defined by our history and culture, then black theologians must excise these false expressions from the black community. It is our task to unmark false prophets and preachers by showing that what they claim contradicts the faith of the people. Passion therefore does not exclude reason. It controls reason by refusing to entertain ideas that are not related to the struggle of freedom.

(4) Because Black Theology is derived from and is dependent upon black religion, the content of the former, like the latter, is liberation. Black Theology is a theology of liberation. On the one hand, this theme is based upon the biblical claim that Jesus came "to set at liberty those who are oppressed" (Luke 4:18 RSV). On the other hand, it is grounded in black people's application of the biblical theme of liberation to their socio-political existence. Thus black slaves sang:

> Children, we shall soon be free
> When the Lord shall appear.
> Give ease to the sick, give sight to the blind,
> Enable the cripple to walk;
> He'll raise the dead from under the earth,
> And give them permission to talk.

If the content of Black Theology is liberation, what then is the method it uses in the analysis of liberation's meaning? Like the content of Black Theology, its method must be derived from the data of black religion. I believe that the best method is what I have chosen to call the "contextual-dialectical" method. To say that Black Theology uses a "contextual-dialectical" method means that I do not believe that there are absolute, universal truths which can be discovered by human reason or disclosed in divine revelation. Truth is a happening, a divine event that invades our history, setting slaves free from bondage. This divine truth is not abstract or objective but is contextual and dialectical. To understand its meaning, we must be in the socio-political context of the liberation struggle. When theological thinking arises out of an historical context, it is of necessity dialectical, that is, paradoxical.

To say that theological thinking is dialectical emphasizes not only the contextual character of truth but also its paradoxical quality. For example, because of the socio-political context of racism in America, some black theologians found it necessary to equate divine revelation with black liberation, even though we did not intend to deny God's universality. Rather we merely intended to affirm that there is no divine universalism that is not at the same time particular. Thus universality and particularity are not abstract attributes of God. On the contrary, they refer to God's concrete presence in history where the oppressed are elected for liberation in order that all peoples universally may know that they are created for freedom.

The event of divine freedom for the oppressed of the land is the content of Black Theology. Methodologically, this gospel can only be described contextually and dialectically. Contextually, because the gospel of freedom is the historical liberation of people. And dialectically, because all theological statements are limited and never absolute. Hence whatever we say about God's liberating presence, it must be revised in different times and contexts.

The dialectical and contextual character of Black Theology is found in its use of black experience, scripture, and Jesus Christ as the starting point of theological analysis. Some of my critics have stated the issue in this manner. "On page 32 of *Black Theology and Black Power,* quoting Ron Karenga, you said that 'The fact that I am Black is my ultimate reality.' But then on page 34 of the same book, you wrote that 'Christianity begins and ends with the man Jesus—his life, death and resurrection.' Which do you *really* mean? Blackness or Jesus Christ? You cannot have it both ways."

This is an important matter, and perhaps the place to begin for clarification is to state emphatically that, like Scripture, the black experience is a *source* of the truth but not the truth itself. Jesus Christ is the truth and thus stands in judgment over all statements about truth. But having said that, we must immediately balance it with another statement, without which the first statement falsifies what it intends to affirm. We must state the other side of the paradox emphatically: There is no truth in Jesus Christ independent of the oppressed of the land—their history and culture. And in America, the oppressed are the people of color—Black, Red and Brown. Indeed it can be said that to know Jesus is to know him as revealed in the struggle of the oppressed for freedom. Their struggle is Jesus' struggle and he is thus revealed in the particularity of their cultural history—their hopes and dreams of freedom.

The difficulty some people have in understanding the relation between

Jesus and the black experience in Black Theology is due partly to their inability to appreciate the dialectical character of theological speech, especially when related to the black struggle for liberation. They use a dialectical model when dealing with such things as divinity and humanity in Jesus Christ or justification and sanctification in St. Paul or John Wesley. But there is a failure of nerve when their abstractions about Jesus are applied to the historical present. Jesus Christ is not a proposition, not a theological concept which exists merely in our heads. He is an event of liberation, a happening in the lives of oppressed people struggling for political freedom. Therefore, to know him is to encounter him in the history of the weak and the helpless. That is why it can be rightly said that there can be no knowledge of Jesus independent of the history and culture of the oppressed. It is impossible to interpret the scripture correctly and thus understand Jesus rightly unless the interpretation is done in the light of the consciousness of the oppressed in their struggle for liberation.

A similar convergence occurs when it is asked whether the black experience exists independently of Jesus Christ. If by Jesus Christ is meant the formal preaching and teachings of white missionaries, at a particular point in time, then the answer is an unqualified "yes." As we must say that Jesus' existence in himself is not a product of culture, so the black experience existed before black people were introduced to Christianity. However that is such an obvious historical fact that we need not debate it further. But if by Jesus Christ is meant "the image of the invisible God, the first-born of all creation, for in him all things were created in heaven and on earth, visible and invisible" (Col. 1:15-16 RSV), then the answer is an unqualified "no." In this context, Jesus is not simply a doctrine or even a particular event limited by time. He is the eternal event of liberation in the divine person who makes freedom a constituent of human existence. There is no existence apart from him because he is the ground of existence without whom nothing is. Therefore, where human beings struggle for freedom and refuse to be defined by unauthorized earthly authorities, there Jesus Christ is present among them. His presence is the sustaining and liberating event in the lives of the oppressed that makes possible the continued struggle for freedom.

From the context of the eternal presence of Christ, the Liberator, emerges the interdependence of Jesus and the black experience as expressed in the lives of many black people. This interdependence is expressed so forcibly and concretely that truly to speak of the black experience is to speak of Jesus. He is the Word in their lives, and thus to speak of their experience as it manifested in the joys and sorrows of black life is to speak of the One they say is the Comforter in time of trouble, "the lily of the valley," and "the bright and morning star."

> He's King of Kings, and Lord of Lords,
> Jesus Christ, the first and the last
> No man works like him.

Others have testified that he is a "bridge over troubled waters," the "One who has been better to us than we have been to ourselves." In *God Struck Me Dead,* a collection of conversion experiences and auto-biographies of ex-slaves, one called him a "time-God"! "He don't come before time; he don't come after time. He comes just on time."[2] And he comes as the preserver of the weak in time of trouble and as the sustaining Spirit of freedom in wretched places. This encounter of Jesus as the Christ of God makes his reality an eternal presence of liberation before and after the slave ships and Middle Passage.

Theologically the convergence of Jesus Christ and the black experience is the meaning of the Incarnation. Because God became man in Jesus Christ, he disclosed the divine will to be with humanity in our wretchedness. And because we blacks accept his presence in Jesus as the true definition of our humanity, blackness and divinity are dialectically bound together as one reality. This is the theological meaning of the paradoxical assertion about the primacy of the black experience and Jesus Christ as witnessed in scripture.

To summarize: The content of Black Theology is liberation, a theme that is derived from black religion's acceptance of the biblical claim that God discloses his presence in the struggle of the poor for freedom. The method which Black Theology uses in its analysis of this liberation theme is contextual and dialectical. This means our thought about liberation is not derived from Euro-American reflections, whether it be Marx or Marcuse. Black Theology's reflection on liberation is derived from the social context of the black struggle of freedom, as found in our prayers, songs and sermons. In these black expressions are disclosed the truth about our struggle. Liberation therefore is not an idea but an event that happens in black history, enabling us to know "We'll soon be free, when de Lord will call us home."

### Notes

1. In *The Journal of Religious Thought* 32 (Fall-Winter 1975): 98-103.
2. Clifton H. Johnson (ed.) *God Struck Me Dead* (Boston: Pilgrim Press, 1969), p. 170.

# Langdon Gilkey

*One outstanding feature of theology throughout the last half of the twentieth century has been ferment in "theological method," which has to do with the bases, ordering, intelligibility, and evaluative criteria of theological reflection itself. The period was first marked by an array of revisionist work on established options, e.g., syntheses of neoorthodox, process, linguistic analysis, and existentialist approaches. It became more searching and "radical," questioning the very possibility of "God-talk," in the late sixties, and since then has generated a vast array of new departures. The career of Gilkey (born 1919) tracked and helped shape these developments.*

*Educated at Harvard and Union Theological Seminary, Gilkey taught at Vassar College and Vanderbilt Divinity School before appointment at the University of Chicago (1963). There he, along with the Roman Catholic theologian David Tracy and other colleagues, led to another, "new" (a "third"?) Chicago School of Theology, oriented toward "public theology." The selection here, from his influential book* Naming the Whirlwind: The Renewal of God-Language *(1969), represents—as its title suggests—a key transition underway not only in his thought or that of the Chicago School but within theology at large.*

## CHRISTIAN DISCOURSE ABOUT GOD[1]

. . .

The first criterion for a valid theology is that any theological statement be a consistent expression of the symbolic forms of the historical community within which the answers are received, experienced, and comprehended through the media of the faith. Theological symbols, such as creation or providence, have not only "felt" meanings in terms of our ordinary secular experience; for felt meanings, however relevant and existential, are blind without symbolic interpretation. Rather, if they are to function as communicating a definite answer to an ultimate ques-

569

tion, the verbal symbols of a particular religious tradition—both with regard to their individual character (for example, that of Creation or of Incarnation) and with regard to the larger system of symbols within which they gain their meaning (for example, in medieval or in Reformation systems of thought)—must have an essential structure of their own, a unique gestalt, an integrity and a logic which has objective status, and which gives to that system of symbols that characterize a particular religion or point of view its "essence" and differentiates it from other religions and points of view. Particular symbols, and especially systems of symbols, say something definite and particular about ultimate issues, which, though never clear and distinct, has a unique essence and so can be delineated; and this uniqueness of each particular symbolic form increases when it enters the whole system of symbols in terms of which an entire religious perspective is expressed. It is because of this definiteness and uniqueness of structural meaning that the symbolic forms of a community *can* be mediatory vehicles of a definite or special form of experience which can provide an answer to an existential question, and an answer sharable in speech, in narration, in kerygma, witness, and reflection alike among a community and a tradition. The appropriation of a symbol both existentially and conceptually, and correspondingly for a symbol to "have meaning," involves, therefore, an *interaction* between the objective gestalt or structure contained in the symbols and the felt meanings of common experience. It is through the intentional structure of the symbol that the unconditioned is experienced, and thus are the felt meanings of experience clarified, illumined, and healed. The first criterion of a valid Christian theology relates, therefore, to those essential—although potentially abstract—"meanings" of the traditional symbols creative of the community's life. Correspondingly, the choice of the symbolic content of a theology and the interpretation or usage of these symbols in theological construction is, in part, to be validated by reference to the original Biblical symbols with which the community began, and the history of their interpretation, their "meaning for" the community which has treasured them. In this sense, every valid theology must justify its own categorial structure of thought first of all in relation to the central symbolic content, eidetically abstracted through historical study, of the Biblical materials and the tradition of life and of reflection which have made up the Church's history. This symbolic content must, to be sure, be reexpressed and reworked in the light of the conceptuality of each age; nevertheless, the first requirement is that a contemporaneously relevant theology express the integral structure of the community's attitudes toward God, the world, history, and man, and thus reflect in its time this community of faith from which the answer has been received.

As we have urged throughout, however, such traditional meanings of a historic symbol, however elegantly elaborated, are empty unless they relate to the stuff of ordinary and contemporary life. Definite symbolic structures, we have said, have meaning only insofar as they thematize the felt experience of the life of the people *for whom* they have meaning. Thus the second criterion for an adequate theology is the relevance of its symbolic content to the deepest problems and issues of human existence as an age experiences those issues, i.e., to the questions of contingency, relativity, temporality, and freedom. For the Biblical and traditional symbols of the community *have* use and, therefore, meaning only as answers to these questions. A theology is to be tested, in the second place, by its relatedness, its relevance, its correlations of symbolic answers to the actual questions of our existence.

This second criterion of relevance to *contemporary* existence is essential for all modes of constructive or systematic theology. For such theology in effect does not ask merely about the "eidetic" meanings of traditional symbols for our revered predecessors in the faith—whether at Sinai, in Jerusalem, at Antioch or Wittenberg. Rather inescapably, if it is to do its work, it must ask about their meaning and validity *for us,* for our time and in our cultural and historical situation. Systematic theology is the effort to understand *our* existence in terms of Christian symbols; thus necessarily, if it is to have a religious function, it seeks to express the meaning and validity of these symbols in relation to the actual world in which we as contemporary men live and think, and in terms of which, as we remarked at the outset, our views of reality, of truth, and of value—and so our sense of meaning—are forged. It is here, in the present world, that we exist and so in which we pose religious questions. If, therefore, symbols are to speak religiously to us, to communicate answers to our own ultimate questions, they must speak to and in this contemporary situation. The corollary to this criterion, then, is that a relevant and "true" theology must be intelligible in terms of all else that is known to be true in our time, and thus to the deliverances of the sciences—physical, social and historical—in so far as we accept and live by those deliverances. In this sense an appropriate "demythologizing" process, appropriate to the scientific Weltanschauung which we actually accept as valid, is inevitably an aspect of any systematic theology which will be meaningful and true for us. If important symbols are not so interpreted in the light of our contemporary view of things, we may be sure that they do not function *religiously,* providing transforming answers to our own most pressing problems, but at best only nostalgically, reminding us of a day when they were meaningful and real to other people.

Thirdly, as we have said, such a symbolic system, mediating historic symbols to contemporary questions, is to be tested and validated by its width of relevance and its adequacy of explanatory power. As a total view of man's being in the world, it should provide categories able to illumine at the deepest level each of man's fundamental interactions with his world, his fellows, and himself. From it should flow intelligible presuppositions or axioms for all of man's creative cultural expressions in social existence, in inquiry, and in the arts. This extension of theological symbols into the totality of human concerns depends, of course, on the elaboration of a "Christian philosophy," in which the primary religious symbolism concerning God, man, time, and the world is extended into more general ontological categories capable of elucidation in relation to all other special fields. A theology that is incapable in this sense of ontological elucidation in the widest philosophical terms is insofar "invalid." The community in the midst of which theology functions, and presumably the theologian himself, are meanwhile participating in and profiting from the full range of cultural existence, political, moral, scientific, and artistic. For this reason alone, that community and its theology should be responsible that its own most fundamental symbolic forms provide an intelligible framework for its own life in this wider world. It is, we believe, an important element within the Christian's conviction of the "truth" of his beliefs that he affirms as well that it is in terms of Christian symbols that the most intelligible foundation can be discovered for the total cultural life of man. Thus it is a part of the task of any theologian that, as best he can, he seek to elucidate this wider intelligibility.

Thus tradition, Biblical and historical, contemporary existential experience, and scope of cultural relevance form the criteria for the assessment of the validity of a theology, and of the set of symbols which it seeks to explicate and interpret. We should recall, however, that, with regard to religious language, any experience of and so claim to validity is an *involved* experience and an *involved* claim. The threefold function of a religious symbol, and so its sole meaningful usage, is, we have said, to point beyond the finite referent of which it is a sign to the sacred and the ultimate that is there manifest; to "disclose" through this manifesta-

572

tion the ultimate ground and meaning of our life, and to answer through this manifestation the ultimate questions and crises of life; and lastly, to provide models and norms by which our freedom, individual and cultural, can guide itself. Each of these three functions presupposes our participation in the symbol as a vehicle of the ultimate and the sacred. If the symbol is to *be* religious for us and so meaningful at all, it must communicate to us an ultimate sacrality that grounds our life, rescues it, and directs it. This *is* its meaning, and the only meaning it can have; and to experience this meaning is to experience the validity of the symbol itself. For in the end, a religious symbol is "true" if it becomes for us a medium of the sacred, and it becomes "false" when that communicative power vanishes. Thus, however important the more objective criteria of tradition, contemporary experience, and width or scope of relevance may be, religious symbols are not validated by these means, for such objective testing communicates no sacral presence to our existence. Religious symbols function as religious symbols and so are known to be true only by those to whom they communicate a religious meaning, i.e., an awareness of an ultimate ground to life's passage and an ultimate answer to life's crises. And such a communication to us inevitably either effects or else presupposes an existential involvement in both the questions that are being asked and the answers that are being received.

A "secular theology," then, will seek to apprehend and interpret secular existence, both creative and ambiguous, through the means of the symbols of its Christian faith. Correspondingly, it will understand the symbolic forms of that faith in the terms of these evident characteristics of man's ordinary life. A relevant theology is man's existence seen in the light of Christian faith, and a relevant faith is one whose symbols are understood in the light of man's ordinary existence—neither one can be comprehended meaningfully without the other.

For secular existence is, as we have shown, unintelligible on its own terms. It cannot understand the facets of ultimacy that suffuse its life; its creativity in the midst of its tragedy be-trays it into either optimism or pessimism, its vitality and autonomy beguiling it into naïveté, its relativity and temporality into despair. These secular elements of existence remain dark and inscrutable on any other terms—and a good theology must point this out. Conversely, the historical symbols or doctrines of faith have no meaning unless this relevance is established throughout their elaboration, and unless their own intrinsic meaning grows out of and is understood in terms of the powers, ambiguities, and crises of ordinary life.

We can, then, perhaps summarize the most important elements in our discussion of Christian discourse about God in the following way.

All religious talk, we have argued, is talk about the ultimate and the sacred as it appears in ordinary experience, that is as it appears in and through the finite, in its experience of itself, of its being in the world and its being in time. Religious discourse is thus *symbolic,* talk about the finite but with regard to its ground, its limits, its ultimate structures, its resources of healing and renewal, and its bases for hope. It is not, therefore, directly talk about God; we cannot know him as he is in himself, and in any case such talk would have no experienced base or content and so would be meaningless. It is talk about the divine *as* it appears in and to us in our experience of finite things as contingent, relative, temporal, and autonomous beings; it is talk about creatures, others and ourselves, as the sacred appears in them. Thus and only thus is it meaningful language, language about a region that is definite to all of us because it is experienced by us all. It is not talk about heaven, but about earth—with regard to its ultimate and sacred ground and limits. Correspondingly, Christian talk about God is language about this ultimate and sacred dimension: our ground, limit, meaning, judge, and resource, in terms of Christian symbols. And those symbols in turn reflect and express those points where *this* apprehension of the divine was manifested in a particular community's life through *those* finite events, persons, media, and symbols. Again, we are talking about the ultimate and sacred dimension of our contingent, relative, transient, and autonomous being; but, as Christians, we know what that ultimacy and sacrality *is,* and so talk about it, as it has manifested itself in *this* history, and so as it is apprehended, conceived, and responded to in and through *these* media and *these* symbols. Thus we use the "Biblical" and "Christian" verbal symbols of creation, providence, covenant, law, judgment, gospel, forgiveness, and new age—and so on—as means with which to conceive the ultimacy and sacrality that appears in all of existence. "God" is this sacred understood in these symbolic terms; Christian God-language is language descriptive of the ultimate which grounds and limits us, but that ultimate apprehended and understood through these symbols.

Again, however, we should be clear, we are talking symbolically as we have defined and used that term. Our direct referent is *not* the divine as it is in itself, or even "God" as he can be imagined or pictured by means of revealed symbols. Such language "about God" quickly loses its touch with experience and so its meaning for us. Rather is our language multivalent, language *about* the finite with regard to what appears in and to our experience, the ultimate or sacral dimension there, but understood in terms of these symbols. Thus the symbol of God as creator refers not to some pictured absolute, but only to the ultimate and sacral ground of our contingency as that ground is apprehended by us in and through our contingency. Providence refers to the ultimate and sacral context of our life's and our history's meaning; judgment refers to the ultimate norm embodied in Jesus by which our life is evaluated; forgiveness refers to the ultimate love resident in him as a man and which accepts us in and through him—and so on. These are not doctrines about a being called God, but doctrines about the creaturely as the sacred manifests itself in and through the creaturely. The *way* we understand the divine in each of the above is very much shaped by the unique "meaning" or structure of the symbol; it is a *Christian* apprehension and understanding. But *what* we understand through these unique symbols and so in this unique way is the appearance of the sacred in and through the finite, and not the sacred by itself.

Symbols in religion are, in the first instance, creatures, men or events through which the sacred acts creatively and manifests itself to men. Correspondingly, the verbal symbols of religion, about which we here speak, are *symbolic* precisely in the sense that they are talk about the finite—creatures, history, men, communities and so on—with regard to their ultimate ground, limit and hope. And the symbol "God" is the way this community, with its experiences and symbolic forms, has apprehended that sacral ultimacy across the entire range of its existence, but centering its delineation of that apprehension on that final event in which the ultimate that is our origin and destiny has manifested itself—in Jesus who is the Christ. In this sense, the task of systematic theology is that of uniting or joining conceptually the Biblical symbols about *God:* as creator, ruler, Judge, Father, Redeemer and Reconciler, with our understanding of *ourselves* as "symbols" through which the sacred appears; for example, of understanding *God's* creation in terms of *our* contingency and its ground. To speak *only* of God is empty; to speak *only* of ourselves is pointless. To talk meaningfully of God is to talk of our existence in contingency and freedom in relation to its divine ground, judge, and redeeming resource, understood symbolically in the terms of our community's life. This by no means answers all our questions about intelligible symbolic language; but at least it relates religious discourse to concrete and contemporary experience without sacrificing either its Biblical or traditional content, its transcendent reference, or its possibility of intelligible ontological and cultural explication.

Our fundamental thesis in this chapter has been that the Christian awareness of God grows out of the wonder and the ambiguity of the ordinary life of man in the world, but that it is an awareness that is finally brought to conscious and definitive form by the central experience of illumination and renewal that comes in the community that witnesses to the Christ. For all of us, this original awareness is *there*, at once elusive and real, absent and present, threatening and reassuring, as the fundamental ground and tone to our ordinary existence—until the knowledge of "faith" illumines and clarifies in part, but only in part, this ever-present mystery. The Christian continues to live, therefore, amidst both the ambiguity and clarity of this situation—for faith clarifies but by no means removes the ambiguities and the threats of our natural existence. Our Christian existence participates in both the worlds we have delineated—that of ambiguity, doubt, and the Void, and that of confidence, meaning, and reconciliation. Finally, from this characteristic situation of Christian life in the present, the strange religious symbols of the immanence and the transcendence of God, on the one hand, and of eschatology, on the other, begin to make sense. We can understand the symbol of the *immanence* of God as the source of our being and meaning in terms of the common, universal, and secular experiences of the reality, wonder and joy of life, of the coherences that experience offers to our inquiries, and of the universally apprehended meaningfulness of life's tasks. Correspondingly, we can understand the symbol of the *transcendence* of God through our continual experience of the elusiveness of that security and meaning, in the experience of the radical relativity of our truth, and in our sense of alienation from forgiveness and from the power to love—of all of which our secular friends, as well as we, are so very much aware. Above all, we can know the divine hiddenness in the Void of insecurity, despair, doubt, guilt, and death, which every human faces—even Jesus himself in his cry from the cross. The transcendence of God is initially experienced in the Void, which is the first terrible face of the divine that, at least in a secular culture, man knows. But then in the joy and acceptance of our contingent being, of our relative life, and of our death, and in the achievement of relative meaning and truth, of love and of community despite our fragmentariness, the renewed immanent presence of God is also known, and we begin to be aware of who that ultimate reality is—and the promise of an end in which God will be all in all takes on concrete, experienced meaning. The beginning of faith then appears in the awareness of the sacred in the profane, of joy and wonder in the midst of insecurity, of meaning and truth in the midst of the meaningless, and of life in the face of death, and it culminates with our understanding and affirmation of their ultimate unity in God.

This dialectic of immanence and transcendence, of hidden presence to all of life and of absence from it when we look for him is, of course, not all of God that we can know, or that the Christian community has believed itself to know. It is only a beginning. "God" here remains perhaps real, deep, but vague and elusive—the mysterious, sacral power from which life comes and which rules our destiny, and the eternity from which we are now separated. When Christian experience and thought move beyond this point, and in the light of those more personal and moral questions raised by our freedom and by our relations to others in community and in history, begin to know the love and acceptance of God in his long relation to his people and especially in the figure of Jesus, then we can say we begin to know the sacred more directly as it is, we begin to know "God." And that knowledge will reflect back on all that has been experienced of the ultimate on the other levels of our existence, shaping our answers to life's dilemmas and so shaping the theological symbols with which we comprehend ourselves, our destiny, and the sacred itself. Then the mysterious source of our being, the dim ruler of our destiny, and the opaque eternity into which we are finally to move, become illumined for us through the law and the love shown in Jesus Christ, and we can begin haltingly, but with some sense of meaning and of certainty, to speak of "God." But that the presence of God is real in secular life, and that our dependence on him makes us search for him even in our most worldly affairs, is true, and thus begins the possibility of knowing the reality of God and of speaking of him in a secular age. Our Biblical symbols, the treasured vehicles of our community's life and faith, can be understood as meaningful and asserted as valid as forthrightly in our secular existence as in any other age—but only if we retain, both in our thought and in our existence, a lively sense of their relatedness to our ordinary secular life.

### Note

1. In *Naming the Whirlwind: The Renewal of God-Language* (Indianapolis and New York: Bobbs-Merrill, 1969), pp. 460-70.

# Thomas J. J. Altizer

*A*ltizer *(born 1927) completed undergraduate and graduate studies at the University of Chicago. Since his Ph.D. in 1955, he has taught at Wabash College (1954–1956), Emory University (1956–1968), and the State University of Stony Brook as professor of English. His early writings of the 1960s reflected his intense encounter with studies of the history and phenomenology of religion, above all the thought of Mircea Eliade. Publication of* The Gospel of Christian Atheism *and, with William Hamilton,* Radical Theology and the Death of God *(both 1966) swept him and his theology into international news coverage and firestorms of controversy known as "the death of God movement." That "movement's" late-1960s efflorescence is less important for the history of theology than the character and influence of Altizer's project of thought, which has been "radical," "death-of-God," "apocalyptic," and at length "deconstructive" as well, and yet "God-intoxicated" and in a peculiar way christocentric.*

*The "death of God" is told of by a post-Reformation Lutheran hymn, post-Kantian idealism, the "mad prophet" of Nietzsche, and to mention only one other, Paul the apostle. Altizer takes the claim seriously, as witness to the self-emptying (kenosis) of God in the crucified Christ, and as such not only a figure of speech but a cultural, historical, cosmic, and theological reality. This conviction and many of Altizer's "standard" themes, as well as his link to "deconstruction," appear in the selection that follows.*

## HISTORY AS APOCALYPSE[1]

V

Just what can it mean to affirm that the end of history has occurred? First, we must note that this is not simply a new or postmodern affirmation, for something very like it lies at the center of the New Testament, even if that center was dislodged and transformed by the historical development and evolution of Christianity. That original Christian center was continually reborn in Christian history, as witness the fullest and most radical expressions of Christian mysticism and Christian apocalypticism. And remarkably enough the very advent of the modern world embodied a comprehensive rebirth of apocalypticism, an apocalypticism extending from romantic poetry to dialectical and idealistic philosophy to revolutionary politics and political action. If we accept Hegel as the primal thinker of modernity, then we can see that apocalypticism and a pure or full historical consciousness go hand in hand, for the full realization of the historical consciousness brings the ancient or premodern world to an end. That historical consciousness in its fullest realization is an absolute or total consciousness, and it can also be named and known as pure self-consciousness, a self-consciousness which is its own creator or ground. Not until Nietzsche's ecstatic discovery of Eternal Recurrence did a pure or total consciousness fully appear as its own ground and source, but that discovery was an interior consummation of nineteenth-century vision and thinking, and it continues to lie before us as perhaps the clearest and most powerful symbolic unveiling of our own interior depths.

Already Hegel conceived the purely inner world as the content of modern art, wherein inwardness shows itself outwardly, yet in such a manner as to triumph over the external by reducing it to relative insignificance. But the Hegel who believed that infinite subjectivity is now the sole habitat of Absolute Spirit is also the Hegel who was persuaded that art no longer counts for us as the highest manner in which truth can realize its existence. No doubt this judgment can no longer stand in the twentieth century, and not only because of the triumphs of twentieth-century art but also and even more deeply because those very triumphs embody a dissolution of self-consciousness in an historically postmodern world. But that dissolution or self-dissolution of self-consciousness is inevitably accompanied by the end of the historical consciousness, and that ending can only be known and realized in consciousness as the end of history itself, the end of the world and actuality of the autonomously existing and acting subject and center of consciousness.

Even if this conception of the end of history is present in Hegel's philosophy of history, and surely present in his logic, it is not fully present, not totally present, as witness the fact that Hegelian language is so comprehensively bound to an interior subjectivity and self-consciousness. Hegel did not live to read the second part of *Faust* or the mature poetry of Hölderlin, nor to encounter his own thinking in a reverse and inverted form in Kierkegaard and Marx, nor to encounter a full expression of that reversal in Nietzsche and late nineteenth-century art and literature. In all of these areas and others pure subjectivity or self-consciousness finally realized itself by ending itself, by ending itself as either a "subject" or "center" of consciousness. Thereafter history could no longer appear and be real as the actualization and realization of an interior subject of consciousness, as interiority fully passed into exteriority, and a new totality is ever more progressively establishing itself which transcends and leaves behind all subjective interiority. Therewith perishes all distinctions between cosmos and consciousness, or selfhood and nature, or nature and history. If an autonomous or self-enclosed nature or world comes to an end with the birth of modern physics, that ending can itself be seen as yet another expression of the end of history, the end of any identity which stands forth and is real by virtue of its own individual presence and actuality.

So it is that the end of history is the death of God, the death of the primal ground of individual presence and actuality, the end or dissolution of the grounding source of all integral and inherent differentiation. Nietzsche's madman asks if there is still any up or down? For now we are continually plunging backward, sideward, forward, and in all directions. That night or infinite nothing into which we have strayed could mythically be named as the chaos prior to the creation. And that is just the reason, mythically considered, why it is no longer possible for us to name God. Nor, of course, can we name ourselves, or name anything whatsoever which is an individual and distinct identity. Yet just as our night is in no sense at all a rebirth of an original innocence, neither is it an impassive or impotent darkness, as witness the incredible power and creativity of modern science and technology. Ours is a darkness of ravaging power, a power without limits, hence the appropriateness of Nietzsche's Dionysian language to name that darkness. However, one of the decisive sources of Nietzsche's Dionysian language is Hegel's *Phenomenology*, and it is significant that Hegel employs the name of Dionysus or Bacchus when he speaks mythically of the power of the negative, as in his most famous aphorism: "The True is thus the Bacchanalian revel in which no member is not drunk."[2]

If the deeper reaches of our darkness embody a Bacchanalian festival, they do so above all in their sheer and total presence, a presence which is not fully or comprehensively realized until the twentieth century. While that presence can now only be actually known or experienced as absence, it is a full presence nonetheless, and is so if only by virtue of the fact that it is actually experienced and known. What Derrida has named as *differance* is present in innumerable forms in twentieth-century science and art. Nothing else is so distinctive of our century, nor is anything of greater significance to us than the sheer fact of this occurrence. Simple identity is what has truly become absent to us, and simple or given identity in all its forms, whether these be subject and object, or matter and spirit, or society and selfhood, or knower and known, no identity whatsoever can any longer stand forth which is only itself. But it is precisely thereby that a total and comprehensive identity is being born in our midst, and that identity is real, as real as modern science and technology, and as modern art, music, and literature, to say nothing of the social and political revolutions of the twentieth century. And it is just because this is a total identity that we can no longer realize it as an historical identity.

Yet if we can no longer know our identity as an historical identity, this very loss of identity can bring a new identity to history itself, and this because we know all too well that our identity is a consequence of historical actuality. If the owl of Minerva flies only with the falling of the dusk, it flies nonetheless, and the very perspective of our night can make possible a new unveiling of a history which has now come to an end. For our darkness is the consummation of history, or the consummation of what can appear and be real to us as history, and thereby history itself passes into a new totality. Now it has always been true that history gains a new identity only as a consequence of the loss of a previous historical identity, and if the end of history has now occurred, that ending could make possible for the first time a total identity of history. Nietzsche's vision of Eternal Recurrence brings such an identity to history, and it was made possible by Nietzsche's historical realization that the totality of consciousness is a consequence of the pure negativity of No-saying or the bad conscience. It is just this historical ground which sets this all too modern or postmodern vision of Eternal Recurrence worlds apart from its premodern counterparts, and it is also its historical ground which makes Nietzsche's language and vision so overwhelmingly real to us.

If Nietzsche was himself destroyed by an ultimate and tragic conflict with a uniquely modern nihilism, that nihilism itself thereafter realized both a universal and an historical expression, and an historical expression giving birth to the twentieth century. How ironic that it was the

581

ecstatic prophet of Eternal Recurrence who first philosophically unveiled the total presence of history, a presence possible only by way of the end of history, or the end of every positive meaning and identity of history. Now we can see that Hegel lived too soon to realize such a totally negative identity of history, even if that identity is both logically and historically present in his own comprehension of pure negativity, for a total negativity can only be real as a consequence of a full and total reversal of consciousness. While such a reversal has its counterpart in an Eastern and Buddhist emptying of consciousness, a pure and total negativity is radically different from a pure emptiness if only because it is actually and immediately present, indeed, historically and irreversibly present, and it is just that final and irreversible presence which brings history to an end.

Nothing so characterizes the actuality which we know as its sheer irreversibility, for the first time past time is wholly lost to consciousness, or lost as a living and a human time, and the nostalgia which we know can never be for an earlier history, but only for a prehistorical and primordial plenum. Derrida is but one of a number of our thinkers who have been obsessed with such nostalgia, but all of them know, and Derrida most clearly and decisively, that this is a hopeless and unrealizable nostalgia, and is so perhaps above all when its goal is named not as a plenum but as an absolute emptiness. For that emptiness is truly and actually possible for no one who is a product of a Western history and consciousness, and it is all too significant that Freud himself named the death instinct as the nirvana principle. The innocent among us may well delight in nostalgic fantasy, but not since Shakespeare has an innocent fantasy passed into poetic language, and from Milton through Proust the only paradise which we have known poetically is a paradise lost. Or, rather, the paradise regained in modern art and poetry is not and cannot be an original paradise. Goethe's Faust may finally be redeemed by union with the Eternal Female, just as Blake's Albion may be redeemed by union with Jerusalem, but the redemptive realm of the Mothers and of Jerusalem is as far removed as possible from the original bliss of a Garden of Eden. But perhaps most significant of all, the paradise which has been named by such fully modern poets as Mallarmé and Yeats, is a paradise which is nameable precisely because it does not and cannot exist.

If the advent of the postmodern world embodies a final and eschatological end of history, then history itself can then appear and be real as paradise just because it no longer exists. For it is the loss of a human

582

time and consciousness, and its final and irretrievable loss, which makes possible the discovery of the totality of lost time, a totality which can only mythically and poetically be named as paradise. True, such a paradise could only be an absent, an empty, or a negative paradise, the very paradise which Kafka poetically and parabolically evoked. But this is the only paradise which has ever actually been present upon our horizon, and it is that paradise which released the actuality and irreversibility of history, an irreversibility culminating in the end of history itself. But is there anything else which we can know and name as grace? For the first time we have been given a grace which is everywhere in history, but it is everywhere in history only when history comes to an end, only when history is no longer actual and real.

Now we can follow Nietzsche's madman and say our *requiem aeternam deo,* our requiem to the God who mercifully no longer exists. That requiem and it alone is our way of knowing the omnipresence of God, an omnipresence which appears and is real only with the dissolution and disappearance of its center. History perishes in that dissolution, but that very perishing unveils the final and ultimate identity of history, an apocalyptic identity which is finally no less and no more than the self-embodiment of God. Such an apocalyptic omnipresence of God in history can never be manifest or real as such so long as history itself remains real, only the end of history can unveil the apocalypse of God. And that apocalypse is inseparable from the end or death of God, the death of the God who is only God, the God who can be named and known as God. Only the eschatological and apocalyptic death or dissolution of the God who is God can unveil the omnipresence of God, and the omnipresence of God in history, an omnipresence which can only occur when history is released as an irreversible actuality, and an omnipresence which can only be manifest as an omnipresence of grace when history itself comes to an end. For only when history comes to an end can history be known as grace, just as the only God who can be known as a totally gracious God is the God who is dead.

Christianity has always known the death of God as the way of absolute grace, for nothing less than the death of God lies behind the symbol of the crucifixion, but not until the birth of the modern world is the death of God fully realized in consciousness and history, a realization which is consummated in an absolute or eschatological explosion of history and consciousness. Now grace is everywhere because it is nowhere, nowhere that is where it is only itself, or where it can be known and named as the grace of God. That absolute necessity or *causa sui* which is the classical Christian identity of God has now passed into the center of the world, and that passage has brought the world to an end, or brought an end to every identity which stands forth only as itself. Such an ending is a fully apocalyptic *parousia* or total presence, and therefore it cannot be known as the presence of God, or even as the omnipresence of God, but only as the death of God, the eschatological end of the God who is God. If the naming of God lies at the very origin of our history, and is the original ground of everything which appears and is real to us as integral and individual identity, then the disintegration and disappearance of individual identity is inseparable from the disappearance and end of everything which we have known and named as God. And that is an apocalyptic and eschatological end, a final and total end, and therefore an end which can only be named by the Christian as the realization of absolute grace.

Yes, history is an absolute presence, and the absolute presence of God, but we can only realize such an absolute or totally gracious identity of history when both God and history finally come to an end. And history comes to an end in and as the death of God, the end of the infinite, and therewith the end of all finitude and limits. An absolute and total nihilism is an inevitable consequence of the end of history or the death of God, and this is a nihilism which historically first appears in Christianity, and as early as Paul. Perhaps nothing is more characteristic of primitive Christianity than its ultimate violation of that which Israel absolutely condemned and condemns, the human pronunciation of the Name of God, a pronunciation which a purely iconoclastic faith must judge to be an absolute assault upon the majesty of the creator. At no point did Jesus more radically assault the guardians of an iconoclastic Law or Torah than in commonly addressing God as Abba or "my father," and this is something new in history, for there is no instance of God being addressed as Abba in the literature of Jewish prayer. Indeed, the Pauline Christ redeems the world from the "curse" of the Torah (Galatians 3:13), a Torah which for Paul was ordained not by God but by the angels, and which at best is a tutoring slave (*paidagogos*) to bring the world to Christ. Freedom in Christ, for either Paul or John, is freedom from the Law, a freedom which was reborn again and again in Christian mysticism and apocalypticism, and which decisively and comprehensively entered Western history in the Protestant Reformation. This is a freedom that was a primal source of what we have known as consciousness and history, and a freedom which finally released itself in the ultimate act of deicide, the murder of the creator and judge.

Hegel could know that deicide as the consummation of the Incarnation, an Incarnation which realized the birth of self-consciousness, a self-consciousness which itself becomes absolute by passing through the death of God. With Nietzsche the willing of the death of God becomes the realization of absolute freedom, the creative transformation of the dreadful accident of "it was" into the destiny of "but thus I willed it," as the majesty of the transcendent creator passes into an all too immanent will to power. Thereby a pure nihilism is released in history, and not simply released in history, but consummated in history, a consummation which brings history to an end. Derrida, as every Jewish theological thinker, can recognize this nihilism as a Christian nihilism, a nihilism which is the inevitable consequence of the absolute presence of the Christian God. History is the eschatological embodiment of that God, a God who becomes absolutely present in the Incarnation, an incarnate or self-conscious presence which releases the finality and irreversibility of history. That finality and irreversibility is actuality itself, an actuality which is undeniable and irresistible, and an actuality which is the kenotic emptying of everything which it enacts.

### Notes

1. In *Deconstruction and Theology*, ed. Thomas J. J. Altizer et al. (New York: Crossroad Publishing, 1982), pp. 168-76.
2. G. W. F. Hegel, *Phenomenology of Spirit*, trans. A. V. Miller (Oxford: Clarendon Press, 1977), p. 27.

# George A. Lindbeck

*Lindbeck (born 1923) has played a first-string role on a team of scholars whose talents and interests have combined to form a "Yale School of Theology" in the later twentieth century. Perhaps the most general and unifying feature of the diverse thinkers associated with this "School" is stress on the primary function(s) of the language of faith distinctive to scripture and historic doctrine within the church as a confessional community. This stress was already prominent at Yale at midcentury, when Lindbeck completed his ministerial and doctoral studies (Ph.D., 1955)—then in the form of linkages between a neoorthodox (especially Barthian) understanding of the task and content of "dogmatics" and the turn in Anglo American analytic philosophy (following the lead of Ludwig Wittgenstein) from linguistic positivism to focus on the use(s) of language. Since that time, one stream of the Yale School has produced and prompted diverse works of "narrative theology," while Lindbeck's course has led to a systemic, "anthropological" model of Christian confessional and doctrinal discourse. His own characterization of his stance as "postliberal" is generally applied to that of the Yale School as a whole.*

*Trained as a medievalist and associated with the World Lutheran Federation, Lindbeck was one of the select group constituting the delegation of church leaders outside the Roman Catholic Church that Pope John XXIII invited to attend the Second Vatican Council (1962–1965). Issues of ecumenicity have been directly related to his reflections on theological language, and are joined in his late but programmatic work* The Nature of Doctrine, *a selection from which follows.*

## RELIGION AND EXPERIENCE: A PRETHEOLOGICAL INQUIRY[1]

### A Cultural-Linguistic Alternative

The description of the cultural-linguistic alternative that I shall now sketch is shaped by the ultimately theological concerns of the present

586

inquiry, but it is consonant, I believe, with the anthropological, socio-logical, and philosophical studies by which it has been for the most part inspired. In the account that I shall give, religions are seen as compre-hensive interpretive schemes, usually embodied in myths or narratives and heavily ritualized, which structure human experience and under-standing of self and world. Not every telling of one of these cosmic stories is religious, however. It must be told with a particular purpose or interest. It must be used, to adopt a suggestion of William Christian, with a view to identifying and describing what is taken to be "more important than everything else in the universe,"[2] and to organizing all of life, including both behavior and beliefs, in relation to this. If the inter-pretive scheme is used or the story is told without this interest in the maximally important, it ceases to function religiously. To be sure, it may continue to shape in various ways the attitudes, sentiments, and conduct of individuals and of groups. A religion, in other words, may continue to exercise immense influence on the way people experience themselves and their world even when it is no longer explicitly adhered to.

Stated more technically, a religion can be viewed as a kind of cultural and/or linguistic framework or medium that shapes the entirety of life and thought. It functions somewhat like a Kantian *a priori*, although in this case the *a priori* is a set of acquired skills that could be different. It is not primarily an array of beliefs about the true and the good (though it may involve these), or a symbolism expressive of basic attitudes, feel-ings, or sentiments (though these will be generated). Rather, it is similar to an idiom that makes possible the description of realities, the formu-lation of beliefs, and the experiencing of inner attitudes, feelings, and sentiments. Like a culture or language, it is a communal phenomenon that shapes the subjectivities of individuals rather than being primarily a manifestation of those subjectivities. It comprises a vocabulary of dis-cursive and nondiscursive symbols together with a distinctive logic or grammar in terms of which this vocabulary can be meaningfully deployed. Lastly, just as a language (or "language game," to use Wittgenstein's phrase) is correlated with a form of life, and just as a cul-ture has both cognitive and behavioral dimensions, so it is also in the case of a religious tradition. Its doctrines, cosmic stories or myths, and ethical directives are integrally related to the rituals it practices, the sen-timents or experiences it evokes, the actions it recommends, and the institutional forms it develops. All this is involved in comparing a reli-gion to a cultural-linguistic system.

Turning now in more detail to the relation of religion and experience, it may be noted that this is not unilateral but dialectical. It is simplistic to say (as I earlier did) merely that religions produce experiences, for the causality is reciprocal. Patterns of experience alien to a given religion can profoundly influence it. The warrior passions of barbarian Teutons and Japanese occasioned great changes in originally pacifistic Christianity and Buddhism. These religions were pressed into service to sanction the values of militaristic societies and were largely transformed in the process. Yet in providing new legitimations for the ancient patterns, they also altered the latter. Presumably the inner experiences as well as the code of behavior of a Zen samurai or a Christian knight are markedly different from those of their pagan or pre-Buddhist predecessors. Yet, as this illustration shows, in the interplay between "inner" experience and "external" religious and cultural factors, the latter can be viewed as the leading partners, and it is this option which the cultural and/or linguistic analyst favors.

It remains true, therefore, that the most easily pictured of the contrasts between a linguistic-cultural model of religion and an experiential-expressive one is that the former reverses the relation of the inner and the outer. Instead of deriving external features of a religion from inner experience, it is the inner experiences which are viewed as derivative.

Thus the linguistic-cultural model is part of an outlook that stresses the degree to which human experience is shaped, molded, and in a sense constituted by cultural and linguistic forms. There are numberless thoughts we cannot think, sentiments we cannot have, and realities we cannot perceive unless we learn to use the appropriate symbol systems. It seems, as the cases of Helen Keller and of supposed wolf children vividly illustrate, that unless we acquire language of some kind, we cannot actualize our specifically human capacities for thought, action, and feeling.[3] Similarly, so the argument goes, to become religious involves becoming skilled in the language, the symbol system of a given religion. To become a Christian involves learning the story of Israel and of Jesus well enough to interpret and experience oneself and one's world in its terms. A religion is above all an external word, a *verbum externum,* that molds and shapes the self and its world, rather than an expression or thematization of a preexisting self or of preconceptual experience. The *verbum internum* (traditionally equated by Christians with the action of the Holy Spirit) is also crucially important, but it would be understood in a theological use of the model as a capacity for hearing and accepting the true religion, the true external word, rather than (as experiential-expressivism would have it) as a common experience diversely articulated in different religions.[4]

As has already been mentioned, part of the strength of a cultural-linguistic outlook is that it can accommodate and combine the distinctive and often competing emphases of the other two approaches. Consider, for example, the insight, foreign to a cognitivist outlook, represented by Paul Tillich's experiential-expressive formula that "religion is the substance of culture, and culture the form of religion"[5]—i.e., religion in the sense of ultimate concern is the vitalizing source of all significant cultural achievements. The alternative here proposed does not deny this, but offers a more complex formulation that transposes the emphases. Religion, one might say, is that ultimate dimension of culture (because it has to do with whatever is taken as most important) which gives shape and intensity to the experiential matrix from which significant cultural achievements flow. The basic imagery in this formulation is closer to Aristotelian hylomorphism than to the idealisms of Schelling or Hegel, by whom Tillich was influenced. In both cases, "form" may be inseparable from experiential "matter," but in a hylomorphic model, form has priority because experience, like matter, exists only insofar as it is informed. In the idealist model, in contrast, experience of a certain kind (i.e., "Spirit" or Geist) has a prior reality that necessarily expresses and fulfills itself in objective cultural and religious forms. In both models the culture-forming power of religious experience can be acknowledged, although in one case the experience is derivative, in the other primordial.

In thus inverting the relation of the internal and external dimensions of religion, linguistic and cultural approaches resemble cognitivist theories for which external (i.e., propositionally statable) beliefs are primary, but without the intellectualism of the latter. A comprehensive scheme or story used to structure all dimensions of existence is not primarily a set of propositions to be believed, but is rather the medium in which one moves, a set of skills that one employs in living one's life. Its vocabulary of symbols and its syntax may be used for many purposes, only one of which is the formulation of statements about reality. Thus while a religion's truth claims are often of the utmost importance to it (as in the case of Christianity), it is, nevertheless, the conceptual vocabulary and the syntax or inner logic which determine the kinds of truth claims the religion can make. The cognitive aspect, while often important, is not primary.

This stress on the code, rather than the (e.g., propositionally) encoded, enables a cultural-linguistic approach to accommodate the experiential-expressive concern for the unreflective dimensions of human existence far better than is possible in a cognitivist outlook. Reli-

589

gion cannot be pictured in the cognitivist (and voluntarist) manner as primarily a matter of deliberately choosing to believe or follow explicitly known propositions or directives. Rather, to become religious—no less than to become culturally or linguistically competent—is to interiorize a set of skills by practice and training. One learns how to feel, act, and think in conformity with a religious tradition that is, in its inner structure, far richer and more subtle than can be explicitly articulated. The primary knowledge is not *about* the religion, nor *that* the religion teaches such and such, but rather *how* to be religious in such and such ways. Sometimes explicitly formulated statements of the beliefs or behavioral norms of a religion may be helpful in the learning process, but by no means always. Ritual, prayer, and example are normally much more important. Thus—insofar as the experiential-expressive contrast between experience and knowledge is comparable to that between "knowing how" and "knowing that"—cultural-linguistic models, no less than expressive ones, emphasize the experiential or existential side of religion, though in a different way.

As a result there is also room for the expressive aspects. The aesthetic and nondiscursively symbolic dimensions of a religion—for example, its poetry, music, art, and rituals—are not, as propositional cognitivism suggests, mere external decorations designed to make the hard core of explicitly statable beliefs and precepts more appealing to the masses. Rather, it is through these that the basic patterns of religion are interiorized, exhibited, and transmitted. The proclamation of the gospel, as a Christian would put it, may be first of all the telling of the story, but this gains power and meaning insofar as it is embodied in the total gestalt of community life and action.

Furthermore, interiorized skill, the skill of the saint, manifests itself in an ability to discriminate "intuitively" (nondiscursively) between authentic and inauthentic, and between effective and ineffective, objectifications of the religion. Having been inwardly formed by a given tradition—by, for example, "the mind of Christ" (1 Cor. 2:16), as Paul puts it—the saint has what Thomas Aquinas calls "connatural knowledge"[6] and by what Newman calls "the illative sense"[7] in matters religious. This is quite different from the reflective and theoretical knowledge of the trained theologian, who employs publicly assessable rules and procedures in seeking to distinguish between the good and the bad, the true and the false. Rather, it is like the grammatical or rhetorical knowledge of a poet such as Homer, who could not enunciate a single rule in either discipline and yet was able to sense as could no one else what conformed or did not conform to the spirit, the unarticulated rules, of the Greek language. On this view, the way a religion functions once it is interiorized is much better described in expressivist than in cognitivist terms.

There is a sense, then, in which experience and expression are no less important in a cultural-linguistic model than in an experiential-expressive one. Nevertheless, the nature of experience and its relation to expression and communication are construed quite differently. This brings us to the conceptual formulation of the major contrast between the two models, which we earlier spoke of in a pictorial fashion as a "reversal of the relation between the inner and outer."

When one pictures inner experiences as prior to expression and communication, it is natural to think of them in their most basic and elemental form as also prior to conceptualization or symbolization. If, in contrast, expressive and communicative symbol systems, whether linguistic or nonlinguistic, are primary—then, while there are of course nonreflective experiences, there are no uninterpreted or unschematized ones. On this view, the means of communication and expression are a precondition, a kind of quasi-transcendental (i.e., culturally formed) *a priori* for the possibility of experience. We cannot identify, describe, or recognize experience qua experience without the use of signs and symbols. These are necessary even for what the depth psychologist speaks of as "unconscious" or "subconscious" experiences, or for what the phenomenologist describes as prereflective ones. In short, it is necessary to have the means for expressing an experience in order to have it, and the richer our expressive or linguistic system, the more subtle, varied, and differentiated can be our experience.

This is a complex thesis, and its full discussion lies beyond the scope of this essay. A crude illustration of what is involved may, however, be helpful. There are reported to be tribal languages that do not discriminate between, e.g., green and blue, and the members of these tribes are reported (erroneously, according to some observers)[8] to have difficulty recognizing the difference between the two colors. They are not color-blind. On the physiological level, their retinas and optic nerves respond differentially to light waves of varying lengths just as ours do, but they lack the verbal categories for experiencing these differences in stimuli. Or, in order to avoid cultural provincialism, one can put the case conversely: we lack the linguistic *a priori* for having the visual experiences that they have.

Whether or not this particular illustration is veridical, it does raise the question of whether language influences domains of human reality that

591

are generally thought of, not simply as prelinguistic, but as preexperiential, e.g., sensory physiological processes to which we as subjects do not have privileged access but of which we can become aware only by external observation of ourselves or others. It seems clear that even the presensory or preperceptual selection and organization of stimuli is not entirely prelinguistic. The classification and categorial patterns embedded in a language, once it has been acquired, help organize the inexperienceably chaotic confusion that bombards our senses. One can even plausibly propose (as have both Noam Chomsky,[9] on theoretical linguistic grounds, and Clifford Geertz,[10] on anthropological-evolutionary ones) that human beings are so thoroughly programmed genetically for language use that apart from acquiring a language they cannot properly develop physiologically as other animals do, but remain peculiarly immature in their sensory and physical competence. Further, once they do learn a language, this shapes the preexperiential physical basis of their conscious experience and activity. Thus language, it seems, shapes domains of human existence and action that are preexperiential. This is one of the senses in which the human being is a psychosomatic unity.

But the position that language (or, more generally, some conceptual and/or symbolic interpretive scheme) is a condition for religious experience need not be based on these perhaps empirically falsifiable speculations. It does not depend, in other words, on the possibility just mentioned that public linguistic categories shape even preexperiential activity. One could also claim that an experience (viz., something of which one is prereflectively or reflectively conscious) is impossible unless it is in some fashion symbolized, and that all symbol systems have their origin in interpersonal relations and social interactions. It is conceptually confused to talk of symbolizations (and therefore of experiences) that are purely private.

There are several ways of arguing this. The most ambitious is Wittgenstein's contention that private languages are logically impossible.[11] If so, the same would have to be said regarding private religious experiences (such as the dynamic state of being unrestrictedly in love), which are purportedly independent of any particular language game. This is not the place to assess this argument. I shall simply note that even those experiential-expressivists—such as Lonergan (or Karl Rahner and David Tracy)—who acknowledge that experience cannot be expressed except in public and intersubjective forms, do seem to maintain a kind of privacy in the origins of experience and language that, if Wittgenstein is right, is more than doubtful.[12]

A more modest argument does not try to demonstrate the impossibility of unthematized yet conscious experience but simply employs Ockham's razor to conclude that there is no need for this hypothesis. One way to make this point is by means of the classic medieval distinction between first and second intentions. As applied to objects (*intentio objectiva*), "animal" in the first intention is this or that creature, Fido or Socrates, in its own actual or possible, imaginary or real being, while in the second intention it is a generic concept embracing many species such as the human and the canine. As applied to mental activities (*intentio formalis*), the first intention is the act whereby we grasp objects, while the second intention is the reflex act of grasping or reflecting on first formal intentions. In the modern philosophical language of consciousness, we are only unthematically (or, in Polanyi's terminology, "tacitly")[13] aware of first intentional activities while we are engaged in them: our attention is focused on objects, not on the subjective experience involved in knowing them. It is only in the second intention that we attend to this experience, that we are focally rather than tacitly aware of it. Yet this does not lead us to suppose that the first-intentional experiences of, for example, attending to Fido or to the logical characteristics of the concept of animal are somehow preverbal or linguistically unstructured. Surely, so the argument goes, the same could be said of religious experiences. They can be construed as by-products of linguistically or conceptually structured cognitive activities of which we are not directly aware because they are first-intentional. The sense of the holy of which Rudolf Otto speaks can be construed as the tacit or unthematic awareness of applying a culturally acquired concept of the holy in a given situation. Similarly, concert pianists tell us that it is disastrous for them to become focally conscious of their fingers while they are playing, but nevertheless their playing (and their sometimes ecstatic experience of playing) depends on their fingering. It seems that the most economical hypothesis is to suppose that the relation between religious experiences and a given culture, language, and form of life is similar. If my application of the notions of first and second intentions is correct, then this is a thesis on which Thomas Aquinas and other medieval Aristotelians (but not all medieval Augustinians)[14] agree with Wittgenstein against post-Cartesian philosophers of consciousness as well as against some professed Thomists such as Lonergan and Rahner. For the Aristotelians, affective experiences (in which would be included a sense of the holy or of absolute dependence) always depend on prior cognition of objects, and the objects available to us in this life are all in some fashion constructed out of (or, in medieval terminology, "abstracted from") conceptually or linguistically structured sense experience.

Many modifications of common ways of thinking about religion follow from abandoning the notion that its source is in prior experience, but I shall mention only two. First, religious change or innovation must be understood, not as proceeding from new experiences, but as resulting from the interactions of a cultural-linguistic system with changing situations. Religious traditions are not transformed, abandoned, or replaced because of an upwelling of new or different ways of feeling about the self, world, or God, but because a religious interpretive scheme (embodied, as it always is, in religious practice and belief) develops anomalies in its application in new contexts. This produces, among other things, negative effects, negative experiences, even by the religion's own norms. Prophetic figures apprehend, often with dramatic vividness, how the inherited patterns of belief, practice, and ritual need to be (and can be) reminded. They discover the concepts that remove the anomalies. Religious experiences in the sense of feelings, sentiments, or emotions then result from the new conceptual patterns instead of being their source.

Thus, if one follows this account, Luther did not invent his doctrine of justification by faith because he had a tower experience,[15] but rather the tower experience was made possible by his discovering (or thinking he discovered) the doctrine in the Bible. To be sure, the experience of justification by faith occasioned by his exegesis then generated a variety of fresh expressive symbolisms, among which Lutherans like especially to mention the music of Johann Sebastian Bach. Without such powerful experiences and their effective expression, the tradition would have neither started nor persisted, yet logically, even if not causally, a religious experience and its expression are secondary and tertiary in a linguistic-cultural model. First come the objectivities of the religion, its language, doctrines, liturgies, and modes of action, and it is through these that passions are shaped into various kinds of what is called religious experience.

A second consequence of this outlook which is particularly important for our immediate purposes is that it raises questions regarding the meaningfulness of the notion that there is an inner experience of God common to all human beings and all religions. There can be no experiential core because, so the argument goes, the experiences that religions evoke and mold are as varied as the interpretive schemes they embody. Adherents of different religions do not diversely thematize the same experience; rather they have different experiences. Buddhist compassion,

Christian love and—if I may cite a quasi-religious phenomenon—French Revolutionary *fraternité* are not diverse modifications of a single fundamental human awareness, emotion, attitude, or sentiment, but are radically (i.e., from the root) distinct ways of experiencing and being oriented toward self, neighbor, and cosmos. The affective features they have in common are part, so to speak, of their raw materials, functions of those feelings of closeness to one's immediate fellows shared by all human beings including Nazis and headhunters. Similarly, the sense of the holy or the sacred that is the identifying mark of religion for much of the experiential-expressive tradition is not a common quality, but a set of family resemblances. There may be some religions in which it is of little or no importance; and even those which emphasize it need not for that reason be similar. It may be as much a mistake to classify them together as to claim that all red things, whether apples, Indians, or the Moscow square belong to the same natural genus. Much the same can be said regarding mystical experiences. What these have in common can be easily understood quite naturalistically as consisting, for example, of the "oceanic feelings" of which Freud spoke.[16] To be sure, in a cultural-linguistic outlook one would add (as Freud did not) that these feelings become ingredients in a wide variety of experiences of the world, of self, and—the believer would say—of God that depend on different perceptual categories (e.g., religious or nonreligious, theistic or nontheistic) and forms of practice (e.g., drug-taking, yoga exercises, contemplative prayer).[17] Thus religion, including mysticism, need not be described as something universal arising from within the depths of individuals and diversely and inadequately objectified in particular faiths; it can at least as plausibly be construed as a class name for a variegated set of cultural-linguistic systems that, at least in some cases, differentially shape and produce our most profound sentiments, attitudes, and awarenesses.

In summary, the alternate model understands religions as idioms for dealing with whatever is most important—with ultimate questions of life and death, right and wrong, chaos and order, meaning and meaninglessness. These are the problems they treat in their stories, myths, and doctrines. They imprint their answers through rites, instruction, and other socializing processes, not only on the conscious mind but in the individual and cultural subconscious. Thus a Balinese, molded by a ceremonial system in which is embedded a partly Hindu and partly animist world view, will fall into a catatonic trance when confronted by types of stimulus that might plunge a Westerner, influenced by a long tradition of biblical monotheism, into strenuous activity.[18] Centuries of ritual reiter-

595

ation of certain definitions of what is ultimately good and true have so shaped these two cultural types that their basic attitudinal reflexes are different even in the absence of belief or of much explicit knowledge of the religious traditions. In the face of such examples, it seems implausible to claim that religions are diverse objectifications of the same basic experience. On the contrary, different religions seem in many cases to produce fundamentally divergent depth experiences of what it is to be human. The empirically available data seem to support a cultural-linguistic rather than an experiential-expressive understanding of the relation of religion and experience.

## Notes

1. In *The Nature of Doctrine: Religion and Theology in a Postliberal Age* (Philadelphia: Westminster Press, 1984), pp. 32-41.
2. William A. Christian, Sr., *Meaning and Truth in Religion* (Princeton University Press, 1964), pp. 60ff. The question of how exactly to define religion is not important for the contrast between the two approaches that we are comparing, provided one insists, as Christian does, that the predicate (e.g., "most important") names a function rather than either a feeling or an experience, on the one hand, or an attribute or a character of the religious object, on the other. The reason for this stipulation is that there appears to be no common experience or attribute that applies within all the things that are normally called religions. David Little and Sumner B. Twiss, *Comparative Religious Ethics* (Harper & Row, 1978), seek to improve on Christian's definition of Religion (p. 56), but their proposal has the disadvantage of doing violence to ordinary usage by giving a functional rather than an experiential or attributive meaning to "sacred" (pp. 59-60).
3. Susanne Langer, *Philosophy in a New Key* (Pelican Books, 1948), pp. 50-51, 83ff.
4. The priority of the *verbum externum* was a major emphasis of the Protestant Reformers against the spiritualists of the sixteenth century, but it was also part of the pre-Reformation tradition. Aquinas, for example, insisted that saving faith comes *ex auditu* (Rom. 10:17). Thus, contrary to some modern interpreters such as Rahner, the notion of "implicit faith" did not for him refer to the *verbum internum* (i.e., an unthematized, preconceptual experience of the divine), but rather presupposed some degree of explicit faith in the *verbum externum*. See Joseph DiNoia, "Implicit Faith, General Revelation and the State of Non-Christians," *The Thomist* 47/2 (1983), pp. 209-41. Cf. George Lindbeck, "*Fides ex Auditu* and the Salvation of Non-Christians: Contemporary Catholic and Protestant Positions," ed. by V. Vajta, *The Gospel and the Ambiguity of the Church* (Fortress Press, 1974), pp. 91-123.
5. Paul Tillich, *Systematic Theology*, Vol. 3 (University of Chicago Press, 1963), pp. 248ff. This is the last of many treatments of the theme by Tillich.
6. Thomas Aquinas, *ST* II-II.45.2; cf. I.1.6, ad 3.
7. John Henry Newman, *An Essay in Aid of a Grammar of Assent* (London, 1870).
8. B. Berlin and P. Kay, *Basic Color Terms* (University of California Press, 1969). Cf. M. Sahlins, "Colors and Cultures," *Semiotica* 16 (1976), pp. 1-22.
9. Noam Chomsky, *Language and Mind,* extended ed. (Harcourt Brace Jovanovich, 1972).
10. Clifford Geertz, "The Growth of Culture and the Evolution of Mind," *The Interpretation of Cultures* (Basic Books, 1973), pp. 55-86.

11. For a comprehensive exposition of Wittgenstein's scattered references see Robert J. Fogelin, *Wittgenstein* (London: Routledge & Kegan Paul, 1980), pp. 153-71.

12. Karl Rahner affirms an experience of the *"Vorgriff auf esse"* which is distinguishable, though not separable, from its categorial, conceptual, or linguistic schematization and is the transcendental condition of all human knowing and willing. See his *Spirit in the World,* tr. by William Dych (Herder & Herder, 1968), pp. 132-236. Cf. George Lindbeck, "The *A Priori* in St. Thomas' Theory of Knowledge," in Robert E. Cushman and Egil Grislis (eds.), *The Heritage of Christian Thought* (Harper & Row, 1965), pp. 41-63, for an evaluation of Rahner's argument that his position is in agreement with that of Aquinas.

　David Tracy's position is structurally similar, although, unlike Rahner, the details of his argument are influenced more by Lonergan than by Marechal. He speaks of the "common human experience" of basic confidence or trust which grounds our commitments to the ultimate meaningfulness or worth of inquiring, deciding, and doing. Religious language and symbols more or less adequately "re-present" and reaffirm this basic experience on the level of self-conscious belief. See *Blessed Rage for Order: The New Pluralism in Theology* (Seabury Press, 1975), esp. pp. 97-103.

　Lonergan, unlike Rahner and Tracy, does not speak of an "experience" of the transcendental conditions for human knowing and willing (inquiry, reflection, and deliberation), nor of religion as the symbolization of "common human experience," but rather of the special religious experience of the gift of God's love (and this is postulated on the basis of theological rather than philosophical considerations). Thus, unlike Tracy and Rahner, he seems to have only theological reasons for rejecting the thesis of the present book that intersubjective communicative systems are the source rather than the product of distinctively human experience, whether religious or nonreligious.

　In view of Lonergan's attack on what he takes to be Wittgenstein's views on private language (*Method in Theology,* pp. 254-56), it might be thought he is committed to prelinguistic experience, but the attack, if I understand it rightly, is based on the misapprehension that a denial of private languages entails a denial of mental acts. According to Peter Geach, *Mental Acts: Their Content and Their Objects* (London: Routledge & Kegan Paul, 1971), Gilbert Ryle makes the converse mistake: he thinks the affirmation of mental acts entails the affirmation of private languages; Aquinas, in contrast, denies private languages yet affirms mental acts (pp. 130-31). If so, the private language argument against prelinguistic experiences would be fully acceptable to Aquinas, but not to Tracy or Rahner, and, to a lesser extent, not to Lonergan.

　The crucial philosophical issue is the validity of transcendental deductions of the necessary conditions of human knowing and willing. If the postulation of such conditions by means of transcendental arguments is valid, then it makes sense to say that one may experience these (e.g., the *Vorgriff auf esse*) prior to, even if not separable from, their thematization by linguistic or other conceptual systems. For a succinct statement of what, as far as I know, is an unanswered objection to transcendental deductions, see Stephan Körner, *Fundamental Questions in Philosophy* (Penguin Books, University Books, 1971), pp. 213ff.

13. The idea of using Polanyi's terminology to say that what is tacit in the first intention becomes focal in the second came to me while reading Robert E. McInnis, "Meaning, Thought and Language in Polanyi's Epistemology," *Philosophy Today* (Spring 1974), pp. 47-67, and "Polanyi's Model of Mental Acts," *The New Scholasticism* 47/2 (1973), pp. 147-80. Neither Polanyi nor McInnis draws the parallel, however.

14. Cf. my article cited in n. 12, above.

15. Assuming that it occurred. This illustration serves, no matter what the truth regarding the much-debated tower experience. What is important for our purposes is the contention that the core of Luther's reformatory breakthrough was an exegetical insight. See George Lindbeck, "Erikson's *Young Man Luther*: A Historical and Theological Reappraisal," *Soundings* 16 (1973), pp. 210-27, reprinted in Donald Capps et al. (eds.), *Encounter with Erikson* (Scholars Press, 1977), pp. 7-28.
16. Sigmund Freud, *Civilization and Its Discontents* (W. W. Norton & Co., 1961), pp. 11-20.
17. On the varieties of mystical experience see R. C. Zaehner, *Mysticism, Sacred and Profane* (Oxford: Clarendon Press, 1957), and Steven Katz, "Language Epistemology, and Mysticism," *Mysticism and Philosophical Analysis*, ed. by S. Katz (London: Sheldon Press, 1978), pp. 22-74.
18. The Balinese reference is to the Rangda-Barong temple dramas, of which one can find a brief description in Geertz, "The Growth of Culture and the Evolution of Mind," in his *The Interpretation of Cultures*, pp. 180f. Cf. his essay on "The Impact of the Concept of Culture on the Science of Man," ibid., pp. 33-55.

# INDEX